Dictionary of Literary Biography • Volume Thirty-seven

American Writers
of the Early Republic

Dictionary of Literary Biography

Documentary Series

Yearbooks

American Writers of the Early Republic

Edited by
Emory Elliott
Princeton University

A Bruccoli Clark Book

Gale Research Company • Book Tower • Detroit, Michigan 48226

11/1985
Ref.

Advisory Board for
DICTIONARY OF LITERARY BIOGRAPHY

Matthew J. Bruccoli and Richard Layman, *Editorial Directors*
C. E. Frazer Clark, Jr., *Managing Editor*

Manufactured by Edwards Brothers, Inc.
Ann Arbor, Michigan
Printed in the United States of America

Copyright © 1985
GALE RESEARCH COMPANY

Library of Congress Cataloging in Publication Data
Main entry under title:

American writers of the early republic.

(Dictionary of literary biography; v. 37)
"A Bruccoli Clark book."
Includes index.
1. American literature—1783-1850—History and criticism. 2. American literature—1783-1850—Bio-bibliography. 3. Authors, American—1783-1850—Biography—Dictionaries. 4. American literature—19th century—History and criticism. 5. Authors, American—19th century—Biography—Dictionaries. I. Elliott, Emory, 1942-   II. Series.
PS208.A44   1985   810'.9'002   84-25901
ISBN 0-8103-1715-X

*This volume is for a few of the scholars
who in recent years have
deepened our understanding and
appreciation of language and literature
in America in the early republic:*

Bernard Bailyn
William L. Hedges
Lewis Leary
Terence Martin
Russel B. Nye
Lewis P. Simpson

Contents

Contents

Plan of the Series

. . . Almost the most prodigious asset of a country, and perhaps its most precious possession, is its native literary product—when that product is fine and noble and enduring.

Mark Twain*

The advisory board, the editors, and the publisher of the *Dictionary of Literary Biography* are joined in endorsing Mark Twain's declaration. The literature of a nation provides an inexhaustible resource of permanent worth. It is our expectation that this endeavor will make literature and its creators better understood and more accessible to students and the literate public, while satisfying the standards of teachers and scholars.

To meet these requirements, *literary biography* has been construed in terms of the author's achievement. The most important thing about a writer is his writing. Accordingly, the entries in *DLB* are career biographies, tracing the development of the author's canon and the evolution of his reputation.

The publication plan for *DLB* resulted from two years of preparation. The project was proposed to Bruccoli Clark by Frederick G. Ruffner, president of the Gale Research Company, in November 1975. After specimen entries were prepared and typeset, an advisory board was formed to refine the entry format and develop the series rationale. In meetings held during 1976, the publisher, series editors, and advisory board approved the scheme for a comprehensive biographical dictionary of persons who contributed to North American literature. Editorial work on the first volume began in January 1977, and it was published in 1978.

In order to make *DLB* more than a reference tool and to compile volumes that individually have claim to status as literary history, it was decided to organize volumes by topic or period or genre. Each of these freestanding volumes provides a biographical-bibliographical guide and overview for a particular area of literature. We are convinced that this organization—as opposed to a single alphabet method—constitutes a valuable innovation in the presentation of reference material. The volume plan necessarily requires many decisions for the placement and treatment of authors who might

properly be included in two or three volumes. In some instances a major figure will be included in separate volumes, but with different entries emphasizing the aspect of his career appropriate to each volume. Ernest Hemingway, for example, is represented in *American Writers in Paris, 1920-1939* by an entry focusing on his expatriate apprenticeship; he is also in *American Novelists, 1910-1945* with an entry surveying his entire career. Each volume includes a cumulative index of subject authors. The final *DLB* volume will be a comprehensive index to the entire series.

With volume ten in 1982 it was decided to enlarge the scope of *DLB* beyond the literature of the United States. By the end of 1983 twelve volumes treating British literature had been published, and volumes for Commonwealth and Modern European literature were in progress. The series has been further augmented by the *DLB Yearbooks* (since 1981) which update published entries and add new entries to keep the *DLB* current with contemporary activity. There have also been occasional *DLB Documentary Series* volumes which provide biographical and critical background source materials for figures whose work is judged to have particular interest for students. One of these companion volumes is entirely devoted to Tennessee Williams.

The purpose of *DLB* is not only to provide reliable information in a convenient format but also to place the figures in the larger perspective of literary history and to offer appraisals of their accomplishments by qualified scholars.

We define literature as the *intellectual commerce of a nation*: not merely as belles lettres, but as that ample and complex process by which ideas are generated, shaped, and transmitted. *DLB* entries are not limited to "creative writers" but extend to other figures who in this time and in this way influenced the mind of a people. Thus the series encompasses historians, journalists, publishers, and screenwriters. By this means readers of *DLB* may be aided to perceive literature not as cult scripture in the keeping of cultural high priests, but as at the center of a nation's life.

DLB includes the major writers appropriate to each volume and those standing in the ranks immediately behind them. Scholarly and critical counsel has been sought in deciding which minor figures to include and how full their entries should be.

*From an unpublished section of Mark Twain's autobiography, copyright © by the Mark Twain Company.

Wherever possible, useful references will be made to figures who do not warrant separate entries.

Each *DLB* volume has a volume editor responsible for planning the volume, selecting the figures for inclusion, and assigning the entries. Volume editors are also responsible for preparing, where appropriate, appendices surveying the major periodicals and literary and intellectual movements for their volumes, as well as lists of further readings. Work on the series as a whole is coordinated at the Bruccoli Clark editorial center in Columbia, South Carolina, where the editorial staff is responsible for the accuracy of the published volumes.

One feature that distinguishes *DLB* is the illustration policy—its concern with the iconography of literature. Just as an author is influenced by his surroundings, so is the reader's understanding of the author enhanced by a knowledge of his environment. Therefore *DLB* volumes include not only drawings, paintings, and photographs of authors, often depicting them at various stages in their careers, but also illustrations of their families and places where they lived. Title pages are regularly reproduced in facsimile along with dust jackets for modern authors. The dust jackets are a special feature of *DLB* because they often document better than anything else the way in which an author's work was launched in its own time. Specimens of the writers' manuscripts are included when feasible.

A supplement to *DLB*—tentatively titled *A Guide, Chronology, and Glossary for American Literature*—will outline the history of literature in North America and trace the influences that shaped it. This volume will provide a framework for the study of American literature by means of chronological tables, literary affiliation charts, glossarial entries, and concise surveys of the major movements. It has been planned to stand on its own as a vade mecum, providing a ready-reference guide to the study of American literature as well as a companion to the *DLB* volumes for American literature.

Samuel Johnson rightly decreed that "The chief glory of every people arises from its authors." The purpose of the *Dictionary of Literary Biography* is to compile literary history in the surest way available to us—by accurate and comprehensive treatment of the lives and work of those who contributed to it.

The *DLB* Advisory Board

Foreword

The decades after the American Revolution have been much studied by historians, but only recently has this period begun to receive the attention that it deserves from literary scholars. Though earlier in this century the great literary historians Moses Coit Tyler and Vernon Louis Parrington each devoted a volume to the literature of the period, the writers of these times never really seem to have captured our imagination. Leon Howard's well-known essay "The Late Eighteenth Century: An Age of Contradictions" (1953) described both the complexity of this period and the problem it presents its critics, while his seminal book *The Connecticut Wits* (1943) identified a small group of writers as representative of the age. One unfortunate result of Howard's book, however, is that too often potential readers of the early-national literature have been convinced that witty poems such as Joel Barlow's *The Hasty-Pudding* (1796) or John Trumbull's *M'Fingal* (1776-1782) are characteristic of a body of work, neoclassical in nature, which many people think of as derivative, imitative, and not truly representative of American literature. While teachers of history have approached these decades as being the "critical period" of American history where the fundamental structures of politics and society took shape, teachers of literature have been inclined to touch briefly, if at all, on these years as they skip from Edward Taylor and Jonathan Edwards to Emerson and Hawthorne.

Fortunately, there have been in recent years a small number of scholar-critics who have questioned inherited assumptions and have participated in an exciting scholarly excavation which has revealed a rich and complex literary culture in the 1780s and 1790s. They have discovered a literary origin that was as crucial to the development of a distinctive American literature as the Bill of Rights and the Constitution were to the creation of our political system. To understand these writings and assess the achievement of the Republic's first men and women of letters, however, it is useful to separate the abundant and varied forms and texts into three categories. There are certainly many works that belong under more than one heading, such as Michel Guillaume Jean de Crevecoeur's *Letters From an American Farmer* (1782) and William Bartram's *Travels* (1791), which qualify as imaginative narratives as well as works of historical and scientific

discourse, but for introductory purposes classification is useful.

The first of these categories includes the writings that have received the most scholarly attention: the political and philosophical essays and documents, such as Thomas Paine's *Common Sense* (1776), Thomas Jefferson's *Notes on Virginia* (1785), the Declaration of Independence and the Constitution, and *The Federalist Papers* of Alexander Hamilton, John Jay, and James Madison, considered by many to be the finest writing of the period. Many students of the period who see the prose essay as its highest form of literary achievement celebrate the works of these writers and the political prose of men such as Philip Freneau and Joel Barlow as their best and most influential. In some ways the magnificence of these prose works has led to an undervaluing of other genres. The religious and oratorical writing of the decades and the studies of language by Noah Webster and Jedidiah Morse should also be included in this class of nonfiction prose. During the last twenty years, historians and literary scholars such as Bernard Bailyn, Edmund Morgan, Sacvan Bercovitch, and Gordon Wood have examined the verbal and ideological continuities that link the political writings of the Revolution and the early Republic to the pamphlets, sermon literature and religious tracts of the early and mid-eighteenth century. Attention to this literary foreground deepens our appreciation of the complex heritage of high and popular culture that gave the prose works of John Adams, Jefferson, and Paine their powerful appeal to a wide spectrum of readers.

Until very recently, the only rival to political discourse as the epitome of literary achievement in the critical decades was the poetry of those so-called Connecticut Wits and a handful of "pre-Romantic" poems by Philip Freneau, such as his well-known lyric "The Wild Honey Suckle." For the poets themselves the period after the Revolution was a time of both excitement and disappointment. In the Rising Glory of America poems (three of which are included in the appendix to this volume), these poets proclaimed the dawning of a new age in America, which would witness not only the glorious establishment of the most productive, successful political and economic system in the world, but would also create an environment in which the arts and letters would reach their highest form. In this spirit Joel

Barlow, Timothy Dwight, and others composed epic poems celebrating the founding of the new nation. By the mid-1790s, however, these writers had come to recognize that whatever benefits the new nation might bestow, increased support for the arts and letters was not to be one of them. A poem such as Barlow's bitter *Advice to a Raven in Russia* (written in 1812) stands in direct contrast to the hopefulness of his *The Prospect of Peace* (written and published in 1778) while the two poems together describe the arc of disillusionment that is also expressed in the oeuvre of Philip Freneau. As a result of this shift, the poetry and the imaginative prose essays of the period took on new dimensions of irony and ambiguity and acquired a questioning, somewhat bemused, comic tone—one that is recognizable in subsequent works of American literature.

Within the last decade, there has developed a new respect for the novels and other narrative forms of this age. While important studies of the works of Royall Tyler and William Dunlap have brought more attention to their plays, the major advances in criticism are occurring in the study of the early American novel. The reputations of Hugh Henry Brackenridge and especially Charles Brockden Brown have been furthered by numerous studies demonstrating the verbal, structural, and thematic complexities of their works and revealing them to be much more consciously artistic than earlier critics had assumed. As this effort to reassess the early novel has proceeded, the canon of American literature has expanded to include works and writers previously overlooked. Writers such as Susanna Rowson, Sarah Wentworth Morton, Hannah Webster Foster, and Olaudah Equiano are now being rediscovered, or sometimes read for the first time. As happened earlier when the critical perspective was broadened to admit the study of the sermon alongside the philosophical writings, now the slave narratives, Gothic novels, and sentimental romances of the period are being explicated with the same energy and attention once expended only on a few poems of Freneau and one or two of Brockden Brown's novels.

This lively reassessment of late-eighteenth century American literature has occurred only because we have had a few great teacher-scholars, such as Harry Hayden Clark, Leon Howard, Edwin Cady, James Woodress, Louis B. Wright, and others, who have inspired their students to dig more deeply and read more closely. Some of the scholars who have contributed to the revival of interest in early American literature are acknowledged on the dedication pages of this volume and the two *Dictionary of Literary Biography* volumes on colonial literature. By placing the name of a scholar at the head of one volume I do not mean to overlook an individual's contributions to the study of other periods as well. For example, Sacvan Bercovitch, Everett Emerson, and Kenneth Silverman have published major works on all areas of early American literature. Such people have kept the fires of American Revolutionary War literature burning even during long cold spells when it seemed that the shrinking space accorded it in anthologies and literary histories would at last extinguish the flames of America's early writers. It is certainly my hope that these three *DLB* volumes on colonial and early national writers will bring new attention and respect to our early literary heritage and encourage others to study it further.

—Emory Elliott

Acknowledgments

This book was produced by BC Research. Karen L. Rood, senior editor for the *Dictionary of Literary Biography* series, was the in-house editor.

Art supervisor is Claudia Ericson. Copyediting supervisor is Joycelyn R. Smith. Typesetting supervisor is Laura Ingram. The production staff includes Mary Betts, Rowena Betts, Kimberly Casey, Patricia Coate, Kathleen M. Flanagan, Joyce Fowler, Judith K. Ingle, Victoria Jakes, Vickie Lowers, Judith McCray, and Jane McPherson. Jean W. Ross is permissions editor. Joseph Caldwell, photography editor, did photographic copy work for the volume.

A project of this magnitude is necessarily the work of many hands, and for such a book to be also of consistent high quality requires the commitment of hearts and minds as well. Credit should go to the contributors who patiently and cheerfully endured too many impersonal form letters from me during our two years of work together. To each of you, a hearty thanks for your goodwill and fine work.

While we would not have this volume without the collective commitment of the contributors, the book certainly would never have seen print without the splendid individual performance of our editor at BC Research, Ms. Karen Rood. Ms. Rood's superb editing skills, her unwavering professionalism, and her genuine scholarly interest in the material were exemplary throughout; she is indeed a person of exceptional talents, and I have been most fortunate to be able to work with her.

Closer to home, I have been able again to count upon the assistance of the mainstay of the Princeton American Studies Program, Mrs. Helen Wright. Aiding me as she has American studies faculty since 1946, Helen helped to organize the complicated assignments for this volume of the *DLB*, and she typed and helped to mail those form letters. During the copyediting stage I received considerable assistance from my research assistant, Ms. Susan Mizruchi, who proved to be a remarkably capable editor as well as the most promising scholar I already knew her to be. Also assisting with final details and in searching for materials for reproduction in the volume has been another graduate student in the Princeton English department, Ms. Elizabeth Dant.

The skillful aid of the reference staff at the John Carter Brown Library at Brown University was essential in providing illustrations for this book. Director Norman Fiering, bibliographer Everett Wilkie, and reference librarian Susan L. Newbury have earned my gratitude.

Valuable assistance was also given by the staff at the Thomas Cooper Library of the University of South Carolina: Lynn Barron, Daniel Boice, Sue Collins, Michael Freeman, Gary Geer, Alexander M. Gilchrist, David L. Haggard, Jens Holley, David Lincove, Marcia Martin, Roger Mortimer, Jean Rhyne, Karen Rissling, Paula Swope, and Ellen Tillett.

Finally, I acknowledge the contribution of those closest to me whose understanding and support are essential to the completion of any project I assume: my children, Scott, Mark, Matthew, Constance, and Laura, and as ever, my wife, Georgia.

American Writers
of the Early Republic

Dictionary of Literary Biography

John Quincy Adams

(11 July 1767-23 February 1848)

Thomas P. Slaughter
Rutgers University

SELECTED BOOKS: *Observations on Paine's Rights of Man* [8 letters], as Publicola (Edinburgh: Printed & sold by J. Dickinson, 1792); enlarged as *An Answer to Pain's Rights of Man* [11 letters] (London: Printed for J. Stockdale, 1793);

An Oration, Pronounced July 4th, 1793, at the Request of the Inhabitants of the Town of Boston, in Commemoration of the Anniversary of American Independence (Boston: Printed by Benjamin Edes & Son, 1793);

An Address, to the Members of the Massachusetts Charitable Fire Society, at their Annual Meeting, May 28, 1802 (Boston: Printed by Russell & Cutler, 1802);

An Oration, Delivered at Plymouth, December 22, 1802. At the Anniversary Commemoration of the First Landing of Our Ancestors, at That Place (Boston: Printed by Russell & Cutler, 1802);

Letters on Silesia, Written During a Tour Through that Country in the Years 1800, 1801 (London: J. Budd, 1804);

An Inaugural Oration, Delivered at the Author's Installation, as Boylston's Professor of Rhetorick and Oratory, at Harvard University, in Cambridge, Massachusetts. On Thursday, 12 June, 1806 (Boston: Printed at the Anthology Office by Monroe & Francis, 1806);

A Letter to the Hon. Harrison Gray Otis, A Member of the Senate of Massachusetts, on the Present State of Our National Affairs; With Remarks upon Mr. Pickering's Letter to the Governor of the Commonwealth (Boston: Published. by Oliver & Munroe, 1808; London: Printed for J. Johnson, 1808);

John Quincy Adams, 1796; portrait by John Singleton Copley (The Museum of Fine Arts, Boston; bequest of Charles Francis Adams)

American Principles. A Review of Works of Fisher Ames . . . (Boston: Published by Everett & Munroe, 1809);

Lectures on Rhetoric and Oratory, Delivered to the Classes of Senior and Junior Sophisters in Harvard Uni-

versity, 2 volumes (Cambridge: Printed by Hilliard & Metcalf, 1810);

Report of the Secretary of State, upon Weights and Measures . . . (Washington, D.C.: Printed by Gales & Seaton, 1821);

An Address Delivered at the Request of a Committee of the Citizens of Washington: On the Occasion of Reading the Declaration of Independence, on the Fourth of July, 1821 (Washington, D.C.: Printed by Davis & Force, 1821; Cambridge: Printed at the University Press by Hilliard & Metcalf and sold by Cummings & Hilliard, 1821);

Answer to W. Sumner's Inquiry on the Importance of the Militia (Boston, 1823);

Letter of the Hon. John Quincy Adams, in Reply to a Letter of the Hon. Alexander Smyth, to His Constituents (Washington, D.C.?, 1823); republished in *Letter of the Hon. John Quincy Adams, in Reply to a Letter of the Hon. Alexander Smyth, to His Constituents. Also the Speech of Mr. Adams on the Louisiana Treaty, Delivered in the Senate of the United States, Nov. 3, 1803. And a Letter from Mr. Jefferson to Mr. Dunbar Relative to the Cession of Louisiana* (Washington, D.C.: Printed by Gales & Seaton, 1828);

Suggestions on Presidential Elections, with Particular Reference to a Letter by William C. Somerville, Esq. (Boston: Cummings, Hilliard, 1825);

Correspondence between John Quincy Adams, Esquire, President of the United States, and Several Citizens of Massachusetts Concerning the Charge of a Design to Dissolve the Union Alleged to Have Existed in That State (Boston: Press of the *Boston Daily Advertiser*, 1829);

An Oration Addressed to the Citizens of the Town of Quincy, on the Fourth of July, 1831, the Fifty-fifth Anniversary of the Independence of the United States of America (Boston: Richardson, Lord & Holbrook, 1831);

An Eulogy: On the Life and Character of James Monroe, fifth President of the United States. Delivered at the Request of the Corporation of the City of Boston, on the 25th of August, 1831 (Boston: Printed by J. H. Eastburn, 1831);

Dermot MacMorrogh, or The Conquest of Ireland; An Historical Tale of the Twelfth Century. In Four Cantos (Boston: Carter, Hendee, 1832);

Speech [suppressed by the previous question] of Mr. John Quincy Adams of Massachusetts, on the Removal of the Public Deposites, and Its Reasons (Washington, D.C.: Printed by Gales & Seaton, 1834);

Oration on the Life and Character of Gilbert Motier de Lafayette. Delivered at the Request of Both Houses of Congress of the United States, Before Them, in

the House of Representatives at Washington, on the 31st of December, 1834 (Washington, D.C.: Printed by D. Green, 1835);

Speech of the Hon. John Q. Adams, of Massachusetts, on His Resolution for the Appointment of a Select Committee to Inquire into the Causes of the Failure of the Fortification Bill at the Last Session of Congress. Delivered Jan. 22, 1836 (Washington, D.C.: Printed by Blair & Rives, 1836);

Speech of John Quincy Adams, on the Joint Resolution for Distributing Rations to the Distressed Fugitives from Indian Hostilities, in the States of Alabama and Georgia. Delivered in the House of Representatives, Wednesday, May 25, 1836 (Washington, D.C.: National Intelligencer Office, 1836);

An Eulogy on the Life and Character of James Madison, Fourth President of the United States, Delivered at the Request of the Mayor, Aldermen, and Common Council of the City of Boston, September 27, 1836 (Boston: American Stationers' Company, 1836; Boston: J. H. Eastburn, city printer, 1836);

Letters from John Adams to His Constituents of the Twelfth Congressional District in Massachusetts. To Which Is Added His Speech in Congress, Delivered February 9, 1837 (Boston: I. Knapp, 1837);

An Oration Delivered before the Inhabitants of the Town of Newburyport, at Their Request, on the Sixty-First Anniversary of the Declaration of Independence, July 4th, 1837 (Newburyport: Printed by Morss & Brewster, 1837);

Speech of John Quincy Adams, of Massachusetts, upon the Right of the People, Men and Women, to Petition; on the Freedom of Speech and of Debate in the House of Representatives of the United States; on the Resolutions of Seven State Legislatures, and the Petitions of More than One Hundred Thousand Petitioners, Relating to the Annexation of Texas to the Union . . . (Washington, D.C.: Printed by Gales & Seaton, 1838);

The Jubilee of the Constitution. A Discourse Delivered at the Request of the New York Historical Society, in the City of New York, on Tuesday, the 30th of April, 1839; Being the Fiftieth Anniversary of the Inauguration of George Washington as President of the United States, on Thursday, the 30th of April, 1789 (New York: S. Coleman, 1839);

A Letter from Ex-President John Quincy Adams to James Henry Hackett, with Hackett's Reply (London: Madeley, 1839); republished as *The Character of Hamlet, by Ex-President Adams and J.H. Hackett* (New York: J. Mowatt, 1844);

A Discourse on Education, Delivered at Braintree, Thurs-

day, Oct. 24, 1839 (Boston: Printed by Perkins & Marvin, 1840);

Argument of John Quincy Adams, Before the Supreme Court of the United States, Appellants, vs. Cinque, and Others, Africans, Captured in the Schooner Amistad, by Lieut. Gedney, Delivered on the 24th of February and 1st of March, 1841 . . . (New York: S. W. Benedict, 1841);

Speech of Mr. John Quincy Adams, on the Case of Alexander McLeod. Delivered in the House of Representatives, September 4, 1841 (Washington, D.C.: Printed by Gales & Seaton, 1841);

The Wants of Man: A Poem (Lowell, Mass.: Amos Upton, 1841);

Mr. Adams' Speech, on War With Great Britain and Mexico: With the Speeches of Messrs. Wise and Ingersoll, to Which It Is in Reply (Boston: Emancipator Office, 1841?);

Address of John Quincy Adams, to his Constituents of the Twelfth Congressional District at Braintree, September 17th, 1842 (Boston: Printed by J. H. Eastburn, 1842);

Address to the Norfolk County Temperance Society, 29 Sept., 1842 (Boston: K. & L. Gould, 1842);

The Social Compact, Exemplified in the Constitution of the Commonwealth of Massachusetts; With Remarks on the Theories of Divine Right of Hobbes and of Filmer, and the Counter Theories of Sidney, Locke, Montesquieu, and Rousseau, Concerning the Nature of Government: A Lecture, Delivered Before the Franklin Lyceum, at Providence, R.I., November 25, 1842 (Providence: Printed by Knowles & Vose, 1842);

The New England Confederacy of MDCXLIII. A Discourse Delivered before the Massachusetts Historical Society, at Boston, on the 29th of May, 1843; in Celebration of the Second Centennial Anniversary of that Event (Boston: Little & Brown, 1843);

An Oration Delivered before the Cincinnati Astronomical Society, on the Occasion of Laying the Corner Stone of an Astronomical Observatory, on the 10th of November, 1843 (Cincinnati: Printed by Shepard, 1843);

Liberty Incomplete . . . Letter from John Quincy Adams . . . Read on the Occasion of the Recent Celebration of West India Emancipation . . . (Boston: J. W. Alden, 1843);

Letters on the Masonic Institution (Boston: Press of T. R. Marvin, 1847);

Poems of Religion and Society (New York: Published by William H. Graham, 1848);

Memoirs of John Quincy Adams, comprising Portions of his Diary from 1795 to 1848, 12 volumes, edited by Charles Francis Adams (Philadelphia: Lippincott, 1874-1877);

Life in a New England Town: 1787, 1788. Diary of John Quincy Adams, While a Student in the Office of Theophilus Parsons at Newburyport, edited by Charles Francis Adams (Boston: Little, Brown, 1903);

Parties in the United States (New York: Greenberg, 1941).

Collections: *Writings of John Quincy Adams,* 7 volumes, edited by Worthington Chauncey Ford (New York: Macmillan, 1913-1917);

The Adams Papers, 26 volumes to date (Cambridge: Harvard University Press, 1961-).

OTHER: *The Duplicate Letters, the Fisheries and the Mississippi, Documents Relating to Transactions at the Negotiation of Ghent,* compiled by Adams (Washington, D.C.: Printed by Davis & Force, 1822);

Henry Adams, ed., *Documents Relating to New-England Federalism. 1800-1815,* includes material by John Quincy Adams (Boston: Little, Brown, 1855).

John Quincy Adams was a United States senator, secretary of state, president, and member of Congress. The eldest son of John and Abigail Smith Adams, he was born in Braintree, Massachusetts. In 1778 he accompanied his father to France, where he studied French and Latin at an academy in Passy, and attended the Latin School of Amsterdam. He matriculated at Leyden University in January 1781, but soon interrupted his studies to serve in Saint Petersburg as secretary to America's minister to Russia. Returning to the Hague in 1783, he resumed the study of classics before returning to the United States, where he entered Harvard as a junior. In 1787, Adams graduated from Harvard and began his legal apprenticeship in Newburyport. He was admitted to the Massachusetts bar in 1790.

In 1779 young Adams began a diary that he continued to keep throughout most of his life. *Memoirs of John Quincy Adams, comprising Portions of his Diary from 1795 to 1848* was published in twelve volumes from 1874 to 1877, and was followed in 1903 by *Life in a New England Town,* his diary for the years 1787-1788. Taken as a whole, the diary is an extraordinary record of places and events experienced during an exceptional life. Adams's first publication, an erudite reply to Paine's *Rights of Man* (1791), which first appeared in the *Columbian Centinel* for June-July 1791 and later as a pamphlet in

Edinburgh (1792) and London (1793), caused a stir at the time partly because the anonymous tract was attributed to the senior Adams. During the 1790s, John Quincy Adams contributed to and translated for a French language newspaper in Boston and wrote a series of political essays under the pseudonyms Publicola, Marcellus, Columbus, and Bosneveld, on the subjects of the French Revolution, the controversy surrounding Charles Genêt's arrival in America as French ambassador in 1793, and the wisdom of American neutrality in European affairs. These literary efforts attracted the favorable attention of President Washington and in 1794 won their author a commission as minister to the Netherlands. On 26 July 1797, while on a diplomatic mission to England, Adams married Louisa Catherine, daughter of Joshua Johnson of Maryland.

In 1803 Adams was elected to the U. S. Senate, where he served less than one full term, until June 1808. His support for President Jefferson's positions on British aggression against neutrals, the *Chesapeake* affair, and the Embargo of 1807 earned him the enmity of fellow Massachusetts Senator Timothy Pickering and other New England Feder-

Louisa Catherine Adams, circa 1824; portrait by Charles Bird King (The Smithsonian Institution, National Collection of Fine Arts)

alists. Pickering was able to bring about the premature election of a new Massachusetts senator, thus forcing Adams to resign from the Senate. He retired temporarily to devote his full time to the chair of rhetoric and oratory at Harvard that he had held since 1803. President Madison appointed him ambassador to Russia in 1809, and from Saint Petersburg in 1811 Adams declined an already confirmed appointment to the U. S. Supreme Court. Beginning in 1814 he served as one of the ambassadors to negotiate an end to the War of 1812 with Great Britain, and he served as Ambassador to the Court of Saint James's until 1817, when he became Madison's secretary of state. In that office he was responsible for conceiving the foreign policy stance that became known as the Monroe Doctrine. In 1824 Adams won a close race for President, one decided in the House of Representatives, and he served a single term before being defeated for reelection by Andrew Jackson.

In some ways, the most distinguished facet of Adams's long career came after his defeat in the 1828 presidential election. On 31 March 1831 he was elected to Congress and served there for eight consecutive terms, eventually dying at his desk. During that time he was an independent voice for such causes as the abolition of slavery and the restraint of imperialistic ambitions in Texas. Some of his most stirring writings came as explanations of his moral stands to his constituents. Among these, the *Address of John Quincy Adams, to his Constituents of the Twelfth Congressional District* (1842) is the most memorable for its explanation of his antislavery principles and its vindication of his twelve years in Congress. Adams's writings have both historical and autobiographical value. Dwelling on links between the classic past and his own times, he also used his experiences and access to public men and public documents fully. His extraordinary memory and erudition make for sometimes dry, but always instructive, reading.

Adams's diary or journal, which he kept assiduously until a few years before his death, is a remarkable contribution to the record of his times, unmatched for its period in breadth and length. The twelve volumes published as *Memoirs of John Quincy Adams* were intended and survive as a monument to the good intentions and noble ideas of a man who, in a moment of deep anguish, contended that in his long life he could remember almost no example of success in any of his major endeavors. Adams sought to leave his son and successive generations a record that would gain him the admiration he felt wanting during his life.

The beginning of Adams's diary, in which he describes setting out with his father on their second journey to France, and diary entries for 16-17 July 1785, in which he describes his return to America to attend Harvard (Massachusetts Historical Society)

John Quincy Adams, 1843; daguerreotype by Philip Haas (The Metropolitan Museum of Art, New York; gift of I. N. P. Stokes and the Hawes family)

Adams's literary productions beyond his diary were prodigious: state papers, speeches, writings on political philosophy, history, autobiography, and polemical tracts are bewildering in number. He even wrote and published poetry, including an epic poem entitled *Dermot MacMorrogh* (1832), perhaps unfortunately for those who have read it and for Adams's literary reputation. It is the *Memoirs of John Quincy Adams,* however, that remains of enduring value for its revelations of the erudition and wisdom of a wise and well-educated man. It documents the experiences of a statesman who participated in the great events and decisions of Europe and America for over sixty years. The literary quality of his writing is high, even by the standards of a family that produced so many great men and women of letters as his.

Biographies:
Josiah Quincy, *Memoir of the Life of John Quincy*

Adams (Boston: Phillips, Sampson, 1858);
James Truslow Adams, *The Adams Family* (Boston: Little, Brown, 1930).

References:
Samuel Flagg Bemis, *John Quincy Adams and the Foundations of American Foreign Policy* (New York: Knopf, 1949);
Bemis, *John Quincy Adams and the Union* (New York: Knopf, 1956);
Kenneth V. Jones, ed., *John Quincy Adams, 1767-1848: Chronology, Documents, Bibliographical Aids* (Dobbs Ferry, N.Y.: Oceana Publications, 1970);
George A. Lipsky, *John Quincy Adams: His Theory and Ideas* (New York: Crowell, 1950).

Papers:
The main collection of the Adams family papers is at the Massachusetts Historical Society.

Richard Alsop

(23 January 1761-20 August 1815)

Carla Mulford
Villanova University

BOOKS: *The Political Green-house, for the Year 1798 . . .*, by Alsop, Lemuel Hopkins, and Theodore Dwight (Hartford: Printed by Hudson & Goodwin, 1799);

A Poem, Sacred to the Memory of George Washington . . . (Hartford: Printed by Hudson & Goodwin, 1800);

The Echo, with Other Poems, by Alsop, Dwight, Mason F. Cogswell, Hopkins, and Elihu Hubbard Smith (New York: Printed at Porcupine Press by Pasquin Petronius [Isaac Riley], 1807);

The Charms of Fancy, A Poem in Four Cantos, edited by Theodore Dwight (New York: Appleton, 1856).

OTHER: John Rodgers Jewitt, *A Narrative of the Adventures and Sufferings of John R. Jewitt: Only Survivor of the Crew of the Ship Boston, during a Captivity of Nearly Three Years Among the Savages of Nootka Sound . . .*, ghostwritten by Alsop (Middletown: Printed by S. Richards, 1815; London: Printed by Rowland Hurst & published by Longman, Hurst, Rees, Orme & Brown, 1816).

TRANSLATIONS: *The Enchanted Lake of the Fairy Morgana. From the Orlando Inamorato of Francesco Berni* (New York: I. Riley, 1806);

The Lovers of La Vendee, or Revolutionary Tyranny. From the French of M. Gosse, 2 volumes (Middletown, Conn.: Printed for I. Riley, 1808);

The Geographical, Natural, and Civil History of Chile by Abbe Don J. Ignatius Molina, 2 volumes (Middletown, Conn.: I. Riley, 1808).

Richard Alsop, miniature by James Sharples

Richard Alsop, poet, satirist, gentleman-financier, was one among a group of writers commonly called the Connecticut or Hartford Wits, a group which also included Joel Barlow, Timothy Dwight, David Humphreys, John Trumbull, Mason Fitch Cogswell, Theodore Dwight, Dr. Lemuel Hopkins, and Elihu Hubbard Smith. Prominent during the last quarter of the eighteenth century, the Connecticut Wits were able, prolific writers who generally sought to glorify America, to defend federal principles of government, and to educate their readers, especially in matters of taste and morality. Although they only occasionally approached the skill of their English models in poetry (such as Pope, Swift, Gray, Churchill, Akenside) and prose (such as Addison and Steele), the group as a whole captured the interests and voiced the ideals and ambitions of their contemporaries. Considered by some readers the most gifted of the wits, Alsop probably had no part in the group's mock-heroic collaboration, *The Anarchiad* (twelve numbers printed sporadically in the weekly *New-Haven Gazette, and the Connecticut Magazine* from 26

October 1786 to 13 September 1787). Alsop was the guiding force, however, in the more distinctive series, *The Echo* (1791-1798). Indeed, Alsop's friend Elihu Hubbard Smith characterized Alsop as the moon shining among lesser lights.

The oldest child of Richard and Mary Wright Alsop, Richard Alsop was born 23 January 1761 in Middletown, Connecticut, where his father prospered as a merchant. Privately tutored and later sent to school in Norwich, Connecticut, he early evidenced literary ability and mastered, in addition to Greek and Latin, the Italian, French, Spanish, and Scandinavian languages. His ready imagination found apt material in modern and classical literature, and, according to one of his four sisters, Alsop as a boy delighted in impersonating favorite heroes from the *Iliad*. He was both genial and curious by nature, and he actively studied natural history, ornithology, and taxidermy. After his father's death in 1777, Alsop studied mathematics for a time with a tutor at Yale but never regularly attended Yale or any other college.

Probably in 1777 Alsop met and began associating with Theodore Dwight and the other young

men who came to be called the Connecticut Wits. While he and his friends imitated the English-wit ideal of a half-century before, Alsop sought also to encourage the newer Gothic spirit by introducing the primitive and exotic in his work. His earliest datable piece (a 1777 manuscript) shows this interest: it is a versification of part of a Saxon poem published in a 1771 issue of the *Ladies Magazine*. And *The Charms of Fancy* (1856), which Alsop had written in large part by his mid-twenties, perhaps too amply demonstrates his admiration for mid-and late-eighteenth-century English writers. His most ambitious poem, *The Charms of Fancy* is a philosophical work in four cantos echoing Mark Akenside's *Pleasures of the Imagination* but demonstrating also Alsop's wide reading in English poetry and prose. Alsop completed it by 1788, probably as he was working on other pieces similarly dealing with remote and exotic lands and lore. In 1793 Elihu Hubbard Smith published in his anthology, *American Poems, Selected and Original*, part of Alsop's unfinished epic of Scandinavian mythology, *The Conquest of Scandinavia*, a versification of the fifth book of *Temora* (1763; written by James Macpherson but attributed by him to the legendary Gaelic warrior-bard Ossian), and a piece of "Runic poetry, *Twilight of the Gods, or the Destruction in the World*, from the 'Edda,' a System of Ancient Scandinavian Mythology." While working on these ambitious projects reflecting his interest in mid- and late-eighteenth-century English modes, Alsop participated in—and most likely guided—the group's more sustained, satiric effort, *The Echo*.

Begun, according to the 1807 edition's preface, during "a moment of literary sportiveness" when its writers decided "to lend their aid to check the progress of false taste in American literature," *The Echo* series, twenty numbers altogether, proceeded from satire of literary "pedantry, affection, and bombast" to satire of individuals—such as the elderly Samuel Adams, Judge Hugh Henry Brackenridge, Massachusetts Governor John Hancock, and the federalists' primary opponent, Thomas Jefferson—and of the French Revolution and American republicans (called Jacobins or Democrats or Republicans interchangeably) in general. Most of *The Echo*'s twenty numbers appeared in Hartford's the *American Mercury* between 8 August 1791 and 20 August 1798. (Numbers thirteen and twenty were published in 1793 and 1798 as broadsides; number nineteen, in Hartford's *Connecticut Courant*.) Although individual numbers of *The Echo* were unsigned, evidence exists that Alsop had a hand in at least two numbers and probably in nearly every

THE

CHARMS OF FANCY:

A Poem,

IN FOUR CANTOS,

WITH NOTES.

BY RICHARD ALSOP.

EDITED FROM THE ORIGINAL MANUSCRIPTS, WITH A BIOGRAPHICAL
SKETCH OF THE AUTHOR,

BY THEODORE DWIGHT.

NEW YORK:
D. APPLETON AND COMPANY,
346 & 348 BROADWAY.
M.DCCC.LVI.

Title page for Alsop's poem about the "visionary Pow'r, whose magic art / With boundless influence rules the feeling heart"

number. In the first number of *The Echo* (8 August 1791) Alsop and Theodore Dwight mocked the grandiose description of a local thunderstorm that had appeared in a July 1791 issue of a Boston paper. With Elihu Hubbard Smith and Dr. Mason F. Cogswell, he also wrote number ten (21 January 1793), which satirically "echoes" a letter in the *Virginia Gazette* (6 December 1792) protesting the name *Jacobin* as it was being applied to the Virginia electors who voted for George Clinton for the vice-presidency in 1792. In addition to mocking the complaint, the authors denounce the French Revolution and Jefferson and Hancock. Its conservative slant guaranteed *The Echo*'s popularity in conservative Connecticut and induced Alsop to collect eighteen of its numbers (omitting numbers two and three) and have his brother-in-law Isaac Riley publish them with ten other poems as *The Echo, with Other Poems* (1807).

Among the other poems in this volume was *The Political Green-house, for the Year 1798*, by Alsop, Lemuel Hopkins, and Theodore Dwight. Originally published as a twenty-four-page pamphlet in 1799, this political satire patterned after the New-Year's verses of the day denounces Jefferson and "Jacobin" republicans, lampoons Joel Barlow (whose republican principles dismayed his former friends) and post-Revolutionary France, and praises Vermont's purging of republicans. So stringent was its position, in fact, that it was read in Congress in January 1799 to demonstrate Connecticut's wish for war with France. Alsop's correspondence during this time, however, reveals a man more temperate than this satire implies, a man genuinely troubled about the contemporary political situation in America. Alsop's popularity and literary eminence earned him an honorary Master of Arts degree from Yale in 1798.

Having spent most of his life primarily in and around Middletown, Connecticut, Alsop decided to travel in 1800 and went not only to New York and Philadelphia but to the West Indies. His younger brother had taken control of the family business, and Alsop evidently sought something that would provide him a definite occupation and income. His bookish inclination finally found satisfaction in the book trade, for by 1801 he had joined his brother-in-law Isaac Riley as a bookseller in New York. From 1801 until his death, Alsop published and sold books in New York and Middletown and was a popular member of literary clubs in both towns.

After the publication of his rather uninspired *A Poem, Sacred to the Memory of George Washington . . .* (1800), Alsop seems to have spent much of his time

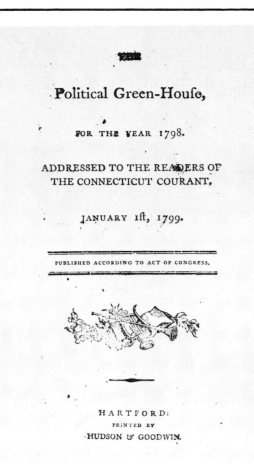

Title page for the anti-Jeffersonian satire that Alsop wrote with Lemuel Hopkins and Theodore Dwight (courtesy of the John Carter Brown Library at Brown University)

translating a variety of works. In 1806, Isaac Riley published *The Enchanted Lake of the Fairy Morgana*, Alsop's translation of part of the *Orlando Inamorato* of Francesco Berni, after the work of the medieval poet Matteo Maria Boiardo. Alsop evidently admired Berni's burlesque style and appreciated his twisting of romance conventions in the "enchanted lake" section, in which the hero, after a succession of adventures, fails to capture the elusive fairy of the lake. Alsop's translation of Berni shows his appreciation of belletristic works; his intent in translating Étienne Gosse's *The Lovers of La Vendee, or Revolutionary Tyranny* (1808), however, was openly political. This French novel in four volumes develops the story of Emily Dorman, her father, and her lover Darcourt as it presents the horrors of the civil war between the peasants of Vendee, France, and the republicans. Concerned about the American republicans' power as Jefferson's second term neared its end, Alsop found Gosse's book "exhibits but too true a picture of the state of La Vendee and the sufferings of the unfortunate inhabitants, during the civil war provoked by the cruelties of the Revolutionary Government." Alsop turned from politics to natural history as he translated Abbé Don Juan Ignatius Molina's two-volume *The Geographical, Natural, and Civil History of Chile* (1808). Alsop's translations during the first decade of the new century thus indicate his varied intellectual interests.

The last important work Alsop wrote was *A Narrative of the Adventures and Sufferings of John R. Jewitt* (1815). An Englishman by birth, Jewitt had been taken captive by Indians at age nineteen and had lived twenty-eight months in 1803-1805 with the natives of Nootka Sound in Vancouver. After his rescue, he came to America and published his diary in 1807 as *A Journal, Kept at Nootka Sound*. In 1813, Jewitt moved to Middletown, met Alsop, and recounted his story for him. Fascinated, Alsop developed and embellished the narrative, creating a tale that captures the characters of the captain and some crewmen from the ship *Boston* and details the habits of the Indians and the character of their leader, Maquina. Alsop's reworked version of Jewitt's journal, with the new title *A Narrative of the Adventures and Sufferings of John R. Jewitt*, was published under Jewitt's name in 1815. That Alsop rather than Jewitt wrote this narrative was a fact not generally known, it seems, until 1860, when Alsop's nephew, Theodore Dwight, answered a query about Jewitt in the *Historical Magazine*, attesting that Alsop had written it. Further evidence of Alsop's authorship was found by his biographer, Karl P. Harrington, who examined Alsop's personal copy of the 1815 edition, which evidently has numerous markings and marginalia, presumably in Alsop's hand, indicating planned corrections, insertions, and additions. But a corrected and enlarged edition never appeared. Alsop's sudden death while visiting relatives in Flatbush, Long Island, prevented his completing the task.

Despite the overwhelming popularity of Alsop's narrative of Jewitt's captivity (it went through about twenty editions), Alsop is probably best remembered for his work with the Connecticut Wits on *The Echo*. Perhaps because of his federalist stance, Alsop has had other pieces attributed to him. Both *Aristocracy: An Epic Poem* (1795) and a somber prose political pamphlet defending the federalists, *An Address to the Freemen of Connecticut* (1803), have been associated with Alsop. No conclusive evidence exists that either work is Alsop's, however, and the tone of the second seems especially uncharacteristic of the genially satiric tone Alsop used in *The Echo* and *The Political Green-house*.

That Alsop is not often read today simply reflects his works' reliance upon the dominating ideas and literary modes of his time. The volume of his writing and its popularity while he lived attest to his ambition and success as the new nation was forming.

Biography:

Karl P. Harrington, *Richard Alsop: A Hartford Wit* (1939; reprinted, Middletown, Conn.: Wesleyan University Press, 1969).

References:

Theodore Dwight, Introduction to *The Charms of Fancy, A Poem in Four Cantos* (New York: Appleton, 1856);

Benjamin Franklin V, Introduction to *The Poetry of the Minor Connecticut Wits* (Gainesville, Fla.: Scholars' Facsimiles and Reprints, 1970);

Franklin, Introduction to *The Prose of the Minor Connecticut Wits*, 3 volumes (Delmar, N.Y.: Scholars' Facsimiles and Reprints, 1974).

Papers:

The largest holdings of Alsop manuscripts, letters, and documents are at Yale, the Connecticut Historical Society, the New-York Historical Society, and the New York Public Library.

Fisher Ames
(9 April 1758-4 July 1808)

Thomas P. Slaughter
Rutgers University

BOOKS: *The Speech of Mr. Ames, in the House of Representatives of the United States, When the Committee of the Whole, on Thursday, April 28, 1796, in Support of the Following Motion: Resolved, That It Is Expedient to Pass the Laws Necessary to Carry into Effect the Treaty Lately Concluded Between the United States and the King of Great-Britain* (Philadelphia: Printed by J. Fenno, 1796);

An Oration on the Sublime Virtues of General George Washington . . . (Boston: Printed for Young & Mims and for Manning & Loring, 1800; London, 1800);

Works of Fisher Ames (Boston: T. B. Wait, 1809); enlarged edition, edited by Seth Ames (Boston: Little, Brown, 1854);

Speeches of Fisher Ames in Congress, edited by Pelham Ames (Boston: Little, Brown, 1871).

Fisher Ames, statesman and author of political tracts, achieved minor literary celebrity because of a series of political essays written between 1787 and his death. The Jeremiah of conservative American politics during the twenty years following 1787, Ames was an articulate spokesman for the most conservative faction of Federalist politicians. He displayed classically inspired oratorical and writing skills in essays memorable as well for their political content.

Fisher Ames was the third of five children born to Deborah Fisher Ames and Nathaniel Ames, astronomer, innkeeper, and physician. His ancestors included William Ames, a Shropshire yeoman who immigrated to Plymouth Colony in 1626, and Captain David Fisher, who personally arrested Governor Edmund Andros during the Glorious Revolution of 1689. According to family tradition, Fisher showed early scholarly promise, and his widowed mother, who ran the family tavern, sacrificed much to enroll him, at the age of twelve, in the Harvard College class of 1774. At Harvard, Ames became a fine scholar and accomplished debater. From 1774 to 1779 he lived at home and taught in local schools. In 1779 he began the study of law as an apprentice in a Boston office and was admitted to the bar in

Stanford University Libraries

Fisher Ames

1781. On 15 July 1792 he married Frances Worthington of Springfield, Massachusetts.

Ames first achieved popular fame for the rabid essays published under the pseudonym Camillus in the *Boston Independent Chronicle* (March 1787), in which he denounced participants in Shays's Rebellion for promoting social disintegration, as he had done even more harshly during the previous year under the pseudonym Lucius Junius Brutus. "Anarchy and government are both before us," he wrote in the Camillus essays, "and in our

Fisher Ames (Independence National Historical Park Collection, Philadelphia)

choice. If we fall, we fall by our folly, not our fate." On the strength of his political jeremiads, Ames was elected first to the state ratifying convention for the national constitution and then to Congress, in an election where he defeated Samuel Adams by a vote of 818 to 521. Reelected by successively greater margins to the second, third, and fourth Congresses (1791-1797), he was an arch Federalist, more vituperatively anti-Republican than any national political of his day. Ames's intolerance for less educated, less wealthy, and less cosmopolitan Americans rang through the halls of Congress, the pages of New England newspapers, and his private correspondence as clarion calls to the defense of public order and maintenance of the status quo. He lived in fear that "our government will be, in fact, a mere democracy, which has never been tolerable, nor long tolerated."

Ames was denounced by his Jeffersonian foes as one of the "paper men" who were self-interested in the Hamiltonian funding system and corrupt for the connection between their financial interests and political views. During 1794 Ames, along with Benedict Arnold and the devil, was burned in effigy in Charleston, South Carolina. His rhetorical ardor had earned the New England Congressman a place in the front rank of liberty's enemies in the eyes of many southern and western Americans.

Several of Ames's speeches before Congress were published and received wide circulation. His speech in defense of Jay's Treaty, delivered in Congress on 28 April 1796 and published in the same year, was later reputed to stand among the greatest oratorical displays given before that body for decades to come. Men well educated in the classics declared it a model of the ancient type.

Ames retired from active political life in 1796, a victim of poor health brought on by what contemporary physicians diagnosed as marasmus or atrophy. The election of Thomas Jefferson in 1800 inspired a renewed fervor in Ames and rekindled his fears of a French-style revolution in America. In "The Dangers of American Liberty" (1805), Ames lamented that "it is the almost universal mistake of our countrymen, that democracy would be mild and safe in America." According to Ames, "the most ferocious of animals when his passions are aroused to fury and uncontrolled, is man; and of all governments, the worst is that which fails to restrain those passions, that is, democracy. It is an illuminated hell." His approximately thirty other essays are, in their political content, generally embroideries on the same themes. Ames feared the rabble, denounced democracy, favored the peaceful rule of the educated and wellborn, and denounced Jeffersonian politicians with every breath until his last at the age of fifty years.

Biography:
Winfred E. Bernhard, *Fisher Ames, Federalist and Statesman, 1758-1808* (Chapel Hill: University of North Carolina Press, 1965).

Papers:
Ames's papers are at the Dedham Historical Society in Dedham, Massachusetts.

James Nelson Barker

(17 June 1784-9 March 1858)

David Robinson
Oregon State University

BOOKS: *The Indian Princess; Or, La Belle Sauvage. An Operatic Melo-drame. In Three Acts* . . . (Philadelphia: Printed by T. & G. Palmer for G. E. Blake, 1808);

Tears and Smiles. A Comedy. In Five Acts . . . (Philadelphia: Printed by T. & G. Palmer for G. E. Blake, 1808);

Marmion; Or, The Battle of Flodden Field. A Drama, In Five Acts . . . (New York: Published by D. Longworth, 1816);

How to Try a Lover. A Comedy. In Three Acts . . . (New York: Published by David Longworth, 1817);

An Oration, Delivered at Philadelphia, Vauxhall Gardens, on the Forty-First Anniversary of American Independence . . . (Philadelphia: Printed by John Binns, 1817);

The Tragedy of Superstition . . . (Philadelphia: Published by A. R. Poole, 1826).

James Nelson Barker, an important early American playwright, was also a prominent political figure in Philadelphia, serving as a mayor of that city and later as comptroller of the U.S. Treasury. His father, John Barker, was influential in Philadelphia politics, also serving as mayor of the city. It is evident that his son felt conflicting desires to have a literary and a political career and that the political duties that he began to assume in his middle thirties finally took precedence over his writing. John W. Crowley has specified the year 1817 as a turning point for Barker. This was the year in which he joined the Board of Aldermen in Philadelphia and thus expressed his recognition that the call to public service and a political career outweighed his desire for a career as an author. As Crowley noted, "Ironically, only in the role that he repudiated (that of author) is he at all remembered now."

Of the five extant plays of Barker, the first two, *Tears and Smiles* (produced in 1807) and *The Indian Princess* (produced in 1808), are notable for the elements of uniquely American materials which they contain. As Arthur Hobson Quinn noted, Barker's choice of American material was neither "accidental" nor "parochial." He was fully committed to a national drama as part of the process of America's cultural fulfillment and felt that a truly national drama had to make use of uniquely American materials. Much of Barker's early career as a playwright involved this nationalistic urge to free America from what he considered its bondage to English cultural domination. *Tears and Smiles*, a comedy of manners in the style of Royall Tyler's *The Contrast* (1787), includes the American rustic Nathan Yank, an important character type in early American drama. As Barker recounted to William Dunlap, he wrote the part at the request of an actor, and he confessed, "The truth is, I had never even seen a yankee at the time." *The Indian Princess* is the first dramatization of Captain John Smith's story of Pocahontas and one of the earliest American plays centering on a native American character. It was rendered, as Barker said, with "as close an adherence to historic truth . . . as dramatic rules would allow of." Pocahontas's dramatic salvation of Captain Smith begins act two of the play, when at the signal for his execution she "presses Smith's head to her bosom" and exclaims, "White man, thou shalt not die; or I will die with thee!"

Barker's use of American characters and materials typifies his outlook as a nationalist in art. He called for the development of an authentic national theater, hoping that "with a free people and under the liberal care of a government such as ours it might tend to keep alive the spirit of freedom." Something of the dilemma of the American playwright can be sensed from the production of Barker's *Marmion* in 1812. The play was adapted from Walter Scott's poem, and the condemnation of England by King James of Scotland in the play was, as Arthur Hobson Quinn noted, a clear reference to strained English-American relations on the eve of the War of 1812:

My lord, my lord, under such injuries,
How shall a free and gallant nation act?
Still lay its sovereignty at England's feet—
Still basely ask a boon from England's bounty—
Still vainly hope redress from England's justice?

Clear as the nationalistic implications were, Bark-

E. BRONSON,

EDITOR OF THE UNITED STATES GAZETTE,

Having departed from the character of a gentleman, in directing an insidious personality in his Gazette of the 7th inst.; and being waited upon for the satisfaction *never refused by gentlemen,* he has proved himself a

COWARD AND POLTROON:

and is thus publicly stigmatized as such to the world.

JAMES N. BARKER.

Oct. 10th, 1809.

Barker had this broadside printed after Enos Bronson accused Barker's father, who was running for mayor of Philadelphia, of "swearing—cursing—employing language, at which a Hottentot would blush, a Christian tremble" during his campaign speeches.

er's authorship was at first kept secret, even from the actors, because as Quinn surmises, the producers were afraid his identity as an American would hurt its draw.

In 1812 Barker's nationalism found another outlet when he entered military service during the War of 1812. He resigned in 1817 and entered a political career which would absorb most of his energies during the rest of his life. After serving as an alderman, he was elected mayor in 1819 and served until the next election in 1821, when he failed to be reelected and resumed his post as alderman. An ardent Democrat and a supporter of Jackson and Van Buren, his support of the national Democratic party eventually took him beyond his Philadelphia politics to national political appointments. In 1838 he was appointed Comptroller of the Treasury by President Van Buren, and though he lost his appointment in 1841, he continued to serve in the Treasury Department until his death in 1858.

The War of 1812 did not completely end his literary career. In 1817, Barker published *How to Try a Lover,* which he called "the only drama I have written with which I was satisfied." A romantic comedy set in Spain, it details the plot of two Spanish counts, Almeyda and Arandez, to deceive their respective son and daughter. The young people, Eugenia and Carlos, are already intended for each other in an arranged marriage, but their fathers try to induce them into falling in love with each other before they learn each other's true identity. The trick is discovered by Eugenia, who makes her father fear it will backfire in a humorous "court of love" scene which ends the play. As judge in the court of love, Eugenia has the power to condemn a man for violating the code of chivalry and thus strip him of his knighthood. In a court scene with much

MARMION;

OR, THE

BATTLE OF FLODDEN FIELD.

A DRAMA,

IN FIVE ACTS.

Performed at the theatres Philadelphia and New-York.

BY J. N. BARKER.

First acted April, 1812.

NEW-YORK :

PUBLISHED BY D. LONGWORTH,
At the Dramatic Repository,
Shakspeare-Gallery.

April 1816.

Title page for Barker's nationalistic adaptation of Walter Scott's poem (courtesy of the Harris Collection of American Poetry and Plays at Brown University)

the English King Charles I, one of whom, after his escape to New England, led the colonists in a battle with hostile Indians. The play attacks religious fanaticism, and that theme is best exemplified by the play's most memorable character, Ravensworth, who has been compared to Hawthorne's Chillingworth in *The Scarlet Letter* (1850). His unyielding thirst for a false justice, arising from his religious fanaticism, eventually leads to the death of his daughter as the play ends. Because of its source, which Cooper and Hawthorne later used, and its criticism of the New England past, the play remains of interest. Barker's talents for humor, however, seemed to surpass those for tragedy. Even considering his accomplishments, one feels that Barker could have secured a much larger place in literary history had not politics become the focus of his career.

Biography:

Paul H. Musser, *James Nelson Barker, 1784-1858* (Philadelphia: University of Pennsylvania Press, 1929).

References:

John W. Crowley, "James Nelson Barker in Perspective," *Educational Theatre Journal*, 24 (December 1972): 363-369;

William Dunlap, *A History of the American Theatre* (New York: Harper, 1832),II: 307-316;

Walter J. Meserve, *An Emerging Entertainment: The Drama of the American People to 1828* (Bloomington: Indiana University Press, 1977), pp. 177-184, 259-263;

Montrose J. Moses, Introduction to *The Indian Princess*, in *Representative Plays by American Dramatists, volume 1, 1765-1819*, edited by Moses (New York: E. P. Dutton, 1918), pp. 565-571;

Arthur Hobson Quinn, *A History of the American Drama: From the Beginning to the Civil War*, revised edition (New York: Crofts, 1936), pp. 136-162;

Quinn, Introduction to *Superstition*, in *Representative American Plays*, edited by Quinn (New York: Century, 1917), pp. 109-112.

pomp and medieval pageantry, Eugenia pretends that she will condemn Carlos, to the horror of their respective fathers. And indeed she does condemn him—to marry her. Thus the play comically avoids a disastrous ending, but not before dispensing a fair amount of comic justice to the meddlesome fathers. The play demonstrates well Barker's facility for comic plotting and characterization.

Barker is perhaps best known for his final play, *Superstition* (produced in 1824). Set in seventeenth-century New England, the play makes use of the story in Thomas Hutchinson's *History of Massachusetts Bay* (1764, 1767, 1828) of the regicides of

Joel Barlow

Cecelia Tichi
Boston University

BIRTH: Redding, Connecticut, 24 March 1754, to Samuel and Esther Hull Barlow.

EDUCATION: Dartmouth College, 1773; B.A., M.A., Yale College, 1778, 1781.

MARRIAGE: 26 January 1781, to Ruth Baldwin.

DEATH: Zarnowiec, Poland, 24 December 1812.

BOOKS: *The Prospect of Peace. A Poetical Composition, Delivered in Yale-College, At the Public Examination, Of the Candidates for the Degree of Bachelor of Arts; July 23, 1778* . . . (New Haven: Printed by Thomas & Samuel Green, 1778);
A Poem, Spoken at the Public Commencement at Yale College, in New-Haven; September 12, 1781 (Hartford: Printed by Hudson & Goodwin, 1781);
An Elegy on the Late Honorable Titus Hosmer, Esq.; One of the Counsellors of the State of Connecticut, A Member of Congress, and a Judge of the Maritime Court of Appeals . . . (Hartford: Printed by Hudson & Goodwin, 1782);
A Translation of Sundry Psalms Which Were Omitted in Doctor Watts's Version; To Which Is Added a Number of Hymns . . . (Hartford: Printed by Barlow & Babcock, 1785);
The Vision of Columbus; A Poem in Nine Books . . . (Hartford: Printed by Hudson & Goodwin, 1787; London: Printed for C. Dilly & J. Stockdale, 1787);
An Oration, Delivered at the North Church in Hartford, at the Meeting of the Connecticut Society of the Cincinnati, July 4th, 1787 . . . (Hartford: Printed by Hudson & Goodwin, 1787);
Advice to the Privileged Orders in the Several States of Europe, Resulting from the Necessity and Propriety of a General Revolution in the Principle of Government. Part I (London: Printed for J. Johnson, 1792; New York: Printed by Childs & Swaine, 1792);
The Conspiracy of Kings; A Poem: Addressed to the Inhabitants of Europe, from Another Quarter of the World . . . (London: Printed for J. Johnson, 1792);
A Letter to the National Convention of France, On the

Joel Barlow, 1807; portrait by Charles Willson Peale

Defects in the Constitution of 1791, and the Extent of the Amendments Which Ought to Be Applied . . . (London: Printed for J. Johnson, 1792);
Advice to the Privileged Orders in the Several States of Europe, Resulting from the Necessity and Propriety of a General Revolution in the Principle of Government. Part II . . . (Paris: Printed at the English Press & sold by Barrois, Senior, 1793; New York: Printed by George Forman for Francis Childs & J. Fellows, 1794; London: Printed & sold by Daniel Isaac Eaton, 1795);
Lettre adressée aux habitans du Piémont, sur les Avantages de la Révolution Française, & la nécessité d'en adopter les principes en Italie (Chambéry, 1793); translated by Barlow as *A Letter, Addressed to the People of the Piedmont, on the Advantages of the French Revolution, and the Necessity of Adopting Its Principles in Italy* (London: Printed & sold by Daniel Isaac Eaton, 1795; New York:

Printed at the Columbian Press by Robertson & Gowan for J. Fellows, 1795);

A Letter to the National Convention of France, on the Defects in the Constitution of 1791, and the Extent of the Amendments Which Ought to Be Applied. To Which Is Added the Conspiracy of Kings, A Poem . . . (New York: Printed by Thomas Greenleaf for J. Fellows, 1793?);

The Hasty-Pudding: A Poem, in Three Cantos . . . (New Haven, 1796);

The Second Warning or Strictures on the Speech Delivered by John Adams, President of the United-States of America at the Opening of the Congress of Said States in November Last (Paris: Printed at the Printing Office of the Social-Circle, 1798);

Joel Barlow to His Fellow Citizens of the United States of America. Letter I. On the System of Policy Hitherto Pursued by Their Government . . . (Paris, 1799?; London: A. Wilson, 1799 or 1800?; Philadelphia: Printed at the Aurora Office, 1800);

Joel Barlow to His Fellow Citizens of the United States. Letter II. On Certain Political Measures Proposed to Their Consideration . . . (Paris, 1800?; Philadelphia: William Duane, 1801);

Letters from Paris, to the Citizens of the United States of America, on the System of Policy Hitherto Pursued by Their Government Relative to Their Commercial Intercourse with England and France, &C. . . . (London: Printed by A. Wilson & by S. Gosnell for James Ridgway, 1800);

Prospectus of a National Institution, to Be Established in the United States (Washington, D.C.: Printed by Samuel H. Smith, 1806);

The Columbiad: A Poem (Philadelphia: Printed for Fry and Kammerer for C. & A. Conrad and for Conrad, Lucas & Co. in Baltimore, 1807; revised edition, Paris: Printed for F. Schoell, 1813; Washington, D.C.: Published by Joseph Milligan, 1825);

Oration Delivered at Washington, July Fourth, 1809 . . . (Washington, D.C.: Printed & published by R. C. Weightman, 1809);

Letter to Henry Gregoire, Bishop, Senator, Compte of the Empire and Member of the Institute of France, in Reply to His Letter on the Columbiad . . . (Washington, D.C.: Printed by Roger Chew Weightman, 1809);

Letter from Joel Barlow, Addressed to the Speaker of the H. of Representatives . . . (Washington, D.C.: Printed by R. C. Weightman, 1811);

A Review of Robert Smith's Address to the People of the United States (Philadelphia: Printed by John Binns, 1811);

The Anarchiad: A New England Poem, by Barlow, David Humphreys, John Trumbull, and Lemuel Hopkins (New Haven: Published by Thomas H. Pease, 1861).

OTHER: *Doctor Watts's Imitation of the Psalms of David, Corrected and Enlarged,* includes psalms and hymns by Barlow (Hartford: Printed by Barlow & Babcock, 1785);

J. P. Brissot de Warville, *New Travels in the United States of America. Performed in 1788,* translated by Barlow (London: Printed for J. S. Jordan, 1792; New York: Printed by T. & J. Swords for Berry & Rogers, 1792);

John Trumbull, *M'Fingal: a Modern Epic Poem, in Four Cantos. The Fifth Edition, With Explanatory Notes,* edited by Barlow (London: Printed for J. S. Jordan, 1792; New York: Printed by John Buel, 1795);

A New Translation of Volney's Ruins; or Meditations on the Revolution of Empires, translated by Barlow and Thomas Jefferson, 2 volumes (Paris: Printed for Levrault, 1802); 1 volume (New York: Printed by & published for Dixon & Sickels, 1828);

Message from the President of the U. States, Transmitting Copies and Extracts from the Correspondence of the Secretary of State, and the Minister Plenipotentiary of the United States at Paris. May 26th, 1812, largely written by Barlow (Washington, D.C.: Printed by R. C. Weightman, 1812).

In the opening years of the nineteenth century, Joel Barlow designed his epic poem, *The Columbiad* (1807), with this end in view: to "encourage and strengthen" republican institutions in the new nation in order ultimately to improve "the condition of human nature." Barlow's purpose was both "moral and political"—and poetical, for he wrote that "this is the moment in America to . . . implant . . . true and useful ideas of glory" and "give direction to poetry, painting, and the other fine arts." It seems ironic that Barlow, who worked to become the American Homer, is now esteemed chiefly for two shorter poems, *The Hasty-Pudding* (1796), a nostalgic recollection of his Connecticut boyhood, and *Advice to a Raven in Russia* (written in 1812, published 1938), an antiwar poem on Napoleon's retreat from Russia. It appears additionally ironic that Barlow, a onetime farm boy turned "politician of the world," should be relegated, in collections of earlier American literature, to the rather provincial fellowship of the Connecticut (or Hartford) Wits, a loose confederation of some ten writers named the Wicked Wits for their sharply satiric (and conservative) views of Revolutionary and Early National America. Yet the importance of Barlow's life and writings lies elsewhere than in the vicissitudes of his literary reputation or in his international sophistication. For Barlow's career, which provides an excellent example of the complex relation of the American writer to his culture, shows a pattern of activist engagement in a national myth central to America since the seventeenth century. In that myth America figures as the nation destined to begin a global epoch of transcendent peace and progress. All of Barlow's major writings embody that myth in Revolutionary and Early National America and place him in a literary-cultural tradition which extends into the twentieth century.

Joel Barlow was descended from prosperous Connecticut yeoman farmers, the first of whom, John Barlow, emigrated from England to New England in the mid seventeenth century. The clapboard, saltbox farmhouse in which Joel grew up was crowded with older brothers and sisters, four stepsiblings from the first marriage of his once-widowed mother, and five additional children fathered by Samuel Barlow, of whom Joel was second-to-last. The hilly Barlow farmstead, on good and ample acreage, brought harvests of rye, oats, Indian corn, potatoes, and turnips. The land, stone-fenced, was worked with oxen and horses. Like their neighbors, the Barlows were largely self-sufficient. Hay was their one cash crop. In verse Barlow later remembered farm life as a continuous round of chores, "from morn to noon, from noon to night" plowing and feeding livestock.

It is probable that Joel, who lived at home until the age of nineteen, received the equivalent of primary and secondary schooling from the Redding minister, the Reverend Nathaniel Bartlett, who was, like most of the Connecticut clergy, a Yale graduate. He maintained a village school and tutored Barlow for a year as a special student to ready him to enter a college preparatory academy. Moor's Indian School, in Hanover, New Hampshire, was the choice of the elder Barlow, a man of limited means, who made a kind of barter business arrangement for Joel's tuition, room, and board, but who died within three months of the boy's matriculation in 1772. Joel remained at the school for the year and entered Dartmouth College the following August. The president of Dartmouth, Eleazar Wheelock, characterized Barlow as a "middling scholar" of "sober, regular, and good behavior." But Barlow's patrimony, conferred at his father's death, enabled the young man to continue his education at Yale in the more urban and sophis-

ticated New Haven, which was evidently more to his taste than rustic New Hampshire. Late in autumn 1774, Barlow entered Yale College, situated in a seaport city of eight thousand souls and the intellectual center of Connecticut.

The Yale curriculum during Barlow's student days consisted of the study of classical languages, mathematics, natural philosophy, and religion. Students recited, in Latin, Cicero's orations and parts of Virgil's *Aeneid*. Over a three-year period undergraduates also translated the New Testament from Greek to Latin. Algebra, astronomy, and geometry were available in accordance with students' capacities, and Barlow, like all his fellow undergraduates, learned natural science from Benjamin Martin's *The Philosophical Grammar* (1735). In theology Yale held fast to its Puritan orthodox lineage, and students studied the works of William Ames and Johannes Wollebuis, and read Jonathan Edwards's *A Careful and Strict Enquiry into the Modern Prevailing Notions of that Freedom of the Will* (1754). William Wollaston's *The Religion of Nature Delineated* (1722) was meant to instill ethics and morality. In his senior year Barlow, like his classmates, studied John Locke's *Essay Concerning Human Understanding*.

Events of the American Revolution obtruded in Barlow's college life. In his freshman year some students foreswore British-taxed tea, and the college militia provided escort to George Washington and his staff when they passed through New Haven. By sophomore year the college community had read and endorsed Thomas Paine's *Common Sense* (1776). News of the first battle at Lexington, then of the bloody loss at Bunker Hill, kept students rapt, as did the news of the Declaration of Independence. Their opportunity to participate arose when the war went badly, and the governor of Connecticut issued a call to arms in response to Washington's request for thousands of men to defend Long Island and New York City. Barlow, along with his fellow students, volunteered. The summer-long Battle of Long Island was lost, and in retreat Barlow returned to New Haven to resume college life. In the dislocations of war, the financially straitened Yale was kept open only by dispersing the students to outlying areas. Barlow and his classmates—among them a future university president, a United States senator, a Secretary of the Treasury, New Hampshire and Vermont supreme court justices, and the prominent lexicographer Noah Webster—all were relocated to Glastonbury, near Hartford, under the guidance of their tutor, Joseph Buckminster. They balked when ordered back to New Haven and, when they graduated, had com-

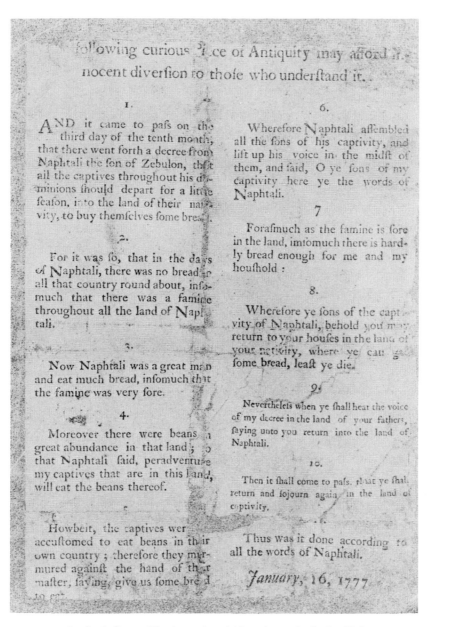

Barlow's first publication, a broadside satire on the food at Yale

pleted just four months' work of the intellectually rigorous senior curriculum. It has been suggested that by missing so much of the emphatically orthodox senior year, Barlow escaped the Connecticut conservatism that ever afterward governed the writings of such other Connecticut Wits as John Trumbull and Timothy Dwight.

Barlow's literary promise may have been detected during his boyhood by his Redding minister. But his earliest extant verse was written at Yale. There he produced a mock-heroic verse on a snowball fight and criticized the undergraduate diet in a

parody about the college president, Naphtali Daggett, cast in language from the book of Canticles ("Now Naphtali was a great man and eat much bread, insomuch that the famine was very sore"). Among such Yale students as Trumbull, Dwight, and David Humphreys, Barlow found encouragement to write poetry. He experimented with different verse forms and with metaphysical and preromantic figures.

No one at Yale served as a good trenchant critic of Barlow's verse. But Barlow, like the other Connecticut Wits, valued Lord Kames's *Elements of*

Criticism (1762), a work then widely circulated in New Haven and a major text of the Scottish commonsense school of criticism. In method Kames promised to move from facts and experiments and "to ascend gradually to principles." He asserted that the nature of man was universal, unrelated to history or to socioeconomic circumstance, and that a universal standard of taste could therefore be applied to the individual. Taste itself, according to Kames, was a moral standard of propriety, of right and wrong. In the fine arts beauty and proportion met the high standard of taste, and the critic's obligation was to condemn the ugly, the disproportionate, the improper. As these views suggest, Kames integrated ideas on art with those on morality and ethics. And Barlow, whose political views later underwent radical transformation, never deviated from the conviction that poetry was preeminently the vehicle for moral guidance.

It is significant that while at Yale Barlow began to think of himself as a poet whose province was America. He was named class poet and at graduation read *The Prospect of Peace* (1778), which President Stiles, no devotee of belles lettres, clocked at twelve minutes' duration. A New Haven printer was so impressed that he published the poem in pamphlet form. But *The Prospect of Peace* was in fact most conventional, its attitude similar to numerous verses presented at graduation ceremonies throughout New England in the 1770s. These were verses filled with optimistic views of the American future. Barlow's commencement poem, however, is a benchmark because it strengthened his resolve to become a poet of America, and because it exploited the millennial themes that Barlow subsequently elaborated in prose and poetry throughout his life, themes which form an enduring and vital part of the American sense of national mission.

It is not surprising—though it is of cultural significance—that Barlow's *The Prospect of Peace* should be virtually indistinguishable from similar efforts by his peers elsewhere. For Barlow, like many of his generation, inherited from his Puritan forebears the belief that the apocalyptic prophesy of the New Testament Book of Revelation was about to be realized. Barlow's ancestors, the New England Puritans, had believed, within this scheme of Christian history, that the final events of earthly time were coming to a close. In method they matched the symbols from Revelation (such as the ten-horned beast, the grapes of wrath, the seven vials) with historical events on earth and adduced God's intention, scheduled in scripture, to bring

THE PROSPECT OF PEACE.

A POETICAL

COMPOSITION,

DELIVERED IN

YALE-COLLEGE,

AT THE

PUBLIC EXAMINATION,

OF THE

CANDIDATES FOR THE DEGREE OF BACHELOR OF ARTS ;

JULY 23, 1778.

By JOEL BARLOW, A. B.

NEW-HAVEN:

PRINTED BY THOMAS AND SAMUEL GREEN,

M,DCC,LXXXVIII.

Title page for the first poem in which Barlow expressed his belief in America's utopian future

human time to a close. They believed that after a period of severe earthly tumult and dissension Christ would return to earth and leash Satan for the duration of the Millennium, one thousand years of peace and harmony, before loosing him for one final great battle that signified the end of the world and the heavenly peace of those called to dwell with God eternally.

Interpretation varied on the specifics of these apocalyptic events. Puritan New England argued, for instance, over whether Christ would return to earth bodily or would solely suffuse it with his spiritual presence. Yet there was consensus that the Millennium was imminent. The Pilgrim Governor William Bradford had been convinced of it, as had the Puritan founders of the Massachusetts Bay Colony and their counterparts in New Haven and the Connecticut outback. Just one decade before Joel Barlow's birth the Reverend Jonathan Edwards had stirred the Connecticut River Valley in the religious revival known as the Great Awakening, one predicated in part upon apocalyptic expectation.

Barlow's commencement poem reveals, as would his subsequent writings, his commitment to a secularized version of that early American millennialism, which held that the thousand years of peace would originate in America and that the colonists bore responsibility for site preparation. For the "drear wastes" of America were conceptually and topographically unsuited to the utopian vision of an American Millennium. Since the seventeenth century, therefore, certain writers had urged environmental change—deforestation of the wilds, damming of streams, town planning—of the kind that would eventually transform the new world into a plausible site of the New Earth, as the Millennium was called in Revelation. Barlow's *The Prospect of Peace* suggests a post-Revolutionary Millennium: "THEN love shall rule, and Innocence adore,/Discord shall cease, and Tyrants be no more." As for the American environment, Barlow paints a pastoral landscape in *The Prospect of Peace*. The plains are furrowed by the plow, and luxuriant vines drop their "clustering fruit." Nature is "kind" and "methodiz'd." Throughout, the context of the poem is Christian, but readers notice that Christ and the celestial figures are more ornamental than fundamental to the work. In fact, the diminishment of doctrinal Christianity in a poem dominated by apocalyptic themes shows Barlow's involvement in the secularization of millennial thought in the American Enlightenment. It shows, additionally, the resilience of such thought even as it anticipates the endurance of Barlow's millennial themes in writings in which politics would take the place of religion.

The presence of the American Millennium in Barlow's poem did not, however, advance his literary career. Upon graduation from Yale, he discovered how problematic was the position of the poet in America. True, his former tutor, Buckminster, had advised him to "encourage and cultivate your turn for poetry," and to that end he had urged Barlow to enter the ministry, apparently the only feasible means of support for a literary man in America at that time. Barlow resisted. He admitted to Noah Webster that "literary accomplishments will not be so much noticed till some time after the [post-Revolutionary] settlement of Peace and the people are more refined." Yet he struck a defiant tone: "Let us show the world a few more examples of men standing on their own merit, and rising in spite of opposition. . . . We are now citizens of the world." His poetic and nationalist ambition is clear

from this couplet: "This new-born Empire should my voice employ/The Muse's transport and the Patriot's joy."

Despite such brave utterance, Barlow was learning that America was not ready to support a poet financially. His search for a wealthy patron was fruitless, and, despite the literary encouragement of his friends, Barlow was soon alternately teaching school (without enthusiasm) and spending terms back at Yale as a graduate student. All the while he sought, in consultation with his friends, an appropriate subject for a major poem. Yet his patrimony was spent and, indebted to his brother for recent loans, Barlow sank into depression ("I have now got to the end of my line. . . . I have nothing to go after, nobody to go to see and nothing to do").

The lifeline arrived in the form of a letter from his Yale friend (and soon-to-be brother-in-law) Abraham Baldwin, inviting Barlow to accept a Revolutionary War chaplaincy. Barlow consented. Weeks of intensive study concluded with the theological examination passed successfully, according to the examining board of Connecticut ministers, who then issued Barlow the necessary license to preach. In autumn 1780 Barlow became the chaplain for the Third Massachusetts Brigade, quartered in northern New Jersey. His principal duty was to preach a Sunday sermon during the months of military activity, May through November. Otherwise Barlow was at liberty, which he used to visit Connecticut friends and to plan his grand poem. In 1779 he had observed to Buckminster that "the discovery of America made an important revolution in the history of mankind," that it "served the purpose of displaying knowledge, liberty, and religion . . . perhaps as much as any human transaction." These were germinal lines for Barlow's *The Vision of Columbus* (1787), the plans for which Washington himself may have heard about when he invited the young chaplain to dinner after having learned of a memorable sermon on patriotism, which Barlow preached following the disclosure of Benedict Arnold's treason.

Barlow's plans for his major long poem took shape through his wartime courtship of Ruth Baldwin, to whom he became secretly engaged in 1779. Connecticut law at that time forbade the courtship of a young woman without her father's consent, and Barlow, a penniless young man as yet uncommitted to a profession, was in no position to approach Ruth's father, Michael Baldwin. The young man, who was admired by women and evidently attracted to them, finally invited "Ruthy" to share in his ambitions: "You know that my plans are large. I want yours to be projected upon the same scale and blended with my own." For both young people the anguish of their interminable engagement proved unendurable. In January 1781 Ruth joined Joel near Hartford at the home of a mutual friend, the Reverend Benoni Upson, who married the couple on the twenty-sixth of the month. The two, soon separated once again, kept their marriage secret for nearly a year, by which time Michael Baldwin had come to think better of the young chaplain who preached so well.

The record of the Barlow marriage, which endured for thirty-one years until Joel Barlow's death, exists in the numerous letters written over years of many separations. The storied happiness of the couple must seem suspect to contemporary readers. Over the years Barlow's endless professions of love and devotion were to sound increasingly perfunctory and clichéd, while Ruth's became tinged with the desperate tones of a woman unable to understand just why she should feel so unhappy amid comfortable circumstances. The American literary record of marital vitality in this period remains that of the Barlows' contemporaries John and Abigail Adams, compared to whom the

Barlows' letters show a progression of distance and estrangement on his part, and of bewilderment and pain on hers.

Yet in the early, happy nuptial years Barlow completed his first important poem, *The Vision of Columbus.* By design it was a "philosophical poem," its scope that of the epic. Barlow had studied the *Aeneid* and was familiar with Milton's *Paradise Lost,* from which he borrowed certain devices. Additionally, he had available Voltaire's *Essay on Epic Poetry* (1727) at an early stage of his planning. It proved fortunate for Barlow that his fellow Connecticut Wit Dwight had preempted the biblical subject for his epic, *The Conquest of Canäan* (1785), which presents the Israelites' struggle as a prophesy and metaphor for the American Revolution. In Dwight's epic the American experience is refracted through biblical events. Behind the figure of Joshua, for example, readers are to recognize Washington.

Barlow, unlike Dwight, moved boldly to partake directly of American materials. His Columbus, a man "educated in all the useful sciences," is "too vigorous and persevering" to rest with "philosophical speculation." The Genoan insists, against adverse conditions, upon making the New World voyage an experiment to test his theory that "the Atlantic ocean must be bounded on the West either by India itself, or by some great continent not far distant from it." Barlow, who conceived Columbus as a figure of heroic action, nevertheless set the poem in the years following Columbus's imprisonment, when the voyages were behind him and he felt himself to be a failure. At this point an angel, much like Michael in *Paradise Lost,* appears to hearten Columbus by showing him the American continents and their future from the top of Mount Vision.

In nine books *The Vision of Columbus* offers lessons in American geography and history and prophesizes the bicontinental American future. Under the angel's tutelage Columbus reviews events of the Renaissance, traces the routes of the explorers, watches settlement patterns, lives through the events of the Revolution, and then sees the distant future in which the sciences and philosophy both bring about moral and material progress.

One unexpected portion of Barlow's *The Vision of Columbus* is the lengthy, two-book account of South American Indian legends, based on information Barlow probably got from Sir Paul Rycault's translations of *The Royal Commentaries of Peru* (1688) by Garcilasso de la Vega, available in the Yale library. Barlow interwove legends of Manco Capac

Ruth Baldwin Barlow; drawing made by Charles de Villette in Paris, probably between 1801 and 1804

and Prince Rocha in order to show the "benevolent and pacific" politics of the ancient civilization of the southern hemisphere. And why?—because Barlow envisioned the ultimate unification of both continents into one nation-state and needed to show the process of enlightened civilization in South America as a counterbalance to the North American Revolution and its heroes. Barlow is so insistent on the point that he suspends the poem in order to present a prose essay on these legends and their significance.

Among the works helpful to Barlow in planning *The Vision of Columbus,* William Robertson's *History of America* (1777) was especially influential because it offered the solution to a problem troubling to the young poet and evident in *The Prospect of Peace.* While his commencement poem proclaimed a post-Revolutionary, millennial America, Barlow knew that the actual American geography belied his vision. An American Millennium was, in material reality, far from being achieved on a continent that was even largely unexplored beyond the Eastern seaboard. Barlow, a practical man, was uneasy with an America poeticized in verbal pictures that were demonstrably at odds with the nation's environmental conditions.

The Scotsman Robertson's book showed Barlow the resolution of the disparity between imagination and the palpable reality of geographic America. For Robertson recognized the environmental difficulties of the North American continent—the harsh climate, impenetrable forests, formidable beasts, noxious insects. In the face of these obstacles to civilization he posed his solution, namely, large-scale Euro-American settlement and technological advances. "The labour and operations of man not only improve and embellish the earth," he writes, "but render it more wholesome and friendly to life." Robertson's position became Barlow's own. The Scotsman, moreover, evidently suggested to Barlow the rightful place of a man of letters in a nation absorbed in practical affairs and yet committed to belief in its millennial destiny. As the epic poet of America, Barlow could be a messianic social planner of the nation, and *The Vision of Columbus* his first efficacious instrument of national guidance.

The impressive list of subscribers to *The Vision of Columbus,* which included Washington, General Lafayette, Benjamin Franklin, and Alexander Hamilton, in addition to many army officers, indicates the success of Barlow's considerable effort to publicize and market his book. He even secured permission, in a symbolic tribute to the monarch of America's ally, to dedicate the work to Louis XVI.

THE

VISION

OF

COLUMBUS;

A POEM IN NINE BOOKS.

BY JOEL BARLOW, ESQUIRE.

HARTFORD:

PRINTED BY HUDSON AND GOODWIN, FOR THE AUTHOR.

M.DCC.LXXXVII.

Title page for Barlow's first important poem, which has been called the first best-selling book in post-Revolutionary America

(*The Vision of Columbus* was published in England without this dedication.) One scholar has remarked that in a modest way *The Vision of Columbus* was "the first American best seller after the Revolution." Yet readers in subsequent generations have unanimously pronounced the work a failure as poetry for its total dissociation of literature from human life. In its own day the poem was probably more respected than read. Its nine-book amplitude and its inexorable march through thousands of lines of heroic couplets nonetheless gave the new nation the power to counter such remarks as that of the English critic Sidney Smith, who sneered, "Who reads an American Book?"

In the years of Barlow's preparation of *The Vision of Columbus* he was variously employed as an editor, bookseller, and lawyer. His chaplaincy had ended with the war. In 1788 he was offered the opportunity to travel in Europe and, so he thought, to make his fortune. His postcollegiate boast of being a citizen of the world seemed about to come true as he accepted a position representing Scioto Associates, a firm established to sell Ohio land to the Europeans. Barlow was, in fact, the dupe of unscrupulous Scioto businessmen who did not have title to the land they were selling. He had no suspicion of their wrongdoing when he sailed, nor for many months afterward.

In Paris Barlow renewed his acquaintance with General Lafayette and met Jefferson, who became a lifelong friend. The land-sales business moved slowly, and once again Barlow resorted to the pen to advance the cause of European settlement of America. His translation of the *New Travels in the United States* (1792), by Brissot de Warville, showed America to great advantage. Brissot, a Girondist who had toured America in 1788 and was guillotined in the French Revolution, had written *Nouveau Voyages dans les États-Unis* (1791) intentionally to instruct post-Revolutionary France. Barlow's translation revised the text in order to minimize the dangers of American settlement and to assert the healthfulness of life in America. He cut passages on water hazards, Indian dangers, and perilous weather. He left intact Brissot's hymns to technological improvement, to bucolic abundance, and to the forthcoming transcontinental empire suffused with liberty—all components of Barlow's millennial America.

Three years after Barlow's arrival abroad, Scioto Associates was disintegrating amid the recriminations of angry, misled French émigrés who returned home with horror stories of Ohio. Though Barlow's finances were precarious, he managed to have Ruth Barlow join him. Exonerated of blame in the Scioto venture, he became intensely involved in revolutionary political issues, while earning some income as a political journalist. In 1790 he was welcomed in England by members of the liberal, pro-Revolutionary group, including Thomas Paine, Richard Price, Joseph Priestley, and Mary Wollstonecraft, all of whom opposed the aristocratic-monarchist position of Edmund Burke's *Reflections on the Revolution in France* (1790).

Among the many rejoinders to Burke, Paine's *Rights of Man* is the best-known. But Barlow's *Advice to the Privileged Orders in the Several States of Europe, Resulting from the Necessity and Propriety of a General Revolution in the Principle of Government* (1792-1793) was a noteworthy contribution. Barlow, his Connecticut conservatism long past, was by the 1790s a radical. *Advice to the Privileged Orders,* a prose work which the British government considered seditious, was addressed to educated, rational intellects, principally those of the upper classes. It argued from

the premise that government of the people was already an accomplished fact, and then attempted "to induce the men who now govern the world to put into practice those principles of the American and French Revolutions."

The work begins with a discussion of such medieval practices as primogeniture and entailment, which are, Barlow argues, instruments of tyranny. His second chapter focuses upon the historically despotic institution of the church (which Barlow carefully distinguishes from religion), after which he proceeds, in chapter three, to indict the standing army as a cause of war. Then Barlow attacks the slow and cumbersome machinery of British jurisprudence which excludes the ordinary citizen from justice. The fifth chapter, published as part two and in Paris in 1793, discusses the evils of indirect taxation.

Stylistically, *Advice to the Privileged Orders* shows Barlow's abilities as a writer of forceful, direct (though sometimes florid) prose, a medium he regrettably undervalued in favor of his poetically leaden couplets. His subsequent antimonarchical verse satire, *The Conspiracy of Kings* (1792), when compared to *Advice to the Privileged Orders,* is utterly lifeless ("From western heav'ns th' inverted orient springs,/The morn of man, the dreadful night of kings").

Yet *The Conspiracy of Kings,* which predicted that the European monarchies would soon fall, proved to be historically accurate. In spring 1792 King Gustavus III of Sweden was assassinated, and Leopold of Austria died. Louis XVI retained mere vestiges of his former power, and France declared war on Austria. Barlow, then in France, was in the thick of it. He had become persuaded that a French revolution would be the salvation of Europe, and when France moved to establish a republican government, Barlow wrote *A Letter to the National Convention* (1792) restating the republican principles to be found in his earlier work.

A Letter to the National Convention was enthusiastically received in France, and Barlow was made an honorary citizen of that nation (as were Paine and Washington). Encouraged by his new prominence, Barlow went to the Savoy to campaign for elective office as deputy. In that same year, 1793, he wrote another letter, this to the people of the Piedmont enumerating the values of the French Revolution and claiming Italy's destiny to be one of republican unity. At this time friends surprised Barlow with a dish of hasty pudding, the cornmeal mush which had been a dietary staple of his boyhood. *The Hasty-Pudding* (1796), the poem occasioned by the

THE

CONSPIRACY OF KINGS;

A POEM:

ADDRESSED

TO THE INHABITANTS OF EUROPE,

FROM ANOTHER QUARTER OF THE WORLD.

Ἀπατήσομαι δὲ τερπνοῖς ἀπας ἐλθῶσι καθεκάστοτε
Οι Νεμοντες πρὸς ἕκαστ γαγαίδας σοφίμασι.
THEOGNIS.

" But they, in footh, muft reafon. Curfes light
" On the proud talent! 'twill at laft undo us,
" When men are gorged with each abfurdity
" Their fubtil wits can frame, or we adopt,
" For very novelty they'll fly to fenfe,
" And we muft fall before the idol, Fafhion."
MYSTERIOUS MOTHER, Act IV.

By JOEL BARLOW, Efq;
AUTHOR OF " ADVICE TO THE PRIVILEGED ORDERS," AND OF " THE VISION OF COLUMBUS,"

LONDON:
PRINTED FOR J. JOHNSON, ST. PAUL'S CHURCH YARD.
1792.

Title page for Barlow's antimonarchial verse satire

dish and by the contours of the Savoy hills and valleys so reminiscent of Connecticut, is considered one of Barlow's best efforts. It receives praise for the whimsical quality of its mock-heroic lines, which, in subtle and varying couplets, detail the making of pudding:

> While the full pail rewards the milk-maid's toil,
> The mother sees the morning cauldron boil;
> To stir the pudding next demands their care;
> To spread the table and the bowls prepare;
> To feed the children as their portions cool,
> And comb their heads and send them off to school.

Recently it has been suggested that *Hasty-Pudding,* more than nostalgic reflection, argues that democratic folkways are the basis for the political democracy of the future.

But democracy was set back in France. In June 1793 Ruth Barlow left England, where her husband's name was now infamous, to join him in Paris for what became the Reign of Terror. Though many of Barlow's friends and acquaintances were executed, he maintained faith in the ultimate success of the revolution. Then, when the republican

government fell, Barlow seized the opportunity both to aid France and to make his fortune at last—as a shipper of goods to that troubled country. His American citizenship put Barlow in a position to act as a neutral agent between the French and divers European suppliers. Barlow, based in Hamburg over the course of a year, 1794-1795, amassed the fortune that made him independently wealthy. His financial success testifies to his having attained a high degree of sophistication, subtlety, and business acumen he had not possessed as a Scioto agent.

Barlow's skills in diplomacy (and intrigue) were thoroughly tested in the following year, 1796, when he accepted a diplomatic mission at the behest of his friends James Madison and David Humphreys to persuade the Dey, ruler of Algiers, to honor a treaty with the United States stipulating that the new nation receive freedom from piracy in the Mediterranean, rights to Algerian ports, and the release of American prisoners who were tortured and enslaved. The one million dollars promised the Dey by the United States Government, under the terms of the treaty, had not arrived, and Barlow's job was to placate the volatile ruler—which he did—until the money arrived.

Barlow was still in France in the final years of the eighteenth century, and fearful that the Feder-

Joel Barlow; portrait by Robert Fulton

alists, then in power in the United States, would precipitate a confrontation between the two nations. A letter expressing his concerns and addressed to his brother-in-law, Abraham Baldwin, at that time a United States senator, miscarried and was published in America in 1801, the effect of which was to make Barlow appear traitorous and to cause a break with his old friends, the Connecticut Wits. When the Jefferson presidency began in 1800, however, Barlow's reputation was restored, and in 1804 Joel Barlow, after seventeen years abroad, returned to America with his wife and purchased a mansion overlooking Rock Creek in Washington, D.C., and renamed it Kalorama ("fine view").

Barlow's significant literary efforts in these later years include unfinished notes and fragments, as well as works published in entirety. Extensive notes remain on his plans, encouraged by Jefferson, to write a history of America, one for which Washington, Monroe, and others would have opened their files, and which would undoubtedly have strengthened Barlow's literary reputation. But Barlow did not complete the history, in part because of involvement in another, fragmentary work, a poem entitled "The Canal: A Poem on the Application of Physical Science to Political Economy." The poem was a collaborative effort with the artist-engineer Robert Fulton, who had become Barlow's protégé in Europe. For "The Canal" Fulton was to supply scientific and technological data and Barlow to provide the poetry. The work is evidently patterned after Constantin de Volney's anticlerical *The Ruins: or, A Survey of the Revolution of Empires* (1793). "The Canal" both hails and tries to hasten the nation's development of technology for socioeconomic coherence and for environmental change. The 290-line fragment "The Canal" (unpublished until the twentieth century) invites engineers and inventors—future Franklins—to become agents of the millennial New Earth.

Barlow tried to further the effort with *Prospectus of a National Institution* (1806), which proposed the establishment of an institution, funded by the federal government, to "combine the two great objects, *research* and *instruction*" in theoretical and technical knowledge. The proposal was not carried out because of expense and the political suspicion, among Federalists, that the institution would nurture their democratic adversaries. Yet Barlow's *Prospectus of a National Institution* anticipated the establishment of the United States service academies and the institutions of higher learning and research based in every state of the union by the

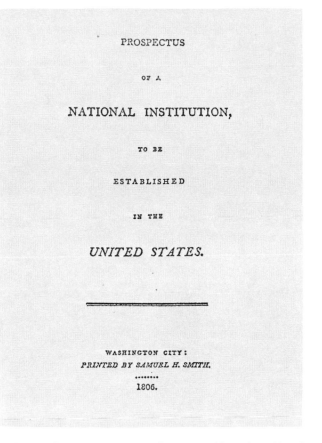

Believing that the American Millenium could not be achieved without the growth of theoretical and technical knowledge, Barlow proposed that the federal government fund an institution for research and instruction.

Morrill Act of the mid-nineteenth century.

Barlow's final major work, *The Columbiad* (1807), combines his engineering activism with the millennial conviction that America must be guided in its gradual transformation to the New Earth. To insure its permanence, Barlow had *The Columbiad* produced in the most expensive available materials and cast it in the heroic couplets which romantic writers were abandoning, but whose dignity and endurance seemed unquestionable to Barlow. As its title suggests, the poem is based on *The Vision of Columbus*, though Barlow worked to replace the genial Christianity of the earlier work with his newer political convictions. The guiding angel of *The Vision of Columbus* gives way to Hesper, a mythological spirit better suited to the agnostic author. And the Christian trinity is replaced by a "holy triad" of "EQUALITY, FREE ELECTION, and FEDERAL BAND," all consonant with the Jeffersonian republicanism which Barlow espoused in his middle and later years.

Readers of *The Columbiad,* for good reason, have found the poem disappointing—"in every way pretentious," as one critic observed. Barlow mistook pomposity for dignity, the sententious for the serious. In places his intentionally exalted rhetoric sounds comic instead, as in these lines on a Revolutionary War naval battle: "There swells the carnage; all the tar-beat floor / Is clogg'd with spatter'd brains and glued with gore."

Barlow kept the characters and situations of his first five books virtually intact from *The Vision of Columbus* and resisted advice to shorten or delete the South American passages (though he did move the interruptive prose essay to his end notes). He expanded the books on the Revolutionary War and its participants in order to emphasize their epic stature. In addition, *The Columbiad* is a more cautionary poem than was its precursor. For Barlow reveals paradoxical views on America. The nation is destined for a glorious millennial future, but it is also subject to backsliding and potential destruction, which Barlow portrays as environmental upheaval. His role, as poet, is to warn the nation and thus to preserve its destiny:

> Think not, my friends, the patriot's task is done,
> Or Freedom safe, because the battle's won.
> Unnumber'd foes, far different arms that wield,
> Wait the weak moment when she quits her shield,
> To plunge in her bold breast the insidious dart,
> Or pour keen poison round her thoughtless heart.

Such passages are the stock-in-trade of *The Columbiad* and are to be found in every book of the poem.

A subtle, psychological change helps to explain why *The Columbiad* emerges as a pretentious poem. Barlow, as a young man, had clearly felt a personal affinity with Columbus, the ambitious and brilliant figure whose genius was long unrecognized but who was destined to greatness. The ambitious but frustrated, postcollegiate Joel Barlow evidently took heart from the example of the Gen-

FRONTISPICE.
COLUMBIAD.

HESPER APPEARING TO
COLUMBUS IN PRISON.

THE

COLUMBIAD.

A Poem,

WITH

THE LAST CORRECTIONS OF THE AUTHOR.

BY JOEL BARLOW.

> Tu spiegherai, Colombo, a un novo polo
> Lontane si le fortunate antenne,
> Ch'a pena seguira con gli occhi il volo
> La Fama, ch'ha mille occhi e mille penne.
> Canti ella Alcide, e Bacco; e di re solo
> Basti a i posteri tuoi, ch' alquanto accenne:
> Che quel poco dara lunga memoria
> Di poema degnissima, e d'istoria.
>   Gierus. Lib. Can. xv.

WASHINGTON CITY:
PUBLISHED BY JOSEPH MILLIGAN, GEORGETOWN.
JUNE 1, 1825.

Frontispiece and title page for the American revised edition of Barlow's republican epic, a prescription for the nation's glorious millennial future

oan who struggled patiently for years to find a patron to support his grand venture. Yet over the years Barlow's feelings changed. In his early fifties his mind was thoroughly utilitarian, and this man of affairs, this internationalist and counselor to presidents, viewed his relation to his poem rather differently. He was now preoccupied with social and spiritual power on a national, even bicontinental, scale, as "The Canal" and *Prospectus of a National Institution* indicate. Barlow's personal affinity shifted, accordingly, from Columbus to Homer, whose *Iliad* and *Odyssey* Barlow believed had exerted the strongest influence on Western civilization to date. Barlow felt that Homer

> with his monumental songs,
> Builds far more durable his splendid throne
> Than all the Pharaohs with their hills of stone.

He thought he could possess Homer's power by working consciously in the epic tradition. *The Columbiad* was Barlow's moral and material epic blueprint for the American New Earth.

One final poem, valued still on a literary basis, remained for Barlow to write. In 1811 he embarked for Europe at the behest of President Madison and Secretary of State James Monroe to try to negotiate a treaty with Napoleon in order to bring France and the United States into closer alliance. He journeyed to the French front lines through a wintry and war-torn Europe, where he sensed the imminent defeat of Napoleon's forces. In feelings of horror and revulsion Barlow wrote *Advice to a Raven in Russia,* a poem whose tone is one of controlled rage. The raven, a "feather'd cannibal," seeks "delicious fare," namely, "human carnage" amply supplied by Napoleon ("He'll make you deserts and he'll bring you blood"). The poem concludes with this imperative, on Napoleon: "Hurl from his blood-built throne this king of woes,/Dash him to dust, and let the world repose."

All readers of *Advice to a Raven in Russia* have wished that its power were evident in Barlow's other poems. Had it been so, then Barlow's stature as a poet would be much higher. This antiwar poem was Barlow's last. In the midst of the retreat of Napoleon's armies from Russia Barlow caught cold from riding in carriages in freezing weather. He developed pneumonia and died in Zarnowiec (near Kracow), Poland, on 24 December 1812.

In American literary history neither Barlow nor the other Connecticut Wits left a legacy re-sumed by others. Barlow had no inkling that in the next generation such writers as Edgar Allan Poe and James Russell Lowell would ridicule *The Columbiad,* or that it would endure more as a literary artifact than as art. Thinking of the poem as a vehicle for ideas rather than as the embodiment of them, he mistakenly thought of a poem as a legislative program, formulated in a medium guaranteed to give it dignity and permanence.

Yet he understood the epic quality of the American national experience, and in retrospect it takes a place on the continuum of writers of the American epic, between Cotton Mather's *Magnalia Christi Americana* (1702) and Walt Whitman's *Leaves of Grass* (1855), continuing through Hart Crane's *The Bridge* (1930) and William Carlos Williams's *Paterson* (1945-1963). In addition, Barlow's utilitarianism, which hearkens in American culture to Franklin, anticipates the aesthetics of functionalism which formed an important movement in the twentieth century. In 1812 Barlow wrote to the engineer Benjamin Latrobe, "Lord Kames's rule that utility always enters into the idea of beauty is wonderfully true in theory, and to render it so in practice is a national object confided in great measure to the engineers and architects of the nation." A full century before the great age of American engineering, Joel Barlow embraced the ethos of utility and, through literature, worked to be the engineer-architect of the nation.

Biographies:

Victor C. Miller, *Joel Barlow: Revolutionist, London, 1791-1792* (Hamburg: de Gruyer, 1932);

Benjamin Zunder, *The Early Days of Joel Barlow, A Connecticut Wit: His Life and Works from 1754 to 1787* (New Haven: Yale University Press, 1934);

James Woodress, *A Yankee's Odyssey* (Philadelphia: Lippincott, 1958).

References:

Arthur L. Ford, *Joel Barlow* (New York: Twayne, 1971);

Leon Howard, *The Connecticut Wits* (Chicago: University of Chicago Press, 1943);

Leo Lemay, "The Contexts and Themes of 'The Hasty-Pudding,' " *Early American Literature,* 17 (Spring 1982): 3-21;

Roy Harvey Pearce, *The Continuity of American Poetry* (Princeton: Princeton University Press, 1961);

Gordon S. Wood, *The Creation of the American Repub-*

lic 1776-1787 (Chapel Hill: University of North Carolina Press, 1969).

Papers:
There are collections of Barlow's papers at the Houghton Library, Harvard University; the Beinecke Library, Yale University; the Pequot Library in Southport, Connecticut; and the Library of Congress.

William Bartram
(9 February 1739-22 July 1823)

Ormond Seavey
George Washington University

BOOK: *Travels through North and South Carolina, Georgia, East and West Florida, the Cherokee Country, the Extensive Territories of the Muscogulges, or Creek Confederacy, and the Country of the Chactaws* ... (Philadelphia: Printed by James & Johnson, 1791; London: Printed for J. Johnson, 1792).

Editions and Collections: *John and William Bartram's America: Selections from the Writings of the Philadelphia Naturalists,* edited by Helen Gere Cruickshank (New York: Devin-Adair, 1957);

The Travels of William Bartram: Naturalist's Edition, edited by Francis Harper (New Haven: Yale University Press, 1958);

William Bartram: Botanical and Zoological Drawings, 1756-1788, edited by Joseph Ewan (Philadelphia: American Philosophical Society, 1968).

OTHER: *Travels in Georgia and Florida, 1773-74: A Report to Dr. John Fothergill,* edited by Francis Harper, *Transactions of the American Philosophical Society,* 33 (November 1943): 121-242.

While the American Revolution was beginning and his countrymen were arguing and arming themselves, William Bartram was making his solitary way across the marshlands and forests of Florida, Georgia, and Alabama collecting botanical specimens. When a group of delegates to the Constitutional Convention of 1787 spent a Sunday off from their deliberations touring the gardens established near Philadelphia by his father, John Bartram, they found William Bartram pottering about the plants in his bare feet. A wonderful anomaly in his place and time, he produced in his long life only

William Bartram; portrait by Charles Willson Peale (Old City Hall, Philadelphia)

one book, *Travels through North and South Carolina, Georgia, East and West Florida.* It remains one of the most impressive and influential works by any early American writer.

Bartram's *Travels,* as its title suggests, does not purport to be an imaginative work. It records the terrain features, flora, and fauna Bartram encountered in three years of wanderings in the South. Bartram was trained as a scientific observer, and his observations have been proved in most cases reliable. The great English scientist Sir Charles Lyell, who covered some of the same area in the middle of the nineteenth century, attested to his accuracy. But the work's lasting importance is literary more than scientific. Bartram's vivid descriptions inspired the English romantic poets, and Thomas Carlyle, in recommending its "floundering eloquence" to Emerson, wrote that all American libraries should keep such a book as a national classic.

Bartram was an unlikely writer, but he was even less suited for the other sorts of activity that his contemporaries valued. He delayed getting his *Travels* into print for fifteen years after he had made the excursions; by then at least some of the discoveries he had first made were credited to others. It is tempting to think of comparisons between Bartram and Thoreau, since both blended philosophical and social commentary with their observation of nature. But Bartram, who was if anything less well-adjusted to his times than Thoreau, never deployed his perceptions of nature against society; perhaps he was too much the Quaker to make war against the world. He was more like his contemporary Hector St. John de Crèvecoeur (Michel Guillaume Jean de Crèvecoeur), a gentle and unpolitical person living in a highly politicized and entrepreneurial society. Nature was filled with wonders for him, but he had no audience near at hand to marvel at them when his book finally appeared. So he spent the remainder of his life as a protected and knowledgeable eccentric, at home in his garden with his travels over.

The son of John Bartram and his second wife, Ann Mendenhall Bartram, William Bartram came to field biology by inheritance. His father had seen the opportunities for marketing American plants and seeds in Europe. Combining diligence as a scientist with a merchant's sense of the profitable, he established the first true botanical garden in America at the family home in Kingsessing, now part of Philadelphia. Though he was self-taught, he managed to carry on an extensive correspondence with European scientific figures, most notably Linnaeus, who acknowledged his achievements in the enterprise of discovering and classifying new species. He was a founding member of the American Philosophical Society along with Benjamin Franklin; their close association began around the early 1740s when Franklin first took an active interest in science.

John Bartram was a Philadelphia Quaker, with an eighteenth-century Quaker's characteristic blend of business acumen and personal mission. Pure scientific speculation, like other aesthetic pursuits, was as foreign to his nature as it would have been to most Quakers. Nature for him was filled with materials of practical use to man. The wilderness was to be subdued for the cultivators of the earth. John Bartram's emphasis was shared by his principal English contacts, Peter Collinson and, later, Dr. John Fothergill, both of them wealthy Quakers with an interest in natural science. Both would later be important patrons of the son's career.

John Bartram broke with the Quakers late in his life and was read out of meeting, but the Quaker heritage passed on to his son. That heritage manifested itself in quite different ways, though, owing to the differing temperaments of the father and the son. Where John Bartram displayed the hardworking, plainspoken, unadorned aspect of Quaker tradition, his son exemplified its otherworldly and mystical side. For William Bartram, as for John Woolman, the world was full of hints of the divine; a benevolent and exquisite artist had contrived these natural scenes, and the most basic response to it all was wonderment. Where his father had looked at animals and plants for their uses, William Bartram looked on them as his fellows. In a letter of 1792, reflecting on the flights of pigeons and woodpeckers, he writes, "Why should the movements of these Creatures afford us any Admonition, or instruction; do they understand any thing of Metaphysics, Astronomy or Philosophy? Why not, I say they are ingenious little Philosophers, & my esteemed Associates."

John Bartram had been self-educated, borrowing books from James Logan and teaching himself the Latin still needed for much scientific reading and correspondence. His son William, though, was sent to the newly founded Academy of Philadelphia, ancestor to the University of Pennsylvania, and it was no doubt there that he acquired the grounding in the classics that can be seen in his *Travels.* Even earlier William had traveled with his father on expeditions of horticultural investigation, and, since he had shown talent as an artist, he sketched plants and animals on their journeys. Writing to Franklin in 1753, Peter Collinson commends "Billys Performances." His father's associates tended to refer to him as Billy, in part because it was the preferred Quaker practice to use first

William Bartram's drawing of the Bartrams' most significant botanical discovery. Last seen growing in the wild in 1803, the plant survives today because the Bartrams planted the seeds in their garden (Fothergill Album, The British Museum).

names, but also because a certain haplessness made the youthful nickname seem appropriate even after the younger Bartram was grown up.

Though young William had showed an aptitude for scientific observation, his father apparently disapproved of the unprofitable and unsystematic way he went about it. In 1756, when William was seventeen, his father withdrew him from the academy and apprenticed him to a merchant in Philadelphia. A few years later, in 1761, William tried to run a trading store on the Cape Fear River in North Carolina, initially under the auspices of his uncle, Colonel William Bartram. After a few years of poor success, he had a chance in 1765 to accompany his father on a journey to the St. John's River in Florida, a recent British acquisition. Apparently liking the area, he remained in Florida and tried to start an indigo and rice plantation; his failure there was even more sudden and drastic than any before. A few years back in Philadelphia brought him no closer to financial success, and by 1772 he was back in the Carolinas, talking about another trip to Florida. During this period he was in contact with Collinson and later with Fothergill in London, sending them drawings he was making of turtles and mollusks.

At last in 1772 Dr. Fothergill intervened and commissioned Bartram to undertake an excursion to Florida collecting plants, seeds, illustrations, and a record of observations, in return for a yearly stipend of £50. Fothergill's instructions were quite detailed, perhaps because he wished to provide firm direction for his erratic protégé. In a letter of introduction to an acquaintance in Charleston, South Carolina, Fothergill described Bartram succinctly: "bred to merchandise, but not fitted to it by inclination at least. He is not quite a systematic botanist. He knows plants and draws prettily." With that assignment and the consent of his father, Bartram set forth in March of 1773 on the nearly four years of wandering which his *Travels* describe.

Once under way, Bartram was hard for his patron to track down. Using Charleston, South Carolina, as his base of operations, Bartram traveled along the coastline into Georgia and later into Florida, up the Savannah River into northern Georgia, and even into Alabama and Louisiana. There does not seem to have been much system or advance planning in his excursions, in part no doubt because he was on his own or with whatever temporary companions he could find along the way. Fothergill's letters reflect his increasing frustration at Bartram's expensive and unproductive rambles. To John Bartram he complained in 1774

that he "must be greatly out of pocket if he does not take some opportunity of doing what I expressly directed, which was to send me seeds or roots of such plants as either by their beauty, fragrance, or other properties might claim attention." By 1776 the Revolution had severed connections between America and England. It was an eye ailment more than any lack of funds that forced Bartram to cut his travels short; he returned to Philadelphia in January of 1777.

Two versions of his travels survive, both apparently drawn from his field journals, which have been lost. He submitted a report to Dr. Fothergill in two installments, totaling 171 manuscript pages. It is hardly more than a rough transcription of field notes, written in the somewhat breathless style of an immediate observer, with frequent misspellings and confusions of expression. In this version he tends to use the common names of plants and animals; in the book version there is a show of erudition in the lists of Latin binomial names. (The manuscript was turned over to the British Museum some time after Fothergill's death in 1780; it was finally edited by Francis Harper of the John Bartram Association and published in the *Transactions of the American Philosophical Society* in 1943.) The other version of his travels took longer to deliver. In the years after he returned to Philadelphia from the South, Bartram worked in the family horticultural business. His father died in the year he returned, and in the following years he worked up his book manuscript. There is reason to believe it was completed early in the 1780s, but it was not until 1791, after negotiations with one publisher had already fallen through, that the book appeared.

In the introduction to the book, Bartram expresses his delight in the diversity of natural phenomena. It is this sense of delight, more than a concern for usable information, that has inspired his travels. "This world, as a glorious apartment of the boundless palace of the sovereign Creator, is furnished with an infinite variety of animated scenes, inexpressibly beautiful and pleasing, equally free to the inspection and enjoyment of all his creatures." Bartram did not have a mind that discriminated among excitements; at one point in the introduction he asserts that nothing is more glorious than the vegetable world, and a few pages later he writes that the animals are just as perfect a manifestation of the divine will. Topics and sometimes even sentences are therefore somewhat disconnected in the introduction, since he has no developing story on which to hang his perceptions. Lists of plants and animals are rushed forward as illustrations for the notions he has in mind. As examples of exalted qualities which are symbolized by trees, he cites the way "the pompous Palms of Florida, and glorious Magnolia, strikes us with the sense of dignity and magnificence; the expansive umbrageous Live Oak with awful veneration; the Carica papaya seems supercilious [*sic*] with all the harmony of beauty and gracefulness; the Lilium superbum represents pride and vanity; Kalmia latifolia and Azalea coccinea exhibit a perfect show of mirth and gaiety." Throughout the book in fact Bartram seems to encounter trees and shrubs with the sort of joyful familiarity that is usually reserved for other humans.

His enthusiasms do not always further his credibility as a scientist. Ornithologists have argued about how much his descriptions of birds can be trusted, and his use of scientific nomenclature is in various places careless. Certainly he gets dates and sightings mixed up; events are transposed from one place to another or from one year to another. Casualness explains these confusions; the precision of scientific observation was really foreign to his nature. Bartram was an artist, and the 1791 edition included nine illustrations of his own. A number of other drawings from the British Museum were pub-

lished in 1968; in these drawings, it has been argued, his sense of composition interferes with his accuracy of depiction. Overall, though, his descriptions have proved to be verifiable; even his encounters with the alligators in book two are consistent with other accounts or with reasonable conjectures.

Bartram found the hand of God everywhere in his travels, and the tension we might anticipate in his travels, between accurate observation and exclamations of praise, did not exist for him. His is an eighteenth-century Quaker version of God, a benevolent master craftsman who instills a moral principle in all things. Even snakes are for Bartram parts of a social and benevolent order; he admires "the dignified nature of the generous though terrible creature," a large rattlesnake whom he had repeatedly passed in the forest. When he meets an Indian renegade in the forest and escapes unharmed, he attributes his escape to an innate moral principle; God, "on these occasions, instantly inspires [the savages], and as with a ray of divine light, points out to them at once the dignity, propriety, and beauty of virtue." The wisdom and orderliness of the created world move him to feel that passivity is the best response to life. "But let us wait and rely upon our God, who in due time will shine forth in

William Bartram's drawing of the alligators he saw in Florida (Fothergill Album, The British Museum)

brightness, dissipate the envious cloud, and reveal to us how finite and circumscribed is human power, when assuming to itself independent wisdom."

Part of the charm of Bartram's narration derives from his reading, which provided him contexts and resonances that enrich the observed scene. The snake bird, a species of cormorant or loon, reminds him of illustrations on Chinese screens, though far more beautiful. "I doubt not but if this bird had been an inhabitant of the Tiber in Ovid's days, it would have furnished him with a subject for some beautiful and entertaining metamorphoses." As he sets out alone toward the territory of the Cherokees, he cannot help comparing his situation to that of Nebuchadnezzar in the book of Daniel, condemned to wander in the wilderness, eating with the beasts and away from human society. Even where he likens his situation to a biblical scene, the parallels are literary and suggestive rather than the insistent similitudes that a Puritan might have sought.

Bartram had a painter's eye for details, and the situations of greatest visual possibilities receive his greatest attention. When he is present at diplomatic negotiations with the Indians, he summarizes briefly, but when he is harassed by alligators on the St. John's River, he is at his vivid best. The scenes in Florida, full of roaring alligators, natural fountains, subterranean rivers, and a rich assortment of other wildlife, are rightly the best-known parts of the book. In 1927 John Livingston Lowes documented in *The Road to Xanadu* the borrowings Coleridge had made from Bartram in "Kubla Khan," including the incense-bearing tree and the twice-five miles of fertile ground. It is clear that Bartram was influenced by contemporary philosophical discussions of aesthetics; he takes special delight in scenes that he can call sublime. Off Cape Hatteras on his way toward Charleston, Bartram's ship had weathered a fierce two-day gale, but he dwells at length on the artistically gratifying aspects of the experience. "There are few objects out at sea to attract the notice of the traveller, but what are sublime, awful, and majestic: the seas themselves, in a tempest, exhibit a tremendous scene, where the winds assert their power, and, in furious conflict, seem to set the ocean on fire. On the other hand, nothing can be more sublime than the view of the encircling horizon, after the turbulent winds have taken their flight, and the lately agitated bosom of the deep has again become calm and pacific; the gentle moon rising in dignity from the east, attended by millions of glittering orbs; the luminous appearance of the seas at night, when all the waters seem transmuted

Bartram delayed publication of his book for so long that some of his important discoveries were originally attributed to others.

into liquid silver; . . . the amplitude and magnificence of these scenes are great indeed, and may present to the imagination, an idea of the first appearance of the earth to man at the creation."

Even in the descriptions he gives of plants, he aims at an aesthetic effect; in describing a species of azaleas he speaks of how the thick clusters of their red and yellow blossoms, when seen from a distance, make the earth appear to be on fire. As a stylist, Bartram sometimes stumbles, as he seeks a language fit to express his enthusiasms. Often the terms he employs derive from pastoral poetry; he is on a "sylvan pilgrimage" among "bowers" and "meads," and the Vale of Keowe in western North Carolina reminds him of the classical fields of Pharsalia or the Vale of Tempe. Yet this vocabulary must also describe scenes of wild danger in a fallen world, and Bartram is too much an artist to neglect depicting the whole complex picture.

The Indian tribes of the Southeast, particularly the Cherokees, Creeks, and Seminoles, are also his subjects. Bartram describes in rather piecemeal fashion their mores and ceremonies. He is partial to the Indians, even describing them at times as exempt from want or desires, contented and free. In the introduction he suggests that intelligent observers should be sent to live among the Indians in order to record their languages and customs; the reports of such observers would enable the government to deal with them better. In his direct dealings with the Indians Bartram reports himself as the same shy, obliging, gentle person he was among whites. The Seminoles called him "Puc Puggy," the flower hunter.

Both his actions and his style reveal Bartram's personality in the *Travels*, and it is Bartram himself, even beyond the innate interest of his discoveries, who gives the book its enduring value. The continuing freshness of his responses and his learned and earnest naiveté make him seem like an Adam exploring a deadly and beautiful paradise; like Adam also, he gives names to things that he sees. He seems to travel primarily alone; other persons figure in the book as hosts—whose hospitality he always acknowledges—or temporary traveling companions. At one point he describes parting from a young craftsman who is on his way to some well-inhabited place where he can earn a living. "Whilst I, continually impelled by a restless spirit of curiosity, in pursuit of new productions of nature, my chief happiness consisted in tracing and admiring the infinite power, majesty and perfection of the great Almighty Creator, and in the contemplation, that through divine aid and permission, I might be instrumental in discovering, and introducing into my native country, some original productions of nature, which might become useful to society." The rejection of the entrepreneurial life and the exalted hopes Bartram entertains for his wanderings make him seem especially young, free of family or work responsibilities to follow wherever his curiosity leads him.

But the travels aged him. He never fully recovered his eyesight after the undiagnosed sickness that he contracted in Alabama. Returned to Philadelphia, he did no more journeying, and after his one book was published, he wrote only a few short pieces on horticultural subjects during the rest of his life. His book received only lukewarm reviews, and no second edition appeared in America during his lifetime; it enjoyed better success in England and Europe, where it appeared in several editions in German, Dutch, and French over the next ten years. Though he was often consulted by botanists and ornithologists, he had no students and developed no theories or methods; unlike his father he made no extensive effort to keep up his standing in the scientific community. When Jefferson, a longtime friend and correspondent, invited him to join the Lewis and Clark expedition, he declined. His own excursions had been much more spontaneous and impressionistic than that expedition would be. Besides, judging from the testimony of visitors in the 1790s and later, Bartram looked like an older man than his age might have suggested. Yet he lived to be eighty-four, never marrying, still working in his father's garden to the end.

The Bartram Gardens can still be visited in Philadelphia, and the Bartram Society works to keep the Bartrams' name remembered. Lowes's book and an edition of the *Travels* introduced by Mark Van Doren produced a modest revival of interest in him during the 1930s. N. Bryllion Fagin's book methodically documents the borrowings of the romantics from Bartram. Francis Harper edited both Bartram's memoranda to Fothergill and the *Travels* itself, with extensive notes and annotated indices in each edition. The botanical and zoological drawings Bartram sent to Collinson and Fothergill have been published by the American Philosophical Society.

In recommending Bartram's *Travels* to Emerson, Carlyle emphasized the peculiarly American character of the book, not only in subject but in style. Bartram sought isolation in the forests and the ecstasy of private communion with wild nature, a pattern so common in American literature that no further examples need to be given. He also meant to be the collector and documenter of the things he saw, in a tradition that extends back to the earliest promotion and travel literature. The *Travels* is not a carefully structured book; it is casually encyclopedic in its frequent lists of plants, trees, and birds. Even as he was traveling, Florida and Georgia were beginning to be transformed by traders and the first plantations; it is fortunate that this scene could still be recorded by someone with Bartram's capacity for wonder.

Bibliography:

Rose Marie Cutting, *John and William Bartram, William Byrd II. and St. John de Crevecoeur: A Reference Guide* (Boston: G. K. Hall, 1976).

Biography:

Ernest Earnest, *John and William Bartram: Botanists and Explorers* (Philadelphia: University of Pennsylvania Press, 1940).

References:

Robert D. Arner, "Pastoral Patterns in William Bartram's Travels," *Tennessee Studies in Literature,* 18 (1973): 133-145;

William Darlington, ed., *Memorials of John Bartram and Humphry Marshall* (Philadelphia: Lindsay & Blakiston, 1849);

Gordon DeWolf, Introduction to *Travels through North and South Carolina, Georgia, East and West Florida* (Savannah: Beehive Press, 1973), pp. v-xx;

N. Bryllion Fagin, *William Bartram: Interpreter of the American Landscape* (Baltimore: Johns Hopkins University Press, 1933);

Richard M. Gummere, "William Bartram, a Classical Scientist," *Classical Journal,* 50 (January 1955): 167-170;

Berta G. Lee, "William Bartram: Naturalist or 'Poet'?," *Early American Literature,* 7 (Fall 1972): 124-129;

John Livingston Lowes, *The Road to Xanadu* (New York: Houghton Mifflin, 1927);

Patricia M. Medeiros, "Three Travelers: Carver, Bartram, and Woolman," in *American Literature, 1764-1789: The Revolutionary Years,* edited by Everett Emerson (Madison: University of Wisconsin Press, 1977): pp. 195-211;

John Seelye, "Beauty Bare: William Bartram and His Triangulated Wilderness," *Prospects: The Annual of American Cultural Studies,* 6 (1981): 37-54;

Bruce Silver, "William Bartram's and Other Eighteenth-Century Accounts of Nature," *Journal of the History of Ideas,* 39 (October-December 1978): 597-614.

Papers:

The primary collection of Bartram letters and manuscripts is at the Historical Society of Pennsylvania. There is also some important Bartram material in the British Museum.

Jeremy Belknap

(4 June 1744-20 June 1798)

Louis P. Masur
Princeton University

See also the Belknap entry in *DLB 30, American Historians, 1607-1865.*

BOOKS: *An Eclogue Occasioned by the Death of the Reverend Alexander Cumming . . .* (Boston: Printed by D. & J. Kneeland for J. Edwards, 1763);

A Plain and Earnest Address from a Minister to a Parishioner, on the Neglect of the Publick Worship, and Preaching of the Gospel . . . (Salem: Sold by Samuel Hall, 1771);

A Sermon on Military Duty, Preached at Dover, November 10, 1772, before His Excellency John Wentworth . . . (Salem: Printed by S. & E. Hall, 1773);

Jesus Christ, The Only Foundation. A Sermon . . . (Portsmouth: Printed by Daniel Fowle, 1779);

The History of New-Hampshire. Volume I. Comprehending the Events of One Complete Century from the Discovery of the River Pascataqua . . . (Philadelphia: Printed by Robert Aitken, 1784; London: Sold by Longman, 1784);

An Election Sermon, Preached before the General Court, of New-Hampshire, At Portsmouth, June 2, 1785 . . . (Portsmouth: Printed by Melcher & Osborne, 1785);

A Sermon, Preached at the Installation of the Rev. Jedidiah Morse, A.M. to the Pastoral Care of the Church and Congregation in Charlestown, on the 30th of April 1789 . . . (Boston: Printed by Samuel Hall, 1789);

The History of New-Hampshire. Volume II. Comprehending the Events of Seventy Five Years, from MDCCXV to MDCCXC . . . (Boston: Printed by Isaiah Thomas & Ebenezer T. Andrews, 1791; London: Sold by Longman, 1791);

The Foresters, An American Tale: Being a Sequel to the History of John Bull the Clothier. In a Series of Letters to a Friend (Boston: Printed by I. Thomas & E. T. Andrews, 1792; revised and enlarged, 1796);

The History of New-Hampshire. Volume III. Containing

Jeremy Belknap; portrait by Henry Sargent (Massachusetts Historical Society)

a Geographical Description of the State; With Sketches of Its Natural History, Productions, Improvements, and Present State of Society and Manners, Laws and Government . . . (Boston: Printed by Belknap & Young, 1792; London: Sold by Longman, 1792);

A Discourse, Intended to Commemorate the Discovery of America by Christopher Columbus; Delivered at the Request of the Historical Society in Massachusetts, on the 23D Day of October, 1792, Being the Completion of the Third Century Since that Memorable Event. To Which Are Added, Four Dissertations . . . (Boston: Printed by Belknap & Hall at the Apollo Press, 1792);

American Biography: Or, An Historical Account of Those Persons Who Have Been Distinguished in America, As Adventurers, Divines, Statesmen, Warriors, Philosophers, Authors, and Other Remarkable Characters . . . , 2 volumes (Boston: Printed by Isaiah Thomas & Ebenezer T. Andrews, 1794, 1798);

Dissertations on the Character, Death & Resurrection of Jesus Christ, and the Evidence of His Gospel; With Remarks on Some Sentiments Advanced in a Book

Intitled "The Age of Reason" . . . (Boston: Printed by Joseph Belknap at the Apollo Press, 1795);

A Sermon, Delivered Before the Convention of the Clergy of Massachusetts, in Boston, May 26, 1796 . . . (Boston: Printed by Samuel Hall, 1796);

A Sermon, Delivered on the 9th of May, 1798, The Day of the National Fast, Recommended by the President of the United States . . . (Boston: Printed by Samuel Hall, 1798);

Two Sermons, Delivered April 27, 1788, on the Institution and Observation of the Sabbath . . . (Boston: Printed for S. Hall and Manning & Loring, 1801);

The Belknap Papers, Collections of the Massachusetts Historical Society, fifth series, 2-3 (1877), sixth series, 4 (1891);

OTHER: *Sacred Poetry. Consisting of Psalms and Hymns, Adapted to Christian Devotion in Public and Private*, compiled, with a preface, by Belknap (Boston: Printed by Joseph Belknap at the Apollo Press, 1795).

Jeremy Belknap, Congregational clergyman and historian, was born at Boston, Massachusetts, to Joseph Belknap, a leather dresser and furrier, and Sarah Byles Belknap, a niece of the Reverend Mather Byles. Originally named Jeremiah by his parents, he later took the shortened form of his name. After graduating from Harvard in 1762 Belknap taught school and studied theology at Milton, Massachusetts, and Portsmouth and Greenland, New Hampshire, before settling at the first Congregational church of Dover, New Hampshire, in 1767. Shortly thereafter he married Ruth Eliot of Boston.

Belknap enthusiastically supported the American Revolution, and he believed that with the birth of a new political order, a new literary order must also arise. In 1780 he wrote, "Why may not a Republic of Letters be realized in America as well as a Republican Government." In 1787, after considering an offer to edit a newly formed magazine in Philadelphia, Belknap accepted a call to the Federal Street Church in Boston and over the next decade established himself as a major literary figure in the early republic.

Belknap is best remembered for his three-volume *The History of New-Hampshire* (1784, 1791, 1792), a project he conceived while still a student at Harvard. Belknap corresponded widely in searching out source material, and he used mostly original documents in writing his account of the rise and progress of New Hampshire. At a time when many Americans viewed the success of the Revolution as a sign of God's providence, Belknap's history relied more on man's reason and judgment than the deity to explain events. The third volume included a brief narrative of Belknap's tour through the White Mountains of New Hampshire in 1784, during which he used scientific instruments to demonstrate that observation and logic, not superstition, explained the enigmas of natural and human history. Although the first volume, published amidst the postwar depression in America, was a financial catastrophe for Belknap, the remaining volumes, which were subsidized by a grant of £50 from the New Hampshire legislature, earned him a substantial profit.

Belknap's literary reputation today rests chiefly on *The Foresters, An American Tale: Being a Sequel to the History of John Bull the Clothier* (1792), published anonymously. An incomplete version appeared originally in the issues of the *Columbian Magazine* between June 1787 and April 1788. In this work of satirical fiction, Belknap borrowed freely from certain British literary conventions. *The Foresters,* which Belknap considered a "historical allegory," tells the story of the settlement of the New World, the origins of the American Revolution, and the formation of the Constitution through the use of allegorical characters. Some, such as John Bull for England and Bull's wife for Parliament, were drawn directly from John Arbuthnot's *The History of John Bull* (1712). Others, such as antifiddlers for antifederalists and rats for speculators, were of Belknap's own invention. For the book version of 1792 Belknap adopted an epistolary form and told the story in a series of sixteen letters from a visitor in the forest (America) to a friend (the second edition added two letters and revised portions of the original text). *The Foresters* sold well throughout the 1790s, but the author's identity remained unknown to the general public.

In the 1790s Belknap also published his two-volume *American Biography* (1794, 1798), a chronologically arranged series of essays on "persons who

THE

H I S T O R Y
of

N E W - H A M P S H I R E.

VOLUME I.

COMPREHENDING THE EVENTS OF ONE COMPLETE CENTURY FROM THE DISCOVERY OF THE RIVER PASCATAQUA.

By JEREMY BELKNAP, A. M.

Member of the American Philosophical Society held at Philadelphia for promoting useful Knowledge.

Tempus edax rerum, tuque invidiofa vetuftas
Omnia deftruitis: vitiataque dentibus ævi
Paulatim lenta confumitis omnia morte.
Hæc perftant.   OVID.

PHILADELPHIA:

PRINTED FOR THE AUTHOR BY ROBERT AITKEN, IN MARKET STREET, NEAR THE COFFEE-HOUSE.

M.DCC.LXXXIV.

Title page for the first volume of Belknap's history of his state (courtesy of the John Carter Brown Library at Brown University)

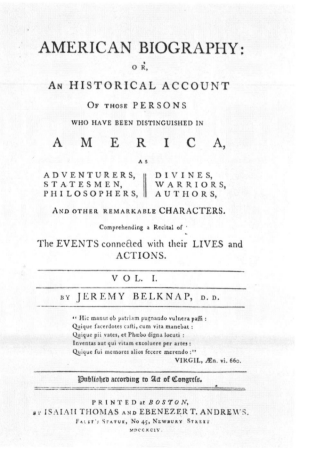

AMERICAN BIOGRAPHY:
OR,

AN HISTORICAL ACCOUNT

OF THOSE PERSONS

WHO HAVE BEEN DISTINGUISHED IN

A M E R I C A,

AS

ADVENTURERS,	DIVINES,
STATESMEN,	WARRIORS,
PHILOSOPHERS,	AUTHORS,

AND OTHER REMARKABLE CHARACTERS.

Comprehending a Recital of

The EVENTS connected with their LIVES and ACTIONS.

VOL. I.

BY JEREMY BELKNAP, D. D.

" Hic manus ob patriam pugnando vulnera paffi :
Quique facerdotes cafti, cum vita manebat :
Quique pii vates, et Phœbo digna locuti :
Inventas aut qui vitam excoluere per artes :
Quique fui memores alios fecere merendo :"
VIRGIL, Æn. vi. 660.

Published according to Act of Congrefs.

PRINTED at BOSTON,
BY ISAIAH THOMAS AND EBENEZER T. ANDREWS.
FAUST's STATUE, No 45, NEWBURY STREET
MDCCXCIV.

Title page for the first volume of Belknap's essays on "persons who have been distinguished in America" (courtesy of the John Carter Brown Library at Brown University)

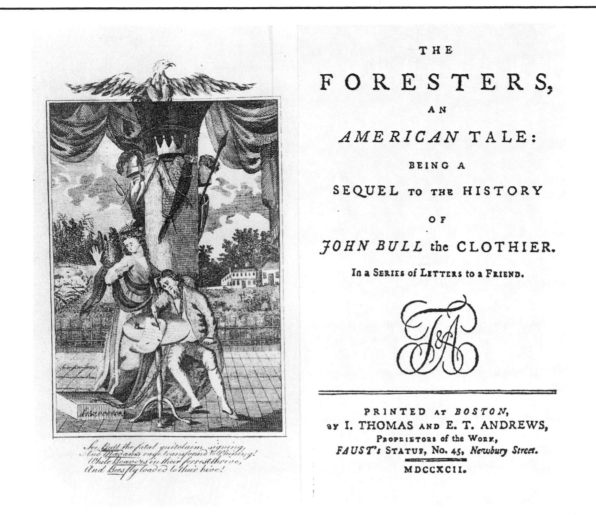

See Bull the fatal quitclaim signing,
And Magna's rage transformed to whistling!
While Beavers in their forrest thrive,
And Bees fly loaded to their hive!

THE

FORESTERS,

AN

AMERICAN TALE:

BEING A

SEQUEL TO THE HISTORY

OF

JOHN BULL the CLOTHIER.

In a SERIES of LETTERS to a FRIEND.

PRINTED AT *BOSTON*,
BY I. THOMAS AND E. T. ANDREWS,
PROPRIETORS of the WORK,
FAUST's STATUE, No. 45, *Newbury Street.*
MDCCXCII.

Frontispiece and title page for Belknap's allegorical satire on American history through the framing of the Constitution

have been distinguished in America." Although many of the entries were repetitive and the work was uneven in scope, one contemporary noted that, prior to these volumes, biography "was a literary path hitherto unexplored in America." Throughout his life, Belknap also contributed to the publications of the American Philosophical Society and the Massachusetts Historical Society, which he helped found in 1791.

Of the many books and sermons he published, contemporaries viewed Belknap's compilation *Sacred Poetry* (1795) as his most important work. The volume served as the most popular hymnbook in New England churches for several decades. Overall, Belknap's career reflected the interrelationship between religion and literature in the early republic. His death at the age of fifty-four inspired one German correspondent, Christopher Ebeling, to lament to an American, William Bently, that "he died, alas, too early for your literature and history."

Letters:

Collections of the Massachusetts Historical Society, fifth series 2-3 (1877); sixth series 4 (1891).

Biography:

Jean Marcou, *Life of Jeremy Belknap, D.D.* (New York: Harper, 1847).

References:

Sidney Kaplan, *"The History of New Hampshire:* Jeremy Belknap as Literary Craftsman," *William and Mary Quarterly,* third series 21 (January 1964): 18-39;

George B. Kirsch, "Jeremy Belknap: Man of Letters in the Young Republic," *New England Quarterly,* 54 (March 1981): 33-53.

Papers:

The largest collection of Belknap's papers is at the Massachusetts Historical Society.

John Bernard

(1756-29 November 1828)

Claudia Johnson
University of Alabama

BOOKS: *Retrospections of the Stage,* edited by Bayle
Bernard (London: Colburn & Bentley, 1830;
Boston: Carter & Hendee, 1832);
Retrospections of America, 1797-1811, edited by Mrs.
Bayle Bernard, with an introduction, notes,
and index by Laurence Hutton and Brander
Matthew (New York: Harper, 1887).

As a man of the theater, John Bernard was
sufficiently well known to receive notice from such
eminent historians of his day as William Dunlap
and William Wood. Estimates of his acting vary:
while some reputable critics disparage his ability as
an actor, Dunlap praises him as the finest comedian
in America, and there seems to be little doubt that
he was popular among audiences on both sides of
the Atlantic. As an author of two posthumously
published works, Bernard is himself a theater historian of significance. His first book is one of the best
of many actors' accounts of London and English
provincial theater in the eighteenth century. His
second work is a rare glimpse of many aspects of
cultural life in America during the federal period.

Retrospections of the Stage (1830) begins with
Bernard's birth in Portsmouth to Ann and John
Bernard, a naval lieutenant, and his youthful fascination with the stage. At seventeen, after a thea-
ter-going trip to London had made him hopelessly
stagestruck, he ran away from home to join what he
calls "a band of dramatic desperadoes." He describes the company's lodgings on tour, theatrical
landladies, and his rise in his profession to become a
member of Covent Garden Theatre, for which he
also wrote two plays. *The Whimsical Ladies* was produced in 1786 and *The British Sailor* in 1786 and
1789. Like many actors, Bernard was active in London club life. He characterizes several of the most
prominent, including the Beefsteak Club, in which
he served as an officer. The story of his life is
frequently interrupted with anecdotes involving his
associates and instructions in the "science of the
stage."

His second memoir, *Retrospections of America,*
(1887), begins where the first ended, with his im-

migration to America in the summer of 1797. The
memoir is an account of his work as an actor and,
occasionally, as a manager during his thirty-one-
year residence in the United States, until 1819 when
he returned to England. Unlike his first book,
which is entirely concerned with matters relating to
the theater, the second contains extensive comment
on nontheatrical life in America: famous American
political and literary figures whom he knew, impressions of cities, states, regions and types, and
American women. Bernard had "an odd sort of
introduction" to George Washington in 1798 at the
scene of a carriage accident near Annapolis. After
he and Washington observed the mishap and got
the vehicle, horse, and victims on their way, they
traveled to Mount Vernon for tea. Bernard was
impressed with Washington's vigorous physical
ability and his willingness to assist directly in this
small crisis rather than sending his servants to help,
as most gentlemen would have done. Through
Washington, who was a lover of the theater, Bernard met Jefferson. The Virginian's broad learning
and plainness of expression impressed Bernard,
whose recollections are chiefly of his conversations
with Jefferson about the French Revolution, the
democratic mission of America, and such varied
people as Mirabeau, Priestley, and Benjamin Rush.
Of particular interest are his frequent, scattered
discussions of the character and plight of American
blacks, the institution of slavery and the slave owner.

Both books, edited from Bernard's journals,
exemplify two of the most popular literary types of
the eighteenth and nineteenth centuries. The first,
as it is arranged by his son Bayle, is in the tradition
of the stage memoir as it later flourished in the
nineteenth century—the chronological sequence,
the anecdotal nature, and the steady focus on the
characters, traditions, and extraordinary life-styles
of theater folk. The second, edited by Mrs. Bayle
Bernard, is in the vein of travel books made popular
by Harriet Martineau, Frances Trollope, and Fanny
Kemble. While the first work has value as a reference, it is less than successful as a personal memoir

JOHN BERNARD AS JACK MEGGOT.

RETROSPECTIONS OF AMERICA

1797–1811

By JOHN BERNARD
SOMETIME SECRETARY OF THE BEEFSTEAK CLUB, AND AUTHOR OF
" RETROSPECTIONS OF THE STAGE "

EDITED FROM THE MANUSCRIPT BY

MRS. BAYLE BERNARD

WITH

AN INTRODUCTION, NOTES, AND INDEX BY

LAURENCE HUTTON AND BRANDER MATTHEWS

ILLUSTRATED

NEW YORK
HARPER & BROTHERS, FRANKLIN SQUARE
· 1887

Frontispiece and title page for Bernard's posthumously published account of his experiences in the American theater

because it fails to present any real sense of the narrator's character. The second book, certainly the more useful, gives the reader the benefit of skillful, firsthand observations and is a standard source for social historians, especially theater historians, of the federal period.

References:

T. Allston Brown, *A History of the New York Stage*, 1 volume (New York: Dodd, Mead, 1903);

William Dunlap, *A History of the American Theatre* (New York: Harper, 1832);

Bernard Hewitt, *Theatre USA, 1668-1957* (New York: McGraw-Hill, 1959);

Francis Hodge, *Yankee Theatre* (Austin: University of Texas Press, 1964);

Laurence Hutton, *Curiosities of the American Stage* (New York: Harper, 1891);

Noah Ludlow, *Dramatic Life As I Found It* (St. Louis: G. I. Jones, 1880);

George C. D. Odell, *Annals of the New York Stage* (New York: Columbia University Press, 1927);

Thomas Clark Pollock, *The Philadelphia Theatre in the Eighteenth Century* (Philadelphia: University of Pennsylvania Press, 1933);

George O. Seilhamer, *History of the American Theatre Before the Revolution* (New York: Harper, 1891);

William Wood, *Personal Recollections of The Stage* (Philadelphia: Henry Carey Baird, 1853).

John Durburrow Blair

(15 October 1759-10 January 1823)

Stephen J. Stedman
Tennessee State University

BOOKS: *A Sermon on the Death of Lieutenant General George Washington, delivered in the Capitol in Richmond* . . . (Richmond: Printed by Merriwether Jones, 1800);

A Sermon on the Impetuosity and Bad Effects of Passion. And the Most Likely Means of Subduing It (Richmond: Printed by Lynch & Southgate, 1809);

Sermons Collected from the Manuscripts of the Late Rev. John D. Blair (Richmond: Printed by Shepherd & Pollard, 1825).

Although John Durburrow Blair's place in literary history depends solely on a relatively small number of published sermons, he also deserves remembrance for the tenor of rational enlightenment which he fostered in most aspects of his life, which, besides the ministry, also included his work as an educator and a patriot. An urbane rationalist who clearly enjoyed the social pleasures of Richmond, where he lived for the last thirty years of his life, Blair was distinctly one of the gentlemen theologians who inhabited most cities in Virginia and surrounding states during the early years of the nineteenth century. Perhaps no single circumstance of his life better illustrates the reasonable temperament of the man than his sharing with Rev. John Buchanan the pastoral duties of St. John's Church in Richmond; for many years they alternated Sundays as preacher to the congregation, which seemed not to mind that Blair was a Presbyterian and Buchanan an Episcopalian. Such easy tolerance says much about early-nineteenth-century Richmond, as well as about the two parsons themselves.

Blair was born in Faggs Manor, Pennsylvania, the son of John Blair, a Presbyterian minister. At sixteen he was graduated from the College of New Jersey, whose president, John Witherspoon, much influenced Blair with his Scots philosophy of Common Sense. In 1780 with President Witherspoon's assistance, Blair was appointed president of Washington-Henry Academy in Hanover County, Virginia, where he taught the classics; he also pastored the nearby Church of Pole Green after being ordained into the Presbyterian ministry in 1785. Apparently seeking a wider circle of enlightened acquaintance, Blair moved in 1790 to Richmond where he opened a school and preached successively at the Old Capitol in the hall of the House of Delegates, in St. John's Church, and finally in the newly erected Presbyterian church on Shockoe Hill. Besides enjoying occasional hunting and fishing expeditions with Buchanan, Blair sought the social pleasures of Richmond society, some thinking that he did so a bit too much for a man of the cloth. Blair argued that he enjoyed these pleasures moderately, that he "used them so as not to abuse them." At any rate, the cultural milieu of the city was such that Blair turned down an offer of the presidency of Hampden-Sydney College in 1796, and he continued the even tenor of his way, occasionally publishing a sermon, until just before his death, when illness forced him to cease preaching.

Blair's medium was the sermon, and it is for his productions in that genre that he is chiefly remembered. However, as published, his sermons do not give the reader a completely accurate idea of the character of the man, whose oral delivery apparently much enhanced their quality. George Munford asserts that the published sermons "were in truth rather full notes of the solid parts of his discourse, which he always embellished and made entertaining by incidents, illustrations, and beautiful imagery." Thus, one must make allowance when reading Blair's sermons for the loss of effect which oral delivery allowed. Even as written, however, Blair's sermons have historical and philosophical, as well as literary and religious, significance.

A Sermon on the Death of Lieutenant General George Washington (1800), besides reflecting Blair's wide reading and exhibiting his poetic prose, remains important as a historical statement. Blair saw in America's first president a spirit of self-sacrifice on which the future hope of the new nation depended. The sermon also offers an optimistic view of the country's future, which is quite characteristic of the time.

Rather different in tone and intention is the only other sermon which was published during Blair's life, *A Sermon on the Impetuosity and Bad Effects of Passion* (1809), later retitled "On Anger" when it was included in Blair's collected sermons. Blair offers in this sermon several nostrums for those wrathfully inclined; additionally, he inserts what amounts to a topical commentary in a long digression on the practice of dueling, in his view an unethical behavior. Some commentators feel that his digression hints at a duel by a colleague, with Buchanan surprisingly being the most likely candidate.

The collected edition of the sermons includes twenty-eight works in addition to the two previously published sermons. Most are on traditional topics, such as sin, the soul, and future punishment, but two of them suggest the minister's mind-set. In "Religion A Reasonable Service" Blair argues that common sense reveals the rational nature of religion, which is "necessary for any enjoyment in life." The extent of his willingness to depend on reason, however, is sharply circumscribed, for in "Of Infidelity" Blair derides those who advocate "free-thinking" and refers to "the age of reason" in which he lives. These phrases undoubtedly allude to Thomas Paine's *The Age of Reason* (1794-1795), the premier deist document of the time. Blair is at some pains to counter the arguments which Paine puts forward. Besides indicating the probable date of this sermon, the references to Paine reveal that Blair was a man fully cognizant of the latest philosophical problems of his time and fully willing to grapple with them head-on if necessary.

As his sermons reveal, John Durburrow Blair will remain significant for his historical and philosophical contributions, as well as for his sometimes poetic style and reasonable orthodoxy.

References:

John Blair Hoge, "Christian Heroism: A Sermon Occasioned by the Death of the Rev. John D. Blair," in *Sermons Collected from the Manuscripts of the Late Rev. John D. Blair* (Richmond: Printed by Shepherd & Pollard, 1825);

George Wythe Munford, *The Two Parsons . . .* (Richmond: J. D. K. Sleight, 1884);

William B. Sprague, ed., *Annals of the American Pulpit* (Newport: Carter, 1858), III: 459-462.

Hugh Henry Brackenridge

James Kelleher
West Chester, State College

See also the Brackenridge entry in *DLB 11, American Humorists, 1800-1950.*

BIRTH: Kintyre, Scotland, 1748, to William Brackenridge (mother's name unknown).

EDUCATION: B.A., College of New Jersey, 1771; M.A., 1774.

MARRIAGES: 1785 to a Miss Montgomery; child: Henry Marie. 1790 to Sabina Wolfe; children: two boys and a girl.

DEATH: Carlisle, Pennsylvania, 25 June 1816.

BOOKS: *A Poem, on the Rising Glory of America; Being an Exercise Delivered at the Public Commencement at Nassau-Hall, September 25, 1771...*, by Brackenridge and Philip Freneau (Philadelphia: Printed by Joseph Crukshank for R. Aitken, 1772);

A Poem on Divine Revelation; Being an Exercise Delivered at the Public Commencement at Nassau-Hall, September 28, 1774 . . . (Philadelphia: Printed & sold by R. Aitken, 1774);

The Battle of Bunkers-Hill. A Dramatic Piece of Five Acts, in Heroic Measure (Philadelphia: Printed & sold by Robert Bell, 1776);

The Death of General Montgomery, at the Siege of Quebec. A Tragedy. With an Ode, in Honour of the Pennsylvania Militia, and the Small Band of Regular Continental Troops, Who Sustained the Campaign, in the Depth of Winter, January, 1777, and Repulsed the British Forces from the Banks of the Delaware . . . (Philadelphia: Printed & sold by Robert Bell, 1777);

Six Political Discourses Founded on the Scripture (Lancaster: Printed by Francis Bailey, 1778);

*An Eulogium of the Brave Men Who Have Fallen in the
    Contest With Great-Britain: Delivered on Monday,
    July 5, 1779 . . .* (Philadelphia: Printed by F.
    Bailey, 1779);

*Narratives of a Late Expedition against the Indians; With
    an Account of the Barbarous Execution of Col.
    Crawford; and the Wonderful Escape of Dr. Knight
    and John Slover from Captivity, in 1782* (Phila-
    delphia: Printed by Francis Bailey, 1783);

Modern Chivalry . . . , part 1, volumes 1 and 2 (Phila-
    delphia: Printed & sold by John M'Culloch,
    1792); revised edition, 1 volume (Philadel-
    phia: J. Conrad, 1804); part 1, volume 3 (Pitts-
    burgh: Printed & sold by John Scull, 1793);
    part 1, volume 4 (Philadelphia: Printed & sold
    by John M'Culloch, 1797); part 1, volumes 3
    and 4, revised edition, 1 volume (Philadelphia
    & Richmond: Jacob Johnson, 1807); part 2,
    volume 1 (Carlisle: Printed by Archibald
    Loudon, 1804); part 2, volume 2 (Carlisle:
    Printed by Archibald Loudon, 1805); parts 1
    and 2, revised edition, 4 volumes (Philadel-
    phia & Richmond: Johnson & Warner, 1815);
    revised again, 2 volumes (Pittsburgh: Patter-
    son & Lambdin, 1819);

*Incidents of the Insurrection in the Western Parts of
    Pennsylvania, in the Year 1794 . . .* (Philadel-
    phia: Printed & sold by John M'Culloch,
    1795);

The Standard of Liberty, An Occasional Paper, as
    Democritus (Philadelphia, 1802?);

Gazette Publications . . . (Carlisle: Printed by Alexan-
    der & Phillips, 1806);

An Epistle to Walter Scott . . . (Pittsburgh: Franklin
    Head Printing Office, 1811?);

Law Miscellanies . . . (Philadelphia: P. Byrne, 1814).

Editions and Collections: *Modern Chivalry,* edited
    by Claude M. Newlin (New York: American
    Book Company, 1937);

Modern Chivalry, edited by Lewis Leary (New
    Haven: College & University Press, 1965);

A Hugh Henry Brackenridge Reader: 1770-1815,
    edited by Daniel Marder (Pittsburgh: Uni-
    versity of Pittsburgh Press, 1970).

Hugh Henry Brackenridge played an impor-
tant role in America's literary and social history. His
career was colorful, remarkably varied, and uniquely American. An immigrant who rose from poverty
to become a justice of the Pennsylvania Supreme
Court, he was also a political essayist, playwright,
preacher, schoolmaster, editor, minor poet, and
satirical novelist. A learned classicist who longed for
the coffeehouses of London, he lived and worked

on the frontier, actively involving himself in the
major political controversies in those turbulent
times when the young democracy was struggling to
define itself. His eccentric personality and the turmoil surrounding his life in politics and the law
often overshadow his importance as a major literary
figure in the post-Revolutionary period. *Modern
Chivalry,* the work on which his reputation rests, is a
satire on democracy, written in installments from
1792 to 1815 and containing, as the author tells us,
"All of which I saw and part of which I was." It was
as Fred Lewis Patee noted, "the first balanced treatment of democracy in America, the first supremely
important book" produced on the Western frontier.

Born in Kintyre, Scotland, in 1748, Brackenridge moved with his family to Pennsylvania in
1753. His father, William Brackenridge, joined
other Scot-Irish immigrants in clearing the land
and farming a frontier settlement in York County
called The Barrens.

The physically demanding labor of farming a
land where Indian raids were a constant danger
never dimmed young Brackenridge's love of learn-

ing. Encouraged by his mother, he attended school at Slate Ridge and later traveled to Fagg's Manor in Chester County in search of books and counseling from the Reverend John Blair. By the age of thirteen he had a command of Latin and a firm grasp on Greek. His inclination toward satire is demonstrated by his early fascination with Horace and later with the dialogues of Lucian: "I acknowledge, indeed, that in my earlier years, and in the course of my academic studies, I had contracted some taste, even habit, this way; owing to my reading the dialogues of Lucian, in the original Greek." This satirical bent advanced further when he read Cervantes, La Sage, and Swift: "I found myself still more inclined to an ironical, ludicrous way of thinking and writing."

At fifteen he taught and advanced his own education at the free school in Gunpowder Falls, Maryland, where his fiery temper and rigorous standards impressed his students and the trustees as well. He stayed five years until, as his son Henry Marie tells us in his "Biographical Notice" (*Southern Literary Messenger*, January 1842), "he had exhausted the sources of learning near him." In 1768 he enrolled in the College of New Jersey, later Princeton University. At Princeton he met and became friends with Philip Freneau and James Madison, two men who, in a sense, represent literature and politics, the twin passions which were to occupy Brackenridge's life.

The curriculum at Princeton suited Brackenridge's love of languages, history, natural philosophy, moral science, mathematics, and oratory. President John Witherspoon's lectures on neoclassical literary theories and Whig political philosophy reinforced his love of the classics and informed his emerging democratic idealism. While advancing himself academically, he also found time to supplement his small income by composing papers for his less talented classmates. Politically, the campus was alive with controversy. The Tories united in the Cliosophic Society, and Brackenridge and his friends formed the Whig Society in opposition. A paper war ensued. The "Satires Against the Tories," written by Brackenridge, Freneau, and Madison, are high-spirited but crude attacks with little attention to literary subtlety. When the vigor of the verbal warfare resulted in public brawling, the college considered disbanding both groups.

In 1770, again in collaboration with Freneau, Brackenridge wrote a fictional narrative in prose entitled "Father Bombo's Pilgrimage to Mecca." Although only fragments of the manuscript are known to exist, Lewis Leary maintains that "if the complete work could be found it would challenge for place as the first novel in America." Daniel Marder suggests that the fragments which do remain may represent America's first work of prose fiction. The narrative's use of the picaro, the dialect of the uneducated Irishmen, and the theme of moderation anticipate *Modern Chivalry*. Brackenridge's debt to Swift is evident in the character of Father Bombo, a picaresque hero who survives in a world of ignorance and superstition by dint of his roguish wit and classical learning. The wily priest also exemplifies characteristics later found in both Captain Farrago and Teague O'Regan, the major figures in *Modern Chivalry*. Like the learned Captain Farrago, Bombo is a "trimmer," a moderate who when faced with extremes on either side, elects the middle course. "I therefore resolved to steer a mean between both for according to that wise Philosopher Ovid, *in medio tutissimus ibis*. The midway is best." Like Teague, he is a confidence man who rises on the shoulders of the ignorant.

On 25 September 1771, Brackenridge and Freneau presented at the Princeton commencement ceremony *A Poem, on the Rising Glory of America*, a poem modeled on Virgil and Milton, which celebrated with unrestrained optimism America's manifest destiny, the inevitable triumph of the new over the old in the arts, science, and commerce. The poem's three speakers, Eugenio, Acasto, and Leander, are flat characters, indistinguishable from each other, and the verse, by Brackenridge's admission, is labored. Brackenridge was to attempt more work in the epic vein before realizing that, for him, prose was "a safer walk," and before his unbridled enthusiasm for the new democracy was dimmed by his experiences on the frontier. The poem, printed in Philadelphia in 1772, was his first published work.

At his graduation in 1771, Brackenridge resisted the call of *A Poem, on the Rising Glory of America* to become a writer—thus contributing to the triumph of American arts—and stayed another year to study for the ministry, more to exercise his gift for oratory than for pietistic reasons. In 1772, with Freneau as his assistant, he taught at an academy in Somerset County, Maryland, returning to Princeton in 1774 to take his master's degree. At commencement he read *A Poem on Divine Revelation*, again, like *A Poem, on the Rising Glory of America*, in the grand style, but adding that, along with art, science, and commerce, Christianity will come to full flower in the New World. An imitation of Milton in its high seriousness and formal verse, it remains little more than an occasional poem revealing the author's limited gifts for the verse epic. *A Poem*

Page from the manuscript for the picaresque narrative on which Brackenridge and Philip Freneau collaborated in 1770

on Divine Revelation was published in Philadelphia in 1774 but received little attention.

Like Freneau, Brackenridge was ardently patriotic and violently anti-British. As the Revolution was gathering force, Brackenridge, having returned to his post in Maryland, wrote two heroic plays, *The Battle of Bunkers-Hill* (1776) and *The Death of General Montgomery* (1777). The former praises the valor of the Americans and their moral victory while the latter tells of British brutality at the siege of Quebec. Both plays are in the grand manner, with more oratory than action, but Brackenridge's outrage is real, and passages of descriptive realism suggest that he was beginning to find his voice.

In 1777, although never officially ordained, Brackenridge joined Washington's army as a chap-lain. He saw himself as a heroic bard whose oratory would inspire patriotic rather than religious zeal. His sermons, "founded on the Scriptures," are passionate denunciations of the British, not Satan, and he makes no pretense that they are otherwise: "I am careful to assure my countrymen that these discourses are what they pretend to be, of a nature chiefly political." Clearly, his long-delayed decision to abandon the pulpit had been made. The real and present danger to the new democracy fed Brackenridge's combative nature, and he marshalled his talents to do battle in the field of human affairs. His attacks on "The Bloody Vestiges of Tyranny" exhibited none of the moderation he was to recommend throughout *Modern Chivalry*.

In 1778, after a year in the army, Bracken-

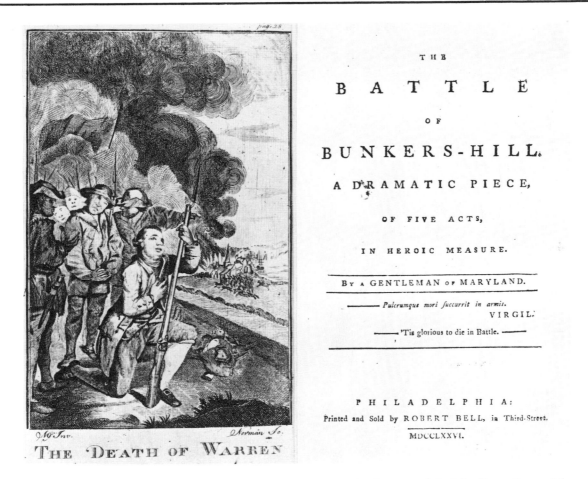

THE

BATTLE

OF

BUNKERS-HILL.

A DRAMATIC PIECE,

OF FIVE ACTS,

IN HEROIC MEASURE.

BY A GENTLEMAN OF MARYLAND.

——— *Pulcrumque mori fuccurrit in armis.*
VIRGIL.

——— 'Tis glorious to die in Battle. ———

PHILADELPHIA:
Printed and Sold by ROBERT BELL, in Third-Street.
MDCCLXXVI.

Frontispiece and title page for Brackenridge's first pro-Revolutionary play (courtesy of the John Carter Brown Library at Brown University)

ridge traveled to Philadelphia, where he published a selection of his sermons entitled *Six Political Discourses Founded on the Scriptures* and where, with a life savings of £1,000, he established the *United States Magazine*. Still imbued with a sense of America's rising glory, Brackenridge ignored the realities of the intellectual marketplace, envisioning a broad-based reading public eager for literature that would entertain and instruct. While acknowledging that the public might "complain that our publication is too highly rated," he assured readers that, with rising inflation, the magazine was actually a bargain. Convinced that Americans "were able to cultivate the *Belles Lettres* even disconnected from Great Britain," he published a monthly "literary coffee house" with frequent contributions from Freneau. The magazine, the first number of which was published in January 1779, failed after one year. In addition to "Beauties of Santa Cruz" and "House of Night" by Freneau, the *United States Magazine* had also presented in monthly install-

ments Brackenridge's short story "The Cave of Vanhest," which Lewis Leary calls "the first native tale set against a realistic background and the first fiction to use the realities of the American Revolution as a theme."

The background of "The Cave of Vanhest" is, indeed, realistic, but the foreground is decidely romantic. The narrator recounts the deaths of soldiers and the sufferings of civilians in the battle around Monmouth at the request of the master of the cave, a learned recluse who, along with his two daughters, has retired from civilization. The congenial company and the romantic environment of the hermit's blissful bower inspire the narrator to musings on his own past, his love for and subsequent disappointments with the muses of art and theology, and his present attachment with "Miss Law, a grave and comely young lady, a little pitted with the small pox." A tone of romantic melancholy pervades the piece and the details are clearly autobiographical: less than a year away from the war and

Frontispiece for The Death of General Montgomery, at the Siege of Quebec

faced with the imminent demise of his magazine, Brackenridge was, at the time of the writing, studying for the bar and considering his remove to the western wilderness. The story's final installment ends with "to be continued."

The failure of the magazine darkened Brackenridge's faith in the ability of the honest husbandman to improve through reading until "He will be capable of any office to which the gale of popularity amongst his countryman may raise him." Brackenridge's anger at "the people who inhabit the region of stupidity" was to fester for a decade until in *Modern Chivalry* he answered the question he had posed earlier in the preface to the first issue of the *United States Magazine:* "For what is a man without taste and the acquirements of genius? An orangutan with the human shape and the soul of a beast."

After completing his study of the law under Samuel Chase of Annapolis, Maryland, Brackenridge was admitted to the bar in December of 1780. Recognizing that Philadelphia was awash with

lawyers and that "there were so many great men before me," he chose the frontier as the best place for a young lawyer to get up in the world. In 1781, he crossed the Alleghenies to the new settlement of Pittsburgh, where his optimism suffered further setbacks. Speaking in the introduction to his magazine, he had recommended to travelers that should they visit abodes beyond the Alleghenies they would "be pleased to find so knowing and polite a people in this embowered residence." What he found was a place without house or street and peopled by rowdy backwoodsmen who would later elect to office the ignorant "Traddle," and ignore the accomplishments of the cultured Philadelphia lawyer.

The harsh realities of life on the frontier temporarily dimmed Brackenridge's desire to produce sophisticated literature. When American troops under a Colonel Crawford were captured, tortured, and killed by Indians, Brackenridge turned to reportage, sending accounts of two survivors back to Eastern readers. *Narratives of a Late Expedition against the Indians,* relating the captivity and escape of Dr. Knight and John Slover, published in 1783, told with graphic realism the dangers of dealing with these "animals vulgarly called Indians." Brackenridge's experiences as a youth in The Barrens of York County had established his antipathy toward the native Americans, and his grim reporting of Indian atrocities was designed to influence Eastern readers away from the European view of the noble savage and toward a realistic appraisal of the dangers Indian raids presented to frontier settlements.

Brackenridge tried his hand one last time at polite letters with *A Masque, Written at the Warm Springs in Virginia, in the Year 1784.* The composition honored General Washington, who was visiting Warm Springs while on tour of his western holdings. Washington's diary for the day of the performance records details of business but no mention of Brackenridge's masque. A year after the event, Brackenridge unsuccessfully opposed Washington's efforts to evict squatters from land he had purchased from a Colonel Groghan. Lawyer Brackenridge maintained, as he had earlier in the *United States Magazine,* that because Indians had no right to land they did not cultivate, Groghan's original purchase of the land was invalid. Brackenridge lost, and the squatters were evicted.

In spite of his avowed contempt for the red man, Brackenridge demonstrated his characteristic unpredictability and independent nature when he defended an Indian accused of murder. "The Trial of Mamachtage," written in 1785 (but not published until 1808, when it appeared in a collection of narratives about the Indians), is the objective account of the trial and execution of a Delaware Indian for the murder of two white men. The narrative reveals an essential nobility in the Indian character and a sympathetic picture of native Americans living in the white man's world. Brackenridge's artistic curiosity and uncompromising integrity is nowhere better illustrated than in "The Trial of Mamachtage."

For the first few years after he settled in Pittsburgh, his law practice prospered. He built a house and married a Miss Montgomery in 1785. A year later, his son Henry Marie was born. His law practice involved him in most of the major political and economic problems facing the frontier settlements, and his political ambitions were rising. He helped to establish the *Pittsburgh Gazette* in 1786: "One of the earliest things which I thought of on going to reside in the Western Country was the encouragement of a public paper." His contributions to the paper were sometimes "ludicrous," but for the most part they were political pieces by which he hoped to advance to public office. His interest in the advancement of the town of Pittsburgh was, however, quite genuine. He wrote well-reasoned arguments for the establishment of a court in Pittsburgh and recommended an academy as the best way to assure an educated electorate. He predicted also a bright economic future for the town: "This Town must in future time be a place of great manufactory, Indeed the greatest on the continent, or perhaps the world." Through his efforts the town got its first bookstore and, in 1786, the Pittsburgh Academy, later the University of Pittsburgh.

Elected to the state assembly on the strength of the wide circulation of his ideas in the *Pittsburgh Gazette*, Brackenridge, following a trait which marked his whole career, voted his independent mind and alienated his backwoods constituency, effectively ending his future hopes for elected office. Confident that he was best qualified to represent the West at the Constitutional Convention in 1787, his bitter defeat at the hands of an Irishman, William Findley, set in motion a literary revenge which would culminate in 1792 with the first volume of *Modern Chivalry*. The first volley in the campaign, delivered in the *Pittsburgh Gazette* of 14 November 1787, was a rhymed satirical attack in which Findley was portrayed as Traddle, an illiterate Irishman unfit for public office. In subsequent issues, ending in June of the following year, Brackenridge wrote letters in which he widened his attack to include not only the demagogic candidate but also the arrogant ignorance of the uninformed vot-

ers. The battle lines were drawn. The threat to the rising glory of democracy came within when the demagogue was swept into office by the "gale of popularity amongst his countrymen." Trained classicist and ardent democrat, Brackenridge looked to satire as a means to restore the natural order of things.

During this period, the evolutionary progress of *Modern Chivalry* took another step forward in the form of *The Modern Chevalier* (first published in *Gazette Publications*, 1806), a long Hudibrastic poem continuing the satire on Traddle and introducing the character of the Chevalier, knight errant and direct antecedent to Captain Farrago. When Brackenridge finally abandoned verse in favor of prose, the vaguely conceived Chevalier became the quixotic John Farrago, and Traddle was transformed in the archetypal parvenu, Teague O'Regan.

The death of his wife in 1788 left Brackenridge with an infant son and a law practice in need of repair. With more practical dispatch than emotion, he married Sabina Wolfe in mid-1790 and promptly sent her off to Philadelphia to "wipe off the rusticities" of the frontier. The couple produced three children, two boys and a girl, who along with their elder brother received a classic education under the tutelage of their father.

Brackenridge was at work on *Modern Chivalry* by the middle of 1790. The first two volumes were published in Philadelphia in 1792. Volume three, the first work in American literature written and printed on the frontier, appeared in Pittsburgh one year later.

Brackenridge could not long remain aloof from public debate and controversy. In Freneau's *National Gazette* he had taken stands against Washington's pro-British policy and against the excise tax. In his enthusiasm for the French cause he returned to the passionate oratory he had used to inflame patriotic emotions during his tenure as chaplain in Washington's army. In a letter "To the President," published in the *National Gazette* of 15 May 1793, Brackenridge responded to the neutrality proclamation by maintaining that neutrality in the struggle against monarchy was impossible, that neutrality was tantamount to desertion. Ironically, when the Whiskey Rebellion began in 1794, Brackenridge found himself caught between loyalty to the federal government and support of Western resistance to Hamilton's excise tax on whiskey produced by frontier farmers. To avoid the open rebellion which threatened the security of the Republic, he sided with the insurrectionists in order to divert the current away from violence by reasonable argument and delay. Although he was successful in defusing the explosive intentions of the frontiersmen, his efforts at moderation earned him enmity from both sides. Hamilton, convinced that Brackenridge had led the rebellion, sent troops to the West. Fearing for his life, Brackenridge put his papers in order, wrote a report explaining his conduct during the affair, and awaited his fate. Hamilton, finding the energy of the rebellion already spent as a result of Brackenridge's mediating strategies, admitted after a brief hearing that the lawyer's conduct had been "horribly misrepresented." Brackenridge was exonerated, but his reputation was under a cloud in both the East and the West.

A year later he again explained his conduct, this time in a 361-page book entitled *Incidents of the Insurrection in the Western Parts of Pennsylvania, in the Year 1794.* Told in clear, direct prose, his dramatic account of the events provides us with an invaluable historical document as well as a penetrating insight into mob psychology, the volatility of the political temper in the young democracy, and, what is most important, insight into the mind of a man of sensibility torn between "treason on the one hand and public odium on the other." Brackenridge places himself at the center of the drama, evaluating the tide of social and psychological forces moving toward rebellion, and examining with scrupulous detail his own struggle to comprehend events, maintain his courage, and restore reason and order among extremists. *Incidents of the Insurrection in the Western Parts of Pennsylvania* is a serious, sober narrative written to restore his reputation. Brackenridge did not, however, stay serious for long. In the fourth volume of *Modern Chivalry*, published in 1797, he makes a final reference to the incident when Teague, a newly appointed excise officer, is tarred and feathered by the mob, and Farrago, for his attempt to explain to the people that their behavior was subversive and "destructive of the first principle of a republican government," is vilified by the administration as an instigator. Captain Farrago is finally "acquitted from the suspicion of having swerved from the duty of a good citizen."

Having rebuilt his reputation after the incidents of the insurrection, Brackenridge, a Jeffersonian, again went against the tide by becoming a leader of the anti-Federalist party at a time when most of the West was leaning toward Federalism. Ironically, it was the *Pittsburgh Gazette,* under the editorship of John Scull, which attacked Brackenridge in his campaign for State Assembly. In need of a platform to counterattack Scull's "Blackguard Journalism," Brackenridge in 1880 established his

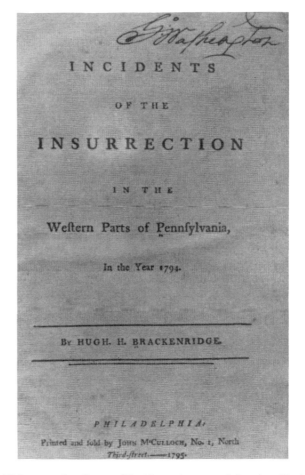

Title page for George Washington's copy of Brackenridge's attempt to explain his behavior during the Whiskey Rebellion (Boston Athenaeum)

own newspaper, *Tree of Liberty.* Brackenridge was defeated in his bid for office, but his efforts helped his party's candidates for Congress and governor and led to his own appointment as a justice of the State Supreme Court. However, even this seemingly secure position was embroiled in controversy. The *Pittsburgh Gazette* continued to ridicule Brackenridge by describing the judge on his opening day of court as "almost 'stark naked' and nearly 'stark mad' from too much tipple." In a later issue, he was pictured as the "biographer of the insurgents" and as a "haberdasher of pronouns." Brackenridge refers to these attacks in part two of *Modern Chivalry,* the opening sections of which examine blackguard journalism and slander, "especially if that slander is of a private, and domestic nature."

By 1804, the ambient anti-intellectualism in the West had manifested itself in hatred for the judiciary, resulting at one point in impeachment proceedings against three justices of the Pennsylvania Supreme Court. Although Brackenridge was not among the three accused, he volunteered to stand with his fellow jurors. The House Committee of Impeachment refused his offer, voting instead to have him removed from the bench for neglect of duty. All four justices were acquitted, but Brackenridge made use of the events by incorporating into part two of *Modern Chivalry* a lengthy defense of the judicial system. Economy, he says in volume one, is the ruling passion of the day and antipathy to laws, lawyers, and judges runs to extremes, "for the people are not always right." He argues that "It may be too soon yet to abolish all law, and jurisprudence."

During the period 1801-1814, while living in Carlisle, Pennsylvania, Brackenridge attempted a "Pennsylvania Blackstone," a study of the adaptability of English law and a defense of the use of English precedents in American courts. Recognizing that a full survey of the legal system was beyond him, he settled for a series of essays, which were collected and published in 1814 under the title *Law Miscellanies*, a valuable contribution to the development of American jurisprudence. Despite efforts such as these, accounts of Brackenridge's career on the bench emphasize more his person than his scholarly accomplishments. Two contemporary observers, Horace Binny and David Paul Brown, both lawyers, recorded impressions of Brackenridge. Brown, cited by Marder, says that the judge was "reserved and misanthropic," alone and shunning company. According to Brown, Brackenridge cared little about his clothes and frequently appeared in court unshaven, his shirt open in the coldest weather, and his hair uncombed. Horace Binny saw the judge charge a jury in his bare feet. Marder, in his study of Brackenridge, quotes from a work published in 1950 to prove the longevity of the legend of Brackenridge the eccentric juror: "He was tall, 'bent in the shoulders,' with a facetious turn of humor that was often at variance with his judicial functions. Careless in dress, often owning only one suit of clothes and no stockings, he was not above kicking off his boots while on the bench and delivering his charge to the jury with bare feet propped on the bar of justice. Once he was seen riding naked through the rain, with his one suit of clothes folded under the saddle, for, he explained 'the storm, you know, would spoil the clothes, but it couldn't spoil me.' Yet this same backwoods political philosopher wrote commentaries on Blackstone, entertained Philip Egalité in his home and was of sufficient stir in the world to have his portrait painted by Gilbert Stuart."

Although busy with his duties on the judiciary, Brackenridge also found time to publish the two volumes of part two of *Modern Chivalry* at Carlisle in 1804 and 1805. No further volumes were to see print, but he continued his observations on public issues in notebooks. Near the end he explains that his book "was not suspended, as to the writing; but only as to the publication." In the last years of his life, Brackenridge was resigned but not bitter. His was a dream deferred, for, in the words of his son, Henry Marie, he was "a man but imperfectly appreciated in his own day, because like others of original cast of intellect, he was ahead of the age, but whose fame is destined to increase, as it becomes more removed from the times in which he lived." In 1815 the author saw through the press a revised edition containing the six volumes previously published as well as material gleaned from notebooks covering the period 1805-1815. Brackenridge died the following year.

The citation from Juvenal which appears on the title page of volume one, part one, of *Modern Chivalry* sets the tone for the entire work: *Quicquid agunt homines, nostri, farrago libelli* ("Whatever men do is the hodgepodge of my book"). The purpose, Brackenridge says, is to examine "all created things and certain others." In the introduction he announces that his book is to be a language experiment only, a model of good writing, "a book without thought or the smallest degree of sense," although he allows that it may yield some amusement. The narrative framework is erected on the travels of Captain John Farrago, a Jeffersonian gentleman farmer (whose surname means "a medley, a conglomeration, a dish of mixed grains"), and his servant, Teague O'Regan, an illiterate Irish immigrant eager to rise up in the world. Farrago, with the ignorant bogtrotter at his heels, travels about the country to observe human nature, and to see firsthand how the newly enfranchised citizens conduct their affairs. The Captain tries vainly to restrain his servant's unbridled ambition but finds that ignorance and a thick brogue are advantages in the eyes of the public when Teague applies for positions as an actor, a minister, a lawyer, and professor of languages. Moreover, the backcountry electorate, heady with their power to elect whomever they please, promote the Irishman to public office and even propose him for membership in the American Philosophical Society. Indeed, he is appointed excise officer by Washington himself and, at the end of part two, will likely become ambassador to Enland.

Perhaps better than any other writer of his generation, Brackenridge understood the full meaning of the democratic experiment, the vitality as well as the dangers inherent in the "rage of mere democracy." His realistic picture of democracy in action is as valuable to the student of American social history as is Tocqueville's objective survey of the principles and promise of self-government in America. A passionate democrat, Brackenridge made himself the devil's advocate, sublimating his experiences in politics and law into writings which illustrated the tyranny of the few and the tyranny of the many, while recommending the proper course between both extremes. However, Brackenridge's public life frequently overshadows his life as a man of letters. His place in American literary history, resting as it does on his one major work, *Modern Chivalry*, is still not firmly established.

According to Mrs. Elvert M. Davis, *Modern Chivalry* "was in its day the most widely read book in the United States," going through edition after edition during the lifetime of the author. Daniel Marder avers that it was "read over the frontier, by some back East and in Europe . . . at least by the king of France." John Quincy Adams said in 1843 that he had read the book as a youth and had "formed a pleasant acquaintance with Captain Farrago and his man Teague." Brackenridge contends that five booksellers made a fortune from his book, adding somewhat extravagantly that in Pennsylvania "there's scarcely a parlour window without a *Modern Chivalry*." In the West, Brackenridge's name was a household word for half a century. In 1835 the *Pittsburgh Literary Examiner* claimed that *Modern Chivalry* was "to the West what *Don Quixote* was to Europe, the humorous textbook of all classes of society." There was, however, little critical response from the literary establishment in the East, owing in part to the fact that, according to the editor of the 1855 edition of part one, "the whole work has never been got up in a manner to give it currency among the higher class of readers." There would be a time, the editor concluded, when *Modern Chivalry* would take its place "among the masterpieces of human genius." A review of modern critical opinion indicates that the time has not yet come.

Daunted by its length (Claude M. Newlin's 1937 edition of the complete work runs to 808 pages) and apparent disorder, critics praise *Modern Chivalry* for its parts, often mistaking a part for the whole. It has been called "a jumbled thesaurus of Americana," a satire modeled on *Don Quixote*, a hodge-podge, our first backcountry book, a sketch, a book of the best American tales written before Charles Brockden Brown's, a Swiftian satire, a forerunner of the novel, a Menippean satire, an anato-

my. To Alexander Cowie it is a book by the "first distinguished American novelist to make substantial use of picaresque technique and of political satire." For Pattee, it is a classic book, but "not because of what its author believed to be its main purpose." Critics make procrustean adjustments to make it a novel, then demonstrate how it falls short. For example William L. Nance says, "It qualifies to some extent as a novel of a semi-picaresque variety." However, because it is a loosely connected series of incidents joined together only by a common character, Edward Park Anderson concludes that it "can scarcely be called the first American novel." Even Daniel Marder, the best of the authorities on Brackenridge, avoids labeling it a novel, picaresque or otherwise. Because novel-centered criticism cannot place *Modern Chivalry* in a convenient pigeonhole, it is generally assumed to be a mutation, an important book, brilliant but seriously flawed.

Modern Chivalry is not a novel nor was it meant to be; however, one must resist the temptation to go immediately to another genre on the assumption that it must therefore be *a* picaresque or *a* comic epic. The prose is modeled on Swift and Sterne. The characters have traceable ancestors. The satiric technique is in a direct line from Menippius, Juvenal, Horace, Lucian, Rabelais, Cervantes, Butler, Swift, and Sterne. The picaresque form was a hybrid, an amalgam of the classical and the modern. It is a picaresque in the sections where there is narrative movement. It is an anatomy of democracy in its didactic lectures, sermons, and scholarly essays. It is a satire in the Menippean manner, through Juvenal and Swift, where it attacks folly and vice, and Horatian satire where the author chides and instructs rather than inflames. Brackenridge's major achievement lies in the way in which he combines the various elements into a unified whole, creating a uniquely American book which captures with robust realism an age that the sentimental novelists and the conservative epic writers scarcely recognized.

Post-Revolutionary political and ethical behavior was the subject and source of *Modern Chivalry*. Judge Brackenridge understood the extreme heterogeneity of his audience. To turn the new leveling democracy away from extremism and toward balance and moderation, he had to appeal at one time to the rowdy backwoodsman and to the literati of the urban centers.

The form and content of *Modern Chivalry* work together to achieve two positions at once: the book is both for something and against something.

Just as Brackenridge used negative and positive polarity in narrative episodes and Platonic dialogues in order to convince readers to select a middle course between extremes, so too, in the book as a whole, he offers alternatives to the three major literary preoccupations of the day: the classical epics of the Connecticut Wits, sentimental novels by and for women, and the Gothic novels, both imported and domestic. Expressed predominantly in a satiric mode, *Modern Chivalry* can safely be called a picaresque anatomy which promotes democratic ideals by satirizing the extremes which threaten them.

The apparent formlessness of *Modern Chivalry*, so disturbing to novel-centered critics, is, for a satiric comic epic, quite conventional. The encyclopedic ramblings, the digressions, interruptions, and changes of pace are integral to the work as a whole. They are part of its rhythm, its medley of lessons on balance. The disorder of *Modern Chivalry* is functional, an ironic parallel to the disorder of the age. In the mixed dish of satire, written for "individuals of all attainments, and of all grades of intellects," variety is a necessity, and the author must appear to be improvising. The cyclical open-endedness of the

book is planned and orchestrated to appeal to an audience intractable to its strictures. The "chaos" of *Modern Chivalry* is deliberate craftsmanship. Controlled disorder is part of its unity.

The first forty-two pages of *Modern Chivalry* are all of a piece, although the presentation seems casual. The themes which unify the book, introduced in these pages, are played and replayed until the lessons are subliminally fixed in the reader's mind. Brackenridge controls his "improvisations" through a pattern of suspensions and returns in which a subject is introduced, left for a time, and then returned to after several buffer chapters intervene. The digressionary material is connected thematically with what went before and what is to follow, allowing the author to play variations on a theme by alternating the serious and the comic.

Critics have been quick to notice in Brackenridge the redundancy of incident and lecture, but few have noticed that he controls and modulates the sequence in order, as he says, "not to exhaust a subject all at once, but to teach it for the present, and introduce it afterwards in a different point of view." The mixture of comedy with moral instruction is necessary because, he says, "it is only by means of amusing that I could get readers; or have an opportunity to reach the public with my lecture."

Brackenridge had to teach the moral that was being abused. He had to assert as well as ridicule. To do so he created the elusive author-narrator. Part oracle, part chorus, this narrator presents the reader a bewildering series of claims and disclaimers, denials and contradictions, but at the center he asserts and maintains a moral and ethical stability. He is the main character who, for fully half the book, occupies center stage. Brackenridge's highly original manipulation of point of view involves the reader in an ambiguous relationship with the author and intensifies the reader's participation in the comic. Superficially the comedy originates in the verbal and situational irony of Teague's efforts to rise to positions for which he is unqualified and the Captain's attempt, sometimes wise, sometimes foolish, to maintain balance. On the highest level, however, it is not Teague but those who trust him who are ridiculed. Teague is beyond redemption, a consistent fool along "humor" lines, unchanged, unchangeable. Farrago is not the simple antithesis of Teague. Teague is at home in a leveling democracy. It is Farrago who is absurd. The Captain wins occasionally, but in the end he is defeated, isolated. Brackenridge's comedy is based on misplaced balance, on incongruity, and it is Farrago, "owing perhaps to his greater knowledge of books than of

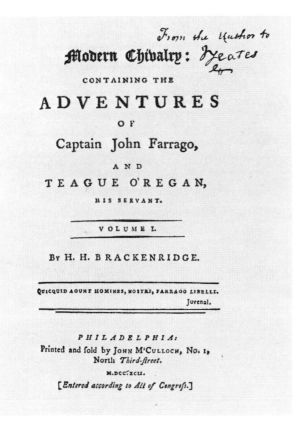

Title page for the first volume of Brackenridge's realistic epic of the unheroic democratic man

the world," who is incongruous on the frontier. It is the incongruity of Farrago's behavior, not Teague's, which carries the ironic humor.

In part two, chapters of reflection become indistinguishable from the narrative because the author no longer insists on the separate identity of Farrago. The assimilation of the Captain with the personality of the narrator is nearly complete at the conclusion. The author, himself a lone classicist among backwoods democrats, claims in his last chapter "that it is not a little owing to this book . . . that a very different state now exists." The irony has pathos in it. The American Yahoos are Yahoos still and the author admits that when an ambassador is sent to England "Teague may be a candidate." The final satiric cut is self-inflicted.

The satire in *Modern Chivalry* is predominantly Horatian, having at its core moral instruction rather than moral indignation. The *saeva indignatio* of Juvenal or Swift is submerged. The satirist saw more clearly that ignorance, anti-intellectualism, and demagoguery could defeat the orderly workings of the American political experiment. The nature of his audience required that he assert as well as attack, amuse in order to instruct. There is, however, a grimace behind the comic mask, an undercurrent of animus toward man's bestial nature. The equation that a man without reason is little more than a beast is introduced early and repeated more than fifty times before the end. The strongest and most complete blast at the irrationality of the public occurs at almost the exact center of the book, delivered by a madman. The attacks are paced throughout the book, building gradually, culminating in the master trope of his satire, animal sufferage.

"The human mind, from defect of attention, or incapacity, cannot be reached all at once." This statement by Brackenridge is central to an understanding of his book, its unity, and the author's artistic control of his audience and his material. His variety is his unity in both matter and method. Having been disappointed with the "honest husbandman" after the failure of the *United States Magazine*, Brackenridge approached him a second time with satire "to revenge himself for injustice, to instruct those in error, and to relieve his oppressed mind." He designed a form uniquely suited to his purpose and his encyclopedic mind. Not even Franklin was more sensitive to the needs and limitations of the reading public than was Brackenridge.

To amuse and instruct over a span of his sprawling volumes, Brackenridge used an astonishing assemblage of masks, tones, and ironic attitudes.

His major achievement is his manipulation of the reader's attention through the multiple and shifting device of the protean author-narrator. The writer announces himself a satirist before the narrative begins. The reader is put on notice early, but because the narrator and the apparent spokesman, Captain Farrago, provides a shifting, unreliable center, the reader is denied a fixed position from which to view the proceedings. Brackenridge's protean shifts of point of view, his alternation from the mask of the learned Olympian, to the backwoods Socrates, to the pragmatic attorney, to the thinly disguised voice of Farrago, keep attention focused on the issue: democracy and the need for balance, moderation, and informed judgment in the exercise of its privileges. Not only do the masks change with astonishing swiftness, but there are also subtle changes in tone within each of the masks. The author-narrator's descriptions of the reasons for writing the book recur like a motif fifty-three times. On twenty-two of these occasions he confesses a serious moral intention. Significantly less often he denies in a mock-serious tone that the book is a satire (five times); calls it an exercise in style only (seven times), a burlesque (once), an adventure narrative (four times), pure nonsense (five times), playful satire (once), and history-memoir-biography (eight times). In short, in one disguise or another, Brackenridge is constantly in touch with the reader explaining his matter and method. On one level, the author-narrator functions as a character and a "character." On another level, he is self-consciously reassuring himself and his reader that his literary schizophrenia is necessary, given his temperament, his time, and his mixed audience. The technique serves as one of several connective tissues which make *Modern Chivalry* a whole piece. These explanatory passages are interspersed throughout the book, complementing or contradicting one another in order to force the reader to be alert not only to the content but to the context of the explanation.

In the very beginning the author lets the reader know that his is no ordinary book. The mockseriousness of his purposes, contradicted in turn by other ironic avowals, leaves the reader only one choice: trust the author-narrator. But Proteus-like, he is not trustworthy. Brackenridge's authornarrator device allows him full play of his learning and wit, and permits him to change his mind, to adjust his attitudes toward contemporary issues as they arise over the twenty-three-year life of his open-ended dialogue.

Suspicious of extremes in art and politics, Brackenridge was an advocate for the balanced view. Like Swift, he was capable of extremes, as his angry wartime sermons against the British demonstrate. And like Swift, he maneuvers his readers into selecting the middle course by presenting mutually unacceptable alternatives. The American satirist knew well Plato's technique of examining a question from several angles through dramatic dialogues in which different points of view are expressed by different characters. By a combination of Plato and Swift, Brackenridge sets up dynamic tensions between opposing positions, forcing the reader to take sides as the combatants argue. A common practice at this point is to have Farrago intervene, offer a moderate solution, and, it would seem, solve the reader's problem. Frequently, however, the author-narrator undercuts Farrago's credibility, leaving the ironic author-narrator the only reliable guide amid confusion. When finally the author-narrator disclaims any responsibility or any purpose other than establishing a model for perfect "stile," the reader is left to his common sense to select a moderate course, usually the only one left after the dust settles. Chapter twelve in volume four of part one shows Brackenridge's technique of dynamic balance at its best.

The effect of the dialectical method of presenting moral ethic strictures is that the reader, alert to the twists and turns of the drama, adjusts and readjusts a movable fulcrum in order to establish balance. Brackenridge, a skillful teacher, keeps his message constantly recurring throughout the length of *Modern Chivalry*. By frustrating the traditional relationship between author and reader, he disturbs the reader's customary stable position and thereby forces a more active involvement in the balancing act. The reader is diverted from externals by dislocations of narrative, but is denied a consistent center by the elusive maneuvers of the ironic author-narrator; thus, the recognition of the need for balance is always in the process of coming into being in the reader's mind.

Implicit in Brackenridge's advocacy of equilibrium is the belief that stasis is impossible in human affairs, especially in the political life of a democracy. The scales are constantly in need of adjustment "as it is the nature of all contraries to run to opposite extremes." Thus it is, as Wendy Martin suggests, that the form of *Modern Chivalry* captures "the fluidity of associative experience and life as an unbroken process." Like *Tristram Shandy*, the book need never end; the cycle repeats itself because folly and ignorance are never vanquished, only temporarily moderated.

In addition to the obvious tensions created by

the author in dramatic scenes of mob violence or in philosophical debates such as one between Farrago and a Quaker on the question of slaveholding, there is the ever-present ambiguous author-narrator. He speaks through all his characters. None, not even Farrago, has a life of his own. Mary S. Mattfield observes that in Brackenridge's alternation between irony and sincerity "extremes are reconciled and the theme of reason is reinforced."

It is perhaps symbolic that a writer whose major preoccupation was balance should also function as the most conspicuous agent for equilibrium between the two great territorial factions in America during the post-Revolutionary period, the East and West. His was the voice of moderation during the Whiskey Rebellion and the controversies over the Federal constitution and Hamilton's economic policies. He saw prophetically the gathering antagonism between East and South. He recommended that the West be encouraged to prosper and thus provide a balance between Eastern and Southern interests. No vague visionary, Brackenridge led the life he wrote about, and it is this life which supplies the robust realism which animates the whole of *Modern Chivalry*.

Although Brackenridge revered the classical epics, he recognized, as his contemporaries did not, that America's epic would have to be different. The new leveling democracy was committed to the common man, to the new over the old, and demanded something unheroic, a contrast epic to balance out aristocratic grandeur with democratic commonplace. "Anyone," Brackenridge averred, "can write the campaign of a great prince. But it would be greater praise to give value to the rambles of privater persons...." The wrecked epics of Timothy Dwight (1785) and Joel Barlow (1787) testified to the futility of imitating Homer's formal verse and royal characters. The new nation had no time for the "specious wonder of Olympus." Consequently, while the Connecticut Wits, whom Vernon L. Parrington characterized as the "self-satisfied embodiment of the outworn," followed classical models and failed, Brackenridge followed Fielding and gave Americans a realistic prose history of an age, his native countryside with a field full of folk.

He employed for his purpose the form of the modern novel, which, with its "supposed travels, conversations, affords great scope, and much freedom, and furnishes an opportunity to enliven with incident." *Modern Chivalry* has the broad sweep of an epic. It is huge, disorderly, like America. Instead of a prince whose genealogy is part of a culture's heritage, we get the Captain and the bogtrotter whose genealogies are unknown. The author admits that if he "were to imitate the action of an epic Poem" he would give the history of the Captain but he knows nothing of his hero's descent or pedigree and he can only guess at the progenitors of Teague. Contrasting his own book with the classical epic, he says, "I must omit, or rather cannot accomplish the dramatic form of the epic, but must proceed in a prosaic way. . . ." Marder observes that "the expanded attitudes of self reflected in *Modern Chivalry* . . . are almost parodies of Homer's heroes." The comic parodies are in keeping with the tone and intention of a contrast epic. They are vital to the nature of an alternative to the lead-plated epics of Dwight and Barlow, both of which were serious to the point of dullness. The cyclical pattern of folly running to extremes followed by a temporary return to reason is repeated over and over again in *Modern Chivalry* and must be repeated as long as human nature is unregenerated.

The book ends on a melancholy note when the author admits that Teague will probably be successful in his quest for public office. This sober realization lends a tragic note to the comedy, universalizes the theme, and raises it above an anatomy of one phase of democracy.

Brackenridge's efforts to produce a realistic epic of the unheroic democratic man have gone unrecognized partly because of his brilliant use of the dynamics of balance. Because he so profoundly understood the precarious equilibrium of the democratic experiment, a one-dimensional representation of the common man was impossible. Crevecoeur said that the American "is a strange heterogeneous assemblage of vices and virtues, and a variety of other principles, forever at war, forever jarring, forever producing some dangerous, some distressing extreme." In its organic open-endedness, Brackenridge's comic prose epic captures the ferment of vices and virtues, of conflicting ideas and manners, in a way hardly possible in the formal verse epic.

Modern Chivalry is a modern epic. To mirror the central paradox of American moral life, idealism versus opportunism, Brackenridge creates two heroes, the idealistic but ineffectual Farrago and the irresponsibly opportunistic but highly effectual Teague. Throughout *Modern Chivalry* the author creates disequilibrated situations and then, through counterpoised arguments or actions, returns everything again to equilibrium. He extends this technique of dynamic balance to include the two main characters, who embody and demonstrate this theme. Farrago is a cultivated gentleman, learned,

with high ethical standards, but he fails in the face of practical reality. Teague is ignorant, ambitious, and confident of his ability to seize the main chance, and he succeeds more often than not. Were it not for the Captain's lies, deceptions, and scare tactics, the bogtrotter would have succeeded in almost all that he attempted. Farrago is an eighteenth-century man of reason who believes in the great chain of being, in congruity, in the eternal fitness of things. Teague, a frontier Scaramouch, is a newly enfranchised democrat, with allegiance to little more than himself and his power to rise up in the world.

Not only is *Modern Chivalry* antidotal to *The Vision of Columbus* and *The Conquest of Canaan* in form, but it is also a more realistic picture because it deals exclusively with the present. The recently completed Revolution is mentioned only in secondary references. His Hogarthian canvas is peopled with a profusion of one-dimensional figures who express viewpoints, then blend back into the crowd. Their behavior shows us the moral and political temper of the age. Brackenridge's epic is about and for the people. The form and content, and the realistic prose style were designed to get it into the hands of those most in need of its instruction.

For the Connecticut Wits, the permanent improvement of the human condition was possible. Brackenridge had a deeper understanding of human nature and of the true nature of the epic, demonstrating through the cyclical order of his book that all lessons must sooner or later be learned over again.

Modern Chivalry is, by degrees, antiepic, antisentimental, and anti-Gothic. It is unique and misunderstood. But if one wishes to know that inchoate period between the Revolution and the romantic period, one has to turn to Brackenridge's Chaucerian portrait of the age. No one else made just such a record. Brackenridge himself, half in jest, half in earnest, asked a question which literary historians have yet to answer: "How many are there in an age that could write such a book as this?"

Biographies:

Henry Marie Brackenridge, "Biographical Notice of H. H. Brackenridge. Late of the Supreme Court of Pennsylvania," *Southern Literary Messenger*, 8 (January 1842): 1-19;

Claude M. Newlin, *The Life and Writings of Hugh Henry Brackenridge* (Princeton: Princeton University Press, 1932);

Daniel Marder, *Hugh Henry Brackenridge* (New York: Twayne, 1967).

References:

J. C. Andrews, "The *Pittsburgh Gazette*—a Pioneer Newspaper," *Western Pennsylvania Historical Magazine* (November 1932): 293-307;

Jay R. Balderson, "A Critical Edition of Hugh Henry Brackenridge's *Modern Chivalry*, Part I," Ph.D. dissertation, University of Iowa, 1972;

Jesse Bier, *The Rise and Fall of American Humor* (New York: Holt, Rinehart & Winston, 1968);

Percy H. Boynton, *Literature and American Life* (New York: Ginn and Company, 1936);

Solon J. Buck and Elizabeth Hawthorn Buck, *The Planting of Civilization in Western Pennsylvania* (Pittsburgh: University of Pittsburgh Press, 1939);

Sargent Bush, Jr., "*Modern Chivalry* and Young's Magazine," *American Literature*, 44 (May 1972): 292-299;

Galen Weare Clough, "The Origin and Development of *Modern Chivalry* and Its Contribution to American Fiction," Ph.D. dissertation, University of Indiana, 1967;

Martha Connor, "Hugh Henry Brackenridge at Princeton University," *Western Pennsylvania Historical Magazine*, 10 (July 1927): 142-162;

Alexander Cowie, *The Rise of the American Novel* (New York: American Book Company, 1948);

A critical estimate of *Modern Chivalry*, in *Literary Examiner and Western Monthly Review*, 1 (1939): 27-29;

Mrs. Elvert M. Davis, "The Bates Boys on the Western Waters," *Western Pennsylvania Historical Magazine*, 29 (1946): 85-138;

Myrl Eakins, "Hugh Henry Brackenridge, Lawyer," *Western Pennsylvania Historical Magazine*, 10 (July 1927): 163-175;

Donald M. Foester, "Homer, Milton and the American Revolt Against Epic Poetry: 1812-1860," *Studies in Philology*, 53 (January 1956): 75-100;

George Martin Galvin, "Hugh Henry Brackenridge and the Popular Press," Ph.D. dissertation, University of Maryland, 1977;

Michael T. Gilmore, "Eighteenth-Century Oppositional Ideology and Hugh Henry Brackenridge's *Modern Chivalry*," *Early American Literature*, 13 (1978): 181-192;

Lynn Haimes, "Of Indians and Irishmen: A Note on Brackenridge's Use of Sources for Satire in *Modern Chivalry*," *Early American Literature*, 10 (1975): 88-92;

Virginia A. Hajek, "The Dramatic Writings of Hugh Henry Brackenridge," Ph.D. dissertation, Loyola University of Chicago, 1971;

Joseph H. Harkey, "The Don Quixote of the Frontier: Brackenridge's *Modern Chivalry*," *Early American Literature*, 8 (1973): 193-203;

W. W. Hoffa, "Language of Rogues and Fools in Brackenridge's *Modern Chivalry*," *Studies in the Novel*, 12 (1980): 289-300;

Leo M. Kaiser, "An Aspect of Hugh Henry Brackenridge's Classicism," *Early American Literature*, 15 (1980-1981): 260-270;

James T. Kelleher, "Hugh Henry Brackenridge: The Art of *Modern Chivalry*," Ph.D. dissertation, University of Pennsylvania, 1973;

Benjamin W. Kennedy, "Hugh Henry Brackenridge: Thoughts and Acts of a Modern Democrat," *West Georgia College Review*, 2, no. 2 (1969): 26-38;

Frances Hoag Kuliash, "Form and Patterning in *Modern Chivalry*," Ph.D. dissertation, University of New Mexico, 1968;

Daniel Marder, ed., *Incidents of the Insurrection* (New Haven: College and University Press, 1972);

Philip Marsh, "Hugh Henry Brackenridge: More Essays in the *National Gazette*," *Western Pennsylvania Historical Magazine*, 29 (1947): 147-152;

Wendy Martin, "On the Road with the Philosopher and the Profiteer: A Study of Hugh Henry Brackenridge's *Modern Chivalry*," *Eighteenth-Century Studies*, 4 (1971): 241-256;

Martin, "The Rogue and the Rational Man: Hugh Henry Brackenridge's Study of a Con Man in *Modern Chivalry*," *Early American Literature*, 8 (1973): 179-192;

Mary S. Mattfield, "*Modern Chivalry*: The Form," part 1, *Western Pennsylvania Historical Magazine*, 50 (1967): 305-326;

Mattfield, "*Modern Chivalry*: The Form," part 2, *Western Pennsylvania Historical Magazine*, 51 (1968): 17-29;

Marcus A. McCorison, "The Rarity of *Modern Chivalry*," *Proceedings of the American Antiquarian Society*, 85 (1975): 309;

Charles E. Modlin, "The Folly of Ambition in *Modern Chivalry*," *Proceedings of the American Antiquarian Society*, 85 (1975): 310-313;

William L. Nance, "Satiric Elements in Brackenridge's *Modern Chivalry*," *Texas Studies in Literature and Language*, 9 (1967): 381-389;

Claude M. Newlin, "Hugh Henry Brackenridge, Writer," *Western Pennsylvania Historical Magazine*, 10 (1928): 224-256;

Vernon L. Parrington, *The Colonial Mind, 1620-1800*, volume 1 of *Main Currents in American Thought* (New York: Harcourt, Brace, 1927);

Fred Lewis Patee, *The First Century of American Literature* (New York: Appleton-Century, 1935);

Arthur Hobson Quinn, *American Fiction: An Historical and Critical Survey* (New York: Appleton-Century, 1936);

Lucille M. Schultz, "Uncovering the Significance of the Animal Imagery in *Modern Chivalry:* An Appreciation of Scottish Common Sense Realism," *Early American Literature,* 14 (1979-1980): 306-311;

J. F. S. Smeal, "The Respective Roles of Hugh Brackenridge and Philip Freneau in Composing *The Rising Glory of America*," *Papers of the Bibliographical Society of America,* 67 (1973): 263-281;

Robert E. Spiller and Harold Blodgett, *The Roots of National Culture* (New York: Macmillan, 1949);

James Lewis Treadway, "The American Picaresque: 1792-1857," Ph.D. dissertation, University of Auburn, 1979;

William E. Vincent, "Hugh Henry Brackenridge: Frontier Commentator," Ph.D. dissertation, University of Maryland, 1974;

Amberys R. Whittle, "*Modern Chivalry:* The Frontier as Crucible," *Early American Literature,* 6 (1971): 263-270;

Mildred Williams, "Hugh Henry Brackenridge as a Judge of the Supreme Court of Pennsylvania," *Western Pennsylvania Historical Magazine,* 10 (1928): 210-233.

Papers:

Brackenridge's papers are scattered among the following institutions: Haverford College, the Historical Society of Pennsylvania, the American Philosophical Society, the Historical Society of Western Pennsylvania, the Library Company of Philadelphia, the Library of Congress, the Boston Public Library, the New York Historical Society, the Berg Collection at the New York Public Library, Princeton University, Dickinson College, and the University of Virginia.

Thomas Branagan

(28 December 1774-12 June 1843)

Michael P. Kramer
University of California at Davis

BOOKS: *A Preliminary Essay on the Oppression of the Exiled Sons of Africa, Consisting of Animadversions on the Impolicy and Barbarity of the Deleterious Commerce and Subsequent Slavery of the Human Species; to which is added, a desultory letter to Napoleon Bonaparte, Anno Domini 1801* (Philadelphia: Printed for the author by John Scott, 1804);

Avenia; or, A Tragical Poem on the Oppression of the Human Species, and Infringement of the Rights of Man. In six books, with notes explanatory and miscellaneous. Written in imitation of Homer's Illiad (Philadelphia: Printed by S. Engles for Silas Engles & for Samuel Wood in New York, 1805);

The Penitential Tyrant; A Juvenile Poem in Two Cantos. To which is prefixed, Compendious Memoirs of the Author (Philadelphia: Printed for the author, 1805); enlarged as *The Penitential Tyrant; or, Slave Trader Reformed: A Pathetic Poem in Four* *Cantos* (New York: Printed & sold by Samuel Wood, 1807);

Serious Remonstrances Addressed to the Citizens of the Northern States, and Their Representatives, Being an appeal to their natural feelings & common sense: Consisting of speculations and animadversions, on the recent revival of the Slave Trade in the American Republic . . . (Philadelphia: Printed & published by Thomas T. Stiles, 1805);

The Flowers of Literature. Being a compendious exhibition of the most interesting geographical, historical, miscellaneous and theological subjects, in miniature. To which are prefixed, preliminary addresses, to parents, teachers and their pupils (Trenton: Printed by James Oram for the author & Daniel Fenton, 1806);

The Excellency of the Female Character Vindicated; Being an Investigation Relative to the Cause and Effects of the Encroachments of Men upon the Rights of Women, and the Too Frequent Degradation and

Consequent Misfortunes of the Fair Sex (New York: Printed by Samuel Wood for the author, 1807);

Political and Theological Disquisitions on the Signs of the Times, relative to the present conquests of France, etc. . . . (Trenton: Printed for the author, 1807);

The Beauties of Philanthropy: or, The Moral Likeness of God Delineated, in Miniature: Being an intellectual mirror for the dignified clergy, as well as the subordinate laiety; To which is added, The Impartiality of Jehovah Vindicated, or, A compendious view of the degradation and destruction of the most celebrated nations of antiquity; With an investigation relative to their downfall . . . (Philadelphia: Printed by Joseph Rakestraw, 1808);

The Curse of Christendom; or, Bigotry and bitterness exposed: Being an answer to the late defamatory publication by the Rev. William White, pastor of the Second Baptist church, Philadelphia, entitled, "Christian Baptism," & c. (Philadelphia: F. Black, 1808);

The Excellency of Virtue, contrasted with the deformity of vice: or, The admonitions of a loving father to his only son, on the most useful, entertaining, and interesting subjects. . . . To which is added, A terrestial paradise displayed; or, the road to happiness and Heaven, strewn with flowers and carpetted with roses, & c. (Philadelphia: Printed by J. Rakestraw for the author, 1808);

An Intellectual Telescope; or, A compendious display of the goodness, glory, and power of God in the starry heavens and the great deep (Philadelphia: Printed by John Cline, 1809);

The Pleasures of Death, contrasted with the miseries of human life; Being a sacred solace on the decease of connections and friends; To which is added the heavenly antidote (Philadelphia: Printed by A. Dickinson for S. Watt, 1809);

A Concise View, of the Principal Religious Denominations, in the United States of America, comprehending a general account of their doctrines, ceremonies, and modes of worship . . . With notes political and philosophical; adapted to the capacities and principles of the youth as well as adults of the American Republic (Philadelphia: Printed by John Cline, 1811);

Rights of God, Written for the Benefit of Man; or, The Impartiality of Jehovah Vindicated. To which is added, A Collection of the Most Precious and Consolatory Scripture Promises, Brought Into One Compendious View, For the Comfort of Believers and The Conviction of Unbelievers (Philadelphia:

Johnston & Cooper/New York: Rowland G. Rogers, 1812);

The Charms of Benevolence, and Patriotic Mentor; Being an essay on the utility and propriety of organizing benevolent associations, for the spiritual and temporal relief of the sick and poor in the United States. To which is added, Solemn admonitions on the present portentious signs of the times: addressed to the people of the United States and particularly the clergy (Philadelphia, 1812); enlarged as *The Charms of Benevolence, and Patriotic Mentor; or The Rights and Privileges of Republicanism Contrasted with the Wrongs and Usurpations of Monarchy* (Philadelphia: Johnston, 1813);

The Celestial Comforter; or, A collection of the most precious and consolatory Scripture promises, introduced in concise but comprehensive sections, for the comfort and support of believers in tribulation and temptation; and particularly to alleviate their pain in sickness, and to illuminate the "valley and shadow of death" with the golden light of eternity. To which is added, A glimpse of the last church of Christ in the world, and the persecution of that church, prior to the commencement of the millenium. Being an apology for the religious sentiments of the author (Philadelphia: Enoch Johnson, 1814);

A Beam of Celestial Light in a Dark, Deluded, and Degenerate Age; or, Epistles consolatory, argumentative, instructive, addressed to The Church of Christ in the wilderness (Philadelphia: Printed for the author, 1814);

A Glimpse of the Sovereign Beneficence, intended to stimulate mankind, To learn from the kindness of God to us all to be kind to one another (Philadelphia: Enoch Johnson, 1815);

A Glimpse of the Beauties of Eternal Truth, contrasted with the deformity of popular error. Intended as a preliminary to the grand centurial jubilee of the reformation of the year 1517, to be celebrated in Denmark and North America, October 31st, 1817 (Philadelphia: For the author, 1817);

The Pleasures of Contemplation, Being a desultory investigation of the harmonies, beauties, and benefits of nature: including a justification of the ways of God to man, and a glimpse of his sovereign beauty (Philadelphia: Eastwick & Stacy, 1817);

The Guardian Genius of the Federal Union; or, Patriotic admonitions on the signs of the times, in relation to the evil spirit of party, arising from the root of all our evils, human slavery (New York: Printed for the author, 1837);

The Beauties of Philanthropy. By a Philanthropist (New York: The author, 1839).

OTHER: *The Pride of Britannia Humbled; or, The Queen of the Ocean Unqueened by the "American Cock Boats"* . . . *Illustrated and Demonstrated by Four Letters Addressed to Lord Liverpool on the late American War by William Cobbett, Esq. To which is added, A Glimpse of the American Victories on Land, on the Lakes, and on the Ocean. With a Persuasive to Political Moderation, Most Respectfully Addressed to the Persons Composing the Two Great Parties in the United States,* compiled, with contributions, by Branagan (New York: T. Boyle/Philadelphia: Wm. Reynolds/Baltimore: J. Campbell, 1815).

Thomas Branagan was an Irish slave trader, privateer, and plantation overseer who, touched by Christ and American rhetoric, dedicated his life at the beginning of the nineteenth century to alleviating the physical and spiritual plight of the new nation's poor and unfortunate. During the early decades of the nineteenth century, he preached relentlessly against oppression and immorality and published prolifically—broadsides, newspaper verse, and more than twenty books—advocating abolition, women's rights, benevolent and relief societies, educational reform, patriotism, and, most broadly, the love of God and man. He wrote in numerous forms and genres, including epic poetry, political and religious tracts, juvenile works, and compendiums of useful knowledge. His checkered life and manifold writings add a fascinating chapter to the history of American literature.

Branagan claimed a "native diffidence" which forbade him "to relate any particulars respecting himself, further than to depict the goodness of God, and his own unworthiness." "Indeed," he complained, "in most biographies there is too much written relative to the big letter I, myself, and too little said for God." Nevertheless, he wrote about himself obsessively in sketches such as his "Compendious Memoirs of the Author" (first published as an introduction to *The Penitential Tyrant,* 1805) and in many autobiographical chapters and confessional passages throughout his writings. The remarkable story that emerges, of past sins and present struggles, serves as a unifying framework for his work, and its considerable drama, told and retold from various and sometimes competing angles, seems to have provided him with the authority he needed to justify and sustain his career.

He was born in Dublin to a Roman Catholic family "of property and respectability." At birth, he was sent to live away from home, under the charge of a nurse—a prevalent practice he later called "one of the greatest misfortunes to civilized society." When he was five years old his mother ("the kindest earthly friend I ever had") died, and his relationship with his father, Thomas, Sr., seems to have been formal at best. At some point an unfeeling stepmother entered the scene. His unhappiness was compounded at seminary school, where he was "flagellated until I was all in a gore of blood," the frequent beatings leaving him "what is generally called a dunce." From the depths of his misfortune, he began to feel "tender impressions of a divine nature." He was so moved by the sight of Dublin's destitute that he vowed to pledge half his fortune to the poor. Frequently attending confession, he even kept a little diary of his sins, "in order to relate them with the more felicity to my confessor." "I was truly," he recalled, "a little zealous devotee." But "the false doctrine inculcated carefully upon my juvenile mind" proved to be "intellectual poison" that turned the naturally compassionate child "blind and bloody minded." "I look back in horror," he wrote, "upon instances of barbarous cruelty, exercised towards innocent and helpless animals by myself in my youth."

When he reached puberty the young Branagan looked toward the sea for escape from his "continual scene of misery." He persuaded his father to allow him to sail to England aboard a ship partly owned by the elder Branagan. Despite a severe bout with seasickness—and in the face of his father's entreaties to continue his education—Thomas resolved to go to sea to see the world. So ended what he called "the sad morning of my life." He was fourteen years old. Soon he was off to Spain, Russia, Prussia, Denmark, and Norway. Branagan gives two versions of his final break with his family. In *A Beam of Celestial Light* (1814), he writes of being forsaken by his father and family (he blames his stepmother) and being forced "to leave home and face a frowning world, helpless, homeless, and almost pennyless." In *The Penitential Tyrant,* however, he recalls being ill-treated on one of his voyages and jumping ship in Portaferry, Ireland, only to be greeted at home by a harsh parental reprimand. "I was so irritated at the reproval," he writes, "that, in a few days after, I left my relatives and friends, without their knowledge and consent." In any case, in 1790, at sixteen years of age, Branagan left port from Liverpool upon a Guineaman bound for West Africa and the slave trade.

"Were I to give a circumstantial account of all the adventures I met with, while on the coast of Africa," he remarks in *The Penitential Tyrant,* "such an account . . . could scarce be contained in a folio volume." To be sure, his experiences would provide him with one of the grand themes of his literary career. But only one particular incident merited the author's mention. After an altercation with the chief mate, Branagan decided to desert the Guineaman to seek his fortune with some other slave traders. He escaped into the jungle, where he was "very cordially received by the negroes, who treated me with the utmost kindness, making me as welcome in their rural abode, as if I had been a dear friend or relative." Sustained by the very people he had come to sell into bondage, Branagan became aware for the first time of the essential humanity and simple nobility of the natives and grew convinced of the enormity of the slave trade. But it would be years before his newfound convictions would effect any change in his life, for he was soon apprehended, returned to his captain, and headed for the Caribbean. "We arrived at our destined port," he concludes the episode, "after throwing many of those unfortunate wretches who composed our cargo overboard, and encountering tremendous gales of wind, with a variety of events peculiar to such voyages, which the brevity of my plan will not allow me to particularize."

The narrative of Branagan's early years in the New World reads like one of the popular adventure novels he would later berate as "idle fopperies and foolish dreams." He sailed throughout the West Indies, escaped "many alarming dangers" off the coast of Georgia, and wandered through the "wildly rude and romantic beauties" of the jungle in Surinam (where, he writes somewhat proudly, he killed an alligator). He was inadvertently deserted by his shipmates and nearly drowned trying to regain the ship. He was twice defrauded of his earnings and found himself stranded in Bermuda without money or friends. "Seeing no better prospect," Branagan then joined the crew of a privateer that cruised off the coast of Hispaniola, attacking and plundering the vessels carrying French refugees from the slave rebellion there. ("Thus they ran," he writes, "from the raging fire into the jaws of the rapacious lion.") But he demurred: "Though I was young at the time, yet I frequently thought that the profession of a privateersman was incompatible with the principles of moral rectitude." So he forsook life on the high seas—and along with it the pirate's booty he had won—for the island of Antigua, where he became an overseer of slaves, rising quickly to the position of chief overseer and to a life of colonial ease: "I became exceeding proud, having an elegant horse to ride upon, a servant to follow me, being cloathed in gay foppish apparel, and

having every accommodation to make life agreeable, and no labour."

While living his sordid, romantic life among slaves and pirates, Branagan seems to have been torn apart by guilt, "making covenants and vows in my own strength, and breaking them as soon as made." In 1792 or 1793, however, "the gracious redeemer had compassion upon me, and blessed me with a sense of his pardoning love and regenerating grace." He gives this account of the experience in *The Penitential Tyrant:* "Being one day at hard labour on board of a sloop, in New Providence, and under pungent conviction for sin, I prayed earnestly to the Almighty, with tears of penitential sorrow, to have compassion upon me, desolate as I was, and rebuke my disorder. After I was done work I laid down on some cedar posts, which was my only bed, and dreamed that I was by some means conveyed imperceptibly to the temple of God, where looking up, I thought I perceived his glory, like a mighty flame of golden light, and while I was gazing on the dazzling sight, I thought a venerable person, which I apprehended was the Son of God, gently placed his hand on my head, and supplicated the Eternal in the most importunate manner for me, in a way which language cannot express; while he thus kept his hand upon my head, he interceded and fervently prayed for me. I seem dissolved in joy, love and gratitude, with the ecstacies of which I awoke. From that, to the present period, the spirit of God never has left striving with me in a peculiar manner."

But only after he was well ensconced on Antigua did he succeed in sanctifying his life. He formally joined a Protestant sect (either Methodist or Moravian), and his dormant sympathy for the African slaves revived. He prayed with them "and took every opportunity to ameliorate their afflictions . . . though frequently in violation of orders I received, forbidding me to shew the least lenity or compassion to them in their sufferings." Finally, his religious convictions joined with "a sense of the villany and barbarity of keeping human beings in such deplorable conditions as I often saw the slave reduced to," convincing him to quit his luxurious life. He returned to Ireland in 1797 to settle the estate of his father, who had died a few years earlier.

Back in Dublin after a seven-year absence, Branagan found no solace in the bosom of his family. Discovering he had forsaken the Catholic church, they "persecuted me as a heretic" and refused to settle his patrimony upon him. Once again cheated, he set sail about a year later for Philadelphia with what was left of his earthly wealth, only to lose that too, through shipwreck and robbery. He arrived almost penniless in the city of brotherly love in 1798 and tried to begin life anew. He married. His wife, Ann, gave birth to a son, Benjamin, in February 1801, but the child died, a "new saint," on 22 October 1802. The Branagans were to have two more sons, in 1803 and 1812. But these, too, died young; the first, William, at age five, the second at one week.

Soon after his arrival, Branagan "became passionately enamored with liberty and America." His evangelical aversion to authority and his reborn sympathy for the poor (underscored by his natural rebelliousness and his destitute condition) were bolstered by the rhetoric of freedom, equality, and independence. But around him he saw poverty, prejudice, slavery, and ignorance, and he bristled at the country's failure to live up to its ideals. In 1801, Branagan set out upon his errand into the urban wilderness of Philadelphia, preaching the gospel "to the poor and the needy, the halt, the maimed, and the blind." In the years to come he would travel up and down the Atlantic coast, delivering his message of God and country, both celebration and lamentation, "on horseback, in the streets, in the highways, in private houses, school houses, and meeting houses." His goal became no less than to "make all America reverberate with my remonstrances."

In 1804, claiming "little learning, less natural capacity, and scarcely common sense," Branagan launched his extraordinary literary career with a powerful antislavery tract, *A Preliminary Essay on the Oppression of the Exiled Sons of Africa*. Drawing upon his own experiences, as well as upon numerous published accounts, he sketches the history of slavery, ancient and modern; details the physical horrors inflicted upon slaves in the British, French, and Dutch colonies; considers "whether the Negroes be a part of the Human Species, capable of intellectual, moral and religious improvement" (favorably reviewing the poetry of Phillis Wheatley along the way); and suggests immediate measures to ameliorate the slaves' conditions, directly addressing both the British Parliament, which had failed to outlaw slavery in their colonies as they did at home, and the legislature of South Carolina, which had recently reinstituted the slave trade in that state. Generically, *A Preliminary Essay on the Oppression of the Exiled Sons of Africa* is a complex, eclectic work, joining poetry to prose, reasoned argument to invective, patriotic oratory to fundamentalist sermonics, graphic description to apocalyptic vision, documented reports to sentimental anecdotes, autobiography to parable. Branagan's purpose, however, is clear and consis-

tent throughout: "to arise and to arise with energy—and strive, though he should strive in vain, to oppose this popular corruption which has too long infected the principles of the inhabitants of Christendom, repugnant to the precepts of moral rectitude, natural reason, and evangelical religion."

As substantial as it is, *A Preliminary Essay on the Oppression of the Exiled Sons of Africa* was intended primarily as a documentary and polemical advertisement for "a work of considerable magnitude in which he has been employed for some years," an American epic in the recent tradition of Timothy Dwight's *The Conquest of Canäan* (1785) and Joel Barlow's *The Vision of Columbus* (1787):

> Awake my muse, the sweet Columbia strain,
> Depict the wars on Afric's crimson plain.
> Sing how the poor, unhappy sable dames
> Are violated at their rural games;
> How Afric's sons surrounded with alarms,
> Die in the cause of liberty, in arms;
> How with their bloody scourge the Christians go
> To Africa, dread ministers of woe;
> How big with war their tilting dungeons ride,
> Like floating castles o'er the yielding tide.
> What pen can half their villainies record?
> What pen can count the slaughters of their sword?
> Give me, my muse, your melancholy bard,
> Give me to paint their guilt and their reward.

Avenia; or, A Tragical Poem on the Oppression of the Human Species, and Infringement of the Rights of Man (1805) is the tale of a beautiful African princess, Avenia, raised in pastoral innocence and splendor, who is cruelly abducted from her wedding celebration by Christian slave traders. Her brother, Louverture, her father, Prince Mondigo, and her lover, Angola, heroically battle to save her; but the evil, technologically advanced Christians triumph, and Avenia is shipped to the West Indies, where she is sold into slavery, raped, and driven to a romantic death, jumping from Caribbean cliffs into the purifying sea below. *Avenia* was an ambitious project. Few had been able to reveal the horrors of slavery to so broad an audience, for, Branagan argued, "it is an undoubted fact, that many will read a performance in poetry; who could not be induced to peruse the same materials, however well arranged and digested, in prose." Certainly, none had written before with quite the same authority: "I write not what I have read or heard, but what I saw; and to my shame I must add, what I did; for in the tragical scene I was an actor."

Admittedly, *Avenia* was written in imitation of

the Iliad (or, to be more precise, of Pope's translation of Homer), but this literary indebtedness only underscored, for Branagan, the political and historical significance of the work: "I thought if the second greatest and most popular poet that ever lived, was tolerated by the vicious Romans in writing an epic poem in imitation of his master and model, the Grecian Bard, and avowedly to gratify the imperial pride and vanity of the destroyer of the Roman republic—I flattered myself that the virtuous Americans would tolerate an unpretending citizen to write a tragic poem, in order to point out the fatal rocks on which all the republics on earth have been shipwrecked; to guard the last remains of republicanism from the attacks of apostate and prostitute politicians; to consolidate, perpetuate, and hand down to posterity as a most sacred deposit, untarnished and adulterated, the liberty and independence their forefathers fought, and sweat, and bled, and died to purchase for them. . . ." Clearly, Branagan considered *Avenia* a magnum opus, not only a significant contribution to the cause of abolition, but a major work of American literature, an affirmation of America's role as the redeemer of the ages and of his own place in the annals of world literature—the democratic heir of a great literary tradition.

When Branagan assumed the mantle of authorship in these early works, he made sure clearly to define his mission. "I have ventured to take the pen in hand," he wrote, "neither for the transitory gain, or fluctuating praise of a sublunary world," but "to contribute my mite towards the suppressing of the growing and alarming evils of these times." Injustice and oppression were his concerns, not style and form: "as I think spontaneously," he later explained, "I write precipitately, and print with few deviations from the MSS." He repeatedly apologized for his "literary inaccuracies and deviations from the radical rules of composition," imploring his readers "to draw a veil over literary errors, and permit the merits of the cause and the purity of my motives to plead my excuse." These self-effacing remarks lay the groundwork for a revisionist literary critique that supported his antislavery argument and, repeated in work after work, constituted a substantial part of his developing remonstrance against American society. The "pedantic style" favored by "logicious cavillers and snarling critics" divided the republic along class lines and smacked of political tyranny. Moreover, those learned, polished writers "who pay so much attention to the arrangement of words" risked losing "the spirit and essence of their matter." Indeed, the

"flowery emblems of fancy, the profound flourishes of rhetoric, the superfluous disquisition of criticism, the majestic brilliancy of diction, and the fascinating flippancy of language" were but visible signs of "the pride and vanity of man's degenerate heart." Branagan's flawed compositions were, to the contrary, "the spontaneous effusions of a grateful heart," reflecting "the unutterable thankfulness I feel to that wise and beneficent Being, who . . . enabled me to relinquish the wages of unrighteousness and to prefer virtue cloathed in rags to vice arrayed in gold." He wanted to distance himself from the elitist literati and to identify with the unlettered multitude. The generic eclecticism of his prose, the repetitiveness of his poetry, the general lack of polish that characterized all his writings—all these, Branagan claimed, were marks of his unwillingness to be shackled by the sinful worldliness of literary and linquistic convention.

To be sure, Branagan did not want simply to cater to popular taste. He wanted to educate, to persuade, and to convert. But it was to a society enthralled with the literature of falsehood and vanity that he offered his antislavery tracts, and he remained cynical concerning his prospects for success. "To my serious strains the ear is shut; and the heart impenetrable," he complained, "while the idle fopperies and the foolish dreams of the romance or the novel, find the readiest access and the kindest entertainment." He presents what amounts to a moralized reader-response theory of popular fiction: "The reader is all attention. He is amused, he is delighted, he is in raptures. Delusory prospects, fanciful scenes open to him, with which he is, at once, astonished and delighted. Every thing he sees is marvellous. Every house is a palace or a cottage; every man an angel or a fiend; every woman a goddess or a fury. Here the scene momentarily varies; and assumes new appearances. Now it is a dreary castle full of spectres and ghosts, robbers and murderers. Next moment it is a beautiful villa or a splendid palace, resounding with the notes of festivity and joy. Now it exhibits the appearance of a loathsome dungeon, with rattling chains and chilly damps. Suddenly it is changed into a beautiful garden with fragrant flowers, blushing parterres, inviting fruits, and melodious songs; by which the juvenile mind is entangled and infatuated. Then succeed adventures, intrigues, rapes, duels, elopements, darts, sighs, groans, armies, murders. Debauchery, in this way, assumes the form and name of gallantry.—Revenge is termed honour. Thus the destruction of the human soul is accomplished; the arts of seduction are practiced, and female innocence is ruined. Thus libertines endeavour, too successfully endeavour, to emancipate mankind from the shackles of religion and morality." Branagan concludes with a single remark that gives rhetorical coherence to his religious, political and literary concerns: "This they call freedom. Fatal freedom!"

We have no record of the influence or success of Branagan's sundry works, but, according to his own testimony, many thousands of copies were printed and distributed. Sometimes he financed publication out of his own limited funds. Sometimes he raised the money through subscriptions or donations. He sold the books cheaply or gave them away. The volumes were often patched together or expanded from handbills or pamphlets of which no copies or records survive. Parts of books were at times lifted, revised and enlarged, and published separately. Individual works frequently went through several editions, sometimes incorporating substantial changes and lengthy additions from his own or others' writings, and then labeled "new and improved." Titles were altered. Although he consistently referred to the works as separate entities, he nevertheless saw them as elements of a single, growing corpus. Their publishing history can be only approximated.

Branagan's commitment to the cause of antislavery, fueled by his guilt-ridden need to atone for the sins of his youth, continued at fever pitch during 1805. Following on the heels of *Avenia,* he published *The Penitential Tyrant,* a grisly, confessional work in heroic couplets:

> Oh! may I never stand where once I stood—
> View hills and dales all red with crimson blood,
> See verdant fields all clotted still with gore,
> Which ne'er were stain'd with human blood before;
> Where mortals wounded pil'd on mortals dead,
> Made verdant green be ting'd with crimson red!
> No more I see that thrice unhappy ground,
> Where heaps of human bones are spread around;
> Hear screams—hear groans—hear agonizing sounds
> Pierce hell—pierce heav'n—pierce earth's remotest
> bounds!
> Alas! my soul the shocking din sustains,
> Which makes the blood hang shiv'ring in my veins!
> Their wrongs I saw and heard, their mighty woes
> I now relate. . . .

With the publication of the poem and its introductory "Compendious Memoirs of the Author," the unsavory story of Branagan's early life and the extent of his involvement in slavery were revealed. With the appearance of *Serious Remonstrances Addressed to the Citizens of the Northern States* (1805), the author's solution to the problem was outlined. Despite his own testimony to black compassion and hospitality, Branagan agreed with Jefferson that a harmonious, integrated society was not feasible. To save the country from the moral and political degradation of the institution of slavery and to remove the real physical danger of a hostile, vengeful black minority, he argues for the colonization of free blacks in part of the Western territories.

In the years following *Serious Remonstrances Addressed to the Citizens of the Northern States,* Branagan turned his attention away from slavery to other aspects of American society, reproving, consoling, and educating his adopted countrymen in what came to be a one-man literary crusade to save the republic from itself. In 1806, sensitive to the personal disadvantages that await the uneducated and fearful of the political dangers that are opened to a democracy of the ignorant, he produced *The Flowers of Literature,* a one-volume compendium of knowledge, addressed to Americans of all social and economic classes—from the "ignorammusses [who] abound in the country" to "persons who are distinguished by their commercial intercourse and consequent riches"—who, for lack of money or time, were unable to pursue a more formal education. In *The Excellency of the Female Character Vindicated* (1807), the author links social injustice and sexual immorality to the tendency of men to consider women "as objects of sensual convenience and domestic accommodation . . . inferior in point of intellectual faculties to the male," condemning fashionmongers and suggesting that women be provided with the benefits of university education. News of the Napoleonic wars prompted *Political and Theological Disquisitions on the Signs of the Times* (1807), a millennialist reading of current events "congenial with reason and the nature of things." The following year Branagan addressed his fellow preachers and writers on their moral responsibility to do away with all traces of selfishness and vanity in *The Beauties of Philanthropy,* a theological meditation on Genesis 1:26-27 ("Let us make man in our own image, after our own likeness. . . ."). After a "defamatory" attack on two sects he had been closely associated with, the Methodists and the Quakers, he published *The Curse of Christendom* (1808), a diatribe against religious bigotry and sectarianism. *The Excellency of Virtue* (1808), a dialogue between "a loving father and his only son," considers the quality of children's literature and includes two noteworthy poems: one, an example of morally healthful fare for American's youth, the author's retelling of the opening chapters of Genesis in doggerel, "The Rise

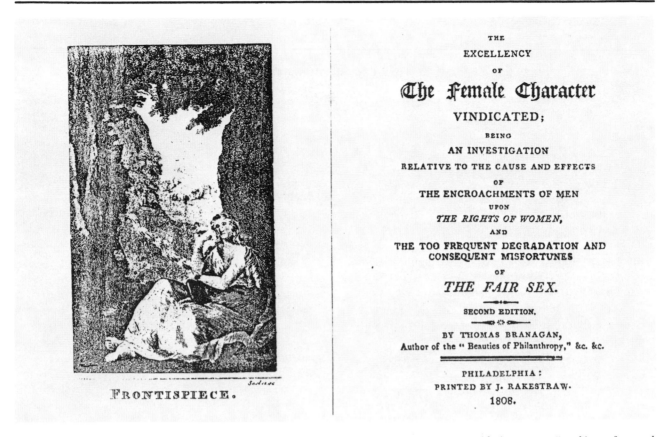

THE
EXCELLENCY
OF
The Female Character
VINDICATED;
BEING
AN INVESTIGATION
RELATIVE TO THE CAUSE AND EFFECTS
OF
THE ENCROACHMENTS OF MEN
UPON
THE RIGHTS OF WOMEN,
AND
THE TOO FREQUENT DEGRADATION AND
CONSEQUENT MISFORTUNES
OF
THE FAIR SEX.

SECOND EDITION.

BY THOMAS BRANAGAN,
Author of the " Beauties of Philanthropy," &c. &c.

PHILADELPHIA :
PRINTED BY J. RAKESTRAW.
1808.

FRONTISPIECE.

Frontispiece and title page for the second edition of the book in which Branagan warns against considering women "as objects of sensual convenience and domestic accommodation . . . inferior in point of intellectual faculties to the male"

and Fall of the Antediluvian World Displayed in Miniature; written in imitation of that ancient Poem, entitled, 'The House that Jack Built' "; the other, ironically, a poignant, if conventional elegy upon the death of his second son, William:

Thy stay was transient in this vale of woe,
  Thy Saviour's bitter cup to taste and die;
Born to endure a moment's pain below,
  And then to travel to the sacred sky.

Recalling his early, vicious life at sea ("as I have been a mariner myself"), he put together in 1809 *An Intellectual Telescope,* an homiletic handbook for sailors on such subjects as astronomy, oceanography, marine biology, and meteorology. And, perhaps more as a comfort to himself than to his readers, Branagan composed a pastoral work with the intentionally macabre title *The Pleasures of Death* (1809).

The years 1810-1814 were a time of tribulation and self-doubt for Branagan. Bearing his cross

through "the wretched lanes and alleys . . . where the devil raged with great fury," he was mocked, assaulted, and threatened with murder. He shrank from his mission to the poor and outcast and suffered through recurring periods of guilt and depression. He quarreled with a fellow minister and withdrew in anger from the denomination he had served since his arrival in Philadelphia. Ann gave birth to a third son, who died within a week. Tormented by sin, distracted from attending to his daily needs, he even contemplated suicide. "Yet in all this time of sorrow and desolation," he wrote in *A Beam of Celestial Light* (1814), "I endeavored to promote the glory of God in my publications." In 1811, he had published *A Concise View, of the Principal Religious Denominations, in the United States of America,* an encyclopedic work, intended as "a persuasive to Christian Moderation," which included entries on Far Eastern religions, as well as a long, detailed essay on Ancient Greek mythology and philosophy. That same year he composed and distributed *The Poetical Apotheosis of Gen. George Washington, the Friend of Man, and Father of His Country,* a poem of epic pretensions that echoes his earlier *Avenia*:

> Awake my muse, the sad Columbian strain,
> Oh! sing the triumph and the deathless fame
> Of Washington! . . . the servant of his God,
> The friend of man, his country's chiefest good.

The pamphlet (no longer extant) was intended to convince his fellow Philadelphians to erect a statue "in front of the State House, representing General Washington on horseback, as large as life; embellished with sculpture emblematical of the revolution," but, to Branagan's surprise, it "sold much worse than any of my works, although I have produced thirteen besides that one, on indifferent subjects! the majority of them have [having] passed through different editions." He reprinted parts of it in *Rights of God* (1812), a theodicy and jeremiad tracing the course of empire and sin which he later credited as being the "only thing I ever did in my life I feel a sure witness in my own mind was pleasing to him [God]" but which also, because of the "naked truths" it contained, "has made me a host of the most deadly foes, and at least helped to leave me without a single friend." *The Charms of Benevolence, and Patriotic Mentor,* published initially in 1812 as a pamphlet advocating the establishment of benevolent societies, grew in 1813 into a full-scale work with added chapters on political philosophy, the science of physiognomy, and the need to provide higher education to those of modest means through the founding of state universities. This period of Branagan's career closes with a consolatory stroll through the Bible, *The Celestial Comforter* (1814), which went quickly through five editions.

In the opening, autobiographical chapter of *A Beam of Celestial Light* Branagan recounts the preceding years of suffering, pointing in particular to a recent "virulent canceric affection" which caused him unbearable physical and spiritual pain. "My ingratitude to God now stared me in the face," he wrote, "like ten thousand infernal gnashing fa[i]ries." When he recovered he entered an intense period of self-purification, of asceticism and withdrawal. He gave up all "strong drink" and became a vegetarian. He fasted for days and "peeled the skin of my back, as broad as the half sheet of paper I am writing upon"—all to expiate the sins of pride and carnality. He came to believe that "the true church of Christ is no w[h]ere on earth to be found, as a community, or body politic," and broke all ties to sects and churches. In order to "avoid all controversy and jangling," he resolved to become "a stranger and pilgrim on earth." Absorbed in his own self-denial, he renewed his appeal to human kindness in *A Glimpse of the Sovereign Beneficence* (1815), and, elated at the American successes during the War of 1812, he put aside his radical separatism to publish *The Pride of Britannia Humbled* (1815), a compilation of William Cobbett's letters on the war and Branagan's own reflections on the "miraculous transactions" on the battlefields and their religious implications. ("The Almighty has most indubitably a predilection for the United States," he maintained, "as he had for his Israelitish theocracy.") He continued to preach, refusing any compensation for his evangelical work, "not even a drink of cold water." Rather than shy away from his mission to society's outcasts, he looked forward enthusiastically to "expose myself to vile and vulgar abuse, and blackguardism; to be spit upon, to be stoned, to be imprisoned, and to be hung as a malefactor, and disturbor of peace and civil liberty."

By 1817, with the publication of *A Glimpse of the Beauties of Eternal Truth* and *The Pleasures of Contemplation,* Branagan seems to have made peace with himself and with his God. He looked back on his turbulent life, especially on the last few lonely years, with a new degree of insight. "Twenty seven years, wandering through a wilderness of calamity" had finally brought him to the realization that his many tribulations—from his mistreatment as a child to the deaths of his children—were so many signs of God's loving kindness, attempts to wean him from a sinful world. He saw self-denial as another form of selfishness and hatred of God. He tacitly rejected the harsher implications of original sin. "Formerly I thought it impossible to please God," he writes; "I now see it is the easiest thing on earth to do." He offered a familiar message, but with a newfound equanimity and hope: "all he requires of me is to love himself above all, and to learn from his kindness to me, to be kind to all his creatures animal and human: and if all men would obey this one simple command, this earth, from that moment, would be changed to a paradise." He calmly looked forward to death, "which, peradventure, will end my cares with this year."

Branagan would live another quarter century, but his creative years, for all intents and purposes, were over. He looked back critically, and with more than a bit of irony, over his literary career: "I have often, too often, attended too much to the jingle of words, have used a redundant phraseology, the flowers of rhetoric, the embellishment of fancy, when I wished to please as well as profit, and, of course, gain the praise of my readers." Even such a recent, purified work as *A Beam of Celestial Light,* though it contained "many most important truths," appeared to Branagan to show "a degree of vanity in the writer," because it was "delivered in the language of prophesy." Now, however, "calamity and the treachery of man has cured me of all such vain and fallacious motives." With a gesture of authorial magnanimity, he announced his intentions "to deposit a collection of my minor works, in nineteen volumes, in the Franklin Philosophical library . . . with the request that if any respectable person or persons, [be] disposed to republish any of them . . . they should be accommodated with a copy." With this he retired, republishing his works from time to time, but composing nothing new.

Ann Branagan died on 28 April 1830. Seven years later Thomas Branagan put together an anthology of his writings with the grandiose title *The Guardian Genius of the Federal Union.* (He added a companion volume in 1839, borrowing his earlier title, *The Beauties of Philanthropy.*) "I have now done with public patronage," he wrote at the close of a revised and updated "Compendious Memoirs." "This volume, like the twenty others from which it has been compiled, I 'cast upon the waters,' and continue in the city of brotherly love in the quiet shades of obscurity." Except for Lewis Leary's 1953 article on the author's life and works, no nineteenth- or twentieth-century work has attempted to relieve that obscurity. Branagan died in Philadelphia of the palsy on 12 June 1843.

Reference:

Lewis Leary, "Thomas Branagan: Republican Rhetoric and Romanticism in America," *Pennsylvania Magazine of History and Biography,* 77 (July 1953): 332-352; reprinted in his *Soundings: Some Early American Writers* (Athens: University of Georgia Press, 1975), pp. 229-252.

Charles Brockden Brown

Bernard Rosenthal
State University of New York at Binghamton

BIRTH: Philadelphia, Pennsylvania, 17 January 1771, to Elijah and Mary Armitt Brown.

MARRIAGE: November 1804 to Elizabeth Linn; children: Charles Brockden, William Linn, Eugene Linn, Mary Caroline.

DEATH: Philadelphia, Pennsylvania, 22 February 1810.

BOOKS: *Alcuin: A Dialogue* (New York: Printed by T. & J. Swords, 1798);

Wieland; Or the Transformation. An American Tale . . . (New York: Printed by T. & J. Swords for H. Caritat, 1798);

Ormond; Or the Secret Witness (New York: Printed by G. Forman for H. Caritat, 1799);

Arthur Mervyn; Or, Memoirs of the Year 1793, part 1 (Philadelphia: Printed & published by H. Maxwell, 1799); part 2 (New York: Printed & sold by George F. Hopkins, 1800);

Edgar Huntly; Or Memoirs of a Sleep-Walker, 3 volumes (Philadelphia: Printed by H. Maxwell, 1799);

Clara Howard; In a Series of Letters (Philadelphia: Printed by H. Maxwell & published by Asbury Dickins, 1801); republished as *Philip Stanley; Or, the Enthusiasm of Love . . . ,* 2 volumes (London: Printed at the Minerva Press for Lane, Newman, 1807);

Jane Talbot, A Novel (Philadelphia: Printed by John Bioren & published by John Conrad, M. & J. Conrad in Baltimore, and Rapin, Conrad & Co. in Washington City, 1801; London: Lane, Newman, 1804);

An Address to the Government of the United States, on the Cession of Louisiana to the French . . . (Philadelphia: Printed by H. Maxwell & published by John Conrad, 1803);

Monroe's Embassy, or, the Conduct of the Government, in Relation to Our Claims to the Navigation of the Missisippi [sic], *Considered* (Philadelphia: Printed by H. Maxwell & published by John Conrad, 1803);

The British Treaty, attributed to Brown (Philadel-
    phia, 1807; enlarged edition, London:
    Printed for John Joseph Stockdale, 1808);
*An Address to the Congress of the United States, on the
    Utility and Justice of Restrictions upon Foreign
    Commerce . . .* (Philadelphia: Printed by John
    Binns & published by C. & A. Conrad, 1809);
The Rhapsodist and Other Uncollected Writings, edited
    by Harry R. Warfel (New York: Scholars' Fac-
    similes & Reprints, 1943);
Memoirs of Stephen Calvert, edited by Hans Borchers
    (Frankfurt am Main, Bern & Las Vegas: Lang,
    1978).
Collection: *The Novels of Charles Brockden Brown,* 7
    volumes (Boston: Published by S. G. Good-
    rich, 1827).

OTHER: C. F. Volney, *A View of the Soil and Climate
    of the United States of America,* translated by
    Brown (Philadelphia: Printed by T & G. Pal-
    mer & published by J. Conrad, 1804);
"A Sketch of the Life and Character of John Blair
    Linn," in *Valerian, a Narrative Poem,* by John
    Blair Linn (Philadelphia: Printed by Thomas
    & George Palmer, 1805), pp. iii-xxiv.

*Portrait by James Sharples, circa January 1798 (Worcester Art
Museum, Worcester, Massachusetts)*

From the years immediately after America
gained its independence from England until long
after, America's literati called for a literature that
would reflect well on the artistic capacities of the
new nation, a literature that could earn the respect
of England even as it treated indigenous themes. In
Charles Brockden Brown, a handful of critics on
both sides of the Atlantic found a writer who
appeared to meet these requirements. While many
scholars have tended to see Brown as a derivative
writer, one who drew heavily on the political ideas
of William Godwin and on the Gothic tradition in
literature, those contemporaries of his who
admired him saw in his works the beginning of an
original American literature of which the new country could be proud. For some Brown's appeal lay in
his depictions of American scenes, whether in writings about plagues in Philadelphia or in those about
battles with Indians in the wilderness. Others felt
the power of his imagination, the sheer force and
energy of his writing. His admirers included William Godwin, who was himself the object of Brown's
admiration, John Keats, Percy Bysshe Shelley, and
Thomas Love Peacock. No American writer of fiction before Brown had achieved such recognition,
and, even though his own countrymen for the most
part ignored his literary efforts he has nevertheless
been historically perceived in America as the pro-

genitor of its fiction. Although such an assessment
of Brown will not bear close scrutiny, he remains as
the first American writer of fiction to have received
recognition as a serious writer. Such prominent
later American writers as Cooper, Hawthorne,
Longfellow, Poe, and Whittier praised his art.

Charles Brockden Brown was born to a Quaker family in Philadelphia on 17 January 1771. His
father was a merchant, descended from a family
whose Quaker roots can be traced to the seventeenth century. His maternal ancestors, the
Armitts, shared a similar heritage. The family business failed, although Brown's father managed to
support his large family, probably through establishing new business activities in real estate.

From about the age of eleven to sixteen,
Brown studied under the tutelage of Robert Proud
at the Friends Latin School in Philadelphia, and
after leaving it he went to work in the Philadelphia
law office of Alexander Wilcocks, without having
attended college. The legal profession seems to
have held little attraction for Brown, but he formed
deep friendships at this time, particularly with Wil-

liam Wood Wilkins and Joseph Bringhurst, both of whom shared Brown's literary interests. The three of them were active in the Belles Lettres Club of Philadelphia, which was formed in 1786 and lasted until 1793. When Wilkins, who had gone on to complete his legal education, died in 1795, Brown lost his closest tie to the profession of law. By then Brown had already declined to complete his own education as a lawyer, and the reason for this decision implies much about him as a writer.

According to his earliest biographer, Paul Allen, Brown rejected the law because he "could not reconcile it [the legal profession] with his ideas of morality to become indiscriminately the defender of right or wrong. Against this he entered a solemn protest, and pursuing the principle to its extreme point, would ask, what must be the feelings of a lawyer if he had become auxilliary to a decision of injustice?" Brown probably should be taken at his word here and when in his description of himself as a writer he calls himself a "moral painter." Although Brown's fiction is not explicitly didactic, his stories rarely stray far from explorations of mor-

al ambiguity. As a young man, he rejected revealed religion and perhaps even Christianity, although he returned to it later in life, but he never rejected his deep commitment to moral concerns. This commitment sometimes brought him to engagements with socially radical issues.

Brown had begun experimenting with the writing of literature even while he studied law. In 1789 a handful of his essays, "The Rhapsodist," were published in *Columbian Magazine* in Philadelphia, and, after abandoning the law a few years later, he dabbled in poetry and fiction. In 1797 he finished a novel called "Sky-Walk." Although he never published it and the manuscript has been lost, parts of it appeared in *Edgar Huntly*. However, in 1798, he began having his work published at a remarkable pace. During this year, he brought out a portion of *Arthur Mervyn*, which appeared in the *Weekly Magazine* (Philadelphia), as well as two complete works, *Wieland* and *Alcuin*.

In *Alcuin*, which he had completed in 1797, one quickly sees Brown's willingness to find a topic in radical thought. Exploring the institution of mar-

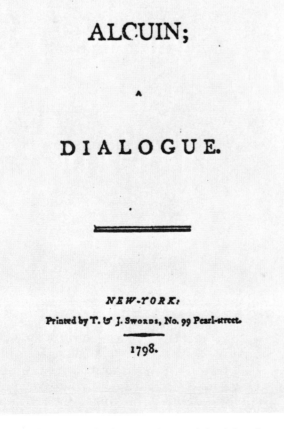

Title page for Brown's book on marriage and the rights of women, and an advertisement by Elihu Hubbard Smith that appeared in the book. Smith had paid for Alcuin's *publication.*

riage and the examination of its usefulness as a social convention, Brown employs the device of a dialogue between a young man named Alcuin and a woman named Mrs. Carter. In the first of the book's two sections Mrs. Carter attacks the constraints of marriage while Alcuin endorses the traditional role of women. In the second part, however, the characters shift their stances and at times reverse their positions. Brown manages to present the whole dialogue without clearly staking out an authorial position on the institution of marriage, but he explores major social questions related to his subject, and his intellectual indebtedness to the radical views of William Godwin and Mary Wollstonecraft is inescapable. Whether Brown declined to take clear sides in the dialogue because it was too risky, or whether it was his purpose to explore the issue rather than advocate a position has been the subject of consideration by his critics. But regardless of his motives, and whatever conclusion one draws about his political stance on the issues before him, Brown produced in *Alcuin* America's first book-length examination of the rights of women.

Whether *Alcuin* should be classified as a work of fiction or as a treatise may be debated. In general, scholars have tended to see *Alcuin* as something of an anomaly. However, no such difficulty occurs with *Wieland,* considered by many to be Brown's best novel. Here, Brown explored the ambiguities of religious belief, just as he had explored uncertainties of marriage in *Alcuin,* but in *Wieland* he managed to find a better balance between intellectual and aesthetic considerations. His tale, as with all his stories, is filled with twists and turns in the plot, quite a few improbabilities, and a relentless exploration of human motives. In *Wieland* these ingredients center on questions of religion and one's proper relation to it. Whether precipitated by religious fanaticism, by inner madness, or by a trick of ventriloquism, or by some combination of these, Wieland, a devoted father and brother, responding to commands that he believes he hears from God, turns on the family he loves, murders his wife and children, and threatens to kill his sister, Clara, the narrator of this tale.

The idea of revealed religion's potential for harm had been with Brown at least as early as 1795 when he wrote a long letter to his friend Joseph Bringhurst, engaging him in a debate on the subject. Brown's position, as indicated in that letter of 24 October, is that moral behavior must be rooted in the individual rather than in the fear of divine retribution. Wieland's behavior stems from his belief that he must follow divine commandments, and

WIELAND;

OR THE

TRANSFORMATION.

AN

AMERICAN TALE.

From Virtue's blisful paths away
The double-tongued are sure to stray;
Good is a forth-right journey still,
And mazy paths but lead to ill.

COPY-RIGHT SECURED.

NEW-YORK:
Printed by T. & J. Swords, for H. Caritat.
—1798.—

Title page for Brown's best-known novel, an examination of the dangers of religious fanaticism

his actions show with graphic horror the consequences of abandoning one's own moral principles to a belief in revealed religion. One may quarrel over whether Brown has fairly tested the proposition in *Wieland,* but his engagement with the issue remains central to the book. It is Brown's handling of this theme that led John Greenleaf Whittier to commend the book's "strength and power."

The year in which Brown had *Wieland* published must have offered an extraordinary test of his will and strength. Not only did he publish *Alcuin* and *Wieland,* but he did so at a time of severe personal trials. In July 1798 he had gone to live in New York, where he shared his living accommodations with Elihu Hubbard Smith, a doctor whom he had met in 1792 and who may have been his closest friend, and another friend, William Johnson. Smith, through an altruistic impulse, had brought to their home an ailing Italian physician who soon died from yellow fever. Shortly afterward, Smith contracted the disease and died, and Brown was stricken as well. Thus Brown was a close witness to the horrors of yellow fever, and his temptation to escape the city was obvious. However, he chose to remain in the midst of the plague, perhaps underestimating its threat.

Brown had been familiar enough with plagues in Philadelphia not to have needed such direct experience for the treatment of the subject in his next two published novels. In Philadelphia, early in 1798, he had begun his serial publication in the *Weekly Magazine* of "The Man at Home," a story drawing on the plague. It is certainly possible, however, that his experience in New York accounted for some of the contents of his published fiction in 1799. That year he had published *Ormond* and part one of *Arthur Mervyn*, both of which make use of the horrors of plague that Brown knew so well. *Edgar Huntly* also appeared that year, and he began publication of a magazine, the *Monthly Magazine and American Review*.

Although the plague is vividly depicted in both the works, *Ormond* depends less on it for a structuring device. Probably the most dramatic plague scene in *Ormond* deals with a secondary character, Martinette de Beauvais, digging a grave in the middle of the night and dragging the body of a plague victim to it for burial. More germane than the plague, however, is the general depiction of a woman as a self-sufficient individual able to cope calmly and decisively with adversity without relying on a man to save the situation. Indeed, if Brown had no other claim to recognition, he would still deserve attention as one of the few early American writers to break from stereotypical representations of women and to present them as having capacities for action according to individual characteristics rather than group stereotypes. It was the heroine of *Ormond*, Constantia, who appealed so greatly to some of Brown's radical European admirers.

Attempting to relate a plot summary of a novel by Brown requires pages of detailed narration and explanation because of the convoluted nature of his tales and because of the rapid introduction of new characters, scenes, and events. However, the dramatic center of *Ormond* rests in the test of wills between Brown's heroine, Constantia, and Ormond, who pursues her. Ultimately, failing to

ORMOND;

OR THE

SECRET WITNESS.

———

BY THE AUTHOR OF WIELAND; OR THE TRANSFORMATION.

———

NEW-YORK:
Printed by G. FORMAN, for H. CARITAT.
—1799.—

Title page for Brown's 1799 tale of attempted rape and murder

win her, Ormond attempts rape. Constantia successfully defends herself with a knife, killing the man who has brought so much grief to her. Rich in its themes, ambitious in what it attempts, *Ormond* explores forbidden topics such as rape and, some critics have suggested, female homosexuality. Inevitably, it probes moral issues, in this case the primary one being the individual's relations to the social conventions of morality.

Arthur Mervyn is perhaps less sensational than *Ormond*, but it also explores forbidden realms, as its hero, Arthur Mervyn, finds in a brothel the woman he will eventually choose for a wife. She is an older Jewish woman, whom Arthur treats as a mother substitute, even to the point of calling her "Mamma." The second part of this book was not published until 1800, more than a year later than the first part (1799). In the first part, Arthur appears to be an innocent young man who comes to the plague-ridden city; he is rescued and taken in by a kindly physician, who, acting on the same principles that Smith did in New York, has stayed in the city. On the basis of Arthur's story of his own life, the physician accepts him as a person of great virtue. In part two, however, Arthur's story is challenged, and

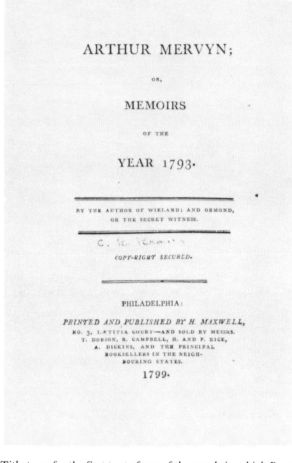

ARTHUR MERVYN;

OR,

MEMOIRS

OF THE

YEAR 1793.

BY THE AUTHOR OF WIELAND; AND ORMOND,
OR THE SECRET WITNESS.

COPY-RIGHT SECURED.

PHILADELPHIA:

PRINTED AND PUBLISHED BY H. MAXWELL,
NO. 3, LÆTITIA COURT—AND SOLD BY MESSRS.
T. DOBSON, R. CAMPBELL, H. AND P. RICE,
A. DICKINS, AND THE PRINCIPAL
BOOKSELLERS IN THE NEIGH-
BOURING STATES.

1799.

Title page for the first part of one of the novels in which Brown drew upon his experiences during plagues in Philadelphia and New York (courtesy of the John Carter Brown Library at Brown University)

the physician, as well as the reader, must choose between two competing versions of Arthur Mervyn, who emerges either as an individual of exemplary virtue or as a confidence man, depending on the view one accepts. One may, of course, find a little of both in Arthur, but a central problem of the book, and at the same time one of its main virtues, concerns the ambiguity of appearances, the difficulty of discerning truth in a world of competing claims. Heavily employing the calamity of plague, Brown vividly depicts the horrors, but also the attractions, of the early American city. For in spite of the plagues that Brown successfully portrays, the city nevertheless emerges as a place of opportunity for the young man from the country, who ultimately chooses its ways over those of his rural youth. Brown tells the story that would dominate so much future literature in his nation, the journey from innocence to experience. His presentation of this

classic American theme, however, with its conflicting views of Arthur's character, emerges as deeply ambiguous.

In *Edgar Huntly* Brown brought another fresh theme to American literature, the portrayal in a novel of the American Indian. As with his other tales, the plot is elaborate, and encounters with Indians represent only a small part of the story. Moreover, in presenting his Indians as only one-dimensional characters, Brown does not succeed in transcending stereotypes as he does with his presentation of women in *Ormond*. The main line of the story, in any case, does not center on Indians. Rather, the tale explores a series of mysteries and confused identities. For a structuring device, Brown employed the idea of sleepwalking. On a literal level, at least, many of the episodes in *Edgar Huntly* hinge on mysteries that become explained with the discovery that actions have occurred during episodes of somnambulism. Many critics of Brown, however, have argued forcefully that the sleepwalking represents a device that merely covers deeper psychological motivations, and many are persuaded that in this tale Brown employs the device of the psychological double.

Whether it was because of his treatment of Indians or for some other reason, *Edgar Huntly* may have had an appeal to his contemporary audience that Brown's other fiction appeared to lack, since in 1801 this novel was republished, making it the only novel of Brown's that reappeared in his lifetime. However, the reason for this printing remains obscure, and its connection to Brown's popularity is inconclusive. Not until 1827 was a collected edition of Brown's novels published in America.

Brown, however, had strived to reach an audience in ways other than through the publication of novels. In 1798 Elihu Hubbard Smith had mentioned to members of the Friendly Club, a group to which Brown belonged, that the time was ripe for the publication of a magazine. Smith's death that year may have prompted his friends into acting on the suggestion. Whether for this or for other reasons, in 1799 Brown, with the help of some of his friends, took on the task of bringing out such a magazine. As editor, Brown made a valiant attempt to make the publication succeed, both through his efforts at raising money and through his editorial work. The *Monthly Magazine and American Review* made its initial appearance in April 1799, and it survived until December 1800. During that time Brown doggedly pursued the task of searching out suitable contributions for the journal. He also contributed heavily from his own writing.

The *Monthly Magazine and American Review* defined itself as a literary and scientific publication, one that eschewed politics on the general principal that too many periodicals already covered political topics. Within this constraint, the *Monthly Magazine* nevertheless managed to cover a wide variety of subjects, including original and reprinted essays. Such stories by Brown as "Thessalonica: A Roman Story" and a fragment from *Edgar Huntly* appeared in the journal. Among other works by Brown to appear in these pages were "On Apparitions" and "Walstein's School of History." The most remarkable work of fiction that Brown published in the *Monthly Magazine* (1799-1800) was *Memoirs of Stephen Calvert*, which can stand alone as a novel even though what appeared in print was only part one of a projected five-part book. Long neglected, the work has appeared in recent years under separate cover.

In *Memoirs of Stephen Calvert* Brown once more takes his reader through psychological labyrinths explored by few other writers. His touching upon the subject of male homosexuality is less ambiguous, though not as fully explored as is his treatment of female homosexuality in *Ormond*. The idea of the double, implicitly suggested in *Edgar Huntly*, receives explicit treatment in this story. In one sense, Brown simply resorts to an old literary ploy of having twins brought up separately with each unaware of the other's existence. But in his hands, the motif lends itself well to psychological examination, and one might argue that he handles his topic with greater subtlety than would Edgar Allan Poe in his "William Wilson," where the idea of the double makes one of its most prominent American appearances. As with some of Brown's other characters, Stephen is haunted by mysterious events that defy comprehension until a single mystery is uncovered. In *Wieland* the mystery had been ventriloquism, in *Edgar Huntly* sleepwalking, and in *Stephen Calvert* an unexpected twin. But in each of these stories, the surface explanation of the mystery serves more complex purposes. And as with his other stories, Brown once more finds an occasion to explore morality and its ambiguities and to confront innocence with experience.

In starting the *Monthly Magazine* Brown had hoped that suitable income could be made from the journal. Scholars have agreed that this hope was misplaced, but less clarity exists as to Brown's response to the failed expectations. In December of 1800, the journal was renamed the *American Review and Literary Journal* and continued publication until 1802. While there is no doubt that Brown con-

tinued to make contributions, primarily as a reviewer, the exact nature of his relation to this journal remains somewhat obscure. Moreover, the task of determining which reviews are his remains to be completed. He left New York in 1800, headed to Philadelphia, and looked for other means to earn money. He soon joined his family in the importing business. Brown seems to have maintained a connection with the family business until 1806, although his primary energies remained directed toward literary enterprises.

In 1801 Brown had two more novels published, *Clara Howard* and *Jane Talbot*. Relative to his previous novels, both these works are less imaginative in their plot structures, and both rely more heavily on the epistolary form. Additionally, neither one employs the kind of bizarre devices, such as ventriloquism or sleepwalking, that Brown had used heavily in earlier fiction. Both works, with some notable exceptions, have been regarded by Brown's critics as his most derivative, least imaginative, and least successful novels, and scholars have tended to believe that the books reflected the running out of Brown's imaginative powers. Yet in both these works Brown continues to explore the problem of morality, its ambiguity, and the deception of appearances. In *Clara Howard* the moral problem centers on the issue of morality based on altruism. The hero, Edward Hartley (called Philip Stanley in texts derived from the first British edition), loves Clara Howard but is engaged to marry Mary Wilmot. Clara, believing that Mary loves Edward, will not marry him and instead insists that her own happiness requires him to marry Mary. This places Edward in the ludicrous position of having to search out and marry a woman, who it turns out does not want him after all, in order to win the respect, if not the hand, of the woman he does want to marry. Fortunately for all the characters, Brown fixes the narrative so that in the end his characters are properly paired. But in the course of this tale, which often seems on the edge of slipping into farce, Brown seriously examines moral assumptions based on altruism, and he explores the limits of such morality, the roots of which may be found in radical ideas emanating from Godwin. In view of Brown's earlier idealization of Godwin, *Clara Howard* may suggest a changing sensibility on Brown's part, one more skeptical of the possibility of human perfectibility.

Brown seems to pursue further a conservative tendency in *Jane Talbot*, where he clearly backs away from the overt hostility he had seemed to show toward religion in *Wieland*. As a result of misunderstandings, unjust accusations, and downright fraud, Henry Colden and Jane Talbot are lovers who are kept apart. Mrs. Fielder, the woman who has raised Jane, acts on evidence available to her that Colden is not only atheistic in his morality, but adulterous in his conduct. Although her belief in his adulterous behavior is eventually proved to be without substance, Mrs. Fielder's understanding of his religious views remains essentially accurate, and, after numerous plot complications, Colden goes to sea and reexamines his moral premises. He returns with a more conventional religion that removes one of the major obstacles to the inevitable happy union with Jane.

For many of Brown's critics, the publication of *Clara Howard* and *Jane Talbot* marked an end to Brown's literary powers. However, Brown's literary interests, including the creation of fiction, continued at a prolific pace. The actual quality of that fiction will be hard to evaluate until a suitable edition of his "History of the Carrils" appears in print. This work, containing more than 100,000 words, appears as segments in the earliest biography of Brown and in the *Literary Magazine and American Register,* a new journal that Brown began to edit in 1803. The "History of the Carrils" is an apparently unfinished family story that spans centuries. It is uncertain whether Brown was still working on it at the time of his death, but its existence demonstrates conclusively that Brown's interest in writing fiction and in experimenting with its forms continued well after the publication of *Clara Howard* and *Jane Talbot.*

From 1803 to 1805 Brown also published serially in the *Literary Magazine* "Memoirs of Carwin the Biloquist." The textual history of this uncompleted story is complex, but apparently the bulk of it was written in 1798 while *Wieland* was in the process of publication. With additional segments probably written when Brown needed material for the *Literary Magazine,* the text of "Memoirs of Carwin the Biloquist" appeared during 1803 through March 1805. Carwin had appeared in *Wieland* as an important but undeveloped character, whose motives for practicing ventriloquism were never clarified, and readers of the novel tend to share the heroine's assessment of him as a monstrous person. However, in "Memoirs of Carwin the Biloquist" he receives more sympathetic and more fully developed treatment from Brown. Whether the Carwin of this tale and the Carwin of *Wieland* may profitably be examined as the same character offers an area for critical examination, but there is no compelling

reason to believe that either tale requires a knowledge of the other.

The year 1803 saw Brown expending his energies in writings other than fiction. In addition to beginning his association with the *Literary Magazine and American Register,* Brown departed from Quaker pacifism to write a pamphlet urging the taking of the Louisiana territory, by force if necessary, and opposing Jefferson's policies, which led to the territory's purchase. Brown seems to have achieved a popularity in the writing of pamphlets that eluded him as a novelist. His work *An Address to the Government of the United States, on the Cession of Louisiana to the French* was quickly reprinted, although in a shortened version. Soon after, Brown published a second pamphlet, which like the first attacked Jefferson's policies toward the Louisiana territory. One possible explanation for Brown's vigorous interest in this issue is that his entrance into the family business gave him a personal economic interest in national expansion. However, a thorough study of Brown's political thought would be required before such a conclusion might be reached.

Brown, however, had interests at this time that were probably more on his mind than the Louisiana dispute, and the outcome was his marriage in November 1804 to Elizabeth Linn. Brown seems to have met Elizabeth Linn and fallen in love with her in 1800. Since Brown died in 1810, their marriage was short, but in that time four children were born to them. The marriage seems to have been a happy one, and Brown apparently got on well with his wife's family. Her brother, John Blair Linn, became a close friend of Brown's, and upon Linn's death, Brown, in 1805, wrote a biographical introduction to Linn's poem *Valerian* (1805). Relations with his own family may have had complications, since Elizabeth Linn was the daughter of a prominent Presbyterian minister. Elizabeth Linn remained with the faith of her father, and it has been speculated that the marriage itself did not take place sooner due to the religious differences of the families. However, the circumstances involving the four-year courtship are sketchy, and Brown's unpublished correspondence has not clarified the matter.

In the year Brown married Elizabeth Linn, he also published, with original notes, a translation of Volney's *A View of the Soil and Climate of the United States of America.* Brown's geographical interest had been an old one, dating back to his childhood, and the translation of Volney represented a continuation of that interest. Indeed, he worked on an origi-

Letter from Brown to his brother-in-law, poet John Blair Linn (Ormond, 1937 edition, ed. Ernest Marchand)

nal book of geography entitled "System of General Geography; Containing a Topographical, Statistical, and Descriptive Survey of the Earth." Brown died before the completion of this study, and the lengthy manuscript has not been found. The history of this manuscript, aside from suggesting the possible loss of a valuable study for geographers, helps offer some insight into the difficulties connected with accurately reconstructing Brown's life. It is known that the manuscript of the book, probably completed (by whom is not known), was extant as late as 1827, and the initial intention of Brown's widow was to have the work published posthumously. To this end she contracted with Paul Allen to complete the study and prepare it for publication. But Allen did not succeed at his task, anymore than he did in writing an authorized biography of Brown. Allen did, however, begin the biography, which was subsequently taken over and completed by Brown's friend William Dunlap. By the time Dunlap received the project, some of the plates were already set, and expense prohibited a thorough rewriting of a biography. Thus, much later biographical information about Brown was based on the Dunlap authorized biography without any realization, until relatively recently, that significant portions of the work were written by Allen and that some items in the work may have been retained on grounds having more to do with economy than accuracy.

Although we may never know the fate of his "Geography," we can be sure that his interest in the subject was a pronounced one. So also, Brown had a keen interest in history, as reflected in the creation of his "History of the Carrils," his attempt at writing historical fiction in epic proportions, and in his various smaller historically related pieces, such as "The Death of Cicero, A Fragment" (which appeared at the end of volume three of *Edgar Huntly*), an attempt in 1803 at writing a play set in Egypt (subsequently destroyed by Brown), and an uncompleted work on Rome. His marriage in 1804 did seem to moderate for a brief time his literary activity, although between 1804 and 1806 he remained occupied with editing the *Literary Magazine and American Register* and, of course, translated Volney's work.

Toward the end of 1807, Brown introduced a new periodical to replace the *Literary Magazine*. The journal was entitled the *American Register, or General Repository of History, Politics, and Science,* and Brown edited five volumes. Although the pages of this journal included literary topics, such as poetry (including Brown's own) and reviews of British and American literature, the main emphasis now reflected Brown's political and historical interests. Essentially, the *Register* was what its name implied. It kept a record of laws and state papers, but it also gave written accounts of contemporary events, such as a report on the duel between Hamilton and Burr. If most of Brown's remaining literary efforts were devoted to the publication of this journal and the writing of his "Geography," he still had time for one more political pamphlet, a document published in 1809, entitled *An Address to the Congress of the United States, on the Utility and Justice of Restrictions upon Foreign Commerce.* This publication reflects Brown's continuing interest in public affairs as his career moved toward its end. Once more, his political position placed him in confrontation with Jefferson, this time on the issue of the embargo that had been placed in an attempt to deal with the war then in progress between England and France. Brown, as did many people with mercantile interests, adamantly opposed the embargo.

During this time, Brown, never a very healthy individual, began to fail. As was customary in his day, he took trips in hopes of restoring his health, but it was to no avail. Apparently a victim of tuberculosis, Brown died, his final days recorded in Dunlap's biography: "On the morning of the nineteenth of February, 1810, it was observed that a change for the worse had taken place. He thought himself dying, and desired to see all his family, and spoke to each in the tenderest and most affectionate manner. He, however, remained in this dying state until the twenty-second, frequently conversing with his friends with perfect possession of his faculties to the last." There is every reason to believe that Brown had long since left behind him the religious radicalism of his earlier days, and the announcement in the *American Daily Advertiser,* 27 February 1810, probably reflected accurately the state of Brown's final days: "he died . . . a Christian, full of the hope of immortality, at peace with himself and with all mankind." He was buried in Philadelphia, in the Friends Burial Ground.

One of the great ironies of Brown's literary career was that he strove so hard to foster and participate in the development of a native American literature, yet his greatest recognition, mostly positive, came from English critics. That Americans paid inadequate attention to him was the subject of numerous essays in America that appeared over the years, but the calls for broader recognition notwithstanding, Brown remained an obscure writer in his native land, appreciated by only a handful of people. In recent years, scholarly interest in him has

Charles Brockden Brown, circa 1809; portrait attributed to William Dunlap (courtesy of Dr. Neil K. Fitzgerald)

increased significantly, and some critics have begun to make claims for him which are probably out of proportion to his actual aesthetic accomplishments. Yet oddly enough, whether seeing in his writing something to be condemned or praised, Brown's critics have generally agreed that his narratives rely heavily on improbabilities, that his characters are not clearly delineated, and that his plots border on the chaotic. For some, these qualities have represented aesthetic flaws; for others they have been signposts of the ambiguities and uncertainties of the human mind and the human heart, examples of style conforming to substance. Whatever the justice of these competing views of him, scholarly interest in Brown has never been greater than at present.

Reliable texts of Brown's major works have been edited at the Bibliographical and Textual Center at Kent State University. In print or forthcoming from the Kent State University Press are *Arthur Mervyn, Clara Howard, Edgar Huntly, Ormond, Jane Talbot, Wieland, Alcuin, Memoirs of Carwin,* and *Stephen Calvert.* The Bibliographical and Textual Center at Kent State also has reproductions of all known Brown manuscripts, except for correspondence with Joseph Bringhurst, which is located at Bowdoin College. Also at Kent State is the manu-

script copy of Daniel Edwards Kennedy's valuable unpublished biography of Brown.

Bibliographies:

Robert E. Hemenway, and Dean H. Keller, "Charles Brockden Brown, America's First Important Novelist: A Check List of Biography and Criticism," *Papers of the Bibliographical Society of America,* 60 (1966): 349-362;

Sydney J. Krause, with assistance of Jane Nieset, "A Census of the Works of Charles Brockden Brown," *Serif,* 3, no. 4 (1966): 27-55;

Paul Witherington, "Charles Brockden Brown: A Bibliographical Essay," *Early American Literature,* 9 (Fall 1974): 164-187;

Charles E. Bennett, "The Charles Brockden Brown Canon," Ph.D. dissertation, University of North Carolina at Chapel Hill, 1974;

Bennett, "The Letters of Charles Brockden Brown: An Annotated Census," *Resources for American Literary Study,* 6 (1976): 164-190;

Patricia Parker, *Charles Brockden Brown: A Reference Guide* (Boston: G. K. Hall, 1980);

Charles A. Carpenter, "Selective Bibliography of Writings about Charles Brockden Brown," in *Critical Essays on Charles Brockden Brown,* edited by Bernard Rosenthal (Boston: G. K. Hall, 1981), pp. 224-239.

Biographies:

William Dunlap, *The Life of Charles Brockden Brown: Together with Selections from the Rarest of His Printed Works, from His Original Letters, and from His Manuscripts Before Unpublished,* 2 volumes (Philadelphia: James P. Parke, 1815);

William Hickling Prescott, "Memoir of Charles Brockden Brown, the American Novelist," in *The Library of American Biography,* edited by Jared Sparks, first series (Boston: Hilliard, Gray, 1834), I: 117-180; republished in Prescott's *Biographical and Critical Miscellanies* (New York: Harper, 1845), pp. 1-56;

Harry R. Warfel, *Charles Brockden Brown, American Gothic Novelist* (Gainesville: University of Florida Press, 1949);

David Lee Clark, *Charles Brockden Brown, Pioneer Voice of America* (Durham: Duke University Press, 1952);

Paul Allen, *The Life of Charles Brockden Brown: A Facsimile Reproduction,* edited by Charles E. Bennett (Delmar, N.Y.: Scholars' Facsimiles and Reprints, 1975); also published as *The Late Charles Brockden Brown,* edited by Robert E.

Hemenway and Joseph Katz (Columbia, S.C.: Faust, 1976).

References:

Alan Axelrod, *Charles Brockden Brown* (Austin: University of Texas Press, 1983);

Michael Davitt Bell, " 'The Double-Tongued Deceiver': Sincerity and Duplicity in the Novels of Charles Brockden Brown," *Early American Literature*, 9 (Fall 1974): 143-163;

Kenneth Bernard, "Arthur Mervyn: The Ordeal of Innocence," *Texas Studies in Literature and Language*, 6 (Winter 1965): 441-459;

Warner B. Berthoff, "Charles Brockden Brown's Historical 'Sketches': A Consideration," *American Literature*, 28 (May 1956): 147-154;

Berthoff, " 'A Lesson on Concealment': Brockden Brown's Method in Fiction," *Philological Quarterly*, 37 (January 1958): 45-57;

A. Carl Bredahl, "Transformation in *Wieland*," *Early American Literature*, 12 (Fall 1977): 177-192;

John Cleman, "Ambiguous Evil: A Study of Villains and Heroes in Charles Brockden Brown's Major Novels," *Early American Literature*, 10 (Fall 1975): 190-210;

Alexander Cowie, "Vaulting Ambition: Brockden Brown and Others," in his *The Rise of the American Novel* (New York: American Book Company, 1948), pp. 69-104;

William Dunlap, *Diary of William Dunlap (1766-1839)*, 3 volumes (New York: New-York Historical Society, 1930);

Emory B. Elliott, "Charles Brockden Brown," in *American Writers: A Collection of Literary Biographies*, supplement 1, edited by Leonard Unger (New York: Scribners, 1979), pp. 124-149;

Norman S. Grabo, *The Coincidental Art of Charles Brockden Brown* (Chapel Hill: University of North Carolina Press, 1981);

William Hedges, "Charles Brockden Brown and the Culture of Contradictions," *Early American Literature*, 9 (Fall 1974): 107-142;

David H. Hirsh, "Charles Brockden Brown as a Novelist of Ideas," *Books at Brown*, 20 (1965): 165-184;

Cynthia S. Jordan, "On Rereading *Wieland*:'The Folly of Precipitate Conclusions,' " *Early American Literature*, 16 (Fall 1981): 154-174;

Arthur G. Kimball, *Rational Fictions: A Study of Charles Brockden Brown* (McMinnville, Oreg.: Linfield Research Institute, 1968);

Sydney J. Krause, "*Ormond:* How Rapidly and How Well 'Composed, Arranged and Delivered,' " *Early American Literature*, 13 (Winter 1978-1979): 238-249;

Krause, "Romanticism in *Wieland*: Brown and the Reconciliation of Opposites," in *Artful Thunder: Versions of the Romantic Tradition in American Literature*, edited by Robert J. DeMott and Sanford E. Marovitz (Kent, Ohio: Kent State University Press, 1975), pp. 13-24;

David Lyttle, "The Case Against Carwin," *Nineteenth Century Fiction*, 26 (December 1971): 257-269;

Ernest Marchand, "The Literary Opinions of Charles Brockden Brown," *Studies in Philology*, 31 (October 1934): 541-566;

Robert Micklus, "Charles Brockden Brown's Curiosity Shop," *Early American Literature*, 15 (Fall 1980): 172-187;

James E. Mulqueen, "The Plea for a Deistic Education in Charles Brockden Brown's *Wieland*," *Ball State University Forum*, 10, no. 2 (Spring 1969): 70-77;

Carl W. Nelson, Jr., "A Just Reading of Charles Brockden Brown's *Ormond*," *Early American Literature*, 8 (Fall 1973): 163-178;

Henri Petter, *The Early American Novel* (Columbus: Ohio State University Press, 1971);

Donald A. Ringe, *Charles Brockden Brown* (New York: Twayne, 1966);

Bernard Rosenthal, ed., *Critical Essays on Charles Brockden Brown* (Boston: G. K. Hall, 1981);

Dieter Schulz, "*Edgar Huntly* as Quest Romance," *American Literature*, 43 (November 1971): 323-335;

Mark Seltzer, "Saying Makes it So: Language and Event in Brown's *Wieland*," *Early American Literature*, 13 (Spring 1978): 81-91;

Elihu Hubbard Smith, *The Diary of Elihu Hubbard Smith (1771-1798)*, edited by James E. Cronin (Philadelphia: American Philosophical Society, 1973);

Paul Witherington, "Benevolence and the 'Utmost Stretch': Charles Brockden Brown's Narrative Dilemma," *Criticism*, 14 (Spring 1972): 175-191;

Witherington, "Brockden Brown's Other Novels: *Clara Howard* and *Jane Talbot*," *Nineteenth-Century Fiction*, 29 (December 1974): 257-272;

Larzer Ziff, "A Reading of *Wieland*," *PLMA*, 77 (March 1962): 51-57.

Papers:
Holdings of Brown manuscript material may be found at the University of Texas at Austin, the University of Virginia, at the Historical Society of Pennsylvania in Philadelphia, and Bowdoin College.

William Hill Brown
(1765-2 September 1793)

Robert D. Arner
University of Cincinnati

BOOKS: *The Power of Sympathy: Or, the Triumph of Nature. Founded in Truth*, 2 volumes (Boston: Printed & sold by Isaiah Thomas, 1789);

The Better Sort: Or, The Girl of Spirit. An Operatical, Comical Farce (Boston: Printed & sold by Isaiah Thomas, 1789);

West Point Preserved or the Treason of Arnold: An Historical Tragedy in Five Acts (Boston, 1797);

Ira and Isabella: or The Natural Children. A Novel, Founded in Fiction (Boston: Published by Belcher & Armstrong, 1807);

Selected Poems and Verse Fables, 1784-1792, edited by Richard Walser (Newark: University of Delaware Press, 1982).

Known to literary history as the author of the first American novel (a claim that has on occasion been challenged), William Hill Brown was also a poet, essayist, and dramatist of some contemporary reputation. Indeed, if Robert Treat Paine, Jr.'s elegy composed shortly after Brown's death is to be believed, Brown was better known as a poet than as a novelist.

The son of a well-known clockmaker, Gawen Brown, and his third wife, Elizabeth Hill Adams Brown, William Hill Brown was born in Boston late in the year 1765. One of his older half brothers, Mather Brown, the son of Gawen Brown and his second wife (a daughter of the Reverend Mather Byles), became a well-known artist. William Hill Brown, who was always in frail health, was encouraged in his literary ambitions by Catherine Byles, one of Mather Brown's mother's unmarried half sisters, who looked on all the Brown children as her family. While attending a Boston boys' school, Brown, whose writings suggest that he read widely in classical, English, and American literature, also helped in his father's clockmaking shop.

Brown's poems have only recently been collected, while his "Reformer" and "Yankee" essays remain buried in the pages of the *Massachusetts Magazine* (1789-1790) and *Columbian Centinel* (1790), respectively. A drama, *West Point Preserved or the Treason of Arnold*, received five professional performances and played to critics who were generally favorable, but the text of the play, which is said to have been published in 1797, has since been lost.

Easily Brown's most popular poem is the thirteen-stanza "Yankee Song," which, with the metrical and stanzaic form, and the refrain, from "Yankee Doodle," celebrates Massachusetts's ratification of the Federal Constitution on 6 February 1788. The poem was printed in the *Pennsylvania Mercury and Universal Advertiser* on 21 February of the same year, then reprinted in the *Columbian Centinel* on 5 March and in the *Worcester Magazine* during the "Second Week in March, 1788"; it is also published under the title "Yankee Doodle" in *Four Excellent New Songs*, printed in New York by John Reid in 1788, and there is abundant evidence of its transcription into commonplace books and even oral transmission. Besides calling the roll of the famous (John Hancock) and the not-so-famous (John Foster Williams) who had a hand in ratifying the Constitution and in directing the festivities that followed, the poem pokes gentle fun at Yankee dialect, praises the American spirit of compromise and the wisdom of majority rule, and ends with an encomium to American agriculture and commerce. After the fashion of John Gay and in keeping with a burgeoning English and American interest in small animals, Brown also composed numerous verse fables, of which "The Two Hares and the Monkey" is probably the most entertaining. Like the novel *Ira and Isabella*, many of these fables (and a few additional prose pieces) were published posthumously in the weekly *Boston Magazine* and its successor, the *Emerald,* for Brown died prematurely after a short illness, in Murfreesborough, North Carolina, where he had gone in 1792 to visit his younger, married sister, Elizabeth Brown Hitchburn, and had stayed on to study law in nearby Halifax. While it is likely that some of the verse fables and other poems were written during Brown's brief stay in North Carolina, none of his work can definitely be attributed to that period of his life.

However Brown's contemporaries may have judged him as a poet, including in their estimation of his abilities the sixteen or so verses he wrote as the libretto for *The Better Sort* (1789), it is *The Power of Sympathy* (1789) on which his fame rests. Using for a subplot a local scandal involving adultery and suicide in the prominent Apthorp and Morton families of Boston, the novel details in a series of letters the reformation of the rake Harrington by the charms of the lovely Harriot, who, he discovers too late, is his sister by a youthful indiscretion of his father's; the power of sympathy, that is, the strong attraction between two people arising from close blood relationships, urges the couple toward incestuous union from which only Harriot's death, followed by Harrington's suicide—an ending prescribed for such cases by Goethe's *The Sorrows of Young Werther* (1774,1787), a copy of which lies on the night table next to Harrington's deathbed—can save them. The action is unabashedly melodramatic, with brief interludes providing Harrington and other characters the opportunity to discourse on the evils of certain kinds of fiction and the virtues of Laurence Sterne's sentiment. Melodrama, however, seems to be the preferred mode of American romance, with its penchant for exploring the dark side of human consciousness in contrast to the bright, enlightenment faith in human reason, and,

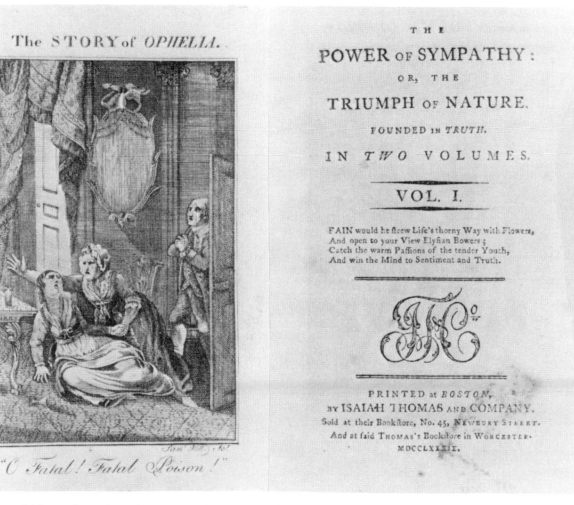

Frontispiece and title page for the first volume of the book that is generally considered the first American novel. The frontispiece depicts an episode from the novel's subplot, which drew upon a scandal that involved the husband and sister of Boston poet Sarah Wentworth Morton.

seen in this way, *The Power of Sympathy*, despite almost incredible narrative awkwardness, is no unworthy ancestor of the great romances of Poe, Melville, and especially Hawthorne and Henry James.

Indeed, the book may have been blacker than its author ever intended, undercutting with its melancholy fable Brown's announced purpose of displaying the evils and evil consequences of seduction: if the power of sympathy is the power of nature, how, one may ask, is it to be successfully combated? More important, is a person who succumbs to so overwhelming a force morally responsible or, as the late-nineteenth-century popular imagination would have it, was he or she more to be pitied than censured?

The confusions that lurk in Brown's first novel accumulate in his second and final book, *Ira and Isabella* (1807), published fourteen years after the author's death. Some readers have regarded the entire work as a travesty, a burlesque narrative "founded on fiction" (as Brown declares in the preface) born of the failure of his initial tale founded on fact to perform its moral mission. The materials of the novel are the same—wayward parents, fallen women, incestuous desires between brother and sister—except that, it turns out at the last minute (and only after the marriage ceremony has been performed), Ira and Isabella are *not* brother and sister because—*mirabile dictu*—one Mr. Savage confesses that Ira is not the child of Isabella's father, Dr. Joseph, but the son of his own illicit relationship with the wayward Lucinda, who seduced him.

Despite the playfulness of Brown's preface, the apparently ironic reversal of the obstacle of incest, and the identification of the woman rather than the man as the seducer, it seems safest to regard *Ira and Isabella* as a hasty work instead of a deliberate parody, the full and final failure of an author who wrote better in his first novel then he probably knew but who, in his second, was betrayed into a confusing and chaotic story that alternately attempted to exploit and to expose existing stylistic and narrative formulae. For the student of American literature and culture, however, this attempt to deal with anarchic impulses of youth and nature within a plot structure and in a stilted, self-consciously literary language that deny freedom in favor of convention is among the most compelling of reasons to continue reading and pondering Brown's novels.

References:

Robert D. Arner, "Sentiment and Sensibility: The Role of Emotion in the Fallen World of William Hill Brown's *The Power of Sympathy,*" *Studies in American Fiction*, 1 (1973): 121-132;

Herbert Ross Brown, *The Sentimental Novel in America 1789-1860* (Durham: Duke University Press, 1940);

Jackson R. Byers, Jr., "Further Verification of the Authorship of *The Power of Sympathy,*" *American Literature*, 43 (1971): 421-427;

Cathy N. Davidson, "*The Power of Sympathy* Reconsidered: William Hill Brown as Literary Craftsman," *Early American Literature*, 10 (1975): 14-29;

Milton Ellis, "The Author of the First American Novel," *American Literature*, 4 (1933): 359-368;

Leslie Fiedler, *Love and Death in the American Novel*, revised edition (New York: Stein & Day, 1966);

Lillie Deming Loshe, *The Early American Novel* (New York: Columbia University Press, 1907);

Terence Martin, *The Instructed Vision: Scottish Common Sense Philosophy and the Origin of American Fiction* (Bloomington: Indiana University Press, 1961);

Martin, "William Hill Brown's *Ira and Isabella*," *New England Quarterly*, 32 (1959): 238-242;

Tremaine McDowell, "The First American Novel," *American Review*, 2 (1933): 73-81;

McDowell, "Last Words of a Sentimental Heroine," *American Literature*, 4 (1933): 359-368;

Henri Petter, *The Early American Novel* (Columbus: Ohio State University Press, 1971);

Richard Walser, "Boston's Reception of the First American Novel," *Early American Literature*, 17 (1982): 65-74;

Walser, "More About the First American Novel," *American Literature*, 24 (1952): 352-357;

Walser, "The North Carolina Sojourn of the First American Novelist," *North Carolina Historical Review*, 28 (1951): 138-155;

J. D. Wilson, "Incest and American Romantic Fiction," *Studies in the Literary Imagination*, 7 (1974): 31-50.

Papers:

A few of Brown's letters are in the Bancroft Library, University of California, Berkeley, and at the Massachusetts Historical Society.

Joseph Stevens Buckminster

(26 May 1784-9 June 1812)

Nancy Craig Simmons
Virginia Polytechnic Institute

BOOKS: *A Sermon Preached at the Church in Brattle Street, Boston, December 18th, 1808. The Lord's Day after the Publick Funeral of His Excellency James Sullivan, Governour of the Commonwealth of Massachusetts* (Boston: Printed by J. Belcher, 1809);

A Sermon, Delivered at the Interment of the Reverend William Emerson, Pastor of the First Church of Christ in Boston, Who Died May 12, 1811 . . . (Boston: Printed by Joseph T. Buckingham, 1811);

Sermon Preached before the Boston Female Asylum, Sept. 1810, 10th Anniversary (Boston, 1814);

Sermons by the Late Rev. J. S. Buckminster (Boston: Printed by J. Eliot, 1814);

Sermons. Now First Published from the Author's Manuscripts (Boston: Carter & Hendee, 1829).

Collection: *The Works of Joseph Stevens Buckminster; with Memoirs of His Life,* 2 volumes (Boston: James Munroe, 1839).

OTHER: "The Poems of Joseph Stevens Buckminster," edited by David Robinson and Lawrence Buell, *Resources for American Literary Study,* 7 (Spring 1977): 41-52.

Joseph Stevens Buckminster was a popular young Boston preacher of "liberal" Christianity when he died, following an epileptic seizure, at the age of twenty-eight. In the seven years that he practiced his vocation Buckminster had accomplished much. He had served as preacher to the Brattle Street Church, the most fashionable congregation in affluent Boston, and written about 250 sermons and some thirty published essays and reviews; he had traveled for a year in Europe, where he collected a library of some 3,000 volumes; he had delivered the 1809 Phi Beta Kappa address at Harvard, had belonged to the Anthology Society and contributed frequently to its journal, and in 1807 had been one of the founders of the Boston Athenaeum. At the time of his death he was preparing for a new position as the first Dexter lecturer in biblical criticism at Harvard. As a result of these activities, Buckminster is remembered primarily

for his influence on emerging American culture: through his preaching, biblical criticism, and interest in letters, books, and scholarship he helped stimulate the development of American Unitarianism and the literary flowering known as the New England Renaissance. Moreover, a success during his lifetime, Buckminster became a legend after his untimely death—a type of New England "saint" and the sign of the dawn of a new era. His sermons, many not published until after his death, were recognized as innovative examples of pulpit oratory. Acclaimed for their literary merit, they were read by at least two generations of New Englanders as models of excellence in prose style. Though his influence is usually noted today, Buckminster's writings are seldom read or reprinted.

Born in Portsmouth, New Hampshire, into an established clerical family (his ancestors included Samuel Stoddard and Elisha Williams, rector of Yale College), young Buckminster was destined for the ministry by his parents, Joseph and Sarah Stevens Buckminster. Joseph was six years old when his mother died, expressing on her deathbed her hope that her only son would become a minister. Already his parents had begun to "cultivate" his mind. Small in stature but intellectually precocious, Buckminster was by all reports an extraordinary child, who began Latin and Greek at the age of four and was soon such an ardent reader that he refused amusements. He was five years old when in his father's absence he began to conduct daily devotions for the family and the Sabbath service for the servants. His father was his earliest teacher, but soon Joseph began to attend Portsmouth Grammar School under the tutelage of an uncle, Amos Tappan. In 1795-1796 he prepared for college at Phillips Exeter Academy. When he entered Harvard in 1797 as a sophomore, Buckminster was the smallest and youngest in his class—but a formidable scholar. The audience at his commencement in 1800 was struck by the contrast between his youthful figure and the maturity and brilliance of his thought as he read his speech "On the Literary Character of Different Nations." Soon after graduation he joined his father's church.

*Joseph Stevens Buckminster; engraving based on a portrait by
Gilbert Stuart*

For the next four years, Buckminster prepared himself for the ministry, stocking his extremely retentive mind by reading widely in theology, philosophy, morals, and general literature. At
the same time, he was teaching, first at Exeter,
where Daniel Webster, two years his senior, was
among his pupils. It was at this time, in the fall of
1802, that Buckminster experienced his first
epileptic attack. In 1803 and 1804 he served as tutor
to the sons of an influential and wealthy Boston
relative, Theodore Lyman. This time of apparent
peace and leisure to pursue his studies masked a
great inner struggle as Buckminster, influenced by
his reading and by his association with James Freeman, Unitarian minister of King's Chapel, Boston,
moved away from the orthodox Calvinism of his
father, with its beliefs in the trinity and original sin,
to a more liberal "rational" Christianity. His central
belief, claimed his friend Samuel Thacher, was
"that the great design of the gospel is, to produce a
moral influence on the human character, to raise it
from the degradation and ruin of sin, and fit it for
the pure and intellectual happiness of heaven." The
question of the younger Buckminster's religious beliefs severely strained the unusually close relationship between the father (who urged Joseph to

study with an Orthodox minister) and the son (who
preferred his own eclectic reading). As a result of
his father's admonitions, young Buckminster
seriously considered abandoning his chosen vocation at this time. Nevertheless, he preached his first
sermon at York, Maine, in the spring of 1804 and
received repeated invitations from the Brattle
Street Church. After preaching to this congregation in October 1804, Buckminster immediately
captivated his audience by his pulpit style, and soon
he was invited to become their pastor. Buckminster
was twenty when he was ordained and installed as
minister to the Brattle Street Church on 30 January
1805.

For the remainder of his life, Buckminster
continued to preach at Brattle Street, with the exception of the year 1806-1807 when he went to
Europe for his health, traveling in England,
Switzerland, Holland, and France with his friend
Thacher. Perhaps because he felt himself under
sentence of early death or incapacitation from his
epilepsy, he worked at a feverish pace. Always interested in philology, he had returned from Europe
with a new interest in German scholarship and
higher criticism of the Bible and with an edition of
Griesbach's Greek New Testament, which he
brought out in its first American edition in 1809.
For the *Monthly Anthology and Boston Review* he wrote
literary and religious essays and retrospective reviews. After Buckminster's return from Europe, his
home became the center for a social and intellectual
circle of gentlemen who met for conversation on
Sunday evenings. His 1809 Phi Beta Kappa
address, "The Dangers and Duties of Men of Letters," laments the decline in American letters and
prophesies the dawn of a new Augustan age. In
1808 Buckminster read an oration on the death of
Massachusetts Governor James Sullivan, and in
1811 he delivered a eulogy at the funeral of the
Reverend William Emerson. His last years were
devoted particularly to biblical criticism as a means
of establishing faith on the internal evidence of
scripture, and his sermons combined the results of
his critical studies with his insights into the moral
nature of man. Gifted, cultivated, urbane, active in
social and cultural endeavors, Buckminster was an
embodiment of the brilliant and adulated young
cleric, a type immortalized by Hawthorne's Arthur
Dimmesdale.

Buckminster's death produced an outpouring
of grief. According to tradition, during the night of
9 June his father, traveling for his own health far
away in Readsboro, Vermont, had a vision of his
dead son. The next day the senior Joseph Buck-

minster died, before he received news of his son's death. Those who knew the young preacher believed that "a mind so richly and splendidly endowed" should not be forgotten; the first collection of his sermons, published in 1814, would be "the only permanent memorial" of what he was and accomplished. In their structure and style, their appeal to reason and the moral nature of man, their combination of objectivity with wonder, Buckminster's sermons indeed stand for the man. Republished frequently in the next quarter century, these very literary productions still demonstrate the rhetorical skill and depth of insight that charmed Buckminster's first Boston audiences.

Despite his short life, Buckminster has traditionally been recognized as a significant early figure in the New England literary renaissance. Lawrence Buell's judicious article, "Joseph Stevens Buckminster: The Making of a New England Saint" (1979), and David Robinson and Lawrence Buell's edition of Buckminster's poetic works (1977) suggest the efforts of recent criticism to demystify Buckminster and assess more accurately his role in American letters.

Biographies:
Samuel C. Thacher, "Memoir of Mr. Buckminster," *The Works of Joseph Stevens Buckminster; with Memoirs of His Life,* volume 1 (Boston: James Munroe, 1839);

Eliza Buckminster Lee, *Memoirs of Rev. Joseph Buckminster D.D. and of His Son, Rev. Joseph Stevens Buckminster* (Boston: Crosby & Nichols, 1849).

References:
Lawrence Buell, "Joseph Stevens Buckminster: The Making of a New England Saint," *Canadian Review of American Studies,* 10 (Spring 1979): 1-29;

Lewis P. Simpson, *The Man of Letters in New England and the South* (Baton Rouge: Louisiana State University Press, 1973), pp. 3-31.

Papers:
The Boston Athenaeum is the major repository for Buckminster's papers, including among its 150 items correspondence, sermons, prayers, the journal for 1803-1806, essays, poems, and sermons. The collections of the Chicago Historical Society include a manuscript for an unpublished sermon.

John Daly Burk

(circa 1772-11 April 1808)

Frank Shuffelton
University of Rochester

BOOKS: *The Trial of John Burk, of Trinity College, For Heresy and Blasphemy* (Dublin, 1794);

Bunker-Hill; or the Death of General Warren: An Historic Tragedy . . . (New York: Printed by T. Greenleaf, 1797);

Female Patriotism, or the Death of Joan d'Arc: An Historic Play . . . (New York: Printed by R. M. Hurtin, 1798);

History of the Late War in Ireland, With an Account of the United Irish Association from the First Meeting at Belfast, to the Landing of the French at Kilala (Philadelphia: Printed by Francis & Robert Bailey, 1799);

An Oration, Delivered on the Fourth of March, 1803, at the Courthouse in Petersburg: to Celebrate the Election of Thomas Jefferson and the Triumph of Re-

publicanism (Petersburg, Va.?: Printed by T. Field, 1803);

The History of Virginia, from Its First Settlement to the Present Day, volumes 1-3 (Petersburg, Va.: Printed for the author by Dickson & Pescud, 1804-1805); volume 4, completed by Skelton Jones and Louis Hue Girardin (Petersburg, Va.: Printed by M. W. Dunnavant, 1816);

Bethlem Gabor, Lord of Transylvania, or The Man Hating Palatine; an Historical Drama (Petersburg, Va.: Printed by J. Dickson for Somervell & Conrad, 1807).

OTHER: *A Selection, from the Ancient Music of Ireland, Arranged for the Flute or Violin: Some of the Most Admired Melodies, Adapted to American Poet-*

ry, Chiefly Composed by John M'Creery, includes an essay and fourteen poems by Burk (Petersburg, Va.: Printed by Yancey & Burton, 1824).

Although the texts of only three of his plays survive, John Daly Burk was one of the major American dramatists at the end of the eighteenth century. *Bunker-Hill* (1797) was amazingly successful in the theaters, and Walter Meserve, the historian of early American drama, has called *Female Patriotism* (1798) "one of the best American plays written in the eighteenth century." Little is known of his early life, and he seems to have had a facility for self-dramatization that may have made an already adventurous life sound even more romantic and mysterious. Probably born in County Cork, Ireland, in 1772 to a Protestant family, he entered Trinity College, Dublin, in June 1792, where in addition to the usual course of studies he became involved with Wolfe Tone's United Irishmen and began writing for an antigovernment newspaper. After the College Board of Senior Fellows expelled him in 1794 for professing atheistic principles, he published *The Trial of John Burk* (1794), where he revealed himself as, if not an atheist, an extreme deist who was defiantly planning to publish a history of "The Horrors of Bigotry and Superstition." Further involvement in secret republican revolutionary societies led to his denunciation to the authorities in 1796, and he was forced to leave the country. Family tradition claimed he escaped arrest by boarding his ship to America disguised as "Miss Daly," a young woman who had given him one of her dresses, and in a characteristically romantic act of gratitude he adopted her name as his own middle name.

He had arrived in Boston by early April 1796, and on 17 February 1797 his play *Bunker-Hill* was first performed at the Haymarket Theater to popular acclaim and critical denigration. William Dunlap later called it "vile trash," but the public flocked to see it, and the Boston run of nine performances brought $2,000 to its author. Despite somewhat sketchily drawn characters, Burk did make a real effort to portray human feeling and moral complexity, even if some of the moral issues are rather clichéd. Abercrombie, a British officer, is torn between a sense of honor that demands loyalty to his uniform and king and a realization of the justice of the American cause, made more poignant by his love for Elvira, a virtuous young patriot. Warren, the American hero, embraces the Revolutionary cause as much from a desire for personal honor and

fame as from patriotic commitment to liberty and national independence. If Abercrombie's dilemma is trite, the presentation of Warren's flawed motives has dramatic possibilities and reflects Burk's independent imagination (also perhaps some naiveté about his Boston audience). This attempt to give depth to his hero also provoked negative responses to the play; when John Adams left the theater, he supposedly told the manager, "Sir, my friend General Warren was a scholar and a gentleman, but your author has made him a bully and blackguard." What undoubtedly caught the public fancy, however, was Burk's spectacular fifth act in which for nearly a quarter of an hour American soldiers, firing from an artificial hill, beat off British troops, accompanied by prodigious amounts of smoke, flame, musket fire, and off-stage blasts of cannon. Patriotic sentiment and a veritable indoor fireworks display were a winning popular combination, but this play's pioneering attempt at realistically portraying action onstage is also theatrically important.

Burk moved on to New York to advise on a run of *Bunker-Hill* at the John Street Theater later in 1797, and there he followed his first dramatic success with *Female Patriotism, or the Death of Joan d'Arc,* a much better play but a public failure when it was produced in the New Theater on 13 April 1798. The poetry and dramatic structure of this play are superior to that of *Bunker-Hill,* and the characters, particularly that of Joan, are more fully and convincingly developed. His Pucella is an Enlightenment heroine who prays to a deist God and is motivated not by divine voices, "a pious fraud / To raise the fainting courage of the land," but by a passion for liberty, "To make all free and equal, *all men kings.*" At the same time, because of her growing love for Chastel and her consequent desire to revert to a traditionally feminine role, she is a genuinely tragic figure caught up in historical crisis and not merely a passive victim of priestcraft and tyranny. The play is full of vigorous, well-paced scenes, but it is the developing character of Joan that structures the dramatic action. Joan's Enlightenment ideals and deistic religion make her almost amusingly anachronistic, but she is an impressively strong and moving heroine. It did not help the chances of *Female Patiotism* to equal the theatrical success of *Bunker-Hill* that it opened at the time of the XYZ affair and a growing public animosity toward France, but the quality of the acting on this occasion was also apparently below the usual standard.

In Boston on 6 October 1796 Burk and Alexander Martin started a newspaper, the *Polar Star and Boston Daily Advertiser,* Boston's first daily, but

HISTORY

OF THE

Late War in Ireland,

WITH

AN ACCOUNT

OF THE

UNITED IRISH ASSOCIATION

FROM THE FIRST MEETING AT *BELFAST*, TO THE
LANDING OF THE FRENCH AT *KILALA.*

BY JOHN BURK.

Quod maxime exitiabile tulere illa tempora, cum primores senatus infimas
etiam delationes exercerent, alii propalam, multi per occultum. *Tacitus.*

Iacuit immensa strages: omnis sexus, omnis ætas: inlustres, ignobiles: disperfi.
aut ..... neque proinquis, aut amicis adfuere, inlacrymare, ne visere
quide diutius dabatur. sed circumjecti custodes, & in mærorem cujusque in-
tenti, corpora putrefacta adsectabantur, dum in Tiberim trahei entur. ubi
fluitantia, aut ripis adpulsa, non cremare quisquam, non contingere. inter-
ciderat fortis humanæ commercium vi metus. *Tacitus.*

O! what are these?
Death's ministers, not men! who thus deal death
Inhumanly to men, and multiply
Ten thousand fold the sin of him who flew
His brother. for of whom such massacre
Make they but of their brethren, men of men!

Milton.

PHILADELPHIA:

PRINTED BY FRANCIS AND ROBERT BAILEY, AT YORICK'S
HEAD, NO. 116, HIGH STREET.
1799.

*Title page for Burk's account of the 1798 rebellion in Ireland
(courtesy of the John Carter Brown Library at Brown University)*

this enterprise ceased two weeks before the opening of *Bunker-Hill.* After moving to New York Burk succeeded Philip Freneau as editor of the *Time Piece,* a republican paper, and in July of 1798 he was indicted under the common law for seditious libel, sharing with Benjamin Franklin Bache the dubious honor of being one of the only two editors so indicted before the passage of the Alien and Sedition Laws. The *Time Piece* had carried on a running series of vigorous attacks on the Federalist political leadership, but the libel charge was specifically prompted by his accusation on 2 July 1798 that President John Adams had altered, in order "to promote certain ends in this country," a letter from Elbridge Gerry on Franco-American relations. Aaron Burr was instrumental in persuading the District Attorney to drop the case on the condition that Burk leave the United States. While he was embracing the republican politics of his adopted country, Burk did not forget his Irish origins, and as he was finding himself in opposition to the Amer-

ican government, he was also following with considerable interest the Irish rebellion of 1798. When he left New York, not departing the country as he was supposed to but going into hiding in Virginia until the election of 1800 removed the danger of prosecution, he gave his publisher his *History of the Late War in Ireland* (1799), an effort at instant history whose shortcomings are perhaps understandable in view of the scarcity of reliable information about these recent events.

In Petersburg, Virginia, he became a lawyer and ardent Jeffersonian, apparently continued to write plays which were produced there, and produced three volumes of his *The History of Virginia* (1804-1805), a notable literary effort in its own right. A number of plays, none surviving, have been dubiously attributed to Burk; he certainly wrote two pantomimes to appear on the same bill with *Bunker-Hill,* and he may have completed scripts for "The Prince of Susa: A Tragedy" and "The Exiles: A Tragedy." His final surviving play, *Bethlem Gabor* (1807), was written for the Thespian Society of

THE

HISTORY OF VIRGINIA,

FROM

ITS FIRST SETTLEMENT

TO

THE PRESENT DAY.

BY JOHN BURK.

VOLUME I.

PETERSBURG, VIRGINIA,
PRINTED FOR THE AUTHOR, BY DICKSON & PESCUD.

1804.

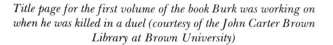

*Title page for the first volume of the book Burk was working on
when he was killed in a duel (courtesy of the John Carter Brown
Library at Brown University)*

Petersburg, in which he took an active part. This Gothic melodrama, which borrows slightly from William Godwin's novel *St. Leon* (1799) and perhaps Charles Brockden Brown's *Wieland* (1798), features an absurd plot full of ruined castles, dungeons, ventriloquism, mirrors, and miraculous reappearances of characters long supposed to be dead. While not devoid of all interest, it is clearly inferior to the earlier plays in terms of structure and character.

Burk's *The History of Virginia* was the first account of the Old Dominion written after it became a state; its Jeffersonian bias guaranteed its favorable reception when first published, and Burk's documentation, partly from materials loaned by Jefferson, ensured its importance after his death. He followed Jefferson in condemning slavery but then apologizing for the Virginians' failure to abolish it, and his long account of the Indians in Virginia reflected Jefferson's own interests in Indian language and customs. Because he was interested in showing the growth of democracy in Virginia as a paradigm for the history of the nation as a whole, he paid particular attention to Bacon's Rebellion and developed the image of Nathaniel Bacon as a liberal hero motivated by "the ardor and

enthusiasm of liberty." He was still at work on the history when on 11 April 1808 he was killed in a duel in Petersburg. The history was taken up by Skelton Jones, himself killed in a duel before its completion, and then finished by Louis Hue Girardin. At his death Burk was at work on a collection of American lyrics to be sung to Irish airs. When this finally appeared in 1824 with music by John M'Creery, it contained an essay on Irish music and fourteen poems by Burk, but by this time he was most often remembered as the historian of Virginia and as a one-time writer for the stage.

References:

Walter J. Meserve, *An Emerging Entertainment* (Bloomington: University of Indiana Press, 1977);

Joseph I. Shulim, *John Daly Burk: Irish Revolutionist and American Patriot. Transactions of the American Philosophical Society*, new series 54, part 6 (1964);

Shulim, "John Daly Burk, Playwright of Libertarianism, From 1796 to 1807," *Bulletin of the New York Public Library*, 65 (September 1961): 451-463.

Mathew Carey

(28 January 1760-3 September 1839)

Alan Axelrod

SELECTED BOOKS: *The Plagi-Scurriliad: A Hudibrastic Poem. Dedicated to Col. Eleazer Oswald* (Philadelphia: Printed & sold by the author, 1786);

Information for Europeans Who Are Disposed to Migrate to the United States. In a Letter from a Citizen of Pennsylvania, to His Friend in Great-Britain (Philadelphia: Printed by Carey Stewart & Co., 1790);

Desultory Account of the Yellow Fever, Prevalent in Philadelphia, and of the Present State of the City (Philadelphia, 1793);

A Short Account of the Malignant Fever, Lately Prevalent in Philadelphia: With a Statement of the Proceedings That Took Place on the Subject in Different Parts of the United States (Philadelphia: Printed

by the author, 1793; improved edition, 1793; London: Printed for J. Johnson, 1794);

Observations on Dr. Rush's Enquiry into the Origin of the Late Epidemic Fever in Philadelphia (Philadelphia: From the press of the author, 1793);

A Short Account of Algiers, and of Its Several Wars against Spain, France, England, Holland, Venice, and Other Powers of Europe, from the Usurpation of Barbarossa and the Invasion of the Emperor Charles V. to the Present Time; with a Concise View of the Origin of the Rupture between Algiers and the United States (Philadelphia: Printed by J. Parker for M. Carey, 1794);

Address of M. Carey to the Public. Philadelphia, April 4, 1794. The Industry Used in Circulating a Libel Against Me, Signed Argus . . . (Philadelphia:

Printed by Mathew Carey, 1794);

Address to the House of Representatives of the United States, on Lord Grenville's Treaty (Philadelphia: Printed by Samuel Harrison for Mathew Carey, 1796);

Fragment, Addressed to the Sons and Daughters of Humanity, as a Citizen of the World (Philadelphia: Printed by Lang & Ustick for Mathew Carey, 1796);

Miscellaneous Trifles in Prose (Philadelphia: Printed by Lang & Ustick for the author, 1796);

A Plumb Pudding for the Humane, Chaste, Valiant, Enlightened Peter Porcupine (Philadelphia: Printed for the author, 1799);

The Porcupiniad. A Hudibrastic Poem . . . , canto 1 (Philadelphia: Printed for & sold by the author, 1799; improved edition, 1799); cantos 2-3 (Philadelphia: Printed for & sold by the author, 1799);

The Columbian Reading Book or Historical Preceptor: A Collection of Authentic Histories, Anecdotes, Characters, &c.&c. Calculated to Incite in Young Minds a Love of Vertue from Its Intrinsic Beauty and a Hatred of Vice from Its Disgusting Deformity (Philadelphia: Printed for Mathew Carey, 1799);

Desultory Reflections, Excited by the Recent Calamitous Fate of John Fullerton. Addressed to Those Who Frequent the Theatre (Philadelphia: Printed by R. Carr for the author, 1802);

Cursory Reflections on the System of Taxation Established in the City of Philadelphia; With a Brief Sketch of Its Unequal and Unjust Operation (Philadelphia: Published by the author, 1806);

Desultory Reflections upon the Ruinous Consequences of a Non-Renewal of the Charter of the Bank of the United States (Washington, 1810);

Nine Letters to Dr. Adam Seybert, Representative in Congress for the City of Philadelphia, On the Subject of the Renewal of the Charter of the Bank of the United States (Philadelphia: Published by the author, 1810; enlarged as *Letters to Dr. Adam Seybert . . .* (Philadelphia: Published by the author, 1811);

Examinations of the Pretensions of New England to Commercial Pre-Eminence. . . (Philadelphia: Printed for M. Carey, 1814);

A Calm Address to the People of the Eastern States, on the Subject of the Representation of Slaves; Representation in the Senate; and the Hostility to Commerce ascribed to the Southern States (Philadelphia: Published by M. Carey, 1814);

The Olive Branch; or, Faults on both sides, Federal and Democratic. A Serious Appeal on the Necessity of Mutual Forgiveness & Harmony, to Save Our Common Country from Ruin (Philadelphia: Pub-

lished by M. Carey, 1814; enlarged, 1815; enlarged again, 2 volumes, 1815; enlarged again, 1815; enlarged again, Philadelphia: M. Carey & Son, 1817);

Reflections on the Consequences of the Refusal of the Banks to Receive in Deposit Southern and Western Bank Notes (Philadelphia, 1815);

Essays on Banking (Philadelphia: Published by the author, 1816);

Reflections on the Present System of Banking, in the City of Philadelphia (Philadelphia: The author, 1817);

Appendix to the Eighth Edition of the Olive Branch: or, Faults on Both Sides, Federal and Democrat (Philadelphia: Printed & published by M. Carey & Son, 1817);

Vindiciae Hibernicae: Or, Ireland Vindicated: An Attempt to Develop and Expose a Few of the Multifarious Errors and Falsehoods Respecting Ireland, in the Histories of May, Temple, Whitelock, Borlase, Rushworth, Clarendon, Cox, Carte, Leland, Warner Macauley, Hume, and Others: Particularly in the Legendary Tales of the Conspiracy and Massacre of 1641 (Philadelphia: Published by M. Carey & Son, 1819);

Three Letters on the Present Calamitous State of Affairs. Addressed to J. M. Garnett, Esq. President of the Fredericksburg Agricultural Society (Philadelphia: M. Carey & Son, 1820);

A View of the Ruinous Consequences of a Dependence on Foreign Markets for the Sale of the Great Staples of this Nation, Flour, Cotton, and Tobacco . . . (Philadelphia: M. Carey, 1820);

The New Olive Branch: or, An Attempt to Establish an Identity of Interest between Agriculture, Manufactures, and Commerce (Philadelphia: M. Carey & Son, 1820);

Address to the Farmers of the United States, on the Ruinous Consequences to Their Vital Interests of the Existing Policy of this Country (Philadelphia: M. Carey & Son, 1821);

An Address to William Tudor, Esq., Author of letters on the Eastern States. Intended to prove the Calumny and Slander of his Remarks on the Olive Branch (Philadelphia: M. Carey & Son, 1821);

Strictures on Mr. Cambreleng's Work, Entitled, An Examination of the New Tariff, as Neckar (N.p., 1821);

Essays on Political Economy; or, the most Certain Means of Promoting the Wealth, Power, Resources, and Happiness of Nations: Applied Particularly to the United States (Philadelphia: H. C. Carey & I. Lea, 1822);

An Appeal to Common Sense and Common Justice; or,

Engraving by John Sartain from a portrait by John Neagle

Irrefragable Facts Opposed to Plausible Theories: Intended to Prove the Extreme Injustice, as Well as the Utter Impolicy, of the Existing Tariff (Philadelphia: H. C. Carey & I. Lea, 1822);

Hamilton, series 1-12 (Philadelphia, 1822-1826);

Desultory Facts, and Observations, Illustrative of the Past and Present Situation and Future Prospects of the United States: Embracing a View of the Causes of the Late Bankruptcies in Boston (Philadelphia: H. C. Carey & I. Lea, 1822); revised as *Facts and Observations, Illustrative of the Past and Present Situation and Future Prospects of the United States . . .* (Philadelphia: H.C. Carey & I. Lea, 1822);

A Desultory Examination of the Reply of the Rev. W. V.

Harold to a Catholic Layman's Rejoinder . . . (Philadelphia: H. C. Carey & I. Lea, 1822);

The Crisis: A Solemn Appeal to the President, the Senate and the House of Representatives and the Citizens of the United States, on the Destructive Tendency of the Present Policy of this Country, on Its Agriculture, Manufactures, Commerce, and Finances (Philadelphia: H. C. Carey & I. Lea, 1823);

Sketch of the Irish Code, Entitled "Laws to Prevent the Growth of Popery:" But Really Intended, and With Successful Effect, to Degrade, Debase, and Enslave the Roman Catholics of Ireland, and to Divest Them of Their Estates . . . (Philadelphia: H. C. Carey & I. Lea, 1823);

A Warning Voice to the Cotton and Tobacco Planters, Farmers, Merchants of the United States, on the Pernicious Consequences to Their Respective Interests of the Existing Policy of the Country (Philadelphia: H. C. Carey & I. Lea, 1824);

Examination of a Tract on the Alteration of the Tariff, written by Thomas Cooper, M.D. (Philadelphia: Printed for H. C. Carey & I. Lea, 1824);

Twenty-one Golden Rules to Depress Agriculture, Impede the Progress of Manufactures, Paralize Commerce, Impair National Resources, Produce a Constant Fluctuation in the Value of Every Species of Property, and Blight and Blast the Bounties of Nature . . . (Philadelphia: H. C. Carey & I. Lea, 1824);

Fifty-One Substantial Reasons Against Any Modification Whatever of the Existing Tariff . . . (Philadelphia: H. C. Carey & I. Lea, 1824);

Address Delivered before the Philadelphia Society for Promoting Agriculture . . . (Philadelphia: Printed by J. R. A. Skerrett, 1824; revised, 1824);

Exhibit of the Shocking Oppression and Injustice Suffered for Sixteen Months by John Randel, Jun., Esq., Contractor for the Eastern Section of the Chesapeake and Delaware Canal . . . (Philadelphia, 1825);

Colbert, series 1-3 (Philadelphia, 1826-1827);

Reflections on the Proposed Plan for Establishing a College in Philadelphia (Philadelphia, 1826);

Reflections on the Subject of Emigration from Europe, with a View to Settlement in the United States . . . (Philadelphia, 1826);

Essays tending to prove the Ruinous Effects of the Policy of the United States on Three Classes, Farmers, Planters and Merchants, as Hamilton (Philadelphia: Printed by J. R. A. Skerrett, 1826);

A Roland for an Oliver. Letters on Religious Persecution: Proving That Most Heinous of Crimes, Has Not Been Peculiar to Roman Catholics . . . (Philadelphia: Dornin, 1826);

Slave Labor in Manufactures, as Hamilton (Philadelphia, 1827);

A Common Sense Address to the Citizens of the Southern States, as Hamilton (Philadelphia, 1828); enlarged as *Common Sense Addresses to the Citizens of the Southern States* (Philadelphia: Printed by Clark & Raser, 1829; enlarged again, 1829);

Emigration from Ireland and Immigration into the United States, as Hamilton (Philadelphia, 1828);

Auto biographical Sketches. In a Series of Letters Addressed to a Friend . . . (Philadelphia: Printed by J. Clarke, 1829);

African Colonization, as Hamilton (Philadelphia, 1829);

The Protecting System, as Hamilton (Philadelphia, 1829);

Essay on Railroads, as Hamilton (Philadelphia, 1830);

Miscellaneous Essays . . . (Philadelphia: Carey & Hart, 1830);

The New Olive Branch. A Solemn Warning on the Banks of the Rubicon, nos. 1-12, as Hamilton (Philadelphia, 1830);

Prospects on and beyond the Rubicon, as Hamilton (Philadelphia, 1830);

Address to the Wealthy of the Land, Ladies as Well as Gentlemen, on the Character, Conduct, Situation, and Prospects, of Those Whose Sole Dependence for Subsistence, is on the Labour of Their Hands (Philadelphia: Printed by W. F. Geddes, 1831); republished as *Appeal to the Wealthy of the Land . . .* (Philadelphia: Printed by L. Johnson, 1833);

The New Olive Branch: Addressed to the Citizens of South Carolina, new series, nos. 1-13, as Hamilton (Philadelphia, 1831);

Brief View of the System of Internal Improvements of the State of Pennsylvania; Containing a Glance at Its Rise, Progress, Retardation,—The Difficulties It Underwent,—Its Present State,—and Its Future Prospects (Philadelphia: Printed by Lydia R. Bailey, 1831);

A Plea for the Poor, nos. 1-3, as Hanway (Philadelphia, 1831-1832);

Reflections on the Causes that Led to the Formation of the Colonization Society: With a View of Its Probable Results . . . (Philadelphia: Printed by W. F. Geddes, 1832);

The Olive Branch. No. III. Or, An Inquiry Whether Any Arrangement is Practicable between the Friends and Opposers of the Protecting System . . . (Philadelphia: Printed by Clark & Raser, 1832);

The Crisis. An Appeal to the Good Sense of the Nation, against the Spirit of Resistance and Dissolution of the Union (Philadelphia: Printed by William F. Geddes, 1832; corrected edition, 1832);

The Dissolution of the Union. A Sober Address to All Those Who Have any Interest in the Welfare, the Power, the Glory, or the Happiness of the United States . . . , as Hamilton (Philadelphia: Printed by J. Bioren, 1832);

Essay on the Dissolution of the Union . . . , as Hamilton (Philadelphia: Printed by L. Johnson, 1832);

The Tocsin: A Solemn Warning against the Dangerous Doctrine of Nullification . . . , as Hamilton (Philadelphia, 1832);

The Olive Branch, No. IV, as Hamilton (N.p., 1832);

Prospects beyond the Rubican . . . , as Hamilton (Philadelphia, 1833);

Prospects beyond the Rubicon . . . , second series, as Hamilton (Philadelphia, 1833);

Collectanea: Displaying the Rise and Progress of the Tariff System of the United States. Also, the Rise, Progress, and Final Triumph of Nullification . . . (Philadelphia: Printed by T. B. Town, 1833; improved edition, 1833);

The Olive Branch Once More, nos. 1-4 (Philadelphia, 1833);

Outline of a System of National Currency; and Substitute for a Bank of the United States, as Colbert (New York: Printed by W. Pearson, 1834);

Female Wages and Female Oppression (Philadelphia, 1835);

Philosophy of Common Sense. Practical Rules for the Promotion of Domestic Happiness . . . (Philadelphia, 1838; improved edition, Philadelphia: Lea & Blanchard, 1838);

The Querist, An Humble Imitation of a work under a similar title published by the celebrated Berkeley, Bishop of Cloyne (Philadelphia, 1839).

OTHER: *The Beauties of Poetry, British and American . . . ,* edited by Carey (Philadelphia: From the press of M. Carey, 1791);

The American Remembrancer; Or, an Impartial Collection of Essays, Resolves, Speeches, &c. Relative, or Having Affinity to the Treaty with Great Britain, 3 volumes, nos. 1-12, edited by Carey (Philadelphia: Printed by Henry Tuckniss for Mathew Carey, 1795-1796);

Select Pamphlets, 3 volumes, pamphlets by Carey and others, collected by Carey (Philadelphia: Published by Mathew Carey, 1796).

Although he was an extraordinarily prolific author, Mathew Carey is less important as a writer than as a publisher who helped to develop the literary taste of the early Republic.

He was born in Dublin, Ireland, the son of Mary and Christopher Carey, a baker who prospered as victualer to the Royal Army and Navy. Timid, solitary, lamed from infancy as a result of his nurse's having dropped him, Mathew Carey was a bookish youth. Against the wishes of his father, who disapproved of reading, Carey apprenticed himself to a Dublin bookseller. A duel between fellow apprentices prompted his first publication, a 1777 essay "On the Subject of Duelling" (published in the *Hibernian Journal*), which gave Carey's master some offense. Two years later the young man offended a party of far greater consequence when he published *To the Roman Catholics*, an anonymous pamphlet protesting against English anti-Catholic discrimination in Ireland. Instead of advancing the Catholic cause, the pamphlet turned Parliament against Catholics. A reward for the arrest of Carey, offered by the conservative Irish Catholic party, occasioned the young man's removal to Paris, where Benjamin Franklin set him up in his print shop at Passy.

Carey returned to Ireland in 1780, editing the *Freeman's Journal* until 1783, when he started his own paper, the *Volunteer's Journal*. Its radical Irish nationalism caused Carey's arrest and imprisonment in 1784. Though he was soon released, the threat of further libel prosecution prompted his immigration to America in September 1784. Settling in Philadelphia, he borrowed $400 from the Marquis de Lafayette to begin, on 25 January 1785,

Carey's Pennsylvania Evening Herald. (In March of that year it became the *Pennsylvania Herald and American Monitor,* and the following year the *Pennsylvania Herald and General Advertiser.*) In 1786 the Democratic Carey lambasted a rival conservative editor in a Hudibrastic verse satire called *The Plagi-Scurriliad,* and the editor, Colonel Eleazer Oswald, challenged Carey to a duel. The young Irishman, who had begun his literary career with an essay against duelling, sustained a serious wound in the thigh.

In September 1786 Carey began the *Columbian Magazine* with four partners, withdrawing in 1787 to begin his own *American Museum, or Repository of Ancient and Modern Fugitive Pieces, Prose and Poetical.* Continued after January 1790 as the *American Museum or Universal Magazine* (through 1792 when it fell victim to high postal rates), it was the first truly significant literary magazine in the United States, numbering Benjamin Franklin, Charles Brockden Brown, Benjamin Rush, Thomas Paine, Philip Freneau, John Trumbull, and Francis Hopkinson among its contributors. In 1790 Carey launched his new book-publishing firm with an edition of the Douay Bible. By 1817 M. Carey and Son had become the largest publishing and distributing firm in the country. Carey published books from many nations and periods, but he concentrated on American works, including books by Susanna Rowson, Noah Webster, Philip Freneau, Washington Irving, Mason Locke Weems, John Neal, and James

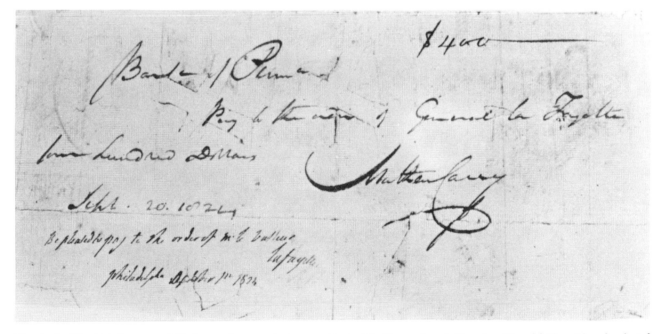

The check with which Carey repaid Lafayette the money he borrowed to start the Pennsylvania Evening Herald *(One Hundred and Fifty Years of Publishing, 1785-1935; Philadelphia: Lea & Febiger, 1935)*

The first issue of Carey's newspaper

Fenimore Cooper. After Carey's retirement in 1824, the firm continued to promote American authors, publishing works by Edgar Allan Poe and William Gilmore Simms.

Carey himself wrote industriously if not brilliantly. The disastrous yellow-fever epidemic of 1793 occasioned *A Short Account of the Malignant Fever, Lately Prevalent in Philadelphia,* which went through four editions in 1793 and 1794. It is a dispassionate work, honest but abstract rather than graphic, relying mainly on statistics and cool observation to make its point. Carey's knowledge of the epidemic was gained during work on a committee he formed to aid the beleaguered population, one of many civic and charitable projects in which Carey, a lifelong philanthropist, was active.

In 1799 Carey published two poems, *A Plumb Pudding for the Humane, Chaste, Valiant, Enlightened Peter Porcupine* and *The Porcupiniad,* abusive Hudibrastic satires directed against William Cobbett, whose hyper-Federalist essays were written under the name of Peter Porcupine. Ironically, though, the contentious Carey was to make his most significant political mark as a peacemaker. His 1814 *The Olive Branch; or, Faults on both sides, Federal and Democratic* was a remarkably successful effort to unite America's political factions against the common British enemy in the War of 1812. Its appeal survived the occasion, the book reaching ten editions by 1818. Carey rightly observed that it was the most popular political work in the United States since Paine's *Common Sense* (1776). Nor was *The Olive Branch* Carey's only essay in conciliation. Throughout the remainder of his career he wrote pamphlets and articles aimed at reconciling North and South and at uniting for the common economic good jarring industrial and agricultural interests. Between 1819 and 1833 he wrote some 59 pamphlets—about 2,322 pages—30 to 40 newspaper essays, 12 to 15 circulars to manufacturers, and 8 to 10 memorials to Congress urging a strong Hamiltonian protectionist economic policy. During his last years, from 1833 until his death from injuries sustained in a carriage accident, Carey turned to essays and pamphlets on subjects of public welfare and charity.

As imaginative literature, the works of Mathew Carey hold little interest. His political satires are brutal rather than witty and too parochial to engage a modern reader. His account of the yellow fever, intentionally dispassionate, lacks the imaginative power of the scenes of the 1793 epidemic in Charles Brockden Brown's *Arthur Mervyn* (1799-1800). *The Olive Branch,* despite moments of eloquence, is a meticulous compendium of documentation, valuable to the historian but not to the reader of literature. Carey's many essays, chiefly on political economy and public charity, were written with the aim of utility rather than pleasure. Still, it was a discerning appreciation of imaginative literature that informed Carey's career as a publisher, the capacity in which he made an indisputably enduring contribution to American letters.

A

PLUMB PUDDING

FOR THE

HUMANE, CHASTE, VALIANT, ENLIGHTENED

PETER PORCUPINE.

BY HIS OBLIGED FRIEND,

MATHEW CAREY.

" His hand will be againſt every man—and every man's hand againſt him.
Gen. xvi. 12.
If " Bleſſed are the peace-makers"—accurſed be Porcupine, the apoſtle of blood.
" Hated by knaves, and knaves to hate,
" Be this my motto—this my fate."

PHILADELPHIA:
PRINTED FOR THE AUTHOR.
Copy right ſecured according to an act of Congreſs.

Title page for one of Carey's Hudibrastic satires (courtesy of the John Carter Brown Library at Brown University)

References:

Earl L. Bradsher, *Mathew Carey: Editor, Author, and Publisher; A Study in American Literary Development* (New York: Columbia University Press, 1912);

Kenneth Wyer Rowe, *Mathew Carey: A Study in American Economic Development* (Baltimore: Johns Hopkins University Press, 1933).

Papers:
The principal depository is the Historical Society of Pennsylvania, with an extensive collection of legal

and business correspondence and records. The Library Company of Philadelphia holds letters and papers relating to Carey's involvement in civic projects. Two additional depositories of correspondence are the Butler Library of Columbia University and the Houghton Library of Harvard.

John Carroll
(8 January 1735-3 December 1815)

Thomas P. Slaughter
Rutgers University

BOOKS: *An Address to the Roman Catholics of the United States of America* (Annapolis: Printed by Frederick Green, 1784; London: Printed for P. Keating, 1785);

An Address from the Roman Catholics of America, to George Washington, esq., President of the United States (London: Printed by J.P. Coglan, 1790);

A Discourse on General Washington; Delivered in the Catholic Church of St. Peter, in Baltimore.—Feb. 22d 1800 (Baltimore: Printed by Warner & Hanna, 1800);

The Catholic Religion Vindicated. Being an Answer to a Sermon Preached by the Rev. Mr. Cuyler, in Poughkeepsie, on the 30th day of July, 1812, the Day Set Apart for Fasting and Prayer in the State of New-York: In Which Sermon the Religion of the Catholics Was so Illiberally Misrepresented as to Require a Vindication (N.p.: Printed for the author, 1812);

The John Carroll Papers, 3 volumes, edited by Thomas O'Brien Hanley (Notre Dame & London: University of Notre Dame Press, 1976).

John Carroll was born in Upper Marlboro, Maryland, to a merchant father, Daniel Carroll, and a mother, Eleanor Darnall Carroll, descended from Lord Calvert, founder of the colony. He was educated at St. Omer's in France, where he was sent at the age of thirteen. Eventually, after two years of study (1753-1755) at the Jesuit novitiate in nearby Watten and three years of study in Liège, he became a member of the Jesuit order of priests who taught at the school.

Carroll was ordained at Liège in 1767 and renounced all claims to his father's estate in favor of his brothers and sisters. During 1771 he toured Europe as a tutor and kept a sketchy diary of his travels. When Pope Clement XIV suppressed the

John Carroll, circa 1776; portrait attributed to Charles Willson Peale (courtesy of The Kennedy Galleries, Inc.)

Society of Jesus in 1773, Carroll obediently left the Continent for England. One year later he returned to his parents' Maryland home at Rock Creek. Carroll was an ardent patriot, but refrained from much active participation in the war. He did, however, accompany American emissaries on an ill-fated journey to Quebec in 1776. During the war years he wrote a "Plan of Reorganization" (1782) urging former Jesuits to reengage themselves actively in the Lord's work, and he participated the following year in a convocation outside Annapolis that petitioned Rome for appointment of a clerical superior for American priests.

Carroll's pamphlet, *An Address to the Roman Catholics of the United States of America* (1784), perhaps his most significant literary accomplishment, was in response to what he considered an intolerant assault on liberty of conscience and the free practice of religion in America. The Reverend Charles Henry Wharton's *Letter to the Roman Catholics of the city of Worcester* (1784) was a widely circulated attack on the doctrines of Roman Catholicism by a former Jesuit priest. Carroll's scholarly retort was a masterful refutation of Wharton's misinformed assaults on Catholicism and a touching plea for religious tolerance and freedom of conscience. In an era of high anti-Catholic prejudice in America, Carroll's reasoned response to Wharton's harangue played an instrumental role in preparing the way for the guarantee of religious liberty that became part of the Bill of Rights attached to the United States Constitution during the 1790s.

In 1789 Carroll established a college at Georgetown, Maryland, so that Catholic boys would have a place of higher education in America. The doors of the college first opened in 1791. Later, after the Jesuits were again recognized by the church, Carroll entrusted the institution to their care. In 1790 Pius VI appointed him the first Catholic bishop of the United States.

Carroll's other major literary accomplishments included a pamphlet defending the cause of religious liberty and a long letter published over the pseudonym Pacificus that appeared in the Philadelphia *Gazette of the United States* on 10 June 1789. Carroll's letter was in response to a letter that had appeared in the newspaper on 9 May in which the author had argued for the exclusion of members of non-Protestant sects from public office and that "the Protestant Religion is the important bulwark of our Constitution." In response Carroll recounted the contributions of Quakers and Roman Catholics to the nation from the time of colonial settlements through the Revolution. He pled for tolerance and respect for the conscience of others.

In 1790 Carroll presided over his first synod.

John Carroll, portrait by Rembrandt Peale

He was instrumental in the founding of St. Mary's College in Baltimore (1803) and Mount St. Mary's College in Emmitsburg (1808). Throughout his life, Carroll was a controversial figure within and without the Church. His attempts to remain conciliatory brought him the distrust of battling ethnic groups, competitive religious orders, and political partisans. All agreed, however, that he was a magnanimous figure, a fine preacher, and an accomplished scholar.

References:

Peter Guilday, *The Life and Times of John Carroll* (New York: Encyclopedia Press, 1922);

Annabelle M. Melville, *John Carroll of Baltimore: Founder of the American Catholic Hierarchy* (New York: Charles Scribners Sons, 1955).

Mason Fitch Cogswell

(17 September 1761-10 December 1830)

Carla Mulford
Villanova University

BOOK: *The Echo, with Other Poems,* by Cogswell, Richard Alsop, Theodore Dwight, Lemuel Hopkins, and Elihu Hubbard Smith (New York: Printed at Porcupine Press by Pasquin Petronius [Isaac Riley], 1807).

Dr. Mason Fitch Cogswell, author and physician, was a less prominent but nonetheless important member of the Connecticut or Hartford Wits, a group which also included Joel Barlow, Timothy Dwight, David Humphreys, John Trumbull, Theodore Dwight, Dr. Lemuel Hopkins, and Elihu Hubbard Smith. The Connecticut Wits were Yale men, products of a conservative culture, who believed in and promoted the glorification of America, federal principles of government (Barlow was the exception here), and instruction in belles lettres. Modeling their work primarily upon the poetry of Pope, Swift, Gray, Churchill, and Akenside and the prose of Addison and Steele, this group sought to establish a literary canon for the growing country. Cogswell seems to have written much in private; his only verifiable published work is his contribution to the group's series, *The Echo,* published serially between August 1791 and August 1798.

The youngest of five children born to the Reverend James and Alice Fitch Cogswell, Mason Fitch Cogswell was born 17 September 1761 in Canterbury, Connecticut. When Cogswell's mother died in 1772, his father moved to Windham, Connecticut, and sent him to live with Samuel Huntington, a lawyer who later became president of the Continental Congress and Governor of Connecticut. With Huntington, Cogswell studied in preparation for attendance at Yale, and he probably entered the college in 1776. He graduated from Yale in 1780, valedictorian of his class at age nineteen. He then studied surgery and medicine with his brother James and, after having been admitted to practice, spent several years in Stamford, Connecticut. Following his brother to New York in 1784, Cogswell trained further in surgery at the Soldier's Hospital and entered business with his brother in 1787. He made a trip through New England in 1788, evidently in search of a locale in which to set up his own

practice. Having married Mary Austin Ledyard in the late 1780s, he finally settled in Hartford as a physician in 1789. By December 1799 his work had become so well known as to cause his election to the Connecticut Academy of Arts and Sciences, and in May 1800 he was also elected to the Academy of Medicine of Philadelphia. Not only did Cogswell introduce in America surgery for removing cataracts from the eye (1803), but he was also instrumental in establishing at Hartford the first deaf and dumb asylum in America (1825), where his daugh-

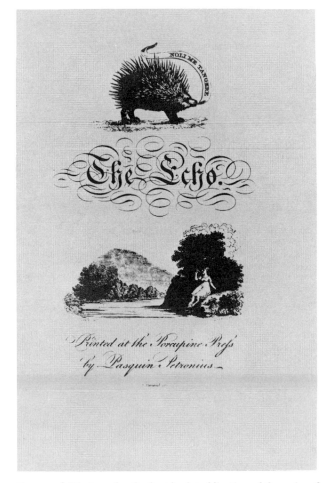

Engraved title page for the first book publication of the series of satires on literary pedantry, bad taste, and republicanism on which Cogswell collaborated with Richard Alsop, Theodore Dwight, Lemuel Hopkins, and Elihu Hubbard Smith

Tisdale pinx!   *Lency sculp!*

a piper had a Cow

page 67.

An illustration for number ten in The Echo *series, the only one of the satires to which Cogswell's contribution can be established with certainty*

ter Alice was one of the first patients.

Probably while he was a student at Yale Cogswell met the group of young men who later became known as the Connecticut Wits. His correspondence indicates that he kept contact with these men after they had all left Yale. He contributed at least in part to *The Echo* series (twenty numbers altogether; seventeen numbers appeared in Hartford's the *American Mercury* between 8 August 1791 and 20 August 1798; two others were published as broadsides; a third appeared in Hartford's *Connecticut Courant*). *The Echo* began as a satire of literary pedantry and bad taste but proceeded to political satire, especially against the American republicans (called Jacobins, Democrats, or Republicans interchangeably) and the French Revolution as well as against individuals such as the elderly Samuel Adams, Judge Hugh Henry Brackenridge, John Hancock, and Thomas Jefferson. Cogswell most likely contributed to more than one number of *The Echo,* but only his contribution to number ten (*American Mercury,* 21 January 1793) can be surely established. A political satire, number ten of *The Echo* mockingly "echoes" a letter in the *Virginia Gazette* for 6 December 1792. The author of the letter protested the name "Jacobin" as it was being applied to the Virginia electors who voted for George Clinton for the 1792 vice-presidency. In addition to mocking the complaint, Cogswell and his coauthors Richard Alsop and Elihu Hubbard Smith denounce the French Revolution and poke fun at Jefferson and Hancock. That more of *The Echo*'s numbers have not been linked to Cogswell attests to his modesty rather than to his lack of interest in the series. His family and friends admired his literary abilities, which were only surpassed by his skill as a surgeon. He died 10 December 1830.

Reference:

Grace Cogswell Root, *Father and Daughter: A Collection of Cogswell Family Letters and Diaries (1772-1830)* (West Hartford, Conn.: American School for the Deaf, 1924).

Papers:

Most of the available Cogswell manuscript material is located at the Connecticut Historical Society and at Yale University.

Tench Coxe
(22 May 1755-16 July 1824)

Hugh J. Dawson
University of San Francisco

BOOKS: *Thoughts Concerning the Bank, of North America, with Some Facts Relating to Such Establishments in Other Countries* (Philadelphia, 1786);

An Address to an Assembly of the Friends of American Manufactures, Convened for the Purpose of Establishing a Society for the Encouragement of Manufactures and the Useful Arts, Read in the University of Pennsylvania on Thursday, the 9th of August, 1787 (Philadelphia: Printed by R. Aitken & Son, 1787);

An Enquiry into the Principles on Which a Commercial System for the United States of America Should Be Founded; To Which Are Added Some Political Observations Connected with the Subject (Philadelphia: Printed & sold by Robert Aitken, 1787);

An Examination of the Constitution for the United States of America . . . (Philadelphia: Printed by Zachariah Poulson, Jr., 1788);

Observations on the Agriculture, Manufactures and Commerce of the United States . . . (New York: Printed by Francis Childs & John Swaine, 1789);

A Brief Examination of Lord Sheffield's Observations on the Commerce of the United States of America (Philadelphia: Carey, Stewart, 1791); enlarged as *A Brief Examination of Lord Sheffield's Observations on the Commerce of the United States. In Seven Numbers. With Two Supplementary Notes on American Manufactures* (Philadelphia: From the press of M. Carey, 1791; London: Philips & Co., 1792);

Reflexions on the State of the Union . . . (Philadelphia: From the press of Mathew Carey, 1792);

A Plan for Encouraging Agriculture, and Increasing the Value of Farms in the Midland and More Western Counties of Pennsylvania . . . (Philadelphia, 1793);

A View of the United States of America, in a Series of Papers, Written at Various Times between the Years 1787 and 1794 . . . (Philadelphia: Printed for William Hall & for Wrigley & Berriman, 1794; London: Printed for J. Johnson, 1795);

The Federalist: Containing some Strictures upon a Pamphlet, Entitled, "The Pretensions of Thomas Jeffer-

son to the Presidency, Examined and the Charges against John Adams, Refuted." Which Pamphlet Was First Published in the Gazette of the United States: in a Series of Essays, under the Signature of "Phocion," 2 parts (Philadelphia: Published by Mathew Carey, 1796);

An Authentic View of the Progress of the State of Pennsylvania, Since the Establishment of the Independence of the United States of America (Philadelphia: Printed by D. Humphreys, 1799);

Strictures upon the letter imputed to Mr. Jefferson, Addressed to Mr. Mazzei, as Greene (N.p., 1800);

To the Republican Citizens of the State of Pennsylvania (Lancaster, Pa., 1800);

An Essay on the Manufacturing Interest of the United States . . . (Philadelphia: Printed by Bartholomew Graves, 1804);

Thoughts on the Subject of Naval Power in the United States of America; and on Certain Means of Encouraging and Protecting Their Commerce and Manufactures (Philadelphia, 1806);

An Examination of the Conduct of Great Britain, Respecting Neutrals . . . , as Juriscola (Philadelphia: Printed by B. Graves, 1807; revised edition, Boston: Printed by Oliver & Munroe, 1808);

An Address to the Citizens of Pennsylvania, on the Situation of our Country; Connected with the Public Conduct of James Ross, a Candidate for the Governmental Chair of Pennsylvania, as a Pennsylvanian (Philadelphia, 1808);

A Memoir on the Subject of a Navigation Act, including the Encouragement of the Manufactory of Boats and Sea Vessels, and the Protection of Mariners (Philadelphia: From the press of T. & G. Palmer, 1809);

A Statement of the Arts and Manufactures of the United States of America, for the Year 1810 (Philadelphia: Printed by A. Corman, 1814);

A Memoir of February, 1817, upon the Subject of the Cotton Wool Cultivation, the Cotton Trade, and the Cotton Manufactories of the United States of America (Philadelphia, 1817);

An Addition, of December, 1818, to the Memoir, of February and August 1817, on the Subject of the Cotton Culture, the Cotton Commerce, and the Cotton Manufacture of the United States . . . (Philadelphia?, 1818).

Tench Coxe was the first American economic theorist to propound a truly national vision. Because of his appreciation of the young nation's industrial potential, he has come to be recognized as a theorist who early foresaw technology's potential for transforming the American economy and perceived, however dimly, its mythic meaning for the emergent society.

The son of William and Mary Francis Coxe, Coxe was born into a well-placed Philadelphia family with distinguished English antecedents. After attending but not graduating from the College of Pennsylvania, he was introduced into a business career when he joined the mercantile firm in which his father was a partner; here he first gained the understanding of business and finance that was to inform his plans for America's development. Although Coxe had shown clear Loyalist sympathies during the Revolution, he was chosen a Whig representative to the Annapolis Convention of 1786 and the Continental Congress of 1788. A year later he became a Federalist and, until he was appointed commissioner of the revenue in 1792, served as assistant secretary of the treasury under Alexander Hamilton, to whose *Report of the Secretary of the Treasury of the United States on the Subject of Manufactures* (1791), Coxe made a major contribution. When in December 1797 John Adams removed him from his position as commissioner of the revenue, Coxe joined the Republicans and served Jefferson's administration as purveyor of public supplies from 1803 until the office was abolished in 1812. Such alterations of allegiance earned him a reputation with some as a rank political adventurer; for Hamilton he was "too cunning to be wise," and John Quincy Adams condemned him as a "wily, winding, subtle, and insidious character."

Coxe married twice. His first wife, the former Catherine McCall of Philadelphia, died only six months after their January 1778 marriage. Four years later Coxe married his cousin, Rebecca Coxe, who lived until 1806 after bearing him eleven children, six of whom survived their father.

Although he was in most respects a dutiful parent, Coxe's optimistic view of the new republic's opportunities led him to plunge his own and his creditors' money into a series of often heedless land speculations in several states. Especially in North Carolina and Pennsylvania, where he bought heavily between 1792 and 1796, his entrepreneurial recklessness left him land poor. A disappointment to his father and for many years the prey of lawyers, he very narrowly skirted the brink of insolvency while serving as a political appointee. Only the good fortune of his inheritances may have saved him from bankruptcy.

If his personality and reputation for political inconstancy kept him from the high offices for which he was so ambitious, Coxe's work as an economist made him an important figure in the shaping of national policies. In all his writings—in his government reports on the national bank, public lands, manufactures, fisheries, commerce, and naval power, as well as in his lectures and general publications—Coxe espoused a mercantilist policy as the best guarantee of American self-sufficiency.

Confident that the new nation had been singled out by providence and believing in inevitable progress, Coxe saw the expanse of American land and the young society's distance from the corruptions of Europe as the best hope of the new age. His 1787 *An Enquiry into the Principles on Which a Com-*

Title page for the address in which Coxe urged that manufacturing was as important as farming in developing a balanced economy (courtesy of the John Carter Brown Library at Brown University)

mercial System for the United States of America Should Be Founded prescribed ways of subduing wanton tastes for foreign luxuries, instituting a fluctuating paper currency, and remedying an ineffectual and disjointed federal government. While carefully observing the pieties due the farming interests, Coxe urged the growth of manufactures as a requisite of the independent country's balanced economy. In his *An Address to an Assembly of the Friends of American Manufactures* (1787), he elaborated his ideas: Favored by a system of sound public credit, manufacturing in the North and cotton raising in the South would combine for national prosperity. American and European inventors would devise labor-saving machinery, and the new economy would draw its workers from among those fugitives from the Old World attracted to "this asylum for mankind." Implicit in Coxe's scheme was a shift in Americans' image of themselves: From being culti-

vators of the soil and coworkers with nature, they would become inventors of the machine and attendants in a technological system. At some points Coxe's argument is a near hymn, in which technology is seen as ennobling what is best in the American environment and freeing manufacture of the drudgery that had made manual and sedentary work so oppressive. His plan promised a happy fusion of machinery with the pastoral ideal. Mechanization was not alien or threatening, but ordained by divine purpose as the means by which industry would harness the fast-falling rivers of the New World. Leo Marx writes that "the speeches of Tench Coxe in the summer of 1787 prefigure the emergence of the machine as an American cultural symbol, that is, a token of meaning and value recognized by a large part of the population."

Coxe's later writings, including his 1791 "Plan for a Manufacturing Society" and other essays collected in *A View of the United States of America* (1794), develop his earlier design with greater explicitness. However, their technical nature makes most of these later writings of interest mainly to economic historians.

Title page for the 1794 collection of Coxe's essays

References:

Jacob Cooke, "Tench Coxe, Alexander Hamilton, and the Encouragement of American Manufactures," *William and Mary Quarterly,* third series 32 (July 1975): 365-392;

Cooke, "Tench Coxe, American Economist: The Limitations of Economic Thought in the Early Nationalist Period," *Pennsylvania History,* 42 (October 1975): 267-289;

Cooke, *Tench Coxe and the Early Republic* (Chapel Hill: University of North Carolina Press, 1978);

Cooke, "Tench Coxe: Tory Merchant," *Pennsylvania Magazine of History and Biography,* 96 (January 1972): 48-88;

Joseph Dorfman, *The Economic Mind in American Civilization* (New York: Viking Press, 1946), I: 253-256, 290-291, 325-326;

Harold Hutcheson, *Tench Coxe: A Study in American Economic Development* (Baltimore: Johns Hopkins University Press, 1938);

Leo Marx, *The Machine in the Garden: Technology and the Pastoral Ideal in America* (New York: Oxford University Press, 1964), pp. 150-169, 180-182.

Papers:

The Coxe papers are at the Historical Society of Pennsylvania.

Michel Guillaume Jean de Crèvecoeur
(31 January 1735-12 November 1813)

John Harmon McElroy
University of Arizona

BOOKS: *Letters From an American Farmer: Describing Certain Provincial Situations, Manners, and Customs, Not Generally Known; and Conveying Some Idea of the Late and Present Interior Circumstances of the British Colonies of North America. Written For the Information of a Friend in England, by J. Hector St. John, A Farmer in Pennsylvania* (London: Printed for Davies & Davis, 1782; Philadelphia: From the Press of Mathew Carey, 1793);

Lettres d'un Cultivateur Américain, Écrites à W.S., Ecuyer, depuis l'année 1770, jusqu'à 1781. Traduites de l'anglois par ***, 2 volumes (Paris: Cuchet, 1784); enlarged edition, 3 volumes (Paris: Cuchet, 1787);

Voyage dans la Haute Pensylvanie et dans l'État de New-York, Par un Membre Adoptif de la Nation Onéida. Traduit et publié par l'auteur des Lettres d'un Cultivateur Américain, 3 volumes (Paris: De l'imprimerie de Crapelet, Chez Maradan, 1801); translated by Clarissa S. Bostelmann (Ann Arbor: University of Michigan Press, 1964);

Sketches of Eighteenth Century America: More "Letters From an American Farmer," edited by Henri L. Bourdin, Ralph H. Gabriel, Stanley T. Williams (New Haven: Yale University Press/London: Oxford University Press, 1923).

A native of France, Michel Guillaume Jean de Crèvecoeur lived half of his adult life in North America and in 1765 became a naturalized citizen of New York. He was a well-proportioned 5 feet 4 inches tall; had reddish-brown hair, tiny freckles, light-brown eyes, a face that was "a little long"; and made "a very handsome appearance." Although first published in Europe, his books are American in subject and setting. All of them are in the eighteenth-century epistolary tradition. His reputation rests on the first of these, *Letters From an American Farmer* (1782), a unified series of expository narratives and the earliest fiction in American literature to express how America differs culturally from Europe. Its chapter "What Is an American?" has been considered the classic statement of American identity. Crèvecoeur's narrative exposition of ideas in *Letters From an American Farmer* is so skillful that many literary historians and critics have mistaken it for an autobiography.

Crèvecoeur based his comparison of American and European cultures mainly on how the acquisition and distribution of property in his adopted country differed from that of Europe. For many centuries property in Europe had been concentrated in autocratic classes and autocratic institutions which were maintained by force and tradition. America, however, had no hereditary ruling class of titled nobility, no established national church, no standing army. Property there was still being rapidly developed from wilderness, and the primary social reality was the expectation that every man would create property for himself. Because of America's inchoate social conditions and immense tracts of undeveloped arable land, labor there had a dignity of opportunity that it could not have in Europe. Crèvecoeur stipulated that these basically different socioeconomic conditions gave Americans different cultural beliefs than Europeans.

Born in Caen, Crèvecoeur received his education at the Jesuit college in that Norman city. His father, Guillaume Jean de Crèvecoeur, was a respected member of the region's minor nobility, and his mother, Marie-Anne-Thérèse Blouet de Crèvecoeur, was a banker's daughter with a better education than most women had in her day. He left Normandy when he was nineteen, going first to England to live with distant relatives; then immigrating, in his twentieth year, to French North America. In Canada, his knowledge of mathematics and draftsmanship enabled him to make his living as a surveyor and cartographer for the colonial militia. He saw service in the wilderness campaigns of the war then being fought in North America between France and Great Britain and in 1757 was present at the surrender of the fort on Lake George, where he witnessed the slaughter of its disarmed British garrison by Indian allies of the French. In 1758, through the influence of noblemen friendly to his father, he was commissioned a lieutenant in a regiment of the regular army of France. The following year, shortly after the battle at Quebec, an action in which he was wounded, he resigned his commission and left Canada to live in the British colonies. During the next decade (between his twenty-fifth and thirty-fifth years), he appears to have traveled through New York, the Ohio region, and Vermont as a surveyor. In 1769 he married Mehitable Tippet, a New York lady from a well-to-do Westchester family, and bought land some thirty miles west of West Point, New York, in Orange County. When the Revolution began six years later, he was the father of a daughter and two sons, an established farmer, and the author of some unpublished manuscripts in English. His attempt to remain neutral during the war caused both the Americans and the British to suspect him of spying, and the British imprisoned him for three months. In September 1780 he left New York for Europe, taking with him his older son, age eight, while his American wife stayed to care for their farm and the two younger

Michel Guillaume Jean de Crèvecoeur, 1786;
portrait by Vallière

children. Seven months after arriving in Great Britain, he sold *Letters From an American Farmer* to a London publisher. In August 1781 he crossed the Channel to the country of his birth, which he had left in 1754.

Letters From an American Farmer consists of twelve fictional epistles organized into a well-defined beginning, middle, and end of nearly equal lengths. Direct reference to the Revolution occurs only at the end of the work, which criticizes the war indirectly by dramatizing the culture it interrupted. In the book an American-born farmer named James Hector St. John, whose paternal grandfather was an English immigrant, relates in letters how he has lived for sixteen years with his family on the frontier, cultivating and enlarging the farm his father established in the forest of central Pennsylvania and bequeathed to him. His correspondent is a London gentleman curious about America and the opinions of Americans. This Englishman, identified as F.B., sets topics for the correspondence and never asks about the Revolution; his letters are not given.

In the form this fiction takes, James's first three epistles, the initial part of his narrative about his American life, are supposedly datable from their internal historical references as communications written between the spring and winter of 1775. Far from expressing concern about the battles in Canada and New England that were fought in these months between American and British forces, these letters tell the history of the American farmer and the peacefulness that have characterized life in America in comparison to Europe's long history of poverty and strife. "Here," James informs F.B. from his farm in the Susquehanna valley, "individuals of all nations are melted into a new race of men, whose labours and posterity will one day cause great changes in the world. Americans are the western pilgrims, who are carrying along with them that great mass of arts, sciences, vigour, and industry which began long since in the east; they will finish the great circle." Uncoerced in America by institutionalized pressures to conform to received beliefs and habits, these former Europeans and their descendants move about freely, marry whom they choose, think their own thoughts, speak as they will, and worship as they believe fitting. James offers the case history of a Scotsman to illustrate what happens to Europe's honest poor when transplanted to America. A peasant family from a notoriously impoverished group of British islands—Andrew the Hebridean, his wife, and teenage son—has increased the small patrimony and life savings they brought with them from the island of Barra by twentyfold after just four years in Pennsylvania. During this time "those new thoughts which constitute an American" (self-respect, a feeling of civic responsibility, confident expectations of being able to improve one's lot in life through steady work) replace Andrew's "European prejudices" of subordination and servility, ingrained by the 1200-year-old traditions of his people. James refers to this change as a "sort of resurrection" and a "great metamorphosis." James believes that because Americans act on "new principles" they "entertain new ideas and form new opinions." "From involuntary idleness, servile dependence, penury, and useless labour"—the characteristics of life in Europe—the American "has passed to toils of a very different nature, rewarded by ample subsistence."

The American farmer's next set of letters illustrates that ideas affect human happiness more than physical conditions. These middle letters describe James's long-ago visits to Martha's Vineyard and Nantucket, two decades before he begins his correspondence with F.B. Though as barren physically as the home of Andrew the Hebridean in Europe, these sand islands off the southern coast of New England supported thriving communities of Quaker seamen when James visited them as a young man in the 1750s, because Quaker ideas formed the basis of a peaceful society of friends having no need for lawyers, priests, police, or rul-

ers. The glory of Martha's Vineyard and Nantucket was that their Quaker magistrates never had to sit in judgment. The American farmer's historical report on these Quaker islands, in his fourth through his eighth letters, is an ironic contrast to the bloody war in America in 1776, the year he evidently composed them.

James's last four letters reveal a change in his feeling about life in America. While his initial letters stress physical conditions and his middle letters stress ideology in explaining differences in human behavior, his concluding letters reveal that slavery and war exist even in America and stipulate that evil is an inherent, inescapable propensity of human nature unaffected by physical conditions or ideology. After witnessing the horribly cruel punishment of a Negro slave in South Carolina, James writes that man is "an animal of prey" whose heroes are "the most successful butchers of the world." This new theme climaxes in the American farmer's last letter. There he explains why he must discontinue his correspondence with F.B. The massacre at Wyoming, Pennsylvania, of noncombatant men, women, and children by Indians under the command of British officers (a historic atrocity in the summer of 1778 incorporated by Crèvecoeur into his fiction) forces James to abandon his farm in fear of death to his family and himself. He hopes that he will be able to keep a love of farming alive among his children during their forced exile in the wilderness with a tribe of peaceful Indians. This final letter in James's correspondence with F.B. is a pathetic reminder of his proud descriptions, in his initial letters, of his happy family life and his satisfaction with the farmer's peaceful round of honorable seasonal toil. The final effect of *Letters From an American Farmer*, therefore, is to call into question the new beginning for mankind in America which the farmer's early letters proclaim.

During Crèvecoeur's two years of asylum in France waiting for the end of the revolution in America so he could rejoin his wife and younger children, he became the protégé of Madame d'Houdetot and the Marquis de Turgot at the French court. In these years he wrote *Lettres d'un Cultivateur Américain* (1784), which is not at all the simple translation of *Letters From an American Farmer* that its title page and introduction suggest but a new composition in French, adapting and incorporating the English materials of Crèvecoeur's first book. *Lettres d'un Cultivateur Américain* is a loose collection of sixty-four letters, sketches, and "anecdotes" (as they are called) instead of a dramatic progression of twelve epistles; its time span is eleven instead of

L E T T E R S

FROM AN

AMERICAN FARMER;

DESCRIBING

CERTAIN PROVINCIAL SITUATIONS,
MANNERS, AND CUSTOMS,

NOT GENERALLY KNOWN;

AND CONVEYING

SOME IDEA OF THE LATE AND PRESENT
INTERIOR CIRCUMSTANCES

OF THE

BRITISH COLONIES

IN

NORTH AMERICA.

WRITTEN FOR THE INFORMATION OF A FRIEN
IN ENGLAND,

By J. HECTOR ST. JOHN,
A FARMER IN PENNSYLVANIA.

LONDON,
PRINTED FOR THOMAS DAVIES IN RUSSEL STREET COVENT-
GARDEN, AND LOCKYER DAVIS IN HOLEORN.
M DCC LXXVII.

Title page for the earliest work of American fiction to express America's cultural difference from Europe (courtesy of the John Carter Brown Library at Brown University)

three years; and the new recipient of James's correspondence is an American instead of an Englishman. The main intention in this much longer, less structured account of America is to display a large amount of information rather than to create an emotionally coherent ideological fiction.

When Crèvecoeur returned to America in the autumn of 1783, it was in the important capacity of French consul to New Jersey, Connecticut, and New York. He discovered that his farm, Pine Hill, had been burned during the closing months of the Revolution, that his wife was dead, and that no one knew what had become of his two children (they were eventually located in Boston). A successful consul, Crèvecoeur supervised the first regular packet service between France and America, promoted an exchange of agricultural products and information between the two former wartime allies, and appreciably increased the existing goodwill between them. During these years he wrote an addi-

tional volume for *Lettres d'un Cultivateur Américain,* enlarging it by half its original length (1787). His active service as consul ended in 1790 with a furlough to France, and he never returned to America. His remaining years were passed almost entirely in France, amid the tumults and dangers of the French Revolution, the Reign of Terror, and the Napoleonic wars. In his mid-sixties he wrote and published yet another book about America, *Voyage dans la Haute Pensylvanie et dans l'État de New-York* (1801), which pretends to be a translation into French of fragments of an English-language manuscript by S.J.D.C., "an adopted member of the Oneida Indians." It describes a trip through the northern and middle parts of the United States in the years following the American Revolution and contains much actual information about postwar economic and political developments in the nascent democracy, word pictures of American landscapes, and depictions of American Indians. This final book of his career is a reaffirmation of belief in America's promise. It praises Americans for having avoided in the aftermath of their revolution "the bloody fury of anarchy."

Crèvecoeur died in the home of his daughter, America-Francès, at Sarcelles, twenty-three years after his last residence in America. An American who had crossed the Atlantic with him in 1787 recalled of his character: "The milk of human kindness circulated in every vein. Mild, unassuming, prompt to serve, slow to censure, extremely intelligent and universally respected and beloved, his society on shipboard could not but be a treasure."

Like Henry David Thoreau, Crèvecoeur published only a few works. But his one book in English, like Thoreau's *Walden,* is a classic representation of American faith in the possibility of renewal, though he doubted that mankind could attain a completely new moral life. Also like Thoreau he rejected wars, political parties, and governments as instruments of human progress. Perhaps because of its pacifist criticism of the American Revolution, *Letters From an American Farmer* was not republished until 1904 in the United States after its first appearance in 1793. Naturally this circumstance retarded Crèvecoeur's reputation. Recognition of his abilities as a creative writer has also been tardy because his success in projecting a living narrator in *Letters From an American Farmer* misled too many readers into evaluating it as an autobiography. This mistake was easy to fall into since he sometimes used in America the surname St. John, though he was never known to have used James or Hector, the first and the middle names of his fictional American farmer. The forth-

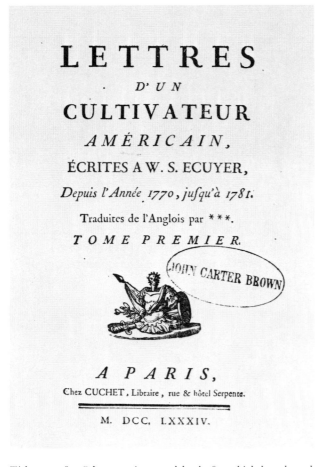

LETTRES

D'UN

CULTIVATEUR

AMÉRICAIN,

ÉCRITES A W. S. ECUYER,

Depuis l'Année 1770, jufqu'à 1781.

Traduites de l'Anglois par ***.

TOME PREMIER.

A PARIS,

Chez CUCHET, Libraire, rue & hôtel Serpente.

M. DCC. LXXXIV.

Title page for Crèvecoeur's second book, for which he adapted and expanded some parts of his first and added a great deal of new material (courtesy of the John Carter Brown Library at Brown University)

coming biography by Gay Wilson Allen and Roger Asselineau should go far toward defining the precise differences between the persona of James the American farmer and the person of Michel Guillaume Jean de Crèvecoeur. The same salutary purpose will be served when Bernard Chevignard of the University of Dijon completes the biographical research incidental to his comparison of the texts of *Letters From an American Farmer* and *Lettres d'un Cultivateur Américain.*

Crèvecoeur's English-language manuscripts published in 1923 under the title *Sketches of Eighteenth Century America* clearly manifest his talent for creative writing. The closet-drama "Landscapes" in this collection is especially noteworthy. Many of the

chapters in his French-language books show the same ability. Though *Lettres d'un Cultivateur Américain* and *Voyage dans la Haute Pensylvanie et dans l'État de New-York,* in comparison to Crèvecoeur's masterpiece, have more of the character of expositions of social and historical facts, their fictional structures are patent. The tendency among twentieth-century analysts and commentators to focus attention only on Crèvecoeur's praise of America in the initial part of *Letters From an American Farmer* has affected appreciation of the artistic wholeness of his masterpiece, a wholeness that comes close to making it the first American novel of ideas; and indeed the first novel of any sort in American literature.

Biography:

Robert de Crèvecoeur, *Saint John de Crèvecoeur: Sa Vie et Ses Ouvrages* (Paris: Librairie des Bibliophiles, 1883).

References:

Percy G. Adams, Introduction to *Crèvecoeur's Eighteenth-Century Travels in Pennsylvania & New York* (Lexington: University of Kentucky Press, 1961);

Everett Emerson, "Hector St. John de Crèvecoeur and the Promise of America," in *Forms and Functions of History in American Literature,* edited by Winfried Flunk, Jurgen Peper, and Willi Paul Adams (Berlin: E. Schmidt, 1981);

Thomas Philbrick, *St. John de Crèvecoeur* (New York: Twayne, 1970);

Howard C. Rice, *Le Cultivateur Américain: Etude sur l'Oeuvre de Saint John de Crèvecoeur* (Paris: Champion, 1932);

Albert E. Stone, Jr., "Crèvecoeur's *Letters* and the Beginnings of an American Literature," *Emory University Quarterly,* 18 (Winter 1962).

Papers:

Crèvecoeur letters are held by the American Philosophical Society, the Beinecke Rare Book and Manuscript Library (Yale University), the Boston Public Library, the Chicago Historical Society, the Connecticut Historical Society, the Library Company of Philadelphia, the Maryland Historical Society, the Massachusetts Historical Society, the New-York Historical Society, and the New York State Library.

John Davis

(6 August 1774-24 April 1854)

Jayne K. Kribbs
Temple University

BOOKS: *A Tribute to the United States. A Poem* (New York: Printed by Robert M. Hurtin, 1798);

The Original Letters of Ferdinand and Elisabeth (New York: Printed & sold by H. Caritat, 1798); translated as *Lettres originals de deux amans habitants de New-York* (New York: H. Caritat, 1798);

Poems, Written at Coosahatchie, in South-Carolina (Charleston, S.C.: Printed by T. C. Cox, 1799);

The Farmer of New-Jersey; or, a Picture of Domestic Life. A Tale (New York: Furman & Loudon, 1800);

Poems, Written Chiefly in South Carolina (New York: H. Caritat, 1801);

The Wanderings of William; or, the Inconstancy of Youth. Being a Sequel to the Farmer of New-Jersey. A Tale (Philadelphia: Printed for R. T. Rawle, 1801);

Adventures of the Mammoth Cheese . . . (Baltimore: W. Pechin, 1802);

Travels of Four Years and a Half in the United States of America; During 1798, 1799, 1800, 1801, and 1802 (Bristol: Printed by R. Edwards & sold by T. Ostell in London & H. Caritat in New York, 1803; New York: Holt, 1909);

Bonaparte and Moreau: A Comparison of Their Military Lives, attributed to Davis (Philadelphia: Printed for the author at the Polygot Office, 1804);

The Philadelphia Pursuits of Literature, a Satirical Poem, as Juvenal Junius (Philadelphia: Printed for the author & sold by John Davis, 1805);

The Story of Poor Dick the Negro (Philadelphia: John Davis, 1805);

Captain Smith and Princess Pocahontas, an Indian Tale (Philadelphia: Printed for the author by T. L. Plowman, 1805; revised edition, Dayton: B. F. Ells & E. M. Strong, 1836);

The Post-Captain; or, the Wooden Walls Well Manned; Comprehending a View of Naval Society and Manners (London: Printed for Thomas Tegg, 1805; Brooklyn: Printed by Spooner & Sleight, 1813);

Walter Kennedy, an American Tale (London: Printed for Longman, Hurst, Rees, & Orme, 1805);

The First Settlers of Virginia, an Historical Novel . . . (New York: Printed by Southwick & Hardcastle for I. Riley, 1805; enlarged, 1806);

The Life of Thomas Chatterton (London: Thomas Tegg, 1806);

Notationes in Virgilium: Complectentes Excerpta Excarminum Principe in Gratium Studiosae Juventutis (Petersburg, Va.: John Dickson, 1807);

Life and Surprising Adventures of the Celebrated John Smith (Pittsburgh: Printed by Cramer, Spear & Eichbaum, 1813);

The American Mariners; or, the Atlantic Voyage . . . (Salisbury: Printed & sold by Brodie & Dowding, 1822);

St. Cross, etc. With the Execution of the Earl of Kent, Before the Castle-Gate at Winchester (Winchester: John Davis, 1836);

Jack Ariel; or, Life on Board an Indiaman, 3 volumes (London: T. C. Newby, 1847; New York: H. Long, 1848).

Collection: *The Poetry of John Davis (1774-1854): With Introduction and Notes,* edited by Jayne K. Kribbs (Ann Arbor: University Microfilms, 1974).

TRANSLATIONS: François René Jean Pommereul, *The Campaigns of General Buonaparte in Italy. During the Fourth and Fifth Years of the French Republic* (New York: Printed for H. Caritat, 1798);

Charles Brockden Brown, *Wieland, ou la Transformation* (New York: Printed for H. Caritat, 1799);

Brown, *Ormond, ou le Témoin Secret* (New York: Printed for H. Caritat, 1799);

Berquin-Duvallon, *Travels in Louisiana and the Floridas, in the Year, 1802, Giving a Correct Picture of Those Countries* (New York: Printed by & for I. Riley, 1806);

The Life and Campaigns of Victor Moreau (New York: I. Riley, 1806; New York: Printed for D. Bliss, 1806);

Original Journals of the Eighteen Campaigns of Napoleon Buonaparte, 2 volumes (London: John Davis, 1816-1817).

John Davis, novelist, poet, translator, and teacher, although not an American by birth or naturalization, owes much of his literary recognition to the United States. His writing career flourished during the twenty-year period (1798-1817) that he traveled up and down the eastern seaboard. In all, he published fifteen prose pieces, four long poetic pieces and collections of poetry; and he published other verses in the leading newspapers and journals in the United States and England. A dedicated and indefatigable worker at the craft of writing, he was convinced that what he wrote had value and that this value would ensure the endurance of his literary work. He was correct in his assumption, at least for a substantial number of years in the early and mid-nineteenth century, especially with regard to four once highly popular books—*Travels of Four Years and a Half in the United States* (1803), *The First Settlers of Virginia* (1805), *The Post-Captain* (1805), and *The American Mariners* (1822).

Born in Salisbury, England, to Ann Gast Davis and James Davis, a wool draper, John Davis apparently enjoyed a fairly pleasant childhood. At fourteen, with only a little formal education and a desire for travel and adventure, Davis sailed to the East Indies and China as a naval assistant for the East India Company. In all Davis spent ten years on the high seas, observing and learning, gathering material that he would later incorporate into most of his major works.

In 1798 love of adventure brought Davis to the United States, where he made the fortunate acquaintance of a young New York bookseller, Hocquet Caritat, who, in effect, launched Davis's literary career. Caritat engaged Davis to translate a number of English works into French, the most notable of these being Charles Brockden Brown's *Wieland* and *Ormond*. Encouraged by the public's reception of these works, Davis ventured into novel writing. After two critical failures, *The Farmer of New-Jersey* (1800) and *The Wanderings of William* (1801), he discovered that he could feed the almost insatiable appetite of Americans and Europeans for travel literature with his *Travels of Four Years and a Half in the United States*. Basically, the book is a record of the author's exploits up and down the eastern seaboard. As the work develops, however, the reader actually comes to know more about the man than about the country he is observing. Davis's love of learning—especially for the ancients, Homer, Horace, and Vergil, and for the classicists of the Augustan Age of literature in England—is evinced time and again. His attitude toward nature

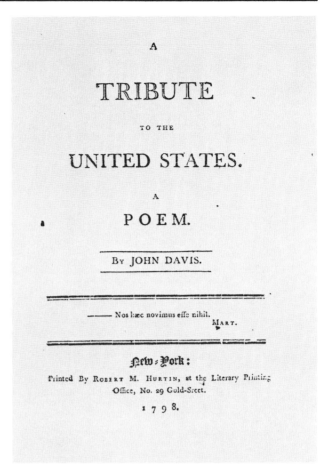

A

TRIBUTE

TO THE

UNITED STATES.

A

POEM.

By JOHN DAVIS.

—— Nos hæc novimus effe nihil. MART.

New-York:
Printed By Robert M. Hurtin, at the Literary Printing Office, No. 29 Gold-Street.
1798.

Title page for Davis's first book (courtesy of the John Carter Brown Library at Brown University)

is a coupling of the eighteenth-century desire for order and the romantic urge for the wild and untrammeled. He seems to lose reader interest in the large sections devoted to Lucas George, his friend and fellow poet, and three distinct episodes also divert the reader from the progress of the work—a description of Jefferson's inauguration and a rendering of the complete text of his inaugural address, a version of the Captain John Smith-Pocahontas legend, and the story of Dick the Negro.

Recognizing the country's enthusiastic response to the Smith-Pocahontas legend and seeing the possibilities for a "best-seller," Davis expanded his forty-page story in *Travels*, first into a seventy-page romance, *Captain Smith and Princess Pocahontas* (1805), and then later that year into *The First Settlers of Virginia, an Historical Novel*. The basis for the story rests on book three of Smith's *The Generall Historie of Virginia, New-England, and the Summer Isles*

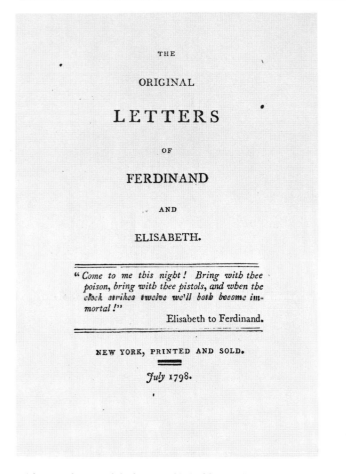

THE

ORIGINAL

LETTERS

OF

FERDINAND

AND

ELISABETH.

"*Come to me this night! Bring with thee
poison, bring with thee pistols, and when the
clock strikes twelve we'll both become immortal!*"

Elisabeth to Ferdinand.

NEW YORK, PRINTED AND SOLD.

July 1798.

*Title page for one of the books published by Davis's mentor, New
York bookseller Hocquet Caritat (courtesy of the John Carter
Brown Library at Brown University)*

(1624) in which Pocahontas, daughter of the Indian
chief Powhatan, rescues the captured Smith from
death by placing her head atop his on the chopping
block. Despite the fact that Davis baldly plagiarized
large sections from Jeremy Belknap's *American
Biography* (1796, 1798) for his tale, he is credited
with fostering a romantic legend that was to become
one of the most popular themes in nineteenth-
century American literature.

The year 1805 also saw the publication of yet
another successful work by Davis, *The Post-Captain;
or, the Wooden Walls Well Manned.* Although the
novel is not widely read today, it was once heralded
as the parent of all American nautical novels,
prompting others to capitalize on their adventures
at sea, to develop a new literary genre. The book
falls into the class of the sentimental novel, yet the
heroes—Captain Bryan Brilliant, Lieutenant Harry Hurricane, and Midshipman Echo—endure no

amorous upsets nor do they cause the discerning
reader of tender sensibilities to drop a tear. There is
no real plot to speak of, and characterization, for
the modern reader, seems shallow. The good
humor and frivolous antics of the characters set the
tone for a basically lighthearted romance. Testimony of the novel's extraordinary popularity is the
fact that new editions were soon published in London, New York, Boston, Brooklyn, and even in
Belfast. The last edition published during Davis's
lifetime appeared in Philadelphia in 1850 as the
twentieth American edition based on the seventh
London edition.

Davis's enormous success as an author dwin-
dled after the initial publication of *The Post-Captain.*
After an abortive attempt at another adventure
story, *Walter Kennedy, an American Tale* (1805), he
settled into the life of a teacher and bookseller, first
in Philadelphia, then in New York. With his regular
contribution of poetry to Joseph Dennie's Philadelphia magazine, the *Port Folio,* his only real contact
with the literary world for a decade or so, his inspiration for writing sustained pieces of literature
seemed to be gone. At last, in 1817, frustrated by his
inability to put together another best-seller and
forced by increasingly pressing financial need,
Davis returned to his hometown of Salisbury, England, where he once again took up the bookseller's
trade, all the while keeping watch on the literary
temper of the time. In 1820 or 1821 he married and
eventually became the father of two daughters. In
1822 he published another effort devoted to the
sea. *The American Mariners; or, the Atlantic Voyage. A
Moral Poem* of 4,500 lines ranks as the third longest
American epic after Timothy Dwight's *The Conquest
of Canäan* (1785; 9,700 lines), and Joel Barlow's *The
Columbiad* (1807; 7,500 lines). Beyond engaging audiences with a dramatic sea story, the six-canto *The
American Mariners* also instructs Davis's British contemporaries in the nobility and sincerity of the
American people. The author clearly states in the
preface to his poem that his primary intention is a
"vindication of the American character from the
aspersions of the Quarterly Reviewers." Americans
are not, he assures these reviewers, the uncivilized
barbarians that they have been painted to be. As a
sojourner for twenty years in the United States,
Davis could write with authority that the malicious
and absurd tales circulating in England were the
results of "an unhappy passion for coarse invective,
clumsy raillery, and vilifying abuse." The poem is
unashamedly patriotic and sympathetic to the
American way of life, without lapsing into sentimentality. There is no bombast, no blatant waving

of banners, no noisy firing of cannons, elements that would have opened the American character and Davis himself to ridicule. The patriotism displayed in the work is tempered with good sense and good humor.

Sometime after the 1822 appearance of *The American Mariners,* Davis and his family moved to nearby Winchester, where he again became a bookseller and stationer. There in 1836 he published his last and perhaps his most enterprising and distinguished poetical work. Written in heroic couplets, *St. Cross, etc. With the Execution of the Earl of Kent, Before the Castle-Gate at Winchester* is a highly dramatic historical narrative of approximately 3,000 lines, focusing primarily on religious and political themes and events of the Winchester area in the fourteenth and fifteenth centuries. Each of the six major divisions in the poem develops a different aspect of medieval life, and each is complete unto itself. The conventions of romanticism are apparent in this work: a sentimental, melancholy interest in the relics of a glorious past; an emotional sympathy with the humble life; a simple desire for unspoiled, "natural" nature; and an interest in Gothicism. These elements, joined with English society's traditional love for its own past, should have assured Davis of a literary success. However, he suffered enormous financial losses from which he never fully recovered.

Ten years later in 1847, at age seventy-three, he wrote his last piece, a novel entitled *Jack Ariel; or, Life on Board an Indiaman,* in what seems to be a desperate attempt to find again the formula that caused his earlier high-seas adventures to stir the public and thus sell. He failed, and in 1854, broken, alone, and seriously ill, Davis died, an inmate at Charterhouse.

Today, recognition of John Davis rests almost solely on two works, *Travels of Four Years and a Half in the United States of America* and *The First Settlers of Virginia.* He wrote vivid and delightful accounts of a post-Revolutionary War America that were to characterize him as the very embodiment of the spirit of adventure and zeal for learning. His *Travels* provides not only a wealth of information on early America but is also the autobiography of a young writer struggling to make a name and a living for himself in an age that discouraged literary enterprise. *The First Settlers of Virginia* presents a dramatic fictional adaptation of one of America's most enduring legends; from Davis's account sprang countless plays, poems, and novels by other authors on the same theme. But for these two works, Davis might well have lapsed into utter obscurity.

> **TRAVELS**
>
> OF
>
> **FOUR YEARS AND A HALF**
>
> IN THE
>
> **UNITED STATES OF AMERICA;**
>
> DURING 1798, 1799, 1800, 1801, and 1802.
>
> DEDICATED BY PERMISSION TO
>
> *THOMAS JEFFERSON, ESQ.*
>
> PRESIDENT OF THE UNITED STATES.
>
> BY JOHN DAVIS.
>
> Je ne connais sur la machine rônde
> Rien que deux peuples différens :
> Savoir les hommes bons, & les hommes méchants.
>
> BEAUMARCHAIS.
>
> *LONDON:*
>
> SOLD BY T. OSTELL, AVE-MARIA-LANE, AND T. HURST,
> PATER-NOSTER-ROW ; B. DUGDALE, AND J. JONES,
> DUBLIN ; AND H. CARITAT, NEW-YORK ;
> FOR
> R. EDWARDS, PRINTER, BROAD-STREET, BRISTOL.
>
> **1803.**

In the preface to his travel book Davis promises that he makes "no mention of my dinner," does not "complain of my bed," does not include drawings of old ruins "which, undeserving of repair, have been abandoned by the possessors," and does not treat common subjects with "magnificent epithets."

References:

Thelma L. Kellogg, *The Life and Works of John Davis,* University of Maine Studies, second series no. 1 (Orono: University of Maine Press, 1924);

Jayne K. Kribbs, Introduction and notes to *The Poetry of John Davis (1774-1854)* (Ann Arbor: University Microfilms, 1974);

Kribbs, "John Davis: A Man for His Time," *Costerus,* new series 3 (1975): 113-145;

Barbara B. Ruf, *John Davis: Poet, Novelist, and Traveler* (Ann Arbor: University Microfilms, 1974).

Samuel Cole Davis

(26 October 1764-31 July 1809)

Steven E. Kagle
Illinois State University

With the exception of John Woolman's well-known *Journal,* a large part of which was rewritten as autobiography proper, the as yet unpublished diary kept by Samuel Cole Davis from 1 April 1808 to 31 July 1809 may be the best Quaker diary written in America.

Davis's family came to the Americas in the seventeenth century and settled in Salem County, New Jersey. The diarist's father, David Davis (1730-1806), married Martha Coles (1736-1780) in September 1762; Samuel was the eldest of their six children. In 1772 the Davis family moved near Haddonfield and was admitted into the Haddonfield Quaker meeting. In June of 1791 Davis married Ann Rowand, an Anglican out of meeting. They had four children: Hannah Cole Davis, Ann Cole Davis, Mary Cole Davis, and Samuel Cole Davis, Jr. Davis drew a large income by renting property which he was given or inherited from his father and from his maternal grandfather, Samuel Coles. Indeed, Davis was so wealthy that, according to one account, he had his own deer park. In the diary, he blamed some of his profligacy and general misbehavior on the leniency of his parents.

The diary begins (after one autobiographical entry) on 1 April 1808. Davis, who by that time had been suffering for a year from a disease diagnosed as cancer, started the work after hearing a voice warning him to "Consider the duration of Eternity . . . [and to recognize that] it was the Lord that sent this affliction." The diary, which he continued until the week of his death, traces the progress of this illness and the process of religious conversion that accompanied it.

These themes alone in a well-written diary could provide enough interesting material to merit publication, but there is more. Davis's spiritual awakening provides the impetus for an ongoing self-analysis that one would be more likely to expect from a diarist of the early twentieth century than one from the early nineteenth century. For example, at one point he not only admitted having committed adultery, but also realized that it was because of his guilt that he had listened to rumors and accused his wife of his own sin. Such entries make an effective self-portrait.

Davis's work has value for those interested in the religious, social, and medical history of America; however, this work is far more important than the facts it contains. Its moving personal portrait gives the reader valuable insights on the way man faces death.

References:

Catherine Soleman Chandler and Elmer Garfield Van Name, *Salem County Historical Society Publications,* 4, no. 1 (1965): 39-40;

Elmer Hutchinson, ed., "Calendar of Wills 1806-1809," *New Jersey Archives,* first series 10: 95;

George R. Prowell, *The History of Camden County, New Jersey* (Philadelphia: L. J. Richards, 1886), p. 727.

Papers:

The Quaker Collection of the Haverford College Library has Davis's papers, including his diary.

Page the 1st

April the first 1808. then laying Down on my
bed I Thought I ~~Received~~ Perceived an Audable or belief voice which
Seemed Plain to my Ears Saying, oh Samuel Consider the
Duration of Eternity why Should the fret and get into
Passions and use bad Language when Dressing thy sore
Remember It was the Lord that has Sent this affliction
On thee? I then thought I would take up a resolution
Let what Should be the Event to Submit to any fate
With as much Patiance and as Strong a resolution to do better
But oh what Frail Beings this of Man Is when he
Is absent from his True guide Conciance. only being
A Little rougher handled by My Doctoress In Cleansing
out of the sore It hurt my Feelings So bad and finding
That Intreating and Begging of her to favour the sore,
But finding no Compassion Shewed, I then Began
With my old way again of using bad and Profane
Speeches, I think Unfielding useage used with anyone
I think is very wrong. x x x x x x x x x x x x x x
First Day, I think I Spent this Day in a good Degree Serious
Second Day, I underwent Such Exceeding Sharp Pains
After Dressing the Sore, as none Can conceive or have
Any Idea of But myself, But Pleas to give me a Degree
of Patiance, O Lord to bear them out, And I hope to be
Truely thankful;   x x x x x x x x x x x x x x
Third Day. My Prayer was answered in a good Degree.
Fourth Day, this Day I Plainly Perceived that the Lord
Answered My Patition in regard to the Dressing and
Handling of my Sore for my Doctoress Seems one of
Little or No feeling Compassion at times when handling
of Sores. —

The first four entries in Davis's diary (Quaker Collection, Haverford College Library)

113

Joseph Dennie

(30 August 1768-7 January 1812)

A. Wheeler Cafarelli
Princeton University

SELECTED BOOKS: *The Lay Preacher, or Short Sermons for Idle Readers* (Walpole, N.H.: Printed & sold by David Carlisle, Jr., 1796);
The Lay Preacher, edited by John E. Hall (Philadelphia: Printed by J. Maxwell & published by Harrison Hall, 1817).

OTHER: *Spirit of the Farmer's Museum and Lay Preacher's Gazette . . . ,* probably edited, with contributions, by Dennie (Walpole, N. H.: Printed by D. & T. Carlisle for Thomas & Thomas, 1801).

Although in his own time Joseph Dennie was known as "the American Addison" for his periodical essays, his most influential literary role was as the editor of the *Port Folio* and several other early American literary periodicals. Despite his political conservatism and his admiration of British literature, Dennie as editor encouraged American literary productivity and raised American literary tastes. Descended from printers on his mother's side and merchants on his father's, Dennie was the only child of Joseph and Mary Green Dennie. Dennie's father was a prosperous merchant, but encroaching insanity led him to retire from business, leaving the family comfortable. Dennie did not receive the large inheritance he might otherwise have expected and frequently fought debt throughout his life. Consequently, Dennie was one of the first Americans, along with Charles Brockden Brown, to make a living as a professional writer.

Dennie spent his early years in Boston at the time of pre-Revolutionary activism, in a family with varied political allegiances. At the outbreak of the Revolution, his father moved the family to Lexington, where Dennie received his elementary education. Unsuccessful in a commercial school, where his family had sent him in an attempt to train him for business, Dennie was then placed with a Loyalist tutor, Rev. Samuel West of Needham, who encouraged his admiration of British literature. At Harvard College, which he entered as a sophomore, his friends described him as unusually interested in literature, but otherwise remiss in his studies; his

Joseph Dennie

rustication for insulting a teacher left him forever resentful toward American education. Upon his graduation in 1790, Dennie moved to Charleston, New Hampshire, where he studied law in the office of Benjamin West, the brother of his former tutor, and was admitted to the bar in March 1794. As his close friend and later collaborator Royall Tyler humorously recounted (*New England Galaxy,* 24 July 1818), Dennie was neither committed to nor well suited for the profession; of his own legal talents Dennie declared, they "are superficial but they are showy." In 1793-1794 Dennie acted briefly as a lay reader for a New Hampshire church. He reported that two churches were willing to await his ordination, but he rejected the ministry as a formal career, although the concept of secular preaching remained with him as an essayist.

Despite this series of false starts, Dennie began to identify his true abilities as a contributor to New England periodicals. The twenty-five extant Farrago essays, written from 1792 to 1795, were a series of lighthearted short pieces on life and manners, inspired by, as he said, "the Goldsmith vivacity in thought, & the Addisonian sweetness in expression." By 1794 Dennie (Colon) and Tyler (Spondee) had started their collaboration on satiric and political paragraphs and verse under the rubric "From the Shop of Colon and Spondee." Dennie felt himself for the first time a success, and in 1795 he went to Boston to write and to gather subscriptions for a literary periodical that would feature his Farrago essays. Dennie's first editorial project, the *Tablet*, a weekly modelled on the *Spectator*, lasted only from 19 May to 11 August 1795, a failure he attributed to the American indifference to belles lettres, a national apathy Dennie worked his entire life to counteract.

Returning to New Hampshire in 1795, Dennie settled in Walpole and began his series of Lay Preacher essays for the *Farmer's Weekly Museum*. The following year he was formally named editor of the publication, gaining notoriety as an effective editor and a vigorous Federalist. The reprinting of his essays by other periodicals, and his publication of a selection of his essays in book form in 1796, *The Lay Preacher, or Short Sermons for Idle Readers,* brought him a national reputation. Using the persona of an older, sedentary country parson, in imitation of Laurence Sterne's *Sermons of Yorick* (1760-1769), the lay preacher retold biblical stories and used scriptural epigraphs at the beginning of each essay to make satiric and "Shandean" observations on politics, manners, and general moral topics such as drinking, fashion, vanity, scandal, and indolence. Although Dennie occasionally had to answer complaints of "tampering with theology," the tone of the essays is more playful than irreverent. Dennie's New England upbringing inclined him to the didactic sermon form and a conservative political Federalism, which were elsewhere becoming obsolete. Nevertheless, in 1803 John Davis described the book as "the most popular work on the American continent."

Well known as the lay preacher, Dennie received offers of editorships in several cities, but since he hoped for political preferment (he had unsuccessfully run for Congress in 1798), he awaited an appointment at a Federalist publication. When in 1799 he was appointed personal secretary to John Adams's Secretary of State Timothy Pickering in Philadelphia, he also accepted editorship of

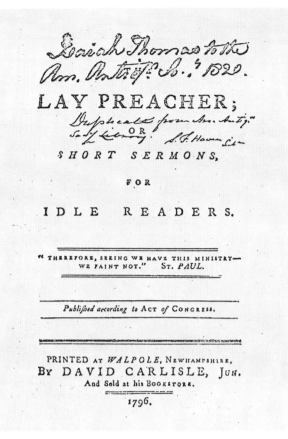

This copy of Dennie's collected essays was presented by printer Isaiah Thomas to the American Antiquarian Society. It was later given or sold to Evert A. Duyckinck, editor of the Cyclopaedia of American Literature *(New York Public Library).*

the *Gazette of the United States.* Both connections were short-lived, but Dennie flourished in the cosmopolitan atmosphere of Philadelphia, which was not only the nation's capital but was fast becoming the literary center of the nation. Dennie assisted Philadelphia's rise to literary preeminence when in 1801 he founded the *Port Folio*, a weekly literary publication whose success under his eleven-year editorship was unparalleled in America.

Dennie edited the magazine under the pseudonym Oliver Oldschool, indicative as he said, of his conservative "moral, political, and literary creed." In addition to original American poetry, criticism, and political essays, the miscellany included travelogues, letters, political synopses, publishing news, and translations of Continental literature, as well as reprints and new material from British authors. In a time when Americans were hostile to British culture, Dennie often praised the eighteenth-century British essayists; somewhat surprisingly, he also printed the poetry of the British romantics. The *Port Folio* drew American contributors from Dennie's political and literary friends, including at the outset John Quincy Adams and Charles Brockden Brown, as well as his literary society, the Tuesday Club, a group of Federalist lawyers with literary ambitions. Dennie was strongly anti-Jacobin and anti-Jefferson; his earlier attacks on Thomas Paine gave way to *Port Folio* attacks on Jefferson and democracy, for which he was charged with treason in 1803 but later acquitted. Like the editors of many other early-nineteenth-century literary publications, Dennie allowed his political beliefs to color his magazine's critical evaluations: Jeffersonian Barlow received a lukewarm commendation for his *Columbiad;* and Freneau's politics were condemned even while the literary quality of his poems was praised. Dennie's reactionary literary and political opinions, unpopular in the emerging Jefferson era, made him unwilling to praise American literature for its own sake. He derided unqualified enthusiasm for American culture and criticized American orthography, education, and government. His early enthusiasm for Benjamin Franklin changed to contempt for Franklin's politics and for the excessive imitation of Franklin's prose, a practice which, he believed, abased American tastes and originality. Although sometimes accused of unfriendliness to American writers, Dennie's chief concern was for America's literary reputation; as an editor, he supported American writers and refined the nation's critical standards.

Despite his politics, Dennie remained a magnet for literary culture throughout his life, attracting *Port Folio* contributors and subscribers up and down the East Coast and on the western frontier. Partly because of frail health and excessive fondness for convivial society, Dennie wrote relatively little, but he remained a visible literary leader in Philadelphia. Washington Irving, whose early pseudonym Jonathan Oldstyle derives from Dennie's, supposedly based his sketch of Launcelot Langstaff (*Salmagundi*, no. 8, 1807) on Dennie. As Dennie's editorial prominence increased, his literary output declined. The 118 Lay Preacher essays were probably written by 1801, although they occasionally appeared through 1808; and as early as 1801 he began republishing in the *Port Folio* nearly all of the Lay Preacher and Farrago essays; many had already appeared more than once in various periodicals. Few unsigned literary or political essays in the *Port Folio* can be reliably assigned to Dennie, for as his early biographer J. E. Hall warned, little fell from Dennie's pen during his *Port Folio* edi-

torship. Aside from republications of earlier essays, Dennie's written contributions were confined to editorial policy statements, short headnotes, and scattered single-paragraph reviews. In 1805 he supervised one volume of an edition of Shakespeare; the authorship or editorship of several political and literary books and pamphlets has been incorrectly attributed to him. In 1809, due to illness and debt, Dennie gave up ownership of the *Port Folio,* and it became a monthly, although Dennie remained as editor. Published in New York and Philadelphia, the *Port Folio* enjoyed a national circulation as the foremost literary magazine in America. After Dennie's death of consumption in 1812, the magazine continued to operate with various editors (who continued to use the pseudonym Oldschool) and with varying levels of success until 1827.

Dennie never married, and his literary reputation did not survive him. In his own lifetime one of the best-known editors and literary celebrities in the nation, Dennie was overshadowed by more productive essayists after his death. Dennie always felt inadequately appreciated in America, and he often considered going to England, where he anticipated an audience who would recognize his talents, but he never went. He planned numerous editions of his essays throughout his life, but only one was published. J. E. Hall published a second selection of Dennie's Lay Preacher essays in 1817; but beyond these two partial collections of Lay Preacher essays, and the inclusion of his work in a few anthologies (including the 1801 *Spirit of the Farmer's Museum and Lay Preacher's Gazette* which Dennie may have edited) almost none of Dennie's fugitive writings have been collected. While Dennie is still considered the major American Addisonian essayist before Washington Irving, his abilities as a writer were limited. His literary influence stemmed chiefly from his role as magazine editor, and in this capacity his reputation as a literary leader was virtually unrivaled in his lifetime. His *Port Folio*'s success as a national literary publication was unheralded in America, and up to that time rarely equaled in England. Dennie encouraged and cultivated American writers, but insisted that Americans achieve literary sophistication. As his epitaph stated, "He devoted his life to the Literature of his Country." By founding the *Port Folio* and bringing together Philadelphia literati, he was a catalyst for American intellectual life; and as an editor and critic, he was a key force in shaping the nation's literature and elevating literary expectations and standards in post-Revolutionary America.

Letters:

The Letters of Joseph Dennie, edited by Laura Green Pedder (Orono, Maine: University Press, 1936).

References:

Joseph T. Buckingham, *Specimens of Newspaper Literature* (Boston: Little, Brown, 1850), II: 74-202;

William Warland Clapp, *Joseph Dennie* (Cambridge, Mass.: John Wilson, 1880);

Harold Milton Ellis, *Joseph Dennie and His Circle,* Studies in English, no. 3 (Austin: University of Texas, 1915);

Ellis, Introduction to *The Lay Preacher,* edited by Ellis (New York: Scholars' Facsimiles, 1943), pp. v-x;

Bruce Granger, *American Essay Serials from Franklin to Irving* (Knoxville: University of Tennessee Press, 1978), pp. 45-163;

John E. Hall, ed., *The Philadelphia Souvenir* (Philadelphia: Printed by William Brown & published by Harrison Hall, 1826), pp. 70-94;

Lewis Leary, "Joseph Dennie on Benjamin Franklin," *Pennsylvania Magazine of History and Biography,* 72 (1948): 240-246;

Leary, *Soundings* (Athens: University of Georgia Press, 1975), pp. 253-270;

Annie Russell Marble, *Heralds of American Literature* (Chicago: University of Chicago Press, 1907), pp. 193-231;

Ellis Paxson Oberholtzer, *The Literary History of Philadelphia* (Philadelphia: George W. Jacobs, 1906), pp. 168-188;

Randolph C. Randall, "Joseph Dennie's Literary Attitudes in the *Port Folio,*" in *Essays Mostly on Periodical Publishing in America,* edited by James Woodress (Durham: Duke University Press, 1973), pp. 57-91;

Albert H. Smyth, *The Philadelphia Magazines and Their Contributors* (Philadelphia: Robert M. Lindsay, 1892).

Papers:

The Chief depository is the Dennie Papers at Harvard University; other letters are in various collections, e.g., Adams Papers and Pickering Papers at the Massachusetts Historical Society.

William Dunlap

Claudia Johnson
University of Alabama

See also the Dunlap entry in *DLB 30, American Historians, 1607-1865.*

BIRTH: Perth Amboy, New Jersey, 11 February 1766, to Samuel and Margaret Sargeant Dunlap.

MARRIAGE: 10 February 1789 to Elizabeth Woolsey; children: John, Margaret Ann.

DEATH: New York, New York, 28 September 1839.

SELECTED BOOKS: *The Father; or, American Shandy-ism. A Comedy, As Performed at the New-York Theatre, by the Old American Company. Written in the year 1788 . . .* (New York: Printed by Hodge, Allen & Campbell, 1789);

Darby's Return. A Comic Sketch. As Performed at the New-York Theatre, November 24, 1789 . . . (New York: Printed & sold by Hodge, Allen & Campbell & sold by Berry & Rogers, 1789);

The Archers or Mountaineers of Switzerland: An Opera, in Three Acts, As Performed by the Old American Company, in New-York; To Which is Subjoined a Brief Historical Account of Switzerland, from the Dissolution of the Roman Empire, to the Final Establishment of the Helvetic Confederacy, by the Battle of Sempach (New York: Printed by T. & J. Swords, 1796);

Tell Truth and Shame the Devil: A Comedy, in Two Acts, As Performed by the Old American Company, New-York, January, 1797, adapted from *Jérôme Pointu,* by A. L. B. Robineau (New York: Printed by T. & J. Swords, 1797);

André: A Tragedy in Five Acts: As Performed by the Old American Company, New-York, March 30, 1798.

To which are added authentic documents respecting Major André; Consisting of letters to Miss Seward, the Cow Chace, Proceedings of the court martial, &c. . . . (New York: Printed by T. & J. Swords, 1798; London: D. Ogilvy & Son, 1799);

The Wild-Goose Chace: A Play, in Four Acts With Songs . . . , adapted from *Der Wildfang*, by Augustus von Kotzebue (New York: Printed & sold by G. F. Hopkins and sold by T. & J. Swords, Gaine & Ten-Eyck, John Black, Alex Somerville . . .* , 1800);

The Virgin of the Sun: A Play, in Five Acts . . . , adapted from *Die Sonnenjungfrau*, by von Kotzebue (New York: Printed & sold by G. F. Hopkins and sold by T. & J. Swords, Gaine & Ten-Eyck, John Black, Alex Somerville . . .* , 1800);

Pizarro in Peru; Or, the Death of Rolla. A Play, in Five Acts . . . , adapted from *Die Spanier in Peru*, by von Kotzebue (New York: Printed & sold by G. F. Hopkins and sold by T. & J. Swords, Gaine & Ten-Eyck, John Black, Alex Sommerville . . .* , 1800);

Abaellino, the Great Bandit. Translated from the German and Adapted to the New-York Theatre . . . , translated and adapted from the dramatic version of *Abällino der Grosse Bandit*, by Johann Heinrich Daniel Zschokke (New York: Printed by L. Nichols & published by D. Longworth, 1802);

The Glory Of Columbia: Her Yeomanry. A Play in Five Acts. The songs, duets, and chorusses, intended for the celebration of the fourth of July at the New-York Theatre (songs, duets, and choruses only, New York: Printed & published by D. Longworth, 1803; published in full, New York: Published by David Longworth, 1817);

Ribbemont; or, The Feudal Baron, A Tragedy in Five Acts. As Performed at the New-York Theatre . . . (New York: Printed & published by D. Longworth, 1803);

The Voice of Nature, a Drama in Three Acts . . . , translated and adapted from *Le Jugement de Salomon*, by L. C. Caigniez (New York: Printed by L. Nichols & published by David Longworth, 1803);

The Wife of Two Husbands. A Drama, in Five Acts. As Performed at the New-York Theatre. Interspersed with Songs, Choruses, Music and Dances . . . , adapted from *La Femme à Deux Maris*, by Guilbert de Pixerécourt (New York: Printed & published by D. Longworth, 1804);

The Dramatic Works of William Dunlap, volume 1 (Philadelphia: Printed by T. & J. Palmer,

1806); volumes 2 and 3 (New York: Published by D. Longworth, 1816);

Fraternal Discord: A Drama, in Five Acts . . . , adapted from *Die Versöhnung*, by von Kotzebue (New York: Published by D. Longworth, 1809);

The Italian Father: A Comedy in Five Acts, By William Dunlap, esq. As performed at the New-York Theatre (New York: Published by D. Longworth, 1810);

Yankee Chronology; Or, Huzza For the Constitution! A Musical Interlude in One Act. To which are added the patriotic songs of The Freedom of the Seas, and Yankee Tars . . . (New York: Published by D. Longworth, 1812);

Memoirs of the Life of George Frederick Cooke, Esquire, Late of the Theatre Royal, Covent Garden. By William Dunlap, esq. Composed principally from journals and other authentic documents, left by Mr. Cooke; and the personal knowledge of the writer, 2 volumes (New York: Published by D. Longworth, 1813; London: Colburn, 1813);

Lovers Vows; a Play, in Five Acts . . . , adapted from *Das Kind der Liebe*, by von Kotzebue (New York: Published by David Longworth, 1814);

The Good Neighbor; an Interlude. In One Act. Altered from a Scene of Iffland's . . . (New York: Published by David Longworth, 1814);

Peter the Great; or, the Russian Mother: A Play, In Five Acts . . . , adapted from *Die Strelizen*, by J. M. Babo (New York: Published by David Longworth, 1814);

A Narrative of the Events Which Followed Bonaparte's Campaign in Russia To the Period of His Dethronement . . . (Hartford: Published by George Sheldon & Co., 1814);

The Life of Charles Brockden Brown: Together with Selections from the Rarest of His Printed Works, From His Original Letters, and from His Manuscripts before Unpublished, 2 volumes (Philadelphia: Published by James P. Parke, 1815); republished as *Memoirs of Charles Brockden Brown, The American Novelist. Author of Wieland, Ormond, Arthur Mervyn, etc. With selections from his original letters, and miscellaneous writings* (London: H. Colburn & Co., 1822);

A Trip to Niagara; Or, Travellers in America. A Farce, In Three Acts. Written for the Bowery Theatre, New-York . . . (New York: Printed & published by E. B. Clayton, 1830);

Address to the Students of the National Academy of Design, at the Delivery of the Premiums, Monday, the 18th of April, 1831 . . . (New York: Printed by Clayton & Van Norden, 1831);

A History of the American Theatre . . . (New York:
    Printed & published by J. & J. Harper, 1832; 2
    volumes, London: R. Bentley, 1832);

*History of the Rise and Progress of the Arts of Design in
    the United States* . . . , 2 volumes (New York:
    Printed by G. P. Scott & Co., 1834);

Thirty Years Ago; or The Memoirs of a Water Drinker . . .
    (New York: Published by Bancroft & Holley,
    1836);

A History of New York, for Schools . . . , 2 volumes
    (New York: Collins, Keese & Co., 1837);

*History of the New Netherlands, Province of New York,
    and State of New York, to the Adoption of the Feder-
    al Constitution* . . . , 2 volumes (New York:
    Printed for the author by Carter & Thorp,
    1839, 1840);

*Diary of William Dunlap (1766-1839) The Memoirs of a
    Dramatist, Theatrical Manager, Painter, Critic,
    Novelist, and Historian* . . . , 3 volumes (New
    York: Printed for the New-York Historical
    Society, 1930);

False Shame and Thirty Years: Two Plays, edited by
    Oral Sumner Coad (Princeton: Princeton
    University Press, 1940).

William Dunlap occupies a place of importance in American letters as a dramatist and historian. Often called the Father of the American Theater, Dunlap was the first professional playwright in
the United States. His first biographer, Oral S.
Coad, is right in claiming that "as a playwright and
manager, he was the dominating personage in our
theatrical affairs at the end of the eighteenth century." Through his frequent choice of native subjects, his frequently expressed patriotic sympathies,
and his written record of the American theater, he
contributed to the infant country's developing
sense of a distinct cultural identity. Dunlap is also a
significant figure in the history of American art,
having been a practicing painter, a founder of the
National Academy of Design, and the author of the
first history of art in America.

Despite his historical importance, Dunlap was
always on the fringes of fame in his lifetime—a
competent but not excellent painter, a respectable
but not highly successful theater manager, a good
but not renowned writer, a friend of the great personalities of his day but not a celebrity himself.
Dunlap was born in America in 1766. As a child of
the American Revolution, he and his work grew
with the new nation, showing evidence from beginning to end of his own democratic sentiments. His
father, Samuel, was able to afford his talented son a
good education, even though plans to give him
training with Benjamin West at his London
Academy went awry when William, having made
the journey to London, failed to enroll. Even at the
early age of seventeen William's reputation as a
painter was such that he was commissioned to do a
portrait of George Washington. After three years in
London, he returned home and shortly entered
theatrical management, to which he had always
been attracted. In 1789, the year of his marriage to
Elizabeth Woolsey, he saw the first production of
two of his plays, the more successful being *The
Father; or, American Shandy-ism,* later entitled *The
Father of an Only Child.* The several plots devised for
this play by the beginning playwright include a
young wife's attempt to interest her wayward husband by making him jealous and an old colonel's
pursuit of an only son he had once thought dead.
The love entanglements of the master and mistress

The Artist Showing a Picture from Hamlet to His Parents, *painting by William Dunlap, circa 1788*
(New-York Historical Society)

and their friends are parallel to those of the rustic servants. The humor comes from what seems to have been amazingly fast-paced action, puns, double entendre, dialect, and comic characters. For example, the attractive young maid, Susannah, is so simple that she thinks mortar shells must be something like oysters, and an insufferable physician bores the other characters with long lectures on his bloodcurdling cases. Although the action is (typical for the times) interrupted occasionally by direct addresses to the audience and songs that have no relevance to the plot, the dialogue is skillfully done.

The play attempts to capture the spirit of Laurence Sterne's *Tristram Shandy* (1759-1767), referred to in the title and on two occasions in the play itself. References are also made to such contemporary issues as American Revolutionary battles, the new Constitution and amendments, national credit, slavery, and America's cultural inferiority, a topic which Royall Tyler had exploited and which Dunlap would return to repeatedly. One American character protests defensively to his English friends, "We claim the same kindred as yourselves

with the heroes, the poets, and the philosophers of England," and the epilogue is a tongue-in-cheek appeal to the audience that, should it want to appear cultured, it had best refrain from any public approval of a native-born playwright.

Dunlap, who would eventually write more than sixty original, adapted, and translated dramas, turned his talents from comedy to history in 1794 with the appearance of *The Fatal Deception, or The Progress of Guilt*, first published as *Leicester, A Tragedy* in volume one of *The Dramatic Works of William Dunlap* (1806). In paying homage to William Shakespeare in the prologue, Dunlap puts his audience on notice that many echoes of Shakespeare's tragedies, particularly *Macbeth*, will be found in the blank-verse play that follows— including a wronged brother, an emasculating wife, a reluctant killer, a kingdom in disarray, and multiple deaths, which are necessary for the play's resolution. Dunlap built an increasingly intricate plot around the return home of the warrior Leicester, who is unaware of his wife's having taken a lover in his absence. In a situation as reminiscent of

THE

FATHER;

O R,

AMERICAN SHANDY-ISM,

A C O M E D Y,

As performed at the NEW-YORK THEATRE,

B Y T H E

OLD AMERICAN COMPANY.

Written in the Year 1788.

*With what fond hope, through many a blisful hour,
We give the foul to fancy's pleasing pow'r.*

CONQUEST OF CANAAN.

N E W - Y O R K:
PRINTED BY HODGE, ALLEN & CAMPBELL:
M,DCC,LXXXIX.

*Title page for Dunlap's first play, which attempts to capture the
spirit of Laurence Sterne's* Tristram Shandy

Agamemnon as *Macbeth,* Leicester's wife, Matilda,
urges her weak, fearful, guilt-ridden lover, Cecil, to
murder her husband. But after Cecil fails miserably
in his attempts to stab and then poison Leicester,
Matilda kills herself, and Leicester kills Cecil. The
darkness of the play arises in large part from its
message that the continuing tragedies that issue
from betrayal cannot be held back, even by
humankind's immense ability and willingness to reform and forgive. As a patriot, Dunlap must have
felt particular satisfaction in the play's success for
despite his use of Shakespeare, he refuses to believe
that American artists must always defer to the British and are incapable of producing tragedy, a chord
that he would strike again and again. As he declares
in his prologue: "And must our music all from
Europe come?/And is there none to strike the lyre
at home?"

In 1796, after having established a reputation

for himself as a successful writer of plays and
sketches, Dunlap bought one-fourth interest in the
Old American Company, the only theater in New
York City. By so doing he joined forces with those
pioneers of the American theater, Lewis Hallam
and John Hodgkinson, both of whom seemed to
have been eager to make use of Dunlap's capital and
his connections, for he had become a leading figure
in literary New York and would include in his circle
of friends Washington Irving, James Fenimore
Cooper, and Charles Brockden Brown. Dunlap
continued to be active in politics as well. As a member of the Friendly Club, he frequently argued
against slavery, putting his principles into action by
working for the New York Manumission Society
and, at his father's death, freeing the slaves he had
inherited.

André, produced in 1798, eighteen years after
the death of the character on which it was based,
shows a strong influence of English heroic drama
and the German playwrights whose plays Dunlap
would continue so frequently to adapt for the stage.
Like the plays Dunlap admired, *André* is notable for
its sentimentality and sensibility.

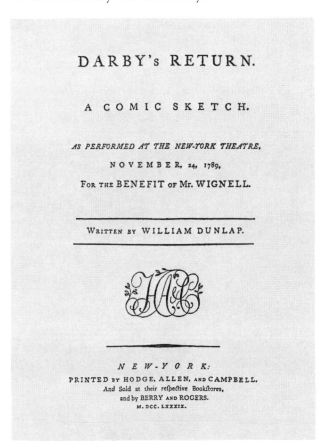

DARBY's RETURN.

A C O M I C S K E T C H.

AS PERFORMED AT THE NEW-YORK THEATRE,

N O V E M B E R, 24, 1789,

FOR THE BENEFIT OF Mr. WIGNELL.

WRITTEN BY WILLIAM DUNLAP.

N E W - Y O R K:
PRINTED BY HODGE, ALLEN, AND CAMPBELL.
And Sold at their respective Bookstores,
and by BERRY AND ROGERS.
M. DCC. LXXXIX.

*Title page for the less successful of the two Dunlap plays produced
at the New-York Theatre in 1789*

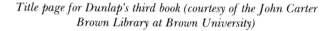

THE

ARCHERS,

OR

MOUNTAINEERS OF SWITZERLAND;

AN OPERA, IN THREE ACTS,

AS PERFORMED BY

THE OLD AMERICAN COMPANY, IN NEW-YORK;

TO WHICH IS SUBJOINED

A BRIEF

HISTORICAL ACCOUNT

OF

S W I T Z E R L A N D,

FROM THE DISSOLUTION OF THE ROMAN EMPIRE,

TO THE FINAL ESTABLISHMENT

OF THE HELVETIC CONFEDERACY,

BY THE

BATTLE OF SEMPACH.

N E W - Y O R K:
Printed by T. & J. SWORDS, No. 99 Pearl-Street.
—1796.—

Title page for Dunlap's third book (courtesy of the John Carter Brown Library at Brown University)

The historical Major John André, whom the youthful Dunlap had observed in military theatricals, was very much like the playwright in his interests in painting, the theater, and the military. Dunlap gives André's story, already well known to his audience, the elegance of blank verse and focuses on the attempt by Captain Bland, a revolutionary army friend of André's, to stay the execution by appeals to General Washington, identified only as "The General." In the ensuing confrontation, patriotism clashes with personal friendship and individual honor. The plot is complicated by British threats to retaliate by executing Bland's father, who is a prisoner of the British. Female characters introduced by Dunlap include the elder Bland's wife and André's lover, both of whom appear to plead for his life. Into the story the politically aware Dunlap is able to weave references to the ideals of the young republic—patriotism, liberty, self-determination, balance, and temperance—all to be defended against the king's tyranny. The play

is remarkable for its simplicity, especially when it is compared to the highly complicated *The Father; or, American Shandy-ism* and *Leicester.* All five acts are set on the day of André's execution; only a few characters represent the entire American army; the scenes are largely encounters between two characters only; and physical action is kept to a bare minimum. Action is outweighed by argument. *André* was the first of many plays about the incident and one of the first of scores of historical plays about the Revolution which remained popular as dramatic material long into the nineteenth century.

Four years later Dunlap introduced Benedict Arnold into a revision of *André* and added farcical scenes and songs, calling the new creation *The Glory of Columbia.* When *The Glory of Columbia* was played as a Fourth of July celebration in Philadelphia in 1807, the company used an old backdrop designed and painted by the real Major André for one of his private theatricals before the Revolution.

In the same year that *André* was produced Dunlap presented what he considered to be one of

ANDRE;

A *TRAGEDY,* IN FIVE ACTS;

AS PERFORMED BY THE OLD AMERICAN COMPANY,

NEW-YORK, MARCH 30, 1798.

TO WHICH ARE ADDED

AUTHENTIC DOCUMENTS

RESPECTING

MAJOR ANDRE;

CONSISTING OF

LETTERS TO MISS SEWARD,

THE

COW CHACE,

PROCEEDINGS OF THE COURT MARTIAL, &c.

COPY RIGHT SECURED.

NEW-YORK:
Printed by T. & J. SWORDS, No. 99 Pearl-street.
—1798.—

Title page for the first of many plays about the notorious Revolutionary War spy John André (courtesy of the John Carter Brown Library at Brown University)

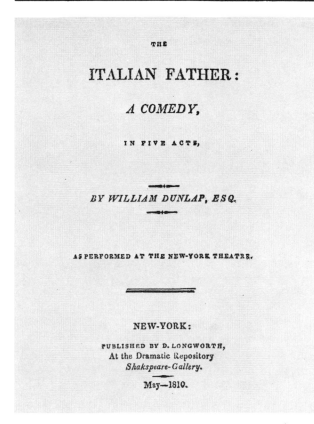

THE

ITALIAN FATHER:

A COMEDY,

IN FIVE ACTS,

BY WILLIAM DUNLAP, ESQ.

AS PERFORMED AT THE NEW-YORK THEATRE.

NEW-YORK:

PUBLISHED BY D. LONGWORTH,
At the Dramatic Repository
Shakspeare-Gallery.

May—1810.

Title page for the play that Dunlap considered one of his best

his best works, *The Italian Father*, a play which owes even more to Thomas Dekker's *The Honest Whore* (1604, 1605) than *Leicester* does to *Macbeth*. Indeed, some critics classify the play as an adaptation. The plot, set in Milan, centers on a young wife, who four years before the action of the play has been driven from her father's house and forced to marry her lover, a rake who has lost all his money and is, in the present action of the play, imprisoned for killing a man in a duel. Father and daughter are reunited in the last act after he comes to her in disguise to test her love for him and her virtue as a wife. Although the play is labeled a comedy and contains in a subplot a fool who plays practical jokes, the main plot is pure melodrama.

At this time in Dunlap's career as a playwright, he turned almost entirely to adaptation, translating some twenty plays by Augustus von Kotzebue alone, only five of which are extant. The most notable of his adaptations are von Kotzebue's *The Stranger, The Virgin of the Sun,* and *Pizarro in Peru;* A. L. B. Robineau's *Tell Truth and Shame the Devil;* and Guilbert de Pixerécourt's *The Wife of Two Husbands.*

Following bankruptcy in 1805 he left the theater and became a traveling painter of miniatures

for a year, then returned as assistant manager at the Park, where his primary job was to be George Frederick Cooke's attendant, seeing as best he could that the well-known British actor appeared at the theater sober. After five years Dunlap left the theater to return to painting and writing. For the remainder of his life he wrote histories and biographies and attempted to make a living at a variety of jobs. By 1813 he had, for one project, not only his own recent bittersweet memories of Cooke but Cooke's letters, journals, and blessing to write a biography. The two-volume book takes the usual chronological form, beginning with Cooke's memories of his childhood. His papers describe his London debut in 1778 and his work with the great actors of his day. After the time when the critics' public humiliation of Cooke drove him from the London stage to America, Dunlap turns from using Cooke's diaries and letters to accounts of his own guardianship of this difficult actor. Dunlap follows the course of Cooke's notorious alcoholism. He would lose his mind for years at a time, often be driven off the stage by boos and hisses during attempts at drunken performances. Finally Dunlap recounts his own frustration after his elaborate schemes to keep Cooke sober failed over and over. The tone and content of the biography are marked by Dunlap's frequently expressed judgments of Cooke. He refused to believe that Cooke was a helpless victim of alcohol because Cooke often chose to be sober for long periods of time, when sobriety would gain something for him that he wanted very badly. Dunlap often quarrels also with the opinions expressed in Cooke's journal, includes his own sermons against drunkenness, and admits that he deliberately left out parts of Cooke's journal and letters for the sole reason that their inclusion would show the actor to be too brutalized.

Even though Dunlap turned increasingly to history, an occasional play came from his pen. In 1812, at the height of the second armed conflict with Britain, one of Dunlap's most famous musical interludes, *Yankee Chronology,* was produced as a Fourth of July celebration. The chief character of the piece is a young boy who has escaped his impressed servitude on a British ship and then volunteered his services on the U.S. *Constitution.* After his account of battle with the *Guerrière,* several patriotic songs are sung to extoll Yankee victories over the British, including an 1812 battle that was won after the interlude was prepared for the stage (the song was written and inserted only days after the battle was waged).

In 1815, during Dunlap's employment as

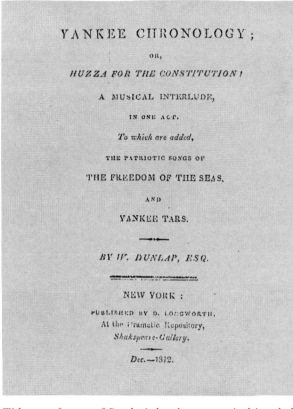

YANKEE CHRONOLOGY;

OR,

HUZZA FOR THE CONSTITUTION!

A MUSICAL INTERLUDE,

IN ONE ACT.

To which are added,

THE PATRIOTIC SONGS OF

THE FREEDOM OF THE SEAS,

AND

YANKEE TARS.

BY W. DUNLAP, ESQ.

NEW YORK :

PUBLISHED BY D. LONGWORTH,
At the Dramatic Repository,
Shakspeare-Gallery.

Dec.—1812.

Title page for one of Dunlap's best-known musical interludes, produced as a Fourth of July celebration at the height of the War of 1812

assistant paymaster for the New York state militia, a job which helped stave off utter poverty for a while longer, he wrote a second biography, this time of his old friend Charles Brockden Brown. The two volumes are comprised largely of verbatim accounts from Brown's own correspondence and lectures. Dunlap arranged these materials, wrote transitions, and included his own critical readings of Brown's novels. Until Harry Warfel's work in 1949, Dunlap's was the only biography of Brown. However, it is also the weakest of Dunlap's works. The lack of discernible focus, the paucity of original comment, coupled with Dunlap's own disappointment with Brown's work, despite their friendship, make it a plodding, uninspiring book which some critics have been reluctant to even designate a biography.

In 1816 Dunlap again began to tour the country as a painter, first concentrating on oil portraits and then, in a style influenced by Benjamin West, on "show pictures" drawn chiefly of Bible scenes. His prevailing interest in the development of American art and his activity in the artistic community led him to found the National Academy of Design in 1826 as an alternative to the already-established but exclusive and ineffectual American Academy of Fine Arts.

Ironically, the last years of Dunlap's life, when he was so ill and poor that his theatrical friends staged two benefits to relieve his poverty, were also his best years as a writer. In this decade he wrote a temperance novel, *Thirty Years Ago; or The Memoirs of a Water Drinker* (1836), *A History of New York, for Schools* (1837), and two works for which he is chiefly remembered: *A History of the American Theatre* (1832) and *History of the Rise and Progress of the Arts of Design in the United States* (1834).

A History of the American Theatre is written largely from Dunlap's own experiences in the theater. His quotation from Colley Cibber, in his preface, is well chosen to show his relationship to his material: "If I have any particular qualification for the task more than another, it is that I am perhaps the only person living (however unworthy) from whom the same material can be collected." After his account of the arrival of the Hallams in America and the introduction of the theater into the cities of the Northeast, Dunlap's memories become his chief source. Even during the Revolution, before Dunlap's profession in the theater began, he had witnessed private and military theatricals in New York City. Into his chronology Dunlap weaves biographical sketches and anecdotes of such pioneers as William Wood, John Bernard, Thomas Wignell, John Hopkinson, Mr. and Mrs. Merry, and many other personalities. He records the names of each company's performers, paying close attention to physical appearance, personality, and professional characteristics. He also inserts a lengthy account of his own life and career. A large part of Dunlap's purpose is to defend the stage against the ignorant attacks to which it was subjected by many religious denominations in America. The fines, prohibition, and licensing are a part of his history. He draws attention to the very real prejudice against actors and the various attempts, especially in Boston and Philadelphia, to kill theater.

However, Dunlap also contends that some grounds exist for public disesteem—excesses in the system of benefit performances, the greed and abusiveness of many managers, the operation of the third tier for prostitutes, and the catering of playwrights and managers to the lowest taste of the public. All of these abuses are, he believes, a direct result of the economic instability of theaters. To correct them, Dunlap recommends sponsorship and financial support of the stage by the state. He also believes that the reputation and tone of the

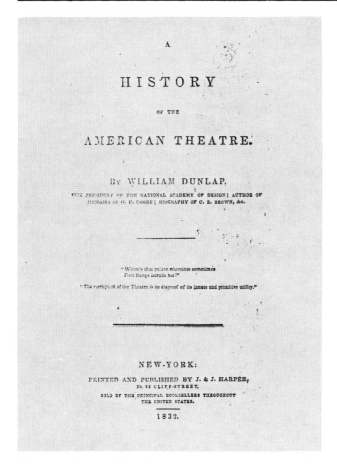

A

HISTORY

OF THE

AMERICAN THEATRE.

By WILLIAM DUNLAP,

VICE PRESIDENT OF THE NATIONAL ACADEMY OF DESIGN; AUTHOR OF
MEMOIRS OF G. F. COOKE; BIOGRAPHY OF C. B. BROWN, &c.

"Where's that palace whereinto sometimes
Foul things intrude not?"

"The corruption of the Theatre is no disproof of its innate and primitive utility."

NEW-YORK:

PRINTED AND PUBLISHED BY J. & J. HARPER,
No. 82 CLIFF-STREET,
SOLD BY THE PRINCIPAL BOOKSELLERS THROUGHOUT
THE UNITED STATES.

1832.

*Title page for one of Dunlap's best-known nondramatic works,
written largely from his own experiences*

stage will be improved with the establishment of academies for training for the stage, as in other professions.

History of the Rise and Progress of the Arts of Design in the United States takes the form of a series of 463 biographical accounts, beginning with John Watson's immigration to the United States in 1715 and following throughout a roughly chronological sequence. Dunlap devotes greater attention to artists whom he regards as particularly important: Benjamin West, Gilbert Stuart, John Trumbull, Samuel F. B. Morse, Henry Inman, Thomas Cole, John James Audubon, and himself. His subjects are painting, engraving, architecture, academies of art, and collections. The history concludes with an annotated list of painters, sculptors, architects, and engravers in pre-1835 America. Dunlap is not reluctant in his history to voice strong opinions about the craft and character of his subjects and proves that he can be a harsh judge. He calls George Catlin "utterly incompetent," and in reference to Catlin's portrait of Governor De Witt Clinton, Dunlap

writes: "He has the distinguished notoriety of having produced the worst full-length portrait which the city of New York possesses." Dunlap is also cool toward John James Audubon: "How much science gains by increasing the picture of a bird beyond that size necessary to display all the parts distinctly, is with me questionable." The author also, as might be expected, makes no secret of his republican sentiments, even in his history of art. He rails against the enslavement of the British artist to a patronage system of wealth and privilege, while lauding art in America because it is maturing as art can only do in a country that listens to the voices of its people.

Thirty Years Ago; or The Memoirs of a Water Drinker, published in 1836, is Dunlap's only novel. As the title suggests, it is a temperance novel whose moral lessons are heavy-handed and whose plots are excessively contrived. The unfortunate water-drinking protagonist, an actor, struggles valiantly against fate, which had dealt him a mother, an aunt, and a wife, all of whom are drunkards. Woven into the fictitious melodrama is the character of George Frederick Cooke whose drunken sprees Dunlap continues to use for his moral lessons.

Dunlap left a further, more personal history in his diary which he kept through the year 1833 and which was first published by the New-York Historical Society in 1930. Of the thirty or more diary volumes written by Dunlap, only eleven have been located. The three that have been made available for publication include a brief life of George Cooke and a chronology of artists and actors from 1793 to 1832. Here for the first time the reader gets a close look at Dunlap's life as an itinerant artist— the poverty, the necessity of exploiting personal contacts, the hustling for commissions, and the nagging uncertainty about ever being paid. The diary is also a source for Dunlap's religious views. In true Federalist fashion, he reveres Thomas Paine, scorns most religious fervor and superstition, including that of his brother-in-law, Timothy Dwight, and attests to a belief in First Cause and religious toleration. In sum, the diary is an invaluable source of information about an artist's mind and the mundane, everyday life in the federal period.

Dunlap's influence is firmly established by virtue of his role as the first professional American playwright, the first American theater historian, and the first American art historian. Although he was not a great author, he was a prolific writer of considerable skill, influence, and versatility, having been one of the few American playwrights in history to master such a broad range of drama: comedy of manners, melodrama, romantic tragedy, musical variety, farce, historical drama, and panorama. With his successful execution of each form, he was able to assure other American playwrights of further possibilities within native drama. As a theater professional, he infused his plays and his philosophy of management with a native spirit, consistently attempting to raise the consciousness and pride of a country suffering from acute feelings of cultural inferiority. Furthermore, Dunlap must receive much of the credit for the eventual acceptance of American theater in a narrowly religious culture suspicious of all theater: Dunlap was able to avoid the subject matter that churchgoers found to be particularly objectionable in eighteenth-century English plays and thereby to diffuse many protests against the theater.

In Dunlap's role as manager, he encouraged the production of American plays, and even went so far as to attempt the exportation of American dramatic talent. As playwright, manager, artist, and historian, he helped develop the artistic tastes of a nation, trying to lead the country away from the embellishment he connected with British privilege and toward the simplicity and honesty which he found to be more in keeping with a democracy.

Like Hawthorne and James after him, Dunlap seemed to sense the importance of having a past in the developing definition of a culture. As a youthful playwright he repeatedly turned the events of his lifetime into history—the plays of his youth and the narratives of his old age.

He is one of those figures who appears to gain even more respect with the passage of time. Writing in 1888, some forty-nine years after Dunlap's death, George O. Seilhamer begrudged Dunlap the distinction of father of the American theater and charged that Dunlap maligned Cooke, that he was ignorant of the theater, and that his statements of fact "are almost always misstatements, either in whole or part." Seilhamer, however, is decidedly in the minority. Theatrical historians such as Richard Moody and Bernard Hewitt have typically had little hesitation about according Dunlap a place of importance in theatrical history. Dunlap has also been well regarded by recent historians of the theater. Although his first biographer, Oral S. Coad, is exceptionally sympathetic to his subject, he expresses in the concluding paragraph of his study what most students of Dunlap's work would acknowledge: "He lived at a time when American art and literature were compelled to struggle for existence, with no popular encouragement and support. . . . He allied himself with the exponents of these pursuits; and throughout a long life, marked often by severe poverty and distress, he remained faithful to the cause which he had espoused."

Bibliography:

Oscar Wegelin, *A Bibliographical Checklist of Plays and Miscellaneous Writings of William Dunlap* (New York: Charles F. Heartman, 1916).

Biographies:

Oscar Wegelin, *William Dunlap and His Writings* (New York: Privately printed, 1904);

Oral S. Coad, *William Dunlap* (New York: Dunlap Society, 1917);

Edward Southern Hipp, *Drama's Father in America, William Dunlap* (Newark, 1934);

William Carroll McGinnis, *William Dunlap* (Perth Amboy, N.J.: City of Perth Amboy, 1956);

Robert H. Canady, *William Dunlap* (New York: Twayne, 1970).

References:

Van Wyck Brooks, *The World of Washington Irving* (New York: Dutton, 1944);

Robert H. Canady, "William Dunlap and the Search for an American Audience," *Midcontinent American Studies Journal,* 4 (Spring 1963): 45-51;

H. E. Dickson, *Arts of the Young Republic: The Age of William Dunlap* (Chapel Hill: University of North Carolina Press, 1968);

David Grimsted, *Melodrama Unveiled: American Theatre and Culture, 1800-1850* (Chicago: University of Chicago Press, 1968);

John Hodgkinson, *A Narrative of His Connection With the Old American Company* (New York: Printed by J. Oram, 1797);

Fred Moramarco, "The Early Dramatic Criticism of William Dunlap," *American Literature,* 40 (January-March 1968): 9-14;

G. C. D. Odell, *Annals of the New York Stage,* 15 volumes (New York: Columbia University Press, 1929-1949);

Phillips Academy, *William Dunlap. Painter and Critic* (Andover, Mass.: Addison Gallery of American Art, 1939);

Arthur Hobson Quinn, *A History of American Drama. From the Beginning to the Civil War* (New York: Harper, 1923), pp. 73-112;

George O. Seilhamer, *A History of the American Theatre,* 3 volumes (Philadelphia: Globe Printing House, 1888-1891);

T. S. Woolsey, "American Vasari," *Yale Review,* 3 (July 1914): 778-789.

Papers:
Manuscripts of value to the student of William Dunlap's work can be found at the Boston Public Library, the Historical Society of Pennsylvania, the Massachusetts Historical Society, the New York State Library, the University of Virginia Library, and the New York Public Library's theater collection.

Timothy Dwight

Vincent Freimarck
State University of New York at Binghamton

BIRTH: Northampton, Massachusetts, 14 May 1752, to Major Timothy and Mary Edwards Dwight.

EDUCATION: B.A., 1769, Yale College; M.A., 1772.

MARRIAGE: 3 March 1777, to Mary Woolsey; eight sons: including Benjamin Woolsey, John, James, Sereno Edwards, William Theodore, Henry Edwin.

DEATH: New Haven, Connecticut, 11 January 1817.

BOOKS: *A Dissertation on the History, Eloquence, and Poetry of the Bible. Delivered at the Public Commencement, at New-Haven* (New Haven: Printed by Thomas & Samuel Green, 1772);
A Valedictory Address to the Young Gentlemen, Who Commenced Bachelors of Arts, at Yale-College, July 25th. 1776 (New Haven: Printed by Thomas & Samuel Green, 1776);
A Sermon, preached at Stamford, in Connecticut, upon the General Thanksgiving, December 18th, 1777 (Hartford: Printed by Watson & Goodwin, 1778);
America: Or, a Poem on the Settlement of the British Colonies; Addressed to Friends of Freedom, and Their Country. By a Gentleman Educated at Yale-College (New Haven: Printed by Thomas & Samuel Green, 1780?);
A Sermon, Preached at Northampton, on the twenty-eighth of November, 1781: Occasioned by the Capture of the British Army, under the Command of Earl Cornwallis (Hartford: Printed by Nathaniel Patten, 1781);
The Conquest of Canäan; a Poem, in Eleven Books . . . (Hartford: Printed by Elisha Babcock, 1785);

Portrait by John Trumbull, 1817 (Yale University Art Gallery. Gift of the Class of 1817. 1817.1)

The Triumph of Infidelity: A Poem (N.p.: Printed in the World, 1788);
Virtuous Rulers a National Blessing. A Sermon, preached at the General Election, May 12th, 1791 . . .

(Hartford: Printed by Hudson & Goodwin, 1791);

A Discourse on the Genuineness and Authenticity of the New-Testament: Delivered at New-Haven, September 10th, at the Annual Lecture, Appointed by the General Association of Connecticut: on the Tuesday before the Public Commencement (New York: Printed by George Bunce, 1794);

Greenfield Hill: A Poem, in Seven Parts . . . (New York: Printed by Childs & Swaine, 1794);

The True Means of Establishing Public Happiness. A Sermon, delivered on the 7th of July, 1795, before the Connecticut Society of Cincinnati . . . (New Haven: Printed by T. & S. Green and sold by I. Beers, 1795);

A Discourse, Preached at the Funeral of the Reverend Elizur Goodrich, D.D. Pastor of the Church in Durham, and One of the Members of the Corporation of Yale-College . . . November 25th, 1797 . . . (New Haven: Printed by T. & S. Green, 1797);

The Nature, and Danger, of Infidel Philosophy, Exhibited in Two Discourses, addressed to the Candidates for the Baccalaureate, in Yale College . . . September 9th, 1797 (New Haven: Printed by George Bunce, 1798);

The Duty of Americans, at the Present Crisis, Illustrated in a Discourse, Preached on the fourth of July, 1798 . . . (New Haven: Printed by Thomas & Samuel Green, 1798);

A Discourse, Delivered at New-Haven, Feb. 22, 1800; on the Character of George Washington, Esq. . . . (New Haven: Printed by Thomas Green and Son, 1800);

A Discourse on Some Events of the Last Century, Delivered in the Brick Church in New Haven, on Wednesday, January 7, 1801 . . . (New Haven: Printed by Ezra Read, 1801);

A Sermon on the Death of Mr. Ebenezer Grant Marsh, Senior-Tutor, and Professor Elect of Languages and Ecclesiastical History, in Yale College, Who Died November 16, 1803 . . . (Hartford: Printed by Hudson & Goodwin, 1804);

The Folly, Guilt, and Mischiefs of Duelling: A Sermon, Preached in the College Chapel at New Haven, on the Sabbath Preceding the Annual Commencement, September, 1804 . . . (Hartford: Printed by Hudson & Goodwin, 1805);

A Sermon Preached at the Opening of the Theological Institution in Andover; and at the Ordination of Rev. Eliphalet Pearson, LL.D. September 28th, 1808 . . . (Boston: Printed by Belcher & Armstrong and published by Farrand, Mallory & Co., 1808);

A Discourse, Occasioned by the Death of His Excellency Jonathan Trumbull, Esq. Governor of the State of Connecticut; and Delivered, at the Request of the General Assembly, in the Brick Church in New-Haven . . . (New Haven: Printed & sold by Oliver Steele & Co., 1809);

The Charitable Blessed. A Sermon, Preached in the First Church in New-Haven, August 8, 1810 . . . (New Haven: Sidney's Press, 1810);

The Dignity and Excellence of the Gospel, Illustrated in a Discourse, Delivered April 8, 1812, at the Ordination of the Rev. Nathaniel W. Taylor, as Pastor of the First Church and Congregation in New-Haven . . . (New York: Printed by J. Seymour, 1812);

A Discourse, in Two Parts, Delivered July 23, 1812, on the Public Fast, in the Chapel of Yale College . . . , part 1 (New York: Printed by J. Seymour, published by Howe and Deforest in New Haven, and sold also by A. T. Goodrich & Co. in New York, 1812); part 2 (New York: Printed by J. Seymour, 1812);

A Sermon, Delivered in Boston, Sept. 16, 1813, before the American Board of Commissioners for Foreign Missions, at Their Fourth Annual Meeting . . . (Boston: Printed by Samuel T. Armstrong, 1813);

Remarks on the Review of Inchiquin's Letters, Published in the Quarterly Review; Addressed to the Right Honorable George Canning, Esquire. By an Inhabitant of New England (Boston: Published by Samuel T. Armstrong, 1815);

An Address, to the Emigrants from Connecticut, and from New-England Generally, in the New Settlements in the United States, by Dwight, Daniel Smith, Lyman Beecher, Aaron Dutton, and Heman Humphrey; signed by Dwight as chairman of the committee appointed by the General Association of Congregational Churches (Hartford: Printed by Peter B. Gleason & Co., 1817);

Theology; Explained and Defended, in a Series of Sermons . . . With a Memoir of the Life of the Author . . . , 5 volumes (Middletown, Conn.: Printed by Clark & Lyman for Timothy Dwight in New Haven, 1818-1819/London: Printed for William Baynes and Son, Paternoster Row, and Thomas Tegg, Cheapside. Sold by H. S. Baynes & Co., Edinburgh; R. Griffin & Co., Glasgow; R. M. Tims, Dublin; and all Booksellers, 1824); republished as Dwight's System of Theology. In Two Volumes. Theology Explained and Defended in a Series of Sermons . . . With a Memoir of the Life of the Au-

thor. (Glasgow: Printed & published by Khull, Blackie & Co. and by A. Fullerton & Co., Edinburgh, 1821);

Travels in New-England and New-York . . . , 4 volumes (New Haven: Printed by S. Converse & published by Timothy Dwight, 1821-1822; London: Printed for W. Baynes & son, 1823); new edition, edited by Barbara Miller Solomon, 4 volumes (Cambridge: Harvard University Press, 1969);

Sermons . . . , 2 volumes (Edinburgh: Waugh & Innes/Glasgow: R. M. Tims/London: James Duncan, 1828; New Haven: Published by Hezekiah Howe and Durrie & Peck, 1828);

President Dwight's Decisions of Questions Discussed by the Senior Class in Yale College, in 1813 and 1814, edited by Theodore Dwight (New York: Jonathan Leavitt/Boston: Crocker & Brewster, 1833).

OTHER: Elihu Hubbard Smith, ed., *American Poems, Selected and Original,* includes poems by Dwight (Litchfield: Printed by Collier & Buel, 1793);

Vernon Louis Parrington, ed., *The Connecticut Wits,* includes poems by Dwight (New York: Harcourt, Brace, 1926; Hamden, Conn.: Archon Books, 1963);

Jane Donahue Eberwein, ed., *Early American Poetry,* includes poems by Dwight (Madison: University of Wisconsin Press, 1978).

PERIODICAL PUBLICATIONS:

Nonfiction:

"The Friend," *New-Haven Gazette, and the Connecticut Magazine,* no. 1, 1 (30 March 1786): 42-43; no. 2, 1 (6 April 1786): 50-51; no. 3, 1 (13 April 1786): 58-60; no. 4, 1 (20 April 1786): 73-74; no. 5, 1 (27 April 1786): 81-82; no. 6, 1 (4 May 1786): 89-90; no. 7, 1 (25 May 1786): 113-114; no. 9 [8?], 1 (8 June 1786): 129-130; no. 9, 1 (15 June 1786): 137-138; no. 11 [10?] (22 June 1786): 145-146; no. 12 [11?], 1 (6 July 1786): 161-163; no. 12, 1 (21 September 1786): 245-246; no. 13, 1 (12 October 1786): 269-270; no. 14, 1 (19 October 1786): 277-278; no. 15, 2 (4 October 1787): 252-253;

"A Historical Account of the Gothic Gospel," *New-Haven Gazette, and the Connecticut Magazine,* 2 (1 March 1787);

"An Essay on the Judgment of History concerning America," *New-Haven Gazette, and the Connecticut Magazine,* 2 (12 April 1787): 59-60;

"Address to the Ministers of the Gospel of every Denomination in the United States," *American Museum,* 4 (July 1788): 30-33;

"Farmer Johnson's Political Catechism," *Mercury and New-England Palladium,* 31 March; 3, 14, 17 April; 8 May 1801;

"Lectures on the Evidences of Divine Revelation," *Panoplist and Missionary Magazine United,* June-December 1810; January-March, June-September 1811; January, March, May 1812; June-August 1813;

"Observations on Language," *Memoirs of the Connecticut Academy of Arts and Sciences,* 1 (1816): 365-386;

"Observations on Light," *Memoirs of the Connecticut Academy of Arts and Sciences,* 1 (1816): 387-391;

"Observations on the Present State of Religion in the World," *Religious Intelligencer,* 10, 17, 24, 31 August; 7, 14 September 1816.

Poetry:

"Columbia; A Song," *Boston Magazine,* 1 (December 1783): 71;

"The Trial of Faith," nos. 12-14 of "The Friend," *New-Haven Gazette, and the Connecticut Magazine,* 1 (21 September; 12, 19 October 1786): 245-246, 269-270, 277-278;

"Address of the genius of Columbia to the members of the continental convention," *American Museum,* 1 (June 1787): 482-484;

"The Seasons Moralized," *American Museum,* 5 (March 1789): 302-303;

"A Song: written in 1771," *American Museum,* 5 (April 1789): 408-409;

"A Hymn Sung at the Public Exhibition of the Scholars, Belonging to the Academy at Greenfield, *American Museum,* 6 (August 1789): 171-172;

"The Critics. A Fable," *Gazette of the United States,* 13 July 1792, p. 2;

"The Maniac of Gadara, An Irregular Ode," *Panoplist and Missionary Magazine United,* November 1816, pp. 526-528.

It is possible to make a modest claim for Timothy Dwight as a poet, but with the proviso that he was a poet only incidentally, in the way of the eighteenth-century man of letters who used the various literary genres selectively in the service of extraliterary ends. He was always something else first, whether teacher, pastor, politician, or college president. His verse (even in representative selections) has disappeared almost entirely from comprehensive college anthologies, and what commen-

Dwight's birthplace in Northhampton, Massachusetts

tary one finds belongs more to historical scholarship than to literary criticism. One recent editor does, however, include Dwight in "a major-figure anthology of American poetry in the colonial and early national periods," the other figures being Anne Bradstreet, Edward Taylor, Philip Freneau, and ·William Cullen Bryant. Jane Donahue Eberwein believes that these five "were all fine writers and made enduring contributions to American literature" and so has "tried to select and emphasize their best poems, confident that literary value transcends historical considerations." Even so, she concedes that "Dwight's main interest for the modern reader may well be his paradoxical situation as a transitional figure who managed, fairly successfully, to express latently Puritan ideas in the language of the Age of Reason."

Timothy Dwight was a member of a network of families that, connected by religious and political interests as well as by blood and marriage, produced many leaders or had ready access to those in power. (In the small world of the early republic such close family ties could yield some odd juxtapositions. When Dwight delivered a notable sermon on the evils of duelling shortly after Alexander Hamilton's death, many were aware that Hamilton's antagonist Aaron Burr was Dwight's first cousin; and Dwight, who believed that a clergyman might justly be dismissed by his congregation for regular theater attendance, was a brother-in-law of the eminent playwright and producer William Dunlap.) His mother was a daughter of the great theologian Jonathan Edwards, and his father, Yale graduate, military man, merchant, and judge of the Court of Common Pleas, was of the fifth generation of Dwights active in the public affairs of Massachusetts. Membership in such an elite was of course no guarantee against reverses in fortune. Jonathan Edwards himself had been dismissed by the Northampton congregation he had served for twenty-three years and gone into virtual exile as a missionary to the Indians on the western Massachusetts frontier, and Dwight's father went into a kind of self-imposed exile, seeking to found a settlement in Mississippi, when loyalty to his magistrate's oath came into conflict with his feelings for the revolutionary sentiments of his neighbors, who suspected him of Tory sympathies—this at the same time that Timothy Dwight left his tutorship at Yale to serve as a chaplain in the First Connecticut Brigade in the bitterly disputed Hudson Valley region during 1777 and 1778. But Dwight did not expect life to be easy, and it is hard to imagine how he would have behaved had he found it so, given his strenuous engagement on many fronts. He had his share of what Perry Miller calls the secret strength of Calvinism—the belief that people in general are about as bad as they can be, which prepares one for the proof to be found in experience. He also had abundant energy and a kind of sturdy optimism about the human capacity for achievement in the face of adversity, qualities that must largely have accounted for his effectiveness in many roles and the regard in which he was held. With equal fervor he could be America's panegyrist or its severest critic, performing never as an alienated writer but always as a spokesman reminding his dominant class of its duties.

Except for a brief period at a local grammar school in Northampton, where he was sent to learn Latin, and a year in the household of a Connecticut clergyman, where he prepared for the Yale entrance examinations, Dwight received his early education at home, largely under his mother's guidance, reading systematically through the works of geography and history (including New England history) in his father's library. Something of a prodigy—he read the Bible fluently at the age of four—he was admitted to Yale at thirteen, having proved that he could read and construe at sight Tully, Vergil, and the Greek Testament, write "true Latin prose," and understand the "Rules of Prosody, and vulgar Arithmetic." Two or three years younger than his classmates, Dwight found the freshman and sophomore studies easy and joined in social activities. On his own he read English literature, especially enjoying Addison and Johnson, and studied the classics in the college library. In his junior year he rose early before the predawn time of compulsory chapel to pursue his self-imposed task of mastering Homer, with harm to his health and lasting damage to his eyesight. Tied with another student for first place, he graduated in 1769.

It was fairly customary for new graduates to teach school prior to professional studies or while awaiting an opportunity in business, but Dwight's two years as a schoolmaster in New Haven proved to be the first step in a lifelong career as a distinguished educator. This early experience must have contributed to his marked success with his Yale students when he assumed a tutorship at the college in 1771. Confirmed in his abilities as a teacher, he later opened his own school at Greenfield, Connecticut, when he was called there as pastor in 1783, and was able to put his theories into practice. While often disdained as a reactionary in politics, Dwight

deserves recognition as a liberal in education. Coeducation at the secondary school level was rare in his day, but Dwight believed that girls were as capable as boys and deserved equal educational opportunities (doubtless the example of his mother remained fresh in his mind). The curriculum at his academy closely paralleled those of the contemporary colleges, and during the dozen years of its existence students came to it not only from New England but from the South as well. An often-noted characteristic of Dwight was his sense of fairness and his belief in persuasion rather than coercion: there was no flogging at his academy, and later as president of Yale he ended the practice according to which older students bullied younger ones into performing menial services for them, and he abolished the system of monetary fines as favoring the richer students, who could easily afford to buy their way out of penalties for infractions of discipline.

On assuming his tutorship at the age of nineteen, Dwight found at Yale a number of like-minded upperclassmen and graduates who shared an enthusiasm for English literature and had literary aspirations. Now remembered collectively as the Connecticut Wits rather than known by their works, these young men constituted the first of those groups that have appeared sporadically on the American college scene down through the Fugitives at Vanderbilt and the Beats at Columbia, warmed by a sense of literary vocation and at odds with the curricular status quo. Dwight and his fellow tutor John Trumbull took the radical step of trying to introduce contemporary English literature as a subject of study, and they encouraged students to write essays and poems. With customary caution, the authorities allowed the innovation as an addition to the regular academic load provided the students had parental consent. Inspiring by example, Dwight and Trumbull collaborated on a series of *Spectator*-like essays, published over a period of months in Boston and New Haven newspapers. Linked closely in New Haven by literary interest and more loosely later by military experience, all the members of the group, still writing, went their separate ways, some to become ministers, David Humphreys to become a leading physician and industrial entrepreneur, Joel Barlow an international radical, Trumbull a lawyer, and Dwight the visible embodiment of established order as president of Yale.

Like many eighteenth-century poets on both sides of the Atlantic, Dwight found his aesthetic in the critical commonplaces of writers from Dryden through Johnson, which were largely codified in two Scottish works, Lord Kames's *Elements of Criticism* (1762) and its successor in Dwight's favor, Hugh Blair's *Lectures on Rhetoric and Belles Lettres* (1783). Not surprisingly, he achieved no technical distinction in the various poetic genres attempted. What is interesting about Dwight's verse is the recurrence in the whole body of his work of motifs that express his central concern, the proper conduct of life to make America worthy of its millennial future and its redemptive role in the world. The shape of works to come is discernible in his first published poem, printed anonymously in New Haven without date (probably 1780). (Dwight had already published sermons under his name; perhaps here he was exercising what he considered to be appropriate genteel anonymity.) Consisting of 346 lines in heroic couplets, the poem bears the title *America: Or, a Poem on the Settlement of the British Colonies; Addressed to Friends of Freedom, and Their Country. By a Gentleman Educated at Yale-College.* It belongs in the category of poems on "the rising glory of America," which takes its name from the actual title of a poem presented jointly by Hugh Henry Brackenridge and Philip Freneau at the

AMERICA:
OR, A
POEM
ON THE SETTLEMENT
OF THE
BRITISH COLONIES;
ADDRESSED
To the Friends of Freedom, and their Country.

By a GENTLEMAN *educated at Yale-College.*

NEW-HAVEN:
Printed by THOMAS and SAMUEL GREEN.

Title page for Dwight's first published poem, a 346-line paeon to America's millennial future

Mary Woolsey Dwight

Princeton commencement of 1772. In his poem Dwight tells the story, familiar in outline to the audience, of how, after centuries in which Asia and Europe had lain "sunk in barbarity," heaven-taught Columbus crossed "unknown pathless seas," and "AMERICA'S bright realms arose to view, / And the *old* world rejoic'd to see the *new*." He reviews the history of settlement, with special attention to "our fathers" who came to New England in the name of freedom, truth, and God, and has good words for the military deeds of Wolfe and Amherst in Canada in a just war that "Heaven itself approved" as it made way for peace and progress in this "Land supremely blessed" and destined for greatness: America's "rising glory shall expand its rays, / And lands and times unknown rehearse their endless praise." But peace is not to be enjoyed without further disruption. A visionary form appears to the poet ("on her sceptre FREEDOM blaz'd in gold") and shows him an American future to which her "Heroes lead the glorious way" through "flames of war" to a period of progress in the arts and sciences and commerce. America will be literally the wonder of the world, which "EUROPE and ASIA with surprize behold." Peace will reign, and "Then, then a heavenly kingdom shall descend,/And Light and Glory through the world extend" until Christ comes in judgment, when nature itself will end, and with it history and time, the saved mounting "to worlds above," there to "Drink streams of purest joy and taste immortal love."

America is less ostensibly the subject of Dwight's most ambitious work, *The Conquest of Canäan; a Poem, in Eleven Books* (1785), a vastly inflated expansion of the narrative in Joshua 7-10, in which chapters Joshua destroys the kingdom of Ai and defeats the five kings who attack the kingdom of Gibeon. This work, in exhaustingly maintained heroic couplets, exemplifies Dwight's belief that to achieve literary greatness for America a poet must attempt the greatest form, the epic. "By the general consensus of criticks," Dwight's admired Samuel Johnson had written, "the first praise of genius is due to the writer of an epick poem, as it requires an assemblage of all the powers which are singly sufficient for other compositions." Johnson had Milton in mind, but the important point is the prestige of

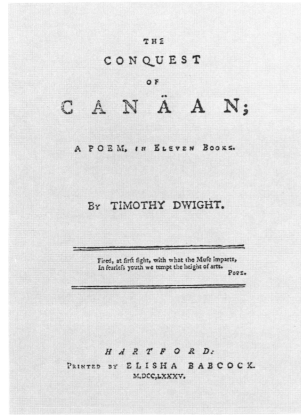

THE

CONQUEST

OF

CANÄAN;

A POEM, IN ELEVEN BOOKS.

BY TIMOTHY DWIGHT.

Fired, at first fight, with what the Muse imparts,
In fearless youth we tempt the height of arts.
                                                    POPE.

HARTFORD:
PRINTED BY ELISHA BABCOCK.
M,DCC,LXXXV.

Title page for Dwight's most ambitious poem, a vastly expanded retelling of Joshua 7-10, in which Joshua is the typological representative for George Washington

the form. Since the epic, however moribund, was still being attempted in England, and (as Robert D. Arner has interestingly suggested) American poets in the wake of the Revolution may have identified the epic as "a literary form appropriate to the birth of a nation," there is little point in dismissing the efforts of Dwight and Barlow and others as evidence of cultural lag. Barlow's choice of Columbus as hero for *The Columbiad* (1807) is readily understandable even today—but why Dwight's choice of Joshua? The question may not have greatly puzzled Dwight's readers, for they could see Joshua as a possible figure for Washington, with the concomitant acceptance of conflict and revolution to effect providential change. They could so see Joshua because they were familiar with the typological exposition of the Bible.

Biblical typology seeks to demonstrate through various correspondences the coherence of the Old Testament and the New: sin and death come into the world through the disobedience of Adam but are conquered through the sacrificial obedience of Christ, the "second Adam"; Isaiah's "suffering servant" who is "despised and rejected of men" is fully revealed in Jesus; Jonah's emergence from the belly of the whale after three days prefigures the descent into hell and the resurrection—and so on through many parallels in which the meaning of the "type" in the Old Testament (like Abraham's readiness to sacrifice his son) is fully comprehended in its "anti-type" in the New (God's sacrifice of his son). Conservatively applied, such interpretation restricts itself to actual events in Bible history, and through study of parallels such as those indicated some conclusions can be drawn about the progress of the spiritual Israel, the true Church, in the world. The world itself is a fallen one, with no place excepted: in the warning words of Roger Williams, "*America* (as *Europe* and all nations) lyes dead in sin." But over the objections of Williams and some English Puritans, John Cotton and his successors viewed America typologically: seen as the anti-type of the flight from Egyptian oppression across the Red Sea to the Promised Land, the Great Migration across the Atlantic to escape oppression could itself serve as a type of signal events in American history to come. To view America this way was, as Sacvan Bercovitch has observed, "to give the kingdom of God a local habitation and a name."

In a typological reading of the Bible, Joshua is not simply a greater leader; he is a type of Jesus. ("Joshua whom the gentiles Jesus call," to use the words Milton gives to the archangel Michael in *Par-*

adise Lost as he shows Adam a vision of history to come, stressing by proximity the root meaning—help or salvation—of both names.) And if America has a typological role beyond the confines of actual biblical history, Joshua can serve as an adumbration of Washington, the "Saviour of his Country" to whom *The Conquest of Canäan* is dedicated. Despite some embarrassment, in that Joshua was an invader and Washington a defender, the figures correspond as leaders in the continuing conflict between the forces of good and the forces of evil as they struggle to establish the just society in the promised land. Like Milton's Adam, Dwight's Joshua is granted a vision of history to come. He is shown a vast region beyond the western seas, "a mighty realm, by heaven design'd/The last retreat for poor, oppress'd mankind," to remain unknown "Till circling years the destin'd period bring" and "a new Moses [Columbus]" "hails a new Canaan's promis'd shores." As Europe sinks into slavery,

> Here union'd Choice shall form a rule divine;
> Here countless lands in one great system join;
> The sway of Law unbroke, unrivall'd grow,
> And bid her blessings every land o'erflow.

When "union'd Choice shall form a rule divine" man's choice will be the expression of God's intention, which is that America shall revive the world:

> Hence, o'er all lands shall sacred influence spread,
> Warm frozen climes, and cheer the death-like shade;
> To Nature's bounds, reviving Freedom reign,
> And Truth, and Virtue, light the world again.

Lest the reader miss the point, Dwight provides a footnote: "Beginning of the millennium. See Isaiah and the other prophets." For the next five hundred lines and more to the end of book ten, Dwight proceeds through the steps of the binding of Satan and the thousand years of peace on earth, the release of Satan at the end of that period, the ensuing last great struggle between good and evil, and God's predestined victory and judgment of all for eternity as time and history end.

America's special role was not merely an obsession of Puritans such as John Cotton, Cotton Mather, Jonathan Edwards, and scores of others who had argued that America's late discovery was part of God's plan to reveal things "in the fullness of time" (just as Augustine had argued in *The City of God* that the incarnation did not take place until the Roman empire had so unified the world that the dissemination of Christianity would be very rapid).

Timothy Dwight, miniature by his brother-in-law William Dunlap

It fascinated as well many other writers long familiar with the idea of *translatio studii*, the passage of civilization over the centuries from the ancient world to western Europe and inevitably to the western hemisphere. In his celebrated "Verses on the Prospect of Planting Arts and Learning in America" (1752), Bishop George Berkeley had predicted there "the rise of empire and of arts," and John Adams could not recall a time when Americans had not lived in that expectation. The fusion of the sacred and the secular strands of this thought in *The Conquest of Canäan* results in a distillation of both millennial and material prospects, occasionally supplying in appeal what the poem lacks in art, as when some lines may suggest at once an Edward Hicks vision of the Peaceable Kingdom and an Enlightenment version of perfectible man.

America's role is still the subject of concern in Dwight's next important poem, *The Triumph of Infidelity*, "Printed in the World" in 1788, with a dedicatory letter "To Mons. de Voltaire." The poem exists in two versions, neither acknowledged by Dwight but both widely known to be by him. The model for it was, as Kenneth Silverman astutely notes, the "rising glory" poem: "Earlier he had traced the growth of America in terms of evolving and decaying empires; now he traces the growth of infidelity in terms of the rise and fall of Satan's 'empire' on earth," beginning with his arrival on America's shores before the close of the Revolution to undertake his subversive work in these "realms of freedom, peace, and virtue." The formal subject of the first part is Satan's review of his hard-won victories in Europe with the aid of "all-subduing Fashion":

> "Let black be white," she said, and white it seem'd
> "Hume a philosopher;" and straight he dream'd
> Most philosophically. At her call,
> Opinions, doctrines, learn'd to rise, and fall;
> Before her, bent the universal knee,
> And own'd her sovereign, to the praise of me.

Satan's first-rate lieutenants, such as Shaftesbury, Hume, and Bolingbroke and lesser ones (his "Tolands, Tindals, Collinses, and Chubbs") have "Help'd fops to folly, and help'd rakes to sin,/And marr'd all sway, by mocking sway divine." The

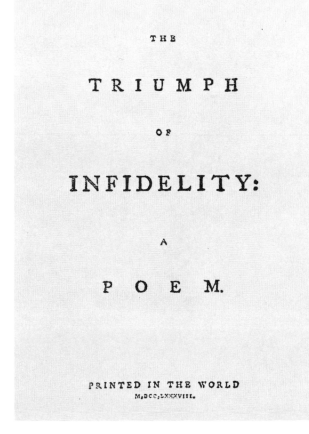

THE

TRIUMPH

OF

INFIDELITY:

A

POEM.

PRINTED IN THE WORLD
M,DCC,LXXXVIII.

Title page for the poem in which Dwight expressed his concern over social forces that he saw as threats to order in the new republic

ostensible subject of the second part is the contest between the unwitting dupes of Satan, the contemporary aging New England theologian Charles Chauncy and his followers on the one hand, and the living spirit of Jonathan Edwards on the other. Chauncy's sin, in Dwight's view, was his teaching that all souls might be saved. But the real subject of both parts of the poem is, to cite Silverman once more, political: *The Triumph of Infidelity* is an "attack against whatever ideas, sects, and personalities Dwight considered friendly to democracy and unfriendly to social order."

The anger and gloominess that pervade *The Triumph of Infidelity* are in marked contrast to the precarious hopefulness of *The Conquest of Canäan*. The Biblical Joshua had more battles before him, but he would be saved; the eighteenth-century reader of Hume or follower of Chauncy very likely would not. Chauncy's thinking could lead to worse than heresy: it could cast doubt on "all sway" by questioning Edwardsean "sway divine." Of course the chosen satiric form of *The Triumph of Infidelity* calls for angry Juvenalian expression, and, though the poem is not a unified work, Dwight's genuine concern is not to be doubted. This concern he was able to express more successfully in *Greenfield Hill* (1794), a pastoral poem which seems to hold out the hope that if America cannot be made safe from democracy right away, perhaps at least Connecticut can be, and in the long run help redeem the nation.

Generally in Dwight's works the private self seems swallowed up in the public man, but here the public and private come together, just as the actual Greenfield Hill of Dwight's experience apparently came close to the ideal projected in his subsequent writings, particularly *Travels in New-England and New-York* (1821-1822). Far from presenting himself as the artist willing to strike an epic blow for the new nation or as the ironist complimenting Voltaire on his success in teaching that "the chief end of man, was to slander his God, and abuse him forever," Dwight sees himself as a sort of man of feeling, who wrote the poem "with no design of publishing it" but "merely to amuse his own mind, and to gain a temporary relief from the pressure of melancholy." A work of nearly 4,500 lines—and copious notes, in which allusions are explained and Connecticut is extolled—*Greenfield Hill* consists of seven parts: "*I. The Prospect. II. The Flourishing Village. III. The Burning of Fairfield. IV. The Destruction of the Pequods. V. The Clergyman's Advice to the Villagers. VI. The Farmer's Advice to the Villagers. VII. The Vision, or Prospect of the Future Happiness of America.*" Dwight's statement that he "designed to imitate, in the several parts, the manner of as many British poets" but that "finding himself too much occupied, when he projected publication, to pursue that design" is a reminder that neoclassical writers apologized not for imitating good models but for not imitating them well enough. (Dwight uses Thomsonian blank verse in the first part, heroic couplets in the second and seventh parts, octosyllabic couplets in the third, fifth, and sixth, and Spenserian stanzas in the fourth part.)

What begins as a "prospect" poem in the tradition of John Denham's *Cooper's Hill* (1642) ends in the already conventional extension of that form in celebrating America's future, with implicit contrasts along the way between European vice and American virtue. Unlike the deserted village of Goldsmith's 1770 poem, which is clearly evoked, Greenfield Hill is a flourishing community where practically all are content, even in some measure the slave ("Lost liberty his sole, peculiar ill,/And fix'd submission to another's will"), who is protected by law from the physical torture permitted in the British West Indies. Those who are not content, like the lazy lounger who has been "The loudest prater in a blacksmith's shop;/The wisest statesman, o'er a drunken cup," have engineered their own fall. Those who leave the village do so not like Goldsmith's people in despair, but in hope to "fix, in untrod fields, another home" in "medial climates" where "cheaper fields the numerous household charm,/And the glad sire gives every son a farm." They are culture bearers, too, planting villages complete with churches and schools: where they are, "There changing neighbours learn their manners mild/And toil and prudence dress th'improving wild." The present tranquility of the village is like tranquil periods in its past history, but that history has included stormy episodes, like the destruction of Fairfield by order of Governor Tryon in July 1779 (which allows Dwight to further the contrast between Europe and America) and the Pequod War. Dwight celebrates the Puritans who braved the combined forces of the Pequod chiefs, worthy opponents who were "Sydneys in zeal, and Washingtons in arms," but contemplation of the destruction of the Pequods and the present plight of the Indians puts a decided check on the rising glory of the nation as the poet calls upon the "Senate august" to "think what nations fill'd the western plain./Where are they?" After admonishing the Senate to "Reflect, be just, and feel for Indian woes severe," he returns to his praise of the Puritans ("Even Pequod foes they view'd with generous eye"), but as William Hedges points out, Dwight

through this and other sections or passages all but poses a question: "The unasked question is, Can the American republic, as the destined successor to the great line of past empires, be expected to retain its virtue? Theoretically of course it can; the millennial empire or republic, by definition, will not fall. But Dwight's Gray-like lingering over images of decay and ruin implicitly jeopardizes the poem's utopian faith." Perhaps the melancholy from which the poet sought temporary relief was real, not just a sentimental indulgence.

However much the fourth part may remind the reader of Lawrence's injunction to trust not the teller but the tale, Dwight's conscious intention is made clear in the fifth and sixth parts, where he is most directly didactic. "As the Writer is the Minister of Greenfield," he says in the introduction, he has his parishioners in mind. "To excite their attention to the truths and duties of Religion . . . is the design of the Fifth Part; and to promote in them just sentiments and useful conduct, for the present life . . . of the Sixth." The teachings of the beloved minister, doubtless Dwight's idealized image of himself, are filially received by the villagers, as are the wise saws of the respected farmer, whose likeness to Franklin's Father Abraham has sometimes been noted. The farmer propounds general principles about observing order and method and dispenses canny practical advice ("When first the market offers well,/At once your yearly produce sell"). Most important, he urges that parents teach their children "to reverence righteous sway" and not to mock those in authority. Where all are literate, even those who do not proceed to college can hope to distinguish themselves, for "APPLICATION MASTERS ALL THINGS." Bringing up children lovingly but firmly, looking to their own tasks, and avoiding contentious litigation, the villagers can achieve happiness.

It is a considerable jump from the "steady habits" of Connecticut to the glorious future of America, one too great for the contemplative poet, but not for the Genius of Long Island Sound, who, rising "from his sapphire bed" and bearing aloft a shield "grav'd with the semblance of his double shore" in the form of likenesses of New Haven and New York, proclaims the spread of the "enduring reign of Peace" and "scepter'd Law," which will let "Man once more, self-ruin'd Phoenix, rise,/On wings of Eden, to his native skies." The Genius of Long Island Sound is a conservative, who knows "How balanc'd powers, in just gradation, prove/The means of order, freedom, peace, and love," and also something of an anti-intellectual, for in his future society not to idle theorizing "But to firm facts, shall human faith be given,/The proofs of Reason, and voice of HEAVEN." The Genius has the last word, but the farmer and the minister leave the lasting impression of a kind of "first" in American poetry—a picture of a specific village, one which exists in actuality and in imagination, embodying the values of the writer, who knows that the glory of America depends upon the strivings of ordinary men and women.

Greenfield Hill, published in 1794, was Dwight's last major poem. Possibly his appointment as president of Yale the following year left him less time for poetry; but since he was a man of incredible energy who always seemed to find time for anything he really wished to do, it is more likely that he felt he had had his say in verse. Although he was sensitive to adverse criticism, his was not the lot of the dedicated poet acutely suffering from a sense of failure; the fact is that poetry, early and late, did not rank highest with Dwight. In *America: Or, a Poem on the Settlement of the British Colonies* it is not poetry that holds first place in that glorious future in which "heaven-born Science every bosom warms,/And the fair Arts unveil their lovely charms," it is Eloquence. Philosophy (that is, natural philosophy, or science), Religion, and History will enlighten man, Poetry will "paint Religion's charms divinely

bright," Sculpture "Bid the fay marble leap to life and breath," and "the canvas glow with living dies" in representations of the physical world, the charms of women, and the boldness of men. And finally there is Eloquence:

> Then Eloquence soft pity shall inspire,
> Smooth the rough breast, or set the soul on fire;
> Teach guilt to tremble at th' Almighty name,
> Unsheath his sword and make his lightnings flame;
> Or reach out grace more mild than falling dews,
> While pale Despair th'n affrighted soul pursues.

The province of eloquence is traditionally oratory, whose end is to effect an action or at least the adoption of an attitude. Dwight has something to say about the relation of oratory to poetry in *A Discourse, Occasioned by the Death of His Excellency Jonathan Trumbull, Esq.* (1809) as he comments on three fields in which men may exercise their powers—fancy, speculation, and action: "The first is peculiarly the province of the Sculptor, the Painter, and the Poet. The Philosopher occupies the second, and the Orator claims them both. The third is peculiarly the scene of effort to the Hero, the Statesman, and the Patriot.... He ... who is employed in acting virtuously, and usefully, fills a nobler sphere of being, than he, who is busied in that course of thinking, from which the action is derived." Trumbull's distinction is that he *"gave the whole vigour of his mind"* to political measures and state decisions: "He was *engrossed* by them, as a Poet by the theme of his song; . . . his life, and his measures, were eminently useful; and deserved, and gained, the approbation of his own mind and that of his country." As Governor of Connecticut, Jonathan Trumbull, Jr., was, so to speak, engaged in the practice of a higher kind of poetry, and in celebrating in seven separate parts of the address Trumbull's practicality, prudence, firmness of mind, attachment to Connecticut "manners and institutions," loyalty to "the religious system of our ancestors," and personal piety, Dwight himself as orator resorts to fancy and speculation in creating the idealized picture of Trumbull as the embodiment of all that a governor must be to inspire the society he leads.

Oratory as a possible field of endeavor was to hold considerable appeal in a later decade for Emerson as a young man contemplating the choice of vocation. It was still an age in which the chief means of moving people to act was the art of persuading them in public assemblies, and for the young Emerson oratory included the pulpit. For Dwight one might almost say that oratory meant

GREENFIELD HILL:

A

P O E M

I N

SEVEN PARTS.

I.   THE PROSPECT.
II   THE FLOURISHING VILLAGE.
III. THE BURNING OF FAIRFIELD.
IV. THE DESTRUCTION OF THE PEQUODS.
V.   THE CLERGYMAN'S ADVICE TO THE VILLAGERS.
VI. THE FARMER'S ADVICE TO THE VILLAGERS.
VII. THE VISION, OR PROSPECT OF THE FUTURE HAPPINESS OF AMERICA.

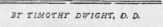

BY TIMOTHY DWIGHT, D. D.

NEW-YORK :—PRINTED BY CHILDS AND SWAINE.
1794

Title page for Dwight's seven-part pastoral poem, the first American poem to depict a specific village

pulpit oratory. Whether preaching to soldiers in the field or to students in the college chapel, delivering an ordination sermon, or addressing notables on a ceremonial occasion, he had about him the ministerial mantle, an outward sign of his inward condition as the *vir bonus* of rhetorical theory from Aristotle and Quintilian on down. He believed that the audience must perceive the orator as a good man, which the orator cannot appear to be unless he really is. (Dwight never at any time doubted that he himself was a good man in fact as well as in theory.) Superficially contrived effects were to be avoided. The pulpit is "no place for wit," a student notebook records Dwight as saying in his rhetoric course; "The language of animated feeling is the best in the world." And animated feeling depends upon personal conviction: "A preacher should in the first place—understand the gospel thoroughly, thus feel it thoroughly—& then study to pour out his knowledge—and form a good delivery. He then will be a good preacher." Forming a good delivery requires practice and self-criticism so that eloquence may achieve its ends. "The great requisites for Eloquence," the notebook reads, "are that what is said should be understood and felt. Instruction and Impression constitute the whole business of Eloquence."

From the close of the Revolution on, Dwight exercised his eloquence in expressions of alarm at the emerging challenges to privilege and power, with the concomitant erosion of respect for social and political authority. He hoped fervently for true leaders in the image of the Trumbull he commemorated, men who in embodying all the virtues might transcend their specified roles, winning public confidence in their effective measures to strengthen religion and curb democracy. In sermons and addresses of the 1790s and the opening years of the new century, Dwight stands as an early complete example of a perennial American type: the political activist who is on the right and knows he is in the right, never doubting the truth of his convictions nor the danger represented by an opposition to be credited with neither purity of motive nor honesty of argument, and identifying his own purposes with those of God, the ultimate source of authority and guarantor of order. Always ready to act on the social implications of his religious beliefs, Dwight did not confine himself to the pulpit but used whatever medium offered and modulated his voice to suit it, thundering from the platform about moral decline, explaining in newspaper articles addressed to farmers and mechanics the reasonableness of clerical leadership in politics, snickering in satirical

essays on Godwinian ideas of perfectibility, even at times stooping as anonymous journalist to sentiments that would be unseemly in the mouth of the candid orator.

Such sustained activity was, in Dwight's view, what the times demanded. A note struck in *A Sermon, Preached at Northampton, on the twenty-eighth of November, 1781: Occasioned by the Capture of the British Army* (1781) was to sound in his works for years: at the flood tide of the Enlightenment, the successful completion of the Revolution had brought America to the threshold of full participation in every advance of human knowledge, but at the same time America was rotting from within. The war had produced "a dissipation of thought, a prostitution of reason, a contempt of religion, a disdain of virtue, a deliberation in vice," all occasioned by the spread of a skepticism that questioned all institutions, its aim being nothing less than the destruction of the kingdom of God. This skepticism had to be confronted and defeated by men newly conscious of their dependence on God and the need for religion. To a certain extent, of course, all of this is what can be expected from any orthodox Christian minister in flush times, warning the proud not to be at ease in Zion. But the spread of skepticism that Dwight and other clergymen of the time spoke of was real, and in a few years their worst fears appeared to be resoundingly confirmed by the French Revolution and its aftermath.

The nature of Dwight's concerns can be gathered from the titles of his sermons, among them *Virtuous Rulers a National Blessing,* a lengthy election sermon delivered before the state legislature in Hartford in 1791, and three New Haven sermons, *The True Means of Establishing Public Happiness* (1795), *The Nature, and Danger, of Infidel Philosophy* (1798), and *The Duty of Americans, at the Present Crisis* (1798). Virtuous rulers, presumably a blessing at any time, were particularly important to Dwight in 1791, the year of the passage of a state law exempting non-Congregationalists from paying dues to the Congregational church (provided that they could certify their regular attendance at other churches). For a century and a half in New England, outstanding clergymen had delivered election sermons to legislative bodies, always paying tribute to the long line of predecessors and dwelling on the awesome responsibilities of those who govern in the sight of God and man. Deploring excessive dependence upon law alone, Dwight now called for a strong national executive who would see as his first duty the support of religion. In *The True Means of Establishing Public Happiness* he turned to the need for institutions which provide for the good society the means to achieve happiness, namely, religious education and public worship. With these properly instituted and supported, Dwight saw hope for an America viewed as Connecticut writ large. This hope gave way in 1797 to the intemperance of an address to the graduating class at Yale, published the following year in expanded form as *The Nature, and Danger, of Infidel Philosophy,* depicting the Reign of Terror as the end result of the wholly secular pursuit of liberty, and to Dwight's gloomy view of what the present crisis required of Americans.

In discussing "infidel philosophy," Dwight descends quickly from moderate reasoning to ad hominem argument, charging thinkers from Aristotle to Thomas Paine with a catalogue of sins ranging from adultery to robbery. The sermon reveals his excited discovery of, and total belief in, the disclosures of Professor John Robison in *Proofs of a Conspiracy against All the Religions and Governments of Europe, Carried on in Secret Meetings of Free Masons, Illuminati, and Reading Societies,* published in London in 1797 and reprinted in Philadelphia the next year. Dwight was sure that the Bavarian Illuminati, or Illuminists, a rationalist sect, had established branches in the United States to carry on their campaign to destroy all civil, familial, and religious institutions "under the pretence of enlarged Philanthropy and of giving mankind liberty and equality." The doctrines of this conspiracy proceed, of course, from the French skeptics, whom Yale students read at their peril. The duty of Americans in the present crisis is to effect a total separation from France (in everything but necessary commerce) and to trust in a God who, now preparing for the millennium, would return the Connecticut clergy to power to do battle with evil.

Convinced that outside agitators (assorted European atheists, deists, communists, and advocates of free love) and inside dupes (the self-made Ethan Allen, the sophisticate Thomas Jefferson, and their ilk) were determined to subvert Christian institutions and so promote anarchy, Dwight was not particularly discriminating in his counterattack. His knee-jerk reactionary response to anything he regarded as emanating from deists or democrats may seem at first blush strange in a man who glorified the American Revolution— something perhaps to be understood in the way of passage from liberal youth to conservative middle age. But then that Revolution was no ordinary revolution, one of the enraged masses rising against their masters, and Dwight had not changed. In his view, shared by many other men in the Puritan tradition,

the American Revolution was a justified defense of liberty—not in the sense of social or egalitarian liberty, but liberty to follow the divine commandments within the framework of New England institutions. In interfering with those institutions the Crown had exceeded the legitimate authority of its stewardship under God; the appeal to arms was a protest against what was essentially a violation of a covenant. Dwight knew what he meant and meant what he said in *The Conquest of Canäan* about the hoped for convergence of God's will and man's act in "union'd choice divine" in America's redemptive mission. Now the task was to prevent Americans from straying from the true path into the dark wood of error.

How to do this was the problem. Dwight could go on reading rationalists (or summaries of their arguments) in order to refute them, or he could proceed by the strategy of encouraging religious revivals, or both. Being Timothy Dwight he did both, but the second was the more effective as it ushered in what has come to be known as the Second Great Awakening. The very term recalls the first, simply known as the Great Awakening, the period of emotional religious revivals of the 1740s that occurred in the Connecticut Valley, initially to the surprise of Jonathan Edwards, who stood in awe of what was happening, and then with his careful encouragement and interpretation. Edwards was a deeply spiritual man whose personal conversion experience and integrity in following out the compelling logic of his convictions shine clear in the chaste and disciplined prose that still moves readers to admiration. Dwight, in marked contrast to his grandfather, left no record of his private religious experience (and among those who had known him no memory of his mentioning one) and was not surprised by a religious phenomenon which was partly of his making. Edwards by his conviction rose above the community that dismissed him; Dwight could not contemplate a life apart from the community in all its aspects. Far from painting himself into a scholarly corner, Dwight constantly thought of religion in relation to social ends and was very busy in what might be termed the engineering of consent. For Edwards, as Kenneth Silverman observes, the key issue had been personal piety; for Dwight "it was becoming *pietas,* social consciousness."

The full and complex story of Dwight's skillful orchestration of the beginnings of a revival movement that was to gather force rapidly and to continue for decades is carefully told by Stephen E. Berk in *Calvinism versus Democracy: Timothy Dwight and the Origins of American Evangelical Orthodoxy,* especially chapter eight, "The Politics of Religion," and chapter nine, "The Contrived Awakening" ("Contrived" is here descriptive, not derogatory). The story is one of the road traveled by Calvinist leaders as they tempered the winds of severe doctrine to flocks increasingly shorn of strictly orthodox belief. It was Dwight's accomplishment that he could continue honestly to believe in and preach the total depravity of man—which satisfied the strictest Calvinist—and yet emphasize the efficacy of religious nurture in preparation for the unmerited grace that God might extend—which relieved the believer to some extent, at least, from the terrifying insecurity to which the unrelenting pursuit of Edwardsean logic had led. If individual repentance and religious nurture were regarded as indeed effectual, the less need then to be concerned with what faction in the power struggles within the established Congregational church of Connecticut was to be considered the true bearer of the ark. And clearly the stress on repentance and nurture made possible ready cooperation among Christian denominations, including Separatists and Episcopalians. (The "Romish" church, though Trinitarian, was generally thought to be a tool of Anti-Christ, though some individual deluded priests might be sincere Christians, and the newly stirring Unitarians were, though in the Christian tradition, not Trinitarian.)

The Congregational churches in Connecticut, though in theory independent, had operated since 1708 under the agreements of the Saybrook Platform, with "consociations" of ministers of churches according to county consulting in the interest of the general good—in effect something like a form of Presbyterial control. During the Great Awakening of the 1740s and its aftermath, factions fought for power in the consociations. Those in control before the Great Awakening, termed later the Old Calvinists, believed in the total depravity of man but also believed that he could do much to prepare for the experience of grace, and they distrusted the emotional subjectivity of the conversion experiences that marked the Great Awakening. The New Divinity men challenged the Old Calvinist position as being hardly distinguishable from justification by works rather than by faith, and they accordingly valued the emotional experience of the convert touched by God's irresistible grace. Eventually the New Divinity men prevailed, and once in power they had to consider means of holding on to it as with noticeable diminution in fervor they learned to operate the stops and levers of the junction of church and state. When Timothy Dwight assumed

his pastorate in Greenfield Hill in 1783 and during the twelve years he spent there, the New Divinity had virtually become an old orthodoxy.

Much as the leaders of the Congregational church (Dwight included) may have wished to look upon Connecticut as their own fiefdom, they were nevertheless aware of frustrations within their church and dangers without. Years of constant preaching of hard-line doctrine had emptied many a church of worshipers who despaired of ever experiencing true conversion, and numbers of those who resented what they perceived as prescriptive consociational control transferred their allegiance to the truly autonomous congregations of the Baptists and Separatists; increasingly, the Episcopal church, with its comparatively humane doctrines, was proving attractive to those tired of ministers more interested in polemical controversy than devoted to pastoral care. And of course there were also those who were unaffiliated with any church, as well as those who did not attend at all, among them the doubters and the indifferent, apparently content to take one world at a time.

Briefly, what Dwight did (in a way entirely characteristic of him in his distrust of abstract thinking and his admiration of practical accomplishment) was to de-emphasize metaphysics in preaching and enlarge the possibilities for cooperative evangelical activity. Man was depraved, but God though sovereign was not totally indifferent and could be the tender parent as well as the just judge. If state churches were going to be disestablished and independent churches deprived of state aid, strong voluntary associations must be in place to carry on the religious education necessary to insure public happiness, which is not to put the community before God but to recognize that without God the community cannot hope for happiness. Using his professorship at Yale to construct his theology and his presidency and personal connections to secure the interest of religious leaders, Dwight was instrumental in setting in motion a series of revivals in the college, in founding and assisting religious magazines and Sunday school societies, and encouraging missionary societies at home (the western frontier provided a field in need of tilling) and abroad, all with an emphasis on doctrinal agreement rather than differences.

New Divinity theology stressed the importance of the touched heart, but Dwight, both by temperament and by his position as virtually the head of an established church, had no desire to see Connecticut Congregationalists stampeded into enthusiasm by emotional exhorters. According to his

The house Dwight lived in while he was president of Yale University

plan, they would be awakened to an appreciation of the dignity and excellence of the gospel by sound leaders exercising the authority of the traditional "learned ministry" through their own evident dedication. His first responsibility was to Yale, that "fountain" from which, he wrote in *Travels in New-England and New-York,* flowed "circuitously indeed, but really and ultimately, the laws of the state and its whole jurisprudence; the rules which form its happy society, and the doctrine and precepts which are inculcated in its churches." He exercised this responsibility directly in his own classes and in his administrative decisions. From his earliest days as a tutor and on through the years of conducting his immensely successful coeducational academy at Greenfield Hill, he had enjoyed his gift for teaching. Tall and dignified, yet approachable, his voice deep and pleasant, Dwight knew how to engage and to dominate the very young men in his classes at Yale, who were already aware of his literary reputation and his prominence in the state, as well as of his brief military history. Warming to his fatherly but firm manner, they were awed by his readiness in refuting the arguments of skeptics and in rendering his "decisions" in their debates on ethical matters. To his artfully restrained appeals to conscience in a series of sermons in the college chapel, they responded with feelings of guilt and repentance, many among them to experience lasting conversions and enter the ministry.

Perhaps more important than enlisting the loyalty of the students was insuring the soundness of religious sentiment in the faculty, which required great caution in hiring. The kind of caution Dwight could exercise and the risks he was willing to take are illustrated in the case of his appointment of Benjamin Silliman as professor of chemistry and natural science. The best professors of science were to be found in Europe; but unlike Jefferson, who a few years later tried to recruit them for his new University of Virginia, Dwight refused to consider them, for as Europeans they might be skeptics, perhaps even infidels. Better to appoint instead a doctrinally sound American—a Yale alumnus—who was not even a scientist and give him the opportunity to become one. Silliman received the call and abandoned his nearly completed legal studies to prepare himself through study in private sessions with scientists in Philadelphia and Princeton and later in courses at the University of Edinburgh.

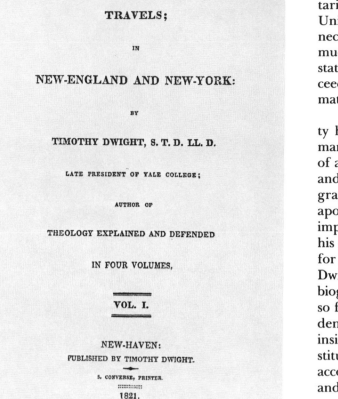

TRAVELS;

IN

NEW-ENGLAND AND NEW-YORK:

BY

TIMOTHY DWIGHT, S. T. D. LL. D.

LATE PRESIDENT OF YALE COLLEGE;

AUTHOR OF

THEOLOGY EXPLAINED AND DEFENDED

IN FOUR VOLUMES,

VOL. I.

NEW-HAVEN:
PUBLISHED BY TIMOTHY DWIGHT.

S. CONVERSE, PRINTER.

1821.

Title page for the first volume of Dwight's impressions of the places he visited between 1796 and 1815

He returned to Yale to begin an outstanding teaching career that was to last for fifty-one years and to establish his name as a geologist. In other less striking instances the same rule applied: doctrinal soundness, yes—but academic excellence, too; and under Dwight, all commentators agree, idolators and detractors alike, Yale was firmly on the path from provincial college to prominent university, with strong graduate departments and professional schools.

It is impossible to overestimate the importance of Yale to Dwight, for he identified with it completely. As a college, it was a true alma mater, guardian and teacher of all that mattered in the religious tradition of New England; as a university, it would work on the frontiers of knowledge in all fields, not least the natural sciences, leading students to an ever-greater understanding of the ways of God with his creation. Harvard might fall to Unitarianism and Andover Theological Seminary have to be founded to protect Massachusetts against

that heresy, but Yale would remain soundly Trinitarian without religious obscurantism: only one Unitarian congregation was to be organized in Connecticut in Dwight's lifetime, a fact which alone tells much about the intricate connection of church and state and his influence in both, an influence proceeding (circuitously indeed, but really and ultimately) from his power base in New Haven.

Dwight's close identification with his university has paradoxically obscured the picture of the man. Early memoirs and biographies, the testimony of actual or academic sons venerating their father and teacher, served as the foundation of a hagiographic tradition in which Dwight reached his apotheosis a century later, with Charles Cuningham implicitly sanctioning his subject's ways because of his good intentions and achievements. It remained for Edmund S. Morgan to notice in the 1960s that if Dwight was the prodigy of energy presented by his biographers, he was also a driven man, even going so far in his consuming ambition to become president of Yale as to disclose in anonymous articles inside information potentially damaging to the institution, an important corrective view taken into account by Kenneth Silverman in his biographical and critical study of Dwight.

Some representative selections excepted, Dwight's published writings are to be found only in their original editions or in facsimile reprints—evidence enough that they have not survived their occasions. "Columbia," the first popular song to make use of the ubiquitous literary name for the new nation, is probably now no better known than *The Conquest of Canäan*, the extreme opposite end of the poetic range. Only two scientific papers (one on language, the other on light) and some hymns were not somehow concerned with issues or personalities of the day. Those writings that were so concerned—poems, addresses, essays, sermons, journeyman pieces from the facile pen of a public man—served their purpose in their time. The grand exception to these observations is *Travels in New-England and New-York*, a four-volume work not published in Dwight's lifetime (it appeared after his death, printed in New Haven in 1821-1822) and recently republished not in facsimile but in Barbara Miller Solomon's excellent, thoroughly annotated edition in a new printing. In the long leading article of the *Quarterly Review* of October 1823, the British critic Robert Southey called it "the most important of Dwight's writings, a work which will derive additional value from time, whatever may become of his poetry and sermons." Here it is possible, one may feel, to encounter Dwight the man more or less directly. That is not to say that there are self-revelations here or any chummy expressions of relief at being able to leave one's public persona behind and take things as they come on the road; coming from Dwight, those would be signals of an experiment in fiction rather than of the record of facts and reflections he intended to set down. In *Travels in New-England and New-York* Dwight writes about what he sees and what he wishes to see in the light of his beliefs, for which he freely argues. The reader encounters abundant descriptive facts and statistics, which may be soon forgotten, and an ordering vision, which will be long remembered. The vision is a hierarchical one of a stable society, in which all recognize the authority of the able few who govern so that the many may enjoy the comfortable circumstances which Franklin called "benevolent mediocrity." Positions of leadership are open to talented men of character industrious enough to attain them, even without a college education. In the knowledge that the health of the society, which is always threatened, depends upon a continuing body of virtuous leaders, the able few are not self-seeking but regard their tasks as almost sacred duties.

The vision just sketched calls *Greenfield Hill* to mind, and of course there are many connections between that poem and *Travels in New-England and New-York*. Much of the interest of the latter work, however, derives from seeing Dwight confront the facts which he may too easily dispose of in the poem. The emigrants of *Greenfield Hill* are praised as the vanguard of waves of New Englanders to come, bringing their values and institutions to the frontier. In *Travels in New-England and New-York* the emigrants are viewed with some ambivalence: frontier opportunities challenge some of the most able and enterprising villagers, but they also attract some of the most shiftless, who are likely to sink into the semisavage state of the frontiersman—good riddance, these latter, for the sake of the village they leave, which will not have to be concerned with providing for an excess and perhaps unemployable population. There is another relation as well to *Greenfield Hill*. For all its pastoral quality, the poem is not one simply in praise of a static agricultural society such as Jefferson had in mind and Crèvecoeur depicted, for the village has a good school and a schoolmaster who tries to broaden the horizons of his charges, some of whom will go west, where eventually "Towns, cities, fanes, shall lift their towery pride," and "Where slept perennial night, shall science rise,/And new-born Oxfords cheer the evening skies." Dwight loved the sight of

an orderly New England village, but he also took pride in the growth of a rising industrial New England town; and often as not, to Dwight an unpeopled landscape was beautiful in a double sense—as the vista before his eyes and as the picture in his mind's eye of how it would appear years hence, neatly arranged in productive fields and dotted with homes and churches and perhaps with water-powered mills. On repeated trips over the same ground he took careful note of increases in population and of the prosperity of enterprises of all sorts, as well as of engineering feats in the way of bridges and canals.

The travels which Dwight records occurred between 1796 and 1815. Undertaken for healthful exercise during his academic vacations, they covered New England from Provincetown (where Dwight and his party were told they were the first people known to have visited the place out of curiosity only) and Boston to the frontiers of Maine and Vermont, and New York (including all of Long Island) from the metropolis to Niagara Falls. What began as a journal soon became a series of notebooks in preparation of a work eventually to be published. The sprawling four-volume work that finally reached readers in a New Haven edition of 1821-1822 and a London edition of 1823 has more of a controlling form than at first meets the eye. The numbered sections are titled not as chapters but as letters, ostensibly to an Englishman but actually, as Dwight says in the preface, to his "own countrymen" as more deserving of information about New England and New York than the uncaring British, who viewed the new country with condescension; as letters to an individual person rather than chapters addressed to the public at large, the sections can vary greatly in style and content, allowing maximum room for the play of Dwight's interests. Another device, or rather technique, is the merging of several journeys in one narrative account: like Thoreau presenting the experience of two years at Walden through the seasonal cycle of one, Dwight can inform the reader about both an original visit and a later one, conveying his sense of the rapidity of change and fascination with the way the scenes before him are becoming a part of history, a very special one at that. He observes in the preface: "The scene is a novelty in the history of man. The colonization of a wilderness by civilized men, where a regular government, mild manners, arts, learning, science, and Christianity have been interwoven in its progress from the beginning, is a state of things of which the eastern continent and the records of past ages furnish neither an example,

Letter to Rufus King in which Dwight asks advice about having Travels in New-England and New-York *published in Great Britain*
(New-York Historical Society)

nor a resemblance." There again is the note of the special nature of America; not now proclaiming its rising glory, Dwight is contented to observe and record the rising in process, still aware of the providential experience of New England and determined, like Cotton Mather a century before him, that it will live in his history.

Formal devices or techniques can unify only so far what Kenneth Silverman has with some justice called a two-thousand-page book imprisoning a good three-hundred-page one trying to get out. What really unifies the work is the vision that permeates the whole. If it is true that the seventeenth-century Puritan New England we think we know is really the New England that Hawthorne imagined in *The Scarlet Letter* (1850), it is also true that the New England village in which even non-Yankees feel at home in their minds—and sometimes confront in startling reality—is in large part the creation of Timothy Dwight, whose *Travels in New-England and New-York* became something of a handbook on the need to keep faith in its virtues. As

he discusses hundreds of communities in New England and in New York (so close in kind to New England that Dwight saw in their union a possible nation) and ponders their history and future prospects, he seems reassured and reassuring, with nothing of the anger or near hysteria of the doomsaying preacher telling the congregation before him that they had justly earned the retribution they were to experience before the millennium could begin. Intent on examining the minute details of forms of local government, church organization, and public education, he freely offers his critical opinions and advice and reports that in general the New England enterprise is going well.

Dwight the celebrant is not the only Dwight one meets in *Travels in New-England and New-York*. There is also the biographer, looking for the connection between life and culture; the student of names on the land, pondering the meaning of the change from Indian to English (and sometimes to another English name in turn), or the coexistence of both Indian and English names; the aesthete, seeking the right terms to describe a landscape and to convey his response to it; the sociologist, interested in the dynamics of social change; the anthropologist, gathering knowledge of the Indians at firsthand and through correspondents as well; the serious amateur scientist who on the basis of his own close observation could draw conclusions that stand up under professional scrutiny (his firsthand observations and hypotheses recorded in *Travels in New-England and New-York* inspired Thoreau's most successful scientific paper, "The Succession of Forest Trees"); the topographer, studying the land and trying to provide it with a geological and a human history.

We can only imagine what might have been Dwight's reaction to the suggestion of recent scholars that the man he most nearly resembles in the range and quality of his interests is Thomas Jefferson, who also produced a classic study of his own region in *Notes on the State of Virginia* (1785). Two of the scholars, Kathryn Whitford, a humanist, and Philip Whitford, a scientist, come to the surprising but well supported conclusion that Dwight was the better scientist of the two, relying on his own careful observations as much as possible rather than on the reports of others, and open-minded enough to modify his conclusions when new evidence seemed to warrant it. It was the believer in revelation who was the more willing to allow for flexibility in the processes of creation, not the deist. (It was Jefferson, not Dwight, who refused to believe in the scientific report of a meteor shower, since stones do not rain from heaven, and who wondered where the mastodon had gone to live, since God would not permit a species to disappear.)

The several Dwights discernible in the *Travels in New-England and New-York* turn out to be the one Dwight after all, more readily understandable through this one most comprehensive and yet most modest of his works than in any of those printed in his lifetime, with the exception perhaps of some passages in *Greenfield Hill*. The protean man that his contemporaries admired for his unlimited curiosity and his energy in doing everything from writing an epic to founding a state academy of arts and sciences moves through New England and New York as inquirer, reporter, moralist, and friend. If in his earlier and other works (as indeed in his profession as clergyman in the years of the journeys themselves) his evangelical vision encompasses ultimately the whole world, here he is most intimately concerned with the part he loved best. Charles Cuningham could not resist closing his biography of Dwight with the sentence "To the end he did his part—for God, for country, and for Yale." But Cuningham might have added that the country was New England.

Biographies:

Benjamin Silliman, *A Sketch of the Life and Character of President Dwight, Delivered as an Eulogium, in New-Haven, February 12, 1817* (New-Haven: Printed by T. G. Woodward & published by Maltby, Goldsmith & Co., 1817);

Sereno E. Dwight, "A Memoir of the Life of the Author," in *Theology Explained and Defended, in a Series of Sermons, by Timothy Dwight . . .* (Middletown, Conn.: Printed by Clark & Lyman, 1818), I: v-lxxi;

William B. Sprague, "Life of Timothy Dwight, President of Yale College," in *The Library of American Biography*, edited by Jared Sparks (Boston: Charles C. Little & James Brown, 1847), Second Series, VI: 225-363;

Charles E. Cuningham, *Timothy Dwight 1752-1817: A Biography* (New York: Macmillan, 1942).

References:

Robert D. Arner, "The Connecticut Wits," in *American Literature 1764-1789: The Revolutionary Years*, edited by Everett Emerson (Madison: University of Wisconsin Press, 1977), pp. 240-245;

Sacvan Bercovitch, *The American Jeremiad* (Madison: University of Wisconsin Press, 1978), pp. 39, 42, 100n, 129, 130;

Stephen E. Berk, *Calvinism versus Democracy: Timothy Dwight and the Origins of American Evangelical Orthodoxy* (Hamden, Conn.: Archon Books, 1974);

Lewis E. Buchanan, "The Ethical Ideas of Timothy Dwight," *Research Studies of the State College of Washington*, 13 (September 1945): 185-189;

John West Davidson, *The Logic of Millennial Thought in Eighteenth-Century New England* (New Haven: Yale University Press, 1977), pp. 19-22, 228-237, 275-293;

Emory Elliott, *Revolutionary Writers: Literature and Authority in the New Republic* (New York: Oxford University Press, 1982), pp. 55-91;

Vincent Freimarck, "Rhetoric at Yale in 1807," *Proceedings of the American Philosophical Society*, 110 (August 1966): 235-255;

Freimarck, "Timothy Dwight's Brief Lives in *Travels in New England and New York*," *Early American Literature*, 8 (Spring 1973): 45-88;

Ralph Henry Gabriel, "Timothy Dwight," in his *Religion and Learning at Yale* (New Haven: Yale

University Press, 1958), pp. 63-82;

Bruce Granger, *American Essay Serials from Franklin to Irving* (Knoxville: University of Tennessee Press, 1978), pp. 102, 163, 235, 236, 249, 250;

John Griffith, "*The Columbiad* and *Greenfield Hill*: History, Poetry, and Ideology in the Late Eighteenth Century," *Early American Literature,* 10 (Winter 1975/6): 235-250;

Nathan O. Hatch, *The Sacred Cause of Liberty: Republican Thought and the Millennium in Revolutionary New England* (New Haven: Yale University Press, 1977), pp. 102-117, 131, 169;

William O. Hedges, "The Old World Yet: Writers and Writing in Post-Revolutionary America," *Early American Literature,* 16 (Spring 1981): 3-18;

Robert David Hoffelt, "Pragmatics of Persuasion and Disciplines of Duty: The Influence of Timothy Dwight in American Preaching," Th.D. dissertation, Princeton Theological Seminary, 1983;

Leon Howard, *The Connecticut Wits* (Chicago: University of Chicago Press, 1943), pp. 81-111, 206-238, 342-401, 416-418;

Charles Roy Keller, *The Second Great Awakening in Connecticut* (New Haven: Yale University Press, 1942), pp. 13-35;

Brooks Mather Kelley, *Yale: A History* (New Haven: Yale University Press, 1974), pp. 116-139;

Lewis Leary, "The Author of *The Triumph of Infidelity,*" *New England Quarterly,* 20 (September 1947): 377-385;

Mason I. Lowance, Jr., *The Language of Canäan: Metaphor and Symbol in New England from the Puritans to the Transcendentalists* (Cambridge: Harvard University Press, 1980), pp. 182, 183, 203-206;

Henry F. May, *The Enlightenment in America* (New York: Oxford University Press, 1976), pp. 260-277;

Edmund S. Morgan, "Ezra Stiles and Timothy Dwight," *Proceedings of the Massachusetts Historical Society,* 72 (1963): 101-117;

Morgan, *The Gentle Puritan: A Life of Ezra Stiles 1727-1795* (New Haven: Yale University Press, 1962), pp. 345-359;

W. F. H. Nicolaisen, " 'A Colony from New England': New York Places and their Names in

Timothy Dwight's *Travels in New England and New York,"* *Names Northeast,* 2 (1980): 100-111;

Vernon Louis Parrington, *Main Currents in American Thought: Volume One, 1620-1820, The Colonial Mind* (New York: Harcourt, Brace, 1927), pp. 358-369;

Abe C. Ravitz, "Timothy Dwight's *Decisions,"* *New England Quarterly,* 31 (December 1958): 514-519;

John F. Sears, "Timothy Dwight and the American Landscape: the Composing Eye in *Travels in New England and New York,"* *Early American Literature,* 11 (Winter 1976-1977): 311-321;

Kenneth Silverman, *A Cultural History of the American Revolution* (New York: Crowell, 1976), pp. 221-235, 483-494, 500-504;

Silverman, Review of *Travels in New England and New York,* edited by Barbara Miller Solomon, *Early American Literature,* 5 (Fall 1970): 73-75;

Silverman, *Timothy Dwight* (New York: Twayne, 1969);

Jack Stillinger, "Dwight's *Triumph of Infidelity*: Text and Interpretation," *Studies in Bibliography,* 15 (1962): 259-266;

Cecelia Tichi, "The American Revolution and the New Earth," *Early American Literature,* 11 (Fall 1976): 202-210;

Ernest Lee Tuveson, *Redeemer Nation: The Idea of America's Millennial Role* (Chicago: University of Chicago Press, 1968), pp. 103-112;

Moses Coit Tyler, *Three Men of Letters* (New York: Putnam's, 1895), pp. 71-127;

Wayne Conrad Tyner, "The Theology of Timothy Dwight in Historical Perspective" (unpublished doctoral dissertation, University of North Carolina at Chapel Hill, 1971);

Kathryn Whitford, "Excursions into Romanticism: Dwight's *Travels,"* *Papers in Language and Literature,* 2 (1966): 225-233;

Kathryn Whitford and Philip Whitford, "Timothy Dwight's Place in Eighteenth-Century American Science," *Proceedings of the American Philosophical Society,* 114 (1970): 60-71.

Papers:

The Dwight family papers are at the Yale University Library.

Jonathan Edwards, Jr.
(26 May 1745-1 August 1801)

Donald Weber
Mount Holyoke College

BOOKS: *The Faithful Manifestation of the Truth, the Proper and Immediate End of Preaching the Gospel. A Sermon Delivered November 5, 1783. At the Ordination of the Reverend Mr. Timothy Dwight, to the Pastoral Office over the Church in Greenfield* (New Haven: Printed by Thomas & Samuel Green, 1783);

Brief Observations on the Doctrine of Universal Salvation, as Lately Promulgated at New-Haven (New Haven: Printed by Meigs, Bowen & Dana, 1784);

The Necessity of Atonement, and the Consistency between That and Free Grace, in Forgiveness. Illustrated in Three Sermons . . . (New Haven: Printed by Meigs, Bowen & Dana, 1785);

Observations on the Language of the Muhhekaneew Indians; In Which the Extent of That Language in North-America Is Shewn; Its Genius Is Grammatically Traced: Some of Its Peculiarities, and Some Instances of Analogy between That and the Hebrew Are Pointed Out . . . (New Haven: Printed by Josiah Meigs, 1788; London: Printed by W. Justins, 1788);

The Salvation of All Men Strictly Examined; and the Endless Punishment of Those Who Die Impenitent, Argued and Defended against the Objections and Reasonings of the Late Rev. Doctor Chauncy, of Boston, in His Book Entitled "The Salvation of All Men," &c. (New Haven: Printed by A. Morse, 1790; Glasgow: Young, 1802);

The Injustice and Impolicy of the Slave Trade, and of the Slavery of the Africans: Illustrated in a Sermon Preached Before the Connecticut Society for the Promotion of Freedom and for the Relief of Persons Unlawfully Holden in Bondage . . . (New Haven: Printed by T. & S. Green, 1791);

All Divine Truth Profitable: Illustrated in a Sermon Preached at Hamden, January 11th, 1792, at the Ordination of the Rev. Dan Bradley, to the Pastoral Charge of the First Church in Whites-Town, in the State of New-York (New Haven: Printed by A. Morse, 1792);

Faith and Good Conscience, Illustrated in a Sermon, Delivered at the Ordination of the Reverend William Brown to the Pastoral Office in the First

Jonathan Edwards, Jr. (Yale University Art Gallery. Bequest of Eugene Phelps Edwards to Jonathan Edwards College. 1938.76)

Church in Glastenbury, on the 27th of June, 1792 . . . (New Haven: Printed for A. Morse, 1792);

The Marriage of a Wife's Sister Considered in a Sermon Delivered in the Chapel of Yale-College, on the Evening After the Commencement. September 12, A.D. 1792; Being the Anniversary Concio ad Clerum (New Haven: Printed by T. & S. Green, 1792);

A Sermon Delivered at the Funeral of the Honorable Roger Shermon [sic] Esq., Senator of the United States of America, Who Deceased the 23 of July 1793 (New Haven: Morse, 1793);

The Necessity of the Belief of Christianity by the Citizens of the State, in Order to Our Political Prosperity; Illustrated in a Sermon, Preached before His Excellency Samuel Huntington . . . (Hartford: Printed by Hudson & Goodwin, 1794);

The Duty of Ministers of the Gospel to Preach the Truth; Illustrated in a Sermon: Delivered at the Ordination of the Rev. Edward Dorr Griffin, A. M., to the Pastoral Charge of the Church in New-Hartford. June 4th, A.D. 1795 (Hartford: Printed by Hudson & Goodwin, 1795);

A Dissertation Concerning Liberty and Necessity; Containing Remarks on the Essays of Dr. Samuel West, and on the Writings of Several Other Authors, on These Subjects (Worcester: Printed by L. Worcester, 1797);

A Farewell Sermon, To the People of Colebrook, Delivered July 14th, 1799 (Suffield, Conn.: Printed by Edward Gray, 1799).

Collection: *The Works of Jonathan Edwards. With a Memoir of His Life and Character, by T. Edwards,* 2 volumes (Andover: Allen, Morrill & Wardwell, 1842).

Jonathan Edwards, Jr., an important figure in the New Divinity movement of American theology in the late eighteenth century, was born in Northampton, Massachusetts, the second son of the Reverend Jonathan and Sarah Pierpont Edwards, but he spent his childhood in Stockbridge, where his father preached to the Indians and wrote his major treatises. In Stockbridge the younger Edwards became fluent in Indian languages: "all my thought ran in Indian," he later recalled. (Edwards eventually published *Observations on the Language of the Muhhekaneew Indians,* 1788.) At the age of ten he was accompanied by the Indian missionary Gideon Hawley to the deeper wilderness of Western New York but returned to Stockbridge soon after the French and Indian War commenced.

In January 1758 the family moved to Princeton, New Jersey, where Jonathan Edwards, Sr., assumed the presidency of the College of New Jersey (later Princeton University). His tenure was brief, however, for he died in March of the same year. Sarah Edwards died the following October. Jonathan Edwards, Jr., entered the College of New Jersey, graduating in 1765, and then studied theology and prepared for the ministry under the care of his father's friend, Joseph Bellamy, at the Bethlehem, Connecticut, "school of the prophets." Edwards returned to Princeton as a tutor in 1767 but left in the wake of John Witherspoon's arrival as president. (Witherspoons's presidency signaled, for those guardians of the Edwardsean tradition, Princeton's "dangerous" embrace of Scottish common-sense principles.) In January 1769, Edwards accepted a call from the White Haven church in New Haven, Connecticut, only after the congrega-

THE

INJUSTICE and IMPOLICY

OF THE

SLAVE TRADE,

AND OF THE

Slavery of the Africans:

ILLUSTRATED IN

A SERMON

PREACHED BEFORE THE CONNECTICUT SOCIETY
FOR THE PROMOTION OF FREEDOM, AND FOR
THE RELIEF OF PERSONS UNLAWFULLY HOL-
DEN IN BONDAGE,

AT THEIR ANNUAL MEETING IN NEW-HAVEN,
SEPTEMBER 15, 1791.

BY JONATHAN EDWARDS, D. D.
PASTOR OF A CHURCH IN NEW-HAVEN.

Printed by THOMAS and SAMUEL GREEN,
M,DCC,XCI.

Title page for a sermon in which Edwards expressed his sympathies with early abolitionists such as Samuel Hopkins and Ezra Stiles (courtesy of the John Carter Brown Library at Brown University)

tion revoked its earlier advocacy of the half-way covenant. In 1770 he married Mary Porter (with whom he had four children). After her death in 1782 he married Mercy Salain in December 1783.

Edwards was dismissed in 1795 over a doctrinal dispute: the church felt that Edwards was too strict in enforcing a demand for public profession of conversion, which had resulted in a dwindling membership. The next year Edwards left for a wilderness pulpit in Colebrook, Connecticut, and, some three years later, at the end of his career, he assumed the presidency of the newly founded evangelical Union College in Schenectady, New York.

Most accounts of the younger Edwards describe him as a stern theologian. "In the pulpit," a nineteenth-century memoirist Calvin Chapin remarked, "he was too profound to be interesting or always intelligible to ordinary minds." In short,

Edwards's career reinforced the stereotype of the aloof, abstract New Divinity ministers who "preached away" their congregations. Edwards the younger is perhaps best remembered as the editor of his father's writings and, with Samuel Hopkins and Ezra Stiles, as an early abolitionist.

But what is most striking in his biography are the similarities in the lives of father and son: both served in prestigious pulpits only to be dismissed for maintaining unpopular doctrines; both did battle with Charles Chauncy over the major religious issues of their time (*The Salvation of All Men Strictly Examined*, 1802, was Edwards's answer to Chauncy's *Divine Glory Brought to View in the Final Salvation of All Men*, 1783); both were exiled to wilderness outposts; and both served in their last days as presidents of evangelical institutions. For most of his life, Edwards the younger labored to defend the legacy of his father.

Biographies:

Tryon Edwards, Memoir of Edwards, in *The Works of Jonathan Edwards* (Andover: Allen, Morrill & Wardwell, 1842), I: ix-xl;

William B. Sprague, *Annals of the American Pulpit* (New York: R. Carter & Brothers, 1857), I-II: 653-660;

Wesley C. Ewert, "Jonathan Edwards The Younger: A Biographical Essay," Th.D. dissertation, Hartford Seminary, 1953;

Robert L. Ferm, *Jonathan Edwards the Younger: A Colonial Pastor, 1745-1801* (Grand Rapids, Mich.: Eerdmans, 1976).

Papers:

The Andover Theological School, Hartford Seminary, and the Sterling Library at Yale University have collections of Edwards's papers.

William Emerson
(6 May 1769-12 May 1811)

Wesley T. Mott
University of Wisconsin

BOOKS: *A Discourse, Delivered in Harvard, July 4, 1794, at the Request of the Military Officers in that Place, Who, With the Militia under Their Command, Were Then Assembled to Commemorate the Anniversary of the American Independence* (Boston: Printed at the Apollo Press by Joseph Belknap, 1794);

Piety and Arms. A Sermon, Preached at the Request of the Ancient and Honourable Artillery Company, in Boston, June 3, 1799; the Anniversary of Their Election of Officers (Boston: Printed by Manning & Loring, 1799);

A Discourse, Delivered Before the Roxbury Charitable Society, at Their Annual Meeting, September 15, 1800 (Boston: Printed by Samuel Hall, 1800);

A Sermon, Preached at the Ordination of the Rev. Robinson Smiley, to the Pastoral Care of the Christian Church and Society in Springfield State of Vermont. September 23, 1801 (Windsor, Vt.: Printed by Nahum Mower, 1801);

An Oration Pronounced July 5, 1802, at the Request of the Inhabitants of the Town of Boston, in Commemoration of the Anniversary of American Independence (Boston: Printed by Manning & Loring, 1802);

A Sermon, on the Decease of The Rev. Peter Thacher, D.D., Pronounced Dec. 31, 1802, in Brattle-Street Church, Boston (Boston: Printed by Young & Minns, 1803);

A Sermon, Delivered March 2, 1803, at the Ordination of the Rev. Thomas Beede, To the Care of the Church of Christ in Wilton (Amherst, N.H.: Printed by Joseph Cushing, 1803);

A Sermon, Delivered in Brattlestreet Church, Boston, on the Sunday after the Interment of Madam Elizabeth Bowdoin, Relict of the late Honourable James Bowdoin, Esq., Who Departed Life May 5, 1803, in the Seventy Second Year of Her Age (Boston: Printed by David Carlisle, 1803);

A Discourse, Delivered Before the Members, of the Boston Female Asylum, September 20, 1805. Being Their Fifth Anniversary (Boston: Printed by Russell & Cutler, 1805);

A Sermon, Delivered to the First Church in Boston, on the Lord's Day after the Calamitous Death of Mr. Charles Austin, Member of the Senior Class in the

University of Cambridge, which Happened Aug. 4, 1806, in the Nineteenth Year of His Age (Boston: Printed at the Emerald Press by Belcher & Armstrong, 1806);

A Discourse, Delivered in the First Church, Boston, on the Anniversary of the Massachusetts Humane Society, June 9, 1807 (Boston: Munroe & Francis, 1807);

A Sermon, Preached at the Ordination of Rev. Samuel Clark, To the Pastoral Care of the First Congregational Society of Christians in Burlington, April 19, 1810 (Burlington, Vt.: Printed by Samuel Mills, 1810);

An Historical Sketch of the First Church in Boston, from Its Formation to the Present Period. To Which Are Added Two Sermons, One on Leaving the Old, and the Other on Entering the New House of Worship (Boston: Munroe & Francis, 1812).

OTHER: *A Selection of Psalms and Hymns, Embracing All the Varieties of Subject and Metre, suitable for Private Devotion, and the Worship of Churches,*

edited by Emerson (Boston: Munroe, Francis, & Parker, 1808).

William Emerson, best known as the father of Ralph Waldo Emerson, was a prominent minister, philanthropist, and man of letters in the burgeoning Boston culture of the young republic.

Born in Concord, Massachusetts, son of the Reverend William Emerson, a Revolutionary chaplain who died of fever returning from Ticonderoga, Emerson was raised by his stepfather, the Reverend Ezra Ripley, whom his mother, Phebe Bliss Emerson, married in 1780. Upon graduating from Harvard College in 1789, he taught grammar school for two years in Roxbury, Massachusetts, before returning briefly to Harvard to study divinity. In 1792 he was ordained minister of the town of Harvard, Massachusetts, where, besides supplementing his pastoral salary by teaching and farming, he delivered a popular July Fourth oration *A Discourse, Delivered in Harvard* (1794; frequently titled "On the American Independence, and the Means of Preserving It") and established the town's first social

Ruth Haskins Emerson

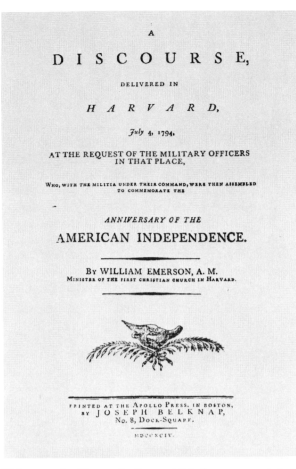

*Title page for Emerson's first published sermon, a popular
Fourth of July discourse (courtesy of the John Carter
Brown Library at Brown University)*

library, a book club whose 100-odd volumes were kept in the minister's house. On 25 October 1796 he married Ruth Haskins of Boston. But he chafed under the constraints of meager income and remoteness from cultured society.

The crucial turning point in Emerson's career was *Piety and Arms* (1799), his sermon preached in Boston before the Ancient and Honourable Artillery Company on 3 June 1799. Expressing the popular fear of the corrupting influence of deism and the excesses of the French Revolution, he declared that Christianity and "liberty" are alike anathema to despotism, that a universal tendency to misuse power requires a strong militia. This performance brought Emerson to the attention of leaders of the First Church in Boston, whose minister had just died, and Emerson was quick to accept their call.

As befitted the minister of one of Boston's

most prestigious churches, Emerson immersed himself in the city's intellectual and social life. Founder of the Christian Monitor Society and cofounder of the Physiological Society, he served as overseer of Harvard College, chaplain of the state senate, member of the school committee, and trustee of the Boston Library Society. He was also an active member of the Massachusetts Historical Society, the Singing, Agricultural, Humane, and Charitable Fire societies, the Boston Philosophical Society, the Wednesday Evening Club, and the American Academy of Arts and Sciences. Though Emerson occasionally berated himself for letting his love of music and society scatter his talents, he relished his busy life.

His most enduring contribution to literary history came when in May 1804 he became editor of the six-month-old *Monthly Anthology*, forerunner of the *North American Review*. To develop material for the journal, Emerson helped establish the Anthology Club, whose book collection became the Boston Athenaeum.

Tall, handsome, refined, Emerson cut a distinguished figure in the pulpit. No religious enthusiast, he took pride in his "melodious voice" and "distinct" delivery, and his dozen published sermons and discourses reflect a similar attention to form and style. Above all, Emerson valued simplicity, whether in expression or doctrine. Though critical of the hairsplitting of contemporary Calvinists, he accepted the notion of universal depravity and regarded earthly existence as an arena of trial and testing.

Emerson is generally regarded as a transitional figure in New England theology, a Congregationalist sympathetic to the emerging Unitarian views, liberal and tolerant in religion but conservative in politics—in short, a scion of enlightened, cultured Boston. Yet this bland stereotype does little justice to the theological tensions Emerson had to reconcile, nor does it capture the intensity of his convictions. Acknowledging that the "age of miracles has passed away," Emerson believed that a minister must employ "Sound reasoning" and other means of moral cultivation to fulfill his office. Discipline was the basis of all worthwhile endeavors—education, letters, charity, and democratic freedom itself. In his universalized version of Christianity, the gospel remained "a rule of life." Human effort, Emerson asserted, would meliorate much of the world's suffering and evil; but the great and indispensable benefit of Christianity, he proclaimed over and over, was the promise of eternal life.

William Emerson's greatest legacy to American letters may well be his fourth child, Ralph Waldo Emerson, who was only eight years old when his father died

Always fond of music, Emerson compiled a carefully indexed *A Selection of Psalms and Hymns* (1808) with the aim of omitting "what savours of party spirit and sectarian notions" and choosing "what is pure, scriptural, and excellent." His most ambitious work, the posthumously published *An Historical Sketch of the First Church in Boston* (1812), shows great industry and familiarity with New England history despite its uneven quality. Emerson's implicit theme is the victory of order and moderation over fanaticism and faction. Though his modern sense of toleration made him decry the "unjus-

tifiable persecution" of Anne Hutchinson, he finally lacked sympathy with her obstinance and "extravagant fancies." Indeed, he perceived a new version of Antinomianism in the "loose, incoherent" sermons of Whitefield revivalism, which stood in contrast to "the cool and moderate strain of preaching" favored by Emerson.

Having survived a severe lung hemorrhage in 1808, William Emerson died of a stomach tumor in 1811. His greatest legacy to American letters may be said to have been the fourth of his eight children. For though Ralph Waldo Emerson, only eight years old when his father died, later recalled him as a stern, remote figure, he attributed to his father his own "formality of manner & speech" as well as "a passionate love for the strains of eloquence."

References:

Gay Wilson Allen, *Waldo Emerson: A Biography* (New York: Viking, 1981), pp. 3-16, 19-20, 23;

James Elliot Cabot, *A Memoir of Ralph Waldo Emerson* (Boston: Houghton, Mifflin, 1887), I: 12-29;

Henry S. Nourse, *History of the Town of Harvard, Massachusetts, 1732-1893* (Harvard, Mass.: Printed for Warren Hapgood, 1894);

Joel Porte, *Representative Man: Ralph Waldo Emerson in His Time* (New York: Oxford University Press, 1979), pp. 99-104, 155-156;

Ralph L. Rusk, *The Life of Ralph Waldo Emerson* (New York: Columbia University Press, 1949), pp. 1-31;

Lewis P. Simpson, ed., *The Federalist Literary Mind: Selections from the 'Monthly Anthology and Boston Review', 1803-1811* (Baton Rouge: Louisiana State University Press, 1962);

William B. Sprague, *Annals of the American Pulpit* (New York: Robert Carter & Brothers, 1865), VIII: 241-246.

Papers:

Emerson's journals, commonplace books, letters, and other materials are among the Emerson family papers at the Houghton Library, Harvard University.

Olaudah Equiano
(Gustavus Vassa)
(circa 1745-circa 1801)

Sondra O'Neale
Emory University

BOOK: *The Interesting Narrative of the Life of Olaudah Equiano, or Gustavus Vassa, the African, Written by Himself,* 2 volumes (London: Printed & sold by the Author, 1789; New York: Printed & sold by W. Durell, 1791).

Editions: *Equiano's Travels: The Interesting Narrative of the Life of Olaudah Equiano or Gustavus Vassa the African,* abridged and edited by Paul Edwards (New York: Praeger, 1967; London: Heinemann, 1967);

The Life of Olaudah Equiano or Gustavus Vassa, The African, 1789: In two volumes with a New Introduction, 2 volumes, edited by Paul Edwards (London: Dawsons of Pall Mall, 1969).

Before the Civil War era, the most influential African abolitionist writer in both America and Britain was Olaudah Equiano. Kidnapped from his native Africa as an adolescent, and pressed into various types of menial labor, Equiano eventually traveled through much of the known world, including the North American continent, the West Indies, and Britain. He triumphed over slavery's adversities and lived to write a brilliant and popularly enduring autobiography that chronicled slavery and race relations from the slave's point of view. Not only is his work a masterful representation of eighteenth-century prose, it is an indispensable contribution to studies of the colonial era, in both Western and African contexts.

According to his biographer Paul Edwards, Equiano—who was taken from his home with his sister in 1756, when he was about eleven years old—was from an Ibo tribe in the North Ika Ibo region of Essaka, Nigeria. He was forced into servitude by several owners as he was being routed toward the Atlantic coast. Separated from his sister for a final time about a year later, he was sold to British slavers who immediately set sail for the American continent.

In the ensuing years Equiano, mastering the craft of seaman, sailed around the world, to everywhere, that is, except the place he most longed to

be, his beloved Africa. His stops included all the slave-trading islands of the West Indies, especially Grenada and Jamaica; England, Ireland and Wales; France; Portugal; Italy and various other Mediterranean countries; most nations of Central America (where he bartered with the Miskito Indians); even the North Pole (where he went as a member of a scientific expedition); and the North American continent, especially Georgia, Virginia, Philadelphia, and New England. Almost as wide ranging as his around-the-world treks were the many jobs he performed: iron smith, ship steward, crewman, cook, clerk, navigator, hairdresser, even amateur scientist. His achievements were phenomenal considering his background as an indigent slave. Nevertheless, Equiano, scarred by his early abduction, expressed a deep sense of displacement and dissatisfaction throughout his autobiography.

Thus the themes in Equiano's narrative are collectively symbolic and interdependent. When, with superb anthropological detail, he faithfully recounts Ibo tribal life, he presents the most-widely disseminated account of eighteenth-century life and values in the African interior told from a nonimperialist viewpoint. When he relates his capture through the eyes of a child who becomes a slave and when he then takes the reader abroad to see exotic sights and strange people, Olaudah articulates the alienation of a people who were misfitted both racially and culturally for life in the Western world and who longed for their own homeland. Authenticating his historic travelogue with painstakingly presented details of slave practices in the Caribbean and American colonies, he speaks with the rare and knowledgeable voice of one who is not only a former slave but who has viewed the institution from various geographical and experiential perspectives firsthand—a qualified and reliable witness to speak for some fifty million Africans who were conscripted to build a world that was hostile to their own survival.

The autobiographical passages are similarly authentic. When he narrates his personal conversion to Christianity, he reveals the individual soul's longing for a God of refuge and comfort, who would save anyone regardless of the supplicant's race or color from storms of life's cruel despair—storms that were made particularly acrimonious by slavery.

One of the difficult tasks of autobiography is to shift the speaker's voice through the various stages of age and experience, but Equiano aptly manages to retain the awe of youthful amazement when he relates his first encounters with Westernization in the spring of 1757. Of first viewing a late sign of winter, he writes: "One morning, when I got upon deck, I saw it covered all over with the snow that fell over-night: as I had never seen any thing of the kind before, I thought it was salt; so I immediately ran down to the mate and desired him, as well as I could, to come and see how somebody in the night had thrown salt all over the deck. He, knowing what it was, desired me to bring some of it down to him: accordingly I took up a handful of it, which I found very cold indeed. . . . I then asked him the use of it, and who made it; he told me a great man in the heavens, called God: but here again I was to all intents and purposes at a loss to understand him. . . ."

Equiano's light, comic style, which still permits subtle political commentary, is an integral and effective part of his artistic narrative voice. For instance he often describes unscrupulous whites who, in a slave society, were able to take advantage of free blacks: "One day I went with a free negroe taylor, named Joe Diamond, to one Mr. Cochran, who was indebted to him some trifling sum; and the man, not being able to get his money, began to murmur. The other immediately took a horse-whip to pay him with it; but, by the help of a good pair of heels, the taylor got off." And in late 1786, when Olaudah wanted to go into the ministry so that he could return to Africa as an African who had accepted the Gospel, he garnered several letters of support from prominent Englishmen and approached the Bishop of London. In recounting the bishop's rebuff, the writer skillfully contrasted the churchman's Christianity with his own: "With these letters, I waited on the Bishop by the Governor's desire, and presented them to his Lordship. He received me with much condescension and politeness; but, from some certain scruples of delicacy, declined to ordain me. My sole motive for thus dwelling on this transaction, or inserting these papers, is the opinion which gentlemen of sense and education, who are acquainted with Africa, entertain of the probability of converting the inhabitants of it to the faith of Jesus Christ, if

the attempt were countenanced by the legislature."

Equiano's autobiography, *The Interesting Narrative of the Life of Olaudah Equiano, or Gustavus Vassa, the African,* was first published in London in 1789. The two-volume work went through eight editions in his lifetime and sixteen additional editions, abridgments, and translations were published before the end of the nineteenth century. Modern readers have been just as enthralled with Equiano's work. Portions are included in many anthologies of eighteenth-century British and American prose and in collections of American and African-American literature. Additionally, Paul Edwards has supervised two editions, one in 1967 and another in 1969; the narrative is also included in Arna Bontemp's 1969 collection of American slave narratives and excerpts from the work are a major strength of Adams and Sanders's *Three Black Writers in Eighteenth-Century England* (1971).

The narrative opens with Equiano's account of tribal culture and politics. With postured aesthetic distance, he details political and military exchanges between warring tribes, including the tradition of slavery for the vanquished. He also describes African communal life: childhood initiation, marriage, social customs, and religion. Like most eighteenth-century black writers, in order to show that Africans were not as far removed from Judeo-Christian foundations as European scions purported, he was particularly careful to correlate African religion to Judaic practice: "And here I cannot forbear suggesting . . . the strong analogy which even by this sketch, imperfect as it is, appears to prevail in the manners and customs of my countrymen and those of the Jews. . . . Indeed this is the opinion of Dr. Gill, who, in his commentary on Genesis, very ably deduces the pedigree of the Africans from Afer and Afra, the descendants of Abraham by Keturah his wife and concubine (for both these titles are applied to her). . . . Like the Israelites in their primitive state, our government was conducted by our chiefs or judges, our wise men and elders; and the head of a family with us enjoyed a similar authority over his household with that which is ascribed to Abraham and the other patriarchs. . . . their religion appeared to have shed upon us a ray of its glory. . . ."

Virginia was Equiano's first stop after he finally sailed from the African coast in 1757. He was sold to Michael Henry Pascal, a rather cruel and sly officer in the Royal Navy. Although the crewmen were at that time calling the young African variously by the names of Jacob or Michael, Pascal insisted on renaming him Gustavus Vassa, after a late Scan-

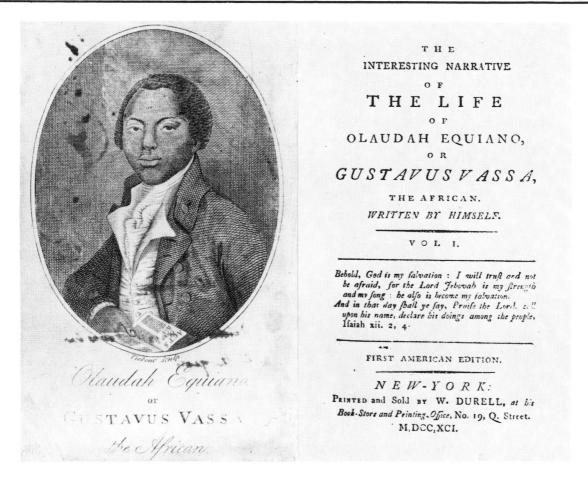

THE
INTERESTING NARRATIVE
OF
THE LIFE
OF
OLAUDAH EQUIANO,
OR
GUSTAVUS VASSA,
THE AFRICAN.
WRITTEN BY HIMSELF.

VOL I.

Behold, God is my falvation : I will truft and not
be afraid, for the Lord Jehovah is my ftrength
and my fong : he alfo is become my falvation.
And in that day fhall ye fay, Praife the Lord, call
upon his name, declare his doings among the people,
Ifaiah xii. 2, 4.

FIRST AMERICAN EDITION.

NEW-YORK:
Printed and Sold by W. DURELL, at his
Book-Store and Printing-Office, No. 19, Q. Street.
M,DCC,XCI.

Frontispiece and title page for the first volume of the American edition of Equiano's autobiography (courtesy of the John Carter Brown Library at Brown University)

dinavian king. Equiano loathed the name and had it changed to a more African nomenclature as soon as he bought his freedom in 1766. On his first voyage with Pascal, Olaudah met young Richard Baker, a scholarly seaman near his age, who not only befriended but tutored him in English language and values which, the narrative painstakingly shows, were startling to the naive youth.

By 1759 Equiano was fully articulate in the English language. He had purchased a Bible, joined a church, and received baptism. With faith in a false promise of freedom at the war's end, he had fought for the British in the Seven Years' War between England and France, and he had closely observed West Indian slave life, suffering cruel reminders that he himself was still a slave. Instead of granting the faithful servant his earned freedom, Pascal, confiscating Equiano's books and other belongings, sold him without notice to the captain of a slave ship that was headed for the West Indies. His eventual new owner, Quaker merchant Robert King, lent

Equiano to Thomas Farmer, a sea captain on his staff. Through Farmer, the precocious youth learned navigation and other supervisory shipboard skills, and, after several years, he had saved enough money to buy his freedom. King, who had acquired Equiano in 1763, for "forty pounds sterling," sold the author his freedom for £70 in 1766 and admitted that he had profited £300 from Equiano's labor during his three years of ownership. King implored Equiano to remain in his employ, so the now-former slave made his second trip to Georgia, where he was almost kidnapped and resold into slavery. In 1768 Equiano returned to England, began an apprenticeship to a hairdresser and also started part-time employment with Dr. Charles Irving, an amateur scientist whom he eventually accompanied on an expedition to the North Pole in 1773. Some of Equiano's most descriptive travel commentary is embedded in his vivid descriptions of the North Pole experience. The adventurers suffered killer whales spouting

Frontispiece for the second volume of the American edition of Equiano's autobiography (courtesy of the John Carter Brown Library at Brown University)

mountains of water upon the ship; the crewmen foolishly tried to attack "sea horses" (probably walruses), and they all barely escaped death from starvation and exposure when the boat struck an iceberg: "On the 28th of June, being in lat. 78, we made Greenland, where I was surprised to see the sun did not set. The weather now became extremely cold; and as we sailed between north and east, which was our course, we saw many very high and curious mountains of ice. . . . The 30th, the captain of a Greenland ship came on board, and told us of three ships that were lost in the ice; however we still held on our course till July the 11th, when we were stopt by one compact impenetrable body of ice. We ran along it from east to west about ten degrees; and on the 27th we got as far north as 80, 37; and in 19 or 20 degrees east longitude from London. On the 29th and 30th of July we saw one continued plain of smooth unbroken ice, bounded only by the horizon. . . ."

Until this point in Equiano's captivating narrative the reader is aware that Equiano had never found lasting comfort or enduring security. However, the harrowing dangers of the Arctic exploration brought Equiano closer to the reality of death than any of his experiences as a slave and seaman: "Our deplorable condition, which kept up the constant apprehension of our perishing in the ice, brought me gradually to think of eternity in such a manner as I never had done before. I had the fears of death hourly upon me, and shuddered at the thoughts of meeting the grim king of terrors in the *natural* state I then was in, and was exceedingly doubtful of a happy eternity if I should die in it."

In another moving section of a work that is filled with touching confessions, Equiano finally bares his loneliness and despair before God and accepts spiritual conversion as the only viable source of security for a displaced African whose race and color rendered him so alien among his peers. Of his conversion, he writes: "I wrestled hard with God in fervent prayer, who had declared in his word that he would hear the groanings and deep sighs of the poor in spirit. I found this verified to my utter astonishment and comfort. . . . It pleased God to enable me to wrestle with him, as Jacob did: I prayed that if sudden death were to happen, and I perished, it might be at Christ's feet." Further relating his conversion to the vicissitudes of race and slavery, he continued: "Now the Ethiopian was willing to be saved by Jesus Christ, the sinner's only surety, and also to rely on none other person or thing for salvation."

In late 1786 Equiano had the opportunity to realize his dream of returning to his beloved Africa. He was appointed commissary for Stores for the Black Poor, a social outreach group of the British antislavery movement that saw returning blacks to Africa as the best way to end the British slave trade. Equiano was to return to Sierra Leone with a group of relocatees, but he was fired within five months, after constant quarrels with the British leader of the expedition. Having only the well-being of the ship's passengers in mind, Equiano, because of his seafaring experience, questioned the honesty and competency of the agent, Joseph Irwin. Equiano's outspoken challenge to Irwin's leadership drew much criticism, but, after exoneration from the maritime bureaucracy, Equiano published gracious responses to Irwin's negative attacks in the British newspapers and thereby regained his status in the abolition movement.

In 1790 Equiano, who was by then totally engaged in the British antislavery movement, petitioned the Queen and the Parliament for an end of slavery: "Your Majesty's well known benevolence and humanity emboldens me to approach your royal presence. . . . I supplicate . . . for millions of my African countrymen, who groan under the lash of tyranny in the West Indies. The oppression and cruelty exercised to the unhappy negroes there, have at length reached the British legislature . . . even several persons of property in slaves in the West Indies, have petitioned parliament against its continuance. . . . surely the more extended the misery is, the greater claim it has to your Majesty's compassion, and the greater must be your Majesty's pleasure in administering to its relief. . . . that they may be raised from the condition of brutes, to which they are at present degraded, to the rights and situation of freemen. . . ."

Equiano finally "surrendered" to a settled life

of matrimony on 7 April 1792, when he married Susan Cullen of Ely County, England. In one of few contemporary mentions of Equiano in British periodicals, *Gentlemen's Magazine* (April 1792) records the nuptials: "At Soham, co. Cambridge, Gustavus Vassa, the African, well known in England as the champion and advocate for procuring a suppression of the slave-trade, to Miss Cullen, daughter of Mr. C. of Ely, in same county." There were two girls born to the couple, Ann Maria and Johanna. (Although one biographer mentions a son, the report is most probably erroneous, as no official record of a boy has been found.)

After finding a modicum of peace and gaining international acclaim from the success of his book and its enormous influence on the antislavery movement in the British Empire, Equiano died in 1801. One of his daughters died a few months afterward. His wife and one remaining daughter withdrew from the London limelight immediately after his death, and no further record of them has been found. What has endured for some two hundred years is *The Interesting Narrative of the Life of Olaudah Equiano*, the most successful prose work written by an African in the Western World until the start of the American Civil War.

References:

Francis D. Adams and Barry Sanders, Introduction to *Three Black Writers in Eighteenth-Century England*, edited by Adams and Sanders (Belmont, Cal.: Wadsworth, 1971);

Bernard W. Bell, "African-American Writers, American Literature, 1764-1789," in *The Revolutionary Years*, edited by Everett Emerson, (Madison: University of Wisconsin Press, 1977);

Arna Bontemps, "The Slave Narrative: An American Genre," *Great Slave Narratives*, edited by Bontemps (Boston: Beacon, 1969);

Benjamin Brawley, "Gustavus Vassa," in his *Early Negro American Writers* (Chapel Hill: University of North Carolina Press, 1935; reprinted, Freeport, N.Y.: Books for Libraries Press, 1968), pp. 56-74;

O. R. Dathorne, "African Writers of the Eighteenth Century," *Black Orpheus*, 18 (October 1965): 51-57;

G. I. Jones, "Olaudah Equiano of the Niger Ibo," in *Africa Remembered: Narratives by West Africans from the Era of the Slave Trade*, edited by Philip D. Curtin (Madison: University of Wisconsin Press, 1967), pp. 60-98;

Charles H. Nichols, "O Wasn't That a Wide River," in *Many Thousands Gone: The Ex-Slaves' Account of Their Bondage and Freedom,* edited by Nichols (Leiden, Netherlands: E. J. Brill, 1963), pp. 5-13;

Marion L. Starkey, *Striving to Make it My Home: The Story of Americans from Africa* (New York: Norton, 1964).

Papers:

Equiano's papers and first editions of his works are held at: The Schomburg Collection, New York Public Library; Library Company, Philadelphia; Ridgeway Brothers, Philadelphia; Boston Public Library; Yale University; Harvard University; Atlanta University; Hornby Collection, Liverpool City Library.

John Filson

(circa 1753-September or October 1788)

Alan Axelrod

BOOK: *The Discovery, Settlement, and Present State of Kentucke: And an Essay Towards the Topography and Natural History of that Important Country . . .* (Wilmington, Del.: Printed by James Adams, 1784; London: Printed for J. Stockdale, 1793).

OTHER: "Two Westward Journeys," *Mississippi Valley History Review,* 9 (1922-1923): 320-330;
"Defeat on the Wabash," *Filson Club History Quarterly,* 12 (1938): 187-199;
"Danger on the Wabash: Vincennes Letters of 1786," *Indiana Magazine of History,* 34 (1938): 456-458.

In his single published work, *The Discovery, Settlement, and Present State of Kentucke* (1784), John Filson wrote the first history of Kentucky and told the story of its first hero, Daniel Boone. Filson came to the frontier from Chester County, Pennsylvania, where he had been born about 1753, the son of Davison Filson. Little is known of his early life. He probably attended West Nottingham Academy in Maryland, where he learned Latin, Greek, French, and surveying, setting up later as an itinerant schoolmaster himself. Tradition has it that Filson's arm was wounded in the Revolution and that after the war he returned to teaching but soon quit because his injury prevented his properly thrashing recalcitrant scholars. There is also evidence, however, that he spent the war years teaching in Wilmington.

Early in the fall of 1783, aged thirty, Filson made his first journey to Kentucky, where he ac-

John Filson (courtesy of the Filson Club)

quired more than 12,000 acres, surveyed the wilderness, and taught school at Lexington. Near Lexington, in the house of Levi Todd, he also wrote a book. *The Discovery, Settlement, and Present State of*

Filson's map of Kentucky, from the first edition of his book

Kentucke was drawn from Filson's firsthand observations as well as from interviews with Todd, Daniel Boone, and other Kentucky pioneers. Doubtless, Filson's principal motive for composition was greed: he wanted to attract settlers to the land in which he had invested so heavily. Like many early American promotion tracts, *The Discovery, Settlement, and Present State of Kentucke* depicts an improbable wilderness Eden; but Filson was also moved by

a more disinterested desire to tell the dramatic story of settlement and to record the phenomena of natural history. The most important part of his book is the Daniel Boone narrative. Though framed as an autobiography dictated to Filson, its learned—at times pedantic—language betrays the schoolmaster's hand. Filson's Boone foreshadows James Fenimore Cooper's Natty Bumppo, the stoic woodsman in love with the land. Like Natty, Boone makes the

THE

DISCOVERY, SETTLEMENT
And prefent State of

K E N T U C K E:

A N D

An ESSAY towards the TOPOGRAPHY,
and NATURAL HISTORY of that important Country:

To which is added,

An A P P E N D I X,
CONTAINING,

I. The ADVENTURES of Col. *Daniel Boon*, one
of the firft Settlers, comprehending every important Occurrence in the political Hiftory of
that Province.

II The MINUTES of the *Piankafhaw* council, held at *Poft St. Vincents, April* 15, 1784.

III. An ACCOUNT of the *Indian* Nations inhabiting within the Limits of the Thirteen United States, their Manners and Cuftoms, and
Reflections on their Origin.

IV. The STAGES and DISTANCES between
Philadelphia and the Falls of the *Ohio*; from
Pittfburg to *Penfacola* and feveral other Places.
—The Whole illuftrated by a new and accurate MAP of *Kentucke* and the Country adjoining, drawn from actual Surveys.

By J O H N F I L S O N.

Wilmington, Printed by JAMES ADAMS, 1784.

Title page for Filson's only book, for which he drew upon interviews with Daniel Boone and other Kentucky pioneers

wilderness safe for settlement, suffering on behalf of civilization the depredations of savage Indians in order to transform a "dark and bloody ground" into Filson's Eden.

Filson left Kentucky for Delaware in 1784 to have his book published in Wilmington, bringing with him the first map of Kentucky based on actual observation. The book and map sold well, though Filson abandoned plans for a second edition when George Washington declined his request for a public endorsement.

During the winter of 1784-1785, Filson taught school in Wilmington and Philadelphia before journeying west again in the spring. Letters and manuscript notes concerning this trip to the Illinois and Kentucky country have been variously collected and published in the twentieth century. It is likely that Filson intended the notes for another book he was planning. In November 1786, he returned to Philadelphia, where, always a litigious man, he was embroiled in lawsuits and burdened by creditors' claims through 1787. In that year he left on a third journey to Kentucky. This final visit was ill-starred. Filson advertised a school in Lexington, but almost certainly never opened it; he searched for silver, but never found it; he studied medicine with a local doctor, but never practiced. Then, in 1788, he became a partner in the founding of a city he wanted to call Losantiville but which came to be called Cincinnati. He disappeared into the wilderness while surveying the town site late in September or early in October 1788, presumably the victim of Shawnee.

The Discovery, Settlement, and Present State of Kentucke was more widely published in Europe than in the United States, but other writers freely plagiarized from it on both sides of the Atlantic, most notably Gilbert Imlay in his popular *A Topographical Description of the Western Territory of North America* (1792). Likely, too, Filson's book did succeed in drawing settlers to Kentucky, though its author, dead on that frontier, enjoyed none of the benefits of settlement. Whatever its immediate effects, the book has made its enduring mark on American literature, culture, and history as the source of the first and most-imitated story of Daniel Boone.

Reference:
John Walton, *John Filson of Kentucke* (Lexington: University of Kentucky Press, 1956).

Papers:
The principal depository for Filson's papers is the Draper Collection at the State Historical Society of Wisconsin, which includes manuscripts from Filson's travels in the Illinois and Kentucky country.

Hannah Webster Foster

(10 September 1758-17 April 1840)

Cathy N. Davidson
Michigan State University

BOOKS: *The Coquette; or, The History of Eliza Wharton; A Novel; Founded on Fact* . . . (Boston: Printed by Samuel Etheridge for E. Larkin, 1797);

The Boarding School; or, Lessons of a Preceptress to her Pupils . . . (Boston: Printed by I. Thomas & E. T. Andrews, 1798).

Hannah Webster Foster's *The Coquette* is probably the finest of the sentimental novels of the early national period. Psychologically astute, well-plotted, and carefully written, the novel portrays sensitively the life and death of Elizabeth Whitman, an accomplished poet of the day. In its depiction of an intelligent and strong-willed heroine, the novel transcends many of the conventions of its time and place.

Born in Salisbury, Massachusetts, the daughter of Grant Webster, a Boston merchant, and Hannah Wainwright Webster, Hannah Webster was sent to boarding school in 1762 after her mother died. Although virtually nothing is known of her childhood and adolescence, comments in *The Boarding School* suggest that she found her own schooling to be exemplary. In 1785 she married the Reverend John Foster, a Dartmouth College graduate who went on to serve as pastor of the First Church in Brighton, Massachusetts. The couple had six children.

The Coquette was published anonymously in 1797 after she had become the mother of one child. The book was an immediate success, one of only two American novels (the other was Susanna Rowson's *Charlotte. A Tale of Truth*, 1791) to be a "bestseller" (purchased by more than one percent of the population) in the decade before 1800. Like virtually all novels of the day, *The Coquette* claimed to be *"Founded on Fact."* The claim was accurate. The novel portrayed sympathetically the recent and much-publicized account of Elizabeth Whitman's elopement and her death while giving birth to an illegitimate child. Although there were numerous speculations about who the father of the child might be, evidence strongly suggests that Pierrepont Edwards was the prototype for Sanford, the

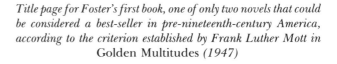

THE

COQUETTE;

OR, THE

HISTORY OF ELIZA WHARTON.

A

NOVEL;

FOUNDED ON FACT.

By a LADY of MASSACHUSETTS.

Boston:

PRINTED BY SAMUEL ETHERIDGE,
FOR E. LARKIN,
No. 47, CORNHILL.

1797.

Title page for Foster's first book, one of only two novels that could be considered a best-seller in pre-nineteenth-century America, according to the criterion established by Frank Luther Mott in Golden Multitudes *(1947)*

rather callow young seducer in the novel. Variously described as "a Chesterfieldian" and a "second Lovelace," Sanford embodies perfectly the traits of the womanizing woman-hater. Not until the final pages of the book, after he has lost wife, family, lover, and fortune, does he see himself for the dubious character he has always been.

Nor does Eliza, for all her obvious intelligence, recognize the depths of his disregard. She immediately perceives that he is flamboyant and perhaps a little shallow, but Foster makes the seducer seem more appealing by contrasting him to a second male character, the Reverend Boyer, who also falls short of Eliza's ideals. Pompous and pedantic, Boyer represents a life of stultifying convention.

The introduction of two opposite male characters adds a new wrinkle to the Richardsonian novel of sentiment which is the ostensible model for *The Coquette*. When the heroine has only one suitor to contend with, her choice becomes the rather simple one of whether she will or will not succumb to his sexual desires. The opposition, then, is between the salacious male character and the virtuous female. But once the female character must choose between men, the reader is forced to weigh carefully the relative merits of representative male characters. To further complicate the moral issues involved here, Foster portrays each male character as less than perfect. Eliza's choices are realistic, and she essentially wants neither. Considering her unsatisfactory alternatives, Eliza at one point laments, "What a pity that the graces and virtues are not oftener united."

Nor is Eliza simply too fussy. Early on she goes to spend time with her friends, the Richmans. Their contented, egalitarian marriage is the ideal after which Eliza aspires. But clearly neither Boyer nor Sanford is a General Richman. Thus, Eliza dallies, choosing neither, until both ultimately reject her. Dejected by finding herself a spinster at the age of thirty-seven, she now has a relationship with Sanford, who has married another woman solely for her fortune. Eliza's act, carefully motivated within the plot, is more an act of calculated self-destruction than coquetry. Her death in childbirth, alone and friendless at a wayside inn, attests to the limitations of her suitors more than to her own lapse of morality.

The Coquette is a moving book, even to the modern reader who finds it easy to dismiss sentimental fiction as inferior art. Numerous modern critics, for example, have noted that Eliza is not a fainting, stereotypical sentimental heroine but a rebel, trying to define herself against the limitations imposed on late-eighteenth-century women. The readers of the time appreciated the novel too. It was reprinted nearly a dozen times by the second quarter of the nineteenth century. H. Horatius Nichols dramatized the novel in 1802 as *The New England Coquette*. The book remained in print until well into the twentieth century and is, in fact, in print today.

Foster's second novel, *The Boarding School*

Title page for Foster's second novel, which advocates better education for women and criticises the double sexual standard (courtesy of the John Carter Brown Library at Brown University)

(1798), was never reprinted nor did it deserve to be. It is didactic and prosaic, lacking in art and ingenuity. However, even in this inferior work Foster proves an important spokeswoman for changing social values. *The Boarding School*, like numerous novels of the day, advocates better female education. More striking, it castigates the double sexual standard, insisting that a girl once seduced is not necessarily a "bad" woman and should not be ostracized by her society. The novel also insists that men be held much more accountable for their sexual behavior and transgressions and be made to share equally the burden of their illicit actions.

Foster did not go on to write other novels, but she did encourage two of her daughters, Eliza Lanesford Cushing and Harriet Vaughan Cheney, to enter literary careers. Foster lived with these daughters in Montreal until her death at the age of eighty-one.

References:

Charles K. Bolton, *The Elizabeth Whitman Mystery* (Peabody, Mass.: Peabody Historical Society, 1912);

Herbert Ross Brown, Introduction to *The Coquette; or, The History of Eliza Wharton,* edited by Brown (New York: Columbia University Press for the Facsimile Text Society, 1939);

Brown, *The Sentimental Novel in America, 1789-1860* (Durham: Duke University Press, 1940), pp. 50-53;

Caroline H. Dall, *The Romance of the Association; Or, One Last Glimpse of Charlotte Temple and Eliza Wharton* (Cambridge, Mass.: Press of John Wilson & Son, 1875);

Cathy N. Davidson, "Flirting with Destiny: Ambivalence and Form in the Early American Sentimental Novel," *Studies in American Fiction* (Spring 1982): 17-39;

Robert L. Shurter, "Mrs. Hannah Webster Foster and the Early American Novel," *American Literature,* 4 (November 1932): 306-308;

James Woodress, *A Yankee's Odyssey: The Life of Joel Barlow* (New York: Lippincott, 1958), pp. 60-64.

Philip Freneau

Richard C. Vitzthum
University of Maryland

BIRTH: New York, 2 January 1752, to Pierre and Agnes Watson Freneau.

EDUCATION: B.A., College of New Jersey (later Princeton University), 1771.

MARRIAGE: 15 April 1790 to Eleanor Forman; children: Helena, Agnes, Catherine, and Margaret.

DEATH: Freehold, New Jersey, 18 December 1832.

BOOKS: *A Poem, on the Rising Glory of America; Being an Exercise Delivered at the Public Commencement at Nassau-Hall, September 25, 1771...,* by Freneau and Hugh Henry Brackenridge (Philadelphia: Printed by Joseph Crukshank for R. Aitken, 1772);

The American Village, A Poem. To Which Are Added, Several Other Original Pieces in Verse... (New York: Printed by S. Inslee & A. Car, 1772);

American Liberty, A Poem... (New York: Printed by J. Anderson, 1775);

A Voyage to Boston. A Poem... (New York: Printed by John Anderson, 1775);

General Gage's Soliloquy (New York: Printed by Hugh Gaine, 1775);

General Gage's Confession, Being the Substance of His Excellency's Last Conference, with His Ghostly Father, Friar Francis... (New York: Printed by Hugh Gaine, 1775);

The British Prison-Ship: A Poem, in Four Cantoes... (Philadelphia: Printed by F. Bailey, 1781);

The Poems of Philip Freneau. Written chiefly during the late war (Philadelphia: Printed by Francis Bailey, 1786);

A Journey from Philadelphia to New-York, By Way of Burlington and South-Amboy. By Robert Slender, Stocking Weaver... (Philadelphia: Printed by Francis Bailey, 1787); republished as *A Laughable Poem; or Robert Slender's Journey from Philadelphia to New York, by Way of Burlington and South Amboy...* (Philadelphia: Printed for Thomas Neversink, 1809);

The Miscellaneous Works of Mr. Philip Freneau... (Philadelphia: Printed by Francis Bailey, 1788);

The Village Merchant: A Poem. To Which Is Added The Country Printer... (Philadelphia: Printed by Hoff & Derrick, 1794);

Poems Written between the Years 1768 & 1794... (Monmouth, N.J.: Printed by the author, 1795);

Letters on Various Interesting and Important Subjects; Many of Which Have Appeared in the Aurora..., as Robert Slender (Philadelphia: Printed by D.

Hogan for the author, 1799);

Poems Written and Published during the American Revolutionary War, and Now Republished from the Original Manuscripts; Interspersed with Translations from the Ancients and Other Pieces Not Heretofore in Print . . . , 2 volumes (Philadelphia: From the press of Lydia R. Bailey, 1809);

A Collection of Poems, on American Affairs, and a Variety of Other Subjects, Chiefly Moral and Political; Written between the Year 1797 and the Present . . . , 2 volumes (New York: Published by David Longworth, 1815);

Some Account of the Capture of the Ship "Aurora" . . . , edited by Jay Milles (New York: M. F. Mansfield & A. Wessels, 1899);

Unpublished Freneauana, edited by Charles F. Heartman (New York, 1918);

The Last Poems of Philip Freneau, edited by Lewis Leary (New Brunswick: Rutgers University Press, 1945);

The Prose of Philip Freneau, edited by Philip M. Marsh (Metuchen, N.J.: Scarecrow, 1955).

Collection: *The Poems of Philip Freneau,* 3 volumes, edited by Fred Lewis Pattee (Princeton: Princeton University Library, 1902, 1903, 1907).

Regarded during his lifetime and for a century after his death chiefly as a political propagandist, Philip Morin Freneau has come to be seen in recent decades as an accomplished informal essayist and as a gifted and versatile lyric poet. His current reputation rests more on the excellence of several dozen nonpolitical or at most quasipolitical poems than on his political writing, which, though good enough on its own grounds to have established him as one of the leading men of letters of the Revolutionary era and important enough from a political point of view to guarantee him a permanent place in American history, has not been the focus of recent favorable reassessments of his literary importance. These reassessments have uncovered a complexity, variety, and richness in his best work which challenge comparison with that of any American poet before Whitman.

Descended from French Huguenot ancestors on his father's side of the family and from Scottish Presbyterians on his mother's, Freneau was born in New York City in 1752 to an orthodox Calvinist heritage fanned to flame by the Great Awakening of the 1740s. Although his father, Pierre Freneau, appears to have taken religion seriously, the main force behind Philip's religious upbringing seems to have been his mother, Agnes Watson Freneau. Af-

ter marrying Pierre Freneau and settling with him in Mount Pleasant, New Jersey, on a farm provided by her parents, Agnes Freneau enrolled her family in the Presbyterian congregation a few miles away in Freehold to which her father and mother already belonged. The minister of this church was William Tennent, Jr., a leader in the mid-century evangelical revival in the mid-Atlantic colonies known as the New Side. Brother of Gilbert Tennent, one of the best-known preachers of the Great Awakening, and son of William Tennent, Sr., founder of the evangelical Log College in Neshaminy, Pennsylvania, William Tennent, Jr., was the director of the grammar school in Manalapan, New Jersey, which Freneau attended during the 1760s. He served also as acting president of the college of New Jersey (now Princeton University) the year Freneau was accepted at that institution to study for the Calvinist ministry and the year his father died.

Freneau's repudiation of the career his father and mother had laid out for him was signalled by a comment he wrote in 1774 in a notebook he was

The Freneau homestead, Mount Pleasant, New Jersey

keeping of his theological studies: "And so, farewell to the study of Divinity—which is, in fact the Study of Nothing!—and the profession of a priest is little better than that of a slothful Blockhead." Until that time he had evidently been trying to conform to his mother's wishes. She had sent him to Princeton at considerable financial sacrifice to the rest of her family, which had been nearly impoverished by her husband's bankruptcy at the time of his death. That Freneau's relationship with his mother was extremely close is suggested by several later facts in his career—his living for long intervals at Mount Pleasant in his mother's household between his graduation from college in 1771 and his marriage in 1790, his return to Mount Pleasant in the late 1790s with his own family to live with Agnes until her death in 1816, and his wish to be buried at Mount Pleasant beneath a gravestone whose reverse side is dedicated to Agnes and which acknowledges his relation to no other human being. Yet his rebellion against the ministerial career his mother had in mind for him and his escapes from a Mount Pleasant dominated by his mother to the sea in 1776, 1783, and again in 1802 suggest that the

relationship was also abrasive and that Freneau's tendency in his poetry to associate land with a superficiality, possessiveness, and constraint that is unmistakably feminine, as opposed to the profundity, freedom, and stoicism of the masculine sea, stemmed in part from unacknowledged feelings of guilt and hostility toward her and women in general.

Another factor that helped deflect Freneau from the ministry may, ironically enough, have been his contact with John Witherspoon at Princeton. Brought from Scotland to Princeton in 1768, the year Freneau matriculated, as president of the college, Witherspoon was, despite his credentials as an Evangelical Calvinist in Scotland, more liberal in religious matters than the New Siders who brought him to Princeton to follow the orthodox footsteps of Jonathan Edwards. He accepted, for example, much of the moral-sense philosophy of Edwards's arch-enemy, Francis Hutcheson, and in his course in moral philosophy at Princeton he taught Freneau and his classmates that belles lettres improved one's moral and aesthetic taste. Witherspoon was also a political liberal, who during the last quarter of the

A

P O E M,

ON THE

RISING GLORY

OF

A M E R I C A;

BEING AN

E X E R C I S E

DELIVERED AT THE PUBLIC COMMENCEMENT AT
NASSAU-HALL, September 25, 1771.

————————

—————*Venient annis*
Sæcula feris, quibus oceannus
Vincula return laxet et ingeus
Pateat tellus, Typhisque novot
Detegat orbes; nec fil.terris
Ultima Thule———

SENECA. MED. ACT iii. v. 375.

PHILADELPHIA:

PRINTED BY JOSEPH CRUKSHANK, FOR R. AITKEN,
BOOKSELLER, OPPOSITE THE LONDON-COFFEE-
HOUSE, IN FRONT-STREET.
M,DCC,LXXII.

*Title page for the graduation poem in which Freneau and Hugh
Henry Brackenridge coined the phrase ("Rising Glory of America") that would come to characterize an important movement in
the literature of the early American republic*

eighteenth century was a leader in the struggle for
independence and nationhood. He appears to have
been one cause of the literary, empirical, and liberal
bent of Freneau's later career.

Yet however liberal he may have been aesthet-
ically, philosophically, and politically, Witherspoon
was no freethinker in religion, and Freneau's first
published piece, a graduation poem he wrote in
1771 with Hugh Henry Brackenridge and had published in 1772 with the title *A Poem, on the Rising
Glory of America,* concludes with a millennial vision
based on Revelations: "A *Canaan* here,/Another
Canaan shall excel the old,/And from a fairer *Pisgah's* top be seen." In 1772, while he was doing
postgraduate study in theology at Princeton, he
published a collection of poems titled *The American
Village,* which strikes several skeptical notes in its
generally orthodox tenor. For instance, the title
poem speculates at one point that death may lead to
"nihility." Although the allusion foreshadows a
bleak theme of nihilism that reaches a climax in
Freneau's poetry of the 1780s, in this early volume

the theme is tempered by conventional religious
attitudes and, more complexly, by a faith that poetic
fancy and the art it produces can somehow compen-
sate for the transiency and impermanence of nature. Lines 87 to 166 of "The American Village"
self-consciously offer an example of such compensation, the speaker first describing an ideal, pastoral community on an imaginary island, then
lamenting the destruction of this imaginary island
by natural causes, and concluding that the poetic
imagination can use the landscapes of America as a
substitute for the ruined island. The entire poem
similarly contrasts American rural life with the decaying village life of Britain that Goldsmith portrayed in 1770 in *The Deserted Village,* idealizes rural
America, and presents it as romantic compensation
for the failed landscapes of England. In concluding
with the wish to settle in an American village in
order to enjoy "heaven born contemplation" inspired by the "aged volumes of some plain divine,"
the speaker continues to pay at least lip service to
religious duty.

Encouraged by the liberal, literate atmosphere of Princeton under Witherspoon, Freneau
in the early 1770s began moving away from what he
apparently felt to be the confining orthodoxy of his
home environment toward a secular literary career.
In 1773 and 1774 he worked as a teacher with
Brackenridge at a Presbyterian academy in Princess
Anne, Maryland, but by 1775 he had given that up,
along with his career in divinity, and drifted to New
York City. There he published a series of poems
that reveal his commitment to the American cause
in the developing war with England and his skill as a
satirist. *General Gage's Soliloquy, A Voyage to Boston,*
and *General Gage's Confession,* written in heroic couplets, are amusing burlesques of the British leaders
in Boston, while "Libera Nos, Domine" parodies the
liturgy of the Mass in galloping anapests, asking
deliverance from Britons in general.

His next move was more decisive. In January
or February 1776 he left North America for a two-
year period of exploring the Caribbean from a
plantation on the island of Santa Cruz. Although he
claimed in an application he submitted in 1832 for a
military pension that during these two years he
helped crew privateers, he is said to have admitted
to an acquaintance in the 1790s that he went to the
Caribbean because he was "averse to enter the
army" and getting "knock'd in the head." There is
no evidence that any of the ships he sailed on saw
military action or tried to run the British blockade
of North America. What is clear is that he chose a
life-style, that of a common sailor, as different from

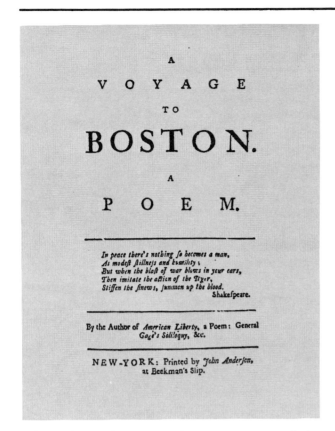

A

V O Y A G E

TO

BOSTON.

A

P O E M.

In peace there's nothing fo becomes a man,
As modeſt ſtillneſs and humility:
But when the blaſt of war blows in your ears,
Then imitate the action of the Tyger,
Stiffen the ſinews, ſummon up the blood.
                                   Shakeſpeare.

By the Author of *American Liberty*, a Poem: General
Gage's Soliloquy, &c.

NEW-YORK: Printed by *John Anderſon*,
at Beekman's Slip.

*Title page for one of the anti-British poems Freneau wrote during
the American Revolution*

that of a clergyman as he could find, in a locale he praised in 1779 in the poem "The Beauties of Santa Cruz" as a paradise of romantic sensuousness and fancy. Furthermore, he met the Bermuda girl who inspired the composite female personality named Amanda in a series of poems published in the 1795 and 1809 collections, and he may have had an affair with her or with one or more other girls. Freneau's appeal to women is indicated not only by his successful courtship of Eleanor Forman, reportedly one of the most beautiful and intelligent New Jersey girls of her day, but also by many hints in his writing of sexual activity.

In any event, when he returned to his mother at Mount Pleasant in the summer of 1778, he had shed the role of pious and dutiful son for that of self-assertive and experienced man of the world. He joined the New Jersey militia and helped crew several blockade runners. Although he saw no significant action, he was obviously ready and willing to fight. He also either had rethought or was in the process of rethinking the romantic escapism of *The American Village* volume and "The Beauties of Santa Cruz," which, although published in Bracken-

ridge's *United States Magazine* in 1779, had been written around the beginning of 1777 when Freneau was still in the West Indies. The tone of this early version of the poem suggests a confused attitude toward the island. Although the narrator tries throughout to convince a presumably reluctant inhabitant of North America to leave his harsh climate and come to the "perpetual green" of "this gay enchanting shore," he admits that "reason's voice must whisper *to the Soul*/That nobler climes for man the Gods design." After praising the soothing, narcotic effect of the island's flora and fauna for 170 lines, he blurts out that he would like to see home again. The final stanza concedes that the responsible northerner will probably prefer staying where he is to joining the narrator on Santa Cruz.

Plainly, Freneau was feeling guilty by 1777 about his escape to a romantic paradise. Although in the poem he clings stubbornly to an idealized landscape that he tries to substitute for the reality of war-torn America, he also reveals his readiness to listen to that "whisper" of "reason's voice" he heard in the Caribbean. His acceptance of the realities of the war is shown by the many propagandistic poems he published during 1779 in the *United States Magazine* as well as by his military service. But the longest and most autobiographical piece of propaganda he ever wrote appeared as a separate pamphlet in the summer of 1781—*The British Prison-Ship*. Based on personal experience, the poem recounts the capture of the brig *Aurora* on 26 May 1780 by the British frigate *Iris* at the mouth of Delaware Bay and the subsequent transfer of the captured Americans, Freneau among them, to the British prison ship *Scorpion* in New York harbor. After three weeks on the *Scorpion*, Freneau caught a fever and was moved to the hospital ship *Hunter*, where he stayed for three more weeks until 12 July when he was paroled and, grotesquely emaciated, allowed to return home to Mount Pleasant.

Virtually all of Freneau's biographers see this imprisonment as a key event in his life. For the first time, it is generally agreed, he personally felt the effects of the British policy against which he had been writing rather breezy burlesques and satires for half a decade. His attempt to tell this story as an epic in heroic couplets is consistent with the seriousness of the poem's tone. Trying through epic form to evoke "sublime" feelings of fear, revulsion, and pity in the reader, Freneau hammers away throughout at the cruelty of his British captors. His earnestness is never in doubt. He pleads, for example, that the prisoners who died on the prison ships be remembered by future Americans: "With gentlest

Title page for the poem in which Freneau described his experiences as a prisoner of war in 1780

footstep press this kindred dust, / And o'er the tombs, if tombs can then be found, / Place the green turf, and plant the myrtle round." That this was a personal vow Freneau took in 1780 and kept for decades afterward is shown by the series of poems he subsequently dedicated to the prison-ship dead. The first of these, published in 1803 in the *New York Weekly Museum* and titled "On Walking over the ground of Long Island, near New-York, where many Americans were interred from the Prison Ships, during the war with Great Britain," one of Freneau's most moving elegies, was republished in revised form in several New York newspapers in 1808 and in his 1809 collection, *Poems Written and Published during the American Revolutionary War.* In his 1815 book, *A Collection of Poems, on American Affairs,* he included another long poem on the subject, "The Tomb of the Patriots."

The main effect of the experience, aside from souring him permanently on England, appears to have been to empty his personal philosophy of whatever youthful romanticism it still had. After recovering his health under his mother's care at

Mount Pleasant, he went to Philadelphia in 1781 to help Francis Bailey edit the *Freeman's Journal,* which until the end of the war in 1783 published dozens of Freneau's poems and essays, all but a handful dealing with the war or some aspect of American politics. His dedication to a single, consistently pursued goal during this period distinguished it from the unfocused pattern of his earlier career. More important, the tone of all his writing, political as well as nonpolitical, is deliberately unillusioned, as though he was trying to put as much distance as possible between his current realism and the earlier escapism of poems like "The American Village" and "The Beauties of Santa Cruz."

His most striking announcement of this new view was a short poem titled "A Moral Thought" that appeared in 1781. The conventionality of the poem's first two stanzas stands in stark contrast to the specificity of a tidal river image in the final two stanzas. Although both halves of the poem argue that experience brings disillusionment, the second half reveals a depth and complexity of feeling missing from the rather vapid generalizations of the first: the muddy river floor exposed by the receding tide evokes a many-leveled, negative response. The hope of waking and rising to a better life voiced in the first two stanzas is undercut by the mud. What really lies beneath the illusoriness of moonlit water is a stifling, alien universe of muck.

Although the theme of disillusionment was generally suppressed in his political writing of the early 1780s, it occasionally breaks through there as well. A case in point is the ending of the 1782 anti-British polemic "Philosophical Reflections," which contradicts the upbeat primitivism of the poem's earlier lines with an image of the illusoriness of all human happiness. Happiness is an "empty circle" that, like the horizon, exists only in the mind. Moreover, chasing this "visionary line" implies a solipsistic skepticism: because human beings impose on the world the meanings and values they would like it to have, they live for the most part in self-made envelopes of delusion.

"The Dying Indian; or the Last Words of Shalum," published 17 March 1784 in the *Freeman's Journal,* suggests how far in this philosophical direction Freneau had traveled by the end of the war. Prefaced by the somber Latin epigraph, "*Debemur morti nos, nostraque*" ("we and our things are owed to death"), the poem recounts speculations about immortality by an Indian who in the final lines dies. As in a number of his other Indian poems, Freneau here uses an Indian speaker for the purpose of commenting on his own Christian civilization. From

From the manuscript for Freneau's prose description of his captivity by the British, written on 14 July 1780 but not published until 1899 (Some Account of the Capture of the Ship "Aurora," 1899)

beginning to end, he has Shalum question the assumptions of the Indian mythology of death. Far from paradisaical, the happy hunting grounds, he fears, are "visionary glades" with "lazy and sad deluding waters," populated by "empty unsubstantial shades." He is contemptuous of the fable makers who tell "Fine tales" of an afterlife, and he asserts that no one "can promise half the tale is true." In view of the well-known religious faith of Indians, Freneau's presentation here of an Indian skeptic "Perplex'd with doubts, and tortur'd with despair" about immortality is designed to suggest to his Christian readers that they too should question their death mythology. Shalum is portrayed as a fearless thinker whose deathbed speech boldly attacks the superstitions of his religion. His intellectual honesty in confessing that neither he nor anyone else knows what happens to human beings after death is underscored by his closing remark that he is approaching death "Without a partner, and with-

out a guide." The lines that immediately follow these end the poem. They are the only ones not spoken by Shalum. Suggesting that death may be annihilation—an "endless sleep" with no awakening— they are the omniscient speaker's blunt confirmation of Shalum's worst fears.

Freneau's sympathy with the intellectual honesty and courage of Shalum-like attitudes by 1784 is evident. He had repudiated the muddled idealism and escapism of his Caribbean adventure in favor of a hard-nosed rationalism that eschewed romantic fancy and easy religious answers. He had come to believe that intellectual growth went hand-in-hand with a stripping away of illusion. Yet a remarkable fact about Freneau as an artist during this and subsequent periods was that he was able to continue writing more conventional material with undiminished verve. The single-minded purpose revealed in his attacks on the British and their American sympathizers produced anything but a single kind of poem. He wrote rousing narrative ballads such as "On the Memorable Victory Obtained by the gallant captain Paul Jones of the *Good Man Richard* over the *Seraphis*" and quiet pastoral elegies such as "To the Memory of the Brave Americans, under General Greene, who fell in the action of September 8, 1781." He could write bloodthirsty invective such as "On the Fall of General Earl Cornwallis" and belly laughs such as "Rivington's Last Will and Testament," "Truth Anticipated," and "Rivington's Confessions." In other words, what Freneau had acquired by the mid-1780s was not only a skepticism that led him toward radical speculation but also a literary professionalism that allowed him to write many kinds of prose and poetry well.

Then, sometime during 1784-1785, something happened that caused him, over the next half-dozen years, to write a score of poems on which his reputation as an important poet chiefly rests. The details of his life between his prison-ship experience in 1780 and his sailing from the Mount Pleasant area as captain of the sloop *Monmouth* on 24 November 1785 are vague. For substantial periods of time between 1781 and 1784 he must have been in Philadelphia helping Bailey produce the *Freeman's Journal,* and by 8 November 1782 he had been appointed as a clerk in the Philadelphia post office. The next solid information we have about him is that on 24 June 1784 he sailed as a passenger on the brig *Dromelly* for Jamaica, went through the worst hurricane to hit the Caribbean in decades, reached Kingston 31 July and left for Philadelphia on 23 September on the brig *Mars,* arriving on 4 November. There are hints that because of an illness during the following winter he may have gone to Pacolet Springs, South Carolina, for a mineral-water cure in the spring of 1785 and on to Charleston that summer or fall to visit his brother Peter, but the evidence is inconclusive. From an experience or group of experiences that occurred roughly between the time of the announcement of the end of the war in Philadelphia in May 1784 and the time of his setting sail on the *Monmouth* as ship captain in November 1785, he developed the poetic style that during the next several years produced masterpieces such as "The Hurricane," "The Vernal Ague," "The Wild Honey Suckle," "Port Royal," "The Departure," "The Indian Burying-Ground," "Hatteras," and "To Cynthia."

We can only speculate as to what this experience was. Tradition has it that some time after his return from the Caribbean in 1778 Freneau fell in love with and proposed to his future wife, Eleanor Forman, but that in 1784 her parents rejected him

because of his poverty, leaving him depressed but determined to prove himself by earning a living at sea. The suggestion has also been made that he sailed to the West Indies in 1784 to woo an old flame from his earlier Caribbean sojourn (the "Amanda" of later editions) but that she either rejected him or died about the time of his visit. Like the "Eleanor" legend, the "Amanda" legend offers an intriguing and by no means implausible explanation for the new, intensely personal quality of certain poems that began appearing in 1785. The two legends, taken together, could also help explain why the bitter depression of many of the poems published between 1785 and 1787 gave way to growing optimism in 1789 and disappeared for good after Freneau's marriage to Eleanor Forman in 1790. And they do not contradict other, less romantic theories that have been advanced—for example, that Freneau found himself at disturbingly loose ends after America made peace with his bitter enemy England or that his experience with the sea, in the 1784 hurricane and afterward as captain, helped darken an already gloomy world view.

Whatever inspired it, the style that first appeared in April 1785 in the magnificent poem "The Hurricane" was, in its fusion of personal incident, symbolic suggestiveness, and philosophical depth, unlike anything Freneau had published to date. Focusing on an event experienced by the speaker, "The Hurricane" proceeds to explore its significance. In contemplating the hurricane's ontological and teleological import, the speaker avoids the overtly philosophical stance of earlier poems such as "A Moral Thought" and "Philosophical Reflections." Instead, he insinuates into a thirty-six-line description of the storm continual hints of deeper meaning.

The most unmistakable of these hints is found in the poem's middle two stanzas.

> While o'er the dark abyss we roam,
> Perhaps, whate'er the pilots say,
> We saw the Sun descend in gloom,
> No more to see his rising ray,
>   But bury'd low, by far too deep,
>   On coral beds, unpitied, sleep!
>
> But what a strange, uncoasted strand
> Is that, where death permits no day—
> No charts have we to mark that land,
> No compass to direct that way—
>   What pilot shall explore that realm,
>   What new Columbus take the helm.

Although the subject of the last two lines in the first

stanza can be "We"—that is, we the sailors may drown and lie unpitied— it can also be "Sun." The ambiguity invites the appalling speculation, one that troubled Freneau throughout his life and especially during the 1780s, that the physical sun could in a metaphoric sense be the victim of a hurricane. Read this way, the lines present the hurricane as a symbol of all the destructive, chaotic, and irrational aspects of nature that Freneau always associated with death and that he here intimates may ultimately destroy all creation. Freneau perhaps meant to underline this meaning with a sardonic pun on the "rising ray" of the "Sun": from this hurricane of destruction no Christian "Sun" (Son) will ever rise. And the "dark abyss" of the stanza's first line is the traditional term for describing a universe void of life or form.

These nihilistic overtones are amplified in the second stanza quoted. Referring back to the "uncoasted strand" not only of "death," where the drowned sailors lie but also of a physical universe reduced to "no day" by the forces of dissolution, the speaker blends an image of ocean depths, the ocean floor serving as the "strand" of some appalling metaphysical "realm," with an image of the hurricane on the surface to evoke a chilling vision of the order of nature. It is a violent, amoral order, indifferent to mankind and inscrutable in terms of ends and origins. In insisting that we have no "charts" or "compass" to help us navigate that order and that no "Columbus" has yet explored it, the speaker confines the scope of human knowledge to empirical reality and denies the traditional claim that knowledge of the supernatural is possible.

Yet the tone of these stanzas and of the poem as a whole is cautious, oblique, and undogmatic. The speaker does not force his ideas on us; the poem can be read simply as a description of a storm. Even the poem's final lines, which further invite us to explore the storm's significance, can be read as referring to nothing but the storm's effect on the ship: "Thus, skill and science both must fall,/And ruin is the lot of all." If these lines are meant to point to cosmic matters, they do so, like the rest of the poem, tentatively. Freneau is not saying that the hurricane *does* symbolize nature but rather that *if* ("Thus") it does, then the poem's grim conclusion is justified. The poem merely offers this conclusion, however powerfully, as one way to interpret a cosmos that remains essentially unknowable.

Evidence that Freneau's voyage to Jamaica in 1784 may have precipitated or helped precipitate the change in style revealed in "The Hurricane" is found in one of his next poems, "Lines Written at

Port-Royal, in the Island of Jamaica." "The Hurricane" was dated July 1784 as the *Dromelly* approached Jamaica, while "Lines Written at Port-Royal" was dated two months later in the middle of his stay on the island. "Lines Written At Port-Royal" echoes the dark speculations of "The Hurricane," giving them even more poignant, personal expression.

The poem opens with the speaker musing somberly on the city's history. Focusing on the earthquake that had a hundred years earlier sunk most of Port Royal into the ocean, he pictures the drowned inhabitants in their eerie, underwater graves and repeatedly contrasts the seedy and decayed Port Royal of the present with its pre-earthquake splendor. Then he alludes to his recent bout with the hurricane and suggests that his reason for sailing to Jamaica was to get literary inspiration. Having failed in this aim, he has fallen into a frame of mind so depressed that at line 83 he suddenly bursts out, "Where shall I go, what Lethe shall I find/To drive these dark ideas from my mind!" Among these "dark ideas" is that of "a half deluded dame" who at some earlier time was seduced by a "British *Paris*" into coming to Jamaica as his wife and was abandoned. The figure of a female abandoned or left waiting on shore by an ocean-going male, which first appears in Freneau's writing at about this time and remains one of its dominant motifs till about 1790, may reflect a web of autobiographical meaning that includes elements of the "Eleanor" and "Amanda" legends and aspects of Freneau's relationship with his mother. Connected as this female figure is in "Lines Written at Port-Royal" and elsewhere with depression on the part of the poem's speaker, it often seems to combine a feeling of guilt in the male speaker over the female's abandonment with a feeling of relief at leaving her behind.

The final twelve lines of "Lines Written at Port-Royal," like "The Hurricane," invite a symbolic reading of the personal experiences the poem has described. They speak of "delusion" being ended by the "burning sands" and "imperious tides" of the area. The "delusion" appears to refer to belief in the stability and permanence of nature itself: nature inevitably destroys mankind's artifacts as well as itself. The poem ends with an ironic prayer to the sea winds in which the speaker asks to be allowed to sail away from Jamaica in good weather as a reward for not complaining about nature's devastation of Port Royal. The speaker has so fully learned his lesson about how nature works, he says, that he accepts nature's destructiveness "without a sigh."

A month after "Lines Written at Port-Royal" first appeared, Freneau published another remarkably interesting poem, "The Lost Sailor," which more resembles "The Dying Indian" than "The Hurricane" or "Lines Written at Port-Royal" in that it consists mainly of the words of someone other than Freneau's characteristic poet-speaker. An old tar named Ralph delivers the poem's seven central stanzas, leaving only the first two stanzas and the final stanza to the Freneauvian "I." Claiming to have met Ralph on a Caribbean island, the speaker presents him through his own words as a quintessential sailor-wanderer—a man who, after urging the speaker never to go to sea, immediately ships out. That Freneau both condescends to and sympathizes with this nautical hypocrite is clear. He treats him ironically, yet he also lets him articulate the doctrine of fortitude that Freneau himself used as the cornerstone of his own philosophy and praised in dozens of subsequent poems. Moreover, Ralph echoes elements of the nihilism heard in "The Hurricane."

If we view Ralph, like Shalum in "The Dying Indian," more as a projection of Freneau's own thought than as a separate person, we see that he embodies in an extreme form the restless, wandering, ocean-going impulses that Freneau acknowledged in an 1800 letter: "I am laying plans and schemes once More to get charge of a vessel in some southern trade where there may be a chance of making something. Every day of my life convinces me that while I live I must be active. A sedentary dull life has a strange effect upon Me. I must be in Motion to be happy—People here think I am mad in again attempting the water." Yet we have also noted Freneau's land-seeking, domestic impulses in his regular returns to his boyhood home and his mother at Mount Pleasant. These are also embodied in Ralph as a feeling of regret over having gone to sea in the first place and as warnings to the speaker not to copy him. He says he was happy on shore with his "Amoranda" and was a fool to leave her for ocean adventures.

But the fact remains that, in straight contradiction to his own advice, Ralph not only did leave his pastoral paradise and Amoranda but at the end of the poem once again flees "the magic of the inchanting shore," as the speaker sarcastically puts it. In regretting his treatment of Amoranda, Ralph is a different kind of sea-going betrayer from the "British Paris" of "Port Royal." He is not so much a victimizer as himself a victim of mysterious, inner compulsions resembling those Freneau confessed in 1800. In calling him "poor Ralph," Freneau pities

rather than condemns his behavior, creating in him a sea-going alter ego he both deprecates and applauds.

"Lines Written at Port-Royal" and "The Lost Sailor" were published in the *Columbian Herald* during Freneau's first voyage as a ship captain, a venture lasting from November 1785 to March 1786 which took him from New Jersey to South Carolina and Georgia and back aboard the forty-ton sloop *Monmouth*. The slackness of the coastal trade kept the *Monmouth* from making another cargo until June, when Freneau captained her again on a month-long cruise to Charleston. It was during this second voyage that *The Poems of Philip Freneau. Written chiefly during the late war* (1786), the first collection of Freneau's poems since *The American Village* volume, appeared. Containing more than four hundred pages, the volume has no clear organizational or thematic center. Its preponderance of war-related, political material seems merely to reflect the fact that Freneau had written more poems of this kind than any other. Its chief interest lies in its revised versions of a number of already-published poems, most notably "The Beauties of

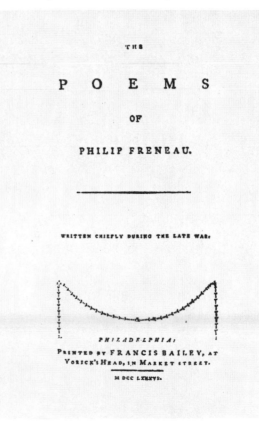

Title page for Freneau's 1786 collection, which demonstrates the pessimism and disillusionment that characterized Freneau's thought after 1780

Santa Cruz," and in several of its new pieces, especially "The Vernal Ague."

The revised poems "The Beauties of Santa Cruz" and "The Vernal Ague" epitomize the pessimism and disillusionment of Freneau's thought after 1780. In contrast to his 1779 predecessor, the speaker of the 1786 version of "The Beauties of Santa Cruz" firmly rejects the island as an ideal, prefacing the poem with these new, devastatingly antiromantic lines:

Sweet orange grove, the fairest of the isle,
In thy soft shade luxuriously reclin'd,
Where, round my fragrant bed, the flowrets smile,
In sweet delusions I deceive my mind.

Later in the poem, he symbolizes the island's delusiveness with the *Animal* flower, which closes like "a deluding dream" if one tries to touch it. More important, he announces, in complete contrast to the central theme of the 1779 version, that he is leaving the island to go to sea. In repudiating the moral hollowness of the island in favor of the harsh but bracing realities of the sea, he echoes Ralph's doctrine of fortitude: on the "inhospitable *main*," as he puts it, "the manly heart alone must conquer." In a 1789 letter, Freneau expressed this stoical doctrine more prosaically: "Indeed, the *sea* is the *best* school for philosophy (I mean of the moral kind;) in thirteen or fourteen years acquaintance with this element, I am convinced a man ought to imbibe more of your right genuine *stoical* stuff, than could be gained in half a century on shore."

Similarly, "The Vernal Ague" depicts a landscape that in the past served the speaker as the "Source of many a golden dream" that "charm'd" him but that now seems hopelessly blighted, its trees "dead," its streams and breezes "disgusting." The speaker, rather than the landscape, has changed. He no longer finds in it the reflection of a benign natural order that he once did. Instead, he sees it from the point of view of the speaker of "A Moral Thought," "The Hurricane," and "Lines Written at Port-Royal"—as a deceptive mask for the destructive forces that appear to dominate nature. The poem concludes with a prayer as somber and ironic as the one at the end of "Lines Written at Port-Royal." Addressed to "Restoring Nature," it deliberately contradicts itself by asking for "aid" from the very force that will eventually destroy both the speaker and "vernal suns" in the "endless winter" of death. All nature can do is "renew" an illusion of natural beauty that will inevitably "fade" when the

speaker dies. It will paint the mind with soothing but deceptive "colours."

The first poem that Freneau published after the 1786 volume echoes these skeptical ideas. On 6 July 1786 the *Columbia Herald* carried the twenty-four-line "The Wild Honey Suckle," one of Freneau's most-celebrated pieces. Its concluding stanza suggests the possibility that the flower's life has no meaning:

From morning suns and evening dews
At first thy little being came:
If nothing once, you nothing lose,
For when you die you are the same;
The space between is but an hour,
The mere idea of a flower.

The nihilism of the thought that the flower may be "nothing" before and after its "hour" of existence complements the skepticism of the thought that the flower exists, in human terms, as a "mere idea" in the mind of the speaker, who in the earlier stanzas is at pains to point out that the flower is "hid" in a "silent dull retreat" and that he alone has perceived its "unseen" branches. Despite these solipsistic notions, the poem does not so much question the flower's independent existence as it does the human ability to comprehend that existence. The flower exists in a nonhuman, unfeeling, unknowing realm where things come and go, exist or cease to exist, meaninglessly. It is the gap between the speaker's concern for the flower and the flower's indifference to the speaker that the poem everywhere stresses. And the corollary question the poem raises, of course, is whether the speaker and the flower share the same fate. For all his percipience and feeling, the speaker suspects he may well follow the flower into blank nonbeing.

When Freneau returned from the midsummer voyage to Charleston during which the 1786 *Poems* and "The Wild Honey Suckle" appeared, he continued having trouble finding cargoes and for the next ten months hung around Philadelphia and Mount Pleasant occupying himself by publishing a few unremarkable poems. Then, in April 1787, just before he embarked for Charleston as captain of a new vessel, the *Industry*, he published one of the most impressive poems of his career. Dated 26 November 1785, or two days into his first voyage as a captain in the merchant marine a year and a half earlier, "The Departure" probably reflects the personal experience, whatever it was, that also motivated "The Hurricane" and "Lines Written at Port-

Royal." Like them, "The Departure" identifies the speaker with a time and place that unequivocally link him to Freneau, encouraging us to read the poem as a personal record. Yet once again the Freneau-speaker avoids idiosyncratic detail in favor of a symbolic mode that invites a multileveled reading. The speaker is a ship captain watching the New Jersey coast slip astern in a cold, autumn sunset, but he is also Everyman contemplating life and death.

His opening stanzas are characteristically somber. They depict the scene in terms of a breeze that "decays," a stillness like the one that "shall be at last," a "dying wave," and fields whose disappearance in the distance promises an end of human "folly." They evoke a sense of death, as though in leaving land the speaker is also leaving illusion and superficiality and confronting what it means to die. Then, in stanzas four and five, the speaker contemplates the seasonal destruction of the forests behind him on shore. The forests are "desolate," "rifled," and "bare." Songbirds and dreaming girls no longer visit them, and the "naked forms" that remain "persuasively, tho' silent, tell,/That at the best they were but drest/Sad mourners for the funeral bell." Whereas the ocean ahead connotes the unknown, inscrutable aspects of death, the forests astern connote its visible effects on nature. To see clearly is by implication to leave the delusions of land in favor of the realism of the sea: the poem is in this sense a departure intellectually from shallowness to depth.

It is also a record of departure from naive idealism to a hard-bitten stoicism. The last four stanzas open with the speaker chiding himself for his lugubriousness over nature's transience. He asserts that "fortitude" is capable of "smoothing the ocean" through force of will. Despite the inevitable disappointments of life, those with fortitude do not need fables of a "first garden" or "golden age," when "all was calm and all serene" to cling to. They can accept the fact that these fantasies have "vanish'd" and that life is an "uncertain road" where, as the poem's final three lines grimly put it, "lost in folly's idle round,/And seeking what shall ne'er be found,/We press to one abode." All that human beings can know is that they must die and that the dreams of earthly happiness they blindly pursue are vain. Yet this knowledge is enough, the poem argues, to satisfy these who are strongminded enough to endure the physical and metaphysical pain of going to sea.

His first two years as a professional ship captain hardly brightened Freneau's outlook. After returning to New Jersey in June 1787 from yet another apparently unprofitable voyage to Charleston, he had to wait six months more for another cargo to develop and, as usual, helped pass the time by writing poetry. Among his efforts were the celebrated "Lines occasioned by a Visit to an old Indian Burying Ground," published in the *American Museum* just before he sailed the *Industry* to Charleston again in late November. More like "The Wild Honey Suckle" than "The Hurricane," "Lines Written at Port-Royal," or "The Departure" in tone, "The Indian Burying Ground" is not set at a time or place that identifies its speaker directly with Freneau himself. Although it may have been inspired by personal experience, it presents a speaker more detached and impersonal than those of Freneau's more clearly autobiographical pieces. It is also more cheerful than they in seeming to concede that the human tendency to self-deception evidenced in the Indian practice of burying the dead in a sitting position is as potent as the rationalism that debunks it. The final stanza denies the validity of the "shadows and delusions" that underlie such myths, yet it also acknowledges that *reason's self* shall bow the knee" to them. Reason is no more influential or effective in human affairs than "timorous Fancy." Although the speaker prefers reason, he seems resigned to the idea that most people do not.

During the month "The Indian Burying Ground" appeared, Francis Bailey announced in the *Freeman's Journal* that a new volume of Freneau's poetry was in press. Five months later, in April 1788, *The Miscellaneous Works of Mr. Philip Freneau* was ready for sale. *The Miscellaneous Works* is different from all of Freneau's other collections in several ways. It is the only one with selections from his prose. That Freneau valued his poetry much more highly than his prose is indicated in his remark to James Madison that he decided not to include prose in his 1809 collection because "any thing I have written in that way is so inferior to the Poetry, that the contrast will be injurious to the credit of the Publication." Although he overstates the case, the self-evaluation is generally valid. While the prose of *The Miscellaneous Works* hardly discredits the book, it is nevertheless overshadowed by poems such as "The Wild Honey Suckle," "The Lost Sailor," "Lines Written at Port-Royal," "The Departure," "The Indian Burying Ground," and many others. In addition, *The Miscellaneous Works* is by far the most personal and least topical collection Freneau ever published. Its poetry and prose are almost wholly nonpolitical: even the "Philosopher of the Forest" essays, selected from the "Pilgrim" series he published in the *Freeman's Journal* in 1782-

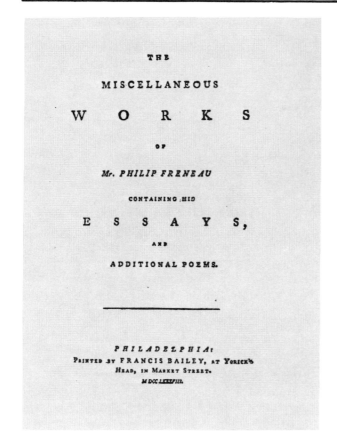

THE

MISCELLANEOUS

W   O   R   K   S

OF

Mr. PHILIP FRENEAU

CONTAINING HIS

E   S   S   A   Y   S,

AND

ADDITIONAL POEMS.

PHILADELPHIA:
PRINTED BY FRANCIS BAILEY, AT YORICK'S
HEAD, IN MARKET STREET.
M DCC LXXXVIII.

Title page for the only collection in which Freneau chose to include selections from his prose along with his poetry. In 1809 he had written to James Madison that his prose was so far inferior to his poetry "that the contrast will be injurious to the credit of the Publication."

1783, are invariably the most literary or philosophical of the original lot. Finally, *The Miscellaneous Works* is unlike his other collections in having a thematic organization.

The book opens with two long, hitherto unpublished poems whose theme is the futility of human ambition. The first, "The Pictures of Columbus," depicts the career of Columbus, the adventurer-discoverer par excellence, as a tragic series of disappointments ending in poverty, disgrace, and death. The second, "The Hermit of Saba," resembles "The Pictures of Columbus" thematically. It portrays a character whose ambition is the reverse of Columbus's in that he wishes to escape all human contact, yet whose plans fail equally tragically. These two narratives of defeat are followed by a poem titled "On the Folly of Writing Poetry" which applies the theme to what Freneau was himself doing in the book and which is in turn followed by "Ariosto's Description of the Gardens in Alcina's

Inchanted Island"—a sixteen-line sonnet that, in ironic contrast to the grim verse preceding it, paints a magic world of peace, harmony, and contentment. These four poems, separated from the next grouping of poems by twenty-five pages of prose, set the tone of stoic resignation to the pain and misfortune of life which dominates the volume.

Among the many poems that reinforce this somber theme, one appearing for the first time in print, "Elegiac Lines," is especially interesting biographically. It memorializes a young woman who has recently died during a separation from a *"Florio* far away," the name Freneau also used for the betrayer in "Lines Written at Port-Royal." Dated "Jamaica, Sept. 1784," the poem lends credence to the "Amanda" legend by serving as another point on the biographical course Freneau obscurely charts in "The Hurricane," "Lines Written at Port-Royal," and "The Departure." Written the same month as "Lines Written at Port-Royal," during Freneau's mysterious 1784 voyage to Jamaica, it hints of an involvement with a woman other than Eleanor Forman and of a reason for the voyage and for his depression at the time. Its themes of disappointment, betrayal, and death reflect the tone of the volume as a whole.

Whatever caused it, this dark period in Freneau's literary career came to an end in early 1788 at about the time he left the sloop *Industry* and took command of a much finer ship, the *Columbia.* For the next year and a half, until November 1789, when he resigned his command in Charleston to return to New York to marry Eleanor Forman and begin a decade of newspaper publishing, Freneau was almost continually busy sailing cargoes up and down the East Coast. His maritime affairs apparently left him little time for writing: he published only four poems, all minor, during the period. Then, between November 1789 and his marriage in New York on 15 April 1790, he published a series of poems that reveal a profound change in mood from the pessimistic stoicism of the mid-1780s to the optimistic deism he professed for the rest of his life.

He expressed the change at first in the oblique, personal style of the earlier ocean lyrics. Several striking poems in late 1789 and early 1790 confront a male ocean wanderer with a female, land-oriented creature toward whom the male has ambivalent feelings. In the first of these, "Hatteras," the male's feelings are not merely ambivalent but hostile. There are actually two males in the poem. The first is the Freneau-narrator, a ship captain waiting at sea off Cape Hatteras for favorable winds. The second is a poor pilot who sails a small boat out from the cape in hopes of a piloting job. Since he is bound for South Carolina, the ship captain needs no pilot but, feeling sorry for him, gives him a drink anyway. What really makes the captain pity the pilot, however, is not his poverty but his wife—a female whom the narrator captures in a single, brilliant image, waving a handkerchief to her husband from shore. Laced with hostile innuendo, the image suggests the narrator's contempt for the emotional excess of waving goodbye to a man venturing only a mile or two to sea. The captain, a true, ocean-going sailor as opposed to the land-hugging pilot, implies that the woman's overblown gesture is motivated more by a wish to supervise her husband and keep him tied to her apron strings than by love. That the captain views the woman and the shore life she represents as suffocatingly prisonlike is plain elsewhere in the poem. He speaks of the pilot as "Condemn'd" to live in "barren wilds" with his "wedded nymph, of sallow hue," a "captive" of her face. Addressing himself to the woman near the end of the poem, he insinuates, in his offer to give her husband all the liquor he has on board to "guard us from your shore," that he is less alarmed by the physical hazards of Hatteras than by the tedium and confinement she symbolizes.

A more oblique—and charming—assessment of femaleness appeared a month later in December 1789. The heroine of this poem is a land bird consistently labeled with feminine pronouns in contrast to the male captain whose ship she suddenly approaches hundreds of miles at sea. Exhaustion forces her to land in the rigging, while fear keeps making her fly away. To the captain's offer of some food she finally responds by flying down and perching nearby, but, "worn with wandering, droop'd her wing,/ And life resign'd in empty air." Freneau uses this touching, doubtless personally observed event to underline the metaphysical as well as physical gulf that he believed separated the harshly masculine, unillusioned, stoical world view he associated with the sea from the soft, irrational, comforting, shallow femaleness he associated with land. The bird-girl belongs with other females in a benevolent pastoral setting, not in the "dismal swelling scene" of "Dread Neptune's wild unsocial sea," where she has, through some pitiless freak of nature, been thrown. In titling the poem "The Wanderer," Freneau stressed the bird's unfitness for her experience by implicitly comparing her to the male sea wanderers in his poetry.

But the most revealing poem of this type that

Freneau wrote in anticipation of his marriage is one he addressed a month later in the 20 January 1790 *Freeman's Journal* directly to his bride-to-be. Although "To Cynthia" nowhere names Eleanor Forman, it includes details that put Cynthia's identity beyond doubt. Cynthia lives in "Monmouth's groves," Monmouth being the New Jersey county where the Freneau and Forman families lived. Also, the fourth stanza speaks of the narrator's being away from Cynthia "too long," from the time he started "wandering" and "sought a deeper, drearier wave" than those of the brooks where Cynthia lives. If the lines refer to the maritime career Freneau began in 1784-1785, they support the "Eleanor" legend by indicating that Freneau had established a serious relationship with her before he went to sea. Finally, the narrator says at the end of the poem that although his ship is frozen in Baltimore harbor, he is waiting for "April showers" to free him so he can sail back to Cynthia. Freneau and Eleanor Forman were married 15 April 1790.

Read as a prothalamium, "To Cynthia" is one of the most biographically and technically interesting poems Freneau ever wrote. The first five stanzas identify his future wife with the delusive and superficial landscapes or creatures he had been portraying in poems as different in purpose as "The Vernal Ague" and "The Wanderer." Cynthia is pictured as sleeping on the banks of a "shallow" stream in a pastoral setting to which the speaker is no longer able to respond. The stream, the moon, the songbirds fail to move him. His explanation for this, already cited, is that he has been away "too long," sailing "deeper, drearier" waters. Freneau seems to be trying to warn Eleanor that he is no longer the romanticist he was when they first met. The metaphor he uses to suggest to her what he is now is the one the poem ends with—his ship being frozen in ice. The hyperbole of having to wait months for the ice to melt and the veiled allusion to their April wedding indicate that Freneau is telling Eleanor that he hopes the marriage will thaw him out philosophically, emotionally, and psychologically. He appears to acknowledge the coldness of his mid-1780s philosophy, but he is still not willing to commit himself fully to the land-based values he has been repudiating for nearly a decade. He says he is "in hopes of April showers," as though he is not sure they will come, and that he is "Reflecting on the spring—and you." Beneath a seemingly trivial surface, "To Cynthia" is a serious, reflective poem that focuses many of the personal meanings Freneau's best work had been accumulating for years.

These three poems and others of the so-called

courtship group that Freneau published in 1789 and 1790 reveal that he was both consciously and unconsciously preparing himself for a radical change in his life. Nearly forty years old, scarred by experience, chilled in philosophical outlook, he decided against being the rootless, sea-going wanderer a part of him wanted to be and in favor of being the responsible, "normal" man of family and substance that his mother, his society, and he himself saw as his "proper" role. The decision involved a sharp change in philosophy. By the beginning of 1790 he had begun publishing extracts from a new poem, *The Rising Empire,* an ambitious effort to define the meaning of America. Although he never finished, he did manage during the next five months to get a half-dozen studies of different American states or regions into print, along with an introductory piece titled "Philosophical Sketch of America." In this introductory poem he for the first time unequivocally commits himself to an optimistically deistical interpretation of nature. Far from questioning the stability or meaningfulness of nature, as he had earlier, he now celebrates a transcendent "creating flame,/All worlds pervading, and through all the same!" It is the "voice" that, shaking "nature's frame," brought from the "vast depth" of the oceans that originally covered America the "new creation" of land. It is the "Almighty power" and the "great disposing power"—a vital and intelligent principle that permeates nature. For the rest of his life, Freneau held to this doctrine in everything he wrote.

An equally lasting change is visible in his poetic style and subject matter after 1790. He abandoned the personal, symbolically suggestive mode of his best work during the 1780s in favor of the more public, straightforward mode he earlier used in his political verse. When he did write figuratively, he tended toward the explicitly allegorical approach of poems such as "Epitaph On a Sea Captain that Shot Himself" (1797), "Esperanza's March" (1809), and "The Brook of the Valley" (1815). Increasingly, he favored also the explicitly philosophical style apparent in the "Philosophical Sketch of America": he included at least a score of new poems in the 1809 and 1815 collections with titles such as "Reflections on the Constitution, or Frame of Nature" (1809), "Science Favourable to Virtue" (1809), "Belief and Unbelief" (1815), and "On the Religion of Nature" (1815). All of these echoed or amplified, with minor variations, the deistical doctrines he had announced in *The Rising Empire.* He returned to public affairs with a zeal not seen in his poetry since the Revolution, first as a

Jeffersonian democrat against the Federalists and for the French Revolution in the early 1790s and again as an anti-British propagandist during the War of 1812.

Although he resumed sailing for a five-year period between 1802 and 1807, Freneau on the whole settled into the usual pattern of husband, father, and provider. During the 1790s he supported his growing family mainly as a newspaper publisher and editor. In 1790-1791 he edited the *New York Daily Advertiser* and then, at the urging of Jefferson and Madison, moved to Philadelphia to establish the *National Gazette,* one of the best-written and most-effective enterprises in early American journalism. Jefferson claimed the newspaper prevented America from "galloping fast into monarchy," and Washington was stung by it into reviling "that rascal Freneau." It served as the national organ of Republican thought until 1793, when Freneau ended it and moved his family to Mount Pleasant to live with his mother. There he sold books, helped run the farm, and in 1795 started a weekly newspaper named the *Jersey Chronicle.* During the same year he edited and personally manufactured on his Mount Pleasant printing press a new collection of his poetry, *Poems Written between the Years 1768 & 1794.*

Set in a chronological sequence that distributed Freneau's poems evenly over the twenty-seven-year period despite the fact that almost all of them had appeared since 1780, the 1795 *Poems* was apparently designed to be the "authorized" edition. Unfortunately, its misleading chronological sequence, its attempt to harmonize several of the finest poems in the 1786 and 1788 collections with his post-1790 optimism through dilutive revision, and its displacement by the 1809 *Poems* as a "final" version limit its usefulness for modern editorial purposes. Its main value lies in its improved versions of poems such as "Hatteras" and "The Wanderer" that had appeared in the newspapers since *The Miscellaneous Works.*

In 1797 and 1798 Freneau undertook his fourth newspaper venture in seven years and the last one of his career, *The Time-Piece; and Literary Companion.* Then he resumed managing the farm at Mount Pleasant until his five-year stint at sea between 1802 and 1807. *Poems Written and Published during the American Revolutionary War,* a rearranged and revised version of the 1795 *Poems* with a score of new poems added, appeared in 1809. In it, as the title indicates, Freneau tried to capitalize on his reputation as Poet of the Revolution, despite the fact that most of its poems have nothing to do with

JERSEY CHRONICLE.

[Vol. I.]   SATURDAY, May 2, 1795.   [Numb. I.]

TO THE PUBLIC.

——Inter sylvas Academi quærere verum.

HOR.

I.

THE JERSEY CHRONICLE will be publish-ed early every SATURDAY Morning;—to be forwarded at the expence of the person or persons sub-scribing, only——

II. The Editor in the Publication of this paper proposes, among other objects, to present his Readers with a complete history of the foreign and domestic events of the Times, together with such essays, re-marks, and observations as shall tend to illustrate the politics, or mark the general character of the age and country in which we live.

III. To the articles of domestic and foreign news will be added, during their sessions, a summary of the proceedings of the General Legislature of the Union, with a sketch of the debates on subjects more particu-larly interesting. A proper attention will also be paid to the proceedings of the State Legislature of New-Jersey, and such Laws and abstracts of Laws inserted as shall appear more immediately interesting to the Community.

IV. All Public Advertisements, Proclamations, notices from heads of departments, public commissioners, &c. shall be carefully republished for the benefit of such inhabitants of this and the adjacent counties as may not have an opportunity of recurring for Information of this sort to other papers published in this and the neighbouring States.

V. Mercantile, and other Advertisements will be thankfully received and inserted at as low a price as in any other Gazette of this State.

VI. A PRICE CURRENT of the most material articles of Export and Import will be inserted once a month, procured from the best authorities in New-York, New-Jersey, and Philadelphia.

VII. The terms of this paper are one DOLLAR and an half, or Twelve Shillings, Yearly: the half of which sum to be paid on the delivery of the first number, or at the conclusion of the first six months, at the option of the person subscribing: the remaining six shillings at the expiration of fifty-two numbers, or ONE YEAR.

NEVER was there a more interesting period than the present, nor ever was there a time with-in the reach of history when mankind have been so generally united in attending to the cultiva-tion of the mind, examining into the natural and political rights of nations, and emancipating themselves from those shackles of despotism which have so long impeded the happiness of the human species, and rendered the rights of the many subservient to the interests of the few.

At this time, when new Republics are forming and new Empires bursting into birth; when the great family of mankind are evidently making their egress from the dark shadows of despotism which have so long enveloped them, & are assum-ing a character suitable to the dignity of their species, the Editor seizes the opportunity to renew his efforts for contributing, in some small degree, to the general information of his fellow citizens in the present history and politics of the world.—No pains shall be spared, on his part, to procure the best, the most authentic, and earliest intelligence from every quarter, and circulating it by every method and means in his power; and to whatever parts his subscription will enable him to do it.

When it is considered that few Advertisements are reasonably to be expected in these more eastern parts of New-Jersey, the terms of subscription will appear low, and, it may be added, are within the power of almost every man who has the will and inclination to encourage literature, promote the interests, or enlarge the ideas of the rising ge-neration, and contribute to the general diffusion of knowledge among his fellow citizens.

Should the publication of The JERSEY CHRO-NICLE be suitably encouraged, the Editor will in due time enlarge the size of the sheet; but that now published on is, in his opinion, every way adequate to an experiment whether the attempt be practicable or not.

PHILIP FRENEAU.

PRINTING OFFICE at *Mount-Pleasant,*

(Near MIDDLETOWN-POINT)—May 1st, 1795.

And of AMERICAN INDEPENDENCE, XIX.

The first issue of the weekly newspaper Freneau started at Mount Pleasant

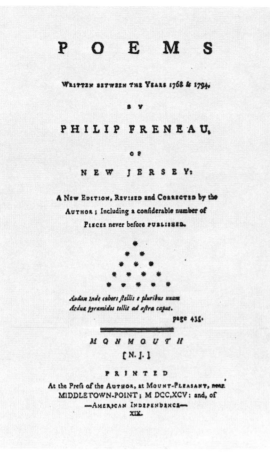

Title page for the collection that Freneau printed himself on his press at Mount Pleasant

the Revolution. It retains the chronological organization of the 1795 *Poems* but disguises the fact by separating the poems into four books whose titles imply a topical rather than chronological structure. In other ways, too, the collection creates more editorial problems than it solves. Although it offers revised, "final" versions of most of the poems Freneau had previously published, many of these versions are even further from the tone and spirit of the originals than in the 1795 *Poems*. The chief value of the 1809 *Poems* lies in its quantitative and qualitative amplification of the "Amanda" poems into one of the most interesting series Freneau created and, of course, in its two dozen new poems.

From the time of his final retirement from the merchant marine in 1807 to the publication of his final book, *A Collection of Poems, on American Affairs*, in 1815, Freneau lived with his family and his mother at Mount Pleasant, helping manage the estate and, as usual, writing poetry. Because the 1815 *Poems* contains only hitherto uncollected

work, it presents far fewer editorial problems than the 1795 or 1809 editions; yet it is also less interesting than they because it lacks all contact with the poetry of the 1780s. Competent but monotonous, its poems reveal how much Freneau's earlier tensions had relaxed. They show a poet far more emotionally and intellectually secure in his sixties than he had been in his thirties. This serenity was temporarily disturbed by his mother's death in 1816 and by the burning down of the Mount Pleasant homestead in 1818. After moving to nearby Freehold, Freneau continued to publish poems occasionally in local newspapers and to earn a modest living from his property until his accidental death in a snowstorm in 1832 at the age of eighty.

Although none of Freneau's post-1790 poems has the intellectual or emotional depth of his best earlier work, a number articulate the confidence and optimism of his deistical philosophy in fresh and effective ways. Among these is "Neversink" (1791), a joyful tribute to the range of hills fronting the Atlantic eight miles east of Mount Pleasant. In the poem, they symbolize the stability, rationality, and trustworthiness of nature. They will metaphorically never sink nor be washed away by the destructiveness Freneau imputed to all nature and especially the ocean in poems such as "The Hurricane" and "The Departure." Also noteworthy is "On Arriving in South Carolina, 1798" (1801). Here Freneau uses the topography of South Carolina to again symbolize the harmony and balance of nature. The rivers of the state are imaged as running from its fecund, western wilderness through the human civilization of its middle regions to the sea in a perfectly integrated pattern of birth, death, and rebirth. A similar sense of what Freneau had come to see as a benign cyclicality in nature pervades a number of poems inspired by his voyages between 1802 and 1807, especially "Stanzas Written at Oratava" (1804) and "On the Peak of Pico" (1815).

In conclusion, the most striking aspect of Freneau's development as a thinker was his movement away from romanticism toward deism at a time when the intellectual tides were running in the opposite direction. After idealizing and romanticizing nature as a young man, he experienced a reaction during his thirties against pastoral escapism so sharp and bitter that it led him to the brink of nihilism. This in turn gave way about the time of his marriage in his late thirties to a reaffirmation of nature's benignity, but the nature he now celebrated was empirical rather than ideal. Unconventionality marks his development as an artist also. Beginning with long, deliberately impersonal

Freneau's grave at Mount Pleasant

poems like "The American Village," "The House of Night," and "The Beauties of Santa Cruz," he then developed, as a result of complex, private experiences, an intensely personal, symbolically compressed type of short lyric rare in his own day though characteristic of most modern poetry. Because he seems to have hit upon this style somewhat unconsciously, in part as means of resolving buried tensions, he neither understood nor valued it fully and after 1790 not only abandoned it but tried to revise it out of some of his finest poems.

This indiscriminateness on Freneau's part may help explain the ambivalence and reservation modern readers express toward his art. Almost without exception, they have failed to value his best work as highly as it deserves, despite the fact that many have sensed something unusually fine in poems such as "The Hurricane," "The Wild Honey Suckle," and "The Indian Burying Ground." Yet Freneau himself was obviously in large part to blame for this state of affairs. He seems not to have recognized his own achievement; he did not sustain it past 1790 and he did not distinguish the poems in which it occurred from any other poems he wrote. In his view, his political and social verse were at least as important. It sometimes seems, in fact, that in revising his best work he tried unconsciously to hide its implications from himself—hardly a surprising psychological phenomenon, given what appears to

have been Freneau's complex psychological make-up. His best art appears thus to have been not only somewhat unintended and incidental but confined to a relatively short period of as yet inadequately explained turmoil in the middle of his life. Granting these limitations, we should nevertheless strive to see beyond them to the complex, fully human Philip Freneau who forged an original poetic mode from his heart's blood.

Biographies:

Lewis Leary, *That Rascal Freneau* (New Brunswick: Rutgers University Press, 1941);

Jacob Axelrad, *Philip Freneau: Champion of Democracy* (Austin: University of Texas Press, 1967).

References:

Nelson F. Adkins, *Philip Freneau and the Cosmic Enigma* (New York: New York University Press, 1949);

Judith Hiltner Bair, "The Newspaper Verse of Philip Freneau: An Edition and Bibliographical Survey," Ph.D. dissertation, University of Maryland, 1979;

Mary W. Bowden, *Philip Freneau* (Boston: Twayne, 1976);

Jeffrey J. Griffith, "When Vernal Suns Forbear to Roll," Ph.D. dissertation, University of Maryland, 1977;

Frank A. Lovelock III, "Philip Freneau's Wildflower: An Analysis of the 'Amanda' Poems," Ph.D. dissertation, University of Maryland, 1981;

Philip M. Marsh, *The Prose of Philip Freneau* (New Brunswick: Scarecrow Press, 1955);

Richard C. Vitzthum, *Land and Sea: The Lyric Poetry of Philip Freneau* (Minneapolis: University of Minnesota Press, 1978).

Francis Walker Gilmer
(9 October 1790-25 February 1826)

Michael A. Lofaro
University of Tennessee

BOOKS: *Sketches of American Orators. By Anonymous. Written in Washington* (Baltimore: Published by Fielding Lucas, Jr., J. Robinson, printer, 1816);

A Vindication of the Laws, Limiting the Rate of Interest on Loans; from the Objections of Jeremy Bentham, and the Edinburgh Reviewers (Richmond: Published by N. Pollard at the Franklin Press, 1820);

Reports of Cases Decided in the Court of Appeals of Virginia from April 10th 1820, to June 28th 1821 (Richmond: Published by N. Pollard at the Franklin Press, 1821);

Sketches, Essays, and Translations (Baltimore: Fielding Lucas, Jun., 1828).

OTHER: John Smith, *The True Travels, Adventures and Observations of Captaine John Smith . . . [and] The Generall Historie of Virginia, New England, and the Summer Iles . . .*, edited by Francis Walker Gilmer, 2 volumes (Richmond: Republished at the Franklin Press, William W. Gray, printer, 1819).

PERIODICAL PUBLICATIONS: "On the Geological Formation of the Natural Bridge of Virginia," *Transactions of the American Philosophical Society,* new series 1 (February 1816): 187-192;

"Reflections on the Institutions of the Cherokee Indians, from Observations Made During a Recent Visit to That Tribe: In a Letter from a Gentleman of Virginia to Robert Walsh, Jan.-June 1st. 1817," *Analectic Magazine,* 12 (July 1818): 36-56.

Francis Walker Gilmer (Bayly-Tiffany Art Museum, University of Virginia)

Francis Walker Gilmer was one of those individuals for whom the predictions of extraordinary achievement in many fields were justified but never fully realized. It was Thomas Jefferson, a critical judge, who best described the potential and growth of his friend with the chronically weak constitution.

Letter to Thomas Jefferson about contributions to establish the college that would become the University of Virginia (Alderman Library, University of Virginia)

In 1815 he said that the young lawyer "will be in future whatever he pleases in either the State, or General Government" and in 1824 that Gilmer was "the best-educated subject we have raised since the Revolution, highly qualified in all the important branches of science, professing particularly that of law."

Francis, the tenth child of Dr. George Gilmer and Lucy Walker Gilmer, was born on 9 October 1790, at Pen Park, an estate across the river from Monticello. Christened Francis Thornton Gilmer, he assumed the name of his uncle Francis Walker after the latter's death in 1806. After his father's death in 1795, Gilmer remained in Albemarle County, Virginia, until he was eighteen as a guest and ward of his neighbors. He entered William and Mary College in 1809, and by January 1811 he was practicing law in Richmond under the tutelage of William Wirt. After moving to Winchester in July 1814, he returned to Richmond in 1818 to take over Wirt's substantial practice, served as the court reporter for the Virginia Court of Appeals (1820-1821), and laid the foundation for an eminent legal career.

Gilmer's writings mirror the range of his erudition. His claim to literary fame is founded upon his *Sketches of American Orators* (1816), one of the first evaluations of the finest practitioners of

America's then widest-spread literary endeavor. His "On the Geological Formation of the Natural Bridge of Virginia," published in the *Transactions of the American Philosophical Society* in 1816, was the first treatise to suggest the still-accepted theory of its formation by erosion due to an underground stream. Gilmer's interest in Virginiana also led to his publishing the first scholarly American editions of John Smith's *True Travels* and *The Generall Historie of Virginia* (1819). Although somewhat a preromantic in taste, Gilmer, in his "Reflections on the Institutions of the Cherokee Indians" (*Analectic Magazine*, July 1818), a result of his 1815 excursion to Georgia, describes the Indians not as noble savages but as a "mixture of insensibility, vulgarity, and vice." In economics, his *A Vindication of the Laws, Limiting the Rate of Interest on Loans* (1820) was a highly esteemed rebuttal of Jeremy Bentham's classic *Defense of Usury*.

With a busy legal career and subsequent illnesses precluding further publication, Gilmer still found the time to serve as Jefferson's commissioner in selecting and securing the six professors who were to be the faculty for the University of Virginia. His successful mission to Europe lasted from May to November 1824. The extremely rough sea voyage back to New York, however, induced an illness from which he would not recover. He died on 25 February 1826, at the age of thirty-five, a little more than four months before his friend Jefferson.

Despite a short life and physical incapacities, Francis Walker Gilmer had become an accomplished lawyer, as well as an author, geologist, economist, botanist, and social scientist. Had he lived, he might have come closest to duplicating the Renaissance-like genius of Thomas Jefferson.

Letters:
Correspondence of Thomas Jefferson and Francis Walker Gilmer, 1814-1826, edited by Richard Beale Davis (Columbia, S.C.: University of South Carolina Press, 1946).

References:
Philip A. Bruce, *History of the University of Virginia, 1819-1919,* 5 volumes (New York: Macmillan, 1920-1922), I: 195, 200, 342-356; II: 25-27, 29, 38-42, 192; V: 4, 231;

Richard Beale Davis, *Francis Walker Gilmer: Life and Learning in Jefferson's Virginia; A Study of Virginia Culture in the First Quarter of the Nineteenth Century* (Richmond, Va.: Dietz Press, 1939);

Davis, *Intellectual Life in Jefferson's Virginia, 1790-1830* (1964; reprinted, Knoxville, Tenn.: University of Tennessee Press, 1972);

Michael A. Lofaro, "Francis Walker Gilmer," in *The Virginia Law Reporters Before 1880,* edited by W. Hamilton Bryson (Charlottesville: University Press of Virginia, 1977), pp. 33-46;

William Peterfield Trent, *English Culture in Virginia: A Study of the Gilmer Letters and an Account of the English Professors obtained by Jefferson for the University of Virginia,* in *Johns Hopkins University Studies in Historical and Political Science,* 7 (May and June 1889): 1-141;

Edgar Woods, *Albemarle County in Virginia* (Charlottesville, Va.: Michie Company, 1901), pp. 206-208.

Papers:
Gilmer's journal and notebook (1815?-1821?) are at Duke University. For other manuscripts see Richard Beale Davis, *Francis Walker Gilmer: Life and Learning in Jefferson's Virginia; A Study of Virginia Culture in the First Quarter of the Nineteenth Century* (Richmond, Va.: Dietz Press, 1939), pp. 392-393.

Alexander Hamilton

Laura Henigman
Columbia University

BIRTH: Nevis, British West Indies, 11 January 1755(?), to Rachel Fawcett Lavien and James Hamilton.

EDUCATION: King's College, New York (admitted 1773).

MARRIAGE: 14 December 1780 to Elizabeth Schuyler; children: Philip, Angelica, Alexander, James Alexander, John Church, William Stephen, Eliza, Philip.

DEATH: New York, New York, 12 July 1804.

SELECTED BOOKS: *A Full Vindication of the Measures of the Congress, from the Calumnies of their Enemies; In Answer to A Letter, Under the Signature of A.W. Farmer. Whereby His Sophistry is exposed, his Cavils confuted, his Artifices detected, and his Wit ridiculed; In A General Address to the Inhabitants of America, And A Particular Address to the Farmers of the Province of New-York* . . . (New York: Printed by James Rivington, 1774);

The Farmer Refuted: or, A more impartial and comprehensive View of the Dispute between Great-Britain and the Colonies, intended as a Further Vindication of the Congress: In Answer to a Letter from A.W. Farmer, intitled A View of the Controversy between Great-Britain and her Colonies . . . (New York: Printed by James Rivington, 1775);

A Letter from Phocion to the Considerate Citizens of New-York, On the Politicks of the Day (New York: Printed by Samuel Loudon, 1784);

A Second Letter from Phocion to the Considerate Citizens of New-York. Containing Remarks on Mentor's Reply (New York: Printed by Samuel Loudon, 1784);

The Federalist: A Collection of Essays, Written in Favour of the New Constitution, as agreed upon by the Federal Convention, September 17, 1787, 2 volumes, by Hamilton, John Jay, and James Madison (New York: Printed & sold by J. & A. M'Lean, 1788; revised and corrected edition, New York: Printed & sold by George F. Hopkins, 1802);

Alexander Hamilton, 1791; portrait by Charles Willson Peale
(Independence National Historical
Park Collection, Philadelphia)

A Defence of the Treaty of Amity, Commerce, and Navigation, Entered into between The United States of America & Great Britain, as it has appeared in the papers under the Signature of Camillus, by Hamilton, Jay, and Rufus King (New York: Printed & sold by Francis Childs & Co. and sold by James Rivington, 1795);

Letters of Pacificus: Written in Justification of the President's Proclamation of Neutrality. Published originally in the Year 1793 (Philadelphia: Printed by Samuel H. Smith, 1796);

Observations on Certain Documents Contained in No. V & VI of "The History of the United States for the Year 1796," in which the Charge of Speculation against Alexander Hamilton, Late Secretary of the

Treasury, is Fully Refuted. Written by himself (Philadelphia: Printed by John Bloren for John Fenno, 1797);

Letter from Alexander Hamilton, Concerning the Public Conduct and Character of John Adams, Esq., President of the United States (New York: Printed by George F. Hopkins for John Lang, 1800);

An Address, to the Electors of the State of New York written by Hamilton, but signed by other Federalists (Albany: Printed by C. R. & G. Webster, 1801);

The Examination of the President's Message, at the Opening of Congress December 7, 1801 (New York: Printed & published at the Office of the *New-York Post*, 1802);

Propositions of Col. Hamilton, of New York, In Convention for Establishing a Constitutional Government for the United States . . . (Pittsfield: Printed by Phineas Allen, 1802).

Collections: *The Papers of Alexander Hamilton,* 27 volumes, edited by Harold C. Syrett and Jacob E. Cooke (New York: Columbia University Press, 1961-1978);

The Law Practice of Alexander Hamilton, 2 volumes, edited by Julius Goebel (New York: Columbia University Press, 1964, 1969).

SELECTED PUBLIC DOCUMENTS: U.S. Treasury Department, *Report of the Secretary of the Treasury to the House of Representatives, Relative to a Provision for the Support of the Public Credit of the United States, in Conformity to a Resolution of the Twenty-First Day of September, 1789. Presented to the House on Thursday the 14th Day of January, 1790 . . . [The Support of Public Credit]* (New York: Printed by Francis Childs & John Swaine, 1790);

U.S. Treasury Department, *December 13, 1790. In obedience to the Order of the House of Representatives, of the Ninth Day of August last, requiring the Secretary of the Treasury to prepare and report, on this Day, such further Provisions as may, in his Opinion be necessary for establishing the Public Credit . . . [The Second Report on the Further Provisions Necessary for Establishing Public Credit . . .]* (New York: Printed by Francis Childs & John Swaine, 1790);

U.S. Treasury Department, *The Secretary of the Treasury having attentively considered the Subject referred to him by Order of the House of Representatives of the fifteenth Day of April last, relative to the Establishment of a Mint, most respectfully submits the Results of his Enquiries and Reflections [Report on a Mint]* (New York: Printed by Francis

Childs & John Swaine, 1791);

U.S. Treasury Department, *Report of the Secretary of the Treasury of the United States, on the Subject of Manufactures. Presented to the House of Representatives, December 5, 1791* (New York: Printed by Childs & Swaine, 1791; London: Printed for J. Debrett, 1793);

U.S. Treasury Department, *Sundry Statements Respecting the Several Foreign Loans, Made under the Authority of the United States . . . [Report on Foreign Loans]* (New York: Printed by Childs & Swaine, 1793);

U.S. Treasury Department, *Report of the Secretary of the Treasury, Read in the House of Representatives of the United States, January 19th, 1795; Containing a Plan for the Further Support of Public Credit . . . [Final Report on the Public Credit]* (Philadelphia: Printed by John Fenno, 1795).

Alexander Hamilton is justly remembered for his creative and energetic contributions to important American institutions in the founding era—to the Constitution, both at the framing convention and in the explanatory *The Federalist,* and to an enduring financial system through his administration as first Secretary of the Treasury. Always acknowledged as one of the giants among the founders, Hamilton is recognized as the designer of vigorous, practical, and forward-looking institutions. But Hamilton's achievements, while appreciated, nevertheless often provoke regret. The democratic principles of the new nation were perhaps better embodied by his more philosophical opponent, Thomas Jefferson; the Federalist program perhaps represented a compromise of those principles with a world of recalcitrant and diffuse regional interests. Hamilton's reputation as an antirepublican, even monarchist, spokesman for privileged banking interests was in force in his own day, which saw its share of political factionalism, intrigue, and mud-slinging. Mixed contemporary opinion has its counterpart in modern ambivalence about Hamilton: was he the hero of the American system, or, as Noah Webster put it, its "evil genius"? Was he the embodiment of lofty principles, or of pragmatic compromise? That ambivalence has its counterpart, too, in the circumstances surrounding Hamilton's birth and death, for the stories of both have achieved near legendary status, and both are infused with irregularities and mysteries that may redound to their subject's credit or to his dishonor. His illegitimate birth and unfortunate early circumstances meant he was a self-made man, but perhaps he remained, as John Adams called him, just a "bastard brat." Throughout his life he was preoccupied with honor, but the circumstances surrounding his duel with Aaron Burr may suggest only that Burr, who for the sake of honor shot him in the early morning hours of 11 July 1804, was merely the greater scoundrel.

Scholars have long considered 1757 the year of Hamilton's birth, but the earlier date of 1755, though it does take away some of his legendary precocity, seems more probable. Hamilton's mother, Rachel Fawcett Lavien of the British West Indies, had left her abusive husband in 1750. She soon began living with James Hamilton, a younger son of a Scotch family and an immigrant to the islands. The two never married, but Rachel bore two children, James and Alexander. The elder James Hamilton abandoned the family in 1765; Rachel died in 1768; and Lavien successfully sued to deprive James and Alexander of the meager estate their mother had left, in favor of her one legitimate son. Whatever his correct birth date, Alexander Hamilton was left without family support at a young age.

Sometime before his mother's death, Hamilton had begun to work as a clerk at Beekman and Cruger, a trading firm in Christiansted, Saint Croix. There he continued, running the business during Nicholas Cruger's six-month absence in New York in 1771-1772. Hamilton's letters to his employer during this period reveal the business acumen that the boy had already acquired. Meanwhile, he had completed some miscellaneous literary productions, including a letter, published in the *Royal Danish American Gazette,* describing a hurricane. The returned Cruger and other islanders evidently found Hamilton's writings, together with his proven aptitude for business, sufficiently impressive that they agreed to finance his education in the northern colonies. Accordingly, later in 1772 he sailed for the North American continent.

Cruger and other of Hamilton's island friends had connections in the New York business community and with the College of New Jersey (later Princeton University). Hamilton stayed with a family in Elizabethtown, New Jersey, for the winter, preparing for entrance at college. In the spring of 1773, he applied to John Witherspoon for admission to Princeton. Witherspoon was impressed with Hamilton's preparation but was unable to grant the young man's request to be admitted with permission to progress through the program at a faster than usual pace. Though he had told one of his sponsors that he preferred the "more republican" Princeton, Hamilton in 1773 entered New York

City's King's College (later Columbia University), which admitted him on his own terms.

At King's, Hamilton evidently considered studying medicine, took part in some debating activities, and made some lifelong friends. Also during this time his first major piece of writing was published. With tensions over British taxation rising, the First Continental Congress had recommended a colonial boycott on trade with Britain. A Tory pamphlet attacking the measure, *Free Thoughts on Congress* by A.W. Farmer (Samuel Seabury), was circulated in New York. Hamilton responded with *A Full Vindication of the Measures of the Congress* (December 1774) and then, to a second pamphlet by Seabury, with *The Farmer Refuted* (February 1775). These two works contain many of the current rebel arguments: warnings against slavery to Parliament, references (especially in *The Farmer Refuted*) to natural rights, insistences on the colonies' independence from a Parliament in which they do not have representatives. Most interesting in light of Hamilton's later writings is his examination of the colonies' place in the British empire. As in his subsequent works, Hamilton's guiding principle for understanding human affairs is self-interest. His comprehensive conception of a mercantilist empire as a large functioning unit with interdependent parts leads him to the conclusion that the profitable American colonies have a good deal of bargaining power within the empire. It is in their interest to boycott; it is in Britain's interest to meet their demands. In *The Farmer Refuted,* he goes even further. If the British do not settle peacefully and instead send troops, the colonies could resist coercive force (by means of skirmishing tactics similar to the program that Washington did in fact use) and could win political independence. As a practical matter, Hamilton concludes, the boycott makes sense.

These practical arguments aside, however, it is notable that in these early writings Hamilton is already thinking continentally. The functional unit, made up of interdependent parts, that makes most sense to him is not the British empire or the separately independent states, but the united American colonies. He argues that the disparity of interests between the colonies and Britain means that the colonies would be better off alone and that the variety of common economic and political interests among the states means that together they should form an interdependent, national unit. Thus, contrary to the Farmer's charge, there is no conflict between the long-range interests of farmers and merchants, of northern states and southern states. It is abundantly clear that the nation Hamilton

Title pages for the pamphlets in which Hamilton responded to Tory Samuel Seabury

imagines is defined by continental boundaries.

Hamilton followed in June 1775 with an essay in the *Rivington's New-York Gazetteer*, "Remarks on the Quebec Bill," which attacked Britain's attempt to retain the loyalties of Canada by allowing it to remain Catholic. The war soon took Hamilton away from pamphleteering, however—and from his formal studies at King's College. Over the next year-and-a-half he trained with a volunteer militia and then was appointed captain of the Provincial Company of Artillery in New York. His company crossed to New Jersey with General Washington and played active roles in the battles of Trenton and Princeton in December 1776 and January 1777. During this time, the young captain came to the favorable attention of the commander in chief. On 1 March 1777 Hamilton was appointed aide-de-camp to Washington with the rank of lieutenant colonel and served on Washington's staff for the next four years.

As a member of the general's staff, Hamilton was at the center of war activity. He knew Lafayette and Von Steuben. He was present during the crisis in September 1780 that exposed Benedict Arnold's treasonous plan to betray West Point; his account,

in a letter to his friend John Laurens, of that discovery and of the subsequent execution of British Major John André is a detailed "inside" report. Washington entrusted him with important military missions, letting him act for him to bring some of the uncooperative American generals into line. Hamilton also assumed primary responsibility for the general's correspondence. In these letters and in others he wrote in his own name to members of the New York Committee of Correspondence, he recorded much important army activity during the war.

His experience in the war seemed to confirm his belief that self-interest would, in the absence of a central coordinator, have consequences detrimental to the whole. The costs to the American side occasioned by generals who would not cooperate with Washington excited his indignation. Deeply aware of the organizational and maintenance problems facing the poorly financed and sometimes near-mutinous continental army, he wrote a report to Washington on how the army might be reorganized. He also believed that Congress as well as the army had to be responsible for giving collective efforts, such as the war, more coherence. He be-

Captain Alexander Hamilton's March 1776 payroll record for his New York artillery company (Manuscript Division, Library of Congress)

came particularly incensed when Congressman Samuel Chase of Maryland used privileged information about the upcoming supply needs of the army to speculate in flour to his private advantage. Over the signature of Publius, Hamilton sent three letters to John Holt's *New York Journal* in October and November 1778, roundly condemning Chase. The letters are sarcastic, expressing outrage at Chase's betrayal of the role of disinterested, large-minded statesman.

Despite his indignation though, Hamilton did believe that self-interest was natural and inescapable; more was required for orderly government than individual good behavior. He early became convinced that much of the maladministration of the war could be attributed to the failure of the Articles of Confederation (drawn up in 1777 and ratified in 1781) to provide Congress with power to raise money, except at the pleasure of the states. While still in the army, Hamilton began his lifelong campaign for a strong and aggressive government. He wrote several private letters to friends in public office urging that Congress act more decisively by

enlisting the aid of moneyed men to establish a national bank and by obtaining a foreign loan in order to finance the war. In a letter to Congressman James Duane (September 1780), he deplored Congressional inactivity, suggesting, as an incipient loose constructionist, that that body should exercise its discretionary powers more boldly, and take financial measures that were, though unpopular with some local interests, essential to the conduct of a long-range, united continental enterprise. With the Articles of Confederation not yet even ratified, he suggested a call for a new convention that would reorganize the government along more practical principles.

Hamilton argued these ideas before the public some time later, in "The Continentalist," a series of six essays published in the *New York Packet* from July 1781 to July 1782. In the first three numbers he argued for increasing the power of the federal government over the states, pointing to the problems of prosecuting the current war with no way for the federal government to raise money. He devoted the last three to explaining that central regulation and

The Surrender of Lord Cornwallis at Yorktown, 19 October 1781; *painting by John Trumbull, circa 1828. Hamilton is standing fourth from right (Yale University Art Gallery. Trumbull Collection. 1832.4).*

promotion of trade were desirable and necessary. Invoking the Greek city-states as bad models, he painted a scenario in which independent, only loosely confederated states guard their local interests jealously and fight among themselves, competing with each other for trade to their collective detriment. He urged his readers to think continentally, putting aside interests that are merely immediate and local: "Unless we can overcome this narrow disposition and learn to estimate measures by their general tendencies, we shall never be a great and happy people, if we remain a people at all." These ideas are central to the nationalist program that came into force, largely through Hamilton's efforts, with the adoption of the Constitution. At this early stage in his public career, Hamilton was already arguing them fairly cogently, but it would take several more years for a majority of political leaders to come around to his program.

Despite his consistency in public affairs, Hamilton's personal life by this time had undergone significant changes. In early 1780, while spending the winter with the army at Morristown, he had met Elizabeth Schuyler, daughter of General Philip Schuyler; he and Elizabeth were married in Albany on 14 December of that year. His alliance with the prominent and wealthy upstate New York Schuyler family would prove valuable to his political career. And by the time he published the first "Continentalist" essay he had left Washington's staff. He had long been anxious to see more direct military action, but Washington had repeatedly denied his aide's requests to be released for field command. In February 1781, Hamilton fancied himself insulted by a reproof from the general and gave notice of his resignation. Despite the general's attempts at reconciliation, Hamilton left Washington's "family" in April. He was granted the command of a battalion, which he led in October in the decisive Yorktown campaign.

Hamilton returned to Albany and his wife immediately after the Yorktown victory. At home he studied law intensively and was admitted to the New York bar after only a few months, in July 1782. As Continental Receiver of Taxes for New York from May to November of that year and then as a delegate from New York to the Continental Congress, Hamilton struggled with the problem of getting the states to provide funds requested by the national government. The issue of continental financing was becoming critical, as the continental army, fearful that they would not be paid, came near mutiny in the early months of 1783 and finally, in June, marched on Philadelphia to threaten Con-

Elizabeth Schuyler Hamilton, 1790 (Library of Congress)

gress, forcing its evacuation to Princeton, New Jersey. Hamilton was active in dealing with this crisis in Congress and continued, during this period, to call in private letters and in proposals to the New York legislature and to the Continental Congress for a new convention that would design a more capable central government.

Having served his one-year term in Congress, Hamilton returned to New York and in November 1783 opened a law office on Wall Street. During the next two years he engaged in a number of activities as a private citizen. He was instrumental in the establishment of the Bank of New York in 1784, and the following year he was a founding member of the Society for the Manumission of Slaves. In his law practice he defended the property rights of Loyalists, an unpopular cause in light of postwar patriotism. In an exchange in the New York press, Hamilton under the pseudonym Phocion condemned proposed anti-Tory legislation, urging "the Considerate Citizens of New York" to avoid the temptation, "in times of heat and violence, to gratify momentary passions" and abridge individual rights. In his briefs for *Rutgers v. Waddington*, an important test case for anti-Loyalist legislation in which Hamilton represented the Tory defendant,

John Adams, Robert Morris, Alexander Hamilton, and Thomas Jefferson conferring at the Continental Congress
(Library of Congress)

he added the nationalist argument that the law depriving his client of the property privileges in question contradicted the terms of the peace settlement with Britain, which as national law must take precedence over local statutes.

Over the next few years, Hamilton continued to make suggestions that a new convention be called. In 1786 he went as a delegate from New York to the Annapolis convention, a meeting suggested by the state of Virginia to discuss possibilities for trade among the states. The Annapolis convention suffered from slight attendance, but the delegates present agreed to return to their respective states with a recommendation that another convention be held in Philadelphia the following May to consider the reorganization of the government. Having meanwhile been elected to the New York Assembly, Hamilton, along with two antifederalist colleagues, was appointed a delegate to that convention.

The deliberations in Philadelphia through the summer of 1787 resulted in the drafting of the Constitution. Hamilton's contributions to the convention were few. Notes taken by Madison and others show that he made an extended speech on the floor on 17 June sounding his old theme of the necessity of centrally concentrated power and a balancing of interests against each other. Some of his specific proposals exceeded by far the centralizing measures finally adopted by the convention—life terms for the executive and senators and an absolute veto for the executive, for example. These proposals, together with memories of his antirepublican language, later provided his enemies with fuel for their accusations that he was a monarchist sympathizer. Most of the Constitution, however, was drafted in Hamilton's absence. He spent six weeks that summer in New York City on private business (soon after his departure from Philadelphia the rest of his delegation left too, thus depriving New York State of a vote at the convention). When Hamilton returned to the convention, the records of floor proceedings show that he served on the Committee of Style, spoke to urge that every delegate sign the finished document, and, unable in the absence of the rest of his own delegation to represent his state officially, signed as an individual, "Mr. Hamilton from New York."

The next step was ratification by the states, and it was in anticipation of strong opposition in the New York legislature that Hamilton produced the writings for which he is best remembered, his contributions to *The Federalist*. There was already a debate about the new Constitution in the press among various pseudonymous writers. Hamilton, James Madison, and John Jay agreed to cooperate in a series of essays for the New York press, all over the same pseudonym, Publius. The first letter from Publius, authored by Hamilton, appeared on 27 October; these papers continued to appear in various newspapers at the rate of several per week until number 77 was published on 4 April 1788. In May, all the essays, together with eight more previously unpublished, were collected in a two-volume set as *The Federalist*.

In the first letter, Hamilton announced the plan for the series. Publius would discuss "The utility of the Union to your political prosperity—The insufficiency of the present Confederation to preserve that Union—The necessity of a government at least equally energetic with the one proposed, to the attainment of this object—The conformity of the proposed Constitution to your new State constitution—and lastly, The additional security which its adoption will afford to the preservation of that species of government, to liberty, and to property." The letters follow this schedule conscientiously. Since Jay fell sick soon after the beginning of the series his contributions were minimal. The authorship of some of the numbers is in dispute, but Hamilton probably wrote about two thirds. He and Madison collaborated closely, probably sometimes exchanging drafts, and in any event, their separate contributions were not substantially divergent. The well-known Federalist number 10, written by Madison, is only one of the several early numbers that argues Hamilton's long-held belief in the necessity of coordinating competing interests and factions under one central government. Later numbers are devoted to explaining the merits of specific measures provided in the Constitution, with Madison writing most of those outlining the distribution of powers between the federal and state governments and the structure of the federal legislature, and Hamilton writing those explaining and justifying the proposed measures pertaining to the army, taxation, and the executive and judiciary departments. To forestall public fears of a repressive central government, Hamilton emphasizes that the strict separation of powers and the express provisions in the Constitution to pay federal officials out of the federal treasury are ways of making the

Title page for Elizabeth Hamilton's copy of volume two of the pro-Constitution essays by Alexander Hamilton, James Madison, and John Jay (Rare Book Division, Library of Congress)

branches independent of each other as well as of the states, and so less liable to corruption. Thus self-interest would be channeled in ways that would protect rather than threaten the public good. Regarding the "vigorous" executive, which had always been a part of the Hamiltonian plan, he adds that despite antimonarchist fears circulating among New Yorkers, the proposed federal executive has more in common with the governor of New York than with the king of England. Another important feature of Hamilton's contributions is his outlining of the principle of judicial review, which established the courts as the final authority for adjudicating the laws.

Although Publius does answer specific anti-federalist arguments and occasionally questions the motives of those making them, he does not attack specific people in vitriolic terms, as, say, the earlier Publius (Hamilton in the anti-Chase letters) did, or as Catullus (Hamilton in the 1792 *Gazette of the United States*, in a newspaper war with Jefferson) would. For the most part, he observes the pledge in Hamilton's Federalist number 1 to maintain a decorous and moderate tone, in keeping with the importance of the issue and with the knowledge that reasonable and wise men may disagree on the most important questions. Hamilton and Madison, in lawyerly fashion, present arguments for the defense which are thorough and comprehensive and which appeal self-consciously, for the most part, to reason and "self-evident fact."

The Federalist probably had little influence on the New York ratifying convention in Poughkeepsie. Hamilton led the federalist minority there in a six-week-long fight that resulted in ratification on 27 July 1788. The antifederalist forces, perhaps persuaded by Hamilton's effective speeches, were finally convinced to ratify the Constitution by the threat of disunion with the other states, and probably most of all by the news, on 21 June, that the requisite nine states had already ratified. *The Federalist*, however, was recognized immediately by contemporaries—including those as divergent in their feelings about Alexander Hamilton as George Washington and Thomas Jefferson—as important commentary on the Constitution. The identity of the authors soon became known, and the essays were reprinted several times during Hamilton's lifetime and numerous times thereafter. Recognized as elucidating the intentions of some of the most active framers of the Constitution, it has continued to influence interpretations of the document.

The next phase of Hamilton's career was devoted to putting the new government in place. In April 1789 Washington became President, and in September he chose Hamilton as the first Secretary of the Treasury. Hamilton assumed the vigorous leadership role that he had long espoused for the executive branch, setting forth in a series of reports to the House of Representatives proposals for establishing the nation's finances on a stable footing. Although there was some opposition in the House to allowing the Secretary of Treasury to play such an active role in the formation of financial policy, many of Hamilton's proposals were eventually adopted.

Hamilton submitted the first of these papers, *The Support of the Public Credit*, to the House in January 1790. Sound credit, he argued, was essential to the new nation; the best way to restore confidence in its credit would be to meet its financial obligations faithfully, in keeping with sound and

George Washington's nomination of Hamilton as Secretary of the Treasury (National Archives)

reputable financial practices. In accordance with this goal, the secretary chose sides in two controversial issues. First, in redeeming securities, he urged that there should be no discrimination made between those that had been bought by speculators and those that had remained in the hands of original investors. Although there was some sentiment against speculators and sympathy for people who had been forced to sell their securities at a loss, Hamilton argued that such discrimination, since it would not honor market principles, would be unfair and would undermine confidence in government securities. Second, Hamilton proposed that the federal government assume the war debts of the states. To arguments that such a measure would be unfair to those states that had already paid their debts, Hamilton replied that only through assumption would the public debt be discharged equitably and efficiently, and in a manner that would instill confidence in the government's credit. By redefining the debt as national and considering the states as one unit, the measure would link the states even more closely together. Finally, to finance the public debt, the secretary proposed another foreign loan to pay back outstanding principal and a duty on liquors and teas.

Hamilton argued that his plan would benefit not only creditors, speculators, and merchants, but the interrelated interests of the whole nation. However, the new government had begun to divide permanently into adversarial factions, and his centralizing proposal met with sharp criticism among antifederalist forces in Congress, with Virginia providing much of the leadership. Hamilton's collaborator on *The Federalist,* James Madison, now led the opposition in the House. The nondiscrimination and assumption measures became law only after the Federalists agreed that the permanent seat of the government would be located on the Potomac.

In spite of antifederalist opposition Hamilton continued to propose—and Congress continued to approve—measures designed to establish stable and favorable financial institutions. His 13 December 1790 report, *The Second Report on the Further Provisions Necessary for Establishing Public Credit [Report on a National Bank],* shows his knowledge of European and American banking principles and experience. Hamilton had to counter a certain amount of general suspicion of banks and began his report with a review of the advantages of such financial institutions: they increase the capital available, they can provide emergency funds for the government, and they facilitate the payment of taxes. He tries to dispel the fears that banks result in the loss of specie and that they cause both unnatural inhibitions and dangerous overextensions of trade. He then outlines a plan for organizing the bank, including partial government shareholding.

The proposed bank engendered heavy opposition, again led by Madison, especially on the grounds that it was beyond the powers of the government to create a corporation. The bill establishing the bank did pass, however, and Washington signed it in February 1791, after receiving a paper from Hamilton defending its constitutionality under the implied powers clause. Hamilton followed with a document usually called *Report on a Mint* (January 1791), which was largely adopted the next year in the Mint Act, which established a mint in Philadelphia and a United States currency with a decimal system based on a bimetallic standard.

Hamilton, then, as his financial proposals consistently show, believed strongly in taking deliberate measures to encourage a vital and growing economy. He had become personally involved in the Society for the Establishment of Useful Manufactures, which was intended to promote manufacturing by private means. His *Report on the Subject of Manufactures* (5 December 1791) was perhaps the most comprehensive and far-reaching official statement of the economy he envisioned. In this extensively researched report, which drew on information gathered from businessmen throughout the country, Hamilton recommended that Congress take measures to encourage the development of domestic manufactures, chiefly by means of public duties. Prosperity need not be reckoned on an agrarian model alone; manufacturers, as well as farmers, were producers, and contributed substantially to the national wealth. Full-scale manufacturing would introduce into society an effective division of labor between farmers and artificers. This division would be economical, would provide extra means of employment and incentive for the industrious, including immigrants, and would help people develop special differentiated talents. Manufactures would encourage the development of efficient machinery and would allow the proliferation of enterprises, which would, in turn, provide a sound basis for the national economy. Nor would all these changes lead to mere arithmetic increases in national wealth. Manufacturing could change the character of society, even "creating, in some instances, a new, and securing, in all, a more certain and steady demand for the surplus value of the soil."

Hamilton was not, as is sometimes claimed, an incipient capitalist—his protectionist scheme put forth in the *Report on the Subject of Manufactures* had more in common with the older, mercantilist system than with a free capitalist economy. But his vision of a growing and changing society, consisting of heterogeneous but interdependent elements developing new products with the help of government intervention in trade, provides an instructive illustration of Hamilton's philosophical divergence from his southern, antifederalist opponents. Their agrarian ideal of a more stable, homogeneous society of self-sufficient, independent farmers brought with it a corresponding suspicion of the centralizing tendency of an active federal government. Thomas Jefferson, the man who was Washington's Secretary of State and who would be Hamilton's lifelong political enemy, was the most thorough exponent of this view. The rivalry between the two approaches to government was played out in the early national period in the factional disputes, both in the Cabinet and in Congress, between the two men and their supporters, the Federalists and antifederalists (eventually called Republicans), and debate over

Alexander Hamilton, 1792; portrait by John Trumbull (New York Chamber of Commerce)

Hamilton's financial program specifically did much to solidify this opposition. On the subject of encouraging manufactures, Congress leaned on the Jeffersonian side, rejecting the suggestions in Hamilton's *Report on the Subject of Manufactures.* Meanwhile, for his part, Hamilton continued fulfilling his duties as Secretary of the Treasury in the active, aggressive manner that he felt was appropriate for a national agency. Throughout 1793 and 1794, Republicans in Congress, suspicious of such executive activism, kept him busy producing documentation of his department's transactions. In response to Congressional directives, he produced a series of reports, beginning with the *Report on Foreign Loans* (3 January 1793). Not satisfied with this accounting, in spring 1793 the Republicans, prodded by Jefferson, tried to impeach him for improper disbursement of funds.

Although these political disputes reflected real philosophical differences between the parties, the arguments were also often merely factional in origin, and quickly became personal as well. A vehement newspaper war in 1792 demonstrates how acrimonious the factions had become. This drawn-out exchange began in July, when Hamilton, signing himself T. L., sent a letter to John Fenno's

Gazette of the United States, a paper generally known to be supported by the Federalist administration and to which Hamilton, at various times, gave private financial assistance. In his letter, Hamilton pointed out the uncomfortable coincidence that the Jeffersonian *National Gazette* was edited by the poet Philip Freneau, who had been appointed official French translator by the State Department. Hamilton charged that Jefferson was, in effect, using government funds to pay not for a clerk for his department but for a sympathetic newspaper. An exchange in the two gazettes continued through the end of the year, Hamilton signing himself variously as Amicus, Fact, Catullus, Metullus, A Plain Honest Man, and other names. He suggested that Jefferson had been only a lukewarm supporter of the Constitution and that his opposition to Hamiltonian economics only confirmed his disloyalty to the government. He accused Jefferson of duplicity in continuing to serve an administration whose policies he opposed, choosing instead to subvert them through concealed patronage of a newspaper campaign. And Hamilton attacked the integrity of the image Jefferson cultivated. In one of the papers signed Catullus (*Gazette of the United States,* 29 September 1792), he wrote, "Mr. Jefferson has hitherto been distinguished as the quiet, modest, retiring philosopher; as the plain, simple, unambitious republican . . . but there is always a *'first time'* when characters studious of artful disguises are unveiled; when the visor of stoicism is plucked from the brow of the epicurean; when the plain garb of Quaker simplicity is stripped from the concealed voluptuary; when Caesar *coyly refusing* the proferred diadem, is seen to be Caesar rejecting the trappings, but tenaciously grasping the substance of imperial domination."

After the French Republic declared war on Britain, Holland, and Spain on 1 February 1795, foreign policy provided more fuel for the conflict. In some ways the party disagreements resolved themselves into whether the United States should have closer ties with France or with England, who both made claims on American allegiance. In the Cabinet, Jefferson, sympathetic to France, opposed the plan to issue the Proclamation of Neutrality, and after its issue (22 April 1793) Hamilton felt constrained to defend the proclamation in the press. In July he published seven letters as Pacificus in the *Gazette of the United States.* Referring to article two of the Constitution, Pacificus wrote that the President had properly exercised an executive function by issuing the proclamation. American neutrality did not violate the 1778 Treaty of Amity and Commerce with France (the basis for French

and American cooperation during the American Revolution), which was explicitly defensive rather than offensive. Moreover, as even the Francophiles admitted, neutrality was clearly in America's best interests. To make a foreign policy decision on any other basis, such as sympathy for liberty, or a "self-denying and self-sacrificing gratitude on the part of a Nation . . . is to misconceive or mistake what usually are and ought to be the springs of National Conduct"—especially since France, in aiding the American Revolution, acted from no love of liberty but from her own interest in weakening Britain. Though Pacificus is generally methodical in his arguments, he does suggest that those opposing the proclamation are disloyal to the United States. Hamilton followed this series with two numbers in the *American Daily Advertiser* (January-February 1794), signed Americanus, in which he denounced French interference in American politics and suggested that given the excesses of the French Revolutionary government, the French cause was not necessarily the "cause of liberty" anyway.

At Jefferson's urging, Madison, as Helvidius, replied in defense of French interests. Meanwhile, though, the conduct of Citizen Genêt, the French ambassador, was embarrassing even the American Francophiles, many of whom agreed with Hamilton that Genêt's aggressive attempts to promote the French war effort against Britain intruded improperly into American politics. In August, Hamilton sent nine letters, signed No Jacobin, to the *American Daily Advertiser* condemning Genêt for outfitting a privateer, *The Little Democrat,* in American ports, in violation of the laws of nations and of the 1778 treaty with France. Most offensive to Hamilton and his party was Genêt's reported intention to appeal for French interests, over the head of the neutrality-proclaiming President, to the American people. In letter number 8 (26 August), Hamilton derides Genêt's "total ignorance of the genius and character of the citizens of this country." Whatever they may do in France, American republicanism is "sober and enlightened . . . rational and orderly," decorous and observant of the authority of elected representatives. He hints again that Genêt's defenders (Jefferson among them) have, at best, misplaced loyalty that could be dangerous.

Hamilton was soon to resign from the Treasury. In 1794, he joined the militia to put down the Whiskey Rebellion, a western protest against the excise tax on liquors. On 19 January 1795 he submitted his *Final Report on the Public Credit* to the House, in which he included a summary of Treasury Department business during his administration as well as a number of recommendations to further secure the public credit. His resignation became official on 31 January, and he returned to his law practice. Hamilton was not yet finished with state business, however. He would serve the Federalist administration again in several important ways.

The other side of the controversy over American relations with France was that Jefferson and his party suspected Hamilton and the Federalists of being too friendly with England. Much of the Republican criticism of Federalist foreign policy surfaced in connection with Jay's Treaty. Even after the Proclamation of Neutrality, both Britain and France continued to interfere with American commerce, each seizing American ships that were engaged in trade with the other. Moreover, the American settlement with Britain at the close of the American Revolutionary War had not fully resolved the question of British rights on the American continent. A continued British presence in the Western Hemisphere, then, was challenging American trading privileges, both on the seas and in the interior. To address the tensions caused by this interference, tensions which seemed likely to lead to war, in 1794 the Federalist administration sent John Jay to England to work out another settlement. As a result of his negotiations, Britain agreed that it would finally evacuate its military outposts in American territory. The United States, for its part, agreed to make good debts from the Revolutionary period as yet unpaid to British merchants. Although some restrictions on American trade remained in place, Britain agreed to curtail some of its interference with the American West Indian trade and to make restitution for seized American ships (though not for impressed American seamen).

When the terms of the Jay Treaty were made public in 1795, the Republicans charged that Jay had made too many concessions to the British. Hamilton sent remarks on the treaty to Washington in July and later that month began submitting letters called "The Defence" to the New York press. Thirty-eight papers signed Camillus appeared over the next six months, first in the New York *Argus, or Greenleaf's New Daily Advertiser,* and then in the New York *Herald; A Gazette for the Country.* Rufus King contributed ten numbers while Hamilton wrote the rest.

Charging that the opponents of the treaty want only to discredit the Federalist administration and eventually to elect Jefferson President, Camillus chides his adversaries for having unreasonably high expectations of the treating process. Although the terms of the treaty are not quite as favorable to

the United States as they might be, they do answer, he says, the major American concerns. They protect American commerce and above all avoid war, the most important objective of any international negotiation. Reviewing the provisions one by one, he finds that they are not so bad anyway. Finally, he defends the treaty against the old charge of unconstitutionality. The treaty, as law of the land, is on a par with legislated statutes, and so no provisions it makes can be said to encroach on legislative prerogatives.

Hamilton continued to be called upon to aid Washington's administration, even to help Washington draft his Farewell Address. He maintained an influence over President Adams's Cabinet officers throughout most of Adams's administration. And, to defend the Federalist party's basically pro-British, anti-French policies, he continued to publish anonymous, increasingly strident denunciations of France. In "The Answer," which appeared in the New York *Minerva* in December 1796, he outlined the ways in which French ministers had tried to interfere in American politics. He continued the theme in a series of six papers called *The Warning,* printed in February and March of 1797 in the *Gazette of the United States & Philadelphia Daily Advertiser.* Seven numbers of *The Stand* were published in the New York *Commercial Advertiser* in April 1798 (around the time the XYZ Affair, in which French diplomats suggested to an American delegation that France could be bribed to stop seizing American ships, was made public). Signing himself Titus Manlius, Hamilton condemns, in near hysterical terms, "the disgusting spectacle of the French Revolution" and French ambitions for "universal empire." He defends the Federalist administration policy generally and suggests again the treachery of certain American leaders sympathetic to France.

As Hamilton's increasing anti-French—and anti-Republican—invective shows, he was becoming, along with many political leaders, more and more involved in the now clearly defined rivalry between the two parties. No longer in administration, no longer charged with shaping new institutions and policies in quite the same way, Hamilton devoted his energies for the rest of his life to wrestling with opponents over political power as much as over particular issues. His major writings over his last years reflect that change.

Most notorious of these writings is Hamilton's 1797 response to a smear campaign against him. In 1792, rumors that the Secretary of the Treasury was using special department information to engage in improper speculations had come to the attention of several officials, including James Monroe. The group confronted Hamilton with the evidence and went away, apparently satisfied with his explanation, promising him that they would not reveal anything that they had learned. Then, in 1797, James Callendar, a journalist associated with the Republican faction, printed the charges in *The History of the United States for 1796: Including a Variety of Interesting Particulars Relative to the Federal Government Previous to that Period.* Hamilton, furious with the apparent breach of trust, came near dueling with Monroe and was forced to publish his answer: *Observations on Certain Documents Contained in No. V & VI of "The History of the United States for the Year 1796," in which the Charge of Speculation Against Alexander Hamilton, Late Secretary of the Treasury, is Fully Refuted. Written by himself.* In this so-called Reynolds Pamphlet he reveals what he had told the delegation five years earlier. "The charge against me is a connection with one James Reynolds for purposes of improper pecuniary speculation. My real crime is an amorous connection with his wife. . . ." James Reynolds was not his agent in improper speculation, he says, but his blackmailer. Acknowledging the grief caused to his wife and family by "so painful an indecorum" as the present publication, he makes a meticulous disclosure of the details of the affair and dealings with the two Reynoldses in order to defend himself "against a more heinous charge." The defense, while frank, is also spirited. Taking passing swipes at Jefferson, Hamilton attributes the publication of the charges to political intrigue, "the spirit of Jacobinism," which would resort to calumny to discredit a political opponent. He refers to the charges contemptuously: Would a department head interested in speculating deal in such relatively small sums as the payments to Reynolds? Would an official abusing his office for his own economic benefit be likely to have the difficulty Hamilton did in raising the sums Reynolds demanded? He appends relevant letters, referring to them in his narrative as exhibits to show that the couple actually colluded to entrap him for purposes of blackmail. To what seems to be a full, detailed disclosure of an embarrassing private lapse in order to protect his integrity as a public servant, the author signs, not some Roman cognomen, but Alexander Hamilton.

The Reynolds Pamphlet did not satisfy his enemies, who claimed that he had merely compromised himself further by revealing the affair without really clearing himself of the corruption charges. Some of them suggested that the story of the adultery was itself a fabrication, that Hamilton

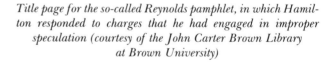

OBSERVATIONS

ON

CERTAIN DOCUMENTS

CONTAINED IN NO. V & VI OF

" THE HISTORY OF THE UNITED STATES
FOR THE YEAR 1796,"

IN WHICH THE

CHARGE OF SPECULATION

AGAINST

ALEXANDER HAMILTON,

LATE SECRETARY OF THE TREASURY,

IS FULLY REFUTED.

WRITTEN BY HIMSELF.

PHILADELPHIA:

PRINTED FOR JOHN FENNO, BY JOHN BIOREN.

1797.

Title page for the so-called Reynolds pamphlet, in which Hamilton responded to charges that he had engaged in improper speculation (courtesy of the John Carter Brown Library at Brown University)

himself wrote the supposed letters from the Reynoldses documenting the sexual affair and blackmail, ineptly disguising them as the productions of less literate writers. Whether honest disclosure or elaborate literary hoax, the Reynolds pamphlet did Hamilton's career no good.

An even more damaging event was his open break with the Adams administration. In 1798 Hamilton was promoted to major general, and in an atmosphere of increasing anti-French hysteria he was given the responsibility to prepare a provisional army, to be commanded by General Washington in the event of a war with France. In 1800, Adams, realizing the extent of Hamilton's influence over his cabinet, removed some cabinet officers and disbanded the army. Hamilton, though insulted, claimed that these events had nothing to do with his disenchantment with Adams as a presidential candidate in 1800. At that time electors could not distinguish their votes for the presidential candidates from their votes for the vice-presidential candidate; the highest vote taker simply became president and the next-highest, vice-president. To avoid a tie between its two candidates, the majority party had to agree to withdraw some votes from the vice-president. Hamilton, perhaps hoping to erode Adams's support among Federalists if not to throw the election to Pinckney, had been suggesting instead that the Federalists support Adams and Pinckney, the vice-presidential candidate, equally in 1800 and said privately that he would prefer Pinckney as President. He wrote, for private circulation among a limited number of Federalist leaders, his *Letter from Alexander Hamilton, Concerning the Public Conduct and Character of John Adams, Esq., President of the United States* (1800). The letter reviews Adams's public career. Conceding that Adams is unquestionably a patriot who has rendered important services to his country, Hamilton nevertheless calls him a political liability, "a man of an imagination sublimated and eccentric; propitious neither to the regular display of sound judgment, nor to steady perseverance in a systematic plan of conduct." His vanity, inconsistency, and impulsiveness, Hamilton says, have, among other things, compromised America's dignity in her strained relations with France and made Adams unfit to be President. After lengthy condemnation and ridicule, Hamilton denies that he is a British partisan or that his motives for opposing Adams are personal. He adds, strangely, that he does not mean that the Federalists should not support Adams for President.

The Republican press—possibly through the agency of Aaron Burr—obtained a copy of the pamphlet and printed excerpts. Hamilton felt forced to authorize publication of the whole, and it came out in October, just as electors were being selected. By publicly airing both substantive and petty divisions among the Federalists, Hamilton damned the party, as it were, out of its own mouth, providing the Republicans with significant campaign material. Both Federalist candidates lost the election of 1800, although Hamilton's letter was by no means the decisive factor. It did, however, divide and embarrass the Federalist party, and it did much to end Hamilton's political influence. The Adams pamphlet had few defenders, even among Hamilton's partisans.

Despite this experience, Hamilton would continue to be interested in elections. The 1800 election resulted not only in the defeat of the Federalist ticket, but in an electoral tie between Jefferson and Burr, the Republican candidates. Hamilton wrote a series of letters to Federalists, urging them to be sure to support Jefferson in the tie-breaking vote in the House. Burr had been Hamilton's political rival in New York, and Hamilton had long before conceived an enmity for him. In his letters now, he called Burr an American Catiline, unscrupulous, ambitious, "bankrupt beyond redemption." Even Jefferson was "by far not so dangerous a man and he has pretensions to character." Given Hamilton's loss of influence by this time, his effect on Jefferson's election is doubtful; but his hatred for Burr had clearly developed to its maturity.

Though no longer in power, Hamilton was asked by New York Federalists to write a campaign document for the New York State gubernatorial election, in which Stephen Van Rensselaer was running against Republican George Clinton. His *An Address, to the Electors of the State of New York* (1801) was published and signed by state Federalists, not including himself. The address covers much old Federalist ground: it attacks Republican sympathies for France, ridiculing the pretensions of the French government to republicanism; it accuses the Republicans of being enemies to the Constitution; it defends the Federalist program, including the Jay Treaty and Hamilton's own funding system; it accuses the Republicans of responsibility for an unpopular direct tax. The by-now-established American two-party system is called no less than "a contest between the tyranny of jacobinism, which confounds and levels every thing, and the mild reign of rational liberty."

Hamilton's last major undertaking for the press was *The Examination of the President's Message, at the Opening of Congress December 7, 1801*, on Jefferson's first annual message to Congress. Eighteen numbers were published between December 1801 and April 1802 in the *New-York Evening Post*, which had been founded recently by Hamilton. Signing himself Lucius Crassus, Hamilton criticized Jefferson's proposals on the issues of war, revenue, immigration, and, most of all, the judiciary system. Jefferson's suggestions that most internal taxes could be abolished and that the number of judgeships could be reduced would, Hamilton emphasized, decrease the public confidence. Attacking Jefferson's seeming fiscal conservatism, he maintained that any excess funds could be used to finance public transportation and communications projects and that a certain amount of federal bureaucracy was necessary to enforce the laws well. Quoting *The Federalist*, he defended the courts against the encroachments of the legislative branch threatened by the proposed repeal of the Judiciary Act of 1801. Once again, he heaped ridicule on his old enemy. Jefferson's proposals were the work of a "pigmy mind," the "schemes of a Philosopher projector" who imagines "that to govern well, is to amuse the wondering multitude with sagacious aphorisms and oracular sayings."

Reduced to something like a political hack writer, Hamilton continued to publish in the *Post*, though his old influence was gone. Meanwhile, Vice-President Burr had lost the favor of the Republican party. Dropped from the 1804 presidential ticket, he attempted to run for governor of New York with Federalist support. An outraged Hamilton did his best to thwart Burr's chances, using whatever influence he had left to remind New York politicians of Burr's "irregular, insatiable ambition," charging him with designing to play the parties against each other.

Burr was soundly defeated, and having heard of Hamilton's remarks, demanded acknowledgment and satisfaction. Hamilton refused to retract or acknowledge his remarks. Stiff notes passed between the two men, and they met in a duel on 11 July 1804, at Weehawken, New Jersey. Hamilton had reason to oppose dueling—his eldest son, Philip, had been killed in a duel only two years before. But he himself had come close to dueling several times previously, and scrupulosity for his honor had led both to his impetuous break with Washington in 1781 and to the publication of the Reynolds pamphlet. Now, he resolved that the encounter with Burr was unavoidable. A few days before the duel, he wrote in his private papers that his "animadversions on the political principles, character, and views of Col. Burr" had been "entertained with sincerity, and uttered with motives and for purposes which might appear to me commendable." They had proceeded from principle, and he could neither deny nor retract them. He also recorded his intention not to fire. On the morning of the duel, Hamilton's pistol did go off, though his partisans maintained that it discharged accidentally, after he had been hit. He lingered on in pain for another day, dying in New York on 12 July. Burr was unhurt.

What was Hamilton defending? Both had by now been repudiated by their respective parties, so the encounter loses at least some of its political significance. Hamilton's early death perhaps was not deeply felt, in material ways, by the nation. But his extensive contributions to American institutions, his ability to imagine a new country, have left a lasting impression.

Bibliography:
Paul Leicester Ford, *Bibliotheca Hamiltoniana. A List of Books Written By, or Relating To, Alexander Hamilton* (New York: Knickerbocker Press, 1886).

Biographies:
Nathan Schachner, *Alexander Hamilton* (New York & London: Appleton-Century, 1946);

Louis M. Hacker, *Alexander Hamilton in the American Tradition* (New York: McGraw-Hill, 1957);

Broadus Mitchell, *Alexander Hamilton*, 2 volumes (New York: Macmillan, 1957, 1962);

John C. Miller, *Alexander Hamilton: Portrait in Paradox* (New York: Harper, 1959);

Jonathan Daniels, *Ordeal of Ambition: Jefferson, Hamilton, Burr* (Garden City: Doubleday, 1970);

Robert A. Hendrickson, *The Rise and Fall of Alexander Hamilton* (New York: Van Nostrand Reinhold, 1981);

Marie B. Hecht, *Odd Destiny: The Life of Alexander Hamilton* (New York: Macmillan, 1982).

References:
Bower Aly, *The Rhetoric of Alexander Hamilton* (New York: Columbia University Press, 1941);

Robin Brooks, "Alexander Hamilton, Melancton Smith, and the Ratification of the Constitution of New York," *William and Mary Quarterly*, third series 24 (July 1967): 339-358;

Ora B. de Vilbiss Davisson, "The Early Pamphlets of Alexander Hamilton," *Quarterly Journal of Speech*, 30 (April 1944): 168-173;

Linda Grant De Pauw, *The Eleventh Pillar: New York State and the Federal Constitution* (Ithaca: Cornell University Press, 1966);

Albert Furtwangler, "Strategies of Candor in the *Federalist*," *Early American Literature*, 14 (Spring 1979): 91-109;

Gilbert L. Lycan, *Alexander Hamilton and American Foreign Policy: A Design for Greatness* (Norman: University of Oklahoma Press, 1970);

Philip Marsh, "Hamilton's Neglected Essays, 1791-1793," *New-York Historical Society Quarterly*, 3 (October 1948): 280-300;

Clinton Rossiter, *Alexander Hamilton and the Constitution* (New York: Harcourt, Brace & World, 1964);

Gerald Stourzh, *Alexander Hamilton and the Idea of Republican Government* (Stanford, Cal.: Stanford University Press, 1970);

Leslie Wharton, *Polity and the Public Good: Conflicting*

Theories of Republican Government in the New Nation (Ann Arbor, Mich.: UMI Research Press, 1980);

William and Mary Quarterly, Hamilton Bicentennial Number, third series 12 (April 1955).

Papers:

The most substantial collection of Hamilton's papers is housed in the Library of Congress. Smaller collections are held by the Columbia University Libraries, the American Antiquarian Society, and the New York Public Library.

Lemuel Hopkins
(19 June 1750-14 April 1801)

Michael Robertson
Princeton University

BOOKS: *The Democratiad. A Poem, in Retaliation, for the "Philadelphia Jockey Club"* (Philadelphia: T. Bradford, 1795);

The Guillotina, or A Democratic Dirge, a Poem . . . (Philadelphia: Published by Thomas Bradford, 1796);

The Political Green-house, for the Year 1798 . . ., by Hopkins, Richard Alsop, and Theodore Dwight (Hartford: Printed by Hudson & Goodwin, 1799);

The Echo, with Other Poems, by Hopkins, Richard Alsop, Theodore Dwight, Mason F. Cogswell, and Elihu Hubbard Smith (New York: Printed at Porcupine Press by Pasquin Petronius [Isaac Riley], 1807);

The Anarchiad: A New England Poem, by Hopkins, David Humphreys, Joel Barlow, and John Trumbull, edited by Luther G. Riggs (New Haven: Published by Thomas H. Pease, 1861).

Lemuel Hopkins was a prominent physician and one of the group of poets known as the Connecticut Wits. Born in Waterbury, Connecticut, the son of Stephen and Dorothy Talmadge Hopkins, he studied medicine under two Connecticut physicians, Dr. Jared Potter of Wallingford and Dr. Seth Bird of Litchfield, and began his own practice in Litchfield in 1776. After serving briefly in the Revolutionary War, he moved to Hartford in 1784, where he practiced medicine for the remainder of his life.

Widely respected in Connecticut as an advocate of progressive medical techniques and as a leading specialist in the treatment of tuberculosis, Hopkins received an honorary M.A. from Yale in

Lemuel Hopkins, 1793; portrait by John Trumbull (Yale University Art Gallery. Gift of Miss Elizabeth Sill. 1914.1)

1784 and was one of the founders of the Connecticut Medical Society.

Hopkins was as well known for his unusual appearance and eccentric manners as for his medical skill. His contemporaries described him to Samuel Goodrich as "long and lank, walking with spreading arms and straggling legs. His nose was long, lean, and flexible; his eyes protruding, and his whole expression a strange mixture of solemnity and drollery." Gifted with a prodigious memory, he could quote at length from any book he had read. His conversation was direct and sardonic, and his actions could be as blunt as his talk. When the sister-in-law of a tubercular patient showed Hopkins some "fever powders" she had bought from a local quack, Hopkins mixed together twelve packets of the supposedly powerful medicine and drank them off in one dose.

Hopkins did much of his writing in collaboration with other members of the loosely constituted literary circle known as the Connecticut Wits, whose first and best-known work was *The Anarchiad,* published in twelve installments in the *New-Haven Gazette* and the *Connecticut Magazine* in 1786-1787. During this period of national uncertainty prior to the framing of the Constitution, Hopkins and collaborators David Humphreys, Joel Barlow, and John Trumbull supported the Federalist movement for a strong national government, attacking mob violence (exemplified by Shays's Rebellion) and paper money as the most serious threats to the Union. A mock-epic modeled on Pope's *Dunciad* and on *The Rolliad* (1784; an English collaborative satire on Pitt and his followers that took its name from John Rolle, a member of Parliament), *The Anarchiad* combines satiric thrusts at Daniel Shays and various political figures with praise of Washington and patriotic homage to the Union.

After 1789 the Connecticut Wits concentrated their venom on the French Revolution and the free-thinking, politically radical ideas it represented. *The Political Green-house, for the Year 1798* (1799), which Hopkins wrote with Richard Alsop and Theodore Dwight, champions Britain in its war against France and labels the opponents of the Federalist party "Jacobins." The poem attacks both Thomas Jefferson and Joel Barlow, a former associate of the Wits who went to Europe, became a friend of Thomas Paine, and went "From preaching Christ, to Age of Reason."

Hopkins also collaborated with Richard Alsop, Theodore Dwight, Mason F. Cogswell, and Elihu Hubbard Smith on *The Echo,* a satiric verse series that appeared in the *American Mercury* and the *Connecticut Courant* from 1791 to 1805. Starting in 1795 he wrote an annual New Year's poem for the *Courant,* satirically reviewing the political events of the preceding year. Hopkins was noted for having the sharpest pen of any of the Connecticut Wits, and two of his satires that were reprinted in book form are zestfully abusive. In *The Democratiad* (1795; originally published in 1795 as number eighteen of *The Echo*) and *The Guillotina* (Hopkins's 1796 New Year's poem), both directed against Jefferson and the Democrats, Hopkins portrays the Democrats as politically seditious and morally corrupt, praises Alexander Hamilton, and ends each poem with a paean to George Washington.

A few short, nonpolitical satiric poems by Hopkins appeared in various periodicals. Two satires on medical charlatans, "Epitaph. On a Patient Cured by a Cancer Quack" (*Connecticut Courant,* 1785) and "Patent Address" (*Connecticut Courant,* 1796), are as sardonic as one would expect from the physician who took a dozen packets of medicine to expose a tuberculosis quack. In "The Hypocrite's Hope" (*New-York Magazine,* 1793), Hopkins urges a program of good works over an empty Calvinist doctrine of faith. As a young man Hopkins was an admirer of Voltaire and other "infidel philosophers," but by 1784, when Ethan Allen published *Reason the Only Oracle of Man,* a critique of the Bible, Hopkins had settled into firm religious convictions; his "On General Ethan Allen" (*American Mercury,* 1786) calls Allen "the seer of Antichrist."

Hopkins's writings were never collected, and it is impossible to be certain of his exact contributions to the many anonymous writings produced by the Connecticut Wits. Apparently little concerned with literary fame, he employed his satiric talents in the service of the Christian and Federalist ideals that he believed were necessary for the survival of the fledgling United States.

References:

Charles W. Everest, *The Poets of Connecticut* (Hartford: Casc, Tiffany & Burnham, 1843);

Howard W. Haggard, "The First Published Attack on Perkinism: An Anonymous Eighteenth Century Poetical Satire," *Yale Journal of Biology and Medicine,* 9 (December 1936): 137-153;

Leon Howard, *The Connecticut Wits* (Chicago: University of Chicago Press, 1943);

Vernon Louis Parrington, Introduction to *The Connecticut Wits,* edited by Parrington (New York: Harcourt, Brace, 1926);

W. R. Steiner, "Dr. Lemuel Hopkins," *Johns Hopkins Hospital Bulletin,* 21 (January 1910): 16-27;

James Thacher, *American Medical Biography* (Boston: Richardson & Lord, 1828; republished, New York: DaCapo Press, 1967), pp. 298-304.

David Humphreys
(10 July 1752-21 February 1818)

William K. Bottorff
University of Toledo

BOOKS: *A Poem Addressed to the Armies of the United States of America,* as a Gentleman of the Army (New Haven: Printed by T. & S. Green, 1780);

The Glory of America; or Peace Triumphant over War: A Poem (Philadelphia: E. Oswald & D. Humphreys, 1783);

A Poem on the Happiness of America: Addressed to the Citizens of the United States (London, 1786; Hartford: Printed by Hudson & Goodwin, 1786);

Select Poems by Col. Humphreys, Aid-de-Camp to Gen. Washington (Philadelphia: Printed by Mathew Carey, 1787);

An Essay on the Life of the Honorable Major-General Israel Putnam: Addressed to the State Society of Cincinnati in Connecticut (Hartford: Printed by Hudson & Goodwin, 1788);

Poems by Col. David Humphreys, Late Aid-de-Camp to His Excellency General Washington (Philadelphia: Printed by Mathew Carey, 1789);

The Miscellaneous Works of David Humphreys (New York: Printed & sold by Hodge, Allen & Campbell, 1790; revised, with differing contents, New York: Printed by T. & J. Swords, 1804);

A Poem on Industry. Addressed to the Citizens of the United States of America (Philadelphia: Printed for M. Carey, 1794);

Considerations on the Means of Improving the Military for Public Defence; In a Letter to His Excellency Governor Trumbull (Hartford: Printed by Hudson & Goodwin, 1803);

A Valedictory Discourse, Delivered before the Cincinnati of Connecticut, in Hartford, July 4th, 1804, at the Dissolution of the Society (Boston: Printed by Gilbert & Dean, 1804);

A Discourse on the Agriculture of the State of Connecticut, and the Means of Making It More Beneficial to the State: Delivered at New-Haven, on Thursday, 12th September, 1816 (New Haven: Printed by T. G. Woodward, 1816);

Letters from the Hon. David Humphreys, F.R.S. *to the Rt. Hon. Sir Joseph Banks . . . Containing Some Account of the Serpent of the Ocean, Frequently*

David Humphreys, circa 1808-1810, portrait by Julian Story (Yale University Art Gallery. Gift of Mrs. David Humphreys. 1830.1)

Seen in Gloucester Bay (New York: Published by Kirk & Mercein, 1817);

The Anarchiad: A New England Poem, by Humphreys, Joel Barlow, John Trumbull, and Lemuel Hopkins, edited by Luther J. Riggs (New Haven: Published by Thomas H. Pease, 1861).

OTHER: Elihu Hubbard Smith, ed., *American Poems, Selected and Original,* includes poems by Humphreys (Litchfield, Conn.: Printed by Collier & Buel, 1793).

David Humphreys was a leading member of the Connecticut Wits, often called the first American school of poets. During the Revolution he attained a reputation as Washington's confidant and was a patriotic poet whose verses were widely read. After the war he wrote a popular, inspirational biography of the Revolutionary War general Israel Putnam. He probably originated the plan for *The Anarchiad,* a series of poems that he wrote with fellow Connecticut Wits Joel Barlow, John Trumbull, and Lemuel Hopkins. Satirizing "faction" and advocating the kind of strong central government that soon emerged from the Constitutional Convention, the poems appeared in the *New-Haven Gazette and Connecticut Magazine* in 1786-1787. In 1793 his works figured prominently in the contents of *American Poems, Selected and Original,* the first anthology of American poetry, edited by Elihu Hubbard Smith, one of the younger Connecticut Wits. Humphreys's revised *Miscellaneous Works* (1804) is one of the earliest, nearly complete collections of the writings of an American author.

Born in Derby, Connecticut, the son of the Reverend Daniel Humphreys and Sarah Riggs Bowers Humphreys, David Humphreys had the usual classical schooling of his time and earned a B.A. at Yale in 1771 and an M.A. in 1774. While at Yale Humphreys met the other major Connecticut Wits, John Trumbull, Timothy Dwight, and Joel Barlow. These men—all considered important poets in their time—encouraged Humphreys toward literary pursuits. (Humphreys organized a literary society at Yale, the Brothers in Unity.) His next course, however, was toward a brief teaching career; he was master at a school in Wethersfield, Connecticut, from 1771 to 1773; and he tutored the children at Philipse Manor, New York, from 1773 to 1776.

With the outbreak of the Revolution, Humphreys joined a New York militia regiment in 1776, later rising in the Sixth Connecticut to the rank of brigade major. He then became, successively, aide to Generals Putnam (1778), Greene (1780), and Washington (June 1780 to the end of hostilities), attaining the rank of lieutenant colonel. He not only served with Washington until 1783, he remained a part of the first president's "family" through Washington's lifetime, living much of the time at Mount Vernon.

Among Humphreys's early poems were those written to encourage the Revolutionary effort and perhaps to enhance his own chances for promotion. "An Elegy on the Burning of Fairfield," for example, condemns the barbarity of British troops and celebrates the dignity of the American people. (He had seen the town's ruins in the fall of 1779.) Humphreys distributed the poem widely and included it

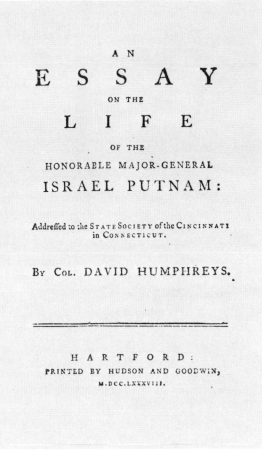

Title page for Humphreys's popular, inspirational biography of one of the generals under whom he served during the Revolution (courtesy of the John Carter Brown Library at Brown University)

in his *Select Poems* (1787) along with "Mount Vernon," an ode "Inscribed to General Washington."

In his biography of Putnam (written in 1788) Humphreys celebrates the archetypal Minute Man and foreshadows some of the romantic motifs of Charles Brockden Brown and Cooper. He had not only known Putnam but had interviewed many others on the subject. Like his earlier collection, *Poems* (1789) includes a variety of neoclassical expressions, ranging from the political and the satirical to the love poem. Finally, his *Miscellaneous Works* (1790) is a full summary of the career of one of our earliest men of letters (this is even more true of the 1804 version). Included are a number of sonnets, a form seldom written in by his contemporaries.

In 1784 Humphreys was appointed by Congress as secretary to the committee to negotiate commercial treaties in Europe, working chiefly under Jefferson. Humphreys's conservative (Federalist) political convictions had not yet fully formed, and he and Jefferson were friends until 1801, when the third president recalled him from his post overseas, ending his diplomatic career. In 1786 he was back in Connecticut, as a member of the state's General Assembly. He was then made colonel of a United States detachment to suppress Shays's Rebellion (one of the phenomena satirized in *The Anarchiad*) in 1787. He spent long periods at Mount Vernon, held other appointments, and was in 1791 named the first United States minister to Portugal. In 1796 he was made minister to Spain, where he took an interest in sheep breeding, and he eventually introduced the Merino breed into Connecticut, improving the American production of high-quality wool. His essay on the breeding of Merino sheep appeared in *The Miscellaneous Works*. In 1797 he married Ann Frances Bulkeley, the daughter of an Englishman who did business at Lisbon. He was a very sociable minister and a good entertainer, at times declaiming his own poems to his guests.

Then, in 1801, he was replaced when Jefferson became president. Back in Connecticut, during the Embargo, Humphreys had the satisfaction of seeing his own woolen and cotton mills thrive. His Humphreysville was an early example of the paternalistic New England mill town. As he grew older, honors came to him from Brown University and Dartmouth College and through membership in the British Royal Society. He was commissioned a brigadier general in the Connecticut militia, in reaction to the War of 1812. In 1815 he wrote and produced a play, *The Yankee in England;* the actors were the boys and young men who worked in his mills. When he died at New Haven he was a respected citizen, merchant, and writer, one of the revered men of the Revolution.

Humphreys was thought of as a significant poet in his lifetime, though no one considered him a great poet. In later times his works have been occasionally reprinted or anthologized, but he has receded into being thought of as a stiff versifier, a somewhat pretentious man, and a very minor figure. His life and writings, especially the 1804 *Miscellaneous Works*, form interesting matter for study by those who would understand the culture of early America.

References:

William K. Bottorff, "Humphreys' 'Ode to Laura': A Lost Satire," *Early American Literature Newsletter*, 2 (Fall 1967): 36-38;

Bottorff, Introduction to *The Miscellaneous Works of David Humphreys (1804)*, edited by Bottorff (Gainesville: Scholars' Facsimiles & Reprints, 1968);

Edward M. Cifelli, *David Humphreys* (Boston: Twayne, 1982);

Leon Howard, *The Connecticut Wits* (Chicago: University of Chicago Press, 1943);

Frank L. Humphreys, *Life and Times of David Humphreys, Soldier—Statesman—Poet, "Belov'd of Washington,"* 2 volumes (New York: Putnam's, 1917);

Julian Mason, "David Humphreys' Lost Ode to George Washington, 1776," *Quarterly Journal of the Library of Congress*, 28 (1971): 29-37.

Papers:

The largest holdings of Humphreys's papers are at the Connecticut Historical Society, the Massachusetts Historical Society, the Historical Society of Pennsylvania, and the Beinecke Rare Book and Manuscript Library at Yale University.

Joseph Brown Ladd

(7 July 1764-2 November 1786)

Georgia Elliott
Princeton University

BOOKS: *An Essay, on Primitive, Latent, and Regenerated Light* (Charleston: Printed & sold by Bowen & Markland, 1786);

The Poems of Arouet (Charleston: Printed by Bowen & Markland, 1786);

The Literary Remains of Joseph Brown Ladd, M.D. Collected by His Sister, Mrs. Elizabeth Haskins of Rhode Island. To Which Is Prefixed, A Sketch of the Author's Life by W. B. Chittenden (New York: H. C. Sleight, Clinton Hall, 1786).

OTHER: *Select Poems on Various Occasions, Chiefly American, Among Which Are Several Wrote by the Celebrated Doctor Ladd,* 2 volumes (Boston: Printed & sold by S. Hall, 1787);

Mathew Carey, ed., *The Beauties of Poetry, British and American . . . ,* includes poems by Ladd (Philadelphia: From the press of M. Carey, 1791);

Carey, ed., *The Columbian Muse, A Selection of American Poetry From Various Authors of Established Reputations. . . ,* includes poems by Ladd (New York: Printed by J. Carey for M. Carey, Philadelphia, 1797).

Joseph Brown Ladd is noteworthy chiefly as a transitional figure. As eighteenth-century classicism withered and the preromantic movement blossomed in Europe, Ladd was receptive to the new trends. With Philip Freneau and Timothy Dwight, he was one of the earliest American writers to be influenced by the English preromantic poets. His popularity in his own time attests to the changing tastes of the American public.

Born the eldest son of Sarah Gardner Ladd and William Ladd, a man of modest means who served as a soldier in the Revolutionary War and as a member of the Rhode Island legislature, Joseph received little formal schooling, but he precociously educated himself with the available books. At ten years of age he had his first poem, "Invocation to the Almighty," published in the *Newport Mercury.* His continuing fascination with books led his father to apprentice him in a printing office in Newport when Ladd was fourteen. There, in addition to his duties, he indulged his adolescent whims by printing his own satiric verses. One such broadside so offended its target, the leading clergyman Dr. Samuel Hopkins, that Dr. Hopkins had Ladd removed from his position by his father.

For the next four years Ladd pursued his studies, especially in the classics, literature, philosophy, and science, under the guidance of Dr. Isaac Senter, who prepared him for his chosen career of medicine. During this period Ladd wrote much of his poetry, primarily love poems addressed to "Amanda," his poetic name for an orphan heiress whose guardians would not permit marriage between the devoted pair. This poetry, which he signed with the name Arouet, suffers from the sentimental excesses of youthful verse.

After completing his studies, Ladd went to South Carolina in 1784 to practice medicine. By all accounts he was a social, literary, and professional success in Charleston. On 4 July 1785 he gave an address on the American Revolution to the governor and other state officials, only the second commemoration of the Declaration of Independence ever to be held in the nation. Excerpts were printed in the *Charleston Columbian Herald.* For the next year and a half, Ladd published poetry and articles in the *Columbian Herald* with regularity and established a firm reputation as a man of letters. His collected poems, *The Poems of Arouet* (1786), sold almost three hundred copies by subscription. In November 1786, only twenty-two years old, he died of wounds suffered in a duel over a frivolous matter.

Ladd should be acknowledged for the role he played in bringing new literary currents into the popular culture. In 1785-1786 he published more than seventy pieces, both poetry and prose, in the *Columbian Herald.* Although he wrote traditional verses in heroic couplets, he also strove to be modern and learned. He published a modernization of one of Thomas Chatterton's Rowley poems and several poems adapted from Ossian. Other poems show the influence of the preromantics Thomas Gray, William Collins, and Oliver Goldsmith. His sentimental love poems to Amanda anticipate the Della Cruscan school with which his poetry is frequently compared.

Eager to impress his countrymen with his new ideas, he brashly published in the *Columbian Herald* of 2 September 1785 an attack on the style of Samuel Johnson in his "Critical Remarks on Dr. Johnson." Similarly in another edition of the *Columbian Herald*, he added a critique of Pope's translation of Homer to the presentation of his own translation of Homer. In many of his articles he paraded the names of important intellectuals such as Newton, Locke, Bacon, and Voltaire, among many others, in a showy display of his knowledge.

Ladd reached the peak of his success with his poetry on nationalistic themes. His most popular poem was the "Prospect of America" (1785), a poem in the tradition of Hugh Henry Brackenridge and Philip Freneau's *A Poem, on the Rising Glory of America* (1772). He even rewrote the book of Psalms into his "new American version." Unfortunately, he died too young to leave a mature body of work, and what remains has more historical significance than literary merit.

References:

Lewis Leary, "A Forgotten Charleston Poet: Joseph Brown Ladd, 1764-1786," *Americana*, 36 (October 1942): 571-588;

Leary, "Ossian in America," *American Literature*, 14 (November 1942): 305-306;

"Literary Odds and Ends," *Proceedings of the American Antiquarian Society*, new series 49 (October 1939): 276.

John Lathrop, Jr.

(13 January 1772-30 January 1820)

John R. Holmes
Kent State University

BOOKS: *An Oration, written at the request of the officers of the Boston Regiment and intended for delivery, October 20, 1794* (Boston: Printed By E. W. Weld & W. Greenough, 1795);

An oration, pronounced July 4, 1796, at the Request of the Inhabitants of the Town of Boston, in Commemoration of the Anniversary of American Independence (Boston: Printed & sold by Benjamin Edes, 1796);

An oration, pronounced on the 4th day of July, 1798, at the Request of a Number of the Inhabitants of Dedham and Its Vicinity, in Commemoration of the Anniversary of American Independence (Dedham, Mass.: Printed at the Minerva Press, 1798);

The Speech of Caunonicus; or, an Indian Tradition: A Poem, with Explanatory Notes (Calcutta: Printed by Thomas Hollingbery, Hircarrah Press, 1802; Boston: Printed & sold by David Carlisle, 1803);

An address, delivered before King Solomon's Lodge, Charlestown, on the Anniversary of St. John the Baptist, June 24, A.L. 5811 (Boston: Printed by Thomas B. Wait & Co. for Russell & Cutler, 1811);

Synopsis for a Course of Lectures, on the Following Branches of Natural Philosophy, viz. Matter, and Its Properties—Mechanics—Electricity—Hydrostasis—Pneumatics, and Astronomy (Boston: Printed by Russell & Cutler, 1811);

A Compendious Treatise on the Use of the Globes, and of Maps; Compiled from the Works of Keith, Ferguson, Adams, Hutton, Bryan, Goldsmith, and Other Eminent Authors; Being a Plain and Comprehensive Introduction to the Practical Knowledge of Geography and Astronomy (Boston: Published by J. W. Burdett & Co. and by W. Wells, 1812);

The Gentleman's Pocket Register, and Free-Mason's Annual Anthology, for the Year of Our Lord 1813 (Boston: Printed by E. G. House & Published by Charles Williams, 1813);

An address, delivered before the Associated Instructers [sic] of Youth in Boston and Its Vicinity, on the First Anniversary of Their Institution, August 19, 1813 (Boston: Printed by John Eliot, 1813);

The Gentleman's Pocket Almanack; and Free-Mason's Vade Mecum. For the Year of Our Lord 1814 (Boston: Printed by Charles Williams, 1814);

A Monody, sacred to the memory of the Rev. John Lovejoy Abbot, A.M., Pastor of the Church in Chauncey-place, Boston; Who Died October 17, 1814, aetat. 31 (Boston: Monroe, Francis & Parker, 1815);

Oration in celebration of peace happily concluded between the United States of America, and Great Britain. Delivered at Boston, March 16, 1815, at the Request of St. John's Lodge; and Sanctioned by the Most Worshipful Grand Master of Massachusetts (Boston: E. G. House & Co., 1815).

OTHER: Mathew Carey, ed., *The Beauties of Poetry, British and American . . .* , includes poems by Lathrop (Philadelphia: From the Press of M. Carey, 1791);

Carey, ed., *The Columbian Muse. A Selection of American Poetry, from Various Authors of Established Reputation*, includes poems by Lathrop (New York: Printed by J. Carey for M. Carey, Philadelphia, 1794);

Benjamin Pollard, *An Address to the Massachusetts Charitable Fire Society; Delivered before the Members at Their Seventeenth Anniversary Meeting, May 31st, 1811*, includes an ode by Lathrop (Boston: Russell & Cutler, 1811);

William Sullivan, *An Oration Delivered before the Washington Benevolent Society of Massachusetts on the Thirtieth Day of April, 1812, Being the Anniversary of the First Inauguration of President Washington*, includes an ode by Lathrop (Boston: Printed by John Eliot, 1812);

Alexander H. Everett, *An Address Delivered before the Massachusetts Charitable Fire Society, at Their Annual Meeting, May 28, 1813*, includes an ode by Lathrop (Boston: Charles Callender, 1813);

Benjamin Whitewell, *An Address to the Members of the Massachusetts Charitable Fire Society; at Their Annual Meeting, May 27, 1814*, includes an ode written by Lathrop for the occasion (Boston: Charles Callender, 1814);

Samuel Kettell, ed., *Specimins of American Poetry, with Critical and Biographical Notices*, volume 2, includes 7 pages of *The Speech of Caunonicus* (Boston: S. G. Goodrich and Co., 1829).

John Lathrop, Jr., poet, lawyer, essayist, editor, orator, and educator, is best known for his lengthy visionary poem *The Speech of Caunonicus* (1802).

Lathrop was born in Boston, son of John and Mary Wheatley Lathrop. His father was pastor of the Second Church in Boston, and a descendant of the Puritan clergyman John Lothropp (1589-1653), first minister of Scituate. He attended Harvard from 1786 to 1789, and two months before graduation published his first poem in the *Massachusetts Magazine* (May 1789). At his commencement, 12 July 1789, he read a poem composed for the occasion. After receiving the baccalaureate degree, Lathrop began his legal training in the office of Christopher Gore, the same office where Daniel Webster later read law. From this time on, however, Lathrop was more successful as a poet than as an attorney, writing occasional verse for friends and for the Boston periodicals. In 1791 his verse was included in *The Beauties of Poetry, British and American*, an anthology compiled and published by Mathew Carey in Philadelphia.

Lathrop was again asked to read a poem at Harvard's 18 July 1792 commencement, where he received his A.M. The following April he married Ann Pierce and moved to Dedham, Massachusetts, where he set up a law practice. But Lathrop soon missed the stimulation of Boston's literary society and returned, apparently without his wife, to live among the wits Robert Treat Paine (a Harvard undergraduate schoolmate who had read a poem at commencement that spring) and Charles Prentiss. This was a prolific period for Lathrop, with many of his verses appearing in the Boston periodicals and in another of Carey's anthologies, *The Columbian Muse* (1794). It was also a productive period for Paine, and early in 1795 a quarrel developed between the two poets, which their younger contemporary S. L. Knapp ascribed to professional jealousy. The quarrel produced at least one satiric barb from Lathrop in the *Boston Gazette*, 5 February 1795:

Should profligate P---e, not quickly refrain,
From preposterous, lewd imprecation;
He justly will find, a Person inclin'd
To cure him of his ill Perturbation.

Lathrop continued to lecture and practice law at this time, and from 10 May to 30 July 1796 edited his own magazine, the *Nightingale*.

Lathrop contributed regularly to the *Federal Boston Gazette* until the end of 1799, when he left the legal profession forever to establish an English school in Calcutta, Wellesley College, where he lectured for the first decade of the nineteenth century.

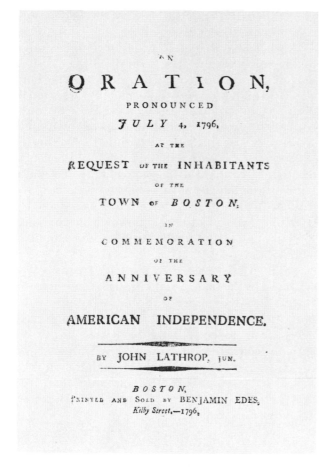

Title page for one of Lathrop's patriotic orations (courtesy of the John Carter Brown Library at Brown University)

He presented a proposal to the Governor-General of India, the Marquess Richard Wellesley, to expand his school into a national academy; but the Court of Directors of the East India Company had frustrated Wellesley's earlier attempts at establishing an English college in Calcutta and continued to refuse funding for that purpose.

Lathrop was married twice more in Calcutta: to Jane Thompson (1801) and Grace Eleanor Harrison (1808). He continued writing essays and poetry in India for the Calcutta *Post* and the *Hircarrah*, and in 1802 the press of the latter newspaper published his best-known poem, *The Speech of Caunonicus; or, an Indian Tradition,* as a quarto volume. Composed, Lathrop says in the preface, "to divert my mind from gloomy contemplations, and melancholy reveries, during a tedious voyage" (that is, the six-month passage from Boston to Calcutta), the poem represents his attempt at writing epic poetry in heroic couplets on an American theme. The speech is the prophetic vision of the aged sachem of the Narragansett tribe, Caunonicus, whom Lathrop likened to the Hebrew prophet Moses:

> At length—serene, CAUNONICUS arose,
> The patriarch sachem of the rude domain!
> Such was the ruler, whom JEHOVAH chose
> To lead from Egypt's land the Hebrew train.

Indeed, *The Speech of Caunonicus* is something of a New World Genesis and Exodus. It begins with the creation of subordinate spirits, then of beasts, including the now-extinct mammoth. Caunonicus digresses for some seventy lines on this great beast, and Lathrop devotes six pages to a note documenting its existence by reports of fossil remains. The beast Lathrop's note documents, however, is a phenomenon of natural history; Caunonicus's is a mythic embodiment of the forces of evil and tyranny. For when God (the Great Spirit, or Coutontowwit) surveys his creation, he finds something amiss wherever Mammoth dwells:

> Thus moved the deity. But vengeful wrath,
> Soon gather'd awful glooms around his path,
> Approaching near to Mammoth's wide domain,
> He view'd the ravage of the tyrant's reign.
> Not the gaunt wolf, nor cougar fierce and wild,
> Escaped the tusks that all the fields despoil'd.

Tyranny in the form of Mammoth is met by divine justice in the form of a thunderstorm:

> Nor did just anger rest. Behold, a storm
> Of sable horror clothe the eternal's form.
> Loud thunders burst while forked lightning dart,
> And each red bolt transfix'd a Mammoth's heart,
> Tall cedars crash'd beneath them falling prone,
> And heaven rebellow'd with their dying groan.

Caunonicus uses the death of Mammoth as an object lesson to would-be tyrants, then goes on to describe the creation of man and woman. His Adam and Eve story is followed by his Cain and Abel story, although the Narragansett Abel is a young maiden named Onega, whose Cain is a rejected suitor. The murderer's arrow had been intended for Onega's lover, Oswego, who is in turn dispatched with a "tomax." The lovers are reunited in paradise, and the murderer is forever exiled.

Again Caunonicus applies the mythic past to the present and, since the sachem's function is partly prophetic, to the future. For the poem is set in 1620, and Caunonicus senses the approach of the English pilgrims toward Plymouth and the end of an era. The rest of the poem, the dying sachem's dark vision of his tribe's future, is remarkable for its imaginative penetration of the Narragansett point of view, although Lathrop undercuts any criticism of the white man in his notes. This is the "Exodus" portion of the Narragansett's oral Bible, but the Indian's years of exile will find no promised land except in death.

> Forced from these groves our vanquished hosts retire,
> Driven by their shining arms and ruthless fire,
> In graceful pride the rubric banner waves,
> And VICTORY triumphs o'er our humble graves.

Yet though "Tremendous flames their brazen engines pour," the pilgrim's most deadly weapon is not the English gun but English rum: "This, shall the arm robust, like sloth, unnerve,/And make the soul from truth and virtue swerve." The Narragansett's world is passing, but Caunonicus envisions the glories of the new empire that will supplant it, and the poem ends, "Thus shall a foreign race achieve their fame,/And on our ruins, raise a deathless name!" The appeal of *The Speech of Caunonicus* is not in the occasional stirring line, though there are a few, but in its Ossianic presentation of the mythic imagination. It is an epic not in length (it is only 526 lines) but in depth of vision and in attempting to encapsulate a culture. The language of the poem matches the grandeur of its scope, though it never varies in intensity, and can thus become tedious. Yet if the verse is not brilliant, it is always competent.

In 1809 Lathrop returned to Boston as preceptor at the Salem Street School, and in 1811 he delivered papers on natural history and moral philosophy selected from his Calcutta lectures. The prospectus for these lectures was published in 1811, and the lectures themselves appeared between 1812 and 1816 in the *Polyanthos*, along with a half-serious column of informal essays called "The Moral Censor," where Lathrop gave pronouncements, often tongue-in-cheek, on such various subjects as slander, old maids, and love poetry. Many, and perhaps all of these comic essays had originally appeared in the Calcutta papers, and they represent his most readable and lively prose. In one installment (July 1813) the Moral Censor reprinted portions of "Sukoontula," Lathrop's versification of the classic Sanskrit drama *Śakuntalā* into heroic couplets. Lathrop claimed to have published the complete work in Calcutta in 1802, but no copies survived. He tried unsuccessfully to begin another literary journal, although he did publish two Masonic almanacs in 1813 and 1814.

When his father died in 1816, Lathrop, discouraged by the failure of his projects, moved to the District of Columbia, where he held a position in the post office until his death. Lathrop's writings have never been collected, and his work was rarely anthologized after his death. His influence on American poetry is negligible, though the publication of his American Indian epic more than fifty years before Longfellow's *Hiawatha* (1855) is a literary curiosity if nothing more.

References:

Thomas Bridgman, *The Pilgrims of Boston and their Descendants* (New York: Appleton, 1856);

Samuel Lorenzo Knapp, *Biographical Sketches of Eminent Lawyers, Statesmen, and Men of Letters* (Boston: Richardson & Lord, 1821);

Lewis Leary, "John Lathrop, Jr. The Quiet Poet of Federalist Boston," *Proceedings of the American Antiquarian Society*, 91 (1981): 39-89.

John Blair Linn

(14 March 1777-30 August 1804)

Alan Axelrod

BOOKS: *Miscellaneous Works, Prose and Poetical* (New York: Printed by Thomas Greenleaf, 1795);

The Poetical Wanderer: Containing, Dissertations on the Early Poetry of Greece, On Tragic Poetry and On the Power of Noble Actions on the Mind. To Which are Added Several Poems (New York: Printed for the author by G. Forman, 1796);

The Death of Washington. A Poem. In Imitation of the Manner of Ossian (Philadelphia: Printed by John Ormrod, 1800);

The Powers of Genius, A Poem, In Three Parts (Philadelphia: Asbury Dickens, 1801; corrected and enlarged edition, Philadelphia: Published by John Conrad, 1802);

A Discourse. Occasioned by the Death of the Reverend John Ewing, D.D. . . .(Philadelphia: From the press of the Late R. Aitken, by Jane Aitken, for John Conrad, 1802);

A Letter to Joseph Priestley, L.L.D. F.R.S. In Answer to His Performance, Entitled Socrates and Jesus Compared (Philadelphia: John Conrad/Baltimore: M. & J. Conrad/Washington: Rapin & Conrad, 1803);

A Letter to Joseph Priestley, L.L.D. F.R.S. In Answer To His Letter, in Defence of His Pamphlet, Entitled Socrates and Jesus Compared (Philadelphia: Printed by H. Maxwell & published by John Conrad/Baltimore: M. & J. Conrad/ Washington: Rapin & Conrad/Norfolk: Bonsal & Conrad/Petersburg: Somervell, Conrad, 1803);

Valerian, A Narrative Poem: Intended, In Part, To Describe the Early Persecutions of Christians, and Rapidly to Illustrate the Influence of Christianity on the Manners of Nations (Philadelphia: Printed by Thomas & George Palmer, 1805).

By the time of his death, at age twenty-seven, John Blair Linn had earned a B.A., two M.A. degrees, and an honorary Doctorate of Divinity. Minister of a prestigious Philadelphia church, he was hailed as a superb pulpit orator, had had a play produced on the New York stage, had written five volumes of poetry, three of prose, and contributed regularly to New York and Philadelphia periodicals.

Linn was born in Big Spring (now Newville), Pennsylvania, the son of Rebecca Blair Linn, the daughter of the Reverend John Blair, and William Linn, a liberal Presbyterian clergyman, who, as his boy was growing up, served as pastor of two important churches, became president of Washington College, regent of the University of the State of New York, acting president of Queens College (now Rutgers University), president of Union College, and chaplain to the U.S. House of Representatives. Young John Blair's early signs of genius promised a life as distinguished as his father's. The boy entered Columbia College at fourteen and was having his verse and prose published in the *New-York Magazine* by the time he was seventeen. At eighteen, in 1795 (the year he received his B.A. degree), he had written enough to fill a volume: *Miscellaneous Works, Prose and Poetical*. The verse here is almost exclusively imitative, drawing upon Ossian (James Macpherson) and the Graveyard Poets and too often absurdly rendering their spirit into stiff neoclassical rhyme and meter. The short prose fiction, likewise, is little more than sentimental pasteboard, but some of the critical essays are of greater interest, particularly "The Young Compositor," republished from the *New-York Magazine*. Defining literary genius as unshackled imagination flowing "naturally," Linn reveals the innovative romantic impulse he was never able to embody successfully in his own verse. But even as unrealized theory, such an aesthetic was new to the literature of the early republic.

Despite the popular and critical success of his first volume, Linn realized that the life of letters was no way to make a living. He read law with Alexander Hamilton for some months, stealing time from his studies in order to assemble a second book, *The Poetical Wanderer*, which appeared in 1796 and is of a piece with his earlier work. Life in New York had also excited in Linn a passion for the stage, and on 16 January 1797 his *Bourville Castle; or, The Gallic Orphan* was produced at the John Street Theater. The play closed after opening night; no manuscript survives.

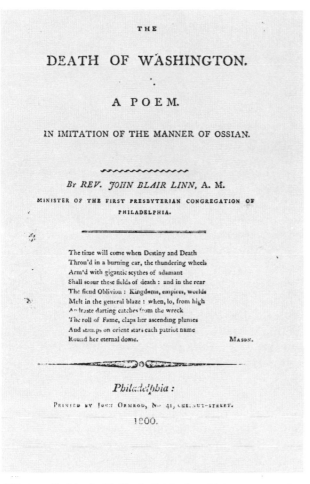

THE

DEATH OF WASHINGTON.

A POEM.

IN IMITATION OF THE MANNER OF OSSIAN.

By REV. JOHN BLAIR LINN, A. M.

MINISTER OF THE FIRST PRESBYTERIAN CONGREGATION OF
PHILADELPHIA.

The time will come when Destiny and Death
Throw'd in a burning car, the thundering wheels
Arm'd with gigantic scythes of adamant
Shall scour these fields of death : and in the rear
The fiend Oblivion : Kingdoms, empires, worlds
Melt in the general blaze : when, lo, from high
Ambrose darting catches from the wreck
The roll of Fame, claps her ascending plumes
And stamps on orient stars each patriot name
Round her eternal dome.

MASON.

Philadelphia :

PRINTED BY JOHN ORMROD, No. 41, CHESNUT-STREET.

1800.

Title page for Linn's third book. Critics found it incongruous that Linn wrote about an American national hero in so-called Celtic verse (courtesy of the John Carter Brown Library at Brown University).

Perhaps discouraged by the failure of his play as well as by the indifference with which *The Poetical Wanderer* had been received, and most definitely tired of the law, Linn left New York City for Schenectady to study theology at Union College. He took his M.A. from Union College in 1797 and another, *in absentia,* from Columbia in spring of the next year. Licensed to preach in fall 1798, he became copastor of Philadelphia's First Presbyterian Church in 1799. Established now, he married Hester Bailey of Poughkeepsie, New York, the same year, and again interested himself in belles lettres, joining a literary society called the Tuesday Club, which included among its members Charles Brockden Brown, the nation's first important novelist; Joseph Dennie, editor of the *Port Folio,* the nation's leading literary periodical; and the young playwright Charles Jared Ingersoll. In 1800, Linn com-

posed a book-length poem titled *The Death of Washington,* but critics were quick to lambaste the incongruity of a panegyric on America's national hero written in imitation of Ossian's languid "Celtic" verse.

Undeterred, Linn published in 1801 what would prove his most popular and critically successful work, *The Powers of Genius.* In this verse essay Linn attempts a kind of anatomy of genius, replete with definition and historical illustration, the object of which is to reconcile the Common-Sense literary aesthetic of such Scots theoreticians as Hugh Blair (whose *Lectures on Rhetoric and Belles Lettres* [1783] dominated early-nineteenth-century American literary criticism) with the protoromantic cult of sensibility. As in his earliest critical essays, Linn sees genius essentially as the operation of liberated imagination. Yet "taste," founded upon accepted canons of correctness, figures as a necessary check on genius. Burdened with such a self-contradictory aesthetic allegiance, Linn produced in *The Powers of Genius* an ambitious, interesting, but barely coherent work.

In 1802, following a sunstroke, the young pastor's health declined. He performed his church offices diligently but in a state of semi-collapse. He continued to write, delivering and publishing a long eulogy on the death of his copastor, John Ewing, and publishing two eloquent replies to Joseph Priestley, whose *Socrates and Jesus Compared* (1803) virtually deified the former while reducing the latter to the level of mere humanity. Linn was at work on *Valerian,* an epic poem about the early Christian martyrs and "the Influence of Christianity on the Manners of Nations," when he succumbed to tuberculosis in 1804. Incomplete, rambling and digressive, *Valerian* was published posthumously with a biographical preface by Charles Brockden Brown, who had become Linn's brother-in-law shortly after the young man's death. Although Linn obviously intended this pious work as his magnum opus, it met with little praise, and at least one early critic, Samuel Kettell in 1829, suggested that it "has little to recommend it to our notice."

"All his performances," Brockden Brown wrote of Linn, "candour compels us to consider as preludes to future exertions, and indications of future excellence." This estimate may well be valid. Linn was a transitional figure who struggled to reconcile an imitative neoclassicism with fitful impulses toward a more original Romanticism. Prolific though Linn's short career was, we can hardly judge his philosophical and aesthetic struggle as a completed life's work.

References:
Charles Brockden Brown, "A Sketch of the Life and Character of John Blair Linn," *Port Folio*, new series 1 (January 1809): 21-29, 129-134, 195-203;

Lewis Leary, "John Blair Linn," in his *Soundings: Some Early American Writers* (Athens: University of Georgia Press, 1975), pp. 175-207;

Leary, "The Writings of John Blair Linn (1777-1804)," *Bulletin of Bibliography*, 19 (1946): 18, 19.

Papers:
The only substantial deposit of Linn's papers, principally correspondence, is at the Historical Society of Pennsylvania.

Anne Home Livingston

(24 February 1763-23 August 1841)

Steven E. Kagle
Illinois State University

BOOKS: *Sacred Records, Abridged in Verse. Consisting of Some of the Parables and Miracles, the Life, Death, Resurrection and Ascension of the Blessed Saviour* (Philadelphia: Printed & published for the author by T. S. Manning, 1817);

Nancy Shippen, Her Journal Book; The International Romance of a Young Lady of Fashion of Colonial Philadelphia, with Letters to Her and About Her, edited by Ethel Armes (Philadelphia & London: Lippincott, 1935).

Anne Home Livingston's reputation as a writer is dependent on her tragic journal which is not only one of the finest diaries of early America but also an important document for women's studies. Anne (Nancy) Home Shippen was born in Philadelphia into one of the more prominent families in colonial America. Her mother, Alice Lee Shippen, was a member of the famous Lee family of Virginia; her father, Dr. William Shippen III, was a prominent physician who would become director of all the American military hospitals during the Revolution and later president of the College of Physicians of the University of Pennsylvania. After the British abandoned Philadelphia in 1778, the Shippens entertained many of the most important members of the colonial army and government. In this setting, Anne's beauty and charm attracted a number of suitors including Albert Otto (later the Compte de Mosloy), a diplomatic secretary. In March 1781, after a romantic courtship, Anne accepted Otto's proposal of marriage, but her father had chosen differently. Dr. Shippen, whose judgment, if not his morals, had already been impeached in a court-

Anne Home Livingston, portrait attributed to Benjamin Trott

martial for speculating on hospital supplies (he was acquitted by one vote), favored another suitor, Colonel Henry Beekman Livingston, an heir to one of the greatest fortunes in America. In only four days

Page from Livingston's journal (Ethel Armes, ed., Nancy Shippen, Her Journal Book, *1935)*

Dr. Shippen deceitfully arranged for a brief separation between Anne and Otto and influenced his daughter to marry Livingston.

Shortly after the marriage, Livingston, the father of several illegitimate children, grew increasingly jealous of his wife. Yet, if her diary can be believed, she had not acted improperly. Livingston, persisting in his accusations, kept his wife a virtual prisoner; even the birth of their daughter did nothing to alter his behavior. Hearing of her husband's plan to bring his illegitimate children to live with them, Anne returned with her child to her parents' home. It was during this crisis that she began her diary. At this point (10 April 1783), Mrs. Livingston was not fully aware of the tragic nature of her situation. Her early entries show that, despite her suffering, the diarist was still living with romantic illusions. For example, she retained the stylized code names, Lord Worthy for her father and Leander for Otto, that she had employed in letters written during her courtship, and she seems to have been still looking to others to provide her "story" with a happy ending. For years she strove for a reconciliation but failed. During this time, Otto had returned to France and come back, married and then widowed. A new future seemed possible if Mrs. Livingston could obtain a divorce, but her husband would only consent if his wife would agree to a permanent separation from their daughter. Anne refused this bargain, and eventually Otto left again for France.

Although they lived many years more, the lives of Anne and her daughter closed. They became increasingly interdependent, religious, and reclusive. During her remaining years, Mrs. Livingston composed poems, including a retelling of portions of the New Testament in verse which she titled *Sacred Records* (1817). Although this work, which she had privately printed, shows her potential, it displays neither the polish nor imagination that would prompt its serious consideration as art. Mrs. Livingston also wrote hymns, letters, and epitaphs, surviving examples of which attest to the sadness and "morbidity" of her existence. She and her daughter were buried in a single grave.

Livingston's journal has a thematic unity exceptional in American diary literature. It was begun in response to the tension of her tragic situation and terminated with her resignation to it. In editing the diary in 1935, Ethel Armes subtitled the work, *The*

International Romance of a Young Lady of Fashion; however, contemporary critics influenced by feminist studies are likely to recognize that Livingston's individual romantic tragedy was very much the result of broader problems stemming from a social order that encouraged or forced women to be dependent on the wills of their fathers and husbands. Seen in this light the diary's significance goes beyond that of one individual's suffering, and Livingston's final actions take on some measure of active heroism rather than passive resignation. Only when Mrs. Livingston had seen through the romantic illusion that some external power would intervene to save her and realized that her choices though limited and unpleasant were her own, could she assume some control of her life.

References:
Steven E. Kagle, *American Diary Literature* (Boston: Twayne, 1979), pp. 92-97;

Randolph Shipley Klein, *Portrait of an Early American Family: the Shippens of Philadelphia* (Philadelphia: University of Pennsylvania, 1975).

Papers:
Livingston's papers are at the Library of Congress.

Samuel Low
(12 December 1765-death date unknown)

Mark R. Patterson
University of Washington

BOOKS: *Winter Display'd, A Poem: Describing the Season in All Its Stages and Vicissitudes; and Occasionally Interspersed with a Variety of Moral and Sentimental Remarks...*, as An American (New York: Printed by Samuel Loudon, 1784);

The Politician Out-Witted, A Comedy, In Five Acts. Written in the Year 1788, as An American (New York: Printed for the author by W. Ross, 1789);

Poems, by Samuel Low, 2 volumes (New York: Printed by T. & J. Swords, 1800).

Samuel Low, New York poet and playwright, achieved a good deal of youthful success only to fall into eventual obscurity. Born on 12 December 1765, in New York City, Low was the fourth child of

John and Susannah Burdet Low and a relative of the prominent merchant brothers Isaac and Nicholas Low. With few opportunities in the nation for an aspiring writer, Low followed his relatives' examples. He worked as a clerk in the Treasury Office until 1794 and as a bookkeeper in the Bank of New York from 1795 to 1803. In 1785 he married Margaret Kip, who bore four children before her death in 1795. Two years later he married Ann Cregier, who bore him a son in 1798. Outside of scattered autobiographical statements in his poetry, little else is known of Low's life.

His slim literary output expresses a definite interest in the new nation's success. His first known publication was *Winter Display'd* (1784), a forty-page poem based on James Thomson's *The Seasons*

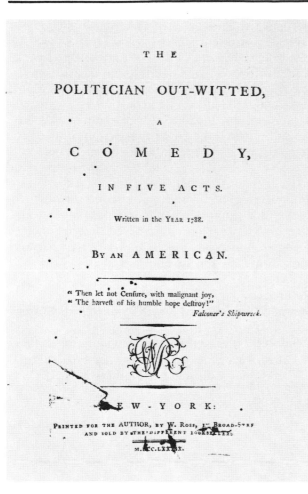

THE

POLITICIAN OUT-WITTED,

A

C O M E D Y,

IN FIVE ACTS.

Written in the YEAR 1788.

BY AN AMERICAN.

" Then let not Cenfure, with malignant joy,
" The harveft of his humble hope deftroy!"

Falconer's Shipwreck.

N E W - Y O R K:

PRINTED FOR THE AUTHOR, BY W. ROSS, IN BROAD-STREET
AND SOLD BY THE DIFFERENT BOOKSELLERS.

M.DCC.LXXXIX.

Title page for Low's only play, in which marriage plans are complicated by the conflict between a Federalist and an anti-Federalist (courtesy of the John Carter Brown Library at Brown University)

(1730). Begun when Low was only sixteen, *Winter Display'd* was later revised extensively for inclusion in the second volume of his *Poems* (1800). During this process he transformed the piece of juvenilia into a longer and more graceful meditation on man's place in the order of nature. Whereas the earlier version ends with the abrupt retreat of winter—"the howling blast is almost o'er, / And spring vouchsafes to visit us once more"—the later version achieves the distinctly religious tone of resurrection: "That man to heav'n at last his flight shall wing, / Where God's bright gift makes eternal Spring."

In 1788, prompted both by Royall Tyler's successful play, *The Contrast* (produced in New York on 16 April 1787), and the political controversy over the Constitution's ratification, Low wrote his only play, *The Politician Out-Witted* (1789). Declared to have been written "by an American," this play combines a number of immediate political issues with a conventionally plotted romance. The conflict between an avowed Antifederalist (Old Loveyet) and Federalist (Trueman) complicates the planned union of Charles Loveyet and Harriet Trueman. Much of the play's humor and nationalistic spirit occur in the contrast between two minor characters: Toupee, a Francophile, and the rustic American, Humphrey. Although successful at recreating the polemical, rumor-filled atmosphere of this critical period, the play stops short of reconciling the opposing sides. The two lovers are finally brought together, but the fathers-in-law remain intractable, suggesting the dangerous factionalism facing the new nation. As Harriet says of her impending marriage, "it is a hazardous expedient, but it is a certain one." It is doubtful that the play was ever produced. William Dunlap mentions that the play was "rejected by the managers" of a New York theater and was "published for their justification by the author."

In 1800, Low published, as he said in his preface, "nearly the whole of his poetic writings" in two volumes. The occasional nature of much of his verse suggests the public ambition he might have had as a poet. Included in these volumes are a number of poems referring to specific national events: "The Constitution" (written during the ratification controversy), "Ode on the Death of General George Washington," "Hymn to Liberty," and poems written for Masonic gatherings. However, as he noted in his preface, he found the necessity of "public business . . . peculiarly inimical to the cultivation of poetic talent." Yet such conflict did not stop his pen; the latest poem in the volume is "Ode for the 4th of July, 1800." In addition to such occasional poems Low wrote more personal and lyric poems to family members, as well as several elegies and epitaphs for friends. Such poems reveal the consistently conventional quality of his writings, even his lighter verse such as "To a Segar." Conservatively moralizing in poems such as "On a small Fish caught by angling," Low nevertheless manages to exhibit a good deal of control of both rhythm and tone. Despite Low's talent, Charles Brockden Brown harshly reviewed the collected poems in his *Monthly Magazine and American Review* (July 1800) as "correct without point or strength; but none of them conspicuous for originality of idea, beauty of simile, ingenuity of description, or harmony of verse."

Low had no further publications after 1800,

and no trace of him in New York exists after 1803. In 1819, William Dunlap described Low as a poet who had "published a volume of bad poems, a bad play, became a drunkard, abandon'd his wife, came South and (as I hope) reformed & became a clergyman of the Church Episcopal." Although this part of Low's biography is unsubstantiated, Dunlap's brief history does suggest a disappointing end to a poet of talent.

Reference:

Lewis Leary, "Samuel Low: New York's First Poet," in his *Soundings* (Athens: University of Georgia Press, 1975), pp. 67-82.

James Madison

Ormond Seavey
George Washington University

BIRTH: Port Conway, Virginia, 16 March 1751, to James and Nelly Conway Madison.

MARRIAGE: 15 September 1794 to Dolley Payne Todd.

EDUCATION: B.A., College of New Jersey (later Princeton University), 1771.

DEATH: Montpelier, Orange County, Virginia, 28 June 1836.

BOOKS: *The Federalist: A Collection of Essays, Written in Favour of the New Constitution, As Agreed upon by the Federal Convention,* by Madison, Alexander Hamilton, and John Jay, 2 volumes (New York: Printed & sold by J. & A. McLean, 1788)—essays 10, 14, 18-20, 37-58, 62, and 63 by Madison;

Letters of Helvidius: Written in Reply to Pacificus, on the President's Proclamation of Neutrality (Philadelphia: Printed by Samuel H. Smith, 1794);

Speech, in the House of Representatives of the Congress of the United States, Delivered January 14, 1794, by James Madison, of Virginia, in Support of His Propositions for the Promotion of the Commerce of the United States, and in Reply to William Smith, of South-Carolina (New York: Printed at Greenleaf's Press, 1794);

An Examination of the British Doctrine Which Subjects to Capture a Neutral Trade Not Open in Time of Peace . . . (Philadelphia?, 1806?; London: Printed for J. Johnson and W. J. & J. Richardson, 1806);

The Reply of Mr. Madison, in Answer to Mr. Rose, in

James Madison as a young man

Discussing the Affair of the Chesapeake (New York: Printed at the Office of the Public Advertiser, 1808);

An Address Delivered before the Agricultural Society of Albemarle, on Tuesday, May 12, 1818 (Richmond: Printed by Shepherd & Pollard, 1818);

Letters on the Constitutionality and Policy of Duties, for the Protection and Encouragement of Domestic Manufactures (Richmond: Printed by T. W. White, 1829);

Considerations in Favour of a National Bank, Independent of Government Influence, with Checks and Balances to Guard against Illegitimate Speculations, and the Dangerous Consequences of a Vicious Administration of Its Affairs (New York, 1834);

Jonathan Bull and Mary Bull (Washington: Printed for Presentation by J. C. M'Guire, 1856).

Editions and Collections: *The Papers of James Madison, Purchased by Order of Congress . . .* , 3 volumes (Washington: Langtree & O'Sullivan, 1840);

Letters and Other Writings of James Madison. Published by Order of Congress, 4 volumes, edited by Philip R. Fendall (Philadelphia: Lippincott, 1865);

The Writings of James Madison, 9 volumes, edited by Gaillard Hunt (New York: Putnam's, 1900-1910);

The Records of the Federal Convention of 1787, 4 volumes, edited by Max Farrand (New Haven: Yale University Press, 1911);

The Federalist, edited by Jacob E. Cooke (Middletown, Conn.: Wesleyan University Press, 1961);

The Papers of James Madison, volumes 1-10, edited by William T. Hutchinson, W. M. E. Rachal, and others (Chicago: University of Chicago Press, 1962-1977); volumes 11- , edited by Robert A. Rutland, Charles F. Hobson, and others (Charlottesville: University Press of Virginia, 1977-).

SELECTED PUBLIC DOCUMENTS: Virginia, General Assembly, *Memorial and Remonstrance, Presented to the General Assembly, of the State of Virginia, at Their Session in 1785, in consequence of a Bill Brought into that Assembly for the Establishment of Religion by Law* (Worcester: Printed by Isaiah Thomas, 1786);

Virginia, General Assembly, *Virginia to wit. In the House of Delegates, Friday, December 21st., 1798. Resolved, That the General Assembly of Virginia doth unequivocally express a firm resolution to maintain and defend the Constitution of the United States, and the Constitution of this State, against every aggression, either foreign or domestic, and that they will support the government of the United States in all measures warranted by the former* (Richmond: Printed by Augustine Davis, 1798);

Virginia, General Assembly, *Report of the Committee*

to Whom Was Committed the Proceedings of Sundry of the Other States . . . (Richmond: Printed for the General Assembly, 1800);

U.S. Department of State, *Letters from the Secretary of State to Mr. Monroe, on the subject of Impressments . . .* (Washington: Printed by order of the House of Representatives; A. & G. Way, printers, 1808).

OTHER: "James Madison's Autobiography," edited by Douglass Adair, *William and Mary Quarterly,* third series 2 (1945): 191-209.

It is not easy to appreciate James Madison's importance to American history. His writing avoided the wit and informality that Franklin excelled in, and he left no record of himself by which he could be more intimately known. He led no armies and gave no stirring speeches; his work as the major contributor to the U.S. Constitution took place in long sessions of intricate negotiations behind closed doors. Even in his greatest published work, *The Federalist,* he was a pseudonymous collaborator with two other men. In his own time and afterward he was thought by many to be a mere subordinate of his older Virginia colleague Thomas Jefferson. His virtues as congressman, secretary of state, and finally as the fourth president were those of prudence, self-control, a broad sense of history, and a loyalty to the republican ideology he held to all his life; none of these will make him seem heroic to an age that looks for originality and easily observable achievements.

Still, if Madison's gifts were more subtle than those of the other leading Founding Fathers, they led to contributions that were in many ways more lasting. The durability of the Constitution is his greatest monument, and since early in the nineteenth century he has been known as the Father of the Constitution. By argument and deft manipulation he was crucial in engineering the Constitution's ratification in the key states of New York and Virginia. As the leading member of the first House of Representatives, he helped to draft and pass the Bill of Rights; he also set in motion the body of procedures and precedents that have governed the operation of Congress ever since. President Washington turned to him repeatedly for advice and speech writing. Later he became Jefferson's close associate in forming what was soon called the Republican party (ancestor to what is now called the Democratic party), and he was elected twice to the Presidency with little opposition. Throughout his life Madison's capacity for closely reasoned

Nelly Conway Madison and James Madison, Sr.; portraits by Charles Peale Polk, 1799 (Maryland Historical Society)

argument and a style of writing well suited for the explication of complex questions won him respectful hearers and readers and an enviable record of political successes. No American did more to make a nation of the contentious states and factions left over from the Revolution, and he achieved what he did in large part by the written word.

He was raised in the rolling hills of the Virginia Piedmont, the oldest son of James Madison, Sr., the most prominent landowner of Orange County. (Until well into middle age the son signed himself "James Madison, Junr.") The Piedmont was still a recently settled area in the 1750s and 1760s, with an economy different from that of the Tidewater region, where the first great tobacco fortunes were made. Madison the son avoided living in the Tidewater, in part because he considered it unhealthful during the summer; his political and personal alliances tended to be in the west or outside of Virginia entirely.

At the age of eleven he went to a school directed by Donald Robertson, a Scottish clergyman who had been educated at the University of Edin-

burgh. The young Madison thus came in contact early with Scottish Enlightenment ideas, probably the most solid and broad-based education available in the English-speaking world in the eighteenth century. After five years at Robertson's school, he spent a year or two at home preparing for college with the Reverend Thomas Martin, a recent graduate of the College of New Jersey (which later became Princeton University). During the late 1760s William and Mary College had slipped into intellectual doldrums, and Princeton's reputation for intellectual and political soundness reached well into Virginia, so Madison traveled north to enroll in 1769.

None of the leaders of the early republic profited better from his formal education than Madison, and Princeton offered probably the best college training to be had in the country. Among his classmates were Philip Freneau, later a close political ally, and Hugh Henry Brackenridge; with them at much the same time were a disproportionate share of the future leaders of the nation. The school's president was John Witherspoon, who had

Page from a notebook that Madison kept at Donald Robertson's school, circa 1766 (Library of Congress)

brought the latest Enlightenment ideas with him from Scotland. Along with a firm grounding in the classical languages, Madison would have learned something about the natural sciences, modern languages, and moral philosophy. Much of the last two years of his education was devoted to exercises in written and oral persuasion. Here and earlier Madison's favored prose model was the essays of Joseph Addison; Addison's *Spectator,* he later wrote, was well suited "to inculcate in youthful minds just sentiments, an appetite for knowledge, and a taste

for the improvement of the mind and manners." Some of Madison's college notebooks survive, and they testify to the methodical way he set about mastering the curriculum. He graduated in 1771 after two years of strenuous study. Witherspoon later remarked that in his years at Princeton Madison never did or said an improper thing.

There is good reason to believe that Madison was not quite such an insufferable paragon. As a member of the American Whig Society, along with Freneau and Brackenridge, he was embroiled in the club's rivalries of wit; Madison's doggerel contributions toward these good-natured contests are unpoetic but lighthearted and particularly scurrilous. Though his formal writing and his conversation on public occasions were uniformly serious, there are many testimonies throughout his life to his lively sense of humor and gift for story-telling. He was short (five feet six inches) and slight of build; early pictures tend to depict him as looking younger than his years. He seems to have trained himself as a public man throughout his years of schooling. Writing in 1774 to his close friend and Princeton classmate, William Bradford of Philadelphia, he claims to have felt an early hankering for belles lettres. But as a maturer man, he writes at twenty-three, he has turned away from those pleasing entanglements: "Poetry, wit and criticism, romances, plays, &c., captivated me much; but I began to discover that they deserve but a small portion of a mortal's time, and that something more substantial, more durable, and more profitable, befits a riper age."

After graduating in September of 1771, Madison stayed around Princeton until the following spring, when he returned home. He seems to have been exhausted by the rigors of study, and his constitution, always rather delicate, took a few years to recover. In the letters he wrote in the early 1770s he talks often about his failed health and his anticipations of an early death. It had been hard for him to leave Princeton behind, and in his letters to Bradford and Freneau he shares their sense of being adrift and without vocation. To Bradford he indicated that he would read law, but the questions that seemed to interest him most were political and philosophical, not the burdensome details of legal practice. At home in Montpelier he was supervising the education of his younger siblings; he was a gentleman-scholar with an education he could make little use of.

The Revolution soon gave him something to do. His father had always been a firm Whig, opposed to the plans for an American bishopric of the Church of England and to the Stamp Act. In 1774 young Madison was appointed to the Orange County Committee of Safety; in 1776 he was a delegate to the convention in Williamsburg that first declared the colonies to be free and independent states. Upon completing the state constitution in May 1776, delegates to the convention became the Virginia Assembly. The following year he was defeated for re-election to the assembly, perhaps because he failed to comply with the traditional practice of supplying barrels of free whiskey on election day. But the assembly elected him to the governor's council, probably a tribute to his already demonstrated ability at the preparing of state papers. Madison made no name for himself as a distinguished public speaker; he had a soft voice and he lacked an impressive manner. But he quickly made himself prominent in every legislative body he ever attended by his political astuteness, his mastery of the questions at hand, and the depth of his theoretical understanding.

In ideology Madison adhered like the majority of his countrymen to the "Country" position, which dictated a suspicion of courts and the trappings of royal power. His lifelong opposition to established or state-supported churches was in part a corollary to that position, and few issues aroused his energies as much as this one. But he combined the "Country" position with an awareness that a national government newly established under republican principles would require adequate powers in order to defend the country and advance the collective interest. The essays of David Hume were a major influence on him, with their arguments for a strong national power.

Sometime in 1776 Madison met Thomas Jefferson and began a collaboration and friendship that lasted fifty years. They lived not far from each other in central Virginia; both were farmers as well as statesmen, and their letters involved agriculture as well as politics. The traditional view has been that Madison was Jefferson's disciple and agent. That view ignores the differing characters and emphases of the two men, whose collaboration was more a matter of compatible concerns than of imitation. Jefferson was an ideologue all his life, a brilliant phrasemaker, a poor administrator and organizer, a philosophe who was as much at home in Paris as at Monticello. Madison knew the enlightened European thinkers only through their writings; he never traveled outside of the United States. He naturally took upon himself details of administration and technical questions that Jefferson had little interest in, and he was more precise and careful as a thinker. Jefferson, the hero of liberalism, was a patrician in his tastes, a bit aloof from all but a few friends. Jefferson's best-known larger work is the *Notes on the State of Virginia* (1785), a tribute to his native state and a defense of the agrarian way of life. Madison's best-known work is his twenty or so essays in *The Federalist* (1788), a brilliantly reasoned defense of national government above sectional interests.

From 1776 to late 1779 Madison served in the governor's council as a sort of cabinet member to Governors Patrick Henry and then Jefferson, carrying on much of the official correspondence re-

Pages from Madison's notes on ancient and modern federal systems. He later expanded upon these notes for three numbers of The Federalist (Irving Brant, James Madison: The Nationalist, 1780-1787, 1948).

quired by a state at war. Beginning in 1780 he was elected a Virginia delegate to the Continental Congress, serving almost continually there for eight years and sometimes in the Virginia legislature as well. While in Congress he turned first to untangling the financial chaos of the national government, which was unable to pay its bills or the troops in the field for lack of contributions from the states. As a member of various committees of Congress he was concerned with preserving the French alliance while still maintaining the American claims to territory in the west and south. Confronted by the powerlessness of Congress under the Articles of Confederation, Madison sought to extend those powers by a free interpretation of the Articles. After prolonged negotiations he was able to persuade the states to relinquish their claims on lands west of

the Appalachians, leaving that area open for new state governments.

Back in Virginia Madison campaigned in 1785 against Patrick Henry's attempt to reintroduce state support for churches. His *Memorial and Remonstrance, Presented to the General Assembly, of the State of Virginia, at Their Session in 1785, in consequence of a Bill Brought into that Assembly for the Establishment of Religion by Law* (published as a broadside in 1785 and as a pamphlet in 1786) set forth fifteen arguments against tax-supported religion. George Mason printed it as a petition to be circulated around the state, and the number of signatures accumulated for the petition prevented any farther moves toward an established church. Like so much of Madison's writing, this petition carried no indication of authorship; it was meant to be signed by its subscribers. Jefferson's Bill for Establishing Religious Freedom (one of the three things he took credit for on his tombstone) was first proposed in 1777 but had not been acted upon; with the momentum from the *Memorial and Remonstrance* Madison was able in 1786 to get the bill passed. In a letter to Jefferson Madison proudly reported his success: "The enacting clauses past without a single alteration, and I flatter myself have in this Country extinguished forever the ambitious hope of making laws for the human mind."

At length the frustrations of serving in a powerless Congress impelled Madison to seek a new design of government. He used the Annapolis Convention of 1786 as a springboard for calling a convention for the following year, supposedly to revise the Articles of Confederation. In fact his intention was to replace them with a new plan. At that convention he began his collaboration with Alexander Hamilton, which would last into the first years of the new government. In the months preceding the convention he drew up for himself two memoranda in preparation for its deliberations, "Of Ancient and Modern Confederacies" and "Vices of the Political System of the United States." The first is a description of ancient and modern federal systems, drawn particularly from his reading of the *Encyclopédie* and other French sources; Madison used these notes later as the basis for his contributions to *The Federalist*, numbers 18, 19, and 20. "Vices of the Political System" examines methodically the structural defects of the Articles of Confederation and ends with a prefiguration of the ideas later set forth in *The Federalist*, number 10, perhaps the key essay of the entire volume. Madison thus arrived at the 1787 convention better prepared than any other delegate.

At the convention the thirty-six-year-old Madison's past service in Congress assured that he would be given a close hearing. He had persuaded Washington to attend, where he would undoubtedly be chosen to preside, so the immense weight of Washington's prestige was already behind whatever result the members might produce. At the beginning of the deliberations Madison drew up what came to be known as the Virginia Plan and had his colleague Edmund Randolph offer it as the basic working document of the Convention. Madison himself both participated actively in the discussion and kept notes; in the evenings he would write out at length what each speaker had said on the basis of those notes. Madison's transcript thus gives us an invaluable and exhaustive record of the thinking that went into the Constitution.

Opposition to the Virginia Plan soon developed, since it proposed representation by population in both houses of its bicameral legislature. Eventually after weeks of contention what has been called the "Great Compromise" was worked out, providing for a House of Representatives reflecting population and a Senate giving equal representation to each state. Madison accepted the compromise with reluctance, realizing that it was necessary to gain the increased national power he saw as crucial. In other details, such as the choice of the president, the selection of the judiciary, and the powers of Congress, Madison's proposals carried. The deliberations were intense through a hot summer, and Madison's sense of the government needed was noticeably more comprehensive and detailed than that of any other delegate.

The Constitution then had to be approved by conventions in each state, and Madison threw himself into the struggle for ratification. Particularly in New York and Virginia the opposition was strong, in New York because of strong local interests. Madison was in New York in late 1787 as a member of the Confederation Congress; while there he joined with Alexander Hamilton and John Jay in a series of periodical letters in defense of the Constitution under the signature Publius. (The name, a common Latin first name, suggests a public or public-spirited man.) The essays first appeared in newspapers from October of 1787 to August of 1788; before the project ended, two volumes of the essays that had thus far appeared were collected in book form. Until 1944 the authorship of the essays had not been worked out precisely, and some questions still remain. It is fairly safe to say that Madison wrote twenty-six of the eighty-five essays by himself and collaborated on three others with Hamilton. Madison's essays, however, were especially significant to the long-term interest of the series.

His first contribution, *Federalist*, number 10, presents his discussion of faction in a republic and argues that an extended republic provides the greatest check on faction. Factions, which he defines as groups actuated by interests of their own opposed to the rights of others or the common interest, could not fail to exist in a free society. "As long as the reason of man continues fallible, and he is at liberty to exercise it, different opinions will be formed." In what Madison called a democracy, by which he meant a pure democracy where every citizen can vote on laws and policies, factions cannot fail to unsettle the state. In a republic, by which he meant a government by elected representatives, the impact of factions is diffused; in a large republic the multitude of special interests will prevent any from an unfair dominance. Thus, he concludes, pointing to the newly designed federal government, "we behold a republican remedy for the diseases most incident to republican government."

Stylistically it is not easy to distinguish Madison's prose from the prose of the other two contributors to *The Federalist*. Each wrote in the balanced Addisonian sentences characteristic of much of the best American writing of the eighteenth century. If it is possible to speak of a stylistic feature that seems more Madisonian, it might be a greater concern for categorization, or what classical rhetoric referred to as the "division" of the subject. There is also at times a certain wry pleasure that he seems to take in his anonymity, such as when (in *Federalist,* number 37) he speculates as a presumed outsider "that the convention must have enjoyed, in a very singular degree, an exemption from the pestilential influence of party animosities—the disease most incident to deliberative bodies and most apt to contaminate their proceedings." Madison had, of course, been present and remembered well the wrangling and factionalism that preceded agreement. Madison's style is often suave and understated. In *Federalist,* number 47, he must deal with objections drawn from "the celebrated Montesquieu" on the mixture of functions among the executive, legislative, and judicial branches. "The British Constitution was to Montesquieu what Homer has been to the didactic writers of epic poetry," Madison writes, deftly pointing beyond Montesquieu to the source of his inspiration, as well as casting doubt on the quality of the imitation. The compliment is elegant and ambiguous; it sets up Madison's next tactic, which is to examine the source of Montesquieu's inspiration. Then follows an examination of the British Constitution (and also, one by one, the American state constitutions) which sidesteps Montesquieu by discovering everywhere the mixture of functions among the separate branches.

The Federalist is organized into two large sections, each published as a volume in the edition of 1788. The first thirty-six papers analyze the inadequacies of the Articles of Confederation and present a general case for a stronger national government. The second half presents a defense of the new Constitution, beginning with a theoretical defense of its republican character, then discussing the parts of the government and their powers one by one. Madison's major contributions to the first half are numbers 10 and 14. In the second half Madison wrote a long series of essays dealing particularly with the Congress and its powers (numbers

37 through 58) while Hamilton was in Albany. (Illness kept Jay from contributing more than six articles.)

Though their travel plans apparently helped to determine who would write, the principal authors wrote on areas congenial to each. For example, Hamilton, a field commander in the Revolution and the future Secretary of the Treasury, wrote on the military weakness of the Articles and on the powers of the executive. Hamilton's emphasis is on the potential greatness of the country, its adventurous spirit, and the future energies of its executive branch. Hamilton rises to a more oratorical tone than Madison employs, with repeated rhetorical questions and phrases in block letters. Madison is more consistently analytical and understated; at points of emphasis he is epigrammatic rather than exclamatory. In *Federalist,* number 51, for instance, he is introducing the controls over concentrations of power in the new Constitution, a balancing of ambitions against ambitions: "But what is government itself but the greatest of all reflections on human nature? If men were angels, no government would be necessary. If angels were to govern men, neither external nor internal controls on government would be necessary. In framing a government which is to be administered by men over men, the great difficulty lies in this: you must first enable the government to control the governed; and in the next place oblige it to control itself. A dependence on the people is, no doubt, the primary control on the government; but experience has taught mankind the necessity of auxiliary precautions." Madison's confidence in human nature was guarded at best, and he had little time for unrealizable ideals, as his tight little *reductio ad absurdum* suggests. The hard details of self-government were his real interest.

The Federalist is a model of lucid exposition, and each individual essay is short enough to appear in an eighteenth-century newspaper. Overall, however, the work is highly complex and subtle; it is a tribute to the electorate of New York in 1788 that they read it and could follow its arguments. (The popularity of the essays when they first appeared is evidenced by their appearance simultaneously in four of the five New York City papers.) *The Federalist* represents in fact a culmination of years of speculation on constitutions for the newly independent states, in part a heritage from the republican and commonwealth theorists of the preceding 150 years.

After making his contributions to the series and finishing his service in the Confederation Congress, Madison left New York for Virginia to organize the campaign for ratification there. He had formidable opponents to expect at the convention: Patrick Henry, Richard Henry Lee, George Mason, Edmund Randolph. His greatest ally in Virginia, Washington, had to remain above the battle, especially since he was universally expected to serve as the president if the Constitution were ratified. Patrick Henry's speeches in the Virginia convention were at one point so eloquent that even the secretary to the convention was spellbound, unable to take notes. Madison by contrast was exhausted and feverish from overwork, and when he spoke in the convention his voice could only be heard by the delegates crowding close to him. Still, his mastery of constitutional questions carried the day, and the Constitution was ratified by a vote of 89 to 79.

In the first Congress Madison was elected to the House of Representatives, the branch of Congress thought likely to be the dominant one. At the same time he continued to serve as an adviser to Washington, consulted continually on matters such as protocol, appointments, and governmental organization. It was Madison who proposed the creation of the departments of state, war, and treasury, each to be headed by a secretary appointable by the president with the advice and consent of the Senate. He also was the principal drafter of the first ten amendments to the Constitution, the Bill of Rights. The absence of a bill of rights had been a major objection against the Constitution; Madison selected the articles from amendments proposed by state ratifying conventions and from the bills of rights already in force in state constitutions. In the case of the First Amendment guarantee against establishments of religion, he had to counteract attempts to weaken the wording. Though each of the provisions has a long history in common law or republican theory, their formulation and place in the Constitution is due to Madison. For these reasons and others Fisher Ames, then a congressman from Massachusetts, called him "our first man."

Madison served in the House of Representatives for the eight years of the Washington administration. His life until this point had consisted of little besides politics; he had little time for the projects and experiments that Franklin and Jefferson had played with on the side. A brief romance in the 1780s had collapsed suddenly. But in 1793 he met a twenty-six-year-old Quaker widow, Dolley Payne Todd, and within a few months they were married. Dolley Madison was charming and buxom, taller than her thin, reserved husband, who was her

Dolley Madison, 1804; portrait by Gilbert Stuart (Pennsylvania Academy of Fine Arts)

senior by seventeen years. For her he remained, in the words of her letter to a friend announcing that he would pay his first call, "the great little Madison"; their marriage was happy for the remaining forty-two years of his life.

During Washington's first term differences arose between Madison and his former collaborator Hamilton, now the secretary of the treasury. Madison disapproved of Hamilton's policy of rewarding speculators in veterans' certificates and of funding the national debt. He also saw the establishment of a national bank as unconstitutional. By 1791 these differences had led to a newspaper war between partisans of the two positions. Madison enlisted the help of his college classmate Philip Freneau and arranged for his appointment in Jefferson's state department so he could print a newspaper in Philadelphia attacking the Hamilton position. Madison himself wrote a number of unsigned essays for Freneau's *National Gazette* on subjects ranging from population and emigration to the property in his rights which every citizen has. Eventually the differences between Madison and Jefferson on the one hand and Hamilton on the other led to the formation of the first national parties, the Republicans and the Federalists.

During the Adams administration Madison was out of the national government for the first extended period since 1780. During those years he was able to remodel Montpelier, where he always returned when he could escape from public business. The Alien and Sedition Acts of 1798 prompted him and Jefferson to draft protests that had a fateful later history. Madison's "Virginia Resolutions" of December 1798, soon passed by the Virginia legislature, argued that the Acts were unconstitutional and that the states "have the right . . . to interpose for arresting the progress of the evil." Jefferson's "Kentucky Resolutions" went beyond denunciation to posit that each state could judge for itself the infractions of the Constitution. In the "Virginia Resolutions" and the subsequent report on the resolution of 1798 which he drafted in 1800 as a member of the Virginia legislature, Madison went as far as he ever did from his basically nationalist principles. In this case he was denouncing acts which infringed on the freedom of speech and the press, but a later generation of Southern politicians would borrow the language of interposition and nullification with the sanction of Madison's and Jefferson's names.

When Jefferson took office as the next president in 1801, he named his old friend as secretary of state. The following eight years were devoted to diplomatic protocol and negotiations with the British and French. The Napoleonic Wars continued with few interruptions through this period; the United States sought to trade with both adversaries without interference. Madison worked closely with Jefferson in formulating what came to be Jefferson's foreign policy. Since the 1770s Madison had inclined toward the French and distrusted England, and the coming of the French Revolution only increased that bias. He saw England as the champion of monarchy and reaction, yet he was wary of Napoleon; the Republicans sought to avoid military entanglements with Europe, even as American merchant ships were ambitiously expanding commercial relationships. The first Jefferson administration saw the negotiations with Napoleon leading to the Louisiana Purchase. Madison and Jefferson coordinated those negotiations, and when Jefferson hesitated at the last moment about the constitutionality of the purchase, Madison insisted that the step be taken. Through these years England was

James Madison, 1804; portrait by Gilbert Stuart
(Colonial Williamsburg, Inc.)

engaged in frequent harassment of American merchant vessels, sometimes even drafting (or "impressing") American seamen to serve in the depleted British Navy. Peaceable means to stop this were tried; in 1806 Madison published anonymously a long pamphlet entitled *An Examination of the British Doctrine Which Subjects to Capture a Neutral Trade Not Open in Time of Peace.* Jefferson imposed in 1807 a total embargo on American shipping to the European belligerents in a futile attempt to pressure them into respecting America's neutral rights. These diplomatic difficulties remained unresolved when Madison succeeded Jefferson as president in 1809.

As a president, Madison remained a believer in the supremacy of the legislative branch, the necessity of avoiding European alliances, and the wisdom of restraining federal power. Later generations of historians who admired a forceful Presidency interpreted this policy as timidity or an intellectual's reluctance to exercise force. Henry Adams, in his magisterial *History of the United States during the Administrations of Jefferson and Madison* (1889-1891),

Certification of Madison's election to the Presidency of the United States (Library of Congress)

presented overall a negative image of Madison as secretary of state and president; his Madison is largely a victim of events.

Until recently the prevailing view has been that Madison was dragged reluctantly into the War of 1812 by war hawks in Congress. Certainly the war message he sent to Congress in June of 1812 is no clarion call to battle. It reviews the recent history of diplomatic efforts to resolve the crisis, notes their failure and the continued English attack on American commerce, and concludes that Congress is now constitutionally charged to decide whether war should be declared. In fact English intransigence in the face of Madison's efforts to negotiate a settlement left the administration little choice. Both of the European powers had offended, but England, as a sea power, was the greater offender. The Republicans had made few preparations for war, despite Madison's rather unemphatic urgings; his secretary of war, like his first secretary of state, filled the post indifferently well. Early humiliating failures by American forces were gradually followed by changes of army leadership, leading to success by the end of the war. Madison had the bizarre fate of being the only president exposed to enemy fire while in office, when a small British detachment routed an army of militiamen and burned the principal public buildings in Washington. With the establishment of peace in 1815 came the end of the Federalists as a political force; their English sympathies and the New England talk of secession left them silent and discredited in the face of what came to be known as the Era of Good Feeling. That period of political tranquillity, lasting from the last years of Madison's administration through the administration of his successor, James Monroe, can be credited in part to the steady and balanced course Madison kept to as president. As his old adversary John Adams wrote to Jefferson, "notwithstand[ing] a thousand Faults and blunders, his Administration has acquired more glory, and established more Union, than all his three Predecessors, Washington Adams and Jefferson, put together."

Madison returned to Montpelier for his retirement, where he was visited as a kind of oracle by people such as Lafayette, Edward Everett, Jared Sparks, James Kirke Paulding, and Harriet Martineau. He had no children except for a stepson, John Payne Todd, whose gambling debts had to be repeatedly paid off. Even in his last years public questions occupied his mind. Jefferson's long correspondence with Adams is clearly the work of someone whose reading and speculations were at

Montpelier after 1811, drawing by J. B. Longacre

last given free rein; Madison's late writing remained that of a statesman. He collaborated with Jefferson in founding the University of Virginia and succeeded him as its rector. He served in 1829 in the Virginia Constitutional Convention, but he was unable to curb the established power of the slaveholding aristocracy, and the compromise he accepted simply confirmed it in its control over Virginia's political life. In his eighties he had to defend his "Virginia Resolutions" of 1798 from the use to which they were being put by South Carolina nullificationists. In 1834 he wrote his "Advice to My Country," two short paragraphs to be read after his death warning against any who would undermine the federal union.

Considering Madison's achievements, it is worth asking why he is less known than others of the Revolutionary generation of comparable importance. Certainly he was honored in his own time and up until the Civil War. Madison, Wisconsin (founded in 1836), and Madison Avenue in New York City are only two of the testimonies to his reputation. But until the middle of the twentieth century he did not have an adequate biography; probably the most influential one published before 1941 was written by Sydney H. Gay, a northern sympathizer with the Federalists who disliked Madison's politics and his origins. In the South Madison was a nagging voice of nationalism in the face of strong sectional tendencies. Even in his own time his calmness and reserve were anomalous in a political scene where displays of personal force and even quarrelsomeness were considered the mark of a substantial figure. Madison did not lay claim to originality in his political thought; he sought rather to be the advocate of tested republican ideas. Even in defending so great an innovation as the Constitution, he commends it as the collective achievement of American political genius. In his style he was unbendingly formal, except in conversation among friends. His restraint in political action, advocacy, and the conduct of life was not the product of inhibitions, so far as his inner life can be discerned; restraint gave him power, enabling his frail body to weather eighty-five years of momentous changes, some of which he brought about himself.

The six volumes of Irving Brant's biography have cleared up misconceptions about Madison left over from the nineteenth century. (Ralph Ketcham's one-volume biography or Brant's own abridgement will serve most students adequately.) The work of Douglass Adair has done much to recapture the subtlety of Madison's thinking; recently Garry Wills has explored Madison's debt to the Scottish Enlightenment in *The Federalist*. Saul Padover and Marvin Meyers have edited useful anthologies of Madison's writings. And eventually the Madison papers, gradually being published by the University of Chicago and the University of Virginia Presses, will reveal "the great little Madison" as fully as his stature deserves.

Biographies:
William C. Rives, *History of the Life and Times of James Madison*, 3 volumes (Boston: Little, Brown, 1859-1868);

Irving Brant, *James Madison*, 6 volumes (Indianapolis: Bobbs-Merrill, 1941-1961); abridged as *The Fourth President: A Life of James Madison* (Indianapolis: Bobbs-Merrill, 1970);

Harold S. Schultz, *James Madison* (New York: Twayne, 1970);

Ralph L. Ketcham, *James Madison* (New York: Macmillan, 1971);

James Madison, A Biography in His Own Words, 2 volumes, edited by Merrill D. Peterson (New York: Newsweek, 1974).

References:
Douglass Adair, *Fame and the Founding Fathers* (New York: Norton, 1974);

Theodore Bolton, "The Life Portraits of James Madison," *William & Mary Quarterly*, third series 8 (January 1951): 25-39;

Marcus Cunliffe, "James Madison," in *The Ultimate Decision: The President as Commander in Chief*, edited by Ernest R. May (New York: Braziller, 1960), pp. 21-53;

Richard Beale Davis, *Intellectual Life in Jefferson's Virginia* (Chapel Hill: University of North Carolina Press, 1964);

John Fiske, "James Madison, the Constructive Statesman," in *Essays Historical and Literary*, volume 1 (New York: Macmillan, 1902), pp. 185-218;

Adrienne Koch, *Jefferson and Madison: The Great Collaboration* (New York: Knopf, 1950);

Koch, *Madison's "Advice to My Country"* (Princeton: Princeton University Press, 1966);

Louis C. Schaedler, "James Madison, Literary Craftsman," *William and Mary Quarterly*, third series 3 (October 1946): 515-533;

Garry Wills, *Explaining America: The Federalist* (Garden City: Doubleday, 1981).

Papers:
Madison's papers are at the Library of Congress.

Samuel Eusebius McCorkle

(23 August 1746-21 June 1811)

M. Jimmie Killingsworth
New Mexico Institute of Mining and Technology

BOOKS: *A Sermon, on the Doctrine and Duty of Sacrificing, First Delivered at an Ordination in New-Providence, Mecklinburg County, North-Carolina, Feb. 2, 1792. And Afterwards, with Some Additions and Alterations at Salim, on Nolichucky, at the Opening of a Commission of the Synod of the Carolinas, Sept. 3d. 1792* (Philadelphia: Printed by William Young, 1794);

A Charity Sermon. First Delivered in Salisbury, July 28: and Afterwards in Other Places in Rowan, and the Counties Adjoining; Particularly at Sugar's Creek, in Mecklenburg County, at the Opening of the Synod of the Carolinas, October 2: and Last at the Meeting of the Hon. the General Assembly in Fayetteville, December, 1793 (Halifax, N.C.: Printed by Abraham Hodge, 1795);

A Sermon, on the Comparative Happiness and Duty of the United States of America, Contrasted with Other Nations, Particularly the Israelites. Delivered in Salisbury, on Wednesday, February 18th: and at Thyatira, on Thursday February 19th, 1795: Being the Day of General Thanksgiving and Prayer, Appointed by the President of the United States (Halifax, N.C.: Printed by Abraham Hodge, 1795);

Four Discourses on the General, First Principles of Deism and Revelation Contrasted, Delivered in Salisbury, and Thyatira, on Different Days in April and May 1797 (Salisbury, N.C.: Francis Coupee & John Slump, 1797);

A Discourse on the Doctrine and Duty of Keeping the Sabbath (Salisbury, N.C.: Printed by John M. Slump at Michael Brown's English and German Printing Office, 1798);

Three Discourses on the Terms of Christian Communion. In the First of Which Certain Principles Are Attempted to Be Established in Order from Them to Deduce in the Ensuing Discourses the Doctrines and Precepts that Ought to Be Made Terms (Salisbury, N.C.: Printed by Francis Coupee & John M. Slump at their English and German Printing Office, 1798);

The Work of God for the French Republic, and Then Her Reformation or Ruin; or, the Novel and Useful Experiment of National Deism, to Us and All Future Ages (Salisbury, N.C.: Printed by Francis Coupee, 1798);

True Greatness. A Sermon on the Death of Gen. George Washington; the Substance of Which Was Delivered at Thyatira on Sunday, January 12th; and Afterwards with Some Additions in Salisbury, Feb. 11, 1800 (Lincolnton, N.C.: Printed by John M. Slump, 1800).

Samuel McCorkle, who was to become one of North Carolina's most prominent preachers and educators in the revolutionary and early national period, was born in Lancaster County, Pennsylvania. His family moved South when he was nine years old and settled in Rowan County, near Salisbury, North Carolina. Young McCorkle received his early education in the classical school of David Caldwell in Guilford County, North Carolina, and eventually attended the College of New Jersey (later Princeton University), from which he graduated in 1772. He immediately began the study of theology and was licensed to preach by the Presbytery of New York. In 1776 he was invited to become the pastor of the Presbyterian church in his home village of Thyatira, North Carolina, a post he was to fill for the rest of his life. During the Revolution, he ardently supported the American cause and became recognized throughout the region as a forceful and learned preacher. He married Margaret Gillespie Steele on 2 July 1776 and with her raised a family of ten children.

McCorkle opened his own classical school in 1785. With its twin emphasis on Christianity and classical scholarship, Zion-Parnassus Academy was well known for its high standards. During the ten years the school was in operation, forty-five future ministers were educated, including six out of seven of the first graduates of the University of North Carolina, which McCorkle, who received a Doctor of Divinity degree from Dickinson College in 1792, was instrumental in founding. He was one of the first trustees and at one time was considered for the office of president. In his *A Charity Sermon* (1795), both a plea for funds for the new university and a statement of his educational principles, he argues that moral society is based on the education of the young, which is the responsibility of the Christian community.

His great sermons of the 1790s are mainly concerned with the moral fabric of the new republic and the Christian's duties in shaping the New World democracy. Though he was a conservative Presbyterian, he did not engage in sectarian squabbles, but instead seemed to address the general Christian community in his battle with external enemies. Particularly he attacked deism, which he saw as the root of social evil in France. In *The Work of God for the French Republic, and Then Her Reformation or Ruin; or, the Novel and Useful Experiment of National Deism* (1798) he concludes that God's cause is ironically furthered by the French government's atrocities, through which the Christian world is made aware of the deficiencies of deistic moral doctrine. The libertinism resulting from deism is also condemned in his *A Sermon, on the Comparative Happiness and Duty of the United States of America* (1795), a patriotic discourse appealing to "revelation and reason." In *Four Discourses on the General, First Principles of Deism* (1797), McCorkle confronts, among others, Thomas Paine, whose *Age of Reason* had just been published. He charges that Paine's book is full of inconsistencies and argues that Christianity is more of a religion of reason than deism is.

McCorkle's fervor for publishing his sermons tapered off toward the end of the century. Perhaps he realized that his closely reasoned discourses with their classical allusions and frequent references to modern historical, ethical, and religious writings were no longer in fashion. An emotional revival, much like the Great Awakening of the previous century, swept through the Carolinas and Tennessee in the early nineteenth century, and the sometimes bizarre "exercises" of this movement were tolerated more than encouraged by the aging McCorkle, who, true to his Scots-Irish heritage, tended to be an "Old Side" Presbyterian. His health failed early in the century, and he died and was buried in Thyatira in 1811.

References:

James F. Hurley and Julia Goode Eagan, *The Prophet of Zion-Parnassus: Samuel Eusebius McCorkle* (Richmond: Presbyterian Committee for Publication, 1934);

William B. Sprague, *Annals of the American Pulpit* (New York: Carter & Brothers, 1858), III: 346-349;

Ernest Trice Thompson, *Presbyterians in the South, Volume One: 1607-1861* (Richmond: John Knox Press, 1963), pp. 82-83, 224, 245, 261.

Jedidiah Morse
(23 August 1761-9 June 1826)

Robert S. Levine
University of Maryland

SELECTED BOOKS: *Geography Made Easy; Being a Short but Comprehensive System of that Useful and Agreeable Science* . . . (New Haven: Printed by Meigs, Bowen & Dana, 1784);

The American Geography; Or, a View of the Present Situation of the United States of America . . . (Elizabeth Town: Printed by Shepard Kollock for the author, 1789; London: Printed for J. Stockdale, 1792);

The History of America . . . (Philadelphia: Printed & sold by Thomas Dobson, 1790);

A Sermon Preached Lord's Day, February 28, 1790, upon the Death of Richard Carey, Esq. . . . (Boston: Printed by Samuel Hall, 1790);

The American Universal Geography . . . , 2 volumes (Boston: Printed by Isaiah Thomas & Ebenezer T. Andrews, 1793);

Elements of Geography . . . (Boston: Printed & sold by I. Thomas & E. T. Andrews, 1795);

The Present Situation of Other Nations of the World, Contrasted With Our Own. A Sermon . . . (Boston: Printed by Samuel Hall, 1795);

The Duty of Resignation under Afflictions, Illustrated and Enforced from the Example of Christ, In a Sermon . . . (Boston: Printed by Samuel Hall, 1796);

The American Gazetteer . . . (Boston: Printed by S. Hall, and by Thomas & Andrews, 1797; London: Printed for J. Stockdale, 1798);

A Description of the Soil, Productions, Commercial, Agricultural and Local Advantages of the Georgia Western Territory... (Boston: Printed by Thomas & Andrews, 1797);

The Character and Reward of a Good and Faithful Servant Illustrated in a Sermon, Delivered at Charlestown, April 29, 1798, the Lord's Day Following the Death and Interment of the Honorable James Russell, Esq.... (Boston: Printed by Samuel Hall, 1798);

A Sermon, Delivered at the New North Church in Boston, in the Morning, and in the Afternoon at Charlestown, May 9th, 1798, Being the Day Recommended by John Adams, President of the United States of America for Solemn Humiliation, Fasting and Prayer (Boston: Printed by Samuel Hall, 1798);

A Sermon Delivered Before the Grand Lodge of Free and Accepted Masons of the Commonwealth of Massachusetts... (Leominster, Mass.: Printed by Charles & John Prentiss, 1798);

A Sermon, Preached at Charlestown, November 29, 1798, on the Anniversary Thanksgiving in Massachusetts... (Boston: Printed by Samuel Hall, 1798);

A Sermon, Exhibiting the Present Dangers, and Consequent Duties of the Citizens of the United States of America. Delivered at Charlestown, April 25, 1799. The Day of the National Fast (Charlestown: Printed & sold by Samuel Etheridge, 1799);

An Address, to the Students at Phillips Academy, in Andover. Delivered July 9, 1799... (Charlestown: Printed by Samuel Etheridge, 1799);

A Sermon Preached before the Humane Society of the Commonwealth of Massachusetts, at Their Semi-Annual Meeting, June 9th, 1801 (Boston: Printed by John & Thomas Fleet, 1801);

A New Gazetteer of the Eastern Continent; or, A Geographical Dictionary: Containing, in Alphabetical Order, A Description of All the Countries, Kingdoms, States, Cities, Towns, Principal Rivers, Lakes, Harbours, Mountains, &c. &c. in Europe, Asia, Africa, and Their Adjacent Islands..., by Morse and Elijah Parish (Charlestown: Printed & sold by S. Etheridge, 1802);

A Sermon, Preached at the Ordination of the Rev. Hezekiah May, to the Pastoral Care of the Second Congregational Church in Marblehead, June 23, 1803... (Charlestown: Printed & sold by Samuel Etheridge, 1803);

A Sermon, Delivered before the Ancient & Honourable

Jedidiah Morse, portrait by Samuel F. B. Morse, circa 1820-1822 (Yale University Art Gallery. Bequest of Josephine K. Colgate, 1968. 3.1)

Artillery Company, in Boston, June 6, 1803... (Charlestown: Printed by S. Etheridge, 1803);

A Compendious History of New England. Designed for Schools and Private Families, by Morse and Parish (Charlestown: Printed & sold by Samuel Etheridge, 1804; London: C. Taylor, 1808);

The True Reasons on Which the Election of a Hollis Professor of Divinity in Harvard College, Was Opposed at the Board of Overseers, Feb. 14, 1805 (Charlestown: Printed for the author, 1805);

A Sermon, Delivered at Charlestown, the Sabbath, after the Interment of Miss Mary Russell, Who Died, July 24, 1806, Aged 53 Years (Charlestown: Printed by J. Howe, 1806);

A Sermon, Preached in Brattle-Street Church, Boston, September 25, 1807, Before the Managers of the Boston Female Asylum, on Their Seventh Anniversary (Boston: Russell & Cutler, 1807);

A Sermon, Delivered, May 18th, 1808, at the Ordination of the Rev. Joshua Huntington... (Boston: Printed by Belcher & Armstrong, 1808);

A Discourse, Delivered at the African Meeting-House, in Boston, July 14, 1808, in Grateful Celebration of the Abolition of the African Slave-Trade, by the

Governments of the United States, Great Britain and Denmark (Boston: Printed by Lincoln & Edmands, 1808);

Signs of the Times. A Sermon, Preached before the Society for Propagating the Gospel among the Indians and Others in North America, At Their Anniversary, Nov. 1, 1810 (Charlestown: Printed by S. T. Armstrong, 1810);

A Sermon Delivered before the Convention of Congregational Ministers in Boston, at Their Anniversary Meeting, May 28, 1812 (Boston: Published by Samuel T. Armstrong, 1812);

A Sermon Delivered at Charlestown, July 23, 1812, the Day Appointed by the Governor and Council of Massachusetts, to Be Observed in Fasting and Prayer Throughout the Commonwealth; In Consequence of a Declaration of War with Great Britain (Charlestown: Printed by S. Etheridge, Jr., 1812);

An Appeal to the Public, on the Controversy Respecting the Revolution in Harvard College, and the Events Which Have Followed It; Occasioned by the Use Which Has Been Made of Certain Complaints and Accusations of Miss Hannah Adams, Against the Author (Charlestown: Printed for the author, 1814);

The Gospel Harvest, Illustrated in a Sermon . . . (Boston: Willis, 1815);

Review of American Unitarianism (Boston: S. T. Armstrong, 1815);

The Christian Ambassador. A Sermon Delivered at the Ordination of Rev. Eliakim Phelps . . . (Brookfield, Mass.: Printed by E. Merriam & Co., 1817);

A Sermon, Delivered before the American Board of Commissioners for Foreign Missions . . . (Boston: Printed by George Clark, 1821);

A Report to the Secretary of War of the United States, on Indian Affairs, Comprising a Narrative of a Tour Performed in the Summer of 1820 . . . (New Haven: Printed by S. Converse, 1822);

A New Universal Atlas of the World . . . , by Morse and Sidney E. Morse (New Haven: Howe & Spaulding, 1822);

Annals of the American Revolution . . . (Hartford, 1824).

The combative and industrious Jedidiah Morse presided over the First Congregational Church of Charlestown, Massachusetts, from 1789 to 1819. During this time Morse emerged as a prominent Federalist supporter and the leading opponent of the Unitarian movement in New En-

gland. While concerning himself with political and theological matters, Morse additionally addressed the plight of the Indian and the problem of slavery, but he achieved his greatest fame for his series of geography textbooks and reference works, which earned him the title Father of American Geography.

Born in Woodstock, Connecticut, to Jedidiah and Sarah Child Morse, Morse was the eighth of ten children, five of whom died in infancy. From his father, a deacon at the First Society of Woodstock and a patriot who served on a committee of correspondence, he learned the paramount importance of religious and civic service. He enrolled at Yale College with the class of 1783 at a time when New Light enthusiasts were challenging the rational orthodoxy of the president, Ezra Stiles. This particular influence at Yale exposed Morse to an evangelical zeal for religion balanced by a rationalistic caution, an approach that would inform his subsequent writings. While studying for the ministry, Morse taught at a girls' school in New Haven, and there he discovered the need for a suitable geography textbook. In 1784 he wrote America's first geography text, *Geography Made Easy,* and in 1787, after his ordination in 1786, he took a pulpit in Midway, Georgia, in part because the position provided him with the opportunity to do further work on his geography. Returning to New York after six months, he preached in the Collegiate Presbyterian Churches of New York in 1788, and on 14 May 1789 he married Elizabeth Ann Breese. Three of their eleven children survived infancy: Sidney Edwards Morse, Richard Cary Morse, and Samuel Finley Breese Morse, the inventor of the telegraph. Elizabeth was the granddaughter of Samuel Finley, president of the Presbyterian College of New Jersey (later Princeton University), and with the help of the Presbyterians, Morse obtained the pulpit of Charlestown's First Congregational Church in 1789.

Installed in Charlestown the day of Washington's inauguration, Morse identified strongly with Washington and the Federalists and was troubled by the rise of Jeffersonian Republicanism. As the Federalists' prestige waned, Morse became convinced that conspirators contributed to the political difficulties of John Adams. In *A Sermon, Delivered at the New North Church in Boston* (1798), Morse became the first clergyman to alert the country to the presumed conspiratorial threat posed by the Bavarian Illuminati, a secret society founded at the University of Ingolstadt in 1776. Relying on a copy of John

By Candlelight, *portrait of Elizabeth Breese Morse by Samuel F. B. Morse, circa 1820 (Yale University Art Gallery. Gift of Richard C. Morse, Ph.D. 1906. 1951. 58.1)*

ism became the overriding concern of his ministry. In the 1790s he initiated an ultimately unsuccessful campaign to create an ecclesiastical association with the Presbyterians that would force the Unitarians from the orthodox fold. But the real crisis for Morse developed in 1803 with the death of David Tappan, the Hollis Professor of Divinity at Harvard. Outraged by the election in 1805 of the Unitarian Henry Ware to replace Tappan as Hollis Professor, Morse, an overseer of the college, responded with *The True Reasons on Which the Election of a Hollis Professor of Divinity in Harvard College, Was Opposed at the Board of Overseers* (1805), which explained Morse's opposition to his election. In this pamphlet Morse provided an overview of Harvard's conservative history, an attack on Ware's Arminianism, and a lament for the dramatic departure from orthodoxy. Morse's dissatisfaction with the outcome of the election signaled the end of his willingness to work with the liberals within the Congregational order.

In 1805 he began the popular and influential *Panoplist*, an evangelical periodical dedicated to up-

Robison's *Proofs of a Conspiracy against All the Religions and Governments of Europe Carried on in the Secret Meetings of Free Masons, Illuminati, and Reading Societies* (1798), Morse declared that this atheistical group caused the French Revolution and now sought to subvert and master American society. Though the Illuminati in fact had been defunct since 1786, Morse's warnings were promptly echoed by a number of leading ministers and contributed to the outbreak of a short-lived popular hysteria. The image of the expedient, conspiring Illuminati found its way into some of Charles Brockden Brown's fiction, most notably *Ormond* and "Memoirs of Carwin." The Illuminati scare was discredited by 1799, but Morse remained true to his Federalist position and soon after Jefferson's election founded the Federalist periodical, the *New England Palladium*.

Morse's energetic and finally misguided response to the erosion of Federalist power no doubt expressed his own unease with the religious situation in New England, as he tried to steer a course between Edwardean New Divinity and liberal Arminianism and was attacked by both sides. The emerging strength of the liberal churches particularly worried Morse, and his effort to combat Unitarian-

GEOGRAPHY
MADE EASY.
BEING A SHORT, BUT COMPREHENSIVE
System
OF THAT VERY USEFUL AND AGREEABLE SCIENCE.
EXHIBITING

In an easy and concise View, the Figures, Motions, Distances, and Magnitudes of the heavenly Bodies :—A general description of the Earth considered as a Planet ; with its grand Divisions into Land and Water, Continents, Oceans, Islands, &c.—The Situation, Boundaries and Extent of the several Empires, Kingdoms, and States, together with an Account of their Climate, Soil, Productions and commerce :—The Number, Genius, and general Character of the Inhabitants :—Their Religion, Government and History :—The Latitude, Longitude, Distances, and Bearings of the principal Places from Philadelphia and London, and a Number of useful Geographical Tables.

Illustrated with two correct and elegant MAPS, one of the World, and the other of the United States, together with a Number of newly constructed Maps, adapted to the Capacities and Understanding of Children.

Calculated particularly for the Use and Improvement of SCHOOLS in the United States.

By JEDIDIAH MORSE, A. B.

" There is not a SON or a DAUGHTER of Adam, but has " some concern in both GEOGRAPHY and ASTRONOMY."
DR. WATTS.

" Among those Studies which are usually recommended to " young People, there can be few that might be improved to " better Uses than Geography." *Essays on various Subjects.*

NEW-HAVEN:
Printed by MEIGS, BOWEN and DANA, in Chapel-Street.
1784

Title page for America's first geography textbook (courtesy of the John Carter Brown Library at Brown University)

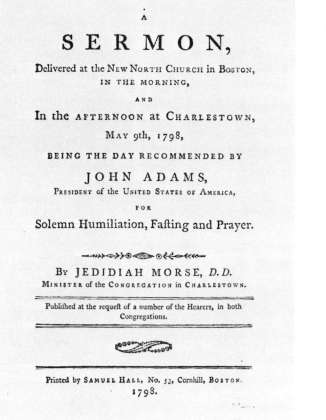

A

SERMON,

Delivered at the New North Church in Boston,
IN THE MORNING,

AND

In the AFTERNOON at CHARLESTOWN,

MAY 9th, 1798,

BEING THE DAY RECOMMENDED BY

JOHN ADAMS,

President of the United States of America,

FOR

Solemn Humiliation, Fasting and Prayer.

By JEDIDIAH MORSE, *D. D.*
MINISTER of the CONGREGATION in CHARLESTOWN.

Publifhed at the requeft of a number of the Hearers, in both
Congregations.

Printed by SAMUEL HALL, No. *53*, Cornhill, BOSTON.
1798.

*Title page for the controversial sermon in which Morse warned
that the Bavarian Illuminati were conspiring to subvert American society. Morse was unaware that the atheistic group had
been defunct since 1786 (courtesy of the John Carter Brown
Library at Brown University).*

holding orthodox principles. In direct response to
the developments at Harvard, Morse in 1808
founded the Andover Theological Seminary and
one year later helped to establish the Park Street
Church in Boston. Morse's outspoken attacks on
liberal religion in the *Panoplist* and in *Review of
American Unitarianism* (1815) prompted William
Ellery Channing to reaffirm the Unitarian position
in *A Letter to the Rev. Samuel C. Thacher, on the Aspersions Contained in a Late Number of the Panoplist*
(1815). The contrast between Morse's polemical
charges and Channing's gentlemanly rejoinder
further strengthened the Unitarian position, and in
1816 a Unitarian defection occurred in Morse's own
church. Concerned that his energies were misspent
on religious controversies and on his geographies,
Morse's parishioners finally requested and received
his resignation in 1819.

Morse's political and theological conflicts centered primarily on New England matters. His geographies on the other hand brought him national,
and even international, renown and are his most
significant literary achievement. Like Jefferson, he
wished to refute those European geographers who
argued that the American continent lacked the
health and vitality of Europe. As he writes in the
preface to *The American Universal Geography* (1793),
"to depend on foreigners, partial to a proverb to
their own country, for an account of the divisions,
rivers, productions, manufactures, navigation,
commerce, literature, improvements, &c. of the
American States, would certainly be a disgraceful
blot upon our literary character." Additionally, he
desired to celebrate social hierarchy and order,
values he believed were central to New England's
republican character. Morse's geographies thus
both situated America and offered guidelines for its
moral well-being. But Morse also possessed a
boundless enthusiasm for the accretion of natural
facts, which help to make his geographies distinc-
tively American.

Morse's textbook, *Geography Made Easy* (1784),
was enthusiastically received and, in revised versions, eventually went through twenty-five print-
ings. In 1789 he published a larger work intended
for home reference, *The American Geography*, which
he later expanded in 1793 to the two-volume *The
American Universal Geography*. (Later editions of
Geography Made Easy drew on these two works.)
Essentially a compilation of gathered information,
The American Universal Geography opens with a detailed astronomical cosmogony and, after providing
a historical overview along with the text of the Constitution, offers precise descriptions of the national
landscape. Morse's writing is empirical and, as his
syntax shows, even a bit poetic: "The Ohio is a most
beautiful river. Its river gentle, waters clear, and
bottom smooth and unbroken by rocks and rapids,
a single instance only excepted. It is one quarter of a
mile wide at Fort Pitt: five hundred yards at the
mouth of the Great Kanhaway: 1200 yards at Louisville; and the rapids, half a mile, in some few places
below Louisville: but its general breadth does not
exceed 600 yards." Morse's passion for precision
does not keep him from speculating about the mysteries of the continent with a genuine awe. For
example, he wonders why oyster shells can be
found in the Savannah River, and after hypothesiz-
ing that the ocean may have left the shells when it
receded in centuries past, allows that he does not
know how or why this process should have occurred. Morse returns to a surer footing when he
describes regional character, celebrating the chari-

table and literate New Englander while condemning the dissipated and slaveholding Southerner. Widely circulated in America and Europe, *The American Universal Geography* secured Morse's reputation as America's great geographer and led to an honorary degree in 1794 from the University of Edinburgh. Morse's industrious reworkings and revisings of his basic texts ensured that his geographies would dominate the field through the early nineteenth century; in 1795 he published a primer, *Elements of Geography*, and in 1797 he published the first of several gazetteers. So pervasive were his texts that Washington Irving recalled them from his school days with annoyance and began his *A History of New York* (1809) with a satirical version of Morse's prefatory cosmogony.

Irving's hostility toward the geographies centered on their all-knowingness, and on their New England evangelical bias. Morse regarded New England as the natural center for evangelical efforts, because, as he argued in *A Compendious History of New England* (1804), written in collaboration with Elijah Parish, New England history was the history of America's spiritual ascent. Morse's evangelical zeal led him to found the New England Tract Society (1814) and to help establish the interdenominational American Bible Society (1816). Both organizations were dedicated to the mass distribution throughout America of religious texts, and both benefited from Morse's entrepreneurial skills.

Soon after his resignation from the First Congregational Church, Morse turned his attention to a different evangelical concern, the problem of America's Indians. He believed that the best way to save the Indians from extermination was to convert them to Christianity and to educate them. Commis-

A

REPORT

TO THE

SECRETARY OF WAR

OF THE UNITED STATES,

ON INDIAN AFFAIRS,

COMPRISING A NARRATIVE OF A TOUR

PERFORMED

IN THE SUMMER OF 1820, UNDER A COMMISSION FROM THE PRESIDENT OF
THE UNITED STATES, FOR THE PURPOSE OF ASCERTAINING, FOR
THE USE OF THE GOVERNMENT, THE ACTUAL STATE OF
THE INDIAN TRIBES IN OUR COUNTRY:

ILLUSTRATED BY A MAP OF THE UNITED STATES; ORNAMENTED BY A
CORRECT PORTRAIT OF A PAWNEE INDIAN.

BY THE REV. JEDIDIAH MORSE, D. D.
Late Minister of the First Congregational Church in Charlestown, near Boston, now resident
in New-Haven.

NEW-HAVEN:

Published by Davis & Force, Washington, D. C.; Cushing & Jewett, Baltimore; W. W. Woodward, and E. Littell, Philadelphia; Spalding & Howe, and R. N. Henry, New-York; E. & E. Hosford, Albany; Howe & Spalding, New-Haven; G. Goodwin & Sons, Hudson & Co. O. D. Cooke & Sons, Hartford; Richardson & Lord, S. T. Armstrong, Lincoln & Edmunds, Cummings & Hilliard, and G. Clark, Boston.

PRINTED BY S. CONVERSE.
1822.

Frontispiece and title page for the report in which Morse urged that American Indians "be raised gradually and ultimately, to the rank, and to the enjoyment of all the rights and privileges of freemen, and citizens of the United States"

sioned in 1820 by the Federal government to study the plight of the Indians and to recommend a national policy, Morse, in *A Report to the Secretary of War of the United States, on Indian Affairs* (1822), urged that the Indians "be raised gradually and ultimately, to the rank, and to the enjoyment of all the rights and privileges of freemen, and citizens of the United States." By contrast, he believed that establishing colonies in Africa for freed blacks was the best solution to the slavery problem, though in *A Discourse, Delivered at the African Meeting-House* (1808) he had expressed the hope that free blacks could adopt the New England way in New England.

Throughout his life, Morse clung tenaciously to his orthodox beliefs and his millennial hope for an orderly Christian republic. His tenacity sometimes clouded his vision, but all of his publications express an honest and scrupulous desire to help shape the national culture and character. His geographies survive as an honorable and prodigious achievement, in their own way an important American epic.

Biographies:

Sidney E. Morse, *Memorabilia in the Life of Jedidiah Morse, D.D., formerly Pastor of the First Church in Charlestown, Mass.* (Boston: A. W. Locke, 1867);

William B. Sprague, *The Life of Jedidiah Morse* (New York: A. D. F. Randolph, 1874);

James King Morse, *Jedidiah Morse: A Champion of New England Orthodoxy* (New York: Columbia University Press, 1939);

Joseph W. Phillips, *Jedidiah Morse and New England Congregationalism* (New Brunswick: Rutgers University Press, 1983).

References:

Sydney A. Ahlstrom, *A Religious History of the American People* (New Haven: Yale University Press, 1972);

Ralph H. Brown, "The American Geographies of Jedidiah Morse," *Annals of the Association of American Geographers*, 31 (1941): 145-217;

K. Alan Snyder, "Foundations of Liberty: The Christian Republicanism of Timothy Dwight and Jedidiah Morse," *New England Quarterly*, 56 (1983): 382-397;

Vernon Stauffer, *New England and the Bavarian Illuminati* (New York: Columbia University Press, 1918);

Conrad Wright, "The Controversial Career of Jedidiah Morse," *Harvard Library Bulletin*, 31 (1983): 64-87.

Papers:

The New-York Historical Society, the New York Public Library, the Historical Society of Pennsylvania, and Yale University have collections of Morse's papers.

Sarah Wentworth Morton

(August 1759-14 May 1846)

Amanda Porterfield
Syracuse University

BOOKS: *Ouâbi; or The Virtues of Nature. An Indian Tale. In Four Cantos,* as Philenia (Boston: Printed by I. Thomas & E. T. Andrews, 1790);

Beacon Hill. A Local Poem, Historic and Descriptive. Book I (Boston: Printed by Manning & Loring for the author, 1797);

The Virtues of Society, A Tale Founded on Fact (Boston: Printed by Manning & Loring for the author, 1799);

My Mind and Its Thoughts, in Sketches, Fragments, and Essays (Boston: Wells & Lilly, 1823).

Sarah Wentworth Morton was described by her biographers in 1931 as "the most noteworthy American poetess . . . between Mrs. Anne Bradstreet and Mrs. Sigourney." In her own time she was renowned for her poetry about the virtues of freedom. Like Anne Bradstreet, Sarah Wentworth Morton wrote about moral ideas and spiritual events. Like Lydia Huntly Sigourney, she wrote poems about and with emotion, but unlike "The Sweet Singer of Hartford," Mrs. Morton's romanticism was tempered by rationalism, and realism

Sarah Wentworth Morton

society, Sarah Wentworth Morton presided over Apthorp House on State Street and, with others of her peers, became the subject of a satirical drama, *Sans Souci, alias Free and Easy:—Or an Evening's Peep in a Polite Circle* (1785).

In 1789, as a twenty-nine-year-old mother of five children, her life again became the subject of literary portrayal because of a domestic tragedy. In August of 1788 her younger sister Frances, who had recently borne a child by Sarah's husband, committed suicide. Five months after Fanny's death *The Power of Sympathy*, the first novel published in America, included as a subplot the thinly veiled story of Fanny's suicide and a frontispiece depicting a young woman seeking death, as Fanny had, through poison. Although Sarah Wentworth Morton never explicitly mentioned her domestic tragedy in her published work, the event is implicit in many of her poems. It may even have prompted her decision to become a serious poet, since emotional pain is a recurrent theme in her poetry and seems to have motivated her creativity.

Mrs. Morton's first poems were published in

Perez Morton (State House, Boston)

organized her sentimentality. In her own time she was heralded by her admirers as "The Sappho of America." A strikingly beautiful woman as well as an American luminary, she was the subject of three portraits painted by Gilbert Stuart.

The third daughter of the wealthy Boston merchant, James Apthorp, and his wife, Sarah Wentworth Apthorp, was baptized Sarah Apthorp at King's Chapel on 29 August 1759 (the exact date of her birth is unknown). In girlhood she took her mother's distinguished family name, becoming Sarah Wentworth Apthorp (later, after her marriage, she used the name Sarah Wentworth Morton). She lived in the Apthorp mansion in Boston until she was ten, when her family moved to Braintree, where the Adams, Quincy, and Hancock families also resided. In 1781 she married Perez Morton, a young lawyer, a political radical, and an ambitious politician, well known for his 1776 oration over the disinterred body of patriot General Joseph Warren. As a prominent young matron in Boston

the *Massachusetts Magazine* (1789-1793) and in the *Columbian Centinel* (1788-1793) under the pseudonym Constantia, a name she chose because it represented her own constancy. When a second Constantia (Judith Sargent Murray) offered her poems for publication and claimed prior ownership of the pen name, Sarah Wentworth Morton changed hers to Philenia Constantia and then to Philenia, the name under which she became best known as a poet. Her first long poem, *Ouâbi; or The Virtues of Nature. An Indian Tale. In Four Cantos* (1790), inspired one of America's first orchestral scores, "The Death Song of an Indian Chief" (1791), by Hans Gram, and also became the basis of Louis James Bacon's drama *The American Indian* (1795). Revolving around the idea that "pain has no terrors to the truly brave," the poem tells of a love triangle involving Azâkia, an Illinois war chief, his wife Zisma, and Celario, a young Anglo-American inspired by Azâkia and in love with Zisma. Celario fights in Azâkia's war until he is wounded and returned to the care of Zisma. At the end of the poem Azâkia chooses to die, an act that retains his dignity and frees Zisma and Celario to love one another without guilt. As the subtitle suggests, the poem explores and extols the moral integrity that might exist outside the conventions of Anglo-American civilization. Although clearly influenced by romanticism, Mrs. Morton's depiction of Indian life is based on historical research and is especially indebted to the *Letters* of William Penn.

In 1797 Sarah Wentworth Morton published *Beacon Hill. A Local Poem, Historic and Descriptive*, celebrating the love of freedom expressed during the American Revolution. As a piece of political philosophy, *Beacon Hill* lies between the Tory predispositions of her father and the Jacobin leanings of her husband. Mrs. Morton believed that social order was best fostered by political freedom and that freedom fostered compassion and justice. The companion volume to *Beacon Hill*, *The Virtues of Society, A Tale Founded on Fact* (1799), was dedicated to Abigail Adams.

During her lifetime, Sarah Wentworth Morton's fame rested on her advocacy of freedom. Perhaps her best-known poem on that subject, which appeared in the *Columbian Centinel* under the title "The African Chief" (1792), includes a description of

> A chief of Gambia's golden shore,
>   Whose arm the band of warriors led;
> Or more—the lord of generous power,
>   By whom the foodless poor were fed.

Title page for Morton's first long poem, which stresses that "pain has no terror to the truly brave" (courtesy of the John Carter Brown Library at Brown University)

> Does not the voice of reason cry,
>   "Claim the first right that nature gave,
> From the red scourge of bondage fly,
>   Nor deign to live a burden'd slave?"

"The African Chief" was republished in school readers and frequently recited by abolitionists in the nineteenth century.

In 1797 the Mortons moved to a house in Dorchester designed by Sarah Wentworth Morton. In 1808 they moved to another house in Dorchester designed by Perez Morton against his wife's aesthetic judgments. She withdrew from publishing between 1807 and 1823 but not from society, for she was celebrated as a literary hostess during these years. In 1823 she published her last volume, *My Mind and Its Thoughts, in Sketches, Fragments, and Essays*. In this collection of occasional and topical writings, the resemblance of her point of view and style to Anne Bradstreet's is most clear, as is her deep involvement in Christianity. In an essay called "The Sexes" she wrote that "it would seem that man was sent into this *breathing world* for the purpose of enjoyment—women for that of trial and of suffering. . . . How then is it possible for her to dispense with the promises, the prospects, the consolations of christianity?"

When her husband died in 1837, Sarah Wentworth Morton returned to Braintree (by then known as Quincy), where she lived until her death at eighty-six and where she was a devoted member of the Episcopal congregation of Christ Church. After her death she was wrongly supposed to be the author of *The Power of Sympathy*, apparently because that work carried the story of her family tragedy. In 1894 that novel was shown to have been written by William Hill Brown, a neighbor of the Mortons in Boston. At the time of the novel's publication in 1789, the Mortons had in fact tried to prevent its distribution.

Biographies:

Louise Gordon Shuttles, "The Life and Works of Sarah Wentworth Morton," M.A. thesis, Columbia University, 1928;

Emily Pendleton and Milton Ellis, *Philenia: The Life and Works of Sarah Wentworth Morton, 1759-1846* (Orono: University of Maine, 1931).

References:

Arthur W. Bayley, "The Real Author of the Power of Sympathy," *Bostonian*, 1 (December 1894);

William K. Bottorff, Introduction to *My Mind and Its Thoughts*, by Sarah Wentworth Morton (Delmar, N.Y.: Scholars' Facsimiles & Reprints, 1975).

Judith Sargent Murray
(1 May 1751-6 July 1820)

James Lawton

BOOK: *The Gleaner. A Miscellaneous Production*, 3 volumes (Boston: Printed by I. Thomas & E. T. Andrews, 1798).

PLAYS: *The Medium; or, The Happy Tea-Party*, Boston, Federal Street Theatre, 2 March 1795; *The Traveller Returned*, Boston, Federal Street Theatre, 9 March 1796.

OTHER: John Murray, *Letters and Sketches of Sermons*, 3 volumes, edited by Judith Sargent Murray (Boston: Joshua Belcher, 1812-1813); John Murray, *Records of the Life of John Murray, written by himself*, edited, with a continuation, by Judith Sargent Murray (Boston: Munroe & Francis, 1816).

PERIODICAL PUBLICATIONS: "Desultory thoughts upon the utility of encouraging a degree of self-complacency, especially in female bosoms," *Gentleman's and Lady's Town and Country Magazine* (October 1784): 251; "Lines, occasioned by the Death of an Infant," *Massachusetts Magazine* (January 1790);

"Verses, wrote at a Period of the American contest, replete with Uncertainty," *Massachusetts Magazine*, 2 (February 1790): 120; "New Epilogue to *The Recruiting Officer*," *Massachusetts Magazine*, 2 (March 1790): 194; "On the Equality of the Sexes," *Massachusetts Magazine*, 2 (March and April 1790): 132ff.; "Lines to Philenia, by Constantia," *Massachusetts Magazine*, 2 (April 1790): 248-249; "Epilogue to *Variety*, a Comedy," *Massachusetts Magazine*, 2 (April 1790); "On the Domestic Education of Children," *Massachusetts Magazine*, 2 (May 1790); "Prologue to *Variety*," *Massachusetts Magazine*, 2 (June 1790): 371; "Apostrophe to the Shade of the justly celebrated founder of Pennsylvania," *Universal Asylum and Columbian Magazine* (19 July 1790); "Prologue to *The West Indian*," *Massachusetts Magazine*, 3 (March 1791): 181-182; "Apology for an Epilogue," *Massachusetts Magazine*, 3 (April 1791): 266; "Valedictory Epilogue," *Massachusetts Magazine*, 3 (April 1791);

"Description of Bethlehem," *Massachusetts Magazine,* 3 (June 1791);

"The Gleaner," *Massachusetts Magazine* (February 1792-August 1794);

"The Repository," *Massachusetts Magazine* (September 1792-July 1794);

"Occasional Epilogue to *The Contrast,*" *Massachusetts Magazine,* 4 (March 1794): 179;

"Reflections in the manner of Hervey—occasioned by the death of an Infant Sister," *Massachusetts Magazine* (June 1794);

"On Rocking a Cradle," *Boston Weekly Magazine,* 1 (30 October 1802);

"Birth Day Invitation," *Boston Weekly Magazine,* 1 (20 November 1802): 16;

"Lines Occasioned by the Departure of a Friend," *Boston Weekly Magazine,* 1 (4 December 1802): 24;

"Death of Saltonstall," *Boston Weekly Magazine,* 1 (15 January 1803): 52;

"Expiring Amity," *Boston Weekly Magazine,* 1 (26 February 1803): 24;

"Blending Spirit with Matter," *Boston Weekly Magazine,* 1 (5 March 1803): 80;

"An Hypothesis," *Boston Weekly Magazine,* 1 (19 March 1803): 88;

"Ode to Time," *Boston Magazine* (14 December 1805).

Judith Sargent Murray, essayist and poet, was born in Gloucester, Massachusetts, the first child of Winthrop and Judith Saunders Sargent. The Sargents were prosperous, public-spirited merchants who were interested in the advancement of education and culture. Thus her parents provided Judith with the same instruction given her brother Winthrop, short of Harvard College. Both she and her brother seemed to have shared a lifelong interest in literature, although he did not pursue it as a career. After military service in the Revolution and Indian wars, he became a Southern planter and politician and was the first governor of Mississippi Territory.

On 3 October 1769, at the age of eighteen, Judith Sargent married Captain John Stevens, a merchant seaman, who built for her, probably with the help of her father, the Gloucester mansion known today as the Sargent-Murray-Gilman-Hough house. They had no children. During the Revolution Captain Stevens fell into financial difficulties from which he never recovered. In 1786, after escaping from his creditors by crawling out a rear window of his house, Stevens sailed for the West Indies without his wife and died on the island of St. Eustache.

Earlier the Sargents and the Stevenses were among the first converts to Universalism when the Reverend John Murray (1741-1815) settled in Gloucester in 1774 and began to gather a congregation for the new faith. Murray became a lodger in Mrs. Stevens's house either shortly before or soon after her husband's death. Their mutual interests drew them together and culminated in their marriage on 6 October 1788.

After her second marriage Judith Sargent Murray turned her attention more fully to her writing. Until then she had published only "Desultory thoughts upon the utility of encouraging a degree of self-complacency, especially in female bosoms" (1784), an essay advocating that young women be allowed to have more self-respect and ambition. She signed this essay Constantia, a pseudonym which she used for all but a few of her published works.

The lack of a suitable magazine combined with the upheavals in her personal life prevented Constantia's work from appearing in print again until 1790. In the fall of 1789 at the age of thirty-eight, Judith Sargent Murray gave birth to her first child, George, who died a few days later. The bereaved mother poured out her grief in verses which appeared in the January 1790 issue of the newly founded *Massachusetts Magazine* under the title "Lines, occasioned by the Death of an Infant." The February issue contained her "Verses, wrote at a Period of the American contest, replete with Uncertainty." This piece is addressed to a brother leaving to join the army and was probably written in 1775 when her brother Winthrop left Gloucester to join Washington's army. The March issue has her "New Epilogue to *The Recruiting Officer,*" written for a performance of the Farquhar play in Gloucester. This poem was the first of several dramatic prologues or epilogues to appear in the *Massachusetts Magazine* for 1790 and 1791. They were written for plays performed in Gloucester, probably for the benefit of the poor, in order to circumvent the Massachusetts statute prohibiting playacting.

These first publications contain the recurring themes, interests, and literary forms which were to dominate the rest of Judith Sargent Murray's writings. Her occasional verse is didactic and marked by the conventional couplet typical of the eighteenth century, which worshiped the poetry of Pope. Her principal effort in the literary field was a series of essays which first appeared in the *Massachusetts Magazine* between February 1792 and August 1794. These "Gleaner" essays provided a broad framework for Mrs. Murray's ideas on female equality and proper education for females and are built

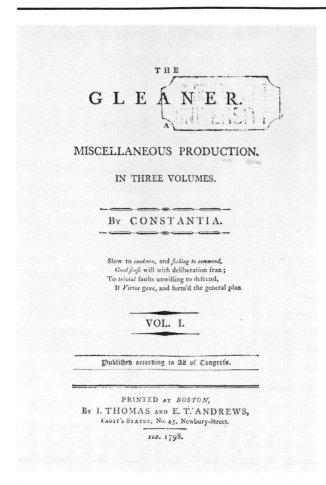

Title page for the first volume of Murray's collected works (courtesy of the John Carter Brown Library at Brown University)

around the story of Margaretta, an orphan adopted by Mr. Vigillius (the Gleaner) and his wife while on a trip to South Carolina. Her education, courtship, and marriage provided ample room for Mrs. Murray to digress on all manner of subjects.

The Murrays moved from Gloucester to Boston in 1793, the same year that the ban on performing plays was repealed. In February of the following year Boston's new Federal Street Theatre was opened with a call for original dramas by Americans. Mrs. Murray, who had already exhibited an interest in drama, was among the first to respond. Her first play, *The Medium; or, The Happy Tea-Party,*

was performed once at the Federal Street Theatre on 2 March 1795. Her second and last play, *The Traveller Returned,* was performed a year later and survived only two performances.

Mrs. Murray's literary efforts after 1796 were turned more to editing. In order to boost family finances, subscriptions were sought for a collected edition of her works. Seven hundred fifty-nine persons agreed to purchase 824 sets at one dollar a volume. The three-volume set was published in 1798 under the general title *The Gleaner.* Aside from several poems published in the *Boston Weekly Magazine* (1802-1803), Mrs. Murray spent her remaining years raising her daughter, Julia Maria, who was born in 1791. She also edited her husband's letters, sermons, and autobiography. His *Letters and Sketches of Sermons* (1812-1813) was published in three volumes, and his autobiography, *Records of the Life of John Murray,* was published in 1816, a year after his death. The final three chapters were written by Mrs. Murray. Unfortunately, the value of these two works is reduced by Mrs. Murray's adherence to notions of editorial propriety prevalent in her age, which allowed her to delete place names and dates as well as personal names.

Upon publication of her husband's autobiography, Judith Sargent Murray moved to Natchez, Mississippi, to live with her daughter, who had married Adam Louis Bingamon, the son of a wealthy planter. She died on 6 July 1820 and was buried in the Bingamon family cemetery.

Reference:

Vena Bernadette Field, *Constantia: A Study of the Life and Works of Judith Sargent Murray, 1751-1820* (Orono, Maine: University Press, 1931).

Papers:

Judith Sargent Murray's manuscripts were stored in an old house on the Bingamon plantation near Natchez, Mississippi, and have been destroyed by mildew. The Massachusetts Historical Society has eight letters written by her; Houghton Library at Harvard University, Fales Library at New York University, and the Historical Society of Pennsylvania each has one of her letters.

Robert Treat Paine, Jr.
(9 December 1773-13 November 1811)

Robert D. Arner
University of Cincinnati

BOOKS: *The Invention of Letters: A Poem, Written at the Request of the President of Harvard University, and Delivered, in Cambridge, on the Day of Annual Commencement, July 15, 1795* (Boston: Printed for the subscribers, 1795);

The Ruling Passion: An Occasional Poem. Written by the Appointment of the Society of the [Phi Beta Kappa] and Spoken, on Their Anniversary, in the Chapel of the University, Cambridge, July 20, 1797 (Boston: Printed by Manning & Loring for the author, 1797);

An Oration, Written at the Request of the Young Men of Boston, and Delivered, July 17th, 1799, in Commemoration of the Dissolution of the Treaties, and Consular Convention, between France and the United States of America (Boston: Printed by John Russell, 1799);

An Eulogy on the Life of General George Washington, Who Died at Mount Vernon, December 14th, 1799 . . . Written at the Request of the Citizens of Newburyport, and Delivered at the First Presbyterian Meeting-House in That Town, January 2nd. 1800 (Newburyport: Printed by Edmund M. Blunt, 1800);

A Monody on the Death of Lieut. General Sir John Moore . . . (Boston: J. Belcher, 1811);

The Works in Verse and Prose of the Late Robert Treat Paine, jun., esq. . . . (Boston: Printed & published by J. Belcher, 1812);

Andromache: or, The Fall of Troy. A Tragedy, in Five Acts (London: Printed for the author & sold by John Lowndes, 1820).

Robert Treat Paine, Jr.

Robert Treat Paine, Jr., was a Federalist essayist, editor, orator, lawyer, and poet whose best-known poem, *Adams and Liberty* (published as a broadside, circa 1798), both capitalized on and contributed to the violently anti-French feeling that built steadily in America during the administration of President George Washington and reached a climax in the demonstrations and legislation following President John Adams's disclosure of the details of the XYZ Affair in the spring of 1798. Paine's prose eulogy on the death of Washington also found a significant, though smaller, national audience, while his *An Oration, Written at the Request of the Young Men of Boston, and Delivered, July 17th, 1799, in Commemoration of the Dissolution of the Treaties, and Consular Convention, between France and the United States of America* (1799) was reviewed in journals in Philadelphia, New York, and other cities. Paine's local reputation, not to say notoriety, rested in large part upon certain controversial anti-Jacobin passages in *The Invention of Letters* (1795), a poem delivered at Harvard upon the receipt of his master's degree in July 1795. As founder and editor of the *Federal Orrery* (1794-1796), Paine was pursued by a mob and challenged to a duel by those whom his anti-Jacobin satires had incensed, experiences that cured him of the itch of editorship for all time. He won yet another sort of local fame for the public and poetical flirtation he carried on, mostly in the pages of Isaiah Thomas's *Massachusetts Magazine,* with the Boston poet Sarah Wentworth Morton, whose poems were published under the pen name Philenia.

For the modern reader, Paine's life unfolds like the plot of a soap opera. The second son of Robert Treat Paine, one of the signers of the Declaration of Independence, and Sally Cobb Paine, he was christened Thomas in honor of the penman of the American Revolution. Blessed with every privilege, he attended Harvard, as would be expected of a scion of Boston society, and received both his bachelor's and master's degrees from that institution. Three of his most popular pieces, the "Valedictory Poem" (21 June 1792), "The Nature and Progress of Liberty" (15 July 1792), and *The Invention of Letters* (15 July 1795), were written for delivery at Harvard Commencement ceremonies. The last contained lines describing Envy as "the *serpent* . . . JACOBIN," which President Willard of Harvard ordered struck from the work as inappropriate to the occasion, but which Paine read anyway, risking the award of his master's degree to do so. Similar independence of action and opinion had previously earned him a four-month suspension from Harvard, and it would eventually lead to a breach with his father. While serving as the clerk of James Tisdale in 1792, Paine had become enamored of the theater and an actress named Eliza Baker, whom he married in February 1795 only to be banned from his father's house as a result.

The opening of Boston's Federal Street Theater in 1793 had been heralded by Paine's prize-winning prologue, a poetical survey of the progress of literature and literacy to their present flourishing state in America, published in *The Works in Verse and Prose* (1812) as "The Prize Prologue: Spoken in the Character of Apollo." Paine became master of ceremonies at the theater but began drinking excessively and fell heavily into debt. Even so, he was appointed by the Phi Beta Kappa Society of Harvard to write a poem for the society's anniversary on 20 July 1797, for which occasion he produced *The Ruling Passion,* considered by his biographer, Charles Prentiss, to be "the longest and most perfect of all his poetical productions." Another invitation, from the Massachusetts Charitable Fire Society in June 1798, led to his best-known work, *Adams and Liberty.* Additional invitations for orations and odes resulted in *An Oration, Written at the Request of*

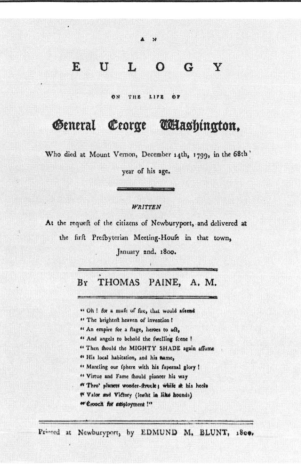

Title page for one of Paine's orations, published before he changed his name (courtesy of the John Carter Brown Library at Brown University)

the *Young Men of Boston,* a speech on the dissolution of diplomatic relations between France and the United States, a eulogy on George Washington written at the request of the town of Newburyport, an ode commemorating First Landing Day written for the Sons of the Pilgrims, and works for other civic, social, and political groups. For these writings, Paine received substantial sums of money, even by present inflated standards. He stopped drinking, paid his debts, and commenced the study and practice of law, all but giving over his attachment to the theater and to poetry. Meanwhile, his elder brother, Robert Treat Paine, Jr., having died of yellow fever in 1798, Paine legally took his brother's name in 1801, in part to end confusion between him and the by-then extremely unpopular author of *The Rights of Man,* in part to honor his father, with whom he was briefly reconciled. Within a short while, however, his fortune reverted; he began to pay court to another actress, one Mrs. Jones, and the death of two of his children within four days of each other in 1804 left him emotionally exhausted. In 1805, he became seriously ill and never entirely recovered. Drifting once again into poverty and debt, he returned to his father's house, where he died in an attic room on 13 November 1811. His funeral was well-attended by many prominent Bostonians.

Through all the vicissitudes of fame and fortune, Paine remained what his staunch friend Charles Prentiss termed a "gospel federalist." With the single and entirely understandable exception of his devotion to George Washington, his vision of America's potential and progress focused solely upon New England; his politics and his patriotism were narrowly parochial, embracing no other region of the infant republic. Nevertheless, because he skillfully manipulated the conventional symbols of patriotism and conflict, he attained a degree of popularity larger than merely local fame. In *Adams and Liberty* images associating America with nature and with a carefully circumscribed version of natural law are repeatedly arrayed against familiar symbols of European tyranny, imperialistic design, and lust for wealth and power: the scepter, the rod, the galling chain of slavery. The refrain in *Adams and Liberty*, despite its rather loud (and perhaps ironic) echoes of "Rule, Britannia," identifies freedom with nature and makes geography itself the divine guarantor of American liberty: "And ne'er shall the sons of Columbia be slaves,/While the earth bears a plant, or the sea rolls its waves." The poem elicits still another standard patriotic response from its historical allusions, with oblique references to Britain's impressment of American seamen and to the incursions of the Barbary pirates against American shipping, very direct references to the French Revolution, and Napoleon's recent conquests. What emerges is a portrait of worldwide collusion against the liberties of America, a theory of international conspiracy based on a vision of history that even today can be counted on to generate powerful emotions of patriotism in the hearts of rank and file Americans.

A repeated allusion in Paine's writing identifies America as God's chosen nation through references to the story of Noah, revealing the typological bias Paine had inherited from his Puritan ancestors. In *Adams and Liberty*, for example, the Constitution as America's "ark of abode" becomes the political antitype of Noah's ark, which transported the patriarch safely from an old world of sin and sorrow to a new one of peace and promise; it is meant to recall as well the Ark of the Covenant, which contained the sacred scripture of the ancient Hebrews as unimpeachable evidence of their special bond with God. Essentially a public poet, Paine fused such political typology with the theory of Northern Translation, that is, the notion that democratic institutions originated among the Teutonic tribes of primitive Germany and, reaching at last the shores of New England, were adapted to American needs. His legacy to American literature lies less in the quality of individual poems than in his contributions to the secular American religion of democracy that emerged with full vigor in the popular mythology of the nineteenth century.

References:

Philip Hale, "A Boston Dramatic Critic of a Century Ago," *Proceedings of the Massachusetts Historical Society*, 59 (1926): 312-324;

Michael L. Lasser, "Thomas Paine and Robert Treat Paine: A Case of Mistaken Identity," *Journal of Rutgers University Library*, 25 (1962): 24-27;

Lewis Leary, "The First Published Poem of Thomas Paine of Boston (i.e., Robert Treat Paine, Jr.): A Note on the Generation Gap in 1786," *New England Quarterly*, 43 (March 1970): 130-134.

Papers:

A major collection of Paine's manuscripts and letters is housed in the Massachusetts Historical Society. Paine's letters are widely scattered, but two significant collections are those at the Rhode Island Historical Society and the Milton S. Eisenhower Library of Johns Hopkins University.

Henry Pattillo
(1726-1801)

Robert W. Hill
Clemson University

BOOKS: *The Plain Planter's Family Assistant; containing an address to husbands and wives, children and servants; with some helps for instruction by catechisms: and examples of devotion for families: with a brief paraphrase on the Lord's Prayer* (Wilmington, Del.: Printed by James Adams, 1787);

Sermons, &c. I. On the Divisions among Christians. II. On the Necessity of Regeneration to future Happiness. III. The Scripture Doctrine of Election. IV. Extract of a Letter from Mr. Whitefield to Mr. Wesley. V. An Address to the Deists (Wilmington, Del.: Printed by James Adams, 1788);

A Geographical Catechism to assist those who have neither maps nor gazeteers to read newspapers, history, or travels with as much of the science of astronomy, and the doctrine of the air as is judged sufficient for the farmer, who wishes to understand something of the works of God around him; and for the studious youth, who have or have not a prospect of further prosecuting those sublime sciences (Halifax, N.C.: Printed by Abraham Hodge, 1796).

A Presbyterian preacher born in Scotland in 1726, Henry Pattillo came to Virginia around 1740. In 1758 he accepted a call from Willis, Bird, and Buck Island, which he served until 1762, leaving when "the people 'being unable to give him a sufficient support.'" On 4 May 1763 at Tinkling Spring he was called to supply Cumberland, Harris Creek, and Deep Creek. In October 1765 he was called by Hawfields, Eno, and Little River, where he began what would be some thirty-five years of service in North Carolina: "in Granville, and in Orange, along the Eno, the eloquent Pattillo taught impressively the wonder-working truths of the gospel of Christ" (*Colonial Records of North Carolina*). Leaving Hawfields in 1774, he became a Bute County (now Warren and Franklin counties) delegate to the first Provincial Congress of North Carolina in 1775.

Also a distinguished educator, Pattillo headed schools at Hawfields and Williamsboro; he was named to help found and to serve on the boards of trustees of Queens College, Charlotte (15 January 1771), Granville Hall Academy (with George Micklejohn, 8 May 1776), and Warrenton Academy (6

January 1787). Of Pattillo's three book-length publications, *The Plain Planter's Family Assistant* (1787) and *A Geographical Catechism* (1796) are notably instructive in matters both theological and secular. *A Geographical Catechism* is frequently called the first textbook written in North Carolina. In these two works Pattillo is persuasive rather than admonitory, his method Socratic rather than expository. Particularly charming are his analogies and figures of speech as he aligns things from one realm of creation with things from another; for example, oceans are like continents, lakes like islands. *The Plain Planter's Family Assistant* includes "The Negroes Catechism," in which, as Guion Griffis Johnson has observed, Pattillo "taught a strange doctrine of racial equality and submission. In answer to the question 'Do you think white folks and negroes all come from one father?,' he had his black pupils give an affirmative reply, 'Because, except for the black skin, and the curled head, their bodies, I believe, are just alike, within and without.'"

In the Latin epigraph to *Sermons, &c.*, Henry Pattillo reveals something of his literary temperament; that is, he advocates rigor in doctrinal necessities, leniency in matters less certain, and Christian love in all things: "*In necessariis unitas; in non-necessariis lenitas; in omnibus charitas.*" Even "An Address to the Deists" tells his clear position with all possible mildness: "The little piece here offered to our *American* brethren, of this unhappy cast, can have no motive, but their advantage; and pleads no merit, but that of offering its hand, where better helps are wanting." While his sermons are distinguished by his Christian charity, Pattillo also makes plain his dedication to Calvinism—"a *moderate* but settled *Calvinist*"—and to the newly blown Americanism. He is troubled by the Methodists' rejection of Calvinist principles and all the more troubled for the admirable piety and strong morality of those followers of John Wesley.

He is anxious to foster and preserve the democratic ideals of America against the condescension of the Old World: "he hopes for the indulgence of his country-men, for whom only, he writes. *Americans* are too deep sufferers, from the destructive

SERMONS, &c.

I. On the Divifions among Chriftians.

II. On the Neceffity of Regeneration to future Happinefs.

III. The Scripture Doctrine of Election.

IV. Extract of a Letter from Mr. *Whitefield*
to Mr. *Wefley.*

V. An Addrefs to the Deifts.

By HENRY PATTILLO, *A. M.* of *Granville,* NORTH-CAROLINA.

*In neceffariis unitas; in non-neceffariis lenitas; in
omnibus charitas.*——
ANON.

WILMINGTON,

Printed by JAMES ADAMS, for
the AUTHOR, 1788.

*Title page for Pattillo's only published sermons, which reveal his
conciliatory manner as well as his Calvinist beliefs (courtesy of the
John Carter Brown Library at Brown University)*

decrees, and sanguinary counsels, of the *right hon-
ourables* and *right reverends* beyond the Atlantick, to
retain that respect for their *stars* and their *mitres,*
which those must shew, who are under the influence of their sovereignty."

Pattillo's conciliatory manner and his generally good judgment made him a diplomat in a difficult time for his Orange and Granville county congregations. At one point he was at a disadvantage
on a committee of the Hillsborough Provincial Congress whose responsibility was to persuade Regula-
tors to break their oaths of allegiance (made for
their amnesty after the battle at Alamance), to urge
them to stop being Tories. On 23 August 1768, he
had cosigned letters to Governor Tryon, praising
his actions at Hillsborough, and to the "Presbyterian inhabitants," urging their cooperation with
Tryon and the civil authorities. Pattillo and George
Micklejohn had preached sermons to troops at
Hillsborough, at the invitation of Tryon, to persuade the righteousness of civil order against the
evil of disorder. Pattillo's sermon has not been preserved, although Micklejohn's was published in
1768.

On another occasion, 4 September 1775, the
Provincial Congress elected him chairman of the
committee of the whole for the purpose of "pur-
porting a Confederation of the United Colonies,"
but the next day he and seven others petitioned
"leave to absent themselves from the Service of the
Congress," feeling that such action was premature
and should only be taken as a last resort. He was
nonetheless elected to the Committee of Safety for
Halifax district just a few days later.

Pattillo's last pastorate was at Nutbush and
Grassy Creek, Granville County, where, beginning
in 1780, he gave "his last labors, ripened by age and
experience."

Reference:

Guion Griffis Johnson, *Ante-Bellum North Carolina:
A Social History* (Chapel Hill: University of
North Carolina Press, 1937).

John Howard Payne

(9 June 1791-9 April 1852)

Jewell B. Parham

Tennessee State University

BOOKS: *Julia, or the Wanderer; A Comedy, in Five Acts. As Performed at the New-York Theatre . . .* (New York: Published by D. Longworth, 1806);

Lovers' Vows; a Play in Five Acts. Altered from the Translations of Mrs. Inchbald and Benjamin Thompson, adapted from *Das Kind der Liebe,* by August von Kotzebue (Baltimore: Printed by George Dobbin & Murphy, 1809);

Juvenile Poems, Principally Written between the Age of Thirteen and Seventeen Years . . . (Baltimore: Printed by R. Gamble & published by Edward J. Coale, 1813); revised as *Lispings of the Muse: a Selection from Juvenile Poems . . .* (London: Privately printed, 1815);

The Magpie or the Maid? A Melo Drama, in Three Acts . . . , translated and adapted, by Payne and Isaac Pocock, from *La Pie Voleuse, ou la Servante de Palaiseau,* by Louis Charles Caigniez and J. Baudouin d'Aubigny (London: Printed for John Miller, 1815; Boston: Printed by Tileston & Weld, 1816);

Accusation; or, the Family D'Anglade: a Play in Three Acts, from the French, with Alterations, adapted from *Le Vol, ou la Famille d'Anglade,* by Frédéric Dupetit-Méré (London: Printed for C. Chapple, 1817; Boston: Printed by J. H. A. Frost & published by West, Richardson & Lord, 1818);

Brutus; or, the Fall of Tarquin. An Historical Tragedy, in Five Acts . . . (London: Published by Richard White; Simpkin & Marshall; Sherwood, Neely & Jones; C. Chapple; and T. Earle, 1818; New York: Published by D. Longworth, 1819; Baltimore: Printed & published by J. Robinson, 1819);

Thérèse, the Orphan of Geneva. A Drama, in Three Acts . . . , translated and adapted from *Thérèse, ou, L'Orpheline de Genève,* by Victor Henri Joseph Brahain Ducange (London: Printed by J. Tabby, Theatre Royal, 1821; London: Theatre Royal, 1821; New York: Published by Murden & Thomson, 1821; New York: Printed by W. Grattan & published by Thomas Longworth, 1821);

Adeline, the Victim of Seduction: a Melo-Dramatic Serious Drama, in Three Acts . . . , translated and adapted from *Valentine, ou la Séduction,* by René Charles Guilbert de Pixérécourt (London: Theatre Royal, 1822; New York: Published by E. M. Murden, 1822);

Ali Pacha; or, The Signet-Ring. A Melo-Drama, in Two Acts . . . (New York: Published by E. M. Murden, 1823);

Clari; or, the Maid of Milan; an Opera, in Three Acts . . . , libretto by Payne, music by Henry R.

Bishop (London: John Miller, 1823; New York: Printed & published at the Circulating Library & Dramatic Repository, 1823);

Charles the Second; or, the Merry Monarch. A Comedy, in Three Acts . . . , translated and adapted, by Payne and Washington Irving, from *La Jeunesse de Henri V,* by Alexandre Duval (London: Printed for Longman, Hurst, Rees, Orme, Brown & Green, 1824; Philadelphia: Printed by Mifflin & Parry & published by Neal & Mackenzie, 1829);

The Fall of Algiers, A New Opera, in Three Acts . . . , libretto by Payne, music by Bishop (London: Published by T. Dolby, 1825);

Love in Humble Life; a Petite Comedy, in One Act, adapted from *Michel et Christine,* by Eugène Scribe and Jean Henri Dupin (London: Thomas Dolby, 1825; New York & Philadelphia: Turner & Fisher, circa 1836);

The Two Galley Slaves; A Melodrama, in Two Acts . . . (London: Thomas Dolby, 1825);

Richelieu: A Domestic Tragedy, Founded on Fact . . . , adapted, by Payne and Irving, from *La Jeunesse du Duc Richelieu ou le Lovelace Français,* by Alexandre Duval (New York: Published by E. M. Murden, 1826);

'Twas I, or The Truth A Lie. A Farce, in Two Acts . . . (New York: Published by E. M. Murden, 1827);

The Lancers: An Interlude, in One Act . . . (London: John Cumberland, circa 1827-1829);

Mrs. Smith: or, the Wife and the Widow. A Farce, in One Act (London: Thomas Hailes Lacy, n.d.);

Peter Smink; or, the Armistice. A Comic Drama, in One Act, adapted from a French play by Payne and Irving (London: Thomas Hailes Lacy, n.d.);

Indian Justice: A Cherokee Murder Trial at Tahlequah in 1840, As Reported by John Howard Payne, edited by Grant Foreman (Oklahoma City: Harlow, 1934);

Trial without Jury & Other Plays, edited by Codman Hislop and W. R. Richardson (Princeton: Princeton University Press, 1940);

The Last Duel in Spain & Other Plays, edited by Hislop and Richardson (Princeton: Princeton University Press, 1940);

John Howard Payne to His Countrymen, edited by Clemens de Baillou (Athens: University of Georgia Press, 1961).

John Howard Payne, the foremost actor-playwright of early American theater, was one of the first American dramatists to win international acclaim. Though his inspiration was foreign (he frequently adapted his plays from English, French, and German sources) and most of his works were written and first performed abroad, Payne's theatrical training and principles were American. Born in New York City to William and Sarah Isaacs Payne, John Howard Payne grew up in Boston and attended the Berry Street Academy, where his father had become headmaster in 1796. In Boston, young Payne's attraction to the stage was nourished by his performance in various school plays. However, when he announced his intention to pursue a professional stage career, his parents sent him to work at the mercantile house of Grant and Bennet Forbes in New York City, in an effort to dispel such a notion. Yet Payne continued to be attracted by the theater, and from 28 December 1805 to 31 May 1806 he published *Thespian Mirror,* one of the earliest reviews of the New York theater. During the same period, his first play, *Julia, or the Wanderer,* was produced at the Park Theatre in New York on 7 February 1806.

Interested friends, especially John E. Seaman, who believed that the fifteen-year-old Payne should continue his education, sent him to Union College in Schenectady, New York, where he remained from July 1806 to November 1808 as a private pupil preparing to enter the sophomore class. While in Schenectady he started another paper, the *Pastime,* which appeared from 2 February 1807 to 18 June 1808. However, after he had a number of misunderstandings with Seaman and his father went bankrupt, incurring heavy financial obligations for the family, young Payne left Union College for a career as an actor and playwright. He made his professional acting debut on 24 February 1809 as Young Norval in *Douglas,* a tragedy by John Home. In that same year he played a number of Shakespearean roles and may have acted in his own play *Lovers' Vows,* an adaptation of a German play by August von Kotzebue.

Over the next few years Payne's acting career took him to cities such as Boston, Providence, Baltimore, Philadelphia, Richmond, Washington, and Charleston, South Carolina. On 17 January 1813 he sailed for Liverpool and remained in Europe for nearly twenty years.

Achieving little success as an actor in England, Payne turned to writing. Although many of the plays he wrote for both New York and London theaters are hackwork, written in the hope of relieving his constant debt, he had occasional critical and popular successes. One of these was his tragedy *Brutus; or, the Fall of Tarquin,* which opened at the Drury Lane Theatre in London on 3 December

Payne made his debut on the New York stage in February 1809 as Young Norval in Douglas, *a tragedy by John Home (engraving of a painting by C. R. Leslie)*

lyric for which Payne is still remembered, "Home, Sweet Home!"

In summer 1823 Payne and his friend Washington Irving began collaborating on a number of plays, two of which were produced with some success. *Charles the Second,* a comedy for which Payne was listed as the sole author, was well received when it opened at the Covent Garden Theatre on 27 May 1824 and is still considered one of the best early-American comedies. *Richelieu: A Domestic Tragedy,* which ran for only six performances after it opened at Covent Garden on 11 February 1826, was once again attributed solely to Payne.

Still in debt, Payne lived in London (sometimes using the name J. Hayward) from autumn 1823 until summer 1825, and in 1826 he was back in London, where from 2 October 1826 until 24 March 1827 he published twenty-six issues of a weekly theater review, *Opera Glass.* He remained in London, in debt, until 16 June 1832, when, with his passage paid for by friends, he sailed for the United States.

Payne discovered that he was well known in

1818 with Edmund Kean as Brutus and Julia Glover as Tullia.

By 1820 Payne was once again in debt after his attempt to act as producer for some of his own plays ended in financial ruin. Taken to Fleet Street debtors' prison, he wrote a melodrama, *Thérèse, the Orphan of Geneva,* which began a successful run at the Drury Lane Theatre on 2 February 1821. Released from prison but still in debt, Payne fled to Paris to avoid his creditors and continued to write plays.

His next important production was *Clari; or, the Maid of Milan,* an opera with a score by Henry R. Bishop, who had written musical arrangements for earlier plays by Payne as well. Opening at the Covent Garden Theatre on 8 May 1823, with Ann Maria Tree in the title role, the opera contains the

Ann Maria Tree sang "Home, Sweet Home" in the premiere of Payne's opera Clari; or The Maid of Milan *at Covent Garden in London on 8 May 1823*

Fair copy of "Home, Sweet Home," made shortly before Payne left for Tunis (American Art Association/Anderson Galleries, sale 4283, 9-10 December 1936)

his native country, but, even after friends organized a special benefit performance of three of his plays, he continued to be in debt. Hoping to launch another magazine, he went to Georgia in September 1835 to gather material for articles on the negotiations between government agents and John Ross, Chief of the Cherokee nation, which eventually resulted in the treaty that removed the Cherokees to the West. While meeting with Ross, Payne was arrested and told to leave the state forever because of his sympathy for the Cherokees and his opposition to the treaty. While his plans for a magazine were never realized, Payne wrote some newspaper articles in support of the Cherokees and began a history of their nation.

In 1842, with the support of Daniel Webster,

Payne was appointed American consul in Tunis by President Tyler. President Polk recalled him in 1845, but he was restored to the post in March 1851 and returned to Tunis, where he died on 9 April 1852.

Much admired by his contemporaries, Payne is now remembered, not for his more than sixty plays, but for his lyric "Home, Sweet Home!," which was popular throughout the nineteenth century and continues to be sung in the twentieth.

Biographies:

Gabriel Harrison, *John Howard Payne, Dramatist, Poet, Actor, and Author of "Home, Sweet Home!":*

His Life and Writings (Philadelphia & London: Lippincott, 1885);

Willis T. Hanson, Jr., *The Early Life of John Howard Payne* (Boston: Printed for the Bibliophile Society, 1913);

Grace Overmyer, *America's First Hamlet* (New York: New York University Press, 1913);

Rosa P. Chiles, *John Howard Payne* (Washington, D.C.: W. F. Roberts, 1930).

Papers:

There are fourteen volumes of Payne's manuscripts in the Edward E. Ayer Collection at The Newberry Library in Chicago.

Thomas Reese
(1742-1796)

Tony Owens
University of South Carolina

BOOKS: *An Essay on the Influence of Religion, in Civil Society* (Charleston: Printed by Markland & M'Iver, 1788);

Steadfastness in Religion, Recommended and Enforced; a Sermon (Philadelphia: Printed by William Young, 1793).

OTHER: *Death the Christian's Gain* and *The Character of Haman,* in *The American Preacher; or a Collection of Sermons from Some of the Most Eminent Preachers, Now Living, in the United States . . . ,* 3 volumes, edited by David Austin (Elizabethtown, N.J.: Printed by Shepard Kollock, 1791).

Respected as a minister and essayist, Thomas Reese was a defender of education, reason, and order in a time and place of social upheaval. Born in Pennsylvania in 1742 to David and Susan Polk Reese, he received a classical education in Mecklenburg County, North Carolina (under Rev. Joseph Alexander and a Mr. Benedict), and graduated from the College of New Jersey (later Princeton) in 1768. Licensed as a Presbyterian minister in 1773, Reese married Jane Harris and accepted the charge of Salem Church at Black River, South Carolina. For almost two decades Reese served Salem as minister, teacher (both at a classical school and a

school for slaves), and unofficial physician. He fathered seven children, two of whom graduated from the College of New Jersey.

The violence of the American Revolution, intensified in South Carolina after the British occupation of Charleston in 1780, disrupted Reese's duties at Salem. After two patriot members of his congregation were murdered, Reese sought temporary refuge in North Carolina. His involvement in these disturbances underlies his best-known work, *An Essay on the Influence of Religion, in Civil Society* (1788). Published in Charleston and reprinted in the *American Museum* (Philadelphia) two years later, this work gained wide popularity and resulted in the College of New Jersey's conferring an honorary doctor of divinity degree upon Reese.

In a clear and logical style, Reese's essay proposes Christianity and education as the foundations of morality and as the only reliable solutions to social lawlessness. Alluding to Aristotle, Homer, Montesquieu, and Locke, Reese confronts the secularism and anticlericalism of his time with an orthodox acceptance of human fallibility. According to Reese, "self-love" as a moral precept is unreliable and makes one vulnerable to desire; the existence of an inborn "moral sense" is uncertain; law and social morality are inadequate. From a rationalist perspective, he portrays God as underlying the

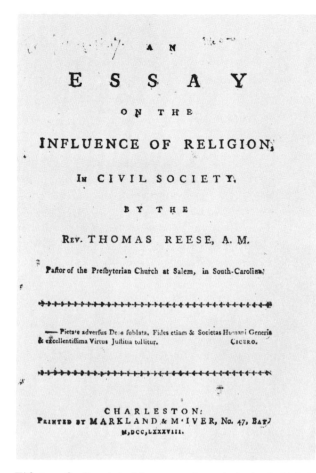

AN

E S S A Y

ON THE

INFLUENCE OF RELIGION,

In CIVIL SOCIETY.

BY THE

Rev. THOMAS REESE, A. M.

Paſtor of the Preſbyterian Church at Salem, in South-Carolina.

━━━━━━━━━━━━━━━━━━━━━━━━━

—— Pietate adverſus Deos ſublata, Fides etiam & Societas Humani Generis
& excellentiſſima Virtus Juſtitia tollitur.   CICERO.

━━━━━━━━━━━━━━━━━━━━━━━━━

CHARLESTON:
PRINTED BY MARKLAND & M'IVER, No. 47, BAY.
M,DCC,LXXXVIII.

Title page for Reese's best-known work, on the basis of which the College of New Jersey granted him an honorary doctorate (courtesy of the John Carter Brown Library at Brown University)

"complicated machine of the universe," as the source for "all beauty, order, and harmony." Stressing behavior rather than doctrine, Reese's sermon recalls the Christian rationalism of Franklin and Jefferson and affirms a "natural religion" as essential to good citizenship. Lamenting (from personal experience) the "barbarian" state of the backcountry, Reese declares that the success of the new nation will be dependent upon the morality of its citizens.

Reese moved to the Pendleton District of South Carolina in 1792, serving the Hopewell-Keowee and Carmel churches until his death in 1796. From these isolated residences, Reese published only three sermons. *Death the Christian's Gain* and *The Character of Haman* were solicited by David Austin for his *The American Preacher* (1791), published in New Jersey. *Steadfastness in Religion* was published in Philadelphia in 1793. Reese's sermons illustrate his scholarship and rationalism. Doctrinally, Reese rejected the New Light evangelicalism of the Tennents and Samuel Davies. Instead he combined the piety of the Great Awakening with an emphasis on restraint and reason. Witnessing the militant enthusiasm of many colonial dissenters, Reese advocated a devout yet orderly support of both religion and nation. Amid the social turmoil and lawlessness of the Carolina backcountry, Thomas Reese attempted in his writings to uphold the classical values of the American Enlightenment and to promote a socially benevolent Christianity. Erudite and persistently logical, he wrote as a patriot without fanaticism, as a rationalist within a context of orthodox religion. Largely on the basis of his 1788 essay, Reese remains a minor yet able spokesman for the Christian rationalism of the American Revolution.

References:

George Howe, *History of the Presbyterian Church in South Carolina* (Columbia, S.C.: Duffie & Chapman, 1870), I: 411-412, 492-493, 593, 636-639;

David Ramsay, *The History of South-Carolina, from its First Settlement in 1670, to the Year 1808* (Charleston, S.C.: Published by David Longworth for the author, 1809), II: 505-507;

R.W. Simpson, *History of Old Pendleton District with a Genealogy of the Leading Families of the District* (Anderson, S.C., 1913), pp. 33-34, 87-90;

J. R. Witherspoon, "Memoirs of the Late Rev'd Thomas Reese," *Southern Presbyterian Review*, 6 (1853): 116-120.

George Richards

(circa 1760-March 1814)

Lewis Leary

University of North Carolina at Chapel Hill

BOOKS: *The Political Passing Bell: An Elegy. Written in a Country Meeting House, April, 1789. Parodized from Gray* . . . (Boston: Printed by Isaiah Thomas & Company, 1789);

The Declaration of Independence: A Poem . . . (Boston: Printed by Isaiah Thomas & E. T. Andrews, 1793);

Operative and Speculative Masonry. A Concise Address, Pronounced before the Venerable Master, Respected Officers, and Beloved Brethren, of St. Andrews Lodge, Boston, Massachusetts; December 27th, anno lucis 5793 (Boston: Printed by Benjamin & John Russell, 1793);

The Cry of the Watchmen of Mount Ephraim! Being the Substance of a Discourse, Delivered at the Universal Meeting-House, in Portsmouth, New-Hampshire: on Thursday, Dec. 25, 1794 . . . (Portsmouth: Printed by John Melcher, 1795);

An Oration on the Independence of the United States of Federated America; Pronounced at Portsmouth, New-Hampshire, July 4, 1795 . . . (Portsmouth, N.H.: Printed & sold by John Melcher, 1795);

The Accepted of the Multitude of His Brethren: An Historical Discourse, in Two Parts; Gratefully Commemorating, the Unparalleled Services, and Pre-Eminent Virtues of General George Washington (Portsmouth: Printed & published by Charles Peirce, 1800);

Watchfulness, Essential to Wisdom, Strength and Beauty . . . (Portsmouth: Printed by John Melcher, 1801);

The Scripture Doctrine of Election, Considered, As Glory to God, in the Highest; and on Earth, as Peace, and Good Will Towards Men: Being the Spirit of a Discourse, Delivered at the Ordination, of Brother Thomas Barnes . . . (Portsmouth: Printed by S. Sewall, 1802);

Light against Light in Three Ranks! A Masonic Discourse Pronounced before the Right Worshipful the Tyrian Lodge, Number XVI at Gloucester, Massachusetts on the Festival of St. John the Baptist. June 24, 5806 (Portsmouth: From the press of S. Whidden, 1806);

Masonic & Social Address, as Pronounced before the Most Worshipful Thomas Thompson, Esq., *G. M. M. and the M. W. the Grand Lodge, of Newhampshire . . . [at] the Laying [of] the Corner Stone of St. John's Episcopal Church, in Ample Form. On the 24th of June, A.L. 5807. By the Grand Chaplain of the Grand Lodge* (Portsmouth: From the press of William Treadwell, 1807?);

Remove Not the Ancient Land Mark! A Masonic Discourse, Pronounced at the Consecration of Ancient Land Mark Lodge and the Installation of Its Officers . . . (Portsmouth: Printed by Samuel Whidden, 1808);

The Feast of Dedication! A Discourse, Delivered in Substance at the New Brick Meeting House Erected by the Universal Society in Salem, Massachusetts, and Publicly Dedicated on Thursday Morning, June 22, 1809 (Salem: Printed by Pool & Palfrey, 1809);

Repent! Repent! or Likewise Perish! The Spirit of an Evening Lecture, February 16, 1812; on the Late Calamity at Richmond, Virginia . . . (Philadelphia: Printed by Lydia R. Bailey, 1812).

OTHER: *Psalms, Hymns and Spiritual Songs; Selected and Original* . . . , compiled by Richards and Oliver W. Lane (Boston: Printed by I. Thomas & E. T. Andrews, 1792);

Hymns and Odes, Composed on the Death of Gen. George Washington . . . , compiled, with contributions, by Richards (Portsmouth: Printed by Charles Peirce, 1800);

William Preston, *Illustrations of Masonry*, edited by Richards (Portsmouth: Printed by W. D. Treadwell, 1804).

George Richards was born in Rhode Island in the late 1750s or early 1760s. There he was introduced to verse-making, and he recalled in later years the "imbecile lays" he had then produced. After the Revolution, he settled in Boston as a schoolmaster and, after 1785, an occasional preacher in Boston's recently organized Universalist church. By the end of 1783, he was a contributor of verse to local periodicals, but his larger literary debut came with the publication in April 1789 of *The*

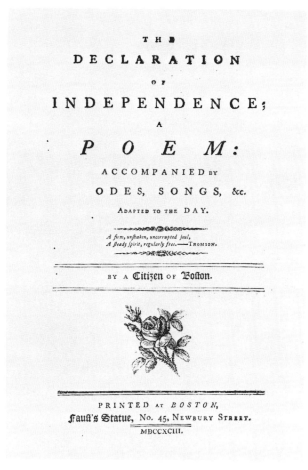

THE

DECLARATION

OF

INDEPENDENCE;

A

P O E M:

ACCOMPANIED BY

ODES, SONGS, &c.

ADAPTED TO THE DAY.

A firm, unshaken, uncorrupted soul,
A steady spirit, regularly free.—THOMSON.

BY A Citizen OF Boston.

PRINTED AT *BOSTON*,
Fauft's Statue, No. 45, NEWBURY STREET.
MDCCXCIII.

Title page for the long poem that Richards recited in Boston, with accompaniment from "a celebrated band" of local musicians, in July 1793 (courtesy of the John Carter Brown Library at Brown University)

Political Passing Bell: An Elegy. Written in a Country Meeting House. A quirky adaptation of the meter and manner of Thomas Gray's *Elegy in a Country Churchyard,* the parody addresses political disruptions in Boston at election time. Two months later, extracts from his long poem "The Zenith of Glory" began to appear in Isaiah Thomas's *Massachusetts Magazine,* and it continued to be published irregularly in eighteen installments through 1792. Richards's intention apparently had been to provide a complete versified history of the American

Revolution. Other verse appeared occasionally in Boston periodicals, and in July 1793 a long and laborious poem, *The Declaration of Independence,* was publicly recited in Boston by its author to the accompaniment of music from "a celebrated band" of local musicians. In the poem the name of every signer of the Declaration was jammed into metronomic rhyme.

Shortly after that reading, Richards moved to Portsmouth, New Hampshire, where he remained until 1808 as preacher at its Universalist church. He became an increasingly active member of the Masonic order, a composer of patriotic and religious songs and odes (especially, after 1800, those dedicated to the memory of George Washington). At this time, or later, he put together materials for a life of Commodore John Manly and published proposals for its publication, but the volume seems not to have appeared. Much of his time was spent in preparation for the 1804 publication of an American "improved" edition of William Preston's *Illustrations of Masonry,* which, since its publication in London in 1772, had become a handbook of Masonic history and practices. From Portsmouth he moved to Philadelphia where, from the spring of 1811 until the spring of 1812, he edited the *Free-Mason's Magazine and General Repository.* Fervently evangelical, in February 1812 he used the disastrous fire that had destroyed the theater in Richmond and killed many of its play-going citizens as the theme for an admonitory address to the people of Philadelphia to *Repent! Repent! or Likewise Perish!* He died, presumably in Pennsylvania, two years later.

References:

Samuel Kettell, "George Richards," in *Specimens of American Poetry,* edited by Kettell (Boston: S. G. Goodrich, 1828), II: 27-28;

A. A. Miner, "The Century of Universalism," in *The Memorial History of Boston,* edited by Justin Winsor (Boston: J. R. Osgood, 1881), III: 488-489;

Lyon N. Richardson, *A History of Early American Magazines, 1741-1789* (New York: Nelson, 1931), pp. 217-223.

Susanna Haswell Rowson
(circa 1762-2 March 1824)

Jenny Franchot
Stanford University

BOOKS: *Victoria. A Novel. In Two Volumes. The Characters taken from real Life, and Calculated to Improve the Morals of the Female Sex, By impressing them with a just Sense of The Merits of Filial Piety* (London: Printed by J. P. Cooke for the author & sold by J. Bew & T. Hookham, 1786);

A Trip to Parnassus; or, The Judgment of Apollo on Dramatic Authors and Performers. A Poem . . . (London: Printed by & for John Abraham, 1788);

The Inquisitor; or, Invisible Rambler, 3 volumes (London: Printed for G. G. J. & J. Robinson, 1788; Philadelphia: Printed & sold by William Gibbons, 1793);

Poems on Various Subjects (London: Printed for G. G. J. & J. Robinson, 1788);

The Test of Honour, A Novel. By a Young Lady, 2 volumes (London: Printed by & for John Abraham, 1789);

Charlotte. A Tale of Truth, 2 volumes (London: Printed for William Lane at the Minerva, 1791; Philadelphia: Printed by D. Humphreys for Mathew Carey, 1794);

Mentoria; or The Young Lady's Friend, 2 volumes (Printed for William Lane at the Minerva, 1791; Philadelphia: Printed for Robert Campbell by Samuel Harrison Smith, 1794);

The Fille de Chambre, A Novel, 3 volumes (London: Printed for William Lane at the Minerva, 1792; Philadelphia: Printed for H. & P. Rice and J. Rice & Co., 1794);

Slaves in Algiers; or, A Struggle for Freedom: A Play, Interspersed with Songs, in Three Acts . . . (Philadelphia: Printed for the author by Wrigley & Berriman, 1794);

Trials of the Human Heart, A Novel, 4 volumes (Philadelphia: Printed for the author by Wrigley & Berriman, 1795);

Reuben and Rachel; or, Tales of Old Times. A Novel (Boston: Printed by Manning & Loring for David West, 1798; London: William Lane, Minerva, 1799);

Miscellaneous Poems (Boston: Printed for the author by Gilbert & Dean, 1804);

Susanna Haswell Rowson

An Abridgment of Universal Geography, Together With Sketches of History. Designed for the Use of Schools and Academies in the United States (Boston: Printed for John West by David Carlisle, 1806);

A Present for Young Ladies; Containing Poems, Dialogues, Addresses . . . (Boston: Printed by E. G. House & published by John West & Co., 1811);

Sarah, or The Exemplary Wife . . . (Boston: Printed by Watson & Bangs & published by Charles Williams, 1813);

Youth's First Step in Geography, Being a Series of Exercises Making the Tour of the Habitable Globe (Boston: Published by Wells & Lilly, 1818);

Biblical Dialogues Between a Father and his Family: Comprising Sacred History, From the Creation to the Death of our Saviour Christ. The Lives of the

Apostles, and the Promulgation of the Gospel; With a Sketch of the History of the Church Down to the Reformation. The Whole Carried on in Conjunction With Profane History, 2 volumes (Boston: Printed by J. H. A. Frost & published by Richardson & Lord, 1822);

Exercises in History, Chronology, and Biography, in Question and Answer. For the Use of Schools. Comprising, Ancient History, Greece, Rome, &c. Modern History, England, France, Spain, Portugal, &c. The Discovery of America, Rise, Progress and Final Independence of the United States (Boston: Published by Richardson & Lord, 1822);

Charlotte's Daughter: or, The Three Orphans. A Sequel to Charlotte Temple (Boston: Printed by J. H. A. Frost & published by Richardson & Lord, 1828).

Susanna Rowson is known today as the author of America's first best-selling novel, *Charlotte. A Tale of Truth* (1791). But in addition to this remarkably popular work, Rowson published nine other novels, two volumes of verse, a lengthy critical poem, five theater pieces, six textbooks, numerous essays, and successful song lyrics. Actress, playwright, novelist, and songwriter, Rowson also founded one of New England's best-known academies for young women. Throughout her varied professional life, Rowson exhibited a Franklinian energy, succeeding in a number of pursuits commonly unavailable to genteel women. Her achievements as an early American writer and public figure belie the modern perception of her as a mere sentimentalist.

Rowson's early years exposed her firsthand to the tumult of the Revolutionary era. She was born in Portsmouth, England, to Susanna Musgrave (or Musgrove) Haswell, who died in childbirth. The motherless Susanna was taken at age five to settle in America with her father, William Haswell, who had by then remarried. Haswell, a revenue collector for the British Royal Navy, remained a Loyalist during the Revolution; his property was soon confiscated, and the impoverished family, after being interned at Hingham and later Abington, was finally deported to England in 1778. Thus by age eighteen, Susanna had experienced stormy transatlantic crossings, the sudden reversal of family fortunes, and the anguish of divided cultural allegiance—events which later figured in her novels of the trials facing young women in the world.

Back in England, Susanna soon showed her gift for attracting the notice of influential people. She became governess to the children of the Duch-

ess of Devonshire and under her patronage published her first novel, *Victoria* (1786), at age twenty-four. That same year she married William Rowson, a merchant and trumpeter in the Royal Horse Guards. Following the failure of his business in 1792, the couple embarked on a stage career. Mrs. Rowson continued to write during this period, publishing her long poem, *A Trip to Parnassus* (1788) and five new novels in rapid succession.

In 1793, the Rowsons accepted Thomas Wignell's offer to join his New Theatre Company just opening in Philadelphia. The Continental Congress's ban against theater had been repealed in 1789, and Philadelphia—a city just recovering from a yellow-fever epidemic—greeted Wignell's company with enthusiasm. As a character actress in a troupe of well-known performers and musicians, Mrs. Rowson also completed her first play before the year was out. With music by America's leading contemporary composer, Alexander Reinagle, Rowson's *Slaves in Algiers, or A Struggle for Freedom* (1794) was an immediate hit. Dealing with the topical issues of Barbary piracy and white slavery, Rowson voices her devotion to American liberty and women's rights, and closes on a bold note: "Women were born for universal sway,/Men to adore, be silent, and obey."

Success came on another front that same year with the publication of her first song, "America, Commerce and Freedom." A sample verse of this popular sea song reveals Rowson at her patriotic best:

> Then under full sail we laugh at the gale
> And the landmen look pale; never heed 'em
> But toss off the glass to a favorite lass
> To America, Commerce and Freedom.

Rowson continued to write lyrics until her death; many of her love songs, ballads, patriotic songs, and dirges were scored by prominent composers of the early national period and achieved immediate popularity.

Having moved to Boston in 1796 to join the Federal Street Theatre Company, Susanna Rowson abandoned the stage a year later to become an educator. The Young Girls' Academy, which she established there and directed for the remaining twenty-five years of her life, was soon enrolling the daughters of New England's elite. The childless Rowson, who had raised her husband's younger sister, Charlotte, his illegitimate son, William, and one adopted daughter as well, poured her energy into this new educational venture. She hired a notable faculty, introduced Boston's first pianoforte, and designed a demanding curriculum for her young American pupils. Never one to let her career interfere with her literary output, Rowson also published two new novels and a series of textbooks for her students. Her work as an editor on the *Boston Weekly Magazine* and her later essays for the *New England Galaxy* increased her reputation in the Boston community all the more.

Throughout her varied career, Rowson dedicated her literary works to the young female reader. Her lifelong concern for educating young girls to become self-reliant and accomplished women informs her tales of feminine adventure and tribulation, her magazine essays, and her textbooks. Rowson saw herself as a didactic realist whose "tales of truth" were meant to educate as well as entertain her readers. Working within the conventions of the sentimental novel, Rowson's fiction proclaims her democratic and Protestant vision. Egalitarianism, familial obedience, and piety were the ideals she advocated for the growth of her beleaguered female heroines into model Republican women.

By the time Rowson published *Charlotte. A Tale of Truth,* better known as *Charlotte Temple,* in 1791 she was a practiced writer whose previous novels showed a competent handling of contemporary genres: the Richardsonian seduction narrative, the digressive sentimental sketches of Laurence Sterne, and the conventional Gothic adventure tale. Her prose, and to a lesser extent her poetry, had met with moderate success. But when *Charlotte* was reprinted in America three years after its publication in England, Rowson, still early in her career, made literary history. Hardly read in England, the novel went through more than two hundred editions by the mid-nineteenth century in America and spawned a "Charlotte cult." Charlotte's supposed tombstone in Trinity Churchyard, New York, became a pilgrimage site for generations of readers.

Overcited and undervalued, the novel has long challenged critics to explain its success. Most likely a roman à clef about Rowson's cousin, John Montrésor, who eloped with a young woman named Charlotte Stanley, Rowson's story of the pathetic Charlotte Temple gave mythic form to the famous scandal. In Rowson's fast-moving narrative, a British soldier, off to fight in the American Revolution, persuades the fifteen-year-old Charlotte to elope with him to America. Abandoned by her lover in New York, Charlotte dies in childbirth, having gained her father's forgiveness in a tearful deathbed reunion. In true sentimental fashion Char-

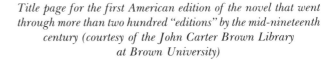

CHARLOTTE

A TALE OF TRUTH.

By Mrs. ROWSON,
OF THE NEW THEATRE, PHILADELPHIA;
AUTHOR OF *VICTORIA, THE INQUISITOR,*
FILLE DE CHAMBRE, &c.

IN TWO VOLUMES.

She was her parent's only joy :
They had but one—one darling child.
ROMEO AND JULIET.

Her form was faultless, and her mind,
Untainted yet by art,
Was noble, just, humane, and kind,
And virtue warm'd her heart,
But ah ! the cruel spoiler came—

VOL. I.

PHILADELPHIA:
PRINTED BY D. HUMPHREYS,
FOR M. CAREY, No. 118, MARKET-STREET.
M.DCC.XCIV.

Title page for the first American edition of the novel that went through more than two hundred "editions" by the mid-nineteenth century (courtesy of the John Carter Brown Library at Brown University)

lotte's aggrieved father refrains from killing her seducer, choosing instead to punish him with guilt: "Look on that little heap of earth, there hast thou buried the only joy of a fond father."

Although Rowson's classic seduction fable, replete with nostalgia for the Old World and indignation over lost innocence, captured the American reading public, her relationship with the critics has always been an uneasy one. As early as 1795, she came under attack by William Cobbett, a celebrated gadfly of the day. Singling out her play, *Slaves in Algiers,* Cobbett bitterly criticized "our American Sappho" for her feminism and her "sudden conversion to republicanism." Since then, Rowson has been generally ignored as yet another "female scribbler." Recently, however, she has benefited from current critical reappraisals of American women writers. Her versatile efforts as novelist, essayist, lyricist, and teacher are increasingly appreciated as a notable contribution to early American culture.

Bibliography:

R. W. G. Vail, "Susanna Haswell Rowson, The Author of Charlotte Temple: A Bibliographical Study," *Proceedings of the American Antiquarian Society*, 42 (April 1932): 47-160.

Biography:

Ellen B. Brandt, *Susanna Haswell Rowson, America's First Best-Selling Novelist* (Chicago, Ill.: Serbra Press, 1975).

References:

William Cobbett, *A Kick for a bite; or, Review upon review; with a critical essay, on the works of Mrs. S. Rowson, in a letter to the editor, or editors, of the American monthly review. 2nd. edition. By Peter Porcupine.* (Philadelphia: Printed by Thomas Bradford, 1796);

Leslie A. Fiedler, *Love and Death in the American Novel,* revised edition (New York: Stein & Day, 1966), pp. 93-98;

Constance Rourke, *The Roots of American Culture and Other Essays* (New York: Harcourt, Brace, 1942), pp. 75-87;

Dorothy Weil, *In Defense of Women: Susanna Rowson (1762-1824)* (University Park & London: Pennsylvania State University Press, 1976).

Papers:

The American Antiquarian Society possesses the largest single holding of Rowson material. The following libraries also have significant Rowson material: New York Public Library, Harvard College Library, Library of Congress, University of Chicago, Boston Public Library, New-York Historical Society, British Museum, Yale University, Brown University, the Watkinson Library at Trinity College, Hartford, and the New York State Library, Albany. The unique copy of the first edition of *Charlotte. A Tale of Truth* is in the Barrett Collection at the University of Virginia.

Benjamin Rush
(4 January 1746-19 April 1813)

Louis P. Masur
Princeton University

BOOKS: *Observations on the Angina Maligna: or, The Putrid and Ulcerous Sore Throat. With a Method of Treating it. By a Lover of Pennsylvania* (Philadelphia: Printed by William & Thomas Bradford, 1769);

A Dissertation on the Spasmodic Asthma of Children: in a Letter to Dr. Miller (London: T. Cadell, 1770);

Syllabus of a Course of Lectures on Chemistry (Philadelphia, 1770);

Sermons to Gentlemen Upon Temperance and Exercise (Philadelphia: Printed by John Dunlap, 1772); republished as *Sermons to the Rich and Studious, on Temperance and Exercise* (London: Edward & Charles Dilly, 1772);

An Address to the Inhabitants of the British Settlements in America, Upon Slave-Keeping (Philadelphia: Printed by John Dunlap, 1773); enlarged as *An Address to the Inhabitants of the British Settlements, on the Slavery of the Negroes in America. The Second Edition. To Which is Added, A Vindica-*

tion of the Address, in Answer to a Pamphlet Entitled, "Slavery not Forbidden in Scripture; or, A Defence of the West-India Planters" (Philadelphia: Printed & sold by John Dunlap, 1773);

Experiments and Observations on the Mineral Waters of Philadelphia, Abington, and Bristol, in the Province of Pennsylvania (Philadelphia: Printed by James Humphreys, junior, 1773);

An Oration, Delivered February 4, 1774, Before the American Philosophical Society, Held at Philadelphia. Containing, an Enquiry into the Natural History of Medicine Among the Indians in North-America, and a Comparative View of their Diseases and Remedies, with Those of Civilized Nations. Together With an Appendix Containing Proofs and Illustrations (Philadelphia: Printed by Joseph Crukshank, 1774);

Observations Upon the Present Government of Pennsylvania. In Four Letters to the People of Pennsylva-

nia (Philadelphia: Printed and sold by Styner & Cist, 1777);

Directions for Preserving the Health of Soldiers . . . (Philadelphia: Printed by John Dunlap, 1778);

The New Method of Inoculating for the Small Pox; Delivered in a Lecture in the University of Philadelphia, Feb. 20th, 1781 (Philadelphia: Printed by Charles Cist, 1781);

Considerations Upon the Present Test-Law of Pennsylvania: Addressed to the Legislature and Freemen of the State (Philadelphia: Printed by Hall & Sellers, 1784);

An Enquiry in to the Effects of Spirituous Liquors upon the Human Body, and Their Influence upon the Happiness of Society . . . (Philadelphia: Thomas Bradford, 1784?; Edinburgh: Printed by H. Inglis, 1791);

Observations Upon the Cause and Cure of the Tetanus . . . (Philadelphia, 1785);

Directions for the Use of the Mineral Water and Cold Bath, at Harrogate, Near Philadelphia (Philadelphia: Printed by Melchior Steiner, 1786);

An Oration, Delivered Before the American Philosophical Society, Held in Philadelphia, on the 27th of February, 1786; Containing an Enquiry into the Influence of Physical Causes Upon the Moral Faculty (Philadelphia: Printed by Charles Cist, 1786; London: Printed for C. Dilly, 1786);

A Plan for the Establishment of Public Schools and the Diffusion of Knowledge in Pennsylvania; To which are Added Thoughts Upon the Mode of Education, Proper in a Republic. Addressed to the Legislature and Citizens of the State (Philadelphia: Printed for Thomas Dobson, 1786);

An Enquiry into the Effects of Public Punishments Upon Criminals, and Upon Society. Read in the Society for Promoting Political Enquiries, Convened at the House of His Excellency Benjamin Franklin, Esquire, in Philadelphia, March 9th, 1787 (Philadelphia: Printed by Joseph James, 1787; London: Dilly, 1787);

Thoughts Upon Female Education, Accommodated to the Present State of Society, Manners and Government in the United States of America. Addressed to the Visitors of the Young Ladies' Academy in Philadelphia, 28 July, 1787, At the Close of the Quarterly Examination (Philadelphia: Printed by Prichard & Hall, 1787);

Observations on the Duties of a Physician, and the Methods of Improving Medicine. Accomodated to the Present State of Society and Manners in the United States. Delivered in the University of Pennsylvania, February 7, 1789, at the Conclusion of a

Course of Lectures Upon Chemistry and the Practice of Physic (Philadelphia: Printed and sold by Prichard & Hall, 1789);

Medical Inquiries and Observations, volume 1 (Philadelphia: Printed and sold by Prichard & Hall, 1789; London, 1789); volume 2 (Philadelphia: Printed by Thomas Dobson, 1793); volume 3 published as *An Account of the Bilious Fever, as It Appeared in the City of Philadelphia, in the Year 1793 . . . Second Edition* (Philadelphia: Printed by Thomas Dobson, 1794); volume 4 (Philadelphia: Printed by Thomas Dobson, 1796); volume 5 (Philadelphia: Printed by Budd & Bartram for Thomas Dobson, 1798);

An Eulogium in Honor of the Late Dr. William Cullen, Professor of the Practice of Physic in the University of Edinburgh; Delivered Before the College of Physicians of Philadelphia, on the 9th of July; Agreeably to their Vote of the 4th of May, 1790 (Philadelphia: Printed by Thomas Dobson, 1790);

Thoughts upon the Amusements and Punishments Which Are Proper for Schools. Addressed to George Clymer . . . (Philadelphia, 1790);

Extract of a Letter from Benjamin Rush, of Philadelphia, to Granville Sharp (London: Phillips, 1792);

An Account of the Sugar Maple Tree, of the United States: and of the Methods of Obtaining Sugar from it; Together with Observations Upon the Advantages, Both Public and Private, of this Sugar; in a Letter to Thomas Jefferson, Esq. Secretary of State of the United States, and one of the Vice-Presidents of the American Philosophical Society. Read in the American Philosophical Society, on the 19 of August, 1791 . . . (Philadelphia: Printed by R. Aitken & Son, 1792);

Considerations on the Injustice and Impolicy of Punishing Murder by Death. Extracted from the American Museum. With Additions (Philadelphia: From the Press of Mathew Carey, 1792); republished as *On the Punishment of Murder by Death* (London: Sold by J. Johnson & J. Phillips, 1793);

An Account of the Causes and Indications of Longevity, and of the State of the Body and Mind in Old Age; With Observations on Its Diseases and Their Remedies (Philadelphia, 1793);

An Enquiry into the Origin of the Late Epidemic Fever in Philadelphia: in a Letter to Dr. John Redman, President of the College of Physicians (Philadelphia: From the Press of Mathew Carey, 1793);

An Account of the Bilious Remitting Yellow Fever, as it Appeared in the City of Philadelphia in the Year 1793 (Philadelphia: Printed by Thomas Dob-

Benjamin Rush; portrait by Charles Willson Peale begun in 1776 and completed in 1781 (courtesy, the Henry Francis du Pont Winterthur Museum; gift of Mrs. Julia B. Henry)

son, 1794; Edinburgh: J. Symington, 1796);

An Eulogium, Intended to Perpetuate the Memory of David Rittenhouse, Late President of the American Philosophical Society, Delivered Before the Society in the First Presbyterian Church, in High-Street, Philadelphia, on the 17th Dec. 1796 (Philadelphia: Printed by Ormrod & Conrad for J. Ormrod, 1796);

Essays, Literary, Moral & Philosophical (Philadelphia: Printed by Thomas & Samuel F. Bradford, 1798; enlarged edition, Philadelphia: Printed by Thomas & William Bradford, 1806);

A Syllabus of a Course of Lectures on the Institutes and Practice of Medicine (Philadelphia: Printed by Thomas & Samuel F. Bradford, 1798);

Observations Upon the Origin of the Malignant Bilious, or Yellow Fever in Philadelphia, and Upon the Means of Preventing It: Addressed to the Citizens of Philadelphia (Philadelphia: Printed by Budd & Bartram, for Thomas Dobson, 1799);

A Second Address to the Citizens of Philadelphia, Containing Additional Proofs of the Domestic Origin of the Malignant Bilious, or Yellow Fever. To Which are Added, Observations, Intended to Shew that a Belief in that Opinion, is Calculated to Lessen the Mortality of the Disease, and to Prevent its Recurrence (Philadelphia: Printed by Budd & Bartram for Thomas Dobson, 1799);

Three Lectures Upon Animal Life, Delivered in the University of Pennsylvania (Philadelphia: Printed by Budd & Bartram, for Thomas Dobson, 1799);

Six Introductory Lectures, to Courses of Lectures, upon the Institutes and Practice of Medicine, Delivered in the University of Pennsylvania (Philadelphia: Printed by H. Maxwell & published by John Conrad, M. & J. Conrad in Baltimore, and Rapin & Conrad in Washington, 1801);

An Inquiry into the Various Sources of the Usual Forms of Summer & Autumnal Disease in the United States, and the Means of Preventing them. To Which are Added, Facts Intended to Prove the Yellow Fever not to be Contagious (Philadelphia: Printed by T. & G. Palmer for J. Conrad & Co., 1805);

Sixteen Introductory Lectures to Courses of Lectures Upon the Institutes and Practice of Medicine, with a Syllabus of the Latter. To Which are Added, Two Lectures Upon the Pleasures of the Senses and of the Mind, With An Inquiry Into Their Proximate Cause . . . (Philadelphia: Printed by Fry & Kammerer & published by Bradford & Innskeep, 1811);

Medical Inquiries and Observations, Upon the Diseases of the Mind (Philadelphia: Published by Kimber & Richardson, 1812);

A Memorial Containing Travels Through Life or Sundry Incidents in the Life of Dr. Benjamin Rush, Born Dec. 24, 1745 (Old Style) Died April 19, 1813; Written by Himself; Also Extracts From his Commonplace Book as well as a Short History of the Rush Family in Pennsylvania . . ., edited by Louis Alexander Biddle (Philadelphia: Published privately at the Sign of the Ivy Leaf, 1905);

The Autobiography of Benjamin Rush; His "Travels Through Life" Together with His Commonplace Book for 1789-1813, edited by George W. Corner (Princeton: Princeton University Press, 1948).

OTHER: William Cullen, *First Lines on the Practice of Physic for the Use of Students . . . ,* volume 1 edited by Rush (Philadelphia: Printed by Steiner & Cist, 1781);

Jean Senac, *A Treatise on the Hidden Nature, and the Treatment of Intermitting and Remitting Fevers,* edited by Rush (Philadelphia: Printed & sold by Kimber, Conrad & Company, 1805);

George Cleghorn, *Observations on the Epidemical Diseases of Minorca. From the Year 1744 to 1749. To Which is Prefixed a Short Account of the Climate, Productions, Inhabitants, and Endemial Distempers of Minorca*, edited by Rush (Philadelphia: Printed by Fry & Kammerer for F. Nichols, 1809);

The Works of Thomas Sydenham . . . , edited by Rush (Philadelphia: B. & T. Kite, 1809);

Sir John Pringle, *Observations on the Diseases of the Army*, edited by Rush (Philadelphia: Printed by Fry & Kammerer, published by Edward Earle and by D. Mallory & Company in Boston, P. H. Nicklin & Company in Baltimore, and J. W. Campbell in Petersburgh, 1810);

William Hillary, *Observations on the Changes of the Air, and the Concomitant Epidemical Diseases in the Island of Barbadoes. To Which Is Added, A Treatise on the Putrid Bilious Fever; and Such Other Diseases as Are Indigenous or Endemial, in the West India Islands, or in the Torrid Zone*, edited by Rush (Philadelphia: Printed by J. Aitken & published by B. & T. Kite, 1811).

Benjamin Rush, physician, scientist, educator, and essayist, was born in Byberry Township near Philadelphia, the son of Susanna Hall Harvey and her second husband, John Rush, a gunsmith and farmer. Rush graduated from the College of New Jersey (now Princeton University) in 1760. From February 1761 to July 1766, he served in Philadelphia as an apprentice to Dr. John Shippen, a distinguished physician. In August of 1766 he left for Edinburgh University, where he received his M.D. in 1768. He continued his studies in London before returning to America in 1769, whereupon the trustees of the College of Philadelphia appointed him the first professor of chemistry. He later served as professor of medicine and clinical practice at the University of Pennsylvania. Perhaps the most influential physician in America, Rush devoted his life to teaching medicine, attending patients, and participating actively in the political and cultural life of the early republic.

To Rush, the study of medicine aimed not only at improving health but at establishing guidelines for the ordering and preserving of the American republic. Cleanliness, exercise, and moderation in drink and diet, the physician believed, would help maintain the virtue of all citizens. Contemporaries appreciated him as a prolific contributor to literary magazines such as the *American Museum* and *Columbian Magazine*, in which he published both

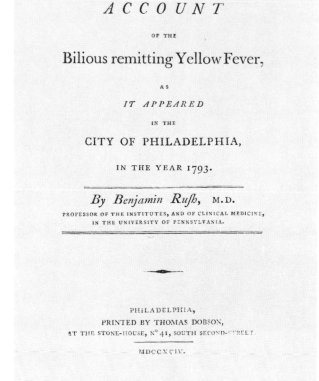

AN

ACCOUNT

OF THE

Bilious remitting Yellow Fever,

AS

IT APPEARED

IN THE

CITY OF PHILADELPHIA,

IN THE YEAR 1793.

By Benjamin Ruſh, M.D.

PROFESSOR OF THE INSTITUTES, AND OF CLINICAL MEDICINE, IN THE UNIVERSITY OF PENNSYLVANIA.

PHILADELPHIA,
PRINTED BY THOMAS DOBSON,
AT THE STONE-HOUSE, N° 41, SOUTH SECOND-STREET.

MDCCXCIV.

Title page for the pamphlet in which Rush provoked a controversy by insisting that yellow fever was of domestic rather than foreign origin (courtesy of the John Carter Brown Library at Brown University)

scientific papers and social commentaries. His medical essays ranged in subject from treatises on smallpox inoculation and the causes of tetanus to inquiries on the effects of "spiritous liquors" and old age. These papers, often delivered orally, published in magazines and sometimes as separate pamphlets, were finally revised and collected in a series of volumes entitled *Medical Inquiries and Observations* (1789-1798).

In one of his most controversial pamphlets, *An Account of the Bilious Remitting Yellow Fever, as it Appeared in the City of Philadelphia in the Year 1793* (1794), Rush defended his belief that yellow fever was of domestic origin and that bloodletting, a common eighteenth-century practice, was the preferred treatment. Many people heaped abuse upon the physician for not agreeing that the disease must have come from abroad, and for failing to stem the

1804. July ~~Died~~ 12th: Died of a wound received in a duel the day before from Col. Burr, Alex.^r Hamilton Esqr the Aid of Washington in the field, & his principal Councillor in the Cabinet while President of the UStates. He was learned, ingenious, & eloquent, & the Object of universal ~~unrivalled~~ Admiration & Attachment of One party, & ~~of~~ hated of ~~the~~ other party which then constituted ~~divided~~ the American people. He was greatly & universally lamented. Funeral Orations were delivered in honor of him in New York & Boston, & funeral ~~sermons~~ Sermons preached upon his death in many churches. mourning was Worne for him by many of the citizens of the principal cities & towns in the UStates. Col Burr visited Philad.^a the week afterwards, went into Company & walked the Streets with ap: =parent unconcern. — Genl Hamilton lost a Son two years before in a duel ~~of~~ which duel he knew, and ~~approved of~~ ———: On his death bed he condemned it ~~duelling~~ in strong terms. —

August 30. 1804 Died suddenly of a rupture of a blood vessel in his lungs the Revd Dr Mc Blair Linn. aged 27. a young man of promising talents. —

The entries from Rush's commonplace book in which he mentions the deaths of Alexander Hamilton and John Blair Linn (American Philosophical Society)

death toll. While many of those who could afford it fled to the safety of the countryside, Rush remained in Philadelphia throughout the epidemic. Of Rush's medical writings, his *Medical Inquiries and Observations, Upon the Diseases of the Mind* (1812) stands as his most important. Published in the year before his death, this volume offered one of the first studies of the causes and treatment of mental illness in America.

As a member of the American Philosophical Society and the society for Promoting Political Enquiries, Rush was at the center of a cohort devoted to advancing the arts and sciences in America; this group also included Benjamin Franklin, David Rittenhouse, and Charles Willson Peale. Rush was deeply committed to improving literary style in America and once remarked in a letter that "the present is an age of simplicity in writing in America. The turgid style of Johnson, the purple glare of Gibbon, and even the studied and thickset metaphors of Junius are all equally unnatural, and should not be admitted into our country." Rush's own style was clear, logical, and purposeful. He eschewed the use of Greek and Latin, developed his arguments point by point, and devoted his work to the creation of a perfect Christian Republic.

As with his medical and scientific papers, Rush's other writings were often presented orally, published in magazines, and printed as pamphlets. Many of these were later collected and revised in *Essays, Literary, Moral & Philosophical* (1798, enlarged 1806). These essays ranged from thoughts on slaveholding, female education, and public schools to enthnological studies of Indians and considerations on public punishments and the death penalty. Many of his essays generated discussion and contributed to changes in society. His commitment to education, for example, helped lead to the 1783 founding of Dickinson College in Carlisle, Pennsylvania. Rush's opposition to capital punishment, to take another case, influenced the passage of a 1794 law that abolished the death penalty in Pennsylvania except for murder in the first degree. Upon Rush's death, John Adams wrote Thomas Jefferson that he knew of "no Character living or dead, who has done more real good in America."

Rush played a role in some of the most important writings to emerge from the Revolutionary and early national period. The young physician was deeply involved in Revolutionary politics in Philadelphia. It was Rush who suggested to Thomas Paine that he title his pamphlet *Common Sense* rather than "Plain Truth." Two days after the publication

of Paine's powerful plea for separation from Great Britain, Rush married sixteen-year-old Julia Stockton, daughter of Richard Stockton. In June 1776, Rush was elected to the Continental Congress; both he and his father-in-law signed the Declaration of Independence. During the Revolutionary War, Rush served as Physician General of the Middle Department. Rush also labored to reconcile the strained friendship between John Adams and Thomas Jefferson, and after four years of cajoling he succeeded in 1812. The resulting correspondence between the two former presidents, which was not published in its entirety until 1959, forms one of the most enlightening contributions in the history of American letters.

Rush's literary reputation today rests chiefly on writings that were not published in his lifetime: his autobiography, *Travels Through Life,* a commonplace book he maintained from 1789-1813, and two volumes of his letters. The autobiography, written in 1800 for his children and never intended for publication, was undertaken in part to vindicate himself from the criticism he received during the yellow fever epidemics of 1793 and 1797. Together, the autobiography, commonplace book, and correspondence provide a fascinating portrait of Rush's life as a physician in Philadelphia and illuminate American politics, society, and culture in the late eighteenth and early nineteenth centuries.

Letters:

Letters of Benjamin Rush, 2 volumes, edited by Lyman H. Butterfield (Princeton: Princeton University Press, 1951);

The Spur of Fame: Dialogues of John Adams and Benjamin Rush, 1805-1813, edited by John A. Schutz and Douglass Adair (San Marino: Huntington Library, 1960).

Biography:

David Freeman Hawke, *Benjamin Rush: Revolutionary Gadfly* (Indianapolis: Bobbs-Merrill, 1971).

References:

George W. Corner, Introduction to *The Autobiography of Benjamin Rush; His "Travels Through Life" Together with His Commonplace Book for 1789-1813* (Princeton: Princeton University Press, 1948);

Donald J. D'elia, "Benjamin Rush: Philosopher of the American Revolution," *Transactions of the American Philosophical Society,* new series 64, part 5 (1974);

James McLachlan, "Benjamin Rush," in *Princetonians, 1748-1768, A Biographical Dictionary*, edited by McLachlan (Princeton: Princeton University Press, 1976), pp. 318-325.

Papers:
The bulk of Rush's papers are located at the Historical Society of Pennsylvania.

Elihu Hubbard Smith
(4 September 1771-19 September 1798)

William K. Bottorff
University of Toledo

BOOKS: *Edwin and Angelina, or the Banditti. An Opera, in Three Acts* (New York: Printed by T. & J. Swords, 1797);

A Discourse, Delivered April 11, 1798, at the Request of and before the New-York Society for Promoting the Manumission of Slaves, and Protesting such of Them as Have Been or May Be Liberated (New York: Printed by T. & J. Swords, 1798);

The Echo, with Other Poems, by Smith, Richard Alsop, Theodore Dwight, Mason F. Cogswell, and Lemuel Hopkins (New York: Printed at Porcupine Press by Pasquin Petronius [Isaac Riley], 1807);

The Diary of Elihu Hubbard Smith (1771-1798), edited by James E. Cronin (Philadelphia: American Philosophical Society, 1973).

OTHER: *American Poems, Selected and Original*, edited by Smith (Litchfield, Conn.: Printed by Collier & Buel, 1793);

"Letters to William Buel. Physician, on the Fever which Prevailed in New-York, in 1795," in *A Collection of Papers on the Subject of Bilious Fevers, Prevalent in the United States for a Few Years Past*, compiled by Noah Webster (New York: Printed by Hopkins, Webb & Co., 1796), pp. 53-144;

"Epistle to Dr. Darwin," in *The Botanic Garden. A Poem in Two Parts. Part I Containing the Economy of Vegetation. Part II The Loves of the Plants. With Philosophical Notes. The First American Edition*, by Erasmus Darwin, edited by Smith (New York: Printed by T. & J. Swords, 1798);

Benjamin Franklin V, ed., *The Poetry of the Minor Connecticut Wits*, includes poems by Smith (Gainesville: Scholars' Facsimiles & Reprints, 1970).

Elihu Hubbard Smith; portrait by James Sharples or Ellen Wallace Sharples (Yale University Art Gallery. Gift to Yale Medical Library through Dr. Herbert Thoms by Mrs. Frances G. Colt.)

One of the most remarkable young men of his day, Elihu Hubbard Smith, in the short twenty-seven years of his life, became a second-generation member of the Connecticut Wits (the first American "school" of poets), editor of the first book-length anthology of American poetry, writer of perhaps the first American comic opera, a biographer, a leading medical figure, and, finally, a martyr to his profession. In the twentieth century Smith has become one of the most written about minor figures in the history of American letters.

Smith was born in Litchfield, Connecticut, to Dr. Reuben Smith and Abigail Hubbard Smith, and, after undergoing tutoring, he entered Yale College at the age of eleven. He took his B.A. degree in 1786—Yale's youngest graduate to that time—with his traditional Christian faith profoundly shaken by freethinking friends and deistical readings. He joined the literary society Brothers in Unity (which had been founded by David Humphreys in 1768). They put on plays, had readings, and exchanged written works. Among his friends—not all freethinkers—were Noah Webster, Mason F. Cogswell, and William Johnson, later his roommate in New York.

In 1787 Smith was sent to Timothy Dwight's academy at Greenfield Hill, where his faith briefly reasserted itself. (Soon Smith adopted deism as his philosophy and held to it for the rest of his life.) He returned home to study pharmacy in his father's apothecary shop and medicine with a local doctor.

Then, in autumn 1790, he went to Philadelphia, where he formally studied medicine under the great Benjamin Rush until February 1791. Smith never completed his medical course work, but was nonetheless called Doctor and practiced medicine from then on. Still in Philadelphia, he began to have light verse and some of the earliest sonnets by an American hand published in the *Gazette of the United States* and the *American Museum or Universal Magazine*. He formed friendships with a number of literary people, including Charles Brockden Brown and Joseph Bringhurst, Jr., and conceived a plan to publish the first book-length, general anthology of American poetry.

Having returned to Litchfield in summer 1791, Smith contributed (with Richard Alsop, Lemuel Hopkins, Theodore Dwight, and Mason F. Cogswell, the minor Connecticut Wits) to *The Echo*, a series of satiric poems with a Federalist bias published in the *American Mercury* and the *Connecticut Current* (both in Hartford), from 1791-1798. When the Hartford Medical Society was founded on 25 September 1792, Smith was the organization's clerk. He then lived in Wethersfield.

In 1793 Smith saw through the press his newly edited volume, *American Poems, Selected and Original*. It contained sixty-five poems, in a variety of verse forms, by some nineteen poets from seven states—chiefly those of the Connecticut Wits. The book

sold more than two hundred copies, but further projected volumes were never forthcoming. The value of *American Poems, Selected and Original* in documenting poetic taste in the new nation is enormous. While the book does have a regional and Federalist bias, some of the poets represented were from elsewhere, and the subscribers pages indicate that the book had a national market.

Smith included in his anthology two of his own poems. One of these, "From a Gentleman, to a Lady, Who Had Presented Him with a Cake Heart," is successful *vers de société*. The burden of the poem is that the lady who has sent the cake heart should surrender instead her own heart in love. The hyperbole used to describe the delight in receiving the valentine (it is "to my soul . . . press'd") complements the serious statement of longing for true love. Smith's little poem, with its subtly handled rhythm and rhyme, is still a delight.

Later that same year, Smith settled permanently in New York, the better to practice his

AMERICAN POEMS

SELECTED AND ORIGINAL.

VOL. I.

LITCHFIELD:
PRINTED BY
COLLIER AND BUEL.

(THE COPY-RIGHT SECURED AS THE ACT DIRECTS.)

Title page for the book that is generally considered the first anthology of American poetry

profession and to move in literary circles. He became affiliated with a hospital in the city, and, in 1796 with two colleagues, he founded and edited the United States' first medical journal, the *Medical Repository*. This was a long-running important contribution to the good health of the Republic's populace.

Smith became a fellow lodger and close friend of Charles Brockden Brown, now also living in New York, and prodded him toward his eventual career as a novelist. It was Smith who privately printed Brown's *Alcuin* (1798) and who no doubt placed with a publisher the manuscript of *Wieland*. Another literary effort by Smith that year was the writing of a series of biographical sketches of American poets, such as Dwight and Joel Barlow. They were published posthumously, in the *Monthly Magazine, and British Register* (July-December 1798), the first notice of any importance to appear about our poets in England.

Furthermore, as far back as 1791, Smith had begun the book for an opera. This work, *Edwin and Angelina, or the Banditti*, was performed in 1796 (with music by Victor Pelissier) and published in 1797. Though not a success at the box office, the piece is in competent blank verse and was perhaps the earliest-written comic opera in the history of the American stage. Smith had many friends in the New York theater, including William Dunlap, who wrote the first American tragedy, and he often attended performances of plays and operas. "I was passionately sensible to music from my earliest moments," Smith wrote in his diary. "Of all other instruments the voice most enchanted me. . . . "

He kept his elaborate diary—of some half a million words—from 1795 to the time of his death. A rich source for intelligent commentary on the era's modes of travel, dress, manners, rural and urban life, religion, medicine, slavery (Smith was antislavery), politics (he was a Federalist), law, theater, commerce, and even marriage and child-rearing (although Smith was a bachelor), it also contains touching remarks on his friendships with Brown, Dunlap, Noah Webster, and others.

Smith was a lover of nature, though he realized that he must live in the city in order to lead the life of doctor and writer. It was the city, with its perennial pestilential outbreaks, that caused his early death—the city which, in his opera, he had called "poisonous." When the yellow fever hit, Smith wrote (as a careful researcher into the disease's cause and treatment), "I compute that about one in ten die; & that not more than one in a hundred would perish, with early attention & faith-

EDWIN AND ANGELINA;

OR

THE BANDITTI.

AN OPERA, IN THREE ACTS.

NEW-YORK:

Printed by T. & J. SWORDS, No. 99 Pearl-street.

—1797.—

Title page for the work that is believed to be the first American comic opera (courtesy of the John Carter Brown Library at Brown University)

ful nursing." His own case proved an exception to his estimate for, upon his giving "faithful nursing," in his own home, to a young colleague, Smith also contracted the malady, which proved fatal to both doctor and patient. Had he not been so diligent in his practice he might well have lived a longer, productive life. Among his last words are these he wrote of his deceased patient: "The history of this most accomplished, & most unfortunate man is calculated to awaken the deepest interest & foster the profoundest regrets." His comment is a fitting epitaph for Smith himself.

In the history of American literature—and in the history of medicine—Elihu Hubbard Smith is certainly a minor figure. Yet his story is rich in material for those who would understand life and letters in early America. He represents the kind of figure who established the very basis of our culture.

Biographies:
"Sketch of the Life and Character of the Late Dr.

Elihu Hubbard Smith, of New-York," *The American Medical and Philosophical Register; or Annals of Medicine, Natural History, Agriculture, and the Arts,* edited by David Hosack and John W. Francis (New York: Published by C. S. Van Winkle, 1814), IV: 391-399;

James Thacher, "Smith, Elihu Hubbard, M.D.," in his *American Medical Biography* (Boston: Richardson & Lord and Cottons & Barnard, 1828), pp. 88-95;

Herbert Thoms, "Elihu Hubbard Smith, Physician, Editor, 'Connecticut Wit,' " *Bulletin of the Society of the Medical History of Chicago,* 3 (1923-1925): 471-478;

Marcia Edgerton Bailey, *A Lesser Hartford Wit, Dr. Elihu Hubbard Smith, 1771-1798,* University of Maine Studies, second series no. 11 (Orono, Maine: University Press, 1928);

James E. Cronin, "The Life of Elihu Hubbard Smith," Ph.D. dissertation, Yale University, 1946.

Charles E. Bennett, "A Poetical Correspondence Among Elihu Hubbard Smith, Joseph Bringhurst, Jr., and Charles Brockden Brown in *The Gazette of the United States,*" *Early American Literature,* 12 (Winter 1977/1978): 277-285;

James E. Cronin, "Elihu Hubbard Smith and the New York Friendly Club, 1795-1798," *PMLA,* 64 (June 1949): 471-479;

Cronin, "Elihu Hubbard Smith and the New York Theater (1793-1798)," *New York History,* 31 (1950): 136-148;

Cronin, "Three Notes on Alexander Hamilton by Elihu Hubbard Smith," *Notes and Queries,* 198 (May 1953): 210, 211;

Michael L. Lasser, "Elihu Smith's All-American Anthology," *Journal of the Rutgers University Library,* 31 (1967): 14-20;

Harry R. Warfel, *Charles Brockden Brown, American Gothic Novelist* (Gainesville: University of Florida Press, 1949), pp. 40-49, 74, 75, 80, 81, 118-123.

References:

M. Ray Adams, "Della Cruscanism in America," *PMLA,* 79 (June 1964): 259-265;

Papers:

Smith's diary and most of his letters are at Yale University.

Samuel Stanhope Smith
(16 March 1751-19 August 1819)

Stephen J. Stedman
Tennessee State University

BOOKS: *A Funeral Sermon on the Death of the Hon. Richard Stockton, Esq., Princeton, March 2, 1781* (Trenton: Printed & sold by Isaac Collins, 1781);

An Essay on the Causes of the Variety of Complexion and Figure in the Human Species. To Which Are Added Strictures on Lord Kaims's Discourse, on the Original Diversity of Mankind (Philadelphia: Printed & sold by Robert Aitken, 1787; Edinburgh: Printed for C. Elliot, 1788; enlarged edition, New Brunswick: Published by J. Simpson, 1810);

Three Discourses, I. On the Guilt and Folly of Being Ashamed of Religion. II. On the Evil of Slander. III. On the Nature and Danger of Small Faults . . . (Boston, 1791);

A Discourse on the Nature and Reasonableness of Fasting, and on the Existing Causes that Call Us to That Duty. Delivered at Princeton, on Tuesday the 6th January, 1795. Being the Day Appointed by the Synod of New-York and New-Jersey to Be Observed as a General Fast . . . (Philadelphia: Printed by William Young, 1795);

The Divine Goodness to the United States of America. A Discourse, on the Subjects of National Gratitude, Delivered in the Third Presbyterian Church in Philadelphia, on Thursday the 19th of February, 1795, Recommended by the President of the United States, to be Observed Throughout the Union as a Day of General Thanksgiving and Prayer (Philadelphia: Printed by William Young, 1795);

A Discourse Delivered on the 22d of February, 1797, at

Samuel Stanhope Smith; portrait by James Sharples
(Princeton University Library)

the Funeral of the Rev. Gilbert Tennent Snowden,
Pastor of the Presbyterian Church of Cranberry, In
the State of New-Jersey (Philadelphia: Printed by
Ormrod & Conrad for John Ormrod, 1797);

Sermons (Newark, N.J.: Printed & sold by Jacob
Halsey, 1799; London: Mawman, 1801);

*An Oration, upon the Death of General George Washing-
ton, Delivered in the State-House at Trenton, on the
14th of January, 1800* (Trenton: Printed by G.
Craft, 1800);

*A Discourse on the Nature, the Proper Subjects, and the
Benefits of Baptism, With a Brief Appendix, on the
Mode of Administering the Ordinance* (Philadel-
phia: B. B. Hopkins & Co., 1808);

*Lectures on the Evidences of the Christian Religion, De-
livered to the Senior Class, on Sundays, in the Afternoon, in the College of New Jersey* (Philadelphia:
Hopkins & Earle, 1809);

*The Resurrection of the Body; In a Discourse, Delivered in
the Presbyterian Church in Georgetown Oct. 22d,
1809* (Washington, 1809);

*On the Love of Praise. A Sermon, Delivered Sept. 23,
1810, Being the Sunday Preceding Commencement*

(New Brunswick: Printed by L. Deare & published by J. Simpson & Co., 1810);

*The Lectures Corrected and Improved, which have been
Delivered for a Series of Years in the College of New
Jersey; on the Subjects of Moral and Political Philosophy* . . . (Trenton: D. Fenton for the author, 1812);

*A Comprehensive View of the Leading and Most Impor-
tant Principles of Natural and Revealed Religion:
Digested in Such Order as to Present to the Pious
and Reflecting Mind, A Basis for the Superstructure of the Entire System of the Doctrines of the
Gospel* (New Brunswick: Printed & published
by Deare & Myer, 1815);

Oratio Inauguralis . . . (Trenton: *edita a* D. & E. Fenton, 1817);

Sermons of Samuel Stanhope Smith . . . (Philadelphia:
S. Potter & Co., 1821).

OTHER: "Continuation to the Treaty of Ghent," by
Smith and others, in *History of the United States*,
by David Ramsay, revised edition (Philadelphia: Published by M. Carey & Son, 1818).

The salient feature of Samuel Stanhope
Smith's career was his effort to unite the rational
and the spiritual. In his capacity as a Presbyterian
minister and as a distinguished educator, Smith
sought to reveal and strengthen the bond which he
believed to exist between the world of the senses
and that of the spirit. He most clearly enunciates
this concern in his well-known *An Essay on the Causes
of the Variety of Complexion and Figure in the Human
Species* (1787), but it is evident in much else which he
wrote and in many of the activities of his life. For
instance, in 1795 Smith was responsible for bringing John Maclean, the first undergraduate teacher
of chemistry and natural science in America, to
Princeton, at that time a bastion of Presbyterian
orthodoxy. Although opposition to Smith's liberal
policies eventually cost him the presidency of the
college, by his action he ensured science a place in
the curricula of American undergraduate studies in
colleges of all religious persuasions.

Born the oldest son of Robert and Elizabeth
Blair Smith in Pequea, Pennsylvania, Smith was
educated at his father's school, concentrating mainly on traditional Greek and Latin studies. At sixteen
he entered the junior class of the College of New
Jersey (now Princeton University) and was graduated in 1769. John Witherspoon, the new president
of the college, exerted considerable influence on
Smith with his Scots Common Sense philosophy.
When Smith later married Witherspoon's daugh-

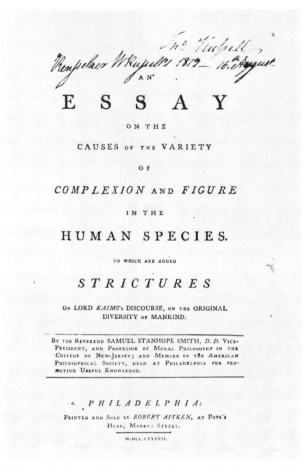

AN

ESSAY

ON THE

CAUSES OF THE VARIETY

OF

COMPLEXION AND *FIGURE*

IN THE

HUMAN SPECIES.

TO WHICH ARE ADDED

STRICTURES

ON LORD *KAIMS*'s DISCOURSE, ON THE ORIGINAL
DIVERSITY OF MANKIND.

BY THE REVEREND SAMUEL STANHOPE SMITH, *D. D.* VICE-
PRESIDENT, AND PROFESSOR OF MORAL PHILOSOPHY IN THE
COLLEGE OF NEW-JERSEY; AND MEMBER OF THE AMERICAN
PHILOSOPHICAL SOCIETY, HELD AT PHILADELPHIA FOR PRO-
MOTING USEFUL KNOWLEDGE.

PHILADELPHIA:

PRINTED AND SOLD BY *ROBERT AITKEN,* AT POPE's
HEAD, MARKET STREET.

M.DCC.LXXXVII.

Title page for the work in which Smith argued for the unity of the human species, as opposed to the separate creation of each race (courtesy of the John Carter Brown Library at Brown University)

ter, Ann, by whom he was to have nine children, he confirmed, as it were, his alignment with rationalist thinking. Following graduation, Smith tutored at his father's school in Pequea, performed missionary work in Virginia, founding the Academy of Hampden-Sydney there in 1776, and returned to Princeton in 1779 as professor of moral philosophy, eventually succeeding Witherspoon as president in 1795.

During his early years at Princeton, Smith wrote and eventually delivered before the American Philosophical Society his most influential work, *An Essay on the Causes of the Variety of Complexion and Figure in the Human Species*, in which he argues for the unity of mankind (as opposed to the argument for the separate creation of each race of mankind) but without recourse to the Bible as a source of authority. Common sense alone, Smith argues, reveals the oneness of our species. Although Smith's

Lamarckian argument has long since been shown to be outmoded, his scientific approach to matters hitherto the sole province of religion marks the essay as an important document in the history of American rationalism.

Although based on traditional thinking, Smith's moral and religious writings also reveal his liberal outlook. In the year of his resignation as president of Princeton he published *The Lectures . . . on the Subjects of Moral and Political Philosophy* (1812), in which he expressed broad-minded opinions on marriage (advocating polygamy in certain situations) and slavery (championing the eventual liberation of all slaves). Smith's sermons were celebrated for their eloquence in his own time and remain some of the best examples of post-Revolutionary War pulpit literature. His *An Oration, upon the Death of General George Washington* (1800) is especially significant, as it reveals a harmonious balance of piety and patriotism.

Samuel Stanhope Smith's life and works remain a significant example of the expanding importance of rationalist thinking in early America. His efforts to unite reason and religion changed the educational process in this country. For this contribution alone Smith deserves remembrance. However, his scientific, moral, and religious writings further enhance his reputation.

References:

David F. Bowers, "The Smith-Blair Correspondence, 1786-1791," *Princeton University Library Chronicle,* 4 (June 1943): 123-134;

M. L. Bradbury, "Samuel Stanhope Smith: Princeton's Accommodation to Reason," *Journal of Presbyterian History,* 48 (1970): 189-202;

Gladys Bryson, "Philosophy and the Modern Social Sciences: The Comparable Interests of the Old Moral Philosophy and the Modern Social Sciences," *Social Forces,* 2 (October 1932): 19-27;

William H. Hudnutt III, "Samuel Stanhope Smith: Enlightened Conservative," *Journal of the History of Ideas,* 17 (October 1956): 540-552;

Winthrop D. Jordan, Introduction to *An Essay on the Causes of the Variety of Complexion and Figure in the Human Species,* edited by Jordan (Cambridge, Mass.: Belknap Press, 1965), pp. vii-liii;

James McLachlan, ed., *Princetonians, 1748-1768: A Biographical Dictionary* (Princeton: Princeton University Press, 1976);

Leroy B. Miles, "Adventures in Persuasion: John Witherspoon, Samuel Stanhope Smith, and Ashbel Green," Ph.D. dissertation, Harvard University, 1967;

Samuel Holt Monk, "Samuel Stanhope Smith: Friend of Rational Liberty," in *The Lives of Eighteen from Princeton,* edited by Willard

Thorp (Princeton: Princeton University Press, 1946), pp. 86-110;

Morton Howison Smith, *Studies in Southern Presbyterian Theology* (Jackson, Miss.: Presbyterian Reformation Society, 1962), pp. 59-63;

William B. Sprague, *Annals of the American Pulpit* (Newport: Carter, 1858), III: 335-345.

Tabitha Gilman Tenney

(7 April 1762-2 May 1837)

Cathy N. Davidson
Michigan State University

BOOK: *Female Quixotism: Exhibited in the Romantic Opinions and Extravagant Adventures of Dorcasina Sheldon* (Boston: Printed by I. Thomas & E. T. Andrews, 1801).

OTHER: *The Pleasing Instructor,* edited, with a preface, by Tenney (Boston, 1799).

Literary historian F. L. Patee has described Tabitha Tenney's *Female Quixotism* (1801) as the most popular novel written in America prior to the publication of *Uncle Tom's Cabin* (1852). Although Patee's statement is something of an exaggeration, *Female Quixotism* did go through at least five editions and was still in print when Harriet Beecher Stowe wrote her landmark book. Tenney's importance is better gauged by her skill rather than her popularity. *Female Quixotism* is remarkable as a satire on the consequences of too much novel reading, as a critique of the American educational system, and as a forerunner of a comic tradition in American fiction.

As is often the case with women who lived in earlier centuries, little is known about Tabitha Tenney's life except as it relates to the lives of her father and her husband. Born in Exeter, New Hampshire, she was descended from some of the first pioneers in the state of New Hampshire, a family that had reached social and professional prominence even before the daughter's success as a writer. Tenney was the oldest of the seven children of Samuel Gilman and Lydia Robinson Giddinge Gilman. Evidence suggests that Tenney remained at home to help care for her siblings after the death of her

father in 1778. Of her schooling and other endeavors during these years we know virtually nothing, except for a few brief glimpses of her personality supplied by one of her peers, the diarist Patty Rogers, whose diary is at the American Antiquarian Society. Rogers, a voluble, excitable young woman, found Tabitha Gilman, in contrast, to be sober, mature, and somewhat disdainful. She did not like her, perhaps because the two women were rivals for the affections of Dr. Samuel Tenney, a medical doctor who had served in the Revolutionary War. After a serious courtship with Patty Rogers, Dr. Tenney abruptly shifted his affections to the more staid Tabitha Gilman. They remained married from 1788 until his death in 1816, living for much of their marriage in Washington, where Dr. Tenney served as a congressman for three consecutive terms, beginning in 1800. It is also worth noting that Patty Rogers may well have been the real-life model for Dorcasina Sheldon, the satirical heroine of *Female Quixotism.* There are remarkable similarities, for example, between the life, the language, and the reading habits of the woman and the character.

Aside from the comments in the Rogers diary, the only information we have of Tenney is that recorded in town and family histories, which invariably describe her as an "accomplished lady." The only record of these accomplishments is the books she produced. *The Pleasing Instructor* (1799) is an anthology of classical literature intended to "inform the mind, correct the manners, or to regulate the conduct." It was also designed to temper "instruction with rational amusement," and, like many similar books, was addressed to young women.

Similarly, *Female Quixotism* is dedicated "To all Columbian Young Ladies, who Read Novels and Romances." Roughly modeled on Charlotte Ramsay Lennox's *The Female Quixote; or, The Adventures of Arabella* (1752), *Female Quixotism* ranges from free-spirited humor to biting satire. The object of satire is sentimentality and particularly the young woman who indulges her sentimental fantasies too much. Equally important, Tenney diverges from her literary model by portraying a character who is less than innocent. In Lennox's book, fiction corrupts. In Tenney's more psychologically astute novel, Dorcasina Sheldon rationalizes her foolishness by conveniently blaming the novels she reads. By shifting the focus in this way, Tenney provides a psychological portrait of a woman who remains trapped in a flighty, frivolous, sentimental adolescence. The device allows Tenney to comment upon the sentimental-novel genre, as well as upon the role late-eighteenth-century women were expected to play.

The book eschews the typical happy ending. Continually duped by various men who hope to trick her out of her fortune, Dorcasina finally realizes her folly. But this sudden glimpse of herself and her life without the comforting delusion of sentiment also leaves her existence bereft of meaning. Her only consolation is that she might now serve as an example to other women: "My fate is singular; and I sincerely wish it may serve as a beacon to assist others, of similar dispositions, to avoid the rock on which I have been wrecked." The tragedy of the book (and tragedy is not too strong a word here) is that Dorcasina could have achieved far more than she did, were it not for social norms that educate women to prefer fantasy over a more realistic awareness of self and others.

It is unfortunate that *Female Quixotism* is no longer in print. It is one of the best examples of early American fiction, and it also adds a new dimension to our understanding of the place of the sentimental novel in American literature of that period. A satire and a critique of society, *Female Quixotism* shows that women writers were not all writing standard sentimental romances.

Female Quixotism was Tabitha Tenney's only novel. After her husband's death in 1816, Tenney returned to Exeter, New Hampshire, and occupied herself mostly with needlework, which was renowned for its originality and intricacy.

References:

Charles H. Bell, *History of the Town of Exeter* (Boston: Press of J. E. Farwell, 1888);

Herbert Ross Brown, *The Sentimental Novel in America, 1789-1860* (Durham, N.C.: Duke University Press, 1940);

Cathy N. Davidson, "Tabitha Tenney," in *American Women Writers,* edited by Lina Maineiro (New York: Ungar, 1982);

Arthur Gilman, *The Gilman Family* (Albany, N.Y.: Joel Munsell, publisher, 1869);

Mary Jane Tenney, *The Tenney Family, or The Descendants of Thomas Tenney of Rowley, Massachusetts, 1638-1890* (Boston: American Printing & Engraving Co., 1891);

Ola Elizabeth Wilson, "Tabitha Gilman Tenney," in *Notable American Women, 1607-1950,* edited by Edward T. James (Cambridge: Harvard University Press, 1971).

James Thacher

(14 February 1754-23 May 1844)

Steven E. Kagle
Illinois State University

BOOKS: *The American New Dispensatory* . . . (Boston: T. B. Wait & Co., 1810);

Observations on Hydrophobia, Produced by the Bite of a Mad Dog, or Other Rabid Animal . . . (Plymouth: J. Avery, 1812);

American Modern Practice; or, A Simple Method of Prevention and Cure of Diseases, According to the Latest Improvements and Discoveries (Boston: E. Read, 1817; revised edition, Boston: Cottons & Barnard,1826);

The American Orchardist; or, A Practical Treatise on the Culture and Management of Apple and Other Fruit Trees . . . (Boston: J. W. Ingraham, 1822; revised edition, Plymouth: E. Collier, 1825);

A Military Journal During the American Revolutionary War, from 1775 to 1783 . . . (Boston: Richardson & Lord, 1823; revised edition, Boston: Cottons & Barnard, 1827);

American Medical Biography: or Memoirs of Eminent Physicians . . . (Boston: Richardson & Lord and Cottons & Barnard, 1828);

A Practical Treatise on the Management of Bees . . . (Boston: Marsh & Capen, 1829);

An Essay on Demonology, Ghosts and Apparitions, and Popular Superstitions. Also an Account of the Witchcraft Delusion at Salem, in 1692 (Boston: Carter & Hendee, 1831);

History of the Town of Plymouth, from Its First Settlement in 1620, to the Year 1832 (Boston: Marsh, Capen & Lyon, 1832; revised and enlarged, 1835).

James Thacher

James Thacher spent most of his life as a practicing physician; however, today his reputation depends on his writings. Few American diaries of the war equal or surpass his as works of literature, and none of these has the scope of his. Thacher is also known for his writings about medical practice in early America. His *American Medical Biography* (1828) was the first major American medical reference work and is still an important historical source.

Although descended from distinguished ancestors who had first settled in America in 1635, Thacher's father, John Thacher, was a farmer of modest means. He probably provided his son only a modest basic education before apprenticing him at the age of sixteen for five years to Dr. Abner Hersey of Barnstable, Massachusetts. Thacher's *American Medical Biography* describes Hersey as "a mere compound of caprice and whim" who "oftener chastened by his frowns than cheered by any expressions of approbation or regard." An adequate practitioner, Hersey had little interest in medical theory, so in this area Thacher was self-taught. When, at twenty-one, Thacher completed his apprenticeship, the first battles of the Revolution were about to be fought. The first entries of his diary, *A Military Journal During the American Revolutionary War, from 1775 to 1783* (1823), deal with this period that brought the first news of fighting at Lexington and Concord. Against the advice of his friends, Thacher decided to enlist in the Continental army and in July 1775 was appointed as a surgeon's mate. During his military service Thacher was involved in or close to many of the most important events of the war, and his diary provides some of the best descriptions of them. Sent first to an army hospital at Cambridge, Thacher treated soldiers injured in the Battle of Bunker Hill and was able to observe actions related to the successful siege of Boston. He cared for the wounded from the American defeat in Canada and the American victory at Saratoga. In winter 1779 he was at Washington's camp at Morristown, where, according to some accounts, the suffering was greater than that at Valley Forge the year before. Thacher witnessed the execution of Major André in 1780 and the defeat and surrender of Cornwallis.

After the war Thacher returned to Massachusetts and married Susan Hayward; they had six children. Thacher started a medical practice in Plymouth, and in 1810 he received an honorary doctorate from Harvard. The same year he published his first book, *The American New Dispensatory*, summarizing current pharmaceuticals and their use. This book was followed by several other works of applied science and history, several of which remained in print through successive new editions. With the exception of his military journal, his most enduring work was his *American Medical Biography*, which, despite significant omissions and inconsistencies, gives a good picture of early American medicine and the men who practiced it. Thacher went beyond the details related to medicine and, as in his journal, provided anecdotes and other details that give the reader a sense of the personalities of his subjects.

Thacher's military journal received considerable praise when it was published in 1823 and is still regarded as among the best and most complete firsthand accounts of the Revolution. Unlike so many diarists of the war, Thacher wrote regular and well-developed entries. This thoroughness is especially significant since the diary spans almost the entire war. Thacher, who had an engaging, although overly florid, prose style, demonstrated a fine eye for detail and an excellent ear for dialogue. He was able to record the war as it was experienced by the participants—from the suffering of the wounded to the panic of a narrow escape, from the

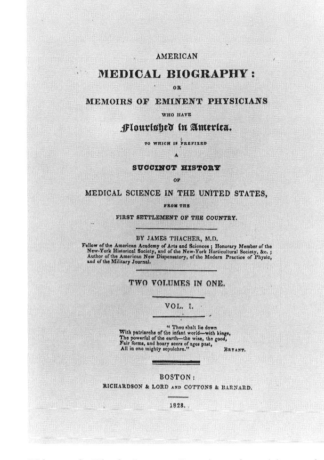

AMERICAN
MEDICAL BIOGRAPHY:
OR
MEMOIRS OF EMINENT PHYSICIANS
WHO HAVE
Flourished in America.
TO WHICH IS PREFIXED
A
SUCCINCT HISTORY
OF
MEDICAL SCIENCE IN THE UNITED STATES,
FROM THE
FIRST SETTLEMENT OF THE COUNTRY.

BY JAMES THACHER, M.D.
Fellow of the American Academy of Arts and Sciences ; Honorary Member of the New-York Historical Society, and of the New-York Horticultural Society, &c. ; Author of the American New Dispensatory, of the Modern Practice of Physic, and of the Military Journal.

TWO VOLUMES IN ONE.

VOL. I.

" Thou shalt lie down
With patriarchs of the infant world—with kings,
The powerful of the earth—the wise, the good,
Fair forms, and hoary seers of ages past,
All in one mighty sepulchre." BRYANT.

BOSTON :
RICHARDSON & LORD AND COTTONS & BARNARD.

1828.

Title page for Thacher's attempt "to animate the aspiring youth to contemplate and admire the virtues, and learn to imitate the noble actions of their ancestors"

beauty of the scenery to the way a bombshell falls. The skills which would later serve him so well as a historian and biographer helped him to give his personal observations a scope unmatched by any American diary of the war.

References:

Steven E. Kagle, *American Diary Literature* (Boston: Twayne, 1979), pp. 121-127;

Stephen W. Williams, *American Medical Biography: or, Memoirs of Eminent Physicians, Embracing Principally Those Who Have Died Since the Publication of Dr. Thacher's Work on the Same Subject* (Greenfield: Printed by L. Merriam & Co., 1845), pp. 565-580.

St. George Tucker

(29 June 1752-10 November 1827)

Homer D. Kemp
Tennessee Technological University

BOOKS: *Reflections on the Policy and Necessity of Encouraging the Commerce of the Citizens of the United States of America, and of Granting Them Exclusive Privileges of Trade,* as Columbus (Richmond: Printed by Dixon & Holt, 1785);

The Knight and Friars. An Historical Tale; After the Manner of John Gilpin . . . (New York: Printed & sold by Eleazer Oswald, 1786);

Liberty, a Poem; on the Independence of America (Richmond: Printed by Augustine Davis, 1788);

Cautionary Hints to Congress, Respecting the Sale of Western Lands, Belonging to the United States, as Columbus (Philadelphia: Printed by William W. Woodward, 1795);

A Letter, to the Rev. Jedediah Morse, A.M., Author of the "American Universal Geography." By a Citizen of Williamsburg (Richmond: Printed by Thomas Nicolson, 1795);

A Dissertation on Slavery: With a Proposal for the Gradual Abolition of It, in the State of Virginia (Philadelphia: Printed for Mathew Carey, 1796);

The Probationary Odes of Jonathan Pindar, esq. a Cousin of Peter's, and Candidate for the Post of Poet Laureat to the C.U.S. In Two Parts . . . (Philadelphia: Printed for Benjamin Franklin Bache, 1796);

Remarks on the Treaty of Amity, Navigation, and Commerce, Concluded between Lord Grenville and Mr. Jay, on the Part of Great Britain and the United States, Respectively . . . , as Columbus (Philadelphia: Printed by Henry Tuchniss for Mathew Carey, 1796);

Examination of the Question, "How far the Common Law of England is the Law of the Federal Government of the United States?" (Richmond: Printed by John Dixon, 1802);

Reflections on the Cession of Louisiana to the United States, as Sylvestris (Washington City: Printed by Samuel Harrison Smith, 1803);

The Crisis: An Appeal to a Candid World, on the War Entered into by the United States of America, Against Great-Britain and Her Dependencies . . . , as Columbus (N.p., 1817);

The Poems of St. George Tucker of Williamsburg, Virgin-

St. George Tucker, 1807; engraving by C. B. Fevret de St. Mémin (Tucker-Coleman Collection, Earl Gregg Swem Library, The College of William and Mary in Virginia)

ia, 1752-1827, edited by William S. Prince (New York: Vantage Press, 1977).

OTHER: *Blackstone's Commentaries: with Notes of Reference, to the Constitution and Laws, of the Federal Government of the United States; and of the Commonwealth of Virginia* . . . , 5 volumes, edited, with an appendix, by Tucker (Philadelphia: Published by William Young Birch & Abraham Small, 1803).

Although he has been remembered best in American history as a judge and as a legal commentator, St. George Tucker has been said to rival Thomas Jefferson in versatility. Tucker's public life, his published works, and his private papers reveal his impressive accomplishments as professor, Revolutionary War soldier and blockade runner, distinguished jurist, inventor, poet, playwright, essayist, political economist, musician, and educational theorist. Few of Tucker's poems were published during his lifetime, but his manuscript papers contain more than 200 poems, three full-length plays, and about thirty Addisonian essays. His *A Dissertation on Slavery* (1796) makes Tucker the most significant writer against slavery in the 1790s, and his comments in his edition of *Blackstone's Commentaries* (1803) are the first legal commentaries on the United States Constitution to appear in this country. In his later essays this thoroughgoing Jeffersonian republican felt a mission to warn Americans of the dangers of losing their original freedoms. Tucker's example of achievement was emulated by his descendants in one of the most important Virginia families of the nineteenth century.

St. George Tucker was born on 29 June 1752, the youngest of six children of Henry and Anne Butterfield Tucker of The Grove, near Port Royal, Bermuda. The Tuckers were one of the oldest aristocratic families in Bermuda, and by 1770 Colonel Tucker had young St. George tutored for entrance into one of the Inns of Court in London. Hard times struck Bermuda in 1771, however, preventing a London legal education. St. George and his two brothers, Thomas Tudor and Nathaniel, immigrated to America that year. While studying law with George Wythe, St. George made many friends and assured himself a place in Williamsburg society. Tucker visited Bermuda in 1775, but returned in 1777 and spent the next three years of the Revolutionary War engaged with Silas Deane in blockade running.

In 1778 Tucker married the wealthy widow Frances Bland Randolph, mother of John Randolph of Roanoke, by whom he had two sons, Thomas Tudor (1780-1848) and Nathaniel Beverly (1784-1851). Although Frances's death in 1788 was to leave Tucker profoundly grief stricken, in 1791 he married the widow Lelia Skipwith Carter. Tucker joined the militia in 1780, saw action at Guilford Courthouse and the Yorktown Campaign, and attained the rank of Lieutenant Colonel. His manuscript journal on the siege of Yorktown is regarded by historians as one of the most important eyewitness accounts of that event.

Tucker wrote verse for more than fifty years and was regarded by his Virginia social circle the equal of the Connecticut Wits. In fact a significant circle of poets was centered on Tucker, who acted from 1779 on as a sort of clearinghouse for his friends' poetry. He penned his patriotic songs, satiric odes, and *vers de société* upon neoclassical models.

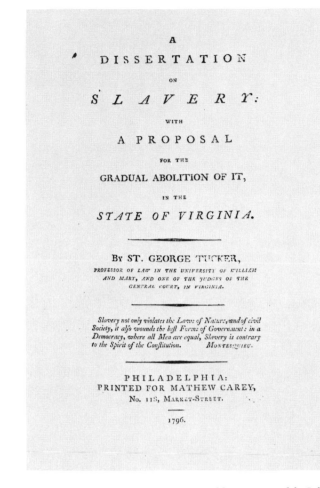

Title page for Tucker's abolitionist pamphlet (courtesy of the John Carter Brown Library at Brown University)

Like his neoclassical models, Tucker looked to poetry for its social value, and he saw his poetry as a vehicle for reminding Americans of the glories and responsibilities of freedom and for expressing his Jeffersonian liberalism. The longest of Tucker's Revolutionary War poems, *Liberty, a Poem; on the Independence of America,* was written during the Yorktown Campaign in 1781 and published in book form in 1788. Here Tucker warned Americans in typical neoclassical style to guard their hard-won liberties. The first of *The Probationary Odes of Jonathan Pindar, esq.* (1796) began to appear anonymously in 1793 in Philip Freneau's *National Gazette* and were traditionally attributed to Freneau. Modeled upon the Peter Pindar poems of John Wolcot, Tucker's odes are effective satire aimed at wealthy Federalist security holders who were speculating with bought-up paper. Richard Beale Davis has said that they are one of the two notable pieces of "satire published by Southerners during the first national period . . . and . . . among the very few in the whole country which dealt with significant national issues."

Not all of Tucker's poetry was devoted to serious or lofty subjects, as the many bawdy pieces in his manuscripts attest. In 1786 he published, without his name, *The Knight and Friars. An Historical Tale*, an American version of Richard Paul Jodrell's *The Knight and Friars* (1785). Jodrell's was a burlesque narrative poem dealing with the grotesque incidents involving the corpse of a libertine monk; Tucker's was a burlesque poem in sixty-five ballad stanzas presenting supposed Virginia character sketches. About 1790 Tucker gathered about a dozen of his verse tales together with the idea of writing a Virginia version of *The Canterbury Tales* to be entitled "The Country Wedding"; however, he never completed it, even though he circulated the poems among his friends and wrote another satiric tale as late as 1820.

It was as a jurist that Tucker was best known to the general public. From his 1788 election to the General Court through his thirteen years as professor of law at the College of William and Mary (1790-1804) and service on the Virginia Court of Appeals (1803-1811) to his appointment by President Madison to the U.S. District Court for Virginia (1813-1827), he was a liberal jurist with strong states' rights leanings and a dedication to the idea of judicial review. Tucker was long known as "the American Blackstone" for his annotated five-volume edition of *Blackstone's Commentaries: with Notes of Reference, to the Constitution and Laws, of the Federal Government of the United States; and of the Commonwealth of Virginia* (1803). The edition, with Tucker's appendix on the American Constitution, was used widely throughout America and remains one of the significant law books of the period.

As an essayist Tucker illustrates well the eighteenth-century writer's impulse toward the didactic. His manuscripts contain twenty holograph essays, written mainly in 1811, for William Wirt's *The Old Bachelor* series; however, it appears that Wirt used only one of Tucker's essays in the series. Tucker's manuscripts reveal that he was planning a "Hermit of the Mountain" series to include his *Old Bachelor* essays and other to-be-written essays. Seven essay-treatises published over two decades consistently show Tucker to be a Jeffersonian, liberal, anti-Adamsonian commentator on· many aspects of American government: *Reflections on the Policy and Necessity of Encouraging the Commerce of the Citizens of the United States of America, and of Granting Them Exclusive Privileges of Trade* (1785), *Cautionary Hints*

Caricature of Tucker drawn by one of his students at The College of William and Mary (Tucker-Coleman Collection, Earl Gregg Swem Library, The College of William and Mary in Virginia)

to Congress, Respecting the Sale of Western Lands, Belonging to the United States* (1795), *A Dissertation on Slavery: With a Proposal for the Gradual Abolition of It* (1796), *Remarks on the Treaty of Amity, Navigation, and Commerce, Concluded between Lord Grenville and Mr. Jay* (1796), *Examination of the Question, "How far the Common Law of England is the Law of the Federal Government of the United States?"* (1802), *Reflections on the Cession of Louisiana to the United States* (1803), *The Crisis: An Appeal to a Candid World, on the War Entered into by the United States of America, Against Great-Britain and Her Dependencies* (1817). It has been suggested by Richard Beale Davis that Tucker may have influenced his friends Jefferson and Madison through his Republican, liberal, anti-Adamsonian comments on aspects and situations of government.

At his death on 10 November 1827, St. George Tucker enjoyed a wide reputation as a distinguished jurist and writer. His son Thomas Tudor was to become a distinguished jurist and U.S. Senator, and his son Nathaniel Beverly was to distinguish himself as a jurist and author, whose novel, *George Balcombe* (1836), received high praise from Edgar Allan Poe. Tucker is a minor figure in American literary history, but, as Richard Beale Davis asserted, "Tucker deserves to be remembered as the Southern poet of the age of the Hartford Wits, a poet who merits comparison and consideration with any of his American contemporaries."

Letters:

"Randolph and Tucker Letters," *Virginia Historical Magazine,* edited by Mrs. George P. Coleman, 42 (January, April 1934): 129-131, 211-221; 43 (January 1935): 41-46.

Biography:

Mary Haldane Coleman, *St. George Tucker, Citizen of No Mean City* (Richmond: Dietz Press, 1938).

References:

Charles W. Coleman, "St. Mémin Portraits: St. George Tucker," *Magazine of American History,* 8 (September 1881): 217-221;

Mary Haldane Coleman, ed., *Virginia Silhouettes: Contemporary Letters Concerning Negro Slavery in the State of Virginia* (Richmond: Dietz Press, 1934);

Richard Beale Davis, *Intellectual Life in Jefferson's Virginia, 1790-1830* (Chapel Hill: University of North Carolina Press, 1964), pp. 245-246, 319-332, 356, 359, 401-402;

Carl Dolmetsch, "The Revolutionary War Poems of St. George Tucker," *Tennessee Studies in Literature,* 26 (1981): 48-65;

Dolmetsch, "Tucker's 'Hermit of the Mountain' Essays: Prolegomenon for a Collected Edi-

tion," *Essays in Early Virginia Literature Honoring Richard Beale Davis,* edited by J. A. Leo Lemay (New York: Burt Franklin, 1977), pp. 257-275;

Jay B. Hubbell, *The South in American Literature, 1607-1900* (Durham, N.C.: Duke University Press, 1954), pp. 148-153;

R. M. Hughes, "Belles of Williamsburg," *William and Mary Quarterly,* first series 10 (April 1930): 172;

William S. Prince, Introduction to *The Poems of St. George Tucker of Williamsburg, Virginia, 1752-1827* (New York: Vantage Press, 1977), pp. 1-33;

Prince, "St. George Tucker as a Poet of the Early Republic," Ph.D. dissertation, Yale University, 1954;

Prince, "St. George Tucker, Bard of the Bench," *Virginia Magazine of History and Biography,* 84 (July 1976): 267-282;

Edward M. Riley, "St. George Tucker's Journal of the Siege of Yorktown, 1781," *William and Mary Quarterly,* third series 5 (July 1948): 375-395;

Henry St. George Tucker, "Patrick Henry and St. George Tucker," *University of Pennsylvania Law Review,* 67 (January 1919): 69-74;

J. Randolph Tucker, "The Judges Tucker of the Court of Appeals of Virginia," *Virginia Law Register,* 1 (March 1896): 789-812.

Papers:

The bulk of St. George Tucker's manuscripts are to be found in the Tucker-Coleman Collection in the Earl Gregg Swem Library of the College of William and Mary. A significant collection of Tucker's letters are in the William Wirt Collection at the Maryland Historical Society.

Royall Tyler

James C. Gaston
U.S. Air Force Academy

BIRTH: Boston, Massachusetts, 18 July 1757, to Royall and Mary Steele Tyler.

EDUCATION: B.A., 1776; M.A., 1779; Harvard College.

MARRIAGE: May 1794 to Mary Hunt Palmer; children: Royall, Jr., John Steele, Mary Whitwell, Edward Royall, William Clark, Joseph Dennie, Amelia Sophia, George Palmer, Charles Royall, Thomas Pickman, and Abiel Winship.

DEATH: Brattleboro, Vermont, 26 August 1826.

BOOKS: *The Contrast, A Comedy in Five Acts* (Philadelphia: From the Press of Prichard & Hall and published by Thomas Wignell, 1790);
The Origin of Evil. An Elegy (N.p., 1793);
The Algerine Captive; or, the Life and Adventures of Doctor Updike Underhill: Six Years a Prisoner Among the Algerines, 2 volumes (Walpole, N.H.: Printed & sold by David Carlisle, jun., 1797; London: Printed for G. & J. Robinson, 1802);
The Georgia Spec; or, Land in the Moon. A Comedy in Three Acts . . . (Boston, 1797);
An Oration, Pronounced at Bennington, Vermont, on the 22d February, 1800. In Commemoration of the Death of General George Washington (Walpole, N.H.: Printed by David Carlisle for Thomas & Thomas, 1800);
The Yankey in London, Being the First Part of a Series of Letters Written by an American Youth, During Nine Months' Residence in the City of London . . . (New York: Printed & published by Isaac Riley, 1809);
Reports of Cases Argued and Determined in the Supreme Court of Judicature of the State of Vermont, 2 volumes (New York: Printed & Published by Isaac Riley, 1809-1810);
The Chestnut Tree or a Sketch of Brattleborough [East Village] at the Close of the Twentieth Century, Being an Address to a Horse-Chestnut Presented to the Author by the Rev. A. L. Baury . . . (North Montpelier, Vt.: Driftwood Press, 1931);
Four Plays by Royall Tyler, edited by Arthur Wallace Peach and George Floyd Newbrough, volume

An 1870 engraving by Samuel Holyer, copied from a miniature on ivory made while Tyler was still alive

15 of *America's Lost Plays,* edited by Barrett H. Clark (Princeton: Princeton University Press, 1941)—includes *The Island of Barrataria, The Origin of the Feast of Purim, Joseph and His Brethren,* and *The Judgement of Solomon;*
The Verse of Royall Tyler, edited by Marius B. Péladeau (Charlottesville: University Press of Virginia, 1968);
The Prose of Royall Tyler, edited by Péladeau (Montpelier & Rutland: Vermont Historical Society/Charles E. Tuttle, 1972).

Royall Tyler came closer than anyone in his generation to answering the post-Revolutionary call for a native American literature. In *The Contrast* (produced on 16 April 1787 and published in 1790), the first commercially successful comedy written in America, and in *The Algerine Captive* (1797), one of the first American novels to be republished in England, he developed comic themes and characters that have informed American literature ever since. He also wrote one of the first American musical plays to be successfully produced (on 19 May 1787), *May Day in Town,* as well as an early fictional travel book, *The Yankey in London* (1809), and at least five more plays, numerous poems, essays, speeches, and sermons, and even a two-volume set of Vermont law reports.

Tyler was born in Boston on 18 July 1757 to a family that had been prominent in Boston politics and business for two generations. His father, a member of the Massachusetts House of Representatives, actively opposed British taxes and the quartering of British troops in Boston. When his father died in 1771, the young man, whose name had been William Clark Tyler until that time, legally took his father's name, Royall.

Tyler entered Harvard in July 1772 and received his Bachelor of Arts degree in July 1776. Three months later Yale awarded him an honorary B.A., at that time a common courtesy between the two schools. After graduation he began to study law, but in summer 1778 he obtained a commission as a major and served as an aide to General John Sullivan when Sullivan unsuccessfully attacked the British in Newport, Rhode Island. After this brief military experience, he returned to his readings in law, obtained a Master of Arts degree at Harvard in 1779, and was admitted to the Massachusetts bar in 1780.

In 1782 he moved to the nearby town of Braintree and rented a room in the home of Richard Cranch, whose wife was a sister of Abigail Adams. The daughter of John and Abigail Adams, also named Abigail (but called Nabby), was seventeen then, and a frequent visitor in the Cranch home. She and Tyler soon began an intense romantic involvement that lasted until 1784 when she and her mother traveled to London to meet her father. For a time the distant lovers remained faithful, but Tyler seldom wrote and Nabby became increasingly interested in an American officer assigned to the diplomatic mission in London. In 1785 she returned Tyler's few letters and his miniature portrait and asked that he do the same with hers.

When his engagement to Nabby ended, Tyler moved from the Cranch home to the Boston home of Joseph Palmer, where he was living when the Daniel Shays Rebellion broke out in Massachusetts. In the summer of 1786, Shays and other angry farmers staged an insurrection, claiming that high taxes, low farm prices, and a restrictive monetary policy were driving them off their lands. In January 1787 the governor appointed Major General Benjamin Lincoln to lead the state militia against Shays, and Tyler became Lincoln's aide. When Lincoln defeated Shays's forces in February, Shays fled into Vermont. Lacking authority to take his state militia into Vermont, Lincoln sent Tyler to persuade Vermont officials not to offer sanctuary to the rebels. Tyler won his case with the Vermont governor and legislature, and he returned to Boston in March. Within a few days, the Massachusetts governor sent him on another diplomatic mission, this time to New York to enlist that state's aid against the rebels.

Tyler arrived in New York on 12 March 1787. Slightly more than one month later, on 16 April, his play *The Contrast* opened at the John Street Theatre, becoming the first American comedy professionally produced in the United States.

How could Tyler have written a successful comedy in such a short time? Some have speculated that he came to the city with the finished play, or a plan for the play, in his pocket, but scholars concede that available evidence simply does not reveal the circumstances of the writing of *The Contrast.* What is known is that Tyler had somehow immersed himself in the dramatic conventions of British comedy by the time he wrote *The Contrast.* For if his play is uniquely American in some respects, those American branches are grafted to a sturdy, thoroughly British comedy of manners. Like the comedies of George Etherege, William Congreve, and especially Richard Sheridan, *The Contrast* satirizes the affected manners and hypocrisies of a sophisticated, urban society. (Sheridan's *The School for Scandal,* 1777, part of which is described in *The Contrast,* was produced in New York nine days after Tyler arrived in the city.) Tyler's play follows the genre in its reliance upon drawing-room dialogue rather than upon action for character revelation, in its use of cunning servants and overheard conversations as devices for advancing the plot, and in its suggestion that true love will eventually overcome the difficulties presented by willful servants and unprincipled rakes. Tyler departs from the genre mainly in his use of distinctly American dialects and in his suggestion that the duplicity of New York society comes more from unsavory European influences than from human nature.

The paragon of virtue in the play is Colonel Henry Manly, a veteran of the Revolutionary War, who has come to New York with his servant Jonathan to petition Congress on behalf of wounded veterans. The play never questions Manly's qualities of courage, loyalty, honesty, and patriotism, nor does it challenge his assertions that the new nation will require such virtues in abundance. It does show, however, through the observations of his worldly sister Charlotte, that even Manly is guilty of a rather benign form of affectation. His transgression lies in his fondness for the sort of overblown rhetoric that filled most public speeches of the day. He is unable to speak of his parents as merely parents, for instance, but calls them "that venerable pair" and "the respectable authors of my

existence,—the cherishers and protectors of my helpless infancy." Charlotte aptly describes Manly's speech: "His conversation is like a rich, old-fashioned brocade,—it will stand alone."

If Manly amused audiences with the excesses of Independence Day rhetoric, his servant Jonathan won them completely with a combination of backwoods Yankee dialect and naive misunderstandings of city ways. Jonathan's response to an effusive greeting shows a characteristic frontier attitude toward the supposed artificiality of city life: "Well, and I vow, too, I am pretty considerably glad to see you," he says, "but what the dogs need of all this outlandish lingo?" Though Jonathan was neither the first rustic Yankee to appear in drama nor the first servant to use a comic dialect, his character-

Frontispiece and title page for the first commercially successful comedy written in America. The frontispiece engraving by Peter Rushton Maverick is based on a picture by William Dunlap.

ization by the popular actor Thomas Wignell was so successful that he soon became the pattern for a number of stage Yankees. Jonathan's influence can be seen, further, in the works of later regional humorists such as Augustus Baldwin Longstreet, Thomas Bangs Thorpe, and even Mark Twain, all of whom relied upon frontier dialects and shrewdly naive backwoodsmen for comic effects.

Contrasting markedly with Colonel Manly and Jonathan are the dissolute dandy, Billy Dimple, and his servant Jessamy. When the play begins, Dimple is the fiancé of Maria, a thoroughly virtuous if excessively sentimental young lady whose father, Van Rough, a wealthy businessman, arranged the engagement to take advantage of Dimple's sizeable inheritance. (To Van Rough, most of life is reducible to the terms of a business transaction. His constant advice to Maria is, "money makes the mare go; keep your eye upon the main chance, Mary.") Since becoming engaged to Maria, Dimple has made an unfortunate trip to England; while there, he squandered his fortune and learned the ways of Chesterfieldian rogues. Maria dislikes his European affectations, but she remains willing to marry him rather than disobey her father. For his part, Dimple cares even less about the marriage than Maria does. He secretly plans to avoid marrying Maria, to marry the wealthy-but-unattractive Letitia, and to take Charlotte, Letitia's beautiful friend and Colonel Manly's sister, for his mistress.

When the dutiful-but-unhappy Maria meets courageous Colonel Manly, they both experience love at first sight. They agree, however, that Maria cannot contradict her father by ending her engagement to Dimple. The progress of true love seems stymied, but the audience knows that a broker has already told Van Rough of Dimple's financial losses, thus ending Van Rough's enthusiasm for the engagement. Soon a series of conveniently overheard conversations notify Letitia, Charlotte, and Manly of Dimple's deceitfulness. In the final scene, Van Rough bestows his daughter and his fortune on Manly, and the colonel reminds all that "probity, virtue, honour" outweigh polished European manners among Americans.

The play was well received from the start. New York reviewers praised it after its first performance on Monday, 16 April 1787, and it was brought to the stage again in New York on 18 April, 2 May, and 12 May. Later that year it was staged in Baltimore (on 12 August) and in Philadelphia (a reading by Wignell on 10 December). When it was published in Philadelphia in 1790, the play's widespread popularity was indicated by the fact that George Washington himself headed the list of subscribers.

Of course reviewers have also found imperfections: the plot is thin; the action is slight; and the harsh treatment of those who imitate European ways is rather unfair in light of the play's own heavy reliance upon conventions of the British comedy of manners. For all its imperfections and its borrowed form, though, most critics have agreed that *The Contrast* is both successful and essentially American. Its setting is American; its central conflict, pitting naive American virtue against sophisticated European manners, reappears in much of the best American literature; and, most important of all, its characters come alive through the diverse sounds of American speech. It is, as Thomas Wignell announced in the prologue on 16 April 1787, "A piece which we may fairly call our own."

After the success of *The Contrast*, Tyler remained in New York long enough to write another work and see it staged. It was *May Day in Town*, a comic opera produced at the John Street Theatre on 19 May. Neither the script nor the music has survived, but the song lyrics were discovered and published in the *Harvard Library Bulletin* in 1975. Tyler apparently wrote new lyrics for a number of popular tunes and connected them in a story about the New Yorkers' common practice of moving household goods from one house to another on May Day. Again he used American vernacular, and again he wrote quickly, for the play was produced less than three weeks after he had witnessed his first May Day in New York. There is no evidence that the play was staged more than once.

Tyler enjoyed his New York celebrity for only a short while before returning to Massachusetts. Three years later, he left Boston for Guilford, Vermont, a growing town where his law practice soon thrived. In 1794 he married Mary Palmer, a daughter of the Joseph Palmer in whose home Tyler had lived at the time of the Shays Rebellion. Also in 1794, he began collaborating with Joseph Dennie of Walpole, New Hampshire, to produce a series of newspaper miscellanies. Dennie, using the pseudonym Colon, contributed mainly humorous essays, and Tyler, writing as Spondee, contributed mainly verse. The column appeared in several New Hampshire papers; one of them, the *Farmer's Weekly Museum*, claimed subscribers in all but three of the states in the union.

Letters from Dennie to Tyler suggest that much of Tyler's newspaper poetry was written as speedily as his drama had been. Perhaps because he wrote hurriedly, Tyler usually confined himself to a few verse forms, strongly favoring tetrameter lines.

Mary Hunt Palmer Tyler

An example of this all-purpose tetrameter line may be seen in the vigorous "Ode Composed for the Fourth of July," which was published in the *New Hampshire and Vermont Journal* on 19 July 1796. This popular ode captures the excitement and sensations of an early Independence Day celebration:

> Squeak the fife, and beat the drum,
> Independence Day has come!
> Let the roasting pig be bled,
> Quick twist off the cockerel's head,
> Quickly rub the pewter platter,
> Heap the nutcakes fried in butter.

As the ode continues, its speaker welcomes various members of the community and encourages all to "drink and dance away / This glorious Independent Day!"

Tyler gained a reputation as a clever versifier from poems like this one, and in *The Origin of Evil*, a poem about Adam and Eve published as a pamphlet in 1793, he showed surprising ability for sensual description. Like much hurried, periodical verse, though, most of Tyler's poems are derivative, and they are often awkward in rhythm and rhyme.

Readers today agree that Tyler's verse is generally undistinguished.

Though most of the Colon and Spondee essays seem to have been written by Joseph Dennie, Tyler did contribute at least fifteen of them. A typical one, "Fine Comb Points," appeared in the *Farmer's Weekly Museum* on 11 April 1797. In this essay Spondee satirizes quack medical remedies by proclaiming a new cure for "common disorders in the head." To relieve infirmities ranging from dandruff to insomnia, Spondee says, the reader need only "Take a fine small tooth comb, pass it through the patient's hair every morning before breakfast, in various directions, for about ten minutes." If the disease is particularly acute, the patient may have to comb his hair in the evening also. Most of Tyler's essays, like this one, are brief, good-natured satirical thrusts at common follies he saw in law, politics, medicine, and manners.

While contributing to Colon and Spondee columns and serving as State's Attorney for Windham County, Vermont, Tyler also found time to write a picaresque novel, *The Algerine Captive*. In 1797 this two-volume work was published in Walpole, New Hampshire. Through most of volume one, Updike Underhill, the Candide-like narrator, recounts his misadventures as a student, a teacher in a country school, and a doctor. First he explains how his youthful studies acquainted him thoroughly with the classics but left him ill suited for work on an American farm: "It was resolved that I should labor on my father's farm; but, alas, a taste for Greek had quite eradicated a love for labor. . . . I gave Greek names to all our farming tools, and cheered the cattle with hexameter verse." Since there is little else he can do, Updike agrees to serve as a teacher. He envisions a peaceful classroom with quiet, respectful young scholars, but his sixty students, most of them younger than seven, bring a different reality: "Perhaps a more ragged, ill bred, ignorant set never were collected for the punishment of a poor pedagogue. To study was impossible."

When the school burns and Updike is mercifully released from his obligations, he enters the profession of medicine. Reality again falls short of sublime expectations as Updike watches a group of colleagues prescribe everything from opium to cobwebs for an unconscious jockey who has fallen from a horse. The doctors eventually abandon the jockey to resolve their disagreements in a fistfight. After eighteen months as a physician, Updike finds himself with neither money nor a stock of drugs. Most of his neighbors prefer to be treated by quacks, and those who do come to Updike neglect to pay their bills. He moves to the South, where he has heard that patients are immensely wealthy, but his practice fares little better there.

Still needing money, offended by the hypocrisy of Southern ministers and by the practice of slavery, he sails to England as a ship's surgeon. After a brief stay in England, he sails again, this time on the *Sympathy*, a slave ship bound for Africa. He is appalled by the crew's talk about slavery on the way to Africa and by their cruelty after they have picked up the slaves. His job is to keep the slaves alive, but he condemns himself for having sold his humane talents to such an awful cause. Seeing that many of the slaves are becoming seriously ill, he obtains permission to take five of the weakest of them ashore to recuperate. While he is ashore, an Algerine (or Algerian) pirate ship drives the *Sympathy* away and returns to capture Updike and his patients. Eleven days later the pirate ship arrives at Algiers, and the first volume ends.

This first half of *The Algerine Captive* obviously is not a story about Updike's captivity in Algeria. It is, however, related to the captivity story of volume two by more than the presence of a common narrator. As Updike moves further from New England, the tone in volume one shifts from amusement at American follies toward outrage at undeniable human wrongs. Tyler exchanges satire, in his caricatures of poor teachers, ignorant students, and quacks, for outright protest in Updike's denunciations of slavery in the American South and on the ironically named ship, *Sympathy*. In volume two, Tyler continues his denunciation of slavery with a firsthand account of one who has been enslaved.

Soon after Updike arrives in Algiers, he is sold and sent to work in a stone quarry. There he is approached by a surprisingly kind supervisor who promises lavish rewards if Updike will renounce Christianity and accept the Mahometan faith. To escape the quarry for a time, Updike agrees to talk about religion with a Mollah. After five days of debate, Updike returns to the quarry with his faith shaken but still intact. Then he becomes seriously ill and is taken to a hospital in Algiers. Soon hospital officials learn of his medical training and put him to work as a physician with freedom to go about the city.

Just as Updike gains this measure of freedom, Tyler interrupts the narrative with a thirteen-chapter digression. He describes the Algerians' history, government, revenue system, military forces, customs, religion, and laws. Then he returns to the narrative long enough for Updike to suffer a terrible disappointment when the money he had been

THE

ALGERINE CAPTIVE;

OR, THE

LIFE AND ADVENTURES

OF

Doctor *UPDIKE UNDERHILL:*

SIX YEARS A PRISONER AMONG THE ALGE-
RINES.

————— By your patience,
I will a round unvarnifhed tale deliver
Of my whole courfe.—————

SHAKESPEARE.

by Royal Tyler.

VOLUME I.

Publifhed according to ACT *of* CONGRESS.

PRINTED AT *WALPOLE*, NEWHAMPSHIRE,
By DAVID CARLISLE, JUN.
AND SOLD AT HIS BOOKSTORE.

1797.

Title page for one of the first American novels to be republished in England

saving for his ransom is lost. To help Updike recover from his disappointment, the hospital director recommends a trip to Medina and Mecca, thus creating the occasion for another digression on Algerian geography and religious practices.

Though these digressions grow tiresome for modern readers, Tyler does redeem them occasionally with a measure of Yankee skepticism, as when Updike pauses to observe a Mahometan saint: "As I had never seen a saint, being bred in a land where even the relics of these holy men are not preserved (for I believe all New England cannot produce so much as a saint's rotten tooth or toenail), I was solicitous to see and converse with this blessed personage." At first Updike is dismayed by the man's filthy appearance; then he is amazed by his foolish speech. Updike recalls the belief that saintly souls inhabit the bodies of seeming idiots, but he concludes, "This saint however did not aspire to the sanctity of a genuine idiot, though I fancy his modesty injured his preferment, for he certainly had fair pretensions."

Updike endures more disappointments and treachery, including being sold again into slavery by a young man who had promised to arrange his escape, before the crew of a Portuguese frigate finally rescues him. Then, after a seven-year absence, he returns to America. His concluding wish is that fellow Americans will learn from his account the value of their freedoms. Americans, he says, must "perceive the necessity of uniting our federal strength to enforce a due respect among other nations."

G. Thomas Tanselle and other students of Tyler have noted that while volume one of *The Algerine Captive* is for the most part a lighthearted, picaresque tale much akin to Hugh Henry Brackenridge's *Modern Chivalry* (1792-1805), volume two has more in common with Indian captivity narratives such as *The Soveraignty & Goodness of God . . . ; Being a Narrative of the Captivity and Restauration of Mrs. Mary Rowlandson* (1682). It differs from the captivity genre mainly in the extent of its expository material about history, religion, government, and customs. Critics agree that this material interrupts and seriously weakens the novel, turning much of the second volume into an anatomy, or compendium of observations about Algeria.

If Tyler violated unity with this material, though, he also played directly to the interests of American readers. From the time when the British navy stopped protecting American shipping (during the Revolutionary War) until the American navy grew strong enough to do so, pirates from the Barbary States were a real and sensational menace. Eighty-five ransomed Americans had returned to the United States only six months before *The Algerine Captive* was published, and the public was eager for information about the homeland of the pirates.

Most readers responded favorably to the novel, but sales were not overwhelming. It was by no means the only book on the subject (Tyler himself obtained material from British and American works on Algeria published in 1769 and 1794), and Tyler's publisher in Walpole, New Hampshire, was poorly situated to reach many American buyers. Despite the remoteness of the publisher, however, the novel gained enough attention to be republished in England in 1802 and 1804 (this time as a magazine serial), and in the United States in 1816.

Only two months after the appearance of *The Algerine Captive,* another of Tyler's plays took the stage. *The Georgia Spec; Or Land in the Moon* was produced on 30 October 1797 at the Haymarket Theatre in Boston. Unfortunately the play has not survived, and we know little about it beyond the facts that it satirized those who speculated in the Yazoo County, Georgia, land scandals, and that it was also produced in New York at the John Street Theatre on 20 and 23 December 1797 and at the New Theatre on 12 February 1798.

For the next several years, Tyler's public service left almost no time for literature. He was elected to the Supreme Court of Vermont in 1801, a position which required him to travel a circuit of trial locations for ten months of the year. He served as an Associate Judge until 1807, when he was elected Chief Justice, and won reelection as Chief Justice every year until 1813. Beginning in 1802, he also served as a trustee of the University of Vermont, and in 1811 the school appointed him professor of jurisprudence.

One of his few literary publications during those years was a small book of letters, *The Yankey in London* (1809), which contains thirteen letters supposed to have been written by an American in England to his friend Frank in the United States (except for one letter addressed to the writer's sister). Each letter is a commentary on some aspect of British life: the English character, the House of Commons, the House of Lords, the language, fashions in clothing, and so on. Not surprisingly, the writer often finds English ways artificial in comparison with their American counterparts. Since Tyler had never visited England, it is perhaps possible to argue that *The Yankey in London* is a work of fiction, but the letters have almost none of the plot or character development normally associated with fiction. Rather, they are a brief series of patriotic essays written with Tyler's characteristic energy in a clear, readable style that matches the naturalness he valued in the best American manners.

Though Tyler won important elective offices in Vermont and gave much of his time to public service, political favor shifted gradually away from him. In 1812 the same state legislature that had elected him twelve times to its Supreme Court chose not to send him to the U.S. Senate. In 1813, they elected another candidate to fill what had been Tyler's position on the court.

Having lost his Supreme Court salary and having allowed his law practice to decline, Tyler soon found himself in serious financial difficulty. He sold his farm home, moved to Brattleboro, and

An early version of "Hymn to the Supreme Being," published in the 28 March 1803 issue of the Reporter *(Royall Tyler Collection, gift of Helen Tyler Brown, Vermont Historical Society)*

obtained an appointment as Register of Probate for his county. Then his health began to fail. He developed a painful, disfiguring facial cancer that gradually deprived him of sight. Eventually he and Mary had to depend upon a son for most of their income. Then in 1822 that son lost his business. From that time until Tyler's death in 1826, the couple depended on the generosity of friends and relatives and a meager income from Mary's sewing.

Through these painful years in Brattleboro, though, Mary kept her husband writing. After failing reelection to the Vermont Supreme Court, Tyler wrote four plays and a 756-line poem, and he attempted a major revision of the first volume of *The Algerine Captive*. None of these final works was produced on stage or published during his lifetime.

The Island of Barrataria, apparently the first of this group to be completed, is a three-act farce based upon the episode from *Don Quixote* in which Sancho Panza governs an island. Tyler adds to the original episode a love story in which Sancho helps a young couple overcome objections of the girl's father to marriage. As in the novel, Sancho is honored by the citizens and offered sumptuous banquets which disappear before he can taste them. He also acts as judge in Barrataria's High Court of Justice, resolving all of his cases comically. Like much of Tyler's earlier writing, this play is both conventional and amusing. If we cannot award it high marks for originality or polish, neither can we fault its energy and satiric wit.

The Chestnut Tree (written in 1824), Tyler's longest poem, contains twenty-three sketches in which townspeople of Brattleboro pass beneath a tree two hundred years after the writer planted it. In this imagined future procession are several of the character types found elsewhere in Tyler's works: wrangling lawyers and doctors, young lovers, playful children. Tyler makes some effort to unify the poem's 186 tetrameter quatrains by bringing every character to the tree and by comparing himself to the tree's original "misshapen seed." Both of them, he says, "Shall in our parent earth be cast/And with new life shall quicken'd be." But in fact the many sketches are only superficially connected by the tree. Though some of its individual characterizations are effective, the poem is weakened by its lack of a unifying theme, its reliance upon stock phrases, and its sometimes monotonous, sometimes awkward metrics.

Tyler seems to have written his last three dramas—*Joseph and His Brethren, The Origin of the Feast of Purim,* and *The Judgement of Solomon*—with no expectation that they would be professionally produced. A line in *Joseph and His Brethren* suggests he intended them to be useful as school plays, but a letter from his wife indicates they served as diversions, perhaps also as religious exercises, for Tyler himself. All of them are brief, blank-verse dramatizations of Old Testament stories. *Joseph and His Brethren,* the longest, effectively depicts the envious brothers who sell Joseph into Egyptian slavery. However, readers often find Joseph himself excessively sentimental and given to long speeches. In *The Origin of the Feast of Purim,* Tyler combines elements from the Book of Haggai and the Book of Esther to intensify an atmosphere of crisis. Queen Esther's maneuvering to prevent destruction of the Jews is doubly suspenseful because it seems to occur at the time that Haggai is urging them to rise up "and prepare forthwith to repossess/The Holy Land." Tyler uses the same technique of combining anachronistic events to build tension for the climactic scene of *The Judgement of Solomon.* By causing the Queen of Sheba's visit to coincide with Solomon's judging of the two women who claim the same child, he puts Solomon's famous wisdom, as well as the women's honesty, on trial. Though no one would claim Tyler's blank verse is masterful in these plays, or that the plays represent the best of his dramatic abilities, they do show that he still had a remarkable sensitivity to the elements of a story that could be dramatized, even in the final months of his life.

His last major project, left unfinished at his death, was a revision of the first volume of *The Algerine Captive* to be called "The Bay Boy." This revision seems to have been the only one he ever undertook, and the completed fragments (published in *The Prose of Royall Tyler,* 1972) suggest it could have become one of his finest works. Updike Underhill remains as the narrator, but his voice is the mature and mellow voice of one who has time to recall warmly the events of his youth in Boston. There is less hurrying from episode to episode, more attention to detail. Some events from the earlier novel are omitted; some are expanded; and several characters and events appear for the first time.

Representative of these additions is the new chapter eight in which Updike falls in love. He sees a "beautiful cherry-cheeked girl" at church and promptly loses both his memory and his appetite. After tolerating him for several weeks, his mother and aunt contrive to cure his lovesickness by arranging for him to surprise the girl in her home. He finds her "seated all in a heap in a low chair . . . her hair unkempt and the big drops of perspiration

A Love Song.

By the fierce flames of Love I'm in a sad taking,
I'm singed like a pig that is hung up for bacon,
My stomach is scorched like an overdone mutton-chop,
That for want of gravy wont afford a single drop.
 Love, love, love is like a dizziness,
  Wont let a poor man go about his business.

My great toes and little toes are burnt to a cinder,
As a hot burning glass burns a dish-cloth to tinder,
A cheese by a hot salamander is roasted,
By beauty Hearts redhot, like a cheese am I toasted.
 Love, love, love is like a dizziness,
  Wont let a poor man go about his business.

Attend all young lovers, who after ladies dandle,
I'm singed like a duck's foot over a candle,
By this that and t'other; I'm treated uncivil,
Like a gizzard I'm peppered, and then made a devil.
 Love, love, love is like a dizziness,
  Wont let a poor man go about his business.

Manuscript for a poem that Tyler wrote during his last years (Royall Tyler Collection, gift of Helen Tyler Brown, Vermont Historical Society)

occasioned by her labors, standing upon her forehead. . . ." A disillusioned Updike hurries home, eats "a whole minced pie," and finds his memory wonderfully recovered. In nostalgic episodes such as this one, the strongly autobiographical work steers clear of sentimentality and provides a vivid picture of New England life in the mid-eighteenth century.

Many readers have wished not only that Tyler had finished "The Bay Boy," but that he had revised his other works with equal care and ability. Like Brackenridge, Barlow, and others of his generation, though, Tyler was a lawyer first and a writer only by avocation. Few lawyers had time to write plays, poems, and novels; fewer still had time to rewrite them.

We may well regret that Tyler was too rushed to realize his full potential as a writer, but such characters as Jonathan, Major Manly, and Updike Underhill continue to delight readers and audiences today as they did in the early national period. With them, Tyler showed that American characters speaking American dialects and concerning themselves with American issues could engage imaginations in this country and abroad. At a time when many were beginning to call for a distinctly American literature, Royall Tyler did more than echo the call. He provided several of our first durable, commercially successful models.

Bibliography:

G. Thomas Tanselle, "Some Uncollected Authors XLII: Royall Tyler, 1757-1826," *Book Collector,* 15 (Autumn 1966): 303-320.

Biographies:

Mary Palmer Tyler, *Grandmother Tyler's Book: The Recollections of Mary Palmer Tyler,* edited by Helen Tyler Brown and Frederick Tupper (New York: Putnam's, 1925);

G. Thomas Tanselle, *Royall Tyler* (Cambridge: Harvard University Press, 1967);

Ada Lou Carson and Herbert L. Carson, *Royall Tyler* (Boston: Twayne, 1979).

References:

Larry R. Dennis, "Legitimizing the Novel: Royall Tyler's *The Algerine Captive,*" *Early American Literature,* 9 (Spring 1974): 71-80;

Katherine Schall Jarvis, "Royall Tyler's Lyrics for *May Day in Town,*" *Harvard Library Bulletin,* 23 (April 1975): 186-198;

Arthur H. Nethercot, "The Dramatic Background of Royall Tyler's *The Contrast,*" *American Literature,* 12 (January 1941): 435-446;

Donald T. Siebert, Jr., "Royall Tyler's 'Bold Example': *The Contrast* and the English Comedy of Manners," *Early American Literature,* 8 (Spring 1978): 3-11;

Roger B. Stein, "Royall Tyler and the Question of our Speech," *New England Quarterly,* 38 (December 1965): 454-474.

Papers:

The bulk of Tyler's papers are in the Royall Tyler collection at the Vermont Historical Society, Montpelier, Vermont.

Noah Webster
(16 October 1758-28 May 1843)

Thomas B. Gustafson
University of Southern California

See also the Webster entry in *DLB 1, The American Renaissance in New England.*

*SELECTED BOOKS: *A Grammatical Institute, of the English Language, Comprising, an Easy, Concise, and Systematic Method of Education, Designed for the Use of English Schools in America. In Three Parts. Part I. Containing, a New and Accurate Standard of Pronunciation* (Hartford: Printed by Hudson & Goodwin for the author, 1783);

A Grammatical Institute of the English Language, Comprising, An Easy, Concise, and Systematic Method of Education, Designed for the Use of English Schools in America. In Three Parts. Part II. Containing a Plain and Comprehensive Grammar . . . (Hartford: Printed by Hudson & Goodwin for the author, 1784);

A Grammatical Institute of the English Language; Comprising an Easy, Concise and Systematic Method of Education; Designed for the Use of Schools in America. In Three Parts. Part III: Containing the Necessary Rules of Reading and Speaking, and a Variety of Essays . . . (Hartford: Printed by Barlow & Babcock for the author, 1785);

Sketches of American Policy. Under the Following Heads: I. Theory of Government. II. Governments on the Eastern Continent. III. American States; or the Principles of the American Constitutions Contrasted with Those of European States. IV. Plan of Policy for Improving the Advantages and Perpetuating the Union of the American States (Hartford: Printed by Hudson & Goodwin, 1785);

The American Spelling Book . . . (Philadelphia: Young & M'Culloch, 1787; revised edition, Philadelphia: Published by Jacob Johnson & Co., 1804);

An American Selection of Lessons in Reading and Speaking. Calculated to Improve the Minds and Refine the Tastes of Youth. . . . Being the Third Part of A Grammatical Institute of the English Language . . . , Greatly Enlarged (Philadelphia:

* Webster's textbooks were frequently revised and abridged. Only significant editions are included in this list.

Noah Webster, 1823; portrait by Samuel F. B. Morse

Printed & sold by Young & M'Culloch, 1787; revised edition, New Haven: From Sidney's Press for I. Beers & Co. and I. Cooke & Co., 1804);

An Examination into the Leading Principles of the Federal Constitution Proposed by the Late Convention Held at Philadelphia. With Answers to the Principle Objections That Have Been Raised Against the System (Philadelphia: Printed & sold by Prichard & Hall, 1787);

An Introduction to English Grammar; Being an Abridgement of the Second Part of the Grammatical Institute (Philadelphia: Printed by W. Young, 1788);

Dissertations on the English Language; With Notes, Historical and Critical. To Which Is Added, By Way of Appendix, An Essay on a Reformed Mode of Spelling, with Dr. Franklin's Arguments on that Subject

(Boston: Printed by Isaiah Thomas & Co. for the author, 1789);

Attention! or, New Thoughts on a Serious Subject; Being an Enquiry into the Excise Laws of Connecticut . . . (Hartford: Printed & sold by Hudson & Goodwin, 1789);

The Little Reader's Assistant . . . (Hartford: Printed by Elisha Babcock, 1790);

A Collection of Essays and Fugitiv Writings. On Moral, Historical, Political and Literary Subjects (Boston: Printed by I. Thomas & E. T. Andrews for the author, 1790);

The Prompter; or A Commentary on Common Sayings and Subjects, Which Are Full of Common Sense, the Best Sense in the World . . . (Hartford: Printed by Hudson & Goodwin, 1791);

Effects of Slavery, on Morals and Industry (Hartford: Printed by Hudson & Goodwin, 1793);

The Revolution in France, Considered in Respect to Its Progress and Effects (New York: Printed & published by George Bunce & Co., 1794);

A Letter to the Governors, Instructors and Trustees of the Universities, and Other Seminaries of Learning, in the United States, on the Errors of English Grammars (New York: Printed by George F. Hopkins for the author, 1798);

An Oration Pronounced before the Citizens of New-Haven on the Anniversary of the Independence of the United States, July 4th 1798 . . . (New Haven: Printed by T. & S. Green, 1798);

A Brief History of Epidemic and Pestilential Diseases; With the Principal Phenomena of the Physical World, Which Precede and Accompany Them, and Observations Deduced from the Facts Stated, 2 volumes (Hartford: Printed by Hudson & Goodwin, 1799; London: Printed for G. G. & J. Robinson, 1800);

Ten Letters to Dr. Joseph Priestly, in Answer to His Letters to the Inhabitants of Northumberland (New Haven: Printed by Read & Morse, 1800);

A Rod for the Fool's Back (New Haven?, 1800);

A Letter to General Hamilton, Occasioned by His Letter to President Adams (New York?, 1800);

Miscellaneous Papers on Political and Commercial Subjects . . . (New York: Printed by E. Belden & Co., 1802);

Elements of Useful Knowledge. Volume I. Containing a Historical and Geographical Account of the United States: For the Use of Schools (Hartford: Printed & sold by Hudson & Goodwin, 1802);

An Oration Pronounced before the Citizens of New Haven, on the Anniversary of the Declaration of Independence; July, 1802 . . . (New Haven: Printed by William W. Morse, 1802);

An Address to the Citizens of Connecticut (New Haven: Printed by J. Walter, 1803);

Elements of Useful Knowledge. Volume II. Containing a Historical and Geographical Account of the United States: For the Use of Schools (New Haven: From Sidney's Press, for the author, 1804);

Elements of Useful Knowledge. Vol. III. Containing a Historical and Geographical Account of the Empires and States in Europe, Asia and Africa, with Their Colonies. To Which Is Added, a Brief Description of New Holland, and the Principal Islands in the Pacific and Indian Oceans. For the Use of Schools (New Haven: Printed by O. Steele & Co. and published by Bronson, Walter & Co., 1806);

A Compendious Dictionary of the English Language (New Haven: From Sidney's Press, 1806);

A Dictionary of the English Language; Compiled for the Use of Common Schools in the United States (New Haven: From Sidney's Press for John & David West in Boston, Brisban & Brannan in New York, Lincoln & Gleason and Oliver D. Cooke in Hartford, and I. Cooke & Co. in New Haven, 1807);

A Philosophical and Practical Grammar of the English Language (New Haven: Printed by Oliver & Steele for Brisban & Brannan, 1807);

A Letter to Dr. David Ramsay, of Charleston, (S.C.) Respecting the Errors in Johnson's Dictionary, and Other Lexicons (New Haven: Printed by Oliver Steele & Co., 1807);

The Peculiar Doctrines of the Gospel, Explained and Defended (New York: J. Seymour, 1809);

History of Animals; Being the Fourth Volume of Elements of Useful Knowledge. For the Use of Schools, and Young Persons of Both Sexes (New Haven: Printed by Walter & Steele and published & sold by Howe & Deforest and Walter & Steele, 1812);

An Oration Pronounced before the Knox and Warren Branches of the Washington Benevolent Society, at Amherst, on the Celebration of the Anniversary of the Declaration of Independence, July 4, 1814 (Northampton: Printed by William Butler, 1814);

A Letter to the Honorable John Pickering, on the Subject of his Vocabulary; or, Collection of Words and Phrases, Supposed to Be Peculiar to the United States of America (Boston: Printed by T. W. White and published by West & Richardson, 1817);

An Address, Delivered before the Hampshire, Franklin and Hampden Agricultural Society, at Their Annual Meeting in Northampton, Oct. 14, 1818

(Northampton: Printed by Thomas W. Shepard & Co., 1818);

A Plea for a Miserable World. I. An Address Delivered at the Laying of the Corner Stone of the Building Erecting for the Charity Institution in Amherst, Massachusetts, August 9, 1820, by Noah Webster, Esq. II. A Sermon Delivered on the Same Occasion, by Rev. Daniel A Clark, Pastor of the First Church and Society in Amherst. III. A Brief Account of the Origin of the Institution (Boston: Printed by Ezra Lincoln, 1820);

Letters to a Young Gentleman Commencing His Education: To Which is Subjoined a Brief History of the United States (New Haven: Printed by S. Converse and sold by Howe & Spalding, 1823);

An American Dictionary of the English Language . . . , 2 volumes (New Haven: Printed by Hezekiah Howe/New York: Published by S. Converse, 1828); republished as *A Dictionary of the English Language*, 12 parts (London: Printed for Black, Young & Young, 1830-1832);

The Elementary Spelling Book; Being an Improvement on the American Spelling Book (New York: Printed by A. Chandler & published by J. P. Haven & R. Lockwood, 1829);

A Dictionary of the English Language; Abridged from the American Dictionary . . . (New York: White, Gallaher & White, 1830);

Biography for the Use of Schools (New Haven: Printed by Hezekiah Howe, 1830);

An Improved Grammar of the English Language (New Haven: Published & sold by Hezekiah Howe, 1831);

History of the United States; to Which Is Prefixed a Brief Historical Account of Our English Ancestors, from the Dispersion of Babel, to Their Migration to America; and of the Conquest of South America, by the Spaniards (New Haven: Printed by Baldwin & Treadway and published by Durrie & Peck, 1832; revised edition, Cincinnati: Published by Corey, Fairbank & Webster, 1835);

Value of the Bible, and Excellence of the Christian Religion: For the Use of Families and Schools (New Haven: Published by Durrie & Peck, 1834);

A Brief View 1. Of Errors and Obscurities in the Common Version of the Scriptures; Addressed to Bible Societies, Clergymen and Other Friends of Religion. 2. Of Errors and Defects in Class-Books Used in Seminaries of Learning; Including Dictionaries and Grammars of the English, French, Greek and Latin Languages; Addressed to Instructors of Youth, and Students, with a Few Hints to Statesmen, Members of Congress, and Heads of Departments. To Which Is Added, 3. A Few Plagiarisms,

Showing the Way in Which Books May Be Made, by Those Who Use Borrowed Capital (New Haven, 1834?);

Instructive and Entertaining Lessons for Youth . . . (New Haven: Published by S. Babcock and Durrie & Peck, 1835);

The Teacher; A Supplement to the Elementary Spelling Book (New Haven: Published by S. Babcock, 1836);

A Letter to the Hon. Daniel Webster, on the Political Affairs of the United States, as Marcellus (Philadelphia: Printed by J. Crissy, 1837);

Mistakes and Corrections. 1. Improprieties in the Common Version of the Scriptures; With Specimens of Amended Language in Webster's Edition of the Bible. 2. Explanations of Prepositions, in English, and Other Languages. These Constitute a Very Difficult Part of Philology. 3. Errors in English Grammars. 4. Mistakes in the Hebrew Lexicon of Gesenius, and In Some Derivations of Dr. Horwitz. 5. Errors in Butter's Scholar's Companion and in Town's Analysis. 6. Errors in Richardson's Dictionary (New Haven: Printed by B. L. Hamlen, 1837);

Appeal to Americans . . . , as Sidney (New York?, 1838?);

Observations on Language, and on the Errors of Class-Books; Addressed to the Members of the New York Lyceum. Also, Observations on Commerce, Addressed to the Members of the Mercantile Library Association, in New York (New Haven: Printed by S. Babcock, 1839);

A Manual of Useful Studies: For the Instruction of Young Persons of Both Sexes, in Families and Schools (New Haven: Printed & published by S. Babcock, 1839);

A Collection of Papers on Political, Literary and Moral Subjects (Boston: Tappan & Dennett/Philadelphia: Smith & Peck, 1843).

OTHER: *The New England Primer, "Amended and Improved . . . ,"* edited by Webster (New York: Printed by J. Patterson, 1789);

John Winthrop, A Journal of the Transactions and Occurrences in the Settlement of Massachusetts and the Other New-England Colonies, from the Year 1630 to 1644, edited by Webster (Hartford: Printed by Elisha Babcock, 1790);

A Collection of Papers on the Subject of Bilious Fevers, Prevalent in the United States for a Few Years Past, edited by Webster (New York: Printed by Hopkins, Webb & Co., 1796);

The Holy Bible, Containing the Old and New Testaments, in the Common Version. With Amendments of the

Language by Noah Webster, LL.D. (New Haven: Published by Durrie & Peck, 1833).

Noah Webster, educator, lexicographer, lawyer, political essayist, and scholar, best remembered for his "Blue-Backed Speller" (*A Grammatical Institute, of the English Language,* part 1, 1783) and *An American Dictionary of the English Language* (1828), devoted his life to educating the young American Republic in hopes of forming its national character. Called "Schoolmaster to America," he wrote the textbooks that directed the early course of American education and helped conserve for the country a common language free of class distinctions. Webster's speller, with its fables, morals, and patriotic sentiments, traveled wherever Americans traveled; an estimated 80 million copies had been sold by 1890. Countless children in every state of the union for many generations were taught to spell Webster's way, to pronounce Webster's way, and perhaps even to think Webster's way. And Webster thought nationally. An early advocate of a strong federal government, he was the first to promote and defend the development of an American language, claiming that a national language would be a bond of national union and the key to cultural independence. He also championed the democratic principle that the general practice of a nation, rather than the opinions of a privileged elite, should be the voice of authority in matters of usage and grammar.

Noah Webster was born in West Hartford, Connecticut, to Noah Webster, a farmer and justice of the peace, and Mercy Steele Webster, a descendant of William Bradford. The fourth of their five children, Webster entered Yale College in 1774, where he was tutored by Timothy Dwight and Ezra Stiles. After graduating in 1778, he studied law while he taught school to support himself; he gained admission to the bar at Hartford in 1781. But faced with slow legal business, he returned to teaching, an unwelcome change for a young man eager for fame. While instructing students in Sharon, Connecticut (July-October 1781), and Goshen, New York (1782-Spring 1783), he took a patriot's dislike to British primers, and conceived of a plan to advance the interests of America and his own reputation. He began writing the textbooks that carried the War for Independence out of the battlefield and into the classroom. Only through a new system of education and a national language, he insisted, could America fulfill its revolutionary destiny and become an independent nation free from the corruption of the Old World.

In 1783 he published his well-known speller as

A

Grammatical Inftitute,

OF THE

ENGLISH LANGUAGE,

COMPRISING,

An eafy, concife, and fyftematic Method of

EDUCATION.

Defigned for the Ufe of *Englifh* Schools

In *A M E R I C A.*

IN THREE PARTS.

PART I.

CONTAINING,

A new and accurate Standard of Pronunciation.

By NOAH WEBSTER, A. M.

Ufus eft Norma Loquendi.   CICERO.

H A R T F O R D :

PRINTED BY HUDSON & GOODWIN,

FOR THE AUTHOR.

Title page for the first edition of Webster's spelling book. The most popular book in Webster's three-part series designed to reform American education, it was revised twice and published under various titles at least 385 times during Webster's lifetime.

part one of *A Grammatical Institute of the English Language,* his new three-part plan for American education. In 1787 it was revised and retitled *The American Spelling Book,* and in 1829 Webster thoroughly revised it once again as *The Elementary Spelling Book.* Known informally as "The Blue-Backed Speller," it was published in at least 385 editions during Webster's lifetime and became the best-selling book ever written by an American. The original text, which did not contain the fables or the major spelling revisions that appeared in later editions, was largely an adaptation of two British works with some added information about United States geography and history, several changes in spelling and pronunciation, and fewer references to the deity.

What made part one of *A Grammatical Institute of the English Language* uniquely American—and revolutionary in its ideology—was its preface, a stirring call for America's political and cultural independence: "Europe is grown old in folly, corruption, and tyranny. . . . For America in her infancy to adopt the present maxims of the old world would be to stamp the wrinkles of decrepid age upon the bloom of youth and to plant the seeds of decay in a vigorous constitution. American glory begins to dawn at a favorable period. . . . We have the experience of the whole world before our eyes; but to receive indiscriminately the maxims of government, the manners, and the literary taste of Europe and make them the ground on which to build our systems in America must soon convince us that a durable and stately edifice can never be erected upon the mouldering pillars of antiquity." In the preface Webster defined the goals of his career and his hopes for America: the young country could mature into an empire of reason if it adopted reforms or new principles in politics, education, and language and developed its own manners and literary tastes. Webster, an enlightened father, would guide that development.

In 1784 Webster published a grammar and in 1785 a reader to complete parts two and three of his *A Grammatical Institute of the English Language*. He based the grammar on Robert Lowth's *A Short Introduction to English Grammar* (1762) and differed most from Lowth in his willingness to accept general usage as a standard of correctness (he sanctioned such expressions as "it is me" and "them horses" and welcomed neologisms). In language and politics, he recognized, vox populi is sovereign; it can amend the rules of grammar just as it can amend the articles and clauses of America's political grammar—the Constitution. But Webster was never one to repose complete trust in the people. Though he maintained that the yeomanry of America spoke truer English than the aristocrats of England because they were less subject to the vagaries of linguistic fashion, he also appealed in his works to the original principles of language as a rule of propriety. In the reader Webster introduced a change in content and design that distinguished it from British readers and set the pattern for later American textbooks, notably William McGuffey's readers. He included selections from American authors (such as John Trumbull, Timothy Dwight, Joel Barlow, and Thomas Paine) and pointedly chose them not only

to form the morals of youths, but to promote republican political ideals: the love of liberty and country and the subordination of self-interest to civic good.

To complete his plan for an elementary education that would establish American ways of speaking and thinking, Webster prepared abridged versions of a speller, grammar, and reader for the youngest pupils. These were published as *The New England Primer, "Amended and Improved"* (1789), a revised version of the popular colonial schoolbook without its rigorous Calvinism, *An Introduction to English Grammar* (1788), and *The Little Reader's Assistant* (1790), which included his "Federal Catechism," a simple explanation of the Constitution. In these books, and throughout his career, Webster gave special attention to the education of youth because he believed that "the only practicable way to reform mankind is to begin with the children" and that "the impressions received in early life usually form the characters of individuals, a union of which forms the general character of a nation." Webster shared this faith in the formative power of education with his contemporaries, and led them in translating it into programs of action.

Encouraged by the initial response to *A Grammatical Institute of the English Language*, Webster toured the country in 1785 and 1786 to promote its sales and the adoption of copyright laws to protect his publishing rights. On the tour he met with many leading citizens and discussed his *Sketches of American Policy* (1785), a four-part political treatise that contained a plan for a stronger central government and ended with a vigorous plea for new cultural, as well as political, bonds of union: "America is an independent empire, and ought to assume a national character." James Madison, who read the work in 1786, later wrote Webster that it was an "early" statement of the ideas that culminated in the Constitution. Webster, always known for his egotism, preferred to think that it was the first and most influential statement, the catalyst of Madison's own plan for union. During the tour Webster also gave lectures on education and language. At the urging of Benjamin Franklin, he published a revised version of his lectures on language in 1789 as *Dissertations on the English Language*. This work, both a polemic for cultural nationalism as well as a treatise on language, reiterated the themes of his textbook prefaces and laid the theoretical foundation for his early dictionary work. Most important, it presented his view that language is a "democratical state" ideally governed by the people in accordance with the laws of language; it charged the King's English with corruption and demanded a revolution to re-

Webster's notes in a copy of the book that James Madison called an early statement of the ideas that culminated in the Constitution
(Robert Keith Leavitt, Noah's Ark: New England Yankees and the Endless Quest, *1947)*

store its purity; it called upon Americans to establish "a national language, as well as a national government," because "our honor" as an "independent nation" and our "political harmony" depend upon it; and it envisioned a time when, through the spread of a uniform tongue in America, "The people of one quarter of this world will be able to associate and converse like children of the same family." America, in his eyes, could repair Babel. And to facilitate that repair, Webster attached to the *Dissertations on the English Language* a radical proposal for spelling reform. In the early 1790s he experimented with these reforms (claiming "Ther iz no alternativ"), but largely abandoned them in later years.

In the late 1780s and 1790s Webster became one of the country's leading political essayists and a prolific author. In 1787 he founded and edited in New York City the *American Magazine,* a general-interest, monthly publication, and he wrote what one historian has termed "an extraordinary series of articles" in defense of the Constitution. When the magazine collapsed in 1788, Webster moved to Hartford and practiced law. In 1789 he married Rebecca Greenleaf, and in 1793 he returned to New York at the request of Alexander Hamilton and John Jay, to edit the *American Minerva,* a daily newspaper (which became the *Commercial Advertiser* in 1787), and in 1794 the *Herald,* a semiweekly (which became the *Spectator* in 1787). For these newspapers Webster wrote essays on almost every conceivable subject, including penal reform, slavery, banking, commerce, education, city planning, forest conservation, the French Revolution, and epidemic dis-

4 Any individual of a family descending in a collateral line;
any descendant from a common parent or stock.

5. _Branches of a bridle._ Two pieces of bent iron which bear
the bit, the cross chains & the curb. *Encyc.*

6 In gothic architecture, the branches of ogives are the arches of
gothic vaults, traversing from one angle to another diag-
onally, & forming a cross between the other arches, which make
the sides of the square, of which the arches are diagonals. *Harris*

7. A warrant or commission given to a pilot. *Laws of Massachu-setts.*

8 A chandelier — — — — — — — — *Ash*

Branch *v.i.* To shoot & spread in branches; as a plant; or as horns. *or to ramify;*

2. To divide into separate parts, or subdivisions; as a mountain; a stream; or a moral subject; to ramify.

3 To speak diffusively; to make many distinctions or
divisions in a discourse; to

4 To have horns shooting out *Milton*

Branch. *v.t.* To divide as into branches; to make subordinate divisions. *Bacon or*

2 To adorn with needle work, representing branches, flowers,
or twigs. *Prior*

Branch'ed *pp.* Divided or spread into branches: separated into subordinate parts: adorned with branches; furnished with branches.

Branch'er *n.* One that shoots forth branches;
2 A young hawk when he begins to leave the nest, & take
to the branches.

Branch'ery *n.* The ramifications or ramified vessels dispersed
through the pulpy part of fruit. *Encyc. Ash.*

Branch'iness *n.* Fulness of branches. —— - *Johnson*

Branch'ing *ppr.* Shooting in branches; dividing into several subordinate parts.

Branch'ing *a.* Loaded with branches coming out without order.
Martyn.

Page from the manuscript for An American Dictionary of the English Language *(Robert Keith Leavitt,* Noah's Ark: New
England Yankees and the Endless Quest, *1947)*

eases. But most important—and not without controversy—he promoted the policies of Washington's administration.

Though viewed as a spokesman for the Federalists, Webster considered himself nonpartisan. One of the prime subjects of his editorial attacks was the growing "party spirit" in the country; another concern was the imprecision of political discourse. His study of the French Revolution and American politics convinced him that there was a close connection between political and linguistic disorders: the misuse of words such as *democracy, republican, free, liberty,* and *equality* had led both nations into errors. Webster's suspicions of these words revealed his own growing conservatism, which began as a distrust of democracy and turned into a passionate dislike. Lacking Thomas Jefferson's faith in rule by popular sovereignty, he increasingly favored restrictions in voting rights, and even advocated in his older age the passage of a federal law requiring that men be denied the vote until they are forty-five. In 1798 he moved to New Haven, and in 1803 he severed connections with both newspapers. For the next forty years he concentrated his energies on literary pursuits and defining words.

Webster's first dictionary, *A Compendious Dictionary of the English Language* (1806), contained 5,000 more words than Samuel Johnson's dictionary and drew much criticism for its inclusion of American neologisms. Anticipating the attack, Webster defended "Americanisms" in his preface as the legitimate outgrowth of new American ideas, customs, laws, and inventions. The culmination of his career as an educator and language reformer was the publication in 1828 of his two-volume *An American Dictionary of the English Language*.

The Webster who wrote the dictionary, however, was a changed man from the Webster who wrote the speller. Once a young radical committed to republican principles, by 1828 he had renounced his early political beliefs as the follies of youth. In 1808 he had an emotional religious experience, which led to his conversion to Calvinism and redirected his focus. In his later years he prepared a revised edition of the Bible and other religious texts, and even his work on the dictionary was as much a personal and a religious quest as a political one; it was in part a quest to repair Babel. For his dictionary Webster compared twenty languages to prepare his etymologies, searching for the "radix" of English words—their origin in the Biblical language of Chaldee. His scriptural literalism led him to ignore the advances made in philology by Franz Bopp and Jacob Grimm. His new etymologies quickly became as irrelevant as his new antidemocratic political views. His 70,000 definitions remained (12,000 more than any previous dictionary of the English language). If the speller was America's Declaration of Linguistic Independence, the dictionary was more of a treaty, in which he asserted that a sameness of language between Britain and America would be desirable, but a difference was inevitable. Ironically, the dictionary was initially received better in England than in America.

At the age of seventy-nine Webster, whose name has now become synonymous with dictionary and whose work has had a more lasting influence on our national language than any other American's, admitted to Daniel Webster that he had "lost nearly all hope of benefiting my country by correcting disorders of our language." But never failing in his quest to shape the character of the nation, Webster participated in the founding of Amherst College in 1821, a school he hoped would provide the intellectual and religious training he endorsed, and he continued writing and revising educational texts until his death in 1843. Today the fame of Webster's dictionary has overshadowed his other contributions as an educator and an essayist, which merit his inclusion among those leaders who helped transform the American colonies into a nation.

Letters:

Letters of Noah Webster, edited by Harry R. Warfel (New York: Library Publishers, 1953).

Bibliography:

Emily Ellsworth Ford Skeel and Edwin H. Carpenter, eds., *A Bibliography of the Writings of Noah Webster* (New York: New York Public Library, 1958).

Biographies:

Emily E. Ford, *Notes on the Life of Noah Webster* (New York: Privately printed, 1912);

Ervin C. Shoemaker, *Noah Webster: Pioneer of Learning* (New York: Columbia University Press, 1936);

Harry R. Warfel, *Noah Webster: Schoolmaster to America* (New York: Macmillan, 1936);

Richard M. Rollins, *The Long Journey of Noah Webster* (Philadelphia: University of Pennsylvania Press, 1980).

References:

Homer D. Babbidge, Jr., Introduction to *Noah Webster: On Being American, Selected Writings, 1783-1828* (New York: Praeger, 1967);

Joseph J. Ellis, *After the Revolution* (New York & London: Norton, 1979);

Joseph H. Friend, *The Development of American Lexicography 1798-1864* (The Hague: Mouton, 1967);

E. Jennifer Monaghan, *A Common Heritage: Noah*

Webster's Blue-back Speller (Hamden, Conn.: Archon Books, 1983).

Papers:
Webster's papers are at the New York Public Library and the Sterling Memorial Library at Yale University.

Mason Locke Weems
(11 October 1759-23 May 1825)

Hugh J. Dawson
University of San Francisco

See also the Weems entry in *DLB 30, American Historians, 1607-1865.*

SELECTED BOOKS: *A History of the Life and Death, Virtues, and Exploits of General George Washington,* anonymous (George-Town, South Carolina: Printed for the Rev. M. L. Weems by Green & English, 1800); enlarged as *The Life of George Washington, with Curious Anecdotes, Equally Honourable to Himself, and Exemplary to His Young Countrymen* (Philadelphia: Printed for the Author by R. Cochran, 1808); republished as *A History of the Life and Death, Virtues and Exploits of General George Washington, with Curious Anecdotes, Equally Honourable to Himself and Exemplary to His Young Countrymen* (Philadelphia & London: Lippincott, 1918);

The True Patriot: or, An Oration, on the Beauties and Beatitudes of a Republic; and the Abominations and Desolations of Despotism . . . (Philadelphia: Printed by William W. Woodward for the author, 1802);

God's Revenge against Murder; or, The Drowned Wife of Stephens Creek. A Tragedy (Augusta, Ga.: Printed by Hobby & Bunce, 1807);

The Life of Gen. Francis Marion in the Revolutionary War, against the British and Tories in South-Carolina and Georgia (Philadelphia: Mathew Carey, 1809);

The Devil in Petticoats, or God's Revenge against Husband Killing, Exemplified in the Awful History of Mrs. Rebecca Cotton (Augusta: Printed by Daniel Starnes, 1810); revised as *The Bad Wife's Looking Glass; or, God's Revenge against Cruelty to Husbands. Exemplified in the Awful History*

tory of the Beautiful but Depraved Mrs. Rebecca Cotton, who Most Inhumanly Murdered Her Husband . . . (Charleston: Printed for the author, 1823);

God's Revenge against Gambling. Exemplified in the Miserable Lives and Untimely Deaths of a Number of

Persons of Both Sexes, Who Had Sacrificed their Health, Wealth, and Honor at the Gaming Tables . . . (Augusta: Hobby & Bunce, 1810);

God's Revenge against Drunkenness; or, The New Drunkard's Looking Glass . . . (Philadelphia, 1812); revised as *The Drunkard's Looking-Glass, Reflecting a Faithful Likeness of the Drunkard in Sundry Very Interesting Attitudes; With Lively Representations of the Many Strange Capers Which He Cuts at Different Stages of His Disease* (Philadelphia?, 1813);

God's Revenge against Adultery, Awfully Exemplified in the Following Cases of American Crim. Con. I. The Accomplished Dr. Theodore Wilson, (Delaware,) who for Seducing Mrs. Nancy Wiley, Had His Brains Blown Out by Her Husband. II. The Elegant James Oneale, Esq. (North Carolina,) who for Seducing the Beautiful Miss Matilda Lestrange, Was Killed by Her Brother (Baltimore: Printed by Ralph W. Pomeroy, 1815);

The Life of Dr. Benjamin Franklin, written Chiefly by Himself . . . (Baltimore: Printed by Ralph W. Pomeroy, 1815); enlarged as *The Life of Benjamin Franklin, with Many Choice Anecdotes and Admirable Sayings of this Great Man* (Philadelphia: Mathew Carey, 1818);

God's Revenge against Duelling; or, The Duellists Looking Glass . . . (Georgetown: Published by E. Weems for the author, 1820; revised, Philadelphia: Printed by J. Bioren for the author, 1821);

The Life of William Penn, the Settler of Pennsylvania, the Founder of Philadelphia, and One of the First Law Givers (Philadelphia: H. C. Carey & I. Lea, 1822).

Parson Weems's claim to a small place in American literary history has often seemed to rest on his having retailed the fabulous story of George Washington and the cherry tree. He is more justly regarded as a writer whose *The Life of George Washington* (1808) transcends its subgenre. Although this edifying biography's starchy simplicity has drawn the derision of generations, critics who have looked beneath its didactic idiom have found revealing testimony to the needs of a society in transition.

Very little is known of Weems's youth. He was born 11 October 1759 at Marshes Seat, Herring Bay, in Maryland's Anne Arundel County, the son of a Scottish farmer who had fathered eighteen earlier children, eleven of them by his second wife, the former Esther Hill. After receiving his early schooling in Maryland, Weems studied medicine in

A

HISTORY,

OF THE LIFE AND DEATH, VIRTUES, AND EXPLOITS,

OF

GENERAL GEORGE WASHINGTON;

DEDICATED

To

MRS. WASHINGTON;

And containing a great many curious and valuable ANECDOTES, tending to throw much light on the *private* as well as *public* life and character, of

THAT VERY EXTRAORDINARY MAN:

THE WHOLE

HAPPILY CALCULATED TO FURNISH A FE**T OF TRUE WASHINGTONIAN ENTERTAINMENT AND IMPROVEMENT, BOTH TO OURSELVES AND OUR CHILDREN.

A wit's a feather, and a chief's a rod; An honest man's the noblest work of God.

Who *noble ends* by *noble means* obtains, Or failing, smiles in exile or in chains; Like good Aurelius let him reign, or bleed Like Socrates, that man is *great* indeed.

PRINTED FOR THE REV. M. L. WEEMS, Of Lodge No. 50, Dumfries, BY GREEN & ENGLISH, GEORGE-TOWN.
(*Price 2s. 3d. only.*)

Title page for the eighty-page pamphlet that Weems later expanded into his best-known biography (courtesy of the John Carter Brown Library at Brown University)

London and possibly in Edinburgh between 1773 and 1776. By one report he was a surgeon in the British navy at the outbreak of the Revolution, but by 1779 he had returned to Maryland. He was again in England from 1781 to 1784, this time preparing for the Anglican priesthood. Following his ordination by the Archbishop of Canterbury in 1784, he returned to America to serve as pastor of a series of parishes in the Chesapeake area. Weems held fixed clerical appointments for less than a decade, and then, after 1792, while remaining a minister, he traveled the Eastern seaboard as an itinerant book salesman. On 2 July 1795 he married Frances Sewall, the daughter of Colonel Jesse Sewall of Bel Air, near Drumfries, in Prince William County, Virginia. The young couple, who would become the parents of ten children, made their home at Drumfries until moving to the Bel Air plantation Mrs. Weems inherited from her father in 1806.

Weems, however, was only occasionally at

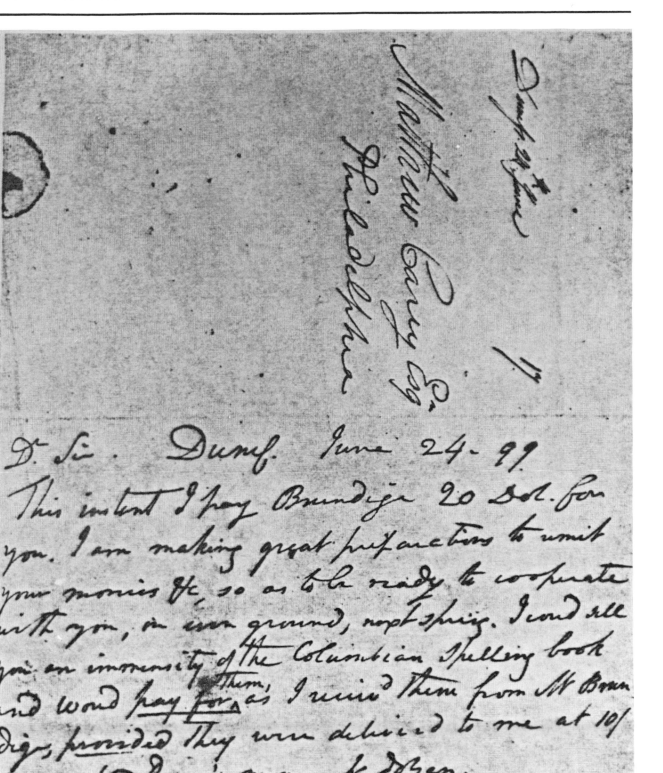

Letter to Mathew Carey in which Weems discusses his biography of George Washington (Paul Leicester Ford, ed., Mason Locke
Weems: His Works and Ways, *1929)*

I have nearly ready for the press 1773, price cheap, or to be christened, "The Beauties of Wash-ington." 'tis artfully drawn up, enlivend with anecdotes, and in my humble opinion, marvel-lously fitted "ad captandum gustum populi Americani!!!" What say you to printing it for me and ordering a copper plate Frontispiece of that HERO, something in this way.

George Washington Esq:

The Guardian Angel of his Country

"Go thy way old George. Die when thou wilt we shall never look upon thy like again"

M. Carey inven. &c

N.B. The whole will make but four sheets and sell like this and at quarter of a dollar. I coud make you a wage of fame and somethings by it.

home. Book-peddling had become his livelihood, and he became the author of many of his wares; besides moralistic pamphlets and *The Life of George Washington*, he wrote exemplary lives of Francis Marion (1809), Benjamin Franklin (1815), and William Penn (1822). He died in Beaufort, South Carolina, on 23 May 1825.

Weems the minister and Weems the peddler were ever at work in Weems the biographer. In his travels as a book purveyor, he saw that the religious and patriotic reading tastes of the new nation might be drawn together and addressed as one. His biographies of the early American heroes became, for Protestant and unchurched readers, equivalents of the sentimental saints' lives popular among some Catholics. His sources were many and varied. He borrowed freely, as in his biography of Franklin, for which he drew heavily on his subject's autobiography. What was new and correct in the life of Marion seems chiefly to have been contributed by the book's intended coauthor, Peter Horry, who withdrew his name when he saw the "romance" that Weems was fashioning. Some of what the biographies tell may be uncritically collected hearsay gathered as his salesman's travels brought Weems into contact with people offering accurate, embellished, or invented memories of his subjects. Much, however, such as the story of the dying Franklin contemplating a picture of Christ, was but his own contrivance. Certainly it was Weems's shameless improvement of history that gave his *The Life of George Washington* its singular appeal. Begun as one of the many tributes that appeared after the venerated hero's death in December of 1799, the biography was expanded as a corrective to the inadequacies Weems perceived in John Marshall's five-volume biography of Washington (1804-1807), which gave only a page to its subject's growing years. The popularity of his own biography was again and again a spur to Weems the imaginative writer. The eighty-page first edition that appeared in 1800 more than tripled in length as the book grew through more than thirty editions—three of them translations into German—by the year of his death. The stories of the cherry tree and the elder Washington's cabbage garden, in which the father plants seeds that come up in the pattern of George's name to teach the Heavenly Father's design in creation, first appeared in the 1806 edition. That such instruction—the first a tale invented by the author, the second a moral lesson cribbed from James Beattie—became enshrined in the American folk consciousness was largely due to the prim earnestness of Weems's telling the "low hortatory" or "juvenile-

homiletic" rhetoric that was employed to persuade the young but has earned the scorn of critics.

The continuing interest of Weems's writings resides not in any intrinsic merit but in their reflection of the widespread American concern with public and private virtue in the decades following the Revolution. An increasingly secular age was more receptive to instructional writings than doctrinal sermons, and in inscribing his *The Life of George Washington* to Thomas Jefferson, Weems expressed his hope that the book would serve as a school text. It came to influence countless readers—Lincoln would tell of its impact on him—especially when its moral anecdotes were mined for McGuffey's readers. The theme of rebellion that runs through the biography of Washington has been read as a transposition of the Revolution and the subsequent intergenerational tensions felt by a society still unsure of itself. Weems's exemplary teachings have been found to incorporate important post-Lockian insights into the nature and improvement of children. Thus young George's disobedience to his father is represented in terms of filial incapacity rather than of moral failure. The accounts of the boy's lapses and his father's corrections are free of the terrifying analogies with original sin so familiar in earlier instruction. Instead Weems presents an understanding father whose admonitions are accompanied by reassurances of parental solicitude. *The Life of Washington* thus mirrors a change from Americans' backward-looking obsession with guilt to the confidence that attended their advance into the nineteenth century.

Letters:

Volumes 2 and 3 of *Mason Locke Weems: His Works and Ways*, 3 volumes, edited by Emily Ellsworth Ford Skeel (New York: Privately printed, 1929).

Bibliography:

Volume 1 of *Mason Locke Weems: His Works and Ways*, 3 volumes edited by Emily Ellsworth Ford Skeel (New York: Privately printed, 1929).

References:

William A. Bryan, "The Genesis of Weems's 'Life of Washington,'" *Americana*, 36 (April 1941): 142-165;

Bryan, *George Washington in American Literature, 1775-1865* (New York: Columbia University Press, 1952);

Marcus Cunliffe, Introduction to *The Life of*

Washington (Cambridge, Mass.: Harvard University Press, 1962);

Cunliffe, "Parson Weems and the Cherry Tree," *Bulletin of the John Rylands Library,* 45 (Autumn 1962): 71-79;

Jay Fliegelman, *Prodigals and Pilgrims: The American Revolution against Patriarchal Authority, 1750-1800* (Cambridge: Cambridge University Press, 1982);

George B. Forgie, *Patricide in the House Divided: A Psychological Interpretation of Lincoln and His Age* (New York: Norton, 1979), pp. 35-49;

Clifford S. Griffin, *Their Brothers' Keepers: Moral Stewardship in the United States, 1800-1865* (New Brunswick: Rutgers University Press, 1960);

Charles A. Ingraham, "Mason Locke Weems: A Great American Author and Distributor of Books," *Americana,* 25 (1930): 469-485;

Harold Kellock, *Parson Weems of the Cherry Tree* (New York: Century, 1928);

Lewis Leary, *The Book-Peddling Parson* (Chapel Hill, N.C.: Algonquin Books, 1984);

Bishop William Meade, *Old Churches, Ministers, and Families of Virginia,* 2 volumes (Philadelphia: Lippincott, 1857);

Mrs. Roswell Skeel, "Mason Locke Weems: A Postscript," *New Colophon,* 3 (1950): 243-249;

Sheldon Sloan, "Parson Weems on Franklin's Death," *Pennsylvania Magazine of History and Biography,* 96 (1972): 369-372;

Bernard Wishy, *The Child and the Republic* (Philadelphia: University of Pennsylvania Press, 1968);

Lawrence C. Wroth, *Parson Weems: A Biographical and Critical Study* (Baltimore: Eichelberger, 1911).

William Wirt
(8 November 1772-18 February 1834)

Alan Axelrod

BOOKS: *The Letters of the British Spy. Originally pub. in the Virginia Argus, in August and September, 1803* (Richmond: Printed by Samuel Pleasants, junior, 1803; London: Printed for Sharpe & Hailes, 1812);

The Two Principal Arguments of William Wirt, esquire, on the Trial of Aaron Burr, for High Treason, and on the Motion to Commit Aaron Burr and Others, for Trial in Kentucky (Richmond: From the press of Samuel Pleasants, jun., 1808);

The Old Bachelor, by Wirt and others (Richmond: Printed at the Enquirer Press for Thomas Ritchie & Fielding Lucas, 1814);

Sketches of the Life and Character of Patrick Henry (Philadelphia: Printed by William Brown & published by James Webster, 1817);

A Discourse on the Lives and Characters of Thomas Jefferson and John Adams, Who Both Died on the Fourth of July, 1826. Delivered, at the Request of the Citizens of Washington, in the Hall of Representatives of the United States, on the Nineteenth October, 1826 (Washington: Printed by Gales & Seaton, 1826);

An Address Delivered Before the Peithessophian and Philoclean Societies of Rutgers College . . . (New Brunswick, N.J.: Rutgers Press, Terhune & Letson, Printers, 1830);

Argument Delivered at Annapolis . . . (Washington: Printed by Gales & Seaton, 1830);

Opinion on the Right of the State of Georgia to Extend Her Laws Over the Cherokee Nation (Printed for the Cherokee Nation at the Office of the *Cherokee Phoenix and Indians' Advocate:* J. F. Wheeler, Printer, 1830);

Address to the People of Maryland (Baltimore: Printed by John W. Woods, 1833).

OTHER: *The Rainbow; First Series. Originally Published in the Richmond Enquirer,* includes two essays by Wirt (Richmond: Published by Ritchie & Worsley, 1804).

Virginia lawyer and man of letters, Attorney General of the United States, William Wirt enjoyed success as an American practitioner of the Addisonian serial essay. He was also the author of a popular, if not wholly reliable, biography of Patrick Henry.

Wirt was born in Bladensburg, Maryland, in 1772 to Jacob and Henrietta Wirt. Orphaned at age eight, he was raised by an uncle and aunt, who enrolled him in a series of classical grammar schools. This education fostered a passion for literature; by age thirteen he was writing poetry in the manner of Pope. One of Wirt's classmates introduced him to Benjamin Edwards (later a member of Congress), who employed the fifteen-year-old boy as a family tutor, giving him the run of an extensive library. He left this service in 1789 for a legal apprenticeship, and three years later he began a distinguished Virginia practice that would bring him into close contact with the likes of Monroe, Madison, and Jefferson. In 1795 he married Mildred Gilmer, the daughter of a well-to-do Albemarle County physician. After her death in 1799, Wirt moved to Richmond and served as Clerk of the Virginia House of Delegates from 1799 until his appointment to the Court of Chancery in 1802. He married Elizabeth Gamble in 1803 and resigned from the Chancery post to return to private practice, the highlight of which was his role in the prosecution of Aaron Burr for treason (1807). Appointed Attorney General for the Virginia District in 1816, he became Attorney General of the United States the following year, holding office for twelve years.

His career as a publishing author began as little more than a respite from the pressures of legal life. Nervous, too, about his wife Elizabeth's approaching confinement, Wirt amused himself by composing ten sketches that appeared serially during 1803 in the *Virginia Argus*. The collected essays were published as *The Letters of the British Spy* later that year and went through ten editions during Wirt's lifetime, spawning a number of imitations. It is difficult to account for the popularity of this casual and slight production, intended more for the admonition and instruction of Virginia's rising generation than for general entertainment. A tepid jeremiad delivered in the guise of ten letters from a British traveler in Richmond, the book rambles into five areas: social and economic inequality in Virginia, the geological evolution of North America, the plight of the Indian, the need for a reawakening of *amor patriae,* and, the fifth and principal topic, a forensic critique of legal, political, and religious eloquence in Virginia.

In 1804-1805 Wirt contributed to a series of philosophical essays run in the *Richmond Enquirer*. These twenty-six essays were a collaborative effort of the Rainbow Association, a Virginia literary and intellectual club of which Wirt was a member. Ten of these essays, including two by Wirt, "On the Condition of Women" and "On Forensic Elo-

Portrait by C. B. Fevret de St. Mémin (The Corcoran Gallery of Art)

quence," were published as *The Rainbow; First Series* in 1804.

Wirt's thriving law practice kept him from further literary work at least until 1810, when, according to his biographer, John Pendleton Kennedy, he began an abortive series of essays called "The Sylph." However, none of these pieces was published, and if a manuscript survives, it has yet to be located.

At the end of 1810 Wirt began another literary project, one that did bear fruit. *The Old Bachelor* was a collaboration with Wirt's friends Dabney and Frank Carr, Dr. Louis Girardin, Richard E. Parker, George Tucker, and Maj. David Watson that ran to twenty-eight numbers in the *Enquirer*. Wirt contributed at least sixteen pieces. For the book-length collection that was published in 1814, Wirt and his friends wrote five additional essays. The series aimed at nothing less than reforming the manners and educating the literary taste of Virginia. Wirt promoted a system of public education meant to foster a Jeffersonian aristocracy of talent and virtue. Despite their didactic purpose, these essays are not mere tracts; their argument is conducted through deft satire and gentle caricature. Richer in characterization and stylistically more polished than *The Letters of the British Spy, The Old Bachelor* nevertheless fell far short of the earlier work's popularity.

After twelve years of fitful labor, Wirt published his *Sketches of the Life and Character of Patrick Henry* in 1817. Intended as the first installment in what the author projected as a "Virginia Plutarch," a series of lives of Virginia's most notable sons, *Sketches of the Life and Character of Patrick Henry* turned out to be Wirt's only exercise in biography and, at that, more valuable as an account of Henry's oratory than of his life. It is through this popular book (fifteen editions by 1859) that we know Henry's "Give me liberty" speech—which some critics have judged more the work of Wirt than of Henry.

Raised on Laurence Sterne, Robert Blair, James Macpherson, and Thomas Gray, William Wirt wrote prose that is valuable as an American example of the preromantic sensibility and as an indication of literary taste in the early Republic. His small body of work forms a transition between the Addisonian serial essay, with its balance of rational discourse and sentimental scene, and the kind of romantic sketch—as fiction, more fully satisfying—practiced by Washington Irving.

References:

Bruce Granger, *American Essay Serials from Franklin to Irving* (Knoxville: University of Tennessee Press, 1978), pp. 182-202;

Jay B. Hubbell, *The South in American Literature: 1607-1900* (Durham: Duke University Press, 1954), pp. 234-242;

John P. Kennedy, *Memoirs of the Life of William Wirt* (Philadelphia: Lea & Blanchard, 1849).

Papers:

Wirt's papers are widely dispersed, but the principal depository is the Library of Congress, with some 900 items, including correspondence, letterbooks, and the manuscript of *Sketches of the Life and Character of Patrick Henry*. The Maryland Historical Society Library holds many letters, essays, legal documents, and other personal papers. The Southern History Collection at the University of North Carolina, Chapel Hill, has autobiographical writings and documents relating to the Henry biography. Two other significant depositories are The Virginia Historical Society and the Earl Gregg Swem Library of the College of William and Mary, which hold literary manuscripts and correspondence.

Appendix

A Crisis of Culture: The Changing Role
of Religion in the New Republic

The Rising Glory of America: Three Poems

A Crisis of Culture: The Changing Role of Religion in the New Republic

Emory Elliott
Princeton University

Until recently few students of American literature recognized the crisis of culture that occurred during the early national period. Only in the last ten to fifteen years has there been a serious challenge to the long-prevailing argument about the formation of American literature alleging that it all really started with Emerson. Although a condescending nod was always given in American literature courses and in book introductions to a few Puritan writers and to the importance of Benjamin Franklin, only exceptional scholars such as Perry Miller and Richard Chase have insisted that an understanding of Emerson, Thoreau, Hawthorne, and Melville requires thorough study of their precursors: those unsung poets and novelists of the late eighteenth century such as Joel Barlow, Hugh Henry Brackenridge, Charles Brockden Brown, Timothy Dwight, and Philip Freneau. Anthologies sometimes exposed students to a few unrepresentative poems of Freneau, but the novels of Brown and Brackenridge were largely unread and the long major poems of Dwight and Barlow were seldom mentioned.[1]

Of course, it must be said at the outset that if the only motive for examining the literature of the past is to appreciate great literary achievement and reap aesthetic pleasure, then the teachers of American literature have been right not to assign *The Columbiad* for study. Aesthetic pleasure is only one of many things to be gained from the study of our literary heritage and from literary works we may learn of the human experience of those who wrote and the world in which they lived. From the study of the careers of our first national writers and close examination of some of their major works, we may gain a clearer understanding of many formative elements of American literature. In the poetry and fiction produced during the critical decades after the Revolution are the earliest signs of the ironies, narrative manipulations, and multileveled ambiguities that would characterize the works of Poe, Hawthorne, and Melville. In the experiences of writers like Freneau and Brown are the seeds of the peculiar relationship between the writer and his audience in American society. By the time Emerson composed his famous essays on the American scholar and the poet, the struggle to establish a role for the man of letters in America had already been fought by this first generation of American writers.

Yet there are many reasons that writers of the Revolution have received so little attention. Not only does the critic have to search for the jewels, but the standards of taste of modern readers have been fashioned by post-Romantic forms and styles. For the most part the first American writers were adhering to literary standards established in the neoclassical period of the eighteenth century. As a result, many of their writings appear antiquated and their subjects and styles are easy marks for ridicule. For this reason the poems of that time that do get anthologized have often been unrepresentative: those few pre-Romantic gems that the editor mined out of volumes of heroic-couplet verse.

Another barrier separating modern readers from the eighteenth-century writers is the intimate relationship between literature and religion that prevailed well beyond the Revolution. Because the clergy and men of letters were striving for similar goals, used many of the same verbal devices, and were sometimes even the same people, the study of the literature of this period involves the reader in matters of theology and religious history as well—a prospect that has not always excited literary critics. Yet the intricate and changing connection between religion and belles lettres is one of the most fascinating aspects of that period, and the moral and spiritual role the American writers inherited became a significant characteristic of those writers and their works.

So fundamental is this connection in American literature that on a deeper level the bond between religious belief and serious literature has remained strong until our own time. In his recent study of American fiction after 1945, *A Literature Without Qualities,* Warner Berthoff has recognized the remarkable persistence of this religious element and has even suggested that the American novelist still sees himself in a clerical role: "In American writing this convergence of secular literary ambition upon essentially religious imperatives runs deep. It is, in one central respect, a *pastoral* model—and by this I do not mean the special set of poetic and mythological conventions descending in western literature from Theocritus and the Virgilian eclogues, but the ministerial pastoralism of the reformed regathered Protestant churches (churches or priesthoods of the single believer, if necessary)."[2]

The continuing debate and confusion over the importance of religious ideas and language upon the formation of an American nationalist ideology has increased the need for a better understanding of the literary works of post-Revolutionary War America. The question of the role of religion in the formation of the republic's ideals is a hotly contested issue that remains unresolved. A provocative and widely respected thesis, elaborated recently by Sacvan Bercovitch, is that religious language and religiously grounded myths about America played a significant role in shaping an ideology of the "American Way of Life." Bercovitch argues that a set of beliefs originally expounded in New England Puritan rhetoric formed the superstructure that encloses virtually all American political and social ideas, even those that appear to be in conflict with one another.[3] Thus, American identity is necessarily a religious identity. Other scholars such as Henry Steele Commager point to the importance of the rules of law, of reason, of political liberalism, which stem from a distinctly non-religious, indeed even anti-religious, tradition of the eighteenth-century Enlightenment from which, in their view, American political and social ideals have derived. For them, religious influences in the last decades of the founding century were quite subordinate to those of classical and modern philosophy, particularly for the leaders who framed the Constitution.[4]

In an attempt to reconcile this debate, Henry May concluded that the function of religion in the minds of the framers was best expressed in *The Federalist #* 10. Madison held that a consensus belief in God would be the essential glue binding all Americans together, while a wide variety of denominations would ensure the general weakness of religion in the realms of politics and society. May's compromise does not succeed, however, because the clash is really between two extremely different methods of historical analysis. Bercovitch and the literary scholars who follow him believe that we can understand the deeper structures of a culture through close study of verbal symbols—image, rhetoric, sermons, fictions, and poems.[5] Incisive readings of these products of the imagination will provide insight into the substratum of our society. At the other extreme, historians trusting direct discourse and the non-symbolic language of official documents and records believe that all we may really know of the past is what people said they did, believed, and intended.

The difficulty with both lines of argument and the evidence for them is that they generalize so broadly about a relatively long period of history in which the lives of individuals and the progress of their ideas underwent many changes and even complete reversals of direction. When we begin to look closely at individual lives and the evolution of particular careers or intellectual activities, the generalizations begin to break down. Religious feeling and unconscious adherence to religious beliefs may exist in an individual who consciously advocates the deistical assumptions of his contemporaries. Or, one person's deepest conviction in the rule of law and reason may be expressed to an audience through symbols of religious expression and myths, as in Thomas Paine's *Common Sense*. Put quite simply, people did not always say what they meant or felt; nor did they always mean what they said. And during this time, called the "Age of Contradictions" by Leon Howard, even poets and preachers contradicted themselves.[6]

The achievement of our first writers has been slighted as well because readers often are not aware of the enormous obstacles these writers faced in creating a literature for the rapidly changing audience of a revolutionary society. Since historians of this period are usually interested in demonstrating those factors that led to stabilization and the containment of the radical tendencies of the Revolution, Americans possess perhaps too limited a sense of the actual ferment of the last decades of the century. Some critics have even argued that Americans have been so obsessed with denying the revolutionary character of the Revolution that they have blinded themselves to its truly rebellious nature.[7]

To understand the conditions in which the writers were working, we need to recognize that the immediate social and psychological effects of the Revolutionary War had all the potential for creating an internal social calamity of the kind that has since occurred in so many revolutionary societies. To say a catastrophe was prevented here because of wise leadership or the rule of law is to identify only one piece of a complex social picture puzzle. Even before the war was over, Americans convinced themselves that the Revolution was not really a revolt but was merely necessary reform, or an inevitable separation or a sacred fulfillment. These myths were consciously created within the rhetoric of the Founding Fathers, who wisely employed such terms to mollify the people's desire for continued changes in social and economic conditions. Once aware of the truly volatile conditions of identity confusion, religious turmoil, and social misdirection that followed upon the war, we may see how easily America could have slipped into the sociological condition of massive despair, cynicism, and anger that has destroyed other post-revolutionary societies.

But containment did occur, and it was furthered by a generation of word-makers—not just the framers of the Constitution but the shapers of the metaphors, articulators of the visions, and the creators of the imaginative projections of America as a nation and of the nature and identity of the American people. The clergymen and poets—the masters of symbolic language—played a role every bit as important, if not more so, as the lawyers and statesmen who crafted the political documents. Writers like Dwight and Freneau approached literature with a sense of religious mission and strove to give America a vision of herself as a promised, New World utopia.

Under the pressures of the changing conditions of the 1780s and 1790s, however, the intimate relationship between religion and literature began to crumble. As religion lost its power to sway people to reform and the ability of the clergy to influence political leaders diminished, some writers, like Brackenridge and Freneau, were less inclined to infuse their works with religious themes and language. In their search for new explanations of the human situation, Freneau, Barlow, and Brown were drawn to the same serious currents of philosophical ideas that would soon inflame the early poetry of Wordsworth and Coleridge. There was even a brief period in the 1780s when the Romantic age of literature as a new religion and the poet as priest might have dawned in America.

With all the moral fervor of eighteenth-century American Calvinism behind them and the expanse of an open cultural horizon before them, these writers saw an opportunity to "make it new" in the fullest sense of the phrase. American writers could confidently dismiss the great classics of literature as secondary and dated because there had been no epoch in history like the present. The classics seemed to have been written on another planet and transmitted to America through eons of time and space; they might provide enjoyment, but the social structure and values they reflected were viewed as completely foreign to the American experience. No

subject more important, no theme more sublime, no material more grandiose could be imagined than American life in the present. It seemed only fitting that the mantle of moral preceptor and intellectual leader now be passed from the clergy to the artists and poets.

The premature and temporary termination of the Romantic fusion of art and religious zeal in these decades occurred for a number of complex reasons. The rapid shift of allegiance of the people from religious and intellectual authorities to the military and political leadership, symbolized in the reverence for George Washington as sage and moral exemplar, undermined the last vestiges of social influence of the literary figures. In addition, business and governmental leaders found it to be in their best interests to discredit the intellectuals and ministers because theology and art often challenged the emergent precapitalist ideology upon which the new economy would be founded. Contrary to the basic truth of the Weber-Tawney thesis that ultimately Protestantism and capitalism were mutually reinforcing, individual clergymen frequently annoyed ambitious merchants with sermons denouncing acquisitiveness and self-interest. To make matters worse, book dealers and buyers remained prejudiced in favor of the literary products from abroad because English books were cheaper and considered more fashionable and entertaining.[8]

In spite of these discouragements, the best writers still fought with religious fervor to save their society from peril. Recognizing the threat of the incipient materialism to all forms of humanistic endeavor, writers such as Barlow, Freneau, Brackenridge, Dwight, and Brown sought to preserve the advances of the Revolution and prevent the slide into moral and cultural degeneracy. While they were in favor of the destruction of the old monarchical order, they each saw, though dimly at first, the weaknesses and flaws of the new republic—consensus, ideology, blind conformity were all to serve the new god of materialism. There would be little place for the expression of genuine human feeling, for passionate commitment to spiritual values, for full dedication to human rights, or for the pleasures of the imagination or aesthetic feelings. As one historian of the period has observed, "This was a society in which nobody played."[9] Fearing that America might become a sterile society which worshiped only the status quo, the writers remained committed to a common goal: to bring art into the marketplace and to use literature to reveal the spiritual meaning and human interests in the practical affairs of life.

Although they were united in their dedication to literature and the life of the mind, these writers also lived in a political world in which they often found themselves at odds with one another over current issues. A questioner of authority from his youth, Freneau spent much of his literary energy and his public life defending the republican policies of Jefferson and attacking the aristocratic inclinations of the Federalists. Joel Barlow underwent a complete change of mind which led him from his early conservatism at Yale to the radicalism of Thomas Paine and William Godwin. The political ideas of Brackenridge and Brockden Brown vacillated between the poles of republican liberalism and the Federalist fear of mobocracy, and these shiftings may be charted in their lives and writings. Those who remained steady on the right throughout their lives or were moved permanently to that position by fears of social decay have been identified as the Connecticut Wits. The members of this group, which included Timothy Dwight, John Trumbull, David Humphreys, Noah Webster, and Lemuel Hopkins, collaborated on or endorsed the anti-republican satire *The Anarchiad* (1786-1787).

No writer could be aloof or detached from politics because the parties themselves were expressions of the deeper identity crisis and divided consciousness of the new nation. On the one side, guilt over rejecting the old culture and fear of freedom led many to serious doubts about the American experiment and toward an impulse to make amends for the slaying of the father and to embrace the old values of the fatherland with even more zeal than during the years before the Revolution. On the other side, the fervor for expansion, growth, unlimited opportunity, and utopian liberty had many yearning to cast off all tethers, certainly those imposed from afar by the federal government. As natural human selfishness of individuals led to exploitation of the political and economic confusion and to rampant land-grabbing schemes, the intellectuals and writers of both persuasions began to search for some means to temper the drive for power and wealth.

Still, opinions differed on the value of religion as a force for inspiring or enforcing social order. At one extreme, the Puritan Old Lights like Dwight were clinging more tightly than ever to the idea that the more political freedom a people possessed the more they required strict religious controls. Without rigid controls human depravity would run wild, and the republic would be destroyed from within by demagogues and criminals. At the other extreme, there were those sons of the Revolution, such as

Paine and later Barlow, who believed that religion was superfluous. For the Enlightenment had ushered in an era of reasoned judgment in which persuasion rather than fear would offset human behavior. As corruption and profligacy actually did increase during the postwar years, the shrewd leaders on all sides, even confirmed Deists, began to recognize the desirability of moderate religious strictures to control the rapaciousness of the people and to further systems of benevolence and philanthropy that might serve as means of distributing the wealth that would naturally come into the hands of the few. Although some resisted, most writers came to share the position that, at least during this period of transition, religion was a social and moral necessity, even if intellectually suspect.

With the possible exception of Dwight, each of these writers was aware, though perhaps vaguely, that current philosophical developments were already challenging the notions of free will and moral choice upon which the new American system was founded. The growing importance of empirical science and materialism was accompanied by a growing skepticism about traditional ideals of morality. There is a remarkable tendency toward naturalism and determinism in the writings of the 1780s and 1790s, especially in the work of Freneau and Brown. They recognized that such skepticism even called into question the legitimacy of the very activity in which they themselves were engaged, for the idea that a literary work could cause people to be moral would soon seem absurd to philosophers and most reflective artists. The role of the public man, whether poet, clergyman, or war hero, would be diminished, for forces rather than people would be perceived as the prime movers of history.[10] It was in reaction to this very denial of human interests that Hawthorne and Melville wrote their great moral romances in the 1850s.

During the period after the Revolution, Charles Brockden Brown was the writer who best understood the psychological consequences and literary implications of the collapse of the Enlightenment epistemology. He saw how the cultural schizophrenia would affect the minds of individuals and how impossible it might become for certain people to live with the irrationality of old religion in a political world that stressed reason and pragmatism. He also recognized how some individuals would react to the fluid economy, which placed only moral restraints on exploitation and used guilt as the only probe to keep men honest. He understood the emotional consequences for the disillusioned individual who discovered the contradiction between the religious and national ideals of benevolence and philanthropy expounded in rhetoric and the realities of disease, crime, and slavery. In his complex psychological fictions Brown expressed the terror of uncertainty that resulted from this new distrust of reason, a theme that was to be at the center of Poe's best fiction and the works of many later American authors.

By 1785, serious writers of both political parties felt that the new order of the republic would be one of fragmentation. As Madison argued in *The Federalist # 10*, order would spring from a consensus that would emerge from a plurality of opinions. Accordingly, the writers realized that traditional literary forms would have to be replaced by structures that would encompass a society of discord and competing voices. The fitting literary embodiment of this disorder would be a form that was more formless. The narrative strategy that Brackenridge used in *Modern Chivalry* with its rambling, picaresque quality was absolutely appropriate to the chaotic and ever-changing conditions of American life, as Mark Twain later recognized when he composed *Huck Finn* and Walt Whitman the many-sectioned *Leaves of Grass*. Indeed, the shifting, accumulating narrative is reflective of the westward movement itself and of the meandering if not unsystematic way that American government and society seemed to many to be organized. Similarly, the several sections and various speakers of Dwight's *Greenfield Hill* reflect a sense of social disjunction within the idyllic frame of a pastoral setting. In both works it is only the voice of the narrator-author (in Dwight's case his voice speaks in the footnotes) that provides reassurance that a mind is in control of the events of the narrative.

For all their failures and disappointments, the poets of this age were poets of vision. It fell to them, regardless of their political or social views, to try to imagine the needs of America in the future. Reared in the Protestant churches and trained for the ministry, these writers carried throughout their lives the conviction that authorship was to a degree a sacred calling. This social mission was so burdensome, however, that it weighted down their poetry with meanings and purposes, duties and moral obligations. Rarely could they find the artistic strength to lift their lines to the heights of fancy. The artistry drowned in the social and political messages they included in an effort to achieve the proper didactic effect.

The writers of the new republic were engaged in a task more difficult than they were capable of understanding: the negotiation of an uncharted intellectual and artistic path from a dominant religious vision of America to a new nationalist ideology. They felt it their duty to express the symbolic meaning of America and the social message of how to live and succeed in American society—how to be an American. Yet they had no literary precedents to help them. As they tried to mediate these difficult problems of identity and national inner conflict, they were also trying to understand their own changing identities. Like a person trying to help a friend through a psychological trauma, who accepts the risk of losing his own grasp on reality, these individual poets were striving to gain mastery over their own inner confusion as they preached to others of their duties.

For each of the writers, the changing attitude toward religion in their society created genuine personal crises. As new philosophical and social theories made traditional religion appear irrelevant for the new society, some writers rejected religion on an intellectual level yet at the same time clung to religion, sometimes unconsciously, on a personal psychological level. Artistically, much of their poetic language was rooted in religious traditions, and when they tried to strip it of religious associations, as Freneau and Barlow did, or to find new symbols to express human experience, they found themselves flailing about in a verbal vacuum.

The story of these writers remains important for understanding the problem of the writer in America ever since. The social and political demands upon the artist in a democratic society are much greater than those in an aristocratic culture where the nobility and a system of patronage ensure the continuation of the arts. The poets who lived through the American Revolution felt an obligation to use their talents to fill the moral and spiritual void left by a declining clergy, to present the social and political ideals of their nation, and to enlighten and inspire their readers with visions of the human condition in a new age and new world. Perhaps a Milton, the poet they all admired, might have been up to the task, but it must be admitted that there were no Miltons in America in the late eighteenth century.

Although they labored heroically, all of the writers of the new republic finally fell short of the victory they desired, some for lack of talent and some for lack of courage. It would be forty years before the ground lost would be regained, and even then the artist in America would continue to be regarded as an outsider, and sometimes as a nuisance, whose interests were most often irrelevant or antagonistic to the ongoing concerns of the commercial society. Given the conditions they faced, the achievement of our early national writers is quite remarkable and demands detailed, sympathetic study.

1. Even the Norton Anthology includes nothing from Dwight and only Barlow's "Hasty-Pudding"; see Sculley Bradley *et al.,* eds., *The American Tradition in Literature,* fourth edition (New York: Norton, 1974).

2. Warner Berthoff, *A Literature Without Qualities* (Berkeley: University of California Press, 1979), p. 17.

3. Sacvan Bercovitch, *The American Jeremiad* (Madison: University of Wisconsin Press, 1979).

4. Henry Steele Commager, *The Empire of Reason: How Europe Imagined and America Realized the Enlightenment* (Garden City: Doubleday, 1977).

5. Henry F. May, *The Enlightenment in America* (New York: Oxford University Press, 1976). Interpreters such as Bercovitch have been strongly influenced by theories of symbolic interpretation established through structural anthropology and best exhibited in the works of Claude Lévi-Strauss, Victor Turner, and Mary Douglas.

6. Leon Howard, "The Late Eighteenth Century: An Age of Contradictions," in *Transitions in American Literary History,* edited by Harry Hayden Clark (Durham: Duke University Press, 1953), pp. 51-89.

7. See Sacvan Bercovitch, "How the Puritans Won the American Revolution," *Massachusetts Review,* 17 (Winter 1976): 597-630.

8. On capitalism and Protestantism see Max Weber, *The Protestant Ethic and the Spirit of Capitalism,* translated by Talcott Parsons (New York: Scribners, 1958). On sales see William Charvat, *The Profession of Authorship in America, 1800-1870,* edited by Matthew J. Bruccoli (Columbus: Ohio State University Press, 1968).

9. An observation made by Yehoshua Arieli, professor of American History at the Hebrew University during a session of a seminar on American culture of the late eighteenth century, National Humanities Center, Research Triangle Park, North Carolina, October 1979.

10. See Richard Sennett, *The Fall of Public Man: The Social Psychology of Capitalism* (New York: Knopf, 1977).

From *Revolutionary Writers: Literature and Authority in the New Republic, 1725-1810,* by Emory Elliott, pp. 6-18. Copyright © 1982 by Emory Elliott. Reprinted by permission of Oxford University Press, Inc.

The Rising Glory of America: Three Poems

No artistic form expressed the optimism and utopian spirit of the new republic as clearly as the "rising glory" poems. The prototype for these patriotic writings was the commencement address that Philip Freneau and Hugh Henry Brackenridge read at their graduation in Princeton in 1771. Their *The Rising Glory of America,* first published in the following year, became a model for Joel Barlow's Yale commencement poem of 1778, *The Prospect of Peace,* as well as a host of other such pieces printed as broadsides and delivered on public occasions. Timothy Dwight's early effort, *America: or, A Poem on the Settlement of the British Colonies* (1780?) is another notable example of the genre.

Articulating a vision of America as a "new Jerusalem," where God's chosen American saints would fulfill the biblical promise of the new millennium, the "rising glory" poems employ biblical types to depict a future America where more efficient government and commerce produce the lei-sure time necessary for the development of all forms of human endeavor. Of particular importance to the poets who composed these verses were the encouragement and support of the arts within the new order, where universal education and the flourishing of colleges would create a love of learning and an appreciation of the arts and literature. Following this course, American culture would soon set the highest standards for the rest of the world.

Though the authors of these patriotic rhapsodies soon became frustrated and disillusioned by the failure of the new nation to achieve this promised glory in the arts, these poems illustrate well the dreams of the most learned and literate of the young republic and the complex ways that religious imagery and political hopes were interwoven in public and private expression.

—Emory Elliott

Hugh Henry Brackenridge and Philip Freneau

The Rising Glory of America
Written 1771

––––––*Venient annis*
Saecula seris, quibus oceanus
Vincula rerum laxet, et ingens
Pateat tellus, Typhisque novos
Detegat orbes; nec sit terris
Ultima Thule.––––––

Seneca. Med. Act III. V. 375.

ARGUMENT.

The subject proposed—The discovery of America by Columbus—A philosophical enquiry into the origin of the savages of America—The first planters from Europe—Causes of their migration to America—The difficulties they encountered from the jealousy of the natives—Agriculture descanted on—Commerce and navigation—Science—Future prospects of British usurpation, tyranny, and devastation on this side the Atlantic—The more comfortable one of Independence, liberty, and peace—Conclusion.

Acasto.

NOW shall the adventurous muse attempt a strain
More new, more noble, and more flush of fame
Than all that went before—
Now through the veil of ancient days renew
The period fam'd when first Columbus touch'd
These shores so long unknown—through various toils,
Famine, and death, the hero forc'd his way,
Thro' oceans pregnant with perpetual storms,
And climates hostile to advent'rous man.
But why, to prompt your tears, should we resume
The tale of *Cortez,* furious chief, ordain'd
With Indian blood to dye the sands, and choak,
Fam'd *Mexico,* thy streams with dead? or why
Once more revive the tale so oft rehears'd
Of *Atabilipa,* by thirst of gold,
(All conquering motive in the human breast)
Depriv'd of life, which not *Peru's* rich ore
Nor *Mexico's* vast mines could then redeem?
Better these northern realms demand our song
Design'd by nature for the rural reign,
For agriculture's toil.—No blood we shed

For metals buried in a rocky waste.
Curs'd be that ore, which brutal makes mankind,
And prompts mankind to shed a brother's blood.

Eugenio.

But whence arose
That vagrant race who love the shady vale,
And choose the forest for their dark abode?—
For long has this perplext the sages skill
To investigate.—Tradition seems to hide
The mighty secret from each mortal eye,
How first these various nations, north and south,
Possest these shores, or from what countries came.—
Whether they sprang from some primaeval head
In their own lands, like Adam in the east,—
Yet this the sacred oracles deny,
And reason, too, reclaims against the thought:
For when the general deluge drown'd the world
Where could their tribes have found security,
Where find their fate, but in the ghastly deep?—
Unless, as others dream, some chosen few
High on the Andes 'scap'd the general death,
High on the Andes, wrapt in endless snow,
Where winter in his wildest fury reigns,
And subtle ether scarce our life maintains.—
But here Philosophers oppose the scheme;
This earth, say they, nor hills nor mountains knew
Ere yet the universal flood prevail'd;
But when the mighty waters rose aloft,
Rous'd by the winds they shook their solid base,
And, in convulsions, tore the delug'd world,
Till by the winds assuag'd, again they fell,
And all their ragged bed expos'd to view.
PERHAPS far wandering toward the northern pole
The streights of Zembla, and the frozen zone,
And where the eastern Greenland almost joins
America's north point, the hardy tribes
Of banish'd Jews, Siberians, Tartars wild
Come over icy mountains, or on floats
First reach'd these coasts, hid from the world beside.—
And yet another argument more strange,
Reserv'd for men of deeper thought, and late,
Presents itself to view:—*In Peleg's*[1] *days,*
(So says the Hebrew seer's unerring pen)

This mighty mass of earth, this solid globe
Was cleft in twain,—*divided* east and west,
While straight between, the deep Atlantic roll'd.—
And traces of indisputable remain
Of this primaeval land, now sunk and lost.—
The islands rising in our eastern main
Are but small fragments of this continent,
Whose two extremities were Newfoundland
And St. Helena.—One far in the north,
Where shivering seamen view with strange surprize
The guiding pole-star glittering o'er their heads;
The other near the southern tropic rears
Its head above the waves—Bermudas' isles,
Cape Verd, Canary, Britain, and the Azores,
With fam'd Hibernia, are but broken parts
Of some prodigious waste, which once sustain'd
Nations and tribes of vanish'd memory,
Forests, and towns, and beasts of every class,
Where navies now explore their briny way.

Leander.

Your sophistry, Eugenio, makes me smile:
The roving mind of man delights to dwell
On hidden things merely because they're hid:
He thinks his knowledge far beyond all limit,
And boldly fathoms nature's darkest haunts—
But for uncertainties, your broken isles,
Your northern Tartars, and your wandering Jews,
(The flimsy cobwebs of a sophist's brain)
Hear what the voice of history proclaims—
The Carthaginians, ere the Roman yoke
Broke their proud spirits, and enslav'd them too,
For navigation were renown'd as much
As haughty Tyre with all her hundred fleets,
Full many a league their vent'rous seamen sail'd
Thro' streight Gibraltar, down the western shore
Of Africa, to the Canary isles
By them call'd Fortunate; so Flaccus[2] sings,
Because eternal spring there clothes the fields
And fruits delicious bloom throughout the year.—
From voyaging here, this inference I draw,
Perhaps some barque with all her numerous crew
Falling to leeward of her destin'd port,
Caught by the eastern *trade*, was hurried on
Before the unceasing blast to Indian isles,
Brazil, La Plata, or the coasts more south—
There stranded, and unable to return,
Forever from their native skies estrang'd
Doubtless they made these virgin climes their own,
And in the course of long revolving years
A numerous progeny from these arose,
And spread throughout the coasts—those whom
  we call
Brazilians, Mexicans, Peruvians rich,

The tribes of Chili, Patagon, and those
Who till the shores of Amazonia's stream.
When first the powers of Europe here attain'd
Vast empires, kingdoms, cities, palaces
And polish'd nations stock'd the fertile land.
Who has not heard of Cusco, Lima, and
The town of Mexico—huge cities form'd
From Europe's architecture; ere the arms
Of haughty Spain disturb'd the peaceful soil.—
But *here*, amid this northern dark domain
No towns were seen to rise.—No arts were here;
The tribes unskill'd to raise the lofty mast,
Or force the daring prow thro' adverse waves,
Gaz'd on the pregnant soil, and crav'd alone
Life from the unaided genius of the ground,—
This indicates they were a different race;
From whom descended 'tis not ours to say—
That power, no doubt, who furnish'd trees, and
  plants,
And animals, to this vast continent,
Spoke into being man among the rest,
But what a change is here!—what arts arise!
What towns and capitals! how commerce waves
Her gaudy flags, where silence reign'd before!

Acasto.

Speak, my Eugenio, for I've heard you tell
The dismal history, and the cause that brought
The first adventurers to these western shores;
The glorious cause that urg'd our fathers first
To visit climes unknown, and wilder woods
Than e'er Tartarian or Norwegian saw,
And with fair culture to adorn that soil
Which never felt the industrious swain before.

Eugenio.

All this long story to rehearse, would tire,
Besides, the sun toward the west retreats,
Nor can the noblest theme retard his speed,
Nor loftiest verse—not that which sang the fall
Of Troy divine, and fierce Achilles ire.
Yet hear a part:—By persecution wrong'd,
And sacerdotal rage, our fathers came
From Europe's hostile shores to these abodes,
Here to enjoy a liberty in *faith*,
Secure from tyranny and base controul.
For this they left their country and their friends,
And dar'd the Atlantic wave in quest of peace;
And found new shores, and sylvan settlements,
And men, alike unknowing and unknown.
Hence, by the care of each advent'rous *chief*
New governments (their wealth unenvied yet)
Were form'd on liberty and virtue's plan.
These searching out uncultivated tracts
Conceiv'd new plans of towns, and capitals,

And spacious provinces—Why should I name
Thee, Penn, the Solon of our western lands;
Sagacious legislator, whom the world
Admires, and mourns: an infant colony,
Nurs'd by thy care, now rises o'er the rest
Like that tall Pyramid in Egypt's waste
O'er all thy neighbouring piles, they also great.
Why should I name these heroes so well known,
Who peopled all the rest from Canada
To Georgia's farthest coasts, West Florida,
Or Apalachian mountains?—Yet what streams
Of blood were shed! what Indian hosts were slain,
Before these days of peace were quite restor'd!

        Leander.

Yes, while they overturn'd the rugged soil
And swept the forests from the shaded plain
'Midst dangers, foes, and death, fierce Indian tribes
With vengeful malice arm'd, and black design,
Oft murder'd or dispers'd these colonies—
Encourag'd, too, by Gallia's hostile sons,
A warlike race, who late their arms display'd
At *Quebec, Montreal,* and farthest coasts
Of *Labrador,* or *Cape Breton,* where now
The British standard awes the subject host.
Here, those brave chiefs, who, lavish of their blood,
Fought in Britannia's cause, in battle fell!—
What heart but mourns the untimely fate of *Wolfe,*
Who, dying, conquer'd!—or what breast but beats
To share a fate like his, and die like him!

        Acasto.

But why alone commemorate the dead,
And pass these glorious heroes by, who yet
Breathe the same air, and see the light with us?—
The dead, Leander, are but empty names,
And they who fall to-day the same to us
As they who fell ten centuries ago—!
Lost are they all that shin'd on earth before;
Rome's boldest champions in the dust are laid,
Ajax and great Achilles are no more,
And *Philip's* warlike son, an empty shade!—
A WASHINGTON among our sons of fame
We boast—conspicuous as the morning star
Among the inferior lights—
To distant wilds Virginia sent him forth—   [1755.
With her brave sons he gallantly oppos'd
The bold invaders of his country's rights,
Where wild *Ohio* pours the mazy flood,
And mighty meadows skirt these subject streams.—
But now, delighting in his elm tree's shade
Where deep *Potowmac* laves the enchanting shore,
He prunes the tender vine, or bids the soil
Luxuriant harvests to the sun display.—
   BEHOLD a different scene—not thus employ'd

Were *Cortez* and *Pizarro,* pride of Spain,
Whom blood and murder only satisfy'd,
And all to glut ambition!—

        Eugenio.

Such is the curse, Acasto, where the soul
Humane is wanting—but we boast no feats
Of cruelty like Europe's murdering breed—
Our milder epithet is merciful,
And each American, true hearted, learns
To conquer, and to spare; for coward souls
Alone seek vengeance on a vanquish'd foe.
Gold, fatal gold, was the alluring bait
To Spain's rapacious tribe—hence rose the wars
From Chili to the Caribbean sea,
Amd Montezuma's Mexican domains:
More blest are we, with whose unenvied soil
Nature decreed no mingling gold to shine,
No flaming diamond, precious emerald,
No blushing sapphire, ruby, chrysalite,
Or jasper red—more noble riches flow
From agriculture, and the industrious swain,
Who tills the fertile vale, or mountain's brow,
Content to lead a safe, a humble life
Among his native hills, romantic shades
Such as the Muse of Greece of old did feign,
Allur'd the Olympian gods from chrystal skies,
Envying such lovely scenes to mortal man.

        Leander.

Long has the rural life been justly fam'd,
And bards of old their pleasing pictures drew
Of flowery meads, and groves, and gliding streams:
Hence, old Arcadia—wood-nymphs, satyrs,
   swains;
And hence Elysium, fancied heaven below!—
Fair agriculture, not unworthy kings,
Once exercis'd the royal hand, or those
Whose virtues rais'd them to the rank of gods.
See old *Laertes*[3] in his shepherd weeds
Far from his pompous throne and court august,
Digging the grateful soil, where round him rise,
Sons of the earth, the tall aspiring oaks,
Or orchards boasting of more fertile boughs,
Laden with apples red, sweet scented peach,
Pear, cherry, apricot, or spungy plumb;
While through the glebe the industrious oxen draw
The earth-inverting plough.—Those Romans too,
Fabricius and Camillus, lov'd a life
Of neat simplicity and rustic bliss,
And from the noisy Forum hastening far,
From busy camps, and sycochants, and crowns,
'Midst woods and fields spent the remains of *life,*
Which full enjoyment only finds for fools.
   HOW grateful, to behold the harvests rise,

And mighty crops adorn the extended plains!—
Fair plenty smiles throughout, while lowing herds
Stalk o'er the shrubby hill or grassy mead,
Or at some shallow river slake their thirst.—
The inclosure now succeeds the shepherd's care,
Yet milk-white flocks adorn the well stock'd farm,
And court the attention of the industrious swain—
Their fleece rewards him well; and when the winds
Blow with a keener blast, and from the north
Pour mingled tempests through a sunless sky
(Ice, sleet, and rattling hail) secure he sits
Warm in his cottage, fearless of the storm,
Enjoying now the toils of milder moons,
Yet hoping for the spring.—Such are the joys,
And such the toils of those whom heaven hath
    bless'd
With souls enamour'd of a country life.

                    Acasto.

Such are the visions of the rustic reign—
But this alone, the fountain of support,
Would scarce employ the varying mind of man;
Each seeks employ, and each a different way:
Strip Commerce of her sail, and men once more
Would be converted into savages—
No nation e'er grew social and refin'd
Till Commerce first had wing'd the adventurous
    prow,
Or sent the slow-pac'd caravan afar,
To waft their produce to some other clime,
And bring the wish'd exchange—thus came, of old,
Golconda's golden ore, and thus the wealth
Of *Ophir* to the wisest of mankind.

                    Eugenio.

Great is the praise of commerce, and the men
Deserve our praise, who spread the undaunted sail,
And traverse every sea—their dangers great,
Death still to combat in the unfeeling gale,
And every billow but a gaping grave:—
There, skies and waters, wearying on the eye,
For weeks and months no other prospect yield
But barren wastes, unfathom'd depths, where not
The blessful haunt of human form is seen
To chear the unsocial horrors of the way—
Yet all these bold designs to Science owe
Their rise and glory—Hail, fair Science! thou,
Transplanted from the eastern skies, dost bloom
In these blest regions—Greece and Rome no more
Detain the Muses on *Cithaeron's* brow
Or old *Olympus,* crown'd with waving woods,
Or *Haemus'* top, where once was heard the harp,
Sweet *Orpheus'* harp, that gain'd his cause below,
And pierc'd the heart of Orcus and his bride;
That hush'd to silence by its voice divine

Thy melancholy waters, and the gales
O *Hebrus!* that o'er thy sad surface blow.—
No more the maids round Alpheus' waters stray,
Where he with *Arethusa's* wave doth mix,
Or where swift *Tiber* disembogues his waves
Into the Italian sea, so long unsung;
Hither they wing their way, the last the best
Of countries, where the arts shall rise and grow,
And arms shall have their day—Even now we boast
A *Franklin,* prince of all philosophy,
A genius piercing as the electric fire,
Bright as the lightning's flash, explain'd so well
By him, the rival of Britannia's sage[4].—
This is a land of every joyous sound,
Of liberty and life, sweet liberty!
Without whose aid the noblest genius fails,
And Science irretrievably must die.

                    Leander.

But come, Eugenio, since we know the past—
What hinders to pervade with searching eye
The mystic scenes of dark Futurity!
Say, shall we ask what empires yet must rise,
What kingdoms, powers, and STATES, where now
    are seen
Mere dreary wastes and awful solitude,
Where melancholy sits, with eye forlorn,
And time anticipates, when we shall spread
Dominion from the north, and south, and west,
Far from the Atlantic to Pacific shores,
And shackle half the convex of the main!—
A glorious theme!—but now shall mortals dare
To pierce the dark events of future years
And scenes unravel, only known to fate?

                    Acasto.

This might we do, if warm'd by that bright coal
Snatch'd from the altar of cherubic fire
Which touch'd Isaiah's lips—or of the spirit
Of Jeremy and Amos, prophets old,
Might swell the heaving breast—I see, I see
A thousand kingdoms rais'd, cities, and men,
Numerous as sand upon the ocean shore!—
The *Ohio* soon shall glide by many a town
Of note; and where the *Missisippi* stream,
By forests shaded, now runs weeping on,
Nations shall grow, and STATES not less in fame
Than Greece and Rome of old!—we too shall boast
Our Alexanders, Pompeys, heroes, kings,
That in the womb of time yet dormant lie,
Waiting the joyous hour of life and light—
O snatch me hence, ye muses, to those days
When through the veil of dark antiquity
Our sons shall hear of us as things remote,
That blossom'd in the morn of days—Alas!

How could I weep that we were born so soon,
Just in the dawning of these mighty times,
When scenes are pregnant with eternity!
Dissentions that shall swell the trump of fame,
And ruin brooding o'er one monarchy!

Eugenio.

Nor shall these angry tumults here subside
Nor murders[5] cease, through all these Provinces,
Till foreign crowns have vanish'd from our view
And dazzle here no more—no more presume
To awe the spirit of fair Liberty—
Vengeance shall cut the thread—and Britain, sure,
Will curse her fatal obstinacy for it!
Bent on the ruin of this injur'd country,
She will not listen to our humble prayers,
Though offer'd with submission.
Like vagabonds, and objects of destruction,
Like those whom all mankind are sworn to hate,
She casts us off from her protection,
And will invite the nations round about,
Russians and Germans, slaves and savages,
To come and have a share in our perdition—
O cruel race, O unrelenting Britain,
Who bloody beasts will hire to cut our throats,
Who war will wage with prattling innocence,
And basely murder unoffending women!—
Will stab their prisoners when they cry for quarter,
Will burn our towns, and from his lodging turn
The poor inhabitant to sleep in tempests!—
These will be wrongs; indeed, and all sufficient
To kindle up our souls to deeds of horror,
And give to every arm the nerves of *Sampson*—
These are the men that fill the world with ruin,
And every region mourns their greedy sway,
Nor only for ambition!—
But what are this world's goods, that *they* for them
Should exercise eternal butchery?
What are these mighty riches we possess,
That they should send so far to finger them—?—
Already have we felt their potent arm—
And ever since that inauspicious day,
When first Sir *Francis Bernard*
His canons planted at the *council door,*
And made the assembly room a home for strum-
    pets,
And soldiers rank and file—e'er since that day
This wretched land, that drinks its children's gore,
Has been a scene of tumult and confusion—!
Are there not evils in the world enough?
Are we so happy that they envy us?
Have we not toil'd to satisfy their Harpies,
King's deputies, that are insatiable;
Whose practice is to incense the royal mind,

And make us despicable in his view?—
Have we not all the evils to contend with
That, in this life, mankind are subject to,
Pain, sickness, poverty, and natural death—
But into every wound that nature gave
They will a dagger plunge, and make them mortal!

Leander.

Enough, enough—such dismal scenes you paint,
I almost shudder at the recollection—
What, are they dogs that they would mangle us?—
To brighter skies I turn my ravish'd view,
And fairer prospects from the future draw—
Here independent power shall hold her sway,
And public virtue warm the patriot breast:
No traces shall remain of tyranny,
And laws, a pattern to the world beside
Be here enacted first.—

Acasto.

And when a train of rolling years are past,
(So sung the exil'd seer in Patmos isle)
A new Jerusalem, sent down from heaven,
Shall grace our happy earth—perhaps this land,
Whose ample breast shall then receive, tho' late,
Myriads of saints, with their immortal king,
To live and reign on earth a thousand years,
Thence called *Millennium.* Paradise anew
Shall flourish, by no second Adam lost.
No dangerous tree with deadly fruit shall grow,
No tempting serpent to allure the soul
From native innocence.—A *Canaan* here,
Another *Canaan* shall excel the old,
And from a fairer *Pisgah's* top be seen.
No thistle here, nor thorn, nor briar shall spring,
Earth's curse before: The lion and the lamb
In mutual friendship link'd, shall browse the shrub,
And tim'rous deer with soften'd tygers stray
O'er mead, or lofty hill, or grassy plain:
Another Jordan's stream shall glide along,
And Siloah's brook in circling eddies flow:
Groves shall adorn their verdant banks, on which
The happy people, free from toils and death,
Shall find secure repose. No fierce disease,
No fevers, slow consumption, ghastly plague,
(Death's ancient ministers) again proclaim
Perpetual war with man: Fair fruits shall bloom,
Fair to the eye and grateful to the taste;
Nature's loud streams be hush'd, and seas no more
Rage hostile to mankind—and, worse than all,
The fiercer passions of the human breast
Shall kindle up to deeds of death no more,
But all subside in universal peace.—

    Such days the world,
And such, AMERICA, thou first shalt have,

When ages, yet to come, have run their round,
And future years of bliss alone remain.

1. Genesis x.25.

2. Hor. Epod. 16.

3. Hom. Odyss. B. 24.

4. Newton.

5. The massacre at Boston, March 5th, 1770, is here more particularly glanced at.

N.B. This Poem is a little altered from the original, (published in Philadelphia in 1772) such parts being only inserted here as were written by the author of these Volumes. A few more modern lines towards the conclusion are incorporated with the rest, being a supposed prophetical anticipation of subsequent events. [Philip Freneau]

Reprinted from *The Poems of Philip Freneau. Written Chiefly during the Late War* (Philadelphia: Printed by Francis Bailey, 1786).

Joel Barlow

The Prospect of Peace

The closing scenes of Tyrants' fruitless rage,
    The opening prospects of a golden age,
The dread events that crown th' important year,
Wake the glad song, and claim th' attentive ear.
    Long has Columbia rung with dire alarms,
While Freedom call'd her injur'd sons to arms;
While various fortune fir'd th' embattled field,
Conquest delay'd, and victory stood conceal'd;
While closing legions mark'd their dreadful way,
And Millions trembled for the dubious day.
    In this grand conflict heaven's Eternal Sire,
At whose dread frown the sons of guilt expire.
Bade vengeance rise, with sacred fury driven,
On those who war with Innocence and Heaven.
    Behold, where late the trembling squadrons
    fled,
Hosts bow'd in chains, and hapless numbers bled,
In different fields our numerous heroes rouse,
To crop the wreath from Britain's impious brows.
    Age following age shall these events relate
'Till Time's old empire yield to destin'd Fate;
Historic truth our guardian chiefs proclaim,
Their worth, their actions, and their deathless
    fame;
Admiring crouds their life-touch'd forms behold
In breathing canvass, or in sculptur'd gold,
And hail the Leader of the favorite throng,
The rapt'rous theme of some heroic song.
    And soon, emerging from the orient skies,
The blisful morn in glorious pomp shall rise,
Wafting fair Peace from Europe's fated coast;
Where wand'ring long, in mazy factions lost,
From realm to realm, by rage and discord driven,
She seem'd resolv'd to reascend her heaven.
    This LEWIS view'd, and reach'd a friendly
    hand,
Pointing her flight to this far-distant land;
Bade her extend her empire o'er the West,
And Europe's balance tremble on her crest!
    Now, see the Goddess mounting on the day,
To these fair climes direct her circling way,
Willing to seek, once more, an earthly throne,
To cheer the globe, and emulate the sun.
With placid look she eyes the blissful shore,
Bids the loud-thundering cannon cease to roar;
Bids British navies from these ports be tost,
And hostile keels no more insult the coast;
Bids private feuds her sacred vengeance feel,

And bow submissive to the public weal;
Bids long, calm years adorn the happy clime,
And roll down blessings to remotest time.
    Hail! heaven-born Peace, fair Nurse of Virtue
    hail!
Here, fix thy sceptre and exalt thy scale;
Hence, thro' the earth extend thy late domain,
'Till Heaven's own splendor shall absorb thy
    reign!
    What scenes arise! what glories we behold!
See a broad realm its various charms unfold;
See crouds of patriots bless the happy land,
A godlike senate and a warlike band;
One friendly Genius fires the numerous whole,
From glowing Georgia to the frozen pole.
    Along these shores, amid these flowery vales,
The woodland shout the joyous ear assails;
Industrious crouds in different labors toil,
Those ply the arts, and these improve the soil.
Here the fond merchant counts his rising gain,
There strides the rustic o'er the furrow'd plain,
Here walks the statesman, pensive and serene,
And there the school boys gambol round the
    green.
    See ripening harvests gild the smiling plains,
Kind Nature's bounty and the pride of swains;
Luxuriant vines their curling tendrils shoot,
And bow their heads to drop the clustering fruit;
In the gay fields, with rich profusion strow'd,
The orchard bends beneath its yellow load,
The lofty boughs their annual burden pour,
And juicy harvests swell th' autumnal store.
    These are the blessings of impartial Heaven,
To each fond heart in just proportion given.
No grasping lord shall grind the neighbouring
    poor,
Starve numerous vassals to increase his store;
No cringing slave shall at his presence bend,
Shrink at his frown, and at his nod attend;
Afric's unhappy children, now no more
Shall feel the cruel chains they felt before,
But every State in this just mean agree,
To bless mankind, and set th' oppressed free.
Then, rapt in transport, each exulting slave
Shall taste that Boon which God and nature gave,
And, fir'd with virtue, join the common cause,
Protect our freedom and enjoy our laws.
    At this calm period, see, in pleasing view,

Art vies with Art, and Nature smiles anew:
On the long, winding strand that meets the tide,
Unnumber'd cities lift their spiry pride;
Gay, flowery walks salute th' inraptur'd eyes,
Tall, beauteous domes in dazzling prospect rise;
There thronging navies stretch their wanton
   sails,
Tempt the broad main and catch the driving
   gales;
There commerce swells from each remotest
   shore,
And wafts in plenty to the smiling store.
     To these throng'd seats the country wide
   resorts,
And rolls her treasures to the op'ning ports;
While, far remote, gay health and pleasure flow,
And calm retirement cheers the laboring brow.
No din of arms the peaceful patriot hears,
No parting sigh the tender matron fears,
No field of fame invites the youth to rove,
Nor virgins know a harsher sound than love.
     Fair Science then her laurel'd beauty rears,
And soars with Genius to the radiant stars.
Her glimmering dawn from Gothic darkness
   rose,
And nations saw her shadowy veil disclose;
She cheer'd fair Europe with her rising smiles,
Beam'd a bright morning o'er the British isles,
Now soaring reaches her meridian height,
And blest Columbia hails the dazzling light!
     Here, rapt in tho't, the philosophic soul
Shall look thro' Nature's parts and grasp the
   whole.
See Genius kindling at a FRANKLIN's fame,
See unborn sages catch th' electric flame,
Bid hovering clouds the threatening blast expire,
Curb the fierce stream and hold th' imprison'd
   fire!
     See the pleas'd youth, with anxious study, rove,
In orbs excentric thro' the realms above,
No more perplex'd, while RITTENHOUSE appears
To grace the museum with the rolling spheres.
     See that young Genius, that inventive soul,
Whose laws the jarring elements control;
Who guides the vengeance of mechanic power,
To blast the watery world & guard the peaceful
   shore.
     And where's the rising Sage, the unknown
   name,
That new advent'rer in the lists of fame,
To find the cause, in secret nature bound,
The unknown cause, and various charms of
   sound?

What subtil medium leads the devious way;
Why different tensions different sounds convey;
Why harsh, rough tones in grating discord roll,
Or mingling concert charms th' enraptur'd soul.
     And tell the cause why sluggish vapors rise,
And wave, exalted, thro' the genial skies;
What strange contrivance nature forms to bear
The ponderous burden thro' the lighter air.
     These last Displays the curious mind engage,
And fire the genius of the rising age;
While moral tho'ts the pleas'd attention claim,
Swell the warm soul, and wake the virtuous flame;
While Metaphysics soar a boundless height,
And launch with EDWARDS to the realms of light.
     See the blest Muses hail their roseate bowers,
Their mansions blooming with poetic flowers;
See listening Seraphs join the epic throng,
And unborn JOSHUAS rise in future song.
     Satire attends at Virtue's wakening call,
And Pride and Coquetry and Dulness fall.
     Unnumber'd bards shall string the heavenly
   lyre,
To those blest strains which heavenly themes
   inspire;
Sing the rich Grace on mortal Man bestow'd,
The Virgin's Offspring and the *filial God;*
What love descends from heaven when JESUS dies!
What shouts attend him rising thro' the skies!
     See Science now in lovelier charms appear,
Grac'd with new garlands from the blooming
   Fair.
See laurel'd nymphs in polish'd pages shine,
And Sapphic sweetness glow in every line.
No more the rougher Muse shall dare disgrace
The radiant charms that deck the blushing face;
But rising Beauties scorn the tinsel show,
The powder'd coxcomb and the flaunting beau;
While humble Merit, void of flattering wiles,
Claims the soft glance, and wakes th' enlivening
   smiles.
The opening lustre of an angel-mind,
Beauty's bright charms with sense superior
   join'd,
Bid Virtue shine, bid Truth and Goodness rise,
Melt from the voice, and sparkle from the eyes;
While the pleas'd Muse the gentle bosom warms,
The first in genius, as the first in charms.
Thus age and youth a smiling aspect wear,
Aw'd into virtue by the leading Fair;
While the bright offspring, rising to the stage,
Conveys the blessings to the future age.
     THESE are the views that Freedom's cause
   attend;

THESE shall endure 'till Time and Nature end.
With Science crown'd, shall Peace and Virtue shine,
And blest Religion beam a light divine.
Here the pure Church, descending from her God,
Shall fix on earth her long and last abode;
Zion arise, in radiant splendors dress'd,
By Saints admir'd, by Infidels confess'd;
Her opening courts, in dazzling glory, blaze,
Her walls salvation, and her portals praise.

    From each far corner of th' extended earth,
Her gathering sons shall claim their promis'd birth.
Thro' the drear wastes, beneath the setting day,
Where prowling natives haunt the wood for prey,
The swarthy Millions lift their wondring eyes,
And smile to see the Gospel morning rise:
Those who, thro' time, in savage darkness lay,
Wake to new light, and hail the glorious day!
In those dark regions, those uncultur'd wilds,
Fresh blooms the rose, the peaceful lilly smiles.
On the tall cliffs unnumber'd *Carmels* rise,
And in each vale some beauteous *Sharon* lies.

    From this fair Mount th' excinded stone shall roll,
Reach the far East and spread from pole to pole;
From one small Stock shall countless nations rise,
The world replenish and adorn the skies.
Earth's blood-stain'd empires, with their Guide the Sun,
From orient climes their gradual progress run;
And circling far, reach every western shore,
'Till earth-born empires rise and fall no more.
But see th' imperial GUIDE from heaven descend,
Whose beams are Peace, whose kingdom knows no end;

From calm Vesperia, thro' th' etherial way,
Back sweep the shades before th' effulgent day;
Thro' the broad East, the brightening splendor driven,
Reverses Nature and illumins heaven;
Astonish'd regions bless the gladdening sight,
And Suns and Systems own superior light.

    As when th' asterial blaze o'er Bethl'em stood,
Which mark'd the birth-place of th' incarnate God;
When eastern priests the heavenly splendor view'd,
And numerous crouds the wonderous sign pursu'd:
So eastern kings shall view th' unclouded day
Rise in the West and streak its golden way:
That signal spoke a Savior's humble birth,
This speaks his long and glorious reign on earth!

    THEN Love shall rule, and Innocence adore,
Discord shall cease, and Tyrants be no more;
'Till yon bright orb, and those celestial spheres,
In radiant circles, mark a thousand years;
'Till the grand *fiat* burst th' etherial frames,
Worlds crush on worlds, and Nature sink in flames!
The Church elect, from smouldering ruins, rise,
And sail triumphant thro' the yielding skies,
Hail'd by the Bridegroom! to the Father given,
The Joy of Angels, and the Queen of Heaven!

Reprinted from *The Prospect of Peace. A Poetical Composition, Delivered in Yale-College, At the Public Examination, of the Candidates for the Degree of Bachelor of Arts; July 23, 1778* (New Haven: Printed by Thomas & Samuel Green, 1778).

Timothy Dwight

America: or, a Poem on the Settlement of the British Colonies

From Sylvan Shades, cool bowers and fragrant
  gales,
    Green hills and murm'ring Streams and
  flowery vales,
My soul ascends of nobler themes to sing;
AMERICA shall wake the sounding string.
Accept, my native Land, these humble lays,
This grateful song, a tribute to thy praise.
    When first mankind o'er-spread great ASIA's
  lands,
And nations rose unnumber'd as the sands,
From eastern shores, where AMOUR rolls his
  streams,
And morning suns display their earliest beams,
TARTARS in millions, swarming on the day,
Thro' the vast western ocean steer'd their way;
From east to west, from north to south they roll,
And whelm the fields from DARIEN to the pole.
    Sunk in barbarity, these realms were found,
And Superstition hung her clouds around;
O'er all, impenetrable Darkness spread
Her dusky wings, and cast a dreadful shade;
No glimpse of science through the gloom appear'd;
No trace of civil life the desert chear'd;
No soft endearments, no fond social ties,
Nor faith, nor justice calm'd their horrid joys:
But furious Vengeance swell'd the hellish mind,
And dark-ey'd Malice all her influence join'd.
Here spread broad plains, in blood and slaughter
  drown'd;
There boundless forests nodded o'er the ground;
Here ceaseless riot and confusion rove;
There savage roarings shake the echoing grove.
Age after age rolls on in deepening gloom,
Dark as the mansions of the silent tomb.
Thus wasting Discord, like an angry sea,
Swept mighty kings and warring worlds away,
And (ages past) succeeding times beheld
The same dire ruin clothe the dreary field.
    At length (COLUMBUS taught by heaven to
  trace
Far-distant lands, through unknown pathless seas)
AMERICA's bright realms arose to view,
And the *old* world rejoic'd to see the *new*.
    When blest ELIZA rul'd th' ATLANTIC main,
And her bold navies humbled haughty SPAIN;
Heaven sent undaunted RALEIGH, ENGLAND's
  pride,

To waft her children o'er the briny tide,
In fair VIRGINIA's fields to fix her throne,
And stretch her sway beneath the falling sun.
    Then CHARLES and LAUD usurp'd despotic
  powers,
And Persecution sadden'd ALBION's shores;
With racks and flames, Religion spread her sway,
BRITONS were learn'd to torture, laws t'obey.
    Forc'd from the pleasures of their native soil,
Where Liberty had lighten'd every toil;
Forc'd from the arms of friends and kindred dear,
With scarce the comfort of one parting tear,
Whilst wives clung round and took a final gaze,
And reverend sires prolong'd the last embrace;
To these far-distant climes our fathers came,
Where blest NEW-ENGLAND boasts a parent's name.
With Freedom's fire their gen'rous bosoms glow'd,
Warm for the truth, and zealous for their GOD;
With these, the horrors of the desart ceas'd;
Without them, ALBION less than desarts pleas'd;
By these inspir'd, their zeal unshaken stood,
And bravely dar'd each danger—to be good;
Th' unfathom'd ocean, roll'd in mighty storms,
Want and Disease in all their dreadful forms,
The freezing blast that roar'd through boundless
  snows,
And War fierce-threat'ning from surrounding foes.
    Yet here Contentment dwelt, and Pleasure
  smil'd,
And rough-brow'd Labour every care beguil'd,
Made fruitful gardens round the forests rise,
And calm'd the horrors of the dreary skies.
    PENN led a peaceful train to that kind clime,
Where Nature wantons in her liveliest prime,
Where mighty *Del'ware* rolls his silver tide,
And fertile fields adorn the river's side.
Peace rul'd his life; to peace his laws inspir'd;
In peace the willing savages retir'd.
The dreary Wilderness, with glad surprise,
Saw spacious towns and golden harvests rise.
    Brave OGLETHROPE in GEORGIA fix'd his seat,
And deep distress there found a calm retreat;
Learning and life to orphans there were given,
And drew down blessings from approving heaven.
    Happy they liv'd, while Peace maintain'd her
  sway,
And taught the furious savage to obey,
Whilst Labour fearless rear'd the nodding grain,

And Innocence securely trod the plain:
But soon, too soon, were spread the dire alarms,
And thousand painted nations rush'd to arms,
War's kindled flames blaz'd dreadful round the
    shore,
And hills and plains with blood were crimson'd o'er,
Where late the flocks rov'd harmless on the green,
Where rising towns and cultur'd fields were seen,
Illimitable desarts met the eye,
And smoking ruins mounted to the sky.
      Oft when deep silent Night her wings had
    spread,
And the vast world lay hid in peaceful shade,
In some lone village mirth led on the hours,
And swains secure to sleep resign'd their powers;
Sudden the fields resound with war's alarms,
And earth re-echoes—arms, to arms, to arms;
Faint through the gloom the murd'ring bands are
    seen;
Disploded thunder shakes the darksome green;
Broad streams of fire from falling structures rise,
And shrieks and groans and shouts invade the
    skies:
Here weeping mothers piercing anguish feel;
There smiles the babe beneath the lifted steel;
Here vig'rous youth from bloody vengeance flies;
There white-hair'd age just looks to heaven, and
    dies.
      The sons of GAUL in yonder northern lands
Urg'd the keen sword and fir'd the painted bands;
Priests, cloath'd in Virtue's garb, destruction
    spread,
And pious fury heap'd the fields with dead.
      Rous'd by increasing woes, our fires bade
    found
The trump of war, and squadrons gather'd round,
Where LOUISBOURG, adorn'd with towering spires,
Defy'd the terror of the BRITISH fires;
Bands, who ne'er heard the thundring cannon's
    roar,
Nor met a foe, nor view'd a wall before,
By Freedom warm'd, with native brav'ry crown'd,
Bade her proud towers be humbled to the ground.
E'en Heaven itself approv'd a war so just;
In Heaven let injur'd nations put their trust.
      Yet still destruction spread around the shore,
And the dire savage bath'd in BRITISH gore,
'Till WOLFE appear'd and led his freeborn bands,
Like a dark tempest to yon GALLIC lands:
Then shook Quebec at his exalted name,
And her high walls already seem'd to flame.
Lo! where deep forests roar with loud alarms,
Th' exalted hero shines in blazing arms;
His squadrons, rolling like the billow'd main,

Dart a bright horror o'er th' embattl'd plain;
Whilst from ascending domes and lofty towers
Pale quivering thousands view the hostile powers.
The BRITISH host, stretch'd out in dark array,
Rush fearless on and sweep their foes away;
From smoky volumes rapid flames aspire,
And bursting cannon set the fields on fire;
Fate swells the sound; whole troops of heroes fall;
And one unbounded ruin buries all.
      As o'er the western dark clouds arise,
Involve the sun and blacken all the skies;
The whirlwinds roar; heaven's awful thunders roll,
And streamy lightnings flash around the pole;
Descending floods along the meadows flow,
And bursting torrents whelm the world below.
      Then glorious AMHERST joins his utmost force,
And tow'rd CANADIA's realms inclines his course;
Immense destruction marks his dreadful way,
And smoking towns spread terror on the day;
O'er all the land one boundless waste is seen,
And blazing hills and gloomy streams between.
The voice of Desolation fills the gales,
And boding Horror sighs along the vales;
Deep in the woods the *savage* world retires,
Far from the thunder and the wasting fires.
At length these realms the BRITISH scepter own,
And bow submissive at great GEORGE's throne.
      Almighty GOD of heaven! thy wondrous ways
Demand loud anthems and eternal praise.
Through earth, through heaven's immeasurable
    rounds,
Thy Greatness beams; thy being knows no bounds.
E'er Time began, unbounded and alone,
Beyond the vast of space thy Glory shone;
'Till that great moment when th' almighty call
From endless darkness wak'd this earthly ball:
Then Being heard his voice, and round the sky
Glow'd the bright worlds, which gild the realms on
    high;
Time then appear'd; the Seasons deck'd his train,
And Hours and Years danc'd joyous o'er the plain;
Millions of morning stars JEHOVAH sung,
And the whole universe with praises rung.
      Yon world of fire, that gives a boundless day,
From thy effulgence darts the burning ray.
Thou bid'st yon starry flames adorn the pole;
Thy word ordains, and circling seasons roll:
At thy command awakes the lovely Spring;
Beauty breaks forth; the hills with music ring:
In Summer's fiercer blaze thy thunders roar;
Nature attends, and trembling realms adore:
When Autumn shines, thy fruits bedeck the plain,
And plenteous harvests joy the humble swain:
On Wintry winds thine awful chariot flies,

When gath'ring storms envelope all the skies;
On Glory thron'd, with flames about thee roll'd;
Light forms thy robes, and clouds thy wheels infold;
Around, ten thousand sparkling angels glow,
Brighten the heavens, and shake the world below.

At thy command, war glitters o'er the plain;
Thou speak'st—and peace revives the fields again,
Vaft empires rise, and cities gild the day;
Thou frown'st—and kings and kingdoms melt
away.
BRITANNIA's happy islands, rais'd by Thee,
Awe the wide world, and rule the boundless sea;
Led by thine arm, WOLFE humbled haughty GAUL,
And glorious AMHERST taught her pride to fall.
May this blest land with grateful praise adore
Such boundless goodness, and such boundless
power.

See heaven-born Peace, descending from the
sky,
Bids discord vanish, and her horrors fly;
The wearied nations hear her gentle voice,
Own her glad sway, and wish for milder joys;
Swift o'er the land, the blissful tidings ring,
The vallies brighten and the nations sing.

As when long night has dwelt on ZEMBLA's
shore,
Where winter reigns, and storms around him roar,
Soon as the rising sun begins to roll,
And gild with fainter beams the frozen pole,
The streams dissolve, the fields no longer mourn,
And raptur'd regions hail his glad return.

Where once dark Superstition fix'd her throne;
Where soul-exalting science never shone;
Where every social joy was drown'd in blood;
Where Hunger ceaseless rang'd the groves for
food;
Where no gay fruits adorn'd the dreary plain;
No mountains brighten'd with the teeming grain;
No flocks nor herds along the hills were seen,
Nor swains nor hamlets chear'd the lonely green:
See num'rous infant slates begin to grow;
See every state with peace and plenty flow;
See splendid towns o'er all the land extend;
The temples glitter and the spires ascend.
The rip'ning harvest waves along the hills,
The orchard blossoms, and the pasture smiles.
Unnumber'd vessels skim the liquid plain,
Search every realm, that hears the roaring main,
And fill'd with treasures, bid our shores behold
The eastern spices and the southern gold.

Celestial science, raptur'd we descry
Refulgent beaming o'er the western sky;
Bright Liberty extends her blissful reign,
With all the graces sparkling in her train:

Religion shines with a superiour blaze,
And heaven-born virtue beams diviner rays;
Justice enthron'd maintains an equal sway,
The poor dwell safely, and the proud obey.

O Land supremely blest! to thee tis given
To taste the choicest joys of bounteous heaven;
Thy rising Glory shall expand its rays,
And lands and times unknown rehearse thine end-
less praise.

As in a lonely vale, with glooms o'erspread,
Retir'd I rov'd, where guiding fancy led,
Deep silence reign'd; a sudden stream of light
Flam'd through the darksome grove & chear'd the
night;
An awful form advanc'd along the ground,
And circling glories cast a radiance round:
Her face divine with sparkling brightness shone
Like the clear splendour of the mid-day sun;
Robes of pure white her heavenly limbs infold,
And on her scepter FREEDOM blaz'd in gold.
"Mortal! attend" (she laid [*sic*] and smil'd sublime)
Borne down the stream of ever rolling time,
View the bright scenes which wait this happy shore,
Her virtue, wisdom, arts and glorious power."

"I see, where Discord thund'ring from afar,
Sounds her shrill trump and wakes the flames of
war;
Rous'd by her voice, vast hosts together driven,
Shake the wide earth, rend air, and darken heaven:
The cannons roar, the fields are heap'd with slain,
And storms of fire are blown along the plain."

"Behold! my Heroes lead the glorious way,
Where warring millions roll in dread array,
Awful as Angels, thron'd on streams of fire,
When trembling nations feel the thund'rer's ire:
Before them, Terror wings the rapid flight,
And Death behind them shrouds whole realms in
night."

"Then, white-rob'd Peace begins her milder
reign,
And all the virtues croud her lovely train.
Lo! heaven-born Science every bosom warms,
And the fair Arts unveil their lovely charms."

"See! blest Philosophy inspires the soul
To roam from land to land, from pole to pole;
To soar beyond the sun, to worlds on high,
Which roll in millions round th' unmeasur'd sky;
To mark the comet thro' his pathless maze,
Whilst his bright glories set the heavens on blaze."

"Her nobler Sister too shall charm the mind
With moral raptures and with truths refin'd;
Religion lead whole realms to worlds of joy,
Undying peace and bliss without alloy."

"See Hist'ry all the scenes of time unveil

And bid my sons attend her wondrous tale!
Led by her voice, behold them mount the throne
And stretch their sway to regions yet unknown!"
　"See all the powers of Poetry unite
To paint Religion's charms divinely bright;
To sing his name, who made yon orbs of fire,
Spread out the sky and form'd th' angelic choir:
Seraphs themselves inspire the sacred lays,
And stoop from heaven to hear their Maker's
　　praise!"
　"See Sculpture mould the rude unpolish'd
　　stone,
Give it new forms and beauties not its own;
Bid the gay marble leap to life and breath,
And call up heroes from the realms of Death!"
　"Behold the canvas glow with living dies,
Tall groves shoot up, streams wind and mountains
　　rise!
Again the fair unfolds a heaven of charms,
And the bold leader frowns in dreadful arms."
　"Then Eloquence soft pity shall inspire,
Smooth the rough breast, or set the soul on fire;
Teach guilt to tremble at th' Almighty name,
Unsheath his sword and make his lightnings
　　flame;
Or reach out grace more mild than falling dews,
While pale Despair th' affrighted soul pursues."
　"Hail Land of light and joy! thy power shall
　　grow
Far as the seas, which round thy regions flow;
Through earth's wide realms thy glory shall
　　extend,
And savage nations at thy scepter bend.
Around the frozen shores thy sons shall sail,
Or stretch their canvas to the ASIAN gale,
Or, like COLUMBUS, steer their course unknown,
Beyond the regions of the flaming zone,
To worlds unfound beneath the southern pole,
Whose native hears Antarctic oceans roll;
Where artless Nature rules with peaceful sway,
And where no ship e'er stemm'd the untry'd
　　way."
　"For thee, proud INDIA's spicy isles shall blow,
Bright silks be wrought, and sparkling diamonds
　　glow;

Earth's richest realms their treasures shall
　　unfold,
And op'ning mountains yield the flaming gold;
Round thy broad fields more glorious ROMES arise,
With pomp and splendour bright'ning all the
　　skies;
EUROPE and ASIA with surprize behold
Thy temples starr'd with gems and roof'd with
　　gold.
From realm to realm broad APPIAN ways shall
　　wind,
And distant shores by long canals be join'd,
The ocean hear thy voice, the waves obey,
And through green vallies trace their wat'ry way.
No more shall War her fearful horrors sound,
Nor strew her thousands on th' embattled
　　ground;
No more on earth shall Rage and Discord dwell,
But sink with Envy to their native hell."
　"Then, then an heavenly kingdom shall de-
　　scend,
And Light and Glory through the world extend;
Th' Almighty Saviour his great power display
From rising morning to the setting day;
Love reign triumphant, Fraud and Malice cease,
And every region smile in endless peace:
Till the last trump the slumbering dead inspire,
Shake the wide heavens, and set the world on fire;
Thron'd on a flaming cloud, with brightness
　　crown'd,
The Judge descend, and angels shine around,
The mountains melt, the moon and stars decay,
The sun grow dim, and Nature roll away;
GOD's happy children mount to worlds above,
Drink streams of purest joy and taste immortal
　　love."

Reprinted from *America: or, a Poem on the Settlement of the British Colonies; Addressed To the Friends of Freedom, and their Country* (New Haven: Printed by Thomas & Samuel Green, 1780?).

Supplementary Reading List

Adair, Douglass. *Fame and the Founding Fathers,* edited by H. Trevor Colbourn. New York: Norton, 1974.

Ahlstrom, Sydney E. *A Religious History of the American People.* New Haven & London: Yale University Press, 1972.

Albanese, Catherine L. *Sons of the Fathers: The Civil Religion of the American Revolution.* Philadelphia: Temple University Press, 1976.

Aldridge, Alfred Owen, ed. *The Ibero-American Enlightenment.* Urbana: University of Illinois Press, 1971.

Appleby, Joyce Oldham. "The Social Origins of American Revolutionary Ideology," *Journal of American History,* 64 (March 1978): 935-958.

Arieli, Yehoshua. *Individualism and Nationalism in American Ideology.* Cambridge: Harvard University Press, 1964.

Bailyn, Bernard. *Education in the Forming of American Society.* Chapel Hill: University of North Carolina Press, 1960.

Bailyn. "Political Experience and Enlightenment Ideas in Eighteenth Century America," *American Historical Review,* 67 (January 1962): 339-351.

Bailyn. "Religion and Revolution: Three Biographical Studies," *Perspectives in American History,* 4 (1970): 85-169.

Bailyn and John Clive. "England's Cultural Provinces: Scotland and America," third series 11 (April 1954): 200-213.

Baldwin, Alice M. *The New England Clergy and the American Revolution.* Durham: Duke University Press, 1928.

Baritz, Loren. *City on a Hill, A History of Ideas and Myths in America.* New York: Wiley, 1964.

Bercovitch, Sacvan. *The American Jeremiad.* Madison: University of Wisconsin Press, 1978.

Bercovitch. *The Puritan Origins of the American Self.* New Haven: Yale University Press, 1975.

Berens, John F. *Providence and Patriotism in Early America.* Charlottesville: University Press of Virginia, 1978.

Berk, Stephen E. *Calvinism versus Democracy: Timothy Dwight and the Origins of American Evangelical Orthodoxy.* Hamden, Conn.: Shoe String Press, 1974.

Bigelow, Gordon F. *Rhetoric and American Poetry of the Early National Period.* Gainesville: University of Florida Press, 1960.

Billias, George A., ed. *Law and Authority in Colonial America: Selected Essays.* Barre, Mass., 1965.

Boorstin, Daniel J. *The Americans: The National Experience.* New York: Random House, 1958.

Bridenbaugh, Carl. *Mitre and Sceptre: Transatlantic Faiths, Ideas, Personalities and Politics, 1689-1775*. New York: Oxford University Press, 1962.

Brooks, Van Wyck. *The World of Washington Irving*. New York: Dutton, 1944.

Brown, Herbert Ross. *The Sentimental Novel in America, 1789-1860*. Durham: Duke University Press, 1940.

Brumm, Ursula. *American Thought and Religious Typology*, translated by John Hooglund. New Brunswick: Rutgers University Press, 1970.

Buel, Richard. *Securing the Revolution: Ideology in American Politics, 1789-1815*. Ithaca: Cornell University Press, 1972.

Cady, Edwin H., ed. *Literature of the Early Republic*. New York: Holt, Rinehart & Winston, 1969.

Calhoun, Daniel. *Professional Lives in America: Structure and Aspiration, 1750-1850*. Cambridge: Harvard University Press, 1965.

Carroll, Peter N., ed. *Religion and the Coming of the American Revolution*. Waltham, Mass.: Blaisdell, 1970.

Charvat, William. *The Origins of American Critical Thought, 1810-1835*. Philadelphia: University of Pennsylvania Press/London: Oxford University Press, 1936.

Charvat. *The Profession of Authorship in America, 1800-1870*, edited by Matthew J. Bruccoli. Columbus: Ohio State University Press, 1968.

Cherry, Conrad. *Nature and Religious Imagination: From Edwards to Bushnell*. Philadelphia: Fortress, 1980.

Cherry, ed. *God's New Israel: Religious Interpretations of American Destiny*. Englewood Cliffs, N.J.: Prentice-Hall, 1971.

Colbourn, H. Trevor. *The Lamp of Experience: Whig History and the Intellectual Origins of the American Revolution*. Chapel Hill: University of North Carolina Press, 1965.

Colbourn, ed. *Fame and the Founding Fathers*. New York: Norton, 1974.

Commager, Henry Steele. *The Empire of Reason: How Europe Imagined and America Realized the Enlightenment*. Garden City: Doubleday, 1977.

Cott, Nancy. *The Bonds of Womanhood: "Women's Sphere" in New England, 1780-1835*. New Haven: Yale University Press, 1977.

Craven, Wesley Frank. *The Legend of the Founding Fathers*. New York: New York University Press, 1956.

Cronin, James E. "Elihu Hubbard Smith and the New York Friendly Club, 1795-1798," *PMLA*, 64 (June 1949): 471-479.

Crowley, J. E. *This Sheba, Self: The Conceptualization of Economic Life in Eighteenth-Century America*. Baltimore: Johns Hopkins University Press, 1974.

Davidson, Philip. *Propaganda and the American Revolution*. Chapel Hill: University of North Carolina Press, 1941.

Davies, Horton. *Worship and Theology in England,* volume 3: *From Watts and Wesley to Maurice, 1690-1850.* Princeton: Princeton University Press, 1961.

Davis, David Brion. *The Problem of Slavery in the Age of Revolution, 1770-1823.* Ithaca: Cornell University Press, 1975.

Davis, Richard Beale. *Intellectual Life of Jefferson's Virginia, 1790-1830.* Chapel Hill: University of North Carolina Press, 1964.

Davis. *Literature and Society in Early Virginia: 1608-1840.* Baton Rouge: Louisiana State University Press, 1973.

Elliott, Emory. "The Dove and the Serpent: The Clergy in the American Revolution," *American Quarterly,* 31 (Summer 1979): 192-197.

Elliott. *Revolutionary Writers: Literature and Authority in the New Republic.* New York: Oxford University Press, 1982.

Elliott, ed. *Puritan Influences in American Literature.* Urbana: University of Illinois, 1979.

Ellis, Joseph J. *After the Revolution: Profiles of Early American Culture.* New York: Norton, 1979.

Emerson, Everett H., ed. *American Literature, 1764-1789.* Madison: University of Wisconsin Press, 1977.

Emerson, ed. *Major Writers of Early American Literature.* Madison: University of Wisconsin Press, 1972.

Fischer, David Hackett. *The Revolution of American Conservatism: The Federalist Party in the Era of Jeffersonian Democracy.* New York: Harper & Row, 1965.

Free, William J. *The Columbian Magazine and American Literary Nationalism.* The Hague: Mouton, 1968.

Friedman, Lawrence J. *Inventors of the Promised Land: Patriotic Crusaders in the White Man's Country, 1786-1840.* New York: Knopf, 1975.

Fritz, Paul Samuel, and David Williams, eds. *The Triumph of Culture: 18th Century Perspectives.* Toronto: A. M. Hakkert, 1972.

Gay, Peter. *The Enlightenment: An Interpretation,* 2 volumes. New York: Knopf, 1966.

Gelpi, Albert J. *The Tenth Muse: The Psyche of the American Poet.* Cambridge: Harvard University Press, 1975.

Gilmore, Michael T., ed. *Early American Literature: A Collection of Critical Essays.* Englewood Cliffs, N.J.: Prentice-Hall, 1980.

Gipson, Lawrence Henry. *The Coming of the Revolution, 1763-1775.* New York: Harper, 1954.

Gohdes, Clarence L. F., ed. *Essays on American Literature in Honor of Jay B. Hubbell.* Durham: Duke University Press, 1967.

Granger, Bruce. *American Essay Serials from Franklin to Irving.* Knoxville: University of Tennessee Press, 1978.

Granger. *Political Satire in the American Revolution, 1763-1783.* New York: Cornell University Press, 1960.

Greene, Evarts B. *The Revolutionary Generation, 1763-1790*. New York: Macmillan, 1943.

Greene, Jack P. "Search for Identity: An Interpretation of the Meaning of Selected Patterns of Social Response in Eighteenth-Century America," *Journal of Social History*, 3 (Spring 1970): 189-220.

Greene. "An Uneasy Connection: An Analysis of the Precondition of the American Revolution," in *Essays on the American Revolution*, edited by Stephen G. Kurtz and James H. Hutson. Chapel Hill: University of North Carolina Press, 1973.

Greene, ed. *The Ambiguity of the American Revolution*. New York: Harper & Row, 1968.

Gummere, Richard M. *The American Colonial Mind and the Classical Tradition*. Cambridge: Harvard University Press, 1963.

Hatch, Nathan. *The Sacred Cause of Liberty: Republican Thought and the Millennium in Revolutionary New England*. New Haven: Yale University Press, 1977.

Hedges, William L. "Toward a Theory of American Literature," *Early American Literature*, 6 (1972): 26-38.

Heimert, Alan. *Religion and the American Mind from The Great Awakening to the Revolution*. Cambridge: Harvard University Press, 1966.

Howard, Leon. *The Connecticut Wits*. Chicago: University of Chicago Press, 1943.

Howard. "The Late Eighteenth Century: An Age of Contradictions," in *Transitions in American Literary History*, edited by Harry Hayden Clark. Durham: Duke University Press, 1953, pp. 51-89.

Howell, Wilbur Samuel. *Eighteenth-Century British Logic and Rhetoric*. Princeton: Princeton University Press, 1971.

Israel, Calvin, ed. *Discoveries & Considerations: Essays on Early American Literature & Aesthetics: Presented to Harold Jantz*. Albany: State University of New York Press, 1976.

Kagle, Steven E. *American Diary Literature: 1620-1799*. Boston: Twayne, 1979.

Kammen, Michael G. *People of Paradox: An Inquiry Concerning the Origins of American Civilization*. New York: Knopf, 1972.

Kammen. *A Season of Youth: The American Revolution and the Historical Imagination*. New York: Knopf, 1978.

Kerber, Linda K. *Federalists in Dissent: Imagery and Ideology in Jeffersonian America*. Ithaca: Cornell University Press, 1970.

Kerber. *Women in the Republic: Intellect and Ideology in Revolutionary America*. Chapel Hill: University of North Carolina Press, 1980.

Ketcham, Ralph L. *From Colony to Country: The Revolution in American Thought, 1750-1820*. New York: Macmillan, 1974.

Knollenberg, Bernhard. *Growth of the American Revolution: 1766-1775*. New York: Free Press, 1975.

Koch, Adrienne. *Power, Morals and the Founding Fathers*. Ithaca: Great Seal Books, 1961.

Koch, ed. *The American Enlightenment: The Shaping of the American Experiment and a Free Society.* New York: Braziller, 1965.

Krout, John Allen, and Dixon Ryan Fox. *The Completion of Independence, 1790-1830.* New York: Macmillan, 1944.

Leary, Lewis. *Soundings: Some Early American Writers.* Athens: University of Georgia Press, 1975.

Leder, Lawrence H., ed. *The Meaning of the American Revolution.* New York: Quadrangle, 1969.

Levin, David. *In Defense of Historical Literature.* New York: Hill & Wang, 1967.

Lockridge, Kenneth. *Literacy in Colonial New England.* New York: Norton, 1974.

Lowance, Mason I., Jr. *The Language of Canaan: Metaphor and Symbol in New England from the Puritans to the Transcendentalists.* Cambridge & London: Harvard University Press, 1980.

Lynen, John F. *The Design of the Present: Essays on Time and Form in American Literature.* New Haven: Yale University Press, 1969.

Maier, Pauline. *From Resistance to Revolution: Colonial Radicals and the Development of American Opposition to Britain, 1765-1776.* New York: Knopf, 1972.

Main, Jackson Turner. *The Social Structure of Revolutionary America.* Princeton: Princeton University Press, 1965.

Martin, Jay. "William Dunlap: The Documentary Vision," in *Theater und Drama in Amerika: Aspekte und Interpretationen,* edited by Edgar Lohner and Rudolf Hass. Berlin: E. Schmidt, 1978.

Martin, Terence. *The Instructed Vision: Scottish Common Sense Philosophy and the Origins of American Fiction.* Bloomington: Indiana University Press, 1961.

Marty, Martin E. *Righteous Empire: The Protestant Experience in America.* New York: Dial, 1970.

May, Henry F. *The Enlightenment in America.* New York: Oxford University Press, 1976.

Mazlish, Bruce. "Leadership in the American Revolution: The Psychological Dimension," in *Leadership in the American Revolution.* Washington, D.C.: Library of Congress, 1974.

McCaughey, Elizabeth P. *From Loyalist to Founding Father: The Political Odyssey of William Samuel Johnson.* New York: Columbia University Press, 1979.

McCleur, J. F. "The Republic and the Millennium," in *The Religion of the Republic,* edited by Elwyn A. Smith. Philadelphia: Fortress, 1970.

McLoughlin, William G. "The Role of Religion in the American Revolution: Liberty of Conscience and Cultural Cohesion in the New Nation," in *Essays on the American Revolution,* edited by Stephen G. Kurtz and James H. Hutson. Chapel Hill: University of North Carolina Press, 1973.

McLoughlin, and Robert N. Bellah, eds. *Religion in America.* Boston: Houghton Mifflin, 1968.

Meserve, Walter J. *An Emerging Entertainment: The Drama of the American People to 1828.* Bloomington: Indiana University Press, 1977.

Meyer, Donald H. *The Democratic Enlightenment.* New York: Putnam's, 1976.

Middlekauff, Robert. "The Ritualization of the American Revolution," in *The Development of an American Culture,* edited by Stanley Coben and Lorman Ratner. Englewood Cliffs, N.J.: Prentice-Hall, 1970.

Miller, John C. *The Federalist Era, 1789-1801.* New York: Harper, 1960.

Miller, Lillian B. *Patrons and Patriotism: The Encouragement of the Fine Arts in the United States, 1790-1860.* Chicago: University of Chicago Press, 1966.

Miller, Perry. *Errand into the Wilderness.* Cambridge: Harvard University Press, 1956.

Monk, Samuel H. *The Sublime: A Study of Critical Theories in XVIII-Century England.* New York: Modern Language Association of America, 1935.

Moore, Frank. *Diary of the American Revolution. From Newspapers and Original Documents,* 2 volumes. New York: Scribners/London: Low, 1860.

Morgan, Edmund S. "The American Revolution Considered as an Intellectual Movement," in *Paths of American Thought,* edited by Arthur M. Schlesinger, Jr., and Morton White. Boston: Houghton Mifflin, 1963.

Morgan. "The Puritan Ethic and the American Revolution," *William and Mary Quarterly,* third series 24 (January 1967): 3-43.

Morgan, and Helen M. Morgan. *The Stamp Act Crisis: Prologue to Revolution.* Chapel Hill: University of North Carolina Press, 1953.

Morgan, Edmund S., ed. *Puritan Political Ideas, 1558-1794.* Indianapolis: Bobbs-Merrill, 1965.

Murrin, John M. "Review Essay," *History and Theory,* 11, no. 2 (1972): 226-275.

Nagel, Paul C. *One Nation Indivisible: The Union in American Thought, 1776-1861.* New York: Oxford University Press, 1964.

Nagel. *This Sacred Trust: American Nationality, 1798-1898.* New York: Oxford University Press, 1971.

Nash, Gary B. *Class and Society in Early America.* Englewood Cliffs, N.J.: Prentice-Hall, 1970.

Nash. *The Urban Crucible: Social Change, Political Consciousness, and the Origins of the American Revolution.* Cambridge: Harvard University Press, 1979.

Needham, H. A., ed. *Taste and Criticism in the Eighteenth Century: A Selection of Texts Illustrating the Evolution of Taste and the Development of Critical Theory.* London: Harrap, 1952.

Neil, J. Meredith. *Toward a National Taste: America's Quest for Aesthetic Independence.* Honolulu: University Press of Hawaii, 1975.

Nye, Russel B. *American Literary History, 1607-1830.* New York: Knopf, 1970.

Nye. *The Cultural Life of the New Nation, 1776-1830.* New York: Harper, 1960.

Nye. *This Almost Chosen People: Essays in the History of American Ideas.* East Lansing: Michigan State University Press, 1966.

Patterson, Samuel White. *The Spirit of the American Revolution as Revealed in the Poetry of the Period: A Study of American Patriotic Verse from 1760 to 1783.* Boston: R. G. Badger, 1915.

Peyre, Henri. *Literature and Sincerity.* New Haven: Yale University Press, 1963.

Pickering, James H., ed. *The World Turned Upside Down: Prose and Poetry of the American Revolution.* Port Washington, N.Y.: Kennikat Press, 1975.

Plumb, H. J. "The Public, Literature and the Arts in the 18th Century," in *The Triumph of Culture: 18th Century Perspectives,* edited by Paul Fritz and David Williams. Toronto: A. M. Hakkert, 1972.

Pocock, J. G. A. *Politics, Language and Time: Essays on Political Thought and History.* New York: Atheneum, 1971.

Pocock. "Virtue and Commerce in the Eighteenth Century," *Journal of Interdisciplinary History,* 3 (Summer 1972-1973): 125-134.

Richardson, Robert D., Jr. *Myth and Literature in the American Renaissance.* Bloomington: Indiana University Press, 1978.

Schlesinger, Arthur M. *Prelude to Independence: The Newspaper War on Britain, 1764-1776.* New York: Knopf, 1958.

Schneider, Herbert W. *A History of American Philosophy.* New York: Columbia University Press, 1963.

Seelye, John. *Prophetic Waters: The River in Early American Life and Literature.* New York: Oxford University Press, 1977.

Sensabaugh, George F. *Milton in Early America.* Princeton: Princeton University Press, 1964.

Shahan, Robert W., and Kenneth R. Merrill. *American Philosophy from Edwards to Quine.* Norman: University of Oklahoma Press, 1978.

Shaw, Peter. *American Patriots and the Rituals of Revolution.* Cambridge: Harvard University Press, 1981.

Shaw. *The Character of John Adams.* Chapel Hill: University of North Carolina Press, 1976.

Shea, Daniel B., Jr. *Spiritual Autobiography in Early America.* Princeton: Princeton University Press, 1968.

Shy, John W. *Toward Lexington: The Role of the British Army in the Coming of the American Revolution.* Princeton: Princeton University Press, 1965.

Shy, ed. *The American Revolution.* Northbrook, Ill.: AHM Press, 1973.

Silverman, Kenneth. *A Cultural History of the American Revolution.* New York: Crowell, 1976.

Silverman, ed. *Colonial American Poetry.* New York: Hafner, 1968.

Simpson, Lewis P. "Federalism and the Crisis of Literary Order," *American Literature,* 32 (1960): 253-266.

Simpson. "Literary Ecumenicalism of the American Enlightenment," in *The Ibero-American Enlightenment,* edited by A. Owen Aldridge. Urbana: University of Illinois Press, 1971.

Simpson. *The Man of Letters in New England and the South.* Baton Rouge: Louisiana State University Press, 1973.

Simpson. "The Printer as a Man of Letters: Franklin and the Symbolism of the Third Realm," in *The Oldest Revolutionary: Essays on Benjamin Franklin,* edited by J. A. Leo Lemay. Philadelphia: University of Pennsylvania Press, 1976.

Sloan, Douglas. *The Scottish Enlightenment and the American College Ideal.* New York: Teachers College Press, Columbia University, 1971.

Slotkin, Richard S. *Regeneration through Violence: The Mythology of the American Frontier, 1600-1860.* Middletown, Conn.: Wesleyan University Press, 1973.

Smith, James Ward, and A. Leland Jamison, eds. *Religion in American Life,* 4 volumes. Princeton: Princeton University Press, 1961-

Spengemann, William C. *The Adventurous Muse: The Poetics of American Fiction, 1789-1900.* New Haven: Yale University Press, 1977.

Spiller, Robert E., ed. *The American Literary Revolution, 1783-1837.* Garden City: Doubleday, 1967.

Sprague, William B. *Annals of the American Pulpit,* 9 volumes. New York: Carter, 1857-1869.

Stein, Roger B. *Seascape and the American Imagination.* New York: Crown, 1975.

Strout, Cushing. *The New Heavens and New Earth: Political Religion in America.* New York: Harper & Row, 1973.

Takaki, Ronald T. *Iron Cages: Race and Culture in Nineteenth-Century America.* New York: Knopf, 1979.

Tichi, Cecelia. *New World, New Earth: Environmental Reform in American Literature from the Puritans through Whitman.* New Haven: Yale University Press, 1979.

Tuveson, Ernest Lee. *The Imagination as a Means of Grace: Locke and the Aesthetics of Romanticism.* Berkeley: University of California Press, 1960.

Tuveson. *Redeemer Nation: The Idea of America's Millennial Role.* Chicago: University of Chicago Press, 1968.

Van Alstyne, Richard W. *Genesis of American Nationalism.* Waltham, Mass.: Blaisdell, 1970.

Watts, Emily Stipes. *The Poetry of American Women from 1632 to 1945.* Austin: University of Texas Press, 1977.

Wiebe, Robert H. *The Segmented Society: An Introduction to the Meaning of America.* New York: Oxford University Press, 1975.

Wills, Garry. *Inventing America: Jefferson's Declaration of Independence.* Garden City: Doubleday, 1978.

Wilson, John F. *Public Religion in American Culture.* Philadelphia: Temple University Press, 1979.

Wood, Gordon S. *The Creation of the American Republic, 1776-1787.* Chapel Hill: University of North Carolina Press, 1969.

Wood. "The Democratization of Mind in the American Revolution," in *Leadership in the American Revolution.* Washington, D.C.: Library of Congress, 1974.

Wood. "Rhetoric and Reality in the American Revolution," *William and Mary Quarterly,* third series 23 (January 1966): 3-32.

Wright, Louis B. *Culture on the Moving Frontier.* Bloomington: University of Indiana Press, 1955.

Wright, Lyle H. *American Fiction, 1774-1850: A Contribution Toward a Bibliography,* revised edition. San Marino: Huntington Library, 1969.

Ziff, Larzer. *Literary Democracy: The Declaration of Cultural Independence in America.* New York: Viking, 1981.

Ziff. *Puritanism in America: New Culture in a New World.* New York: Viking, 1973.

Contributors

Robert D. Arner .... *University of Cincinnati*
Alan Axelrod .... *New York, New York*
William K. Bottorff .... *University of Toledo*
A. Wheeler Cafarelli .... *Princeton University*
Cathy N. Davidson .... *Michigan State University*
Hugh J. Dawson .... *University of San Francisco*
Emory Elliott .... *Princeton University*
Georgia Elliott .... *Princeton University*
Jenny Franchot .... *Stanford University*
Vincent Freimarck .... *State University of New York at Binghamton*
James C. Gaston .... *U.S. Air Force Academy*
Thomas B. Gustafson .... *University of Southern California*
Laura Henigman .... *Columbia University*
Robert W. Hill .... *Clemson University*
John R. Holmes .... *Kent State University*
Claudia Johnson .... *University of Alabama*
Steven E. Kagle .... *Illinois State University*
James Kelleher .... *West Chester State College*
Homer D. Kemp .... *Tennessee Technological University*
M. Jimmie Killingsworth .... *New Mexico Institute of Mining and Technology*
Michael P. Kramer .... *University of California at Davis*
Jayne K. Kribbs .... *Temple University*
James Lawton .... *Brookline, Massachusetts*
Lewis Leary .... *University of North Carolina at Chapel Hill*
Robert S. Levine .... *University of Maryland*
Michael A. Lofaro .... *University of Tennessee*
Louis P. Masur .... *Princeton University*
John Harmon McElroy .... *University of Arizona*
Wesley T. Mott .... *University of Wisconsin*
Carla Mulford .... *Villanova University*
Sondra O'Neale .... *Emory University*
Tony Owens .... *University of South Carolina*
Jewell B. Parham .... *Tennessee State University*
Mark R. Patterson .... *University of Washington*
Amanda Porterfield .... *Syracuse University*
Michael Robertson .... *Princeton University*
David Robinson .... *Oregon State University*
Bernard Rosenthal .... *State University of New York at Binghamton*
Ormond Seavey .... *George Washington University*
Frank Shuffelton .... *University of Rochester*
Nancy Craig Simmons .... *Virginia Polytechnic Institute*
Thomas P. Slaughter .... *Rutgers University*
Stephen J. Stedman .... *Tennessee State University*
Cecelia Tichi .... *Boston University*
Richard C. Vitzthum .... *University of Maryland*
Donald Weber .... *Mount Holyoke College*

Cumulative Index

Dictionary of Literary Biography, Volumes 1-37
Dictionary of Literary Biography Yearbook, 1980-1983
Dictionary of Literary Biography Documentary Series, Volumes 1-4

Cumulative Index

DLB before number: *Dictionary of Literary Biography*, Volumes 1-37
Y before number: *Dictionary of Literary Biography Yearbook*, 1980-1983
DS before number: *Dictionary of Literary Biography Documentary Series*, Volumes 1-4

A

Abbot, Willis J. 1863-1934 ....DLB29

Abbott, Jacob 1803-1879......................................DLB1

Abbott, Robert S. 1868-1940 ....DLB29

Abercrombie, Lascelles 1881-1938 ....DLB19

Abse, Dannie 1923- DLB27

Adair, James 1709?-1783? DLB30

Adamic, Louis 1898-1951 ....DLB9

Adams, Douglas 1952- Y83

Adams, Franklin P. 1881-1960 ....DLB29

Adams, Henry 1838-1918......................................DLB12

Adams, James Truslow 1878-1949.....................DLB17

Adams, John 1734-1826 ....DLB31

Adams, John Quincy 1767-1848 ....DLB37

Adams, Samuel 1722-1803 ....DLB31

Ade, George 1866-1944...............................DLB11, 25

Adeler, Max (see Clark, Charles Heber)

AE 1867-1935..DLB19

Agassiz, Jean Louis Rodolphe 1807-1873 ....DLB1

Agee, James 1909-1955...............................DLB2, 26

Aiken, Conrad 1889-1973.....................................DLB9

Ainsworth, William Harrison 1805-1882 ....DLB21

Akins, Zoë 1886-1958 ....DLB26

Albee, Edward 1928- DLB7

Alcott, Amos Bronson 1799-1888 ....DLB1

Alcott, Louisa May 1832-1888...............................DLB1

Alcott, William Andrus 1798-1859.......................DLB1

Aldington, Richard 1892-1962 ....DLB20, 36

Aldis, Dorothy 1896-1966.....................................DLB22

Aldiss, Brian W. 1925- DLB14

Alexander, James 1691-1756...............................DLB24

Algren, Nelson 1909-1981 ....DLB9; Y81, 82

Alldritt, Keith 1935- DLB14

Allen, Ethan 1738-1789 ....DLB31

Allen, Hervey 1889-1949......................................DLB9

Allen, James 1739-1808 ....DLB31

Allen, Jay Presson 1922- DLB26

Josiah Allen's Wife (see Holly, Marietta)

Allingham, William 1824-1889............................DLB35

Allott, Kenneth 1912-1973 ....DLB20

Allston, Washington 1779-1843............................DLB1

Alsop, George 1636-post 1673 ....DLB24

Alsop, Richard 1761-1815 ....DLB37

Alvarez, A. 1929- DLB14

Ames, Fisher 1758-1808 ....DLB37

Ames, Mary Clemmer 1831-1884.......................DLB23

Amis, Kingsley 1922- DLB15, 27

Amis, Martin 1949- DLB14

Ammons, A. R. 1926- DLB5

Anderson, Margaret 1886-1973 ....DLB4

Anderson, Maxwell 1888-1959............................DLB7

Anderson, Paul Y. 1893-1938............................DLB29

Anderson, Poul 1926- DLB8

Anderson, Robert 1917- DLB7

Anderson, Sherwood 1876-1941 .... DLB4, 9; DS1

Andrews, Charles M. 1863-1943 ....DLB17

Anhalt, Edward 1914- DLB26

Anthony, Piers 1934- DLB8

Archer, William 1856-1924................................DLB10

Arden, John 1930- DLB13

Arensberg, Ann 1937- Y82

Arlen, Michael 1895-1956.................................DLB36

Arnold, Edwin 1832-1904................................DLB35

Arnold, Matthew 1822-1888..............................DLB32

Arnow, Harriette Simpson 1908- DLB6

Arp, Bill (see Smith, Charles Henry)

Arthur, Timothy Shay 1809-1885 ....DLB3

Asch, Nathan 1902-1964................................DLB4, 28

Ashbery, John 1927- DLB5; Y81

G

I

J

K

M

Q

R

T